polytekton Design

1978-1989

Drawing
Photography
Graphic Design
Painting
Etching
Ceramics
Architectural Projects
Architexts
Design-Build Work

Obvious Press
918 5th Street
Ames, IA, 50010-5906
USA
www.obviouspress.com

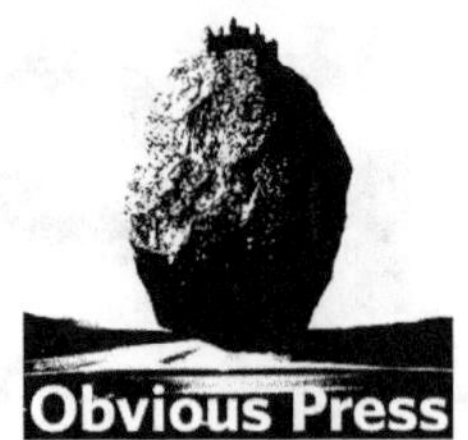

First published in 2010, second edition 2017

For information address Obvious Press, 922 5th Street, Ames, IA 50010-5906 or write to editor@obviouspress.com

Paperback edition ISBN-13: 978-1-941892-31-2
ISBN-10: 1-941892-31-0

Graphic design, layout, and typesetting by 918studio.com
Cover image, flipped horizontally © 1962 by Walter Mücke.

Table of Contents

For Miriam,
the butterflies,
and all the dignified donkeys

Prologue

Design is always a negotiation between the private and the public. In that space of opposition between the individual and society, creative inquiry—and design is that, too—offers an antidote to business-as-usual, to *stasis.* And design always moves, transforms, and remakes the world, at all scales, continuously. Until we become part of humus under our feet there is no escape from the environmental envelope that surrounds us or even the interior space of our bodies that is increasingly transformed by designed bio-objects.

And design is on my mind, even in those least self-conscious times, when, early in the morning while still half asleep I catch myself thinking about the space around me as the daylight oozes through the translucent paper strip along the upper wall of the bedroom, and the ceiling color slowly changes from a dark gray to a lighter shade of pale green. I'm lying there, wondering how to finish the joint between the wall and the ceiling that's still unfinished. That is design, too: the certainty of change.

Chance

My official profession, that to which I profess, is architecture, and the field caught me by surprise. I entered the art of building or *Baukunst,* as we say in German, sideways and in stages—through the related arts—mostly by drawing, painting, and photography, and only later by transforming and designing the environments around other clients.

The best way to understand the world is to initially make it strange to oneself. In 1979 I said good-bye to Germany for the first time, and started my own non-European *grand tour* through Canada, the United States, and Mexico. Along the way I learned about the materiality of the built environment by painting King Ludwig's *Neuschwanstein* castle on a house of another German emigrant in Bowden, Alberta, picked flowers and apples in an orchard owned by a retired VW car dealer—who liked to support other young German immigrants—near Watsonville, California, and repaired apartment buildings on the south side of Chicago with carpenter Phil Beaver who had studied philosophy at the University of Chicago.

The first time I approached architecture in a conventional sense was out of necessity: Miriam and I needed a new place to live after we had moved out of the *Turmhof* farmstead commune outside the small hamlet of Entrup near Lemgo, Germany in 1982. At that time our 'site' was a used circus trailer we had bought from a retired carny for 1200 DM.

Even in the commune we had set ourselves initially apart from the main group by claiming the most remote space in the drafty attic of the farmstead, and transforming it into an adequate but not particularly comfortable living space. I would classify that design project as proto-architectural. At least we knew and responded to basic physics—heat rises—by building our bed on stilts.

The second time around I thought it useful to work for professionals when I interned as a designer for three weeks at *Planen+Bauen*, a small architecture office (now defunct), in Lemgo. At that time I had just read the passive-solar handbook by Edward Mazria. *Planen+Bauen* was not ready for the revolution. They let me draw passive solar buildings with large southern glass expanses on thick vellum sheets with rapidographs on one of the drawing desks in the office. Then, after doing some calculations, one of the architects promptly informed me that my house designs would never work because the night-time heat loss would offset the daytime solar gains of the south-facing spaces. Realizing that professional architects were not yet ready for something as transformative as passive solar designs, I finished out my three weeks and went back to the circus trailer—parked at the water-powered sawmill across from the *Turmhof*—for a few more years of doing what I thought was best: observing and learning from what surrounded me.

Living and working at the old sawmill was a welcome counterpart to working on paper in the architecture office. In this outcast zone on the periphery of convention and society I learned about dimensions, mass, gravity, levers, coldness, dampness, and the beauty of light and shadow.

During those times there was a directness to our life; actions had immediate consequences, and usually found quick solutions: we decided to make the used circus trailer into our main living quarters. It was quite small, even for two love birds, and we added two even smaller construction trailers as satellites to our living space. The experience we made renovating the larger trailer helped us transform the two smaller vehicles into a music room and a painting studio, respectively.

While Miriam was teaching piano in the nearby town of Bad Salzuflen and at the University of Bielefeld, I worked with the other sawmill inhabitants—a small group of commune emigrés including Manfred and Artus—on renovating the mill building and taking care of our animal menagerie (chicken, ducks, goats, rabbits) while also repairing and maintaining our vehicle park (a Citroën 2CV6, a Renault 4, and a small 1950s-vintage Deutz tractor).

As a shade-tree mechanic I honed my three-dimensional understanding of mechanical parts and their relations to each other. Taking apart a disc brake, changing a carburator, or swapping out a two-cylinder engine on a Citroën 2CV became an exercise in spatial calisthenics that no doubt taught me, hands on, much more about leverage, distance differentiation, and angular dimensions than I learned later at the university. Around this time I realized that, quite often, practice precedes theory, followed by more practice.

At some point I realized my affinity for architecture. Unofficially I had always been designing, and yes, from early childhood I played with Legos, and play I did, happily making all kinds of objects and spaces, from the age of about five up to my early teens. My magnus opus was a model of a Galaxy C5 aircraft that used almost all available Lego pieces I had at the time. And I was proud as anyone about being able to build something that complex, even if it was anything but able to fly. This capacity to work in the face of futility has cost me countless hours but I've also immensely enjoyed wasting time while gaining dexterity and insight into how something comes together or apart.

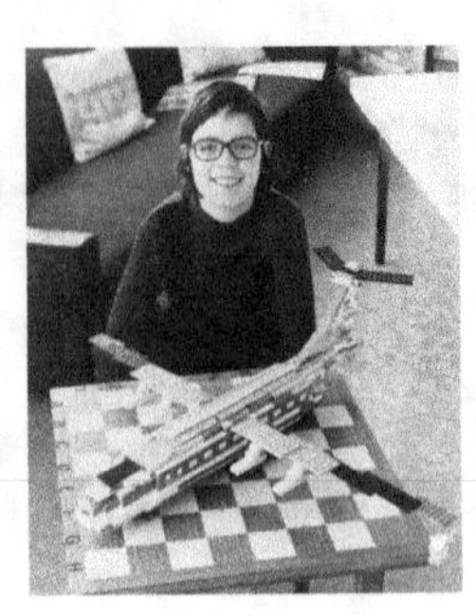

In addition to some affinity what has aided my architectural design is the capacity to find my way using a survey map. Often I intentionally look for alternate ways to reach a place I know at a certain location. This exploratory tendency, perhaps it's just curiosity, helps me explore new places, like cities, neighborhoods, buildings, or even people. And for a student of design there is nothing better than to experience the environment hands-on, physically, and mentally. All the senses combined give a much more nuanced understanding of a space than the visual crutch provided by images in a magazine or online. That means, of course, an admission of the inadequateness of what you hold in your hands to serve as an accurate reflection of my work.

My official architectural career started in 1986 when I took my first studio in the Summer II session at the University of Florida School of Architecture. I was already a semester late entering the program but Professor Martin Gunderson was kind enough to let me into the program on probation, and I never looked back, earning a Bachelor of Design in 1989 and a professional Master of Architecture in 1991. After an invitation by the then new chair Robert Segrest and his colleague/wife Jennifer Bloomer I taught design studios and computer applications and drawing courses for a year at Iowa State University. Toward the end of the first semester it became clear to me that I didn't feel ready to go into teaching full time. I applied to three schools for Ph.D. programs: MIT, Princeton, and McGill. MIT was not interested, McGill accepted me but only as an advanced Masters student in a provisional Ph.D. program that had not been established yet, and Princeton said 'yes' as well; Princeton it was.

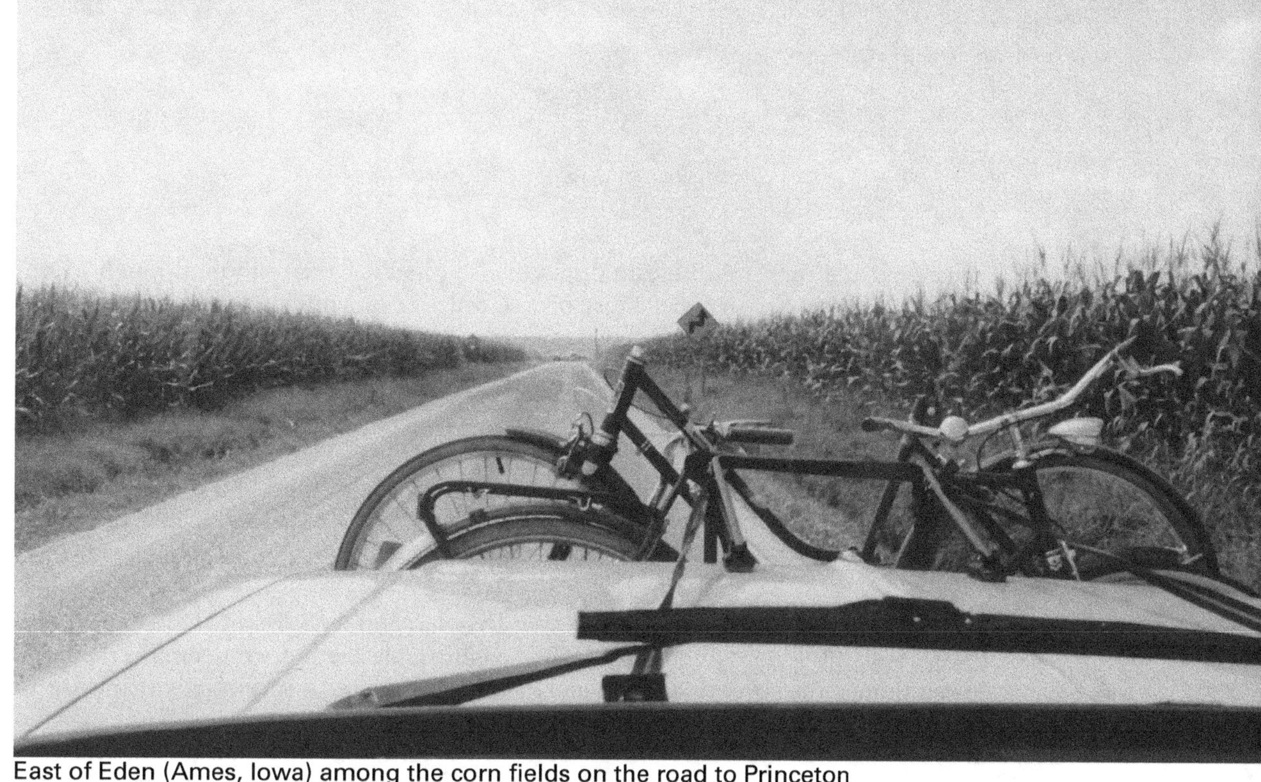

East of Eden (Ames, Iowa) among the corn fields on the road to Princeton

When Miriam and I rolled into the tiny tony east coast town with our overloaded 1984 short-bed Dodge pickup truck in the fall of 1992 (Bob Segrest said something about *The Grapes of Wrath* when we left Ames, Iowa), we felt like the Beverly Hill Billies, but without the money. For the next two years I shuttled back and forth between our post-WW II apartment at 218-C Harrison Street and Firestone Library, and spent the rest of my time reading and writing while Miriam played the organ at Witherspoon Presbyterian church on Sundays, and in between finished her Ph.D. in Musicology, on leave from the University of Florida. Design of the applied kind (what I had been doing until then) was actively discouraged by Princeton's architecture faculty, and so you will find little conventional design work between 1992 and 1994 in Volume 2 of this portfolio. However, I did write a handful of publishable papers, and, for someone like me, whose mother tongue is not English, writing is always a kind of designing-with-language. After finishing my generals exam in the middle of January 1995, I went back to Iowa State University to begin my professional and professorial career of teaching, lecturing, and designing in earnest.

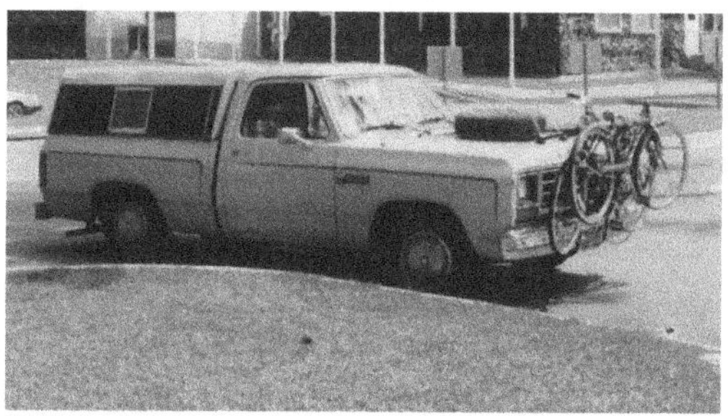

Pickup truck

Logic and Method

Since the mid-1970s I have explored design through a wide variety of media, shifting my focus from one to the other. Unlike my life, however, this book (Volume 1 and its successors, Volumes 2 and 3) is organized by years with self-explanatory indicators at the bottom of each page, and by material/representational identifiers (in the upper left corner of each spread)—from drawing via photography, graphic design, painting, etching, ceramics, architectural projects, and architexts (written+drawn investigations) to design+build work. The alert reader will notice in that sequence a subtle shift from 2D to 3D designs.

Much of the early work—until I entered the professional design program at the University of Florida—falls under the category of derivative production: I studied, borrowed from, and interpreted the work of other artists and makers, adding my own interpretation in the process. Later, during my official design training phase, there was, of course, the pressure to create original work, but I still suspect that most of the time we learn is to cloak our references with more finesse. Truly unprecedented design is rare and only one option; the other is to acknowledge and revel in the historical context that is part of the DNA of any design, and my doctorate in architectural history and theory won't allow me to let go of what preceded my work.

Acknowledgments

Even though the cover bears the name *polytekton*, this book, and the subsequent volumes, would not have been possible without the input of many minds. First and foremost I thank my wife and partner of many years, Miriam Zach, for her love, graciousness, and unwavering support. Very early on in our relationship she was the one to point out my talent of imagining spaces in 3D (an absolute prerequisite for any serious designer, and one that is not that common among architects, as one of my most important teachers, Harry Merritt, once told me). Next in line I have to mention my parents, Irma and Walter Mücke who, with a certain prejudice for the first male and eventual middle child to come along, offered much freedom to do as I pleased, giving encouragement where needed, and allowing me to make mistakes, and learn from them. Our adoptive American parents, Bob and Millie Ramey, helped us financially and philosophically when Miriam and I were both students by hiring us as weekend gardeners for their round house, and I've been trying to repay them ever since. Bill Knack and his wife Ruth Eckdish-Knack were the first to show me the material side of architecture when I helped them renovate their railroad apartment on the southside of Chicago in the spring of 1980. I still seem to have the taste of demolished plaster on lathe in my nose. Bob Segrest and Jennifer Bloomer saw my potential for graduate studies, and, as junior faculty, helped me along when it mattered. My hero and doctor father Georges Teyssot continues to be a source of inspiration.

Finally, I thank those through whom I will live on: my students and colleagues who are too numerous to mention, but they know who they are.

About the Cover

As a middle child between two older and one younger sister—as well as mostly female cousins on both sides of my parents—I grew up surrounded by women. That has influenced who I became: I feel comfortable around women, and the book cover represents a very minor thankyou to all the women of the universe for being who they are, for making the rest of us possible—and for running this world, even if most men don't know, understand, or appreciate that fact.

Why Polytekton?

When I checked the domain name for www.polymath.com, it was already taken. Perhaps the elision of *poly* and *tecton* would work? Alas, www.polytecton.com was taken as well; so I tried the Greek spelling, and that was still available. *Polytekton* became my new identity. The word has multiple meanings: nom de plume and identity container for a variety of venues. The word derives from the Greek *polus* 'much,' *polloi* 'many,' and the Greek *tektonikos*, from *tektōn* 'carpenter, builder.' I am the builder/maker of many things.

If you have any comments about this volume, drop me a line addressed to mikesch@polytekton.com

1978

Drawing

pencil on paper

Theme + Variation

In a KQED Forum episode from Thursday, January 28, 2010, Michael Krasny interviewed Patti Smith, and she described her method of working, i.e. how she would take material from other artists and then interpret it, adding her own take in the process. That's how she wrote and performed her music, poetry and visual art.

Until I heard the interview I had thought about my designs as derivatives rather than as interpretations of other artists' work but after listening to Patti Smith—and who am I to argue with her— it made sense: the drawings I did in the late 1970s were collages of resonant images that other people had created, or photographs I had taken along my travels. The drawings were interpretations of those earlier works, symbolic hybrids with augmented meanings that helped me to externalize the demons and angels in my head. Drawing became a therapy for staying sane.

In the summer of 1978 we travelled to France with a group of friends. I was in love with S. who, it turned out later, was not really that into me. As an aspiring artist with bohemian tendencies and an immature cerebrum I didn't know any better and kept on projecting my *agape* onto S., making drawings full of symbols that were more meaningful to me than her.

The drawing on the right is based on several photographs I took during our vacation in France near Bordeaux.

The sunflowers have continued to stay with me....

completed drawing (23.4" x 33.1") >

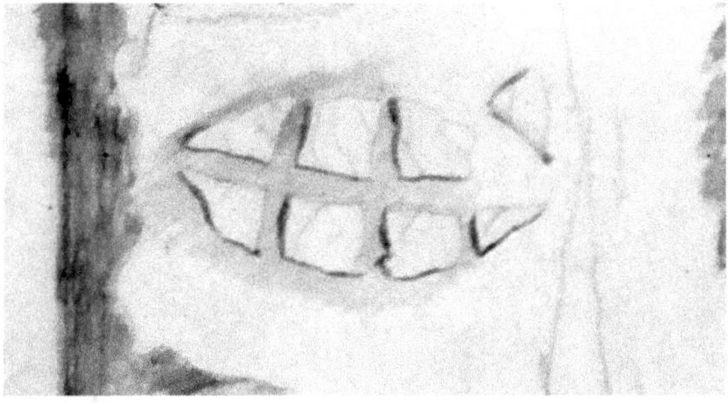

details: 1/8 of a bay leaf ^

details: the glasses that would make the trip across the Atlantic ocean >

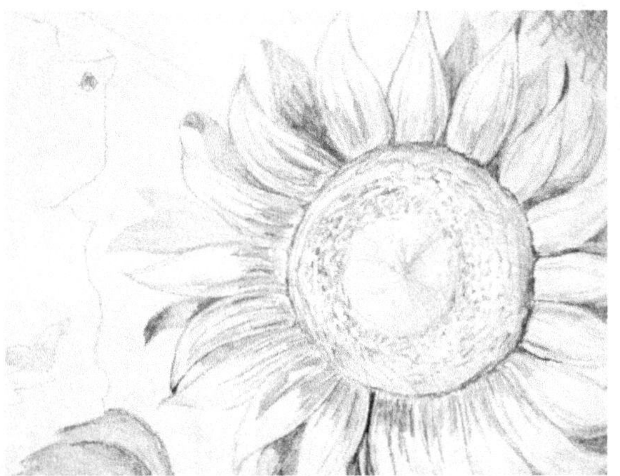

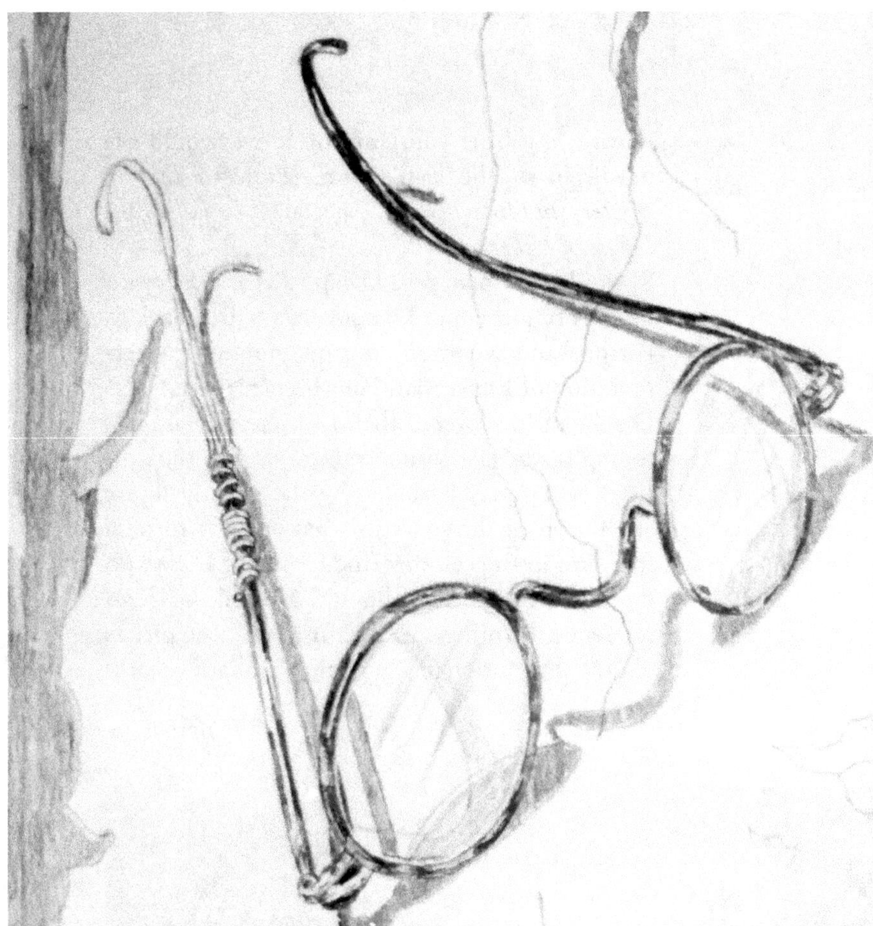

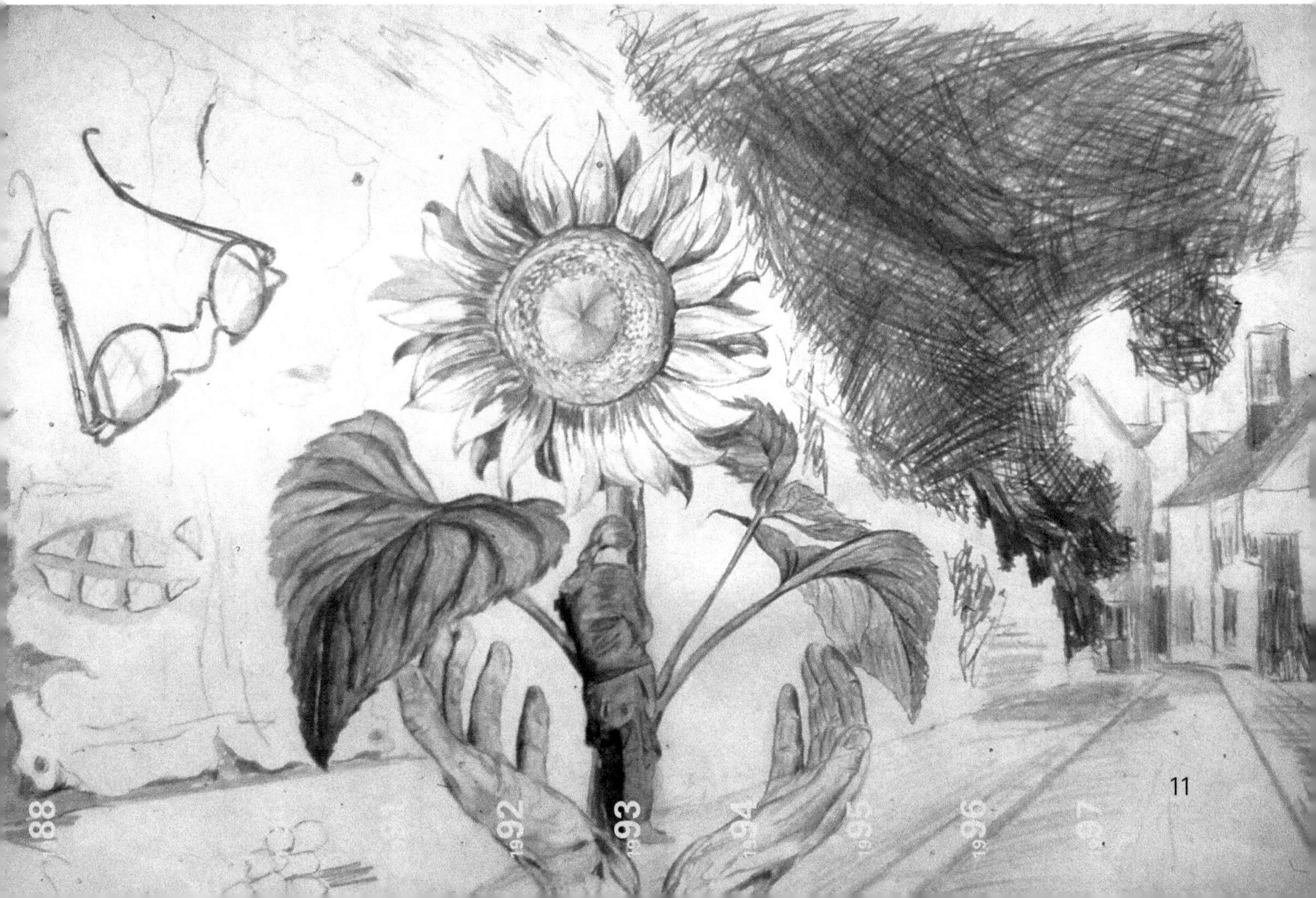

Drawing

pencil on paper

During my brief courtship of S. we would often listen to The Alan Parsons Project's *Tales of Mystery and Imagination,* especially *The Fall of the House of Usher* groove.

S. would also play Bob Dylan's *Lay Lady Lay* on her record player but I would always drift back to Parsons' and Woolfson's stormy symphonic interpretation of Edgar Alan Poe's literary piece.

On the inside cover of their LP were several photographs staged as visual counterparts to the music. I was especially taken by the ghostly figure at the top of the stairs in what appears to be a mansion in the country (the House of Usher, no doubt). I added the cello and a profile of S. to reference the otherworldly music, and the piece's ending dissolution in a gigantic dissonant accord.

details >

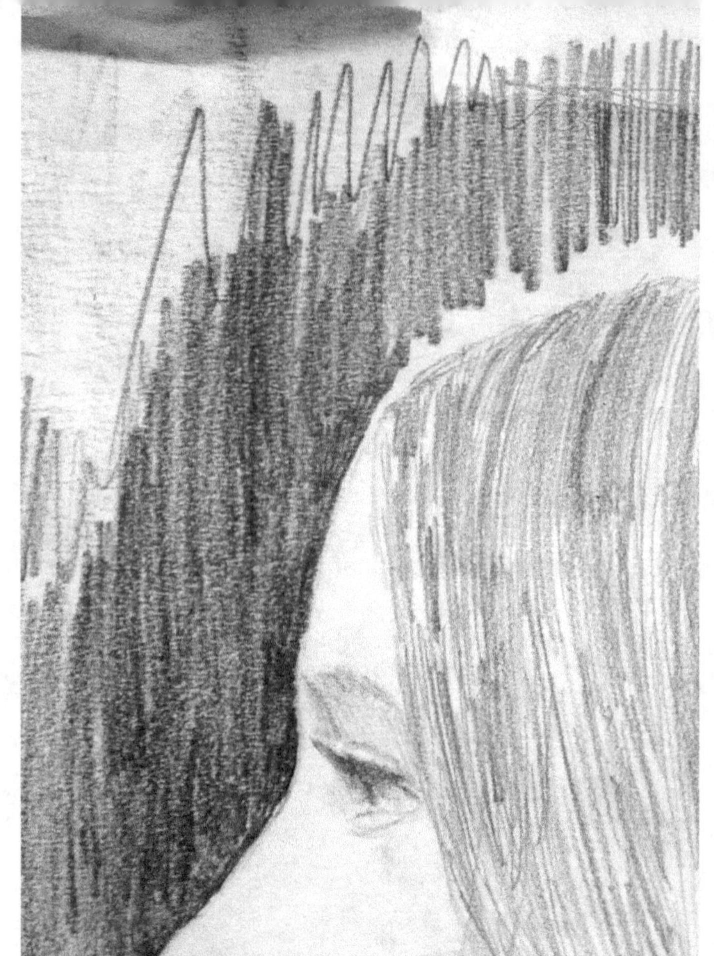

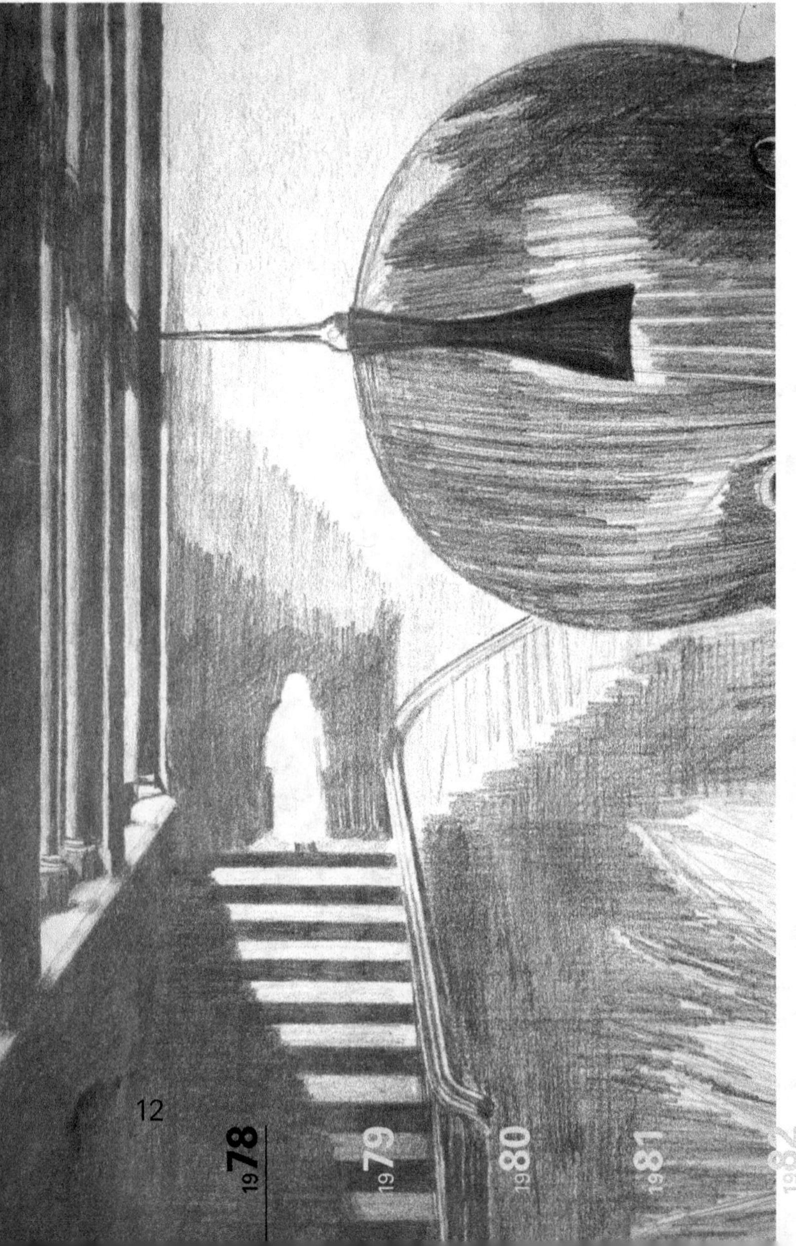

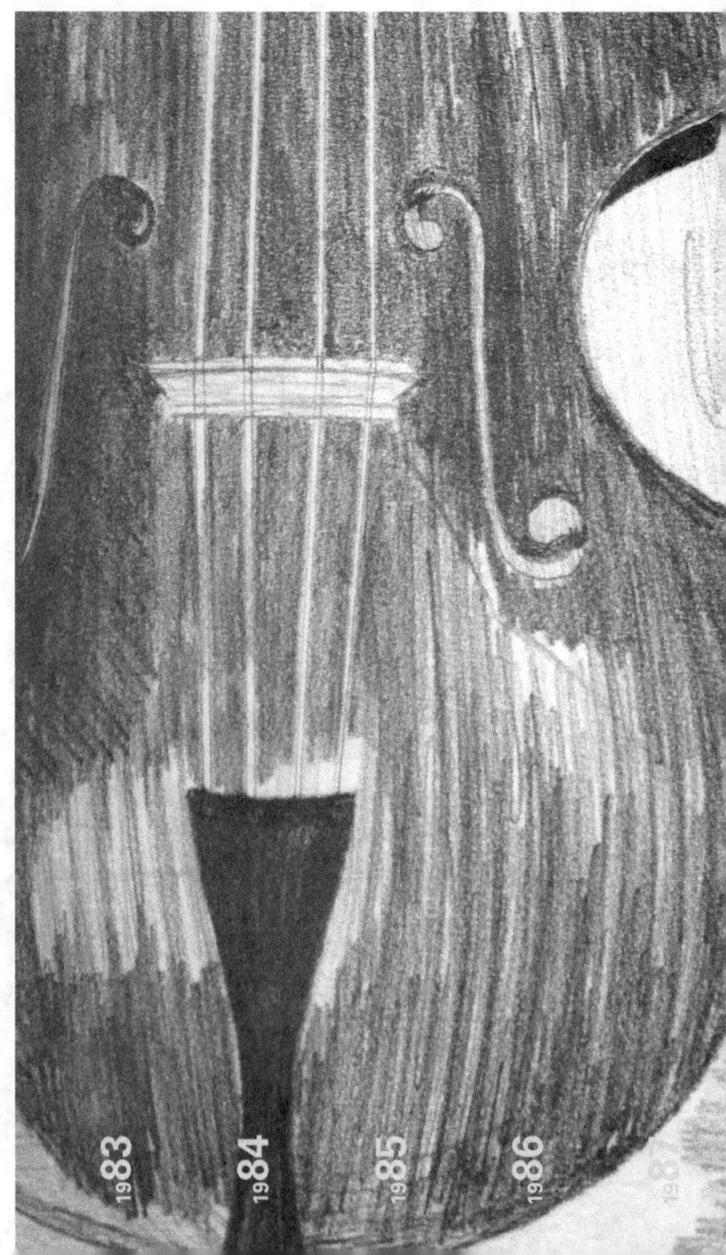

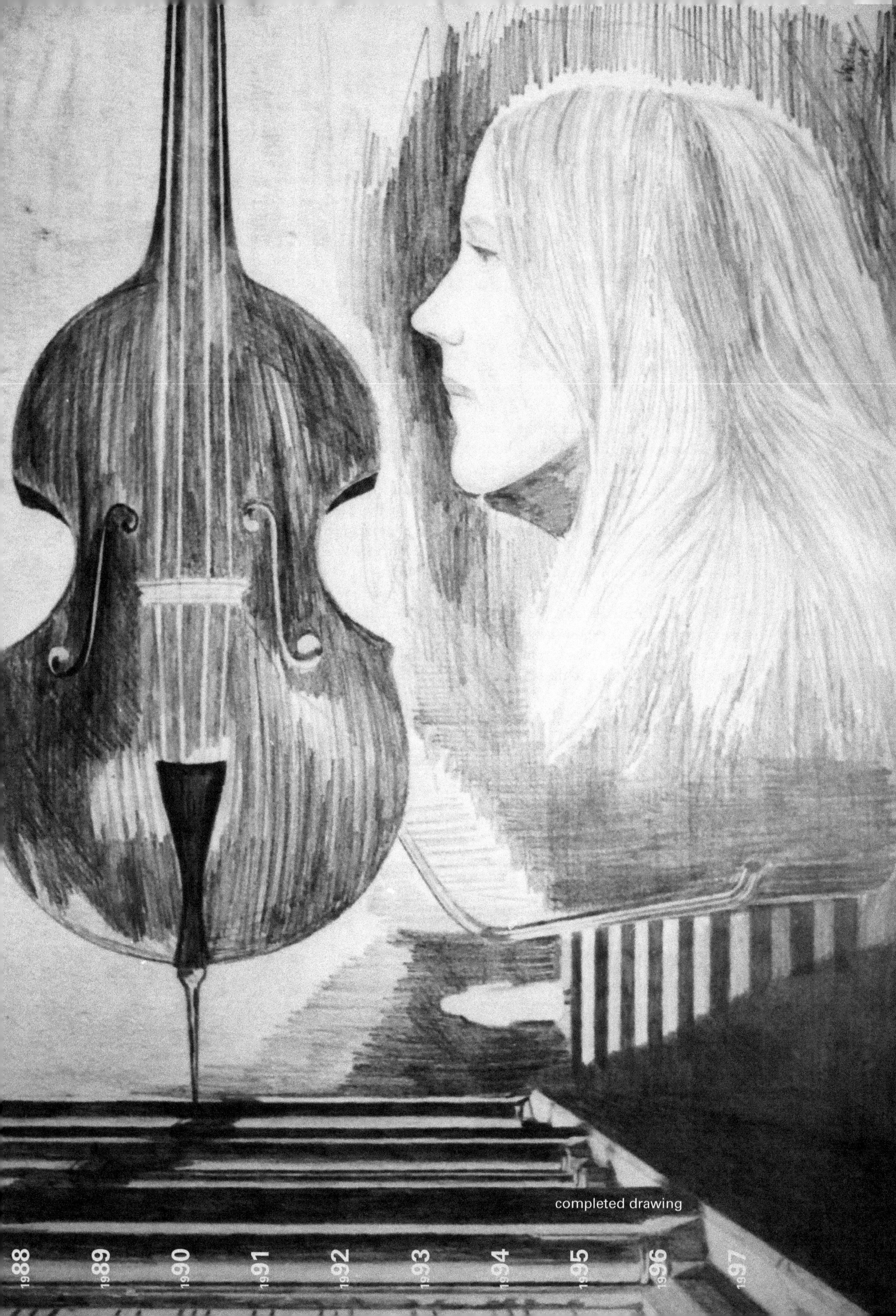
completed drawing
1988
1989
1990
1991
1992
1993
1994
1995
1996
1997

Drawing with Light

The experience of life is not congruent with its representation in photography (literally drawing with light; look it up.), or, for that matter, any form of representation.

All I have left of my early amateur years of transforming the world around me are images (mostly photographs), and a few stories. Everything else is gone: there is, for example, no visual record of my attempt to repair that Renault 5 of an acquaintance in the Breite Strasse in Lemgo right in front of the liquor store where I worked as a clerk for a few weeks before taking off for the United States from Brussels on June 11, 1979; or the face of the alcoholic homeless man who would come into the store every day for his fix, drowning out the painful memories of his daughter's untimely death when she was run over by a car at a crosswalk, or so he told me.

I assume that my first exposure to photography happened while I was tagging along with my father on Sundays to the newspaper, the local *Lippische Landeszeitung*, where he worked. At other times I would go with him to soccer games (he held various jobs at the paper, from journalist to executive sports editor) and he would undoubtedly carry a silver aluminium suitcase with camera gear. During the late 1970s and early 1980s I worked in the newspaper's darkroom on Saturdays and Sundays, developing films brought in by the other reporters. This was the time of black & white film, so after I had developed the images for the other reporters, I would work on my own prints, often out of boredom while waiting for more films to develop as they sat steeping in their chemicals (to the right is a self portrait I took in the office adjacent to the darkroom). During the week other photographers would use the lab and I tended to feel like a visitor, which gave me license to experiment. We used Ilford film and paper at the time, and I remember recycling the white Ilford cardboard boxes to hold my own prints.

I haven't developed a film in ages ... and I miss the smell of the chemicals.

Ilford photo paper boxes

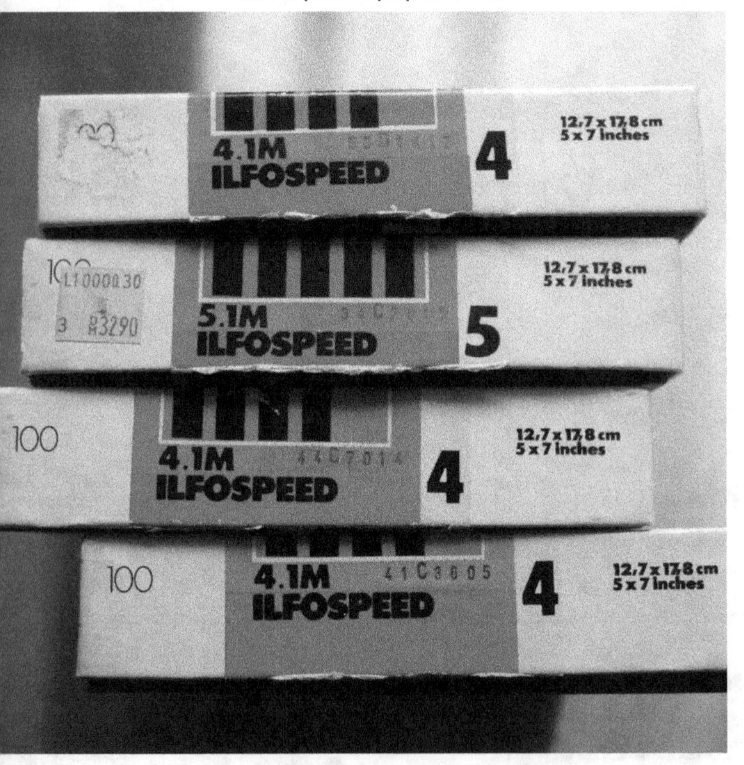

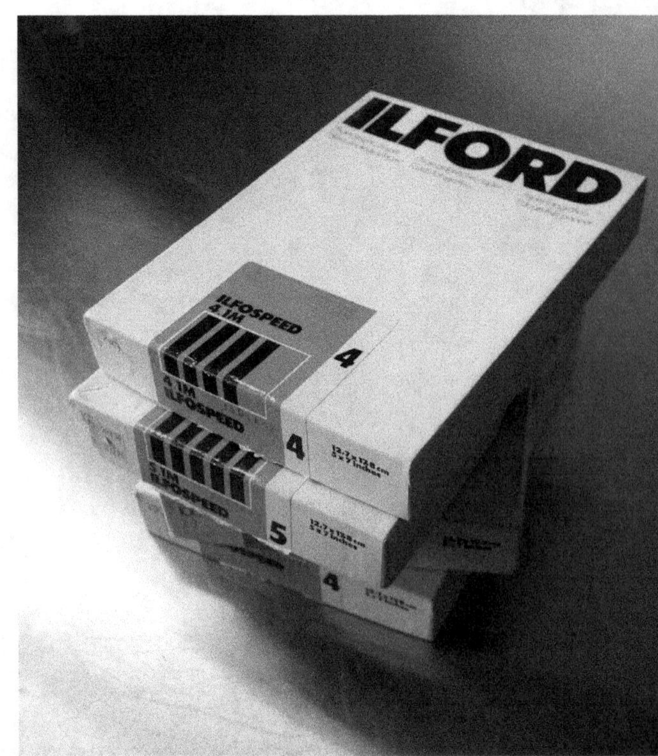

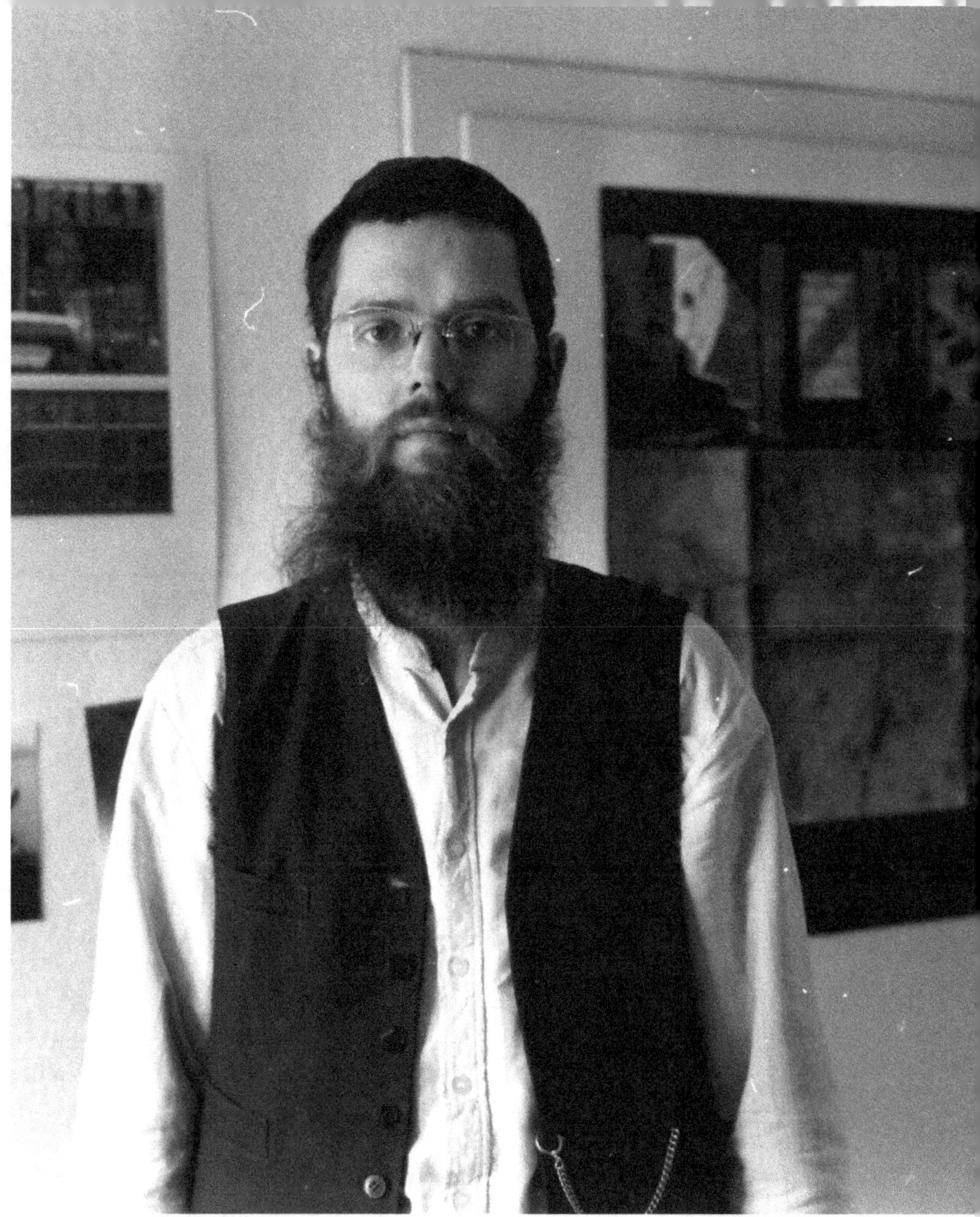

Looking toward the darkroom door in the *Landeszeitung* newspaper photo lab in my Rabbi outfit and do (fresh for the summer).

Photography

Different

In need to make travel money for a summer vacation I followed my older sister Beate during the spring break of 1978 to *Hallig Hooge*, an odd place in the North Sea that, during a storm, turns into an atoll but at other times resembles an island surrounded by a levee. Tourists and sick children come here to breathe the salty air, eat cod, and get well—perhaps. I came to work in a restaurant to make money for a trip with friends to France later in the summer. After a single week of selling overpriced fried flounders and doing dishes in a commercial kitchen for too little money, I quit and moved up the geographical chain to the real island of Föhr. There I quickly found a better-paying job as a sous-chef in a restaurant on the *Sandwall*. I stayed for two more weeks to the delight of the owner who gave me a bonus on my last day (I think she thought of me as a son she never had).

In between I loitered on the beach and watched the garden-chess action on the *Sandwall*, the main pedestrian drag for tourist dandies. One late afternoon, a few days before my departure, I was standing at the edge of the chess board, next to a young man, O., who started to comment about the two middle-aged players. Soon we struck up a conversation that led to a loose friendship over the next few years during which time I would take the photographs on the following pages. I visited Föhr mostly during the off-season between the winter holidays and new year, during those times when few tourists grace the island, and my melancholic id could merge with the exterior beauty of a deserted environment.

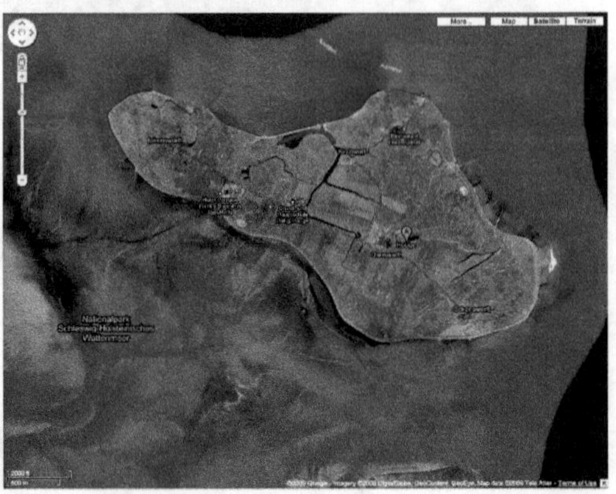

In my romantically inclined mind Föhr became one of those places that I would call a spiritual home away from home, a place where I could see myself live out the rest of my life. There were other places I felt home: *Bergkirchen*, for example, or that round, thatch-covered hut in Föhr (see image on the right), our trailer (Da Capo) and my studio trailer, the windmills we visited in the UK and the Netherlands, some of the houses in the *Freilichtmuseum* in Detmold, the old customs house on Lake Michigan (just south of Navy Pier in Chicago), the abandoned house between Loholz and Istorf off of the Kirchheider Strasse.

This kind of projected habitation, i.e. the virtual appropriation of other people's residences, still plays an important role in my representational production. Part of that, I'm sure, is a vivid imagination, the other is a certain restlessness and dissatisfaction with the status quo.

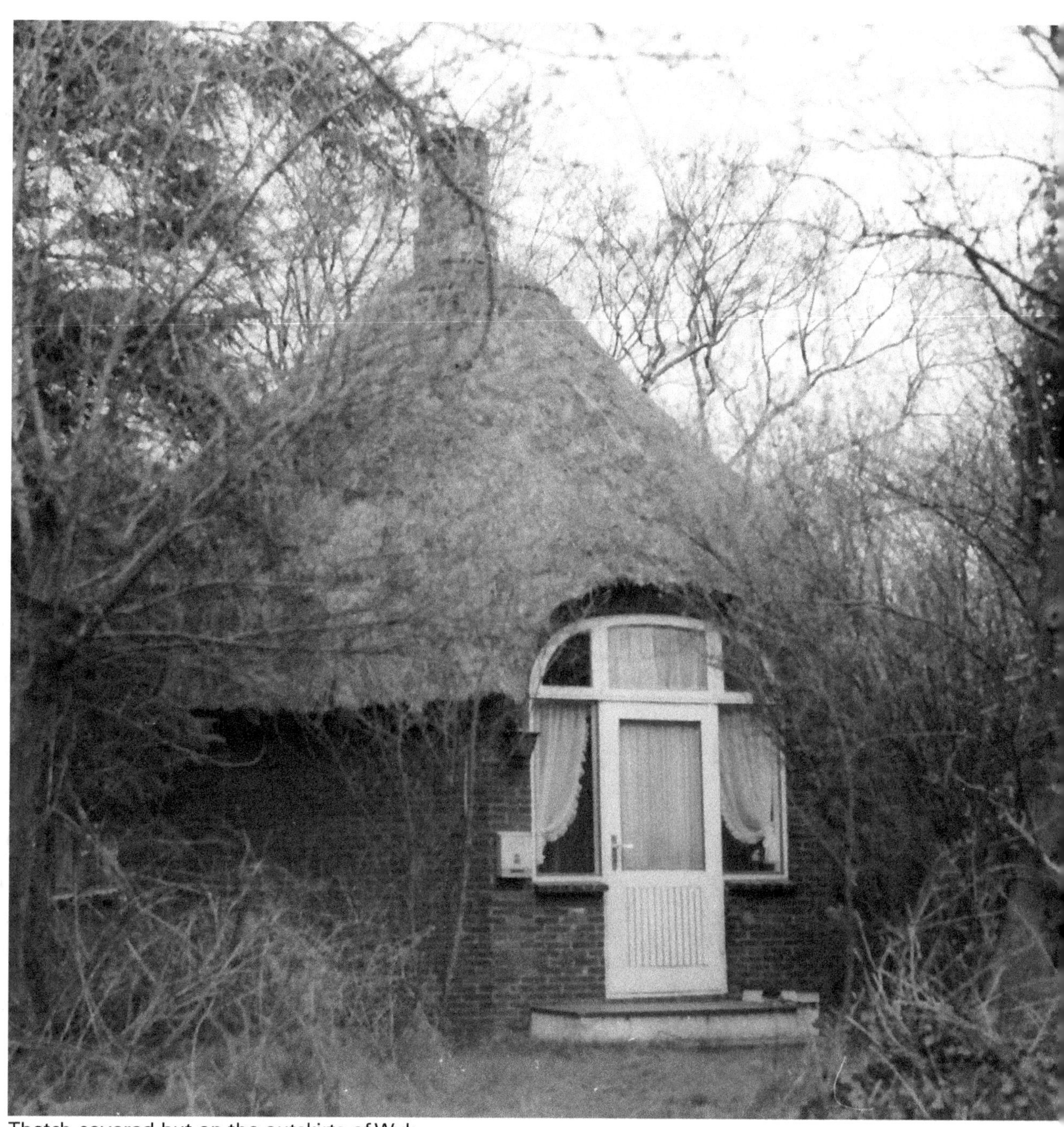
Thatch-covered hut on the outskirts of Wyk

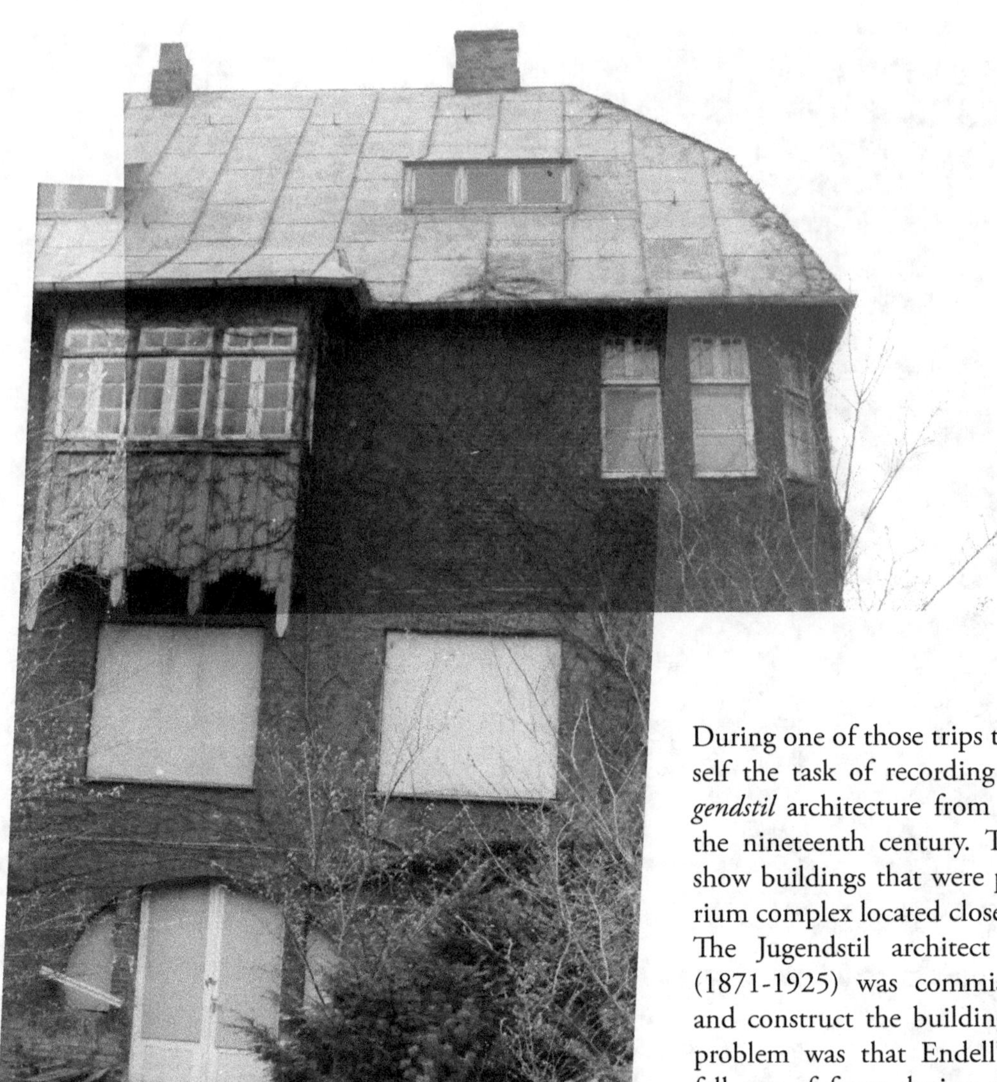

During one of those trips to Föhr I set myself the task of recording endangered *Jugendstil* architecture from the late part of the nineteenth century. The photographs show buildings that were part of a sanatorium complex located close to the beach.
The Jugendstil architect August Endell (1871-1925) was commissioned to plan and construct the buildings in 1898. The problem was that Endell's building style fell out of favor during the Third Reich, and that some of the politicians of the city government on Föhr identified closely with Nazi philosophies. All of this lead after the second World War to a joint movement of local politicians and builders to tear down the complex and build some high-rise apartment buildings that would create accomodation for tourists and revenue for the city. But another interest group proposed to restore the buildings as well as an adjoining park and declare the whole complex a national landmark. The city government and the owner had not anticipated any

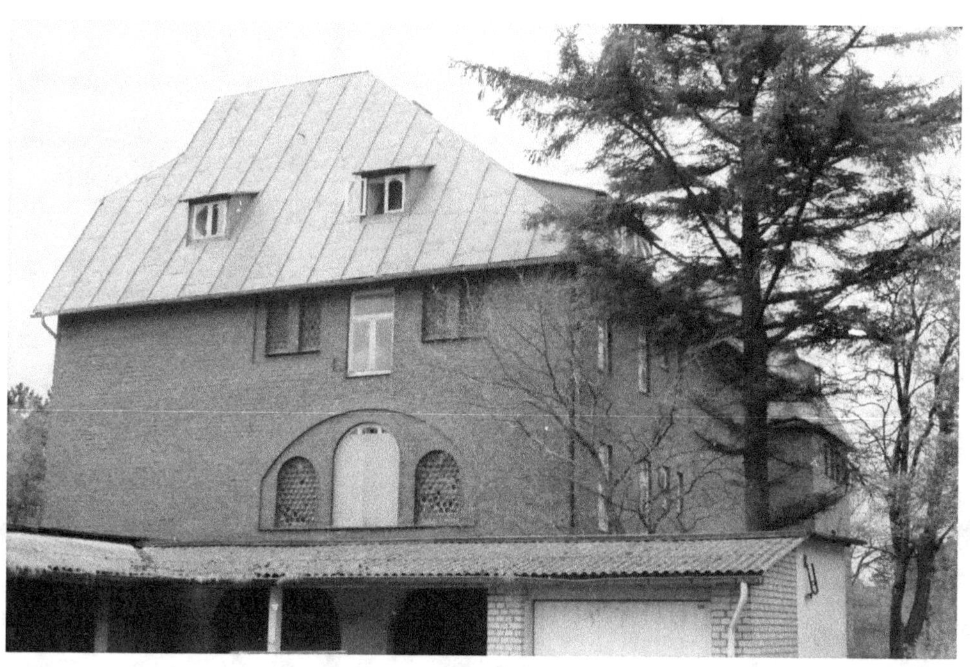

problems and worked from then on hard to help nature destroy the buildings. Windows were deliberately smashed. There were several cases of arson. The humid and salty air in conjunction with hard winters were literally eating away the buildings. The buildings were finally destroyed in 1991.

The photographs show the general disrepair of the buildings in 1978, yet they also reveal the particular details of creative *Jugendstil* architecture. My goal then was to record with my camera the buildings which were most likely to be torn down. Of special interest is the low-relief sculpture on one of the walls. The relief was taken off the wall in 1979 when it was not clear whether the buildings would survive, and is now on display in the Kunsthalle Kiel.

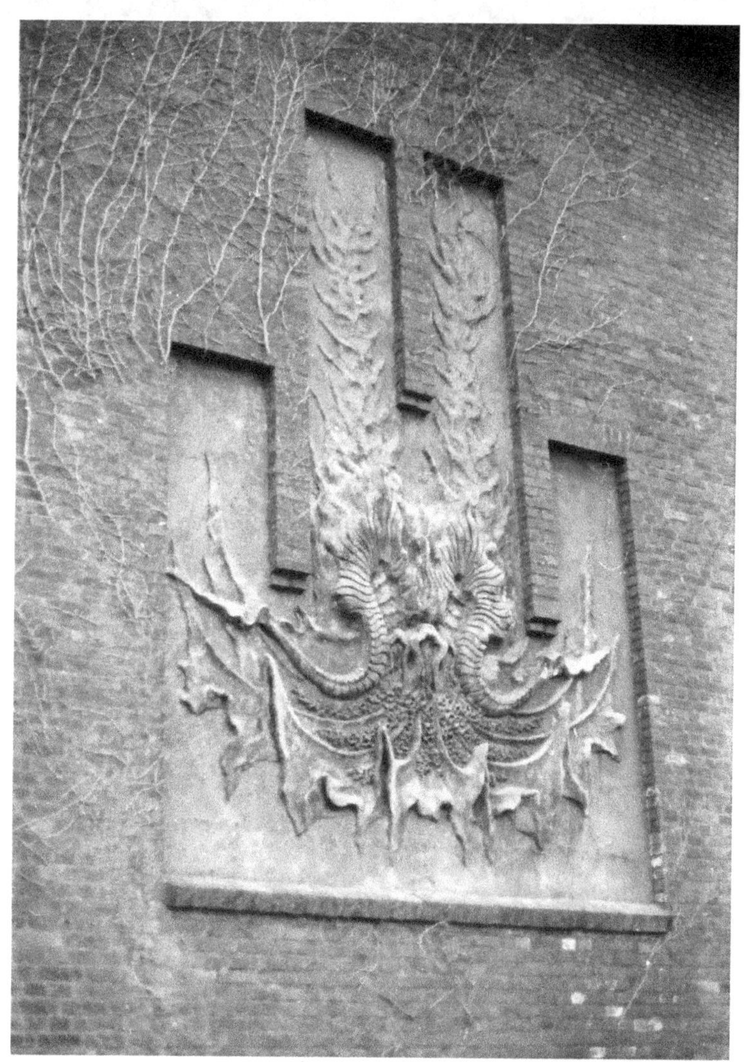

When we went for a walk on Föhr one foggy winter morning the air was full of melancholy. The lack of visual distance, the disappearance of the horizon, made my mind fill in the absences with thoughts of past events and future possibilities. The longing remained just that but it was beautiful. The fog, like snow, muffles sound and in that quietness the dialogue between nature and self is foregrounded.

1988 1989 1990 1991 1992 1993 1994 1995 1996 1997

1979

Drawing

pencil on paper

Death on my mind; death and a beautiful woman whose name is Catherine Deneuve

completed drawing >

details of drawing

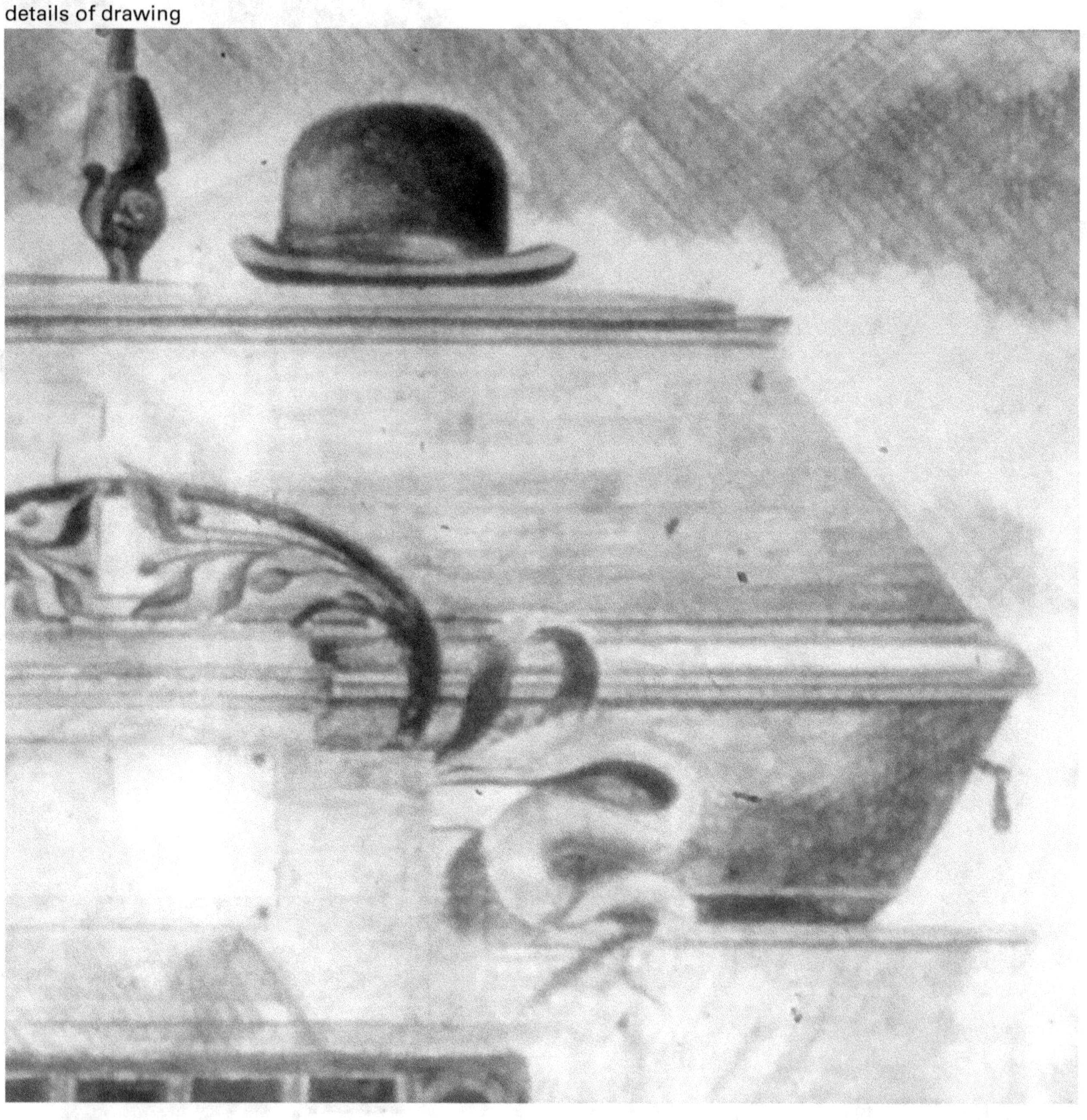

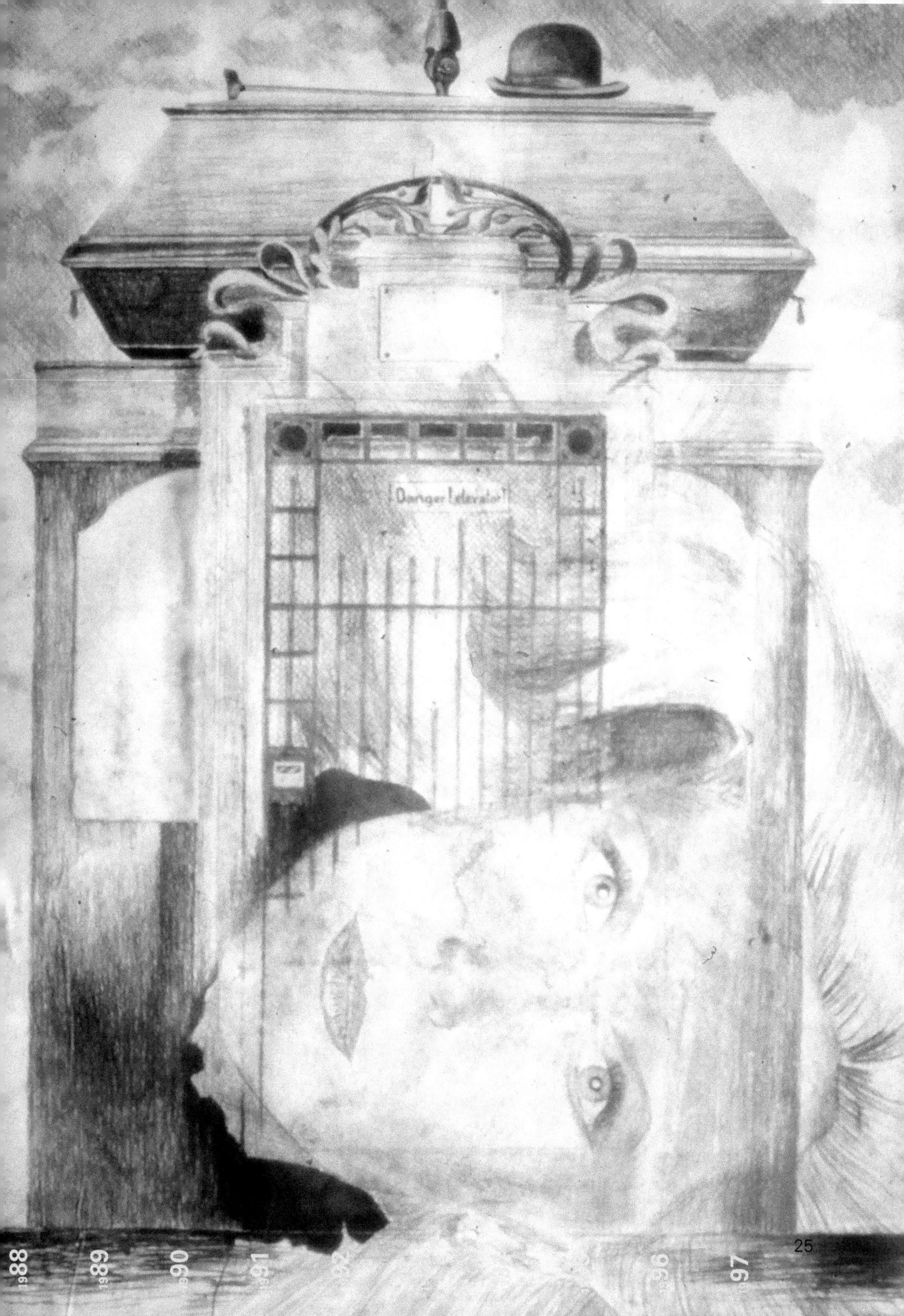

Drawing

pencil on Arché paper

André Heller
"..als ich das erste mal begriff daß wir nicht an der fähigkeit zu sterben, sondern an der unfähigkeit zu leben zugrundegehen."

"..that is when I understood for the first time that we won't perish because of our ability to die but due to our incapacity to live."

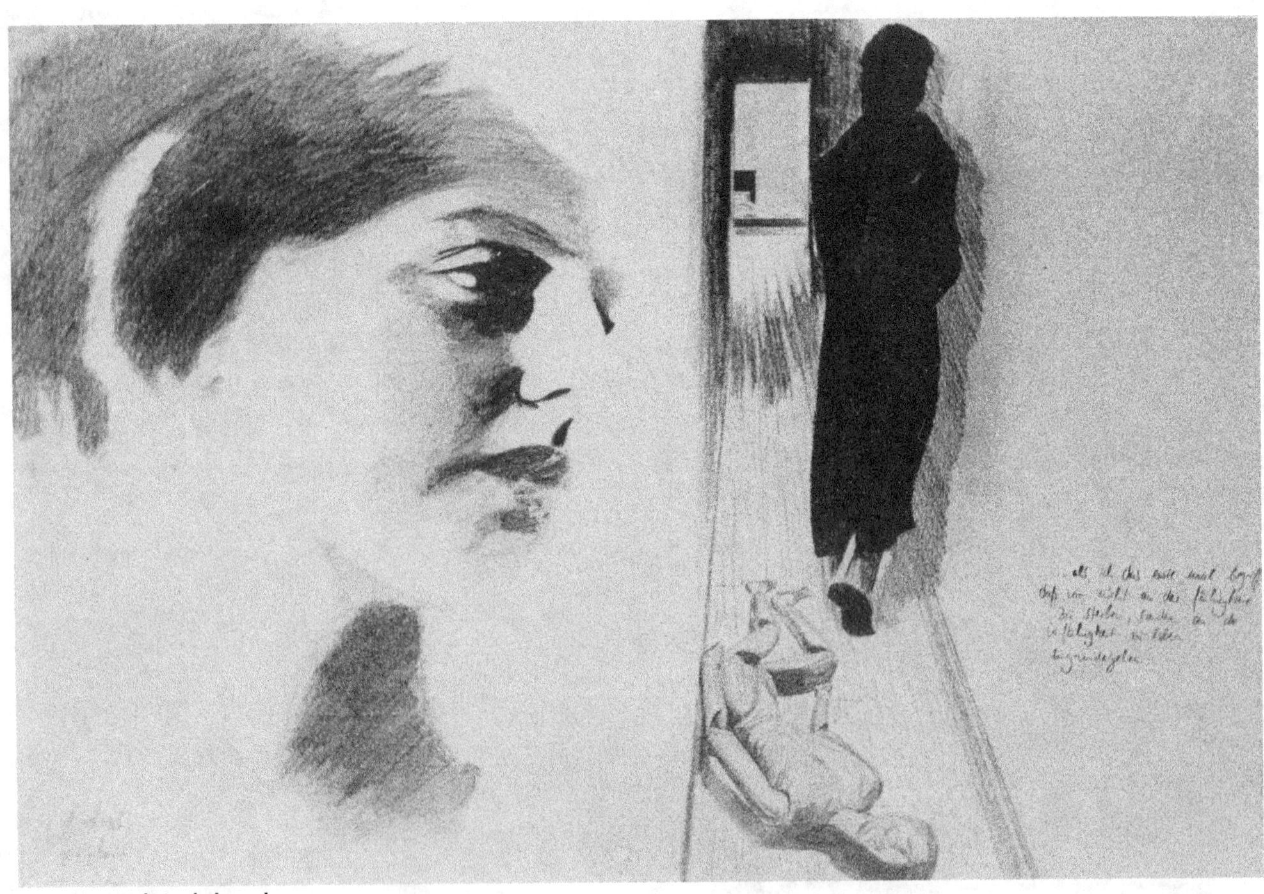

completed drawing

pencil on carton

Thus quoth the raven, plus a top hat, and a floating egg coaxed by a hand, based on Alan Parsons Project's *Tales of Mystery and Imagination* which is, of course, based on Edgar Allen Poe's story of the same title

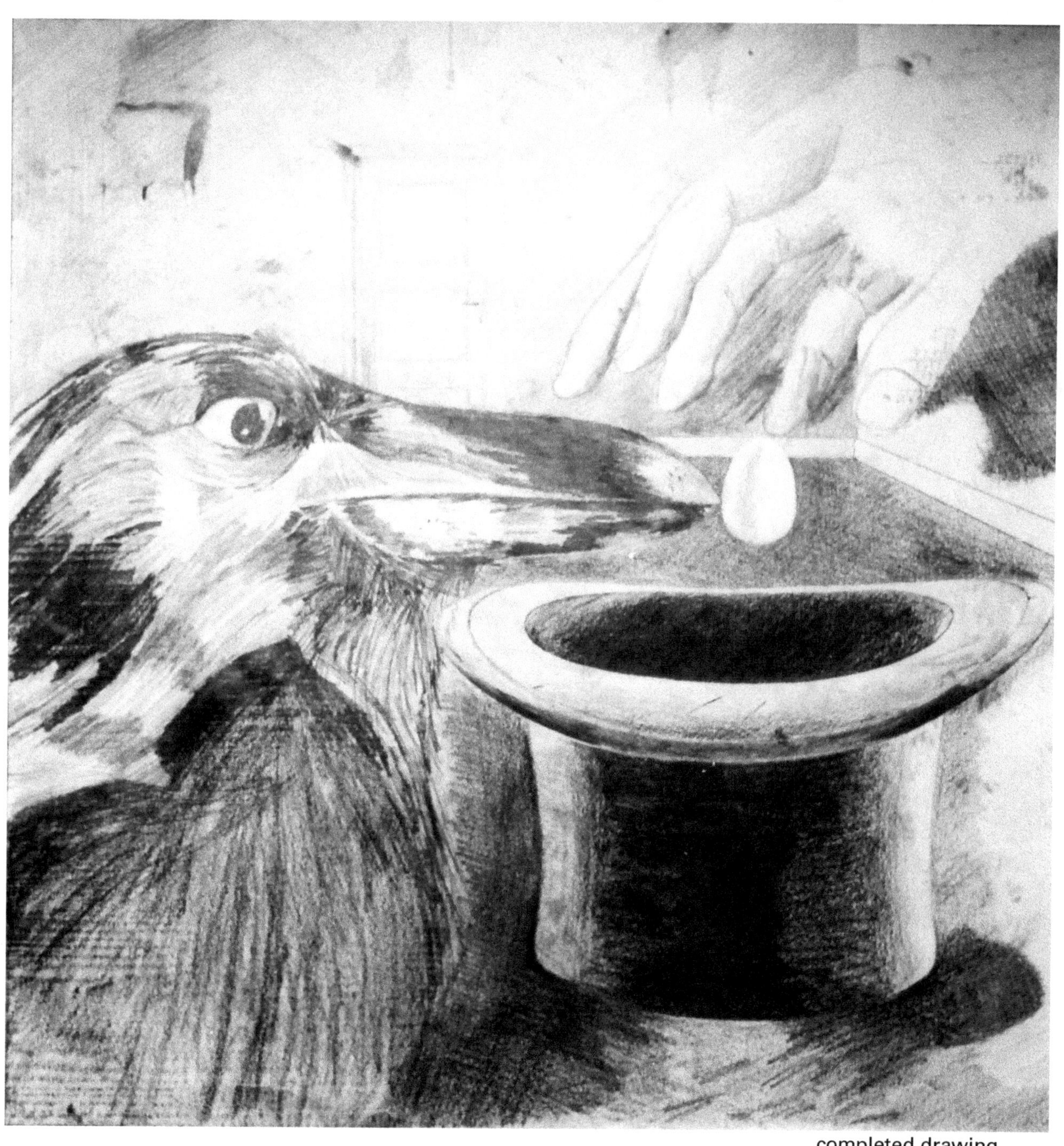

completed drawing

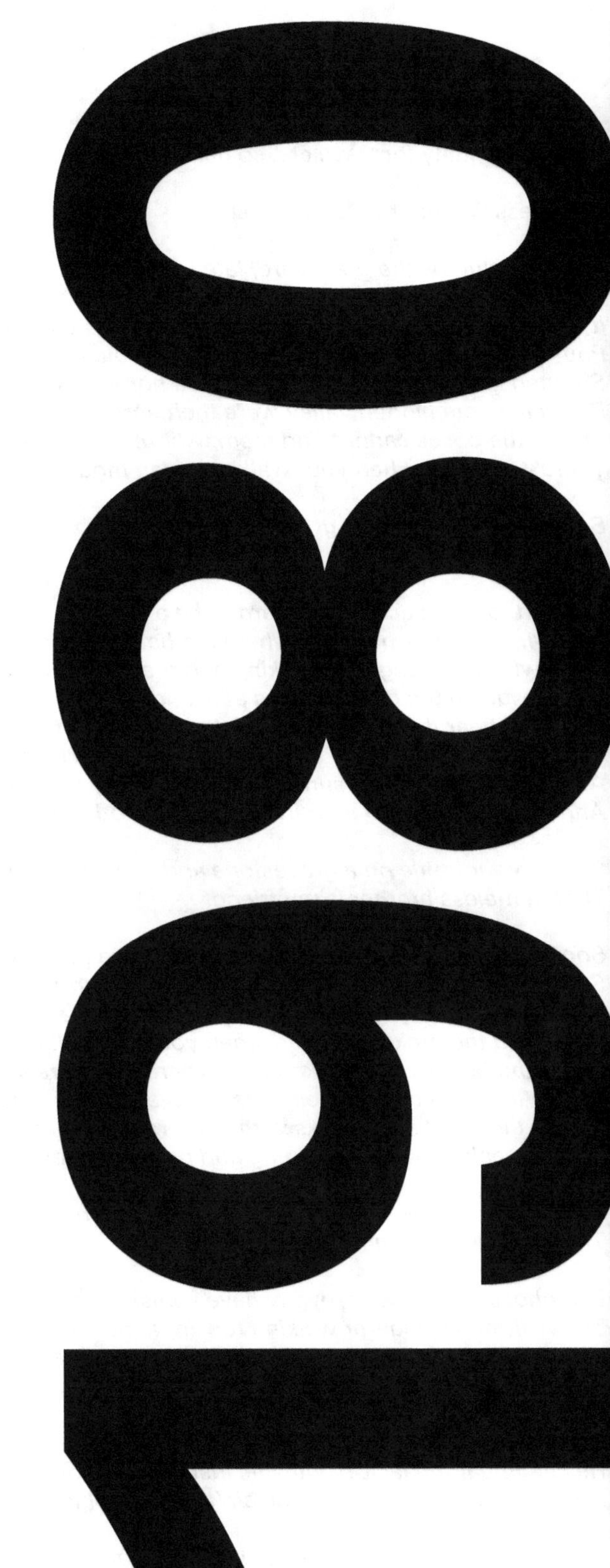
1980

Drawing

I have an affinity for travelers, so here are the lyrics for

Homeless Brother by Don McLean

I was walking by the graveyard, late last Friday night,
I heard somebody yelling, it sounded like a fight.
It was just a drunken hobo dancing circles in the night,
Pouring whiskey on the headstones in the blue moonlight.
So often have I wondered where these homeless brothers go,
Down in some hidden valley were their sorrows cannot show,
Where the police cannot find them, where the wanted men can go.
There's freedom when your walking, even though you're walking slow.

Smash your bottle on a gravestone and live while you can,
That homeless brother is my friend.

It's hard to be a pack rat, it's hard to be a 'bo,
But living's so much harder where the heartless people go.
Somewhere the dogs are barking and the children seem to know
That Jesus on the highway was a lost hobo.
And they hear the holy silence of the temples in the hill,
And they see the ragged tatters as another kind of thrill.
And they envy him the sunshine and they pity him the chill,
And they're sad to do their living for some other kind of thrill.

Smash your bottle on a gravestone and live while you can,
That homeless brother is my friend.

Somewhere there was a woman, somewhere there was a child,
Somewhere there was a cottage where the marigolds grew wild.
But somewhere's just like nowhere when you leave it for a while,
You'll find the broken-hearted when you're travelling jungle-style.
Down the bowels of a broken land where numbers live like men,
Where those who keep their senses have them taken back again,
Where the night stick cracks with crazy rage, where madmen don't pretend,
Where wealth has no beginning and poverty no end.

Smash your bottle on a gravestone and live while you can,
That homeless brother is my friend.

The ghosts of highway royalty have vanished in the night,
The Whitman wanderer walking toward a glowing inner light.
The children have grown older and the cops have gripped us tight,
There's no spot round the melting pot for free men in their flight.
And you who live on promises and prosper as you please,
The victim of your riches often dies of your disease,
He can't hear the factory whistle, just the lonesome freight train's wheeze,
He's living on good fortune, he ain't dying on his knees.

Smash your bottle on a gravestone and live while you can,
That homeless brother is my friend.
That homeless brother is my friend.

pencil on paper

Unfinished drawing in one of my many attempts to deal with the history of my father's desire, and failure, to emigrate, and my pacifist position, derived from my grandfather losing his eyesight and left hand during World War II.

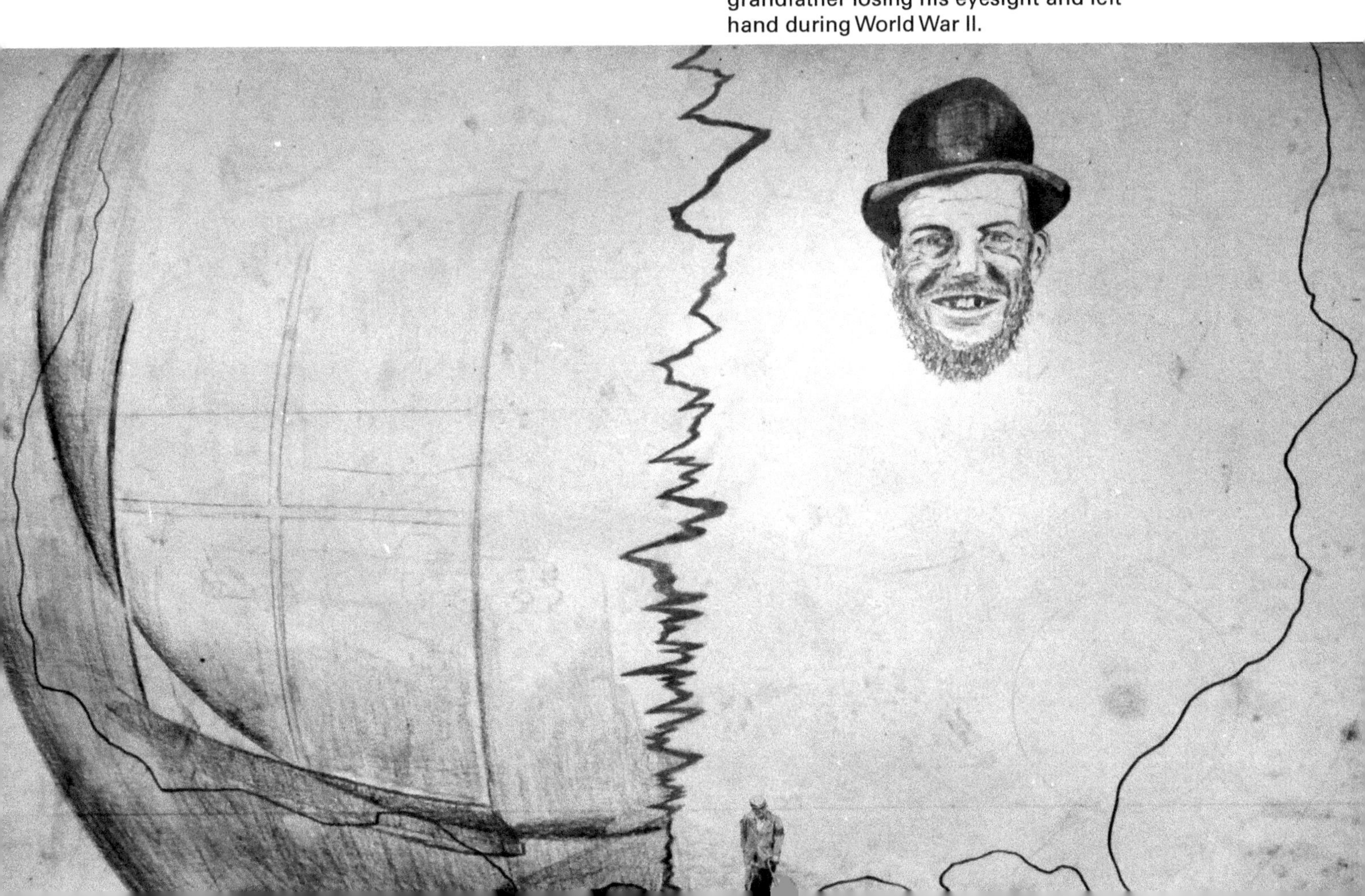

Painting

oil on canvas

When I first met Miriam on the southside of Chicago in the winter of 1980 at Crossroads, I began to think of an appropriate painting that might express the complexity of my emotions. Hobo's Dream was the answer.

Hobo's Dream in situ

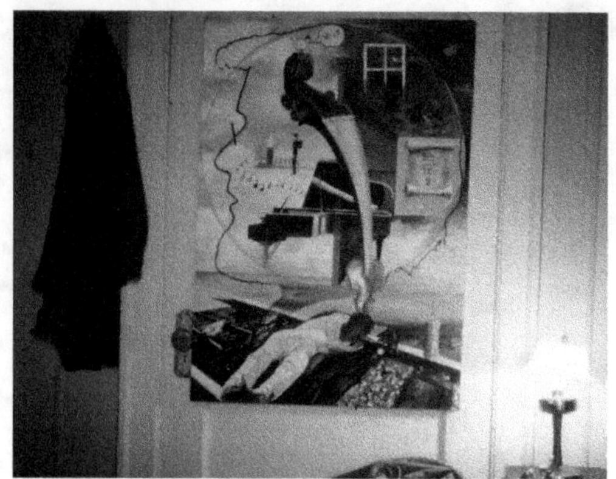

Hobo's Dream

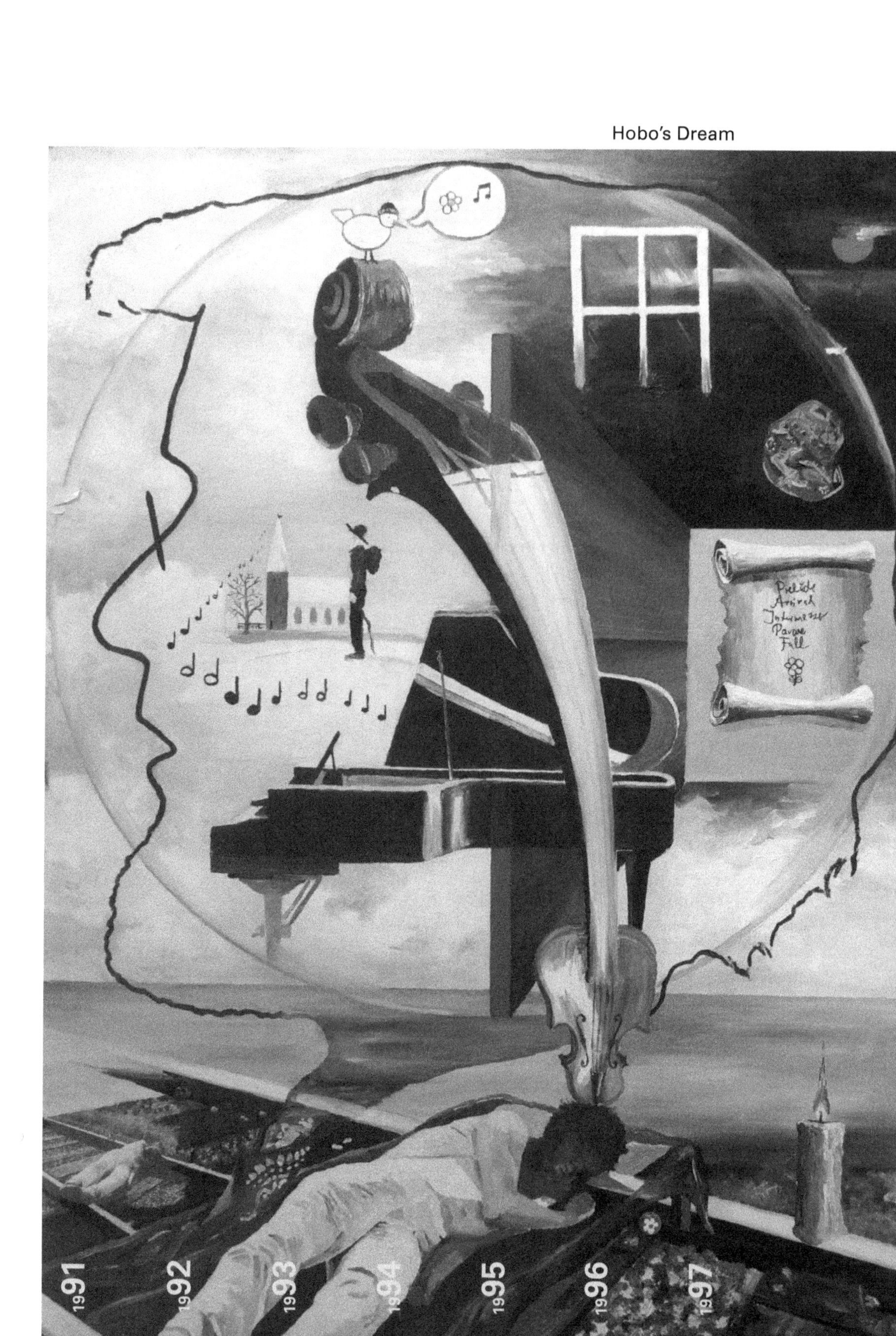

Painting

oil on wood board

S. Daydreaming, after the painting *Träumerei* (see below) from 1906 by Heinrich Vogeler (1872-1942) >

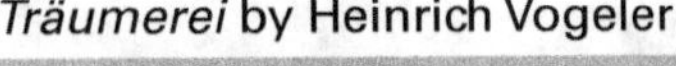

Träumerei by Heinrich Vogeler

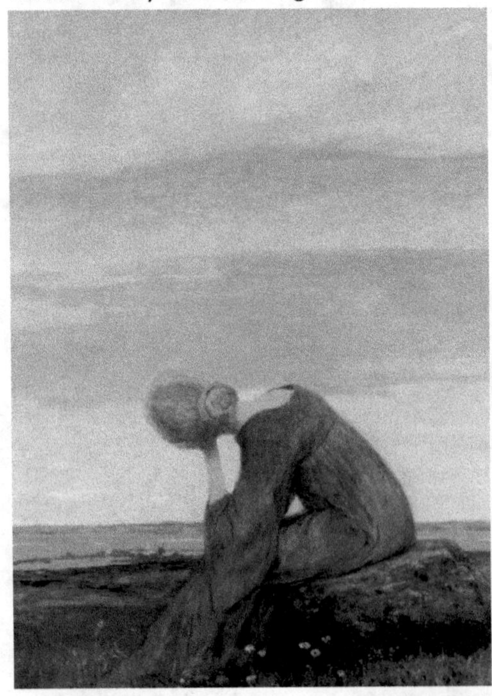

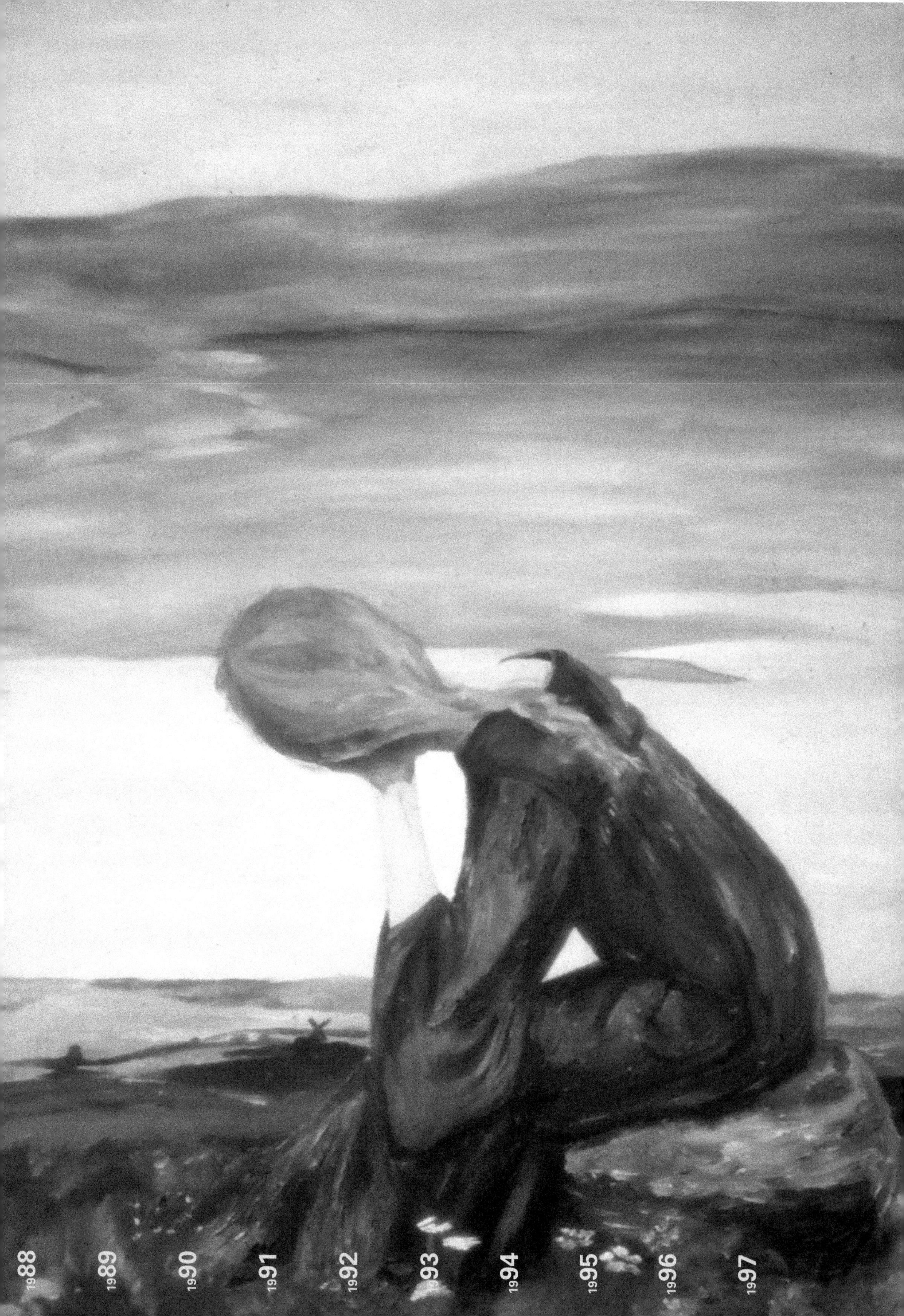
1988
1989
1990
1991
1992
1993
1994
1995
1996
1997

1981

Photography

After returning to Germany in the Summer of 1980 I began my civil service, in lieu of military service, in late Fall at the Wiehmbeck orphanage near Lemgo. By the Spring of 1981 I had become used to the children and their problems, and had learned quite a bit from working with the manager of the orphanage on maintenance projects in the complex.

Painting a car from one of the staff with the children (photo by Miriam Zach)

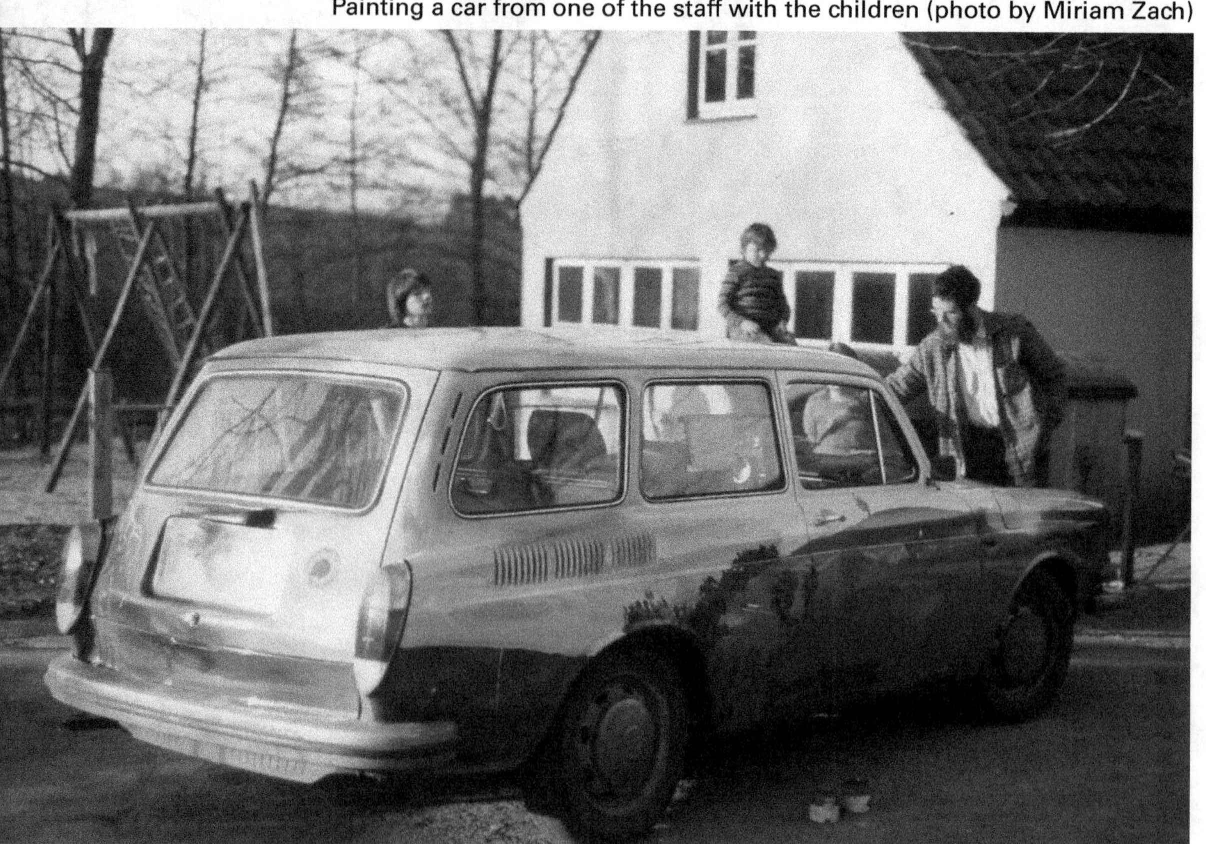

Oliver Knauer and children in the smoking room at Wiembeck orphanage while I'm trying to paint another still life
(photo by Miriam Zach)

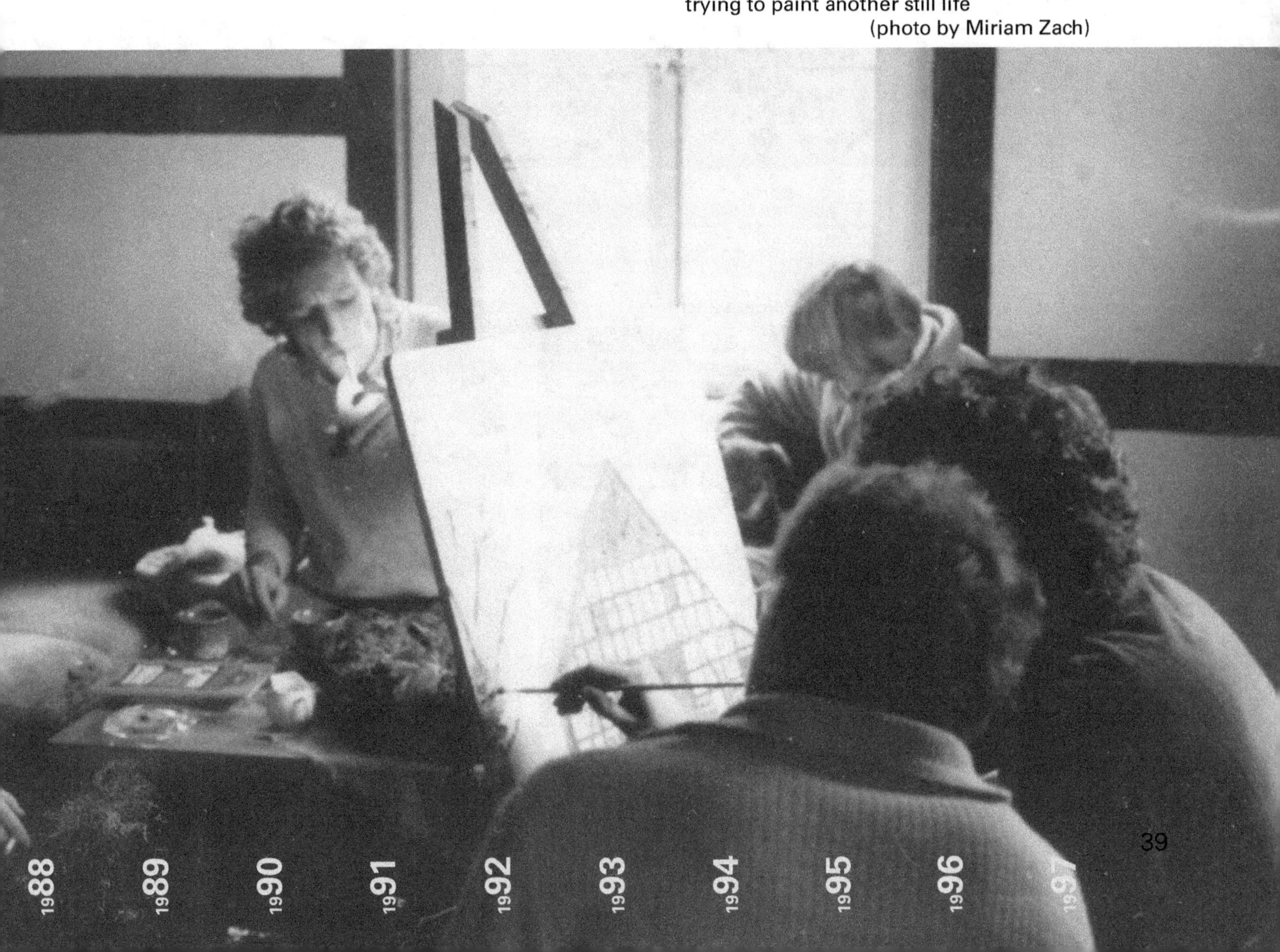

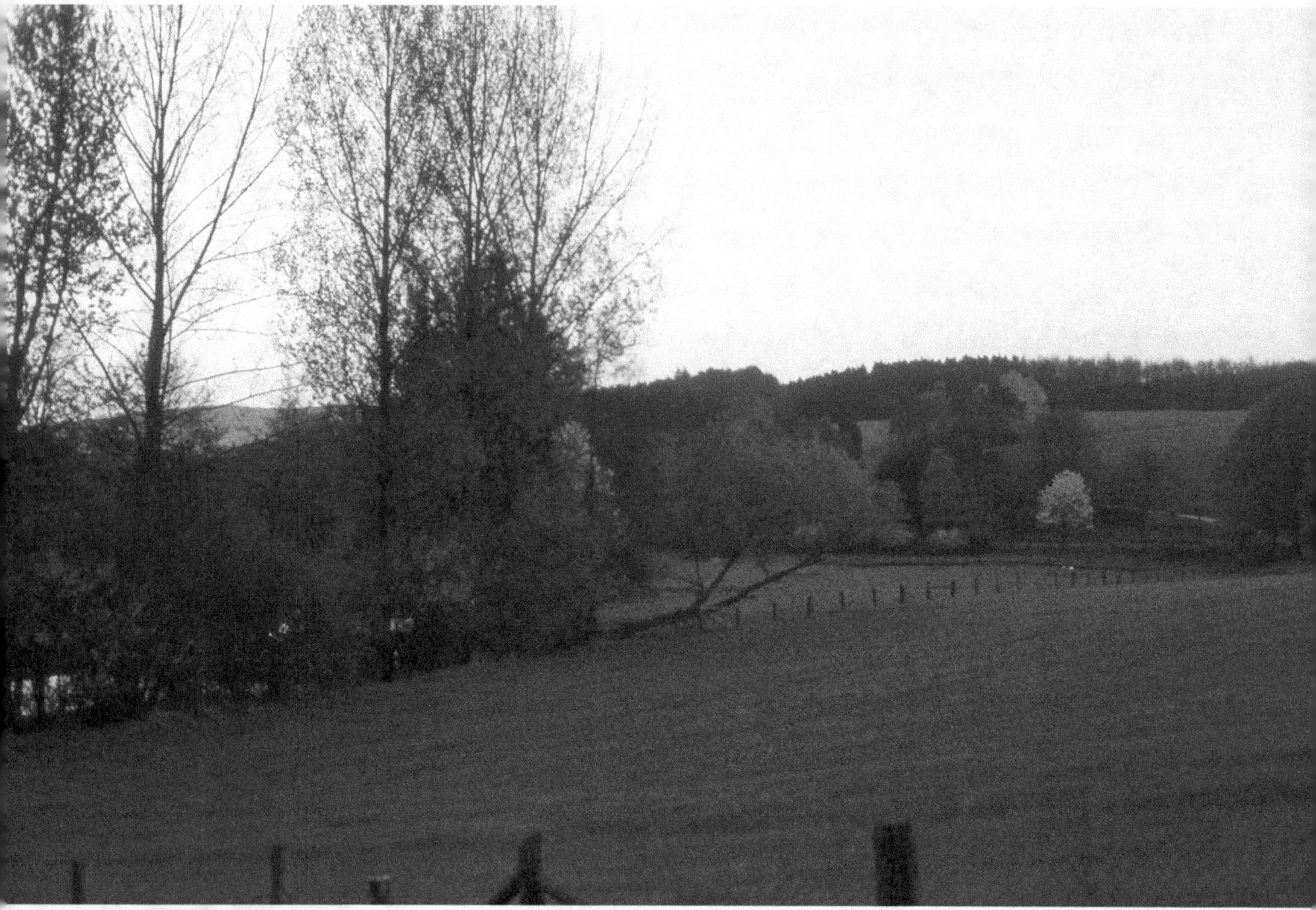

Photography

Near Wiembeck

Foosball at the orphanage (photo by Miriam Zach)

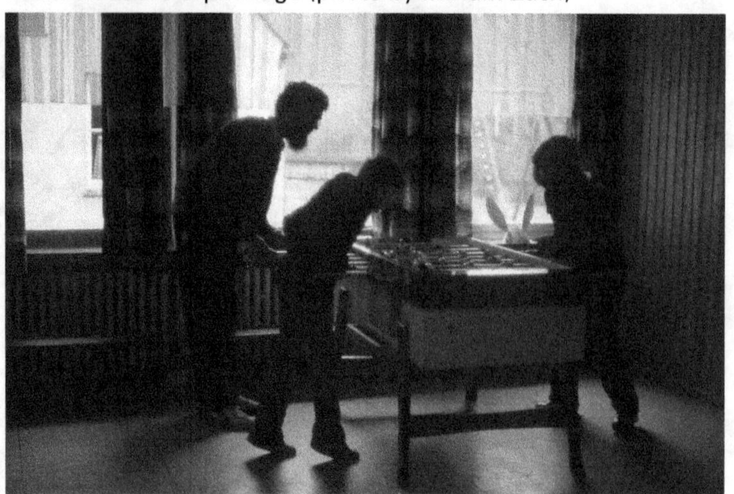

Main building of the orphanage

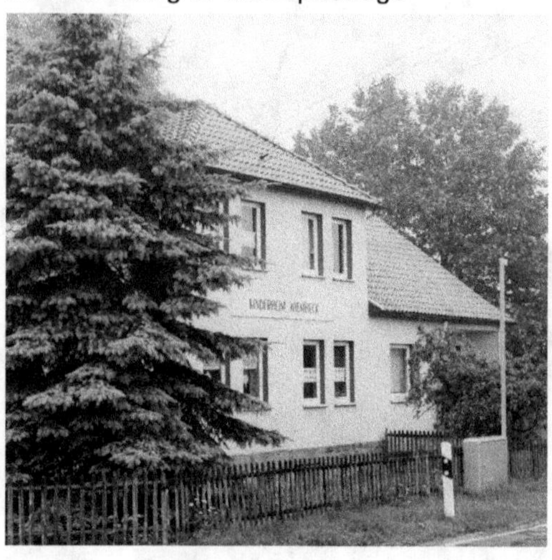

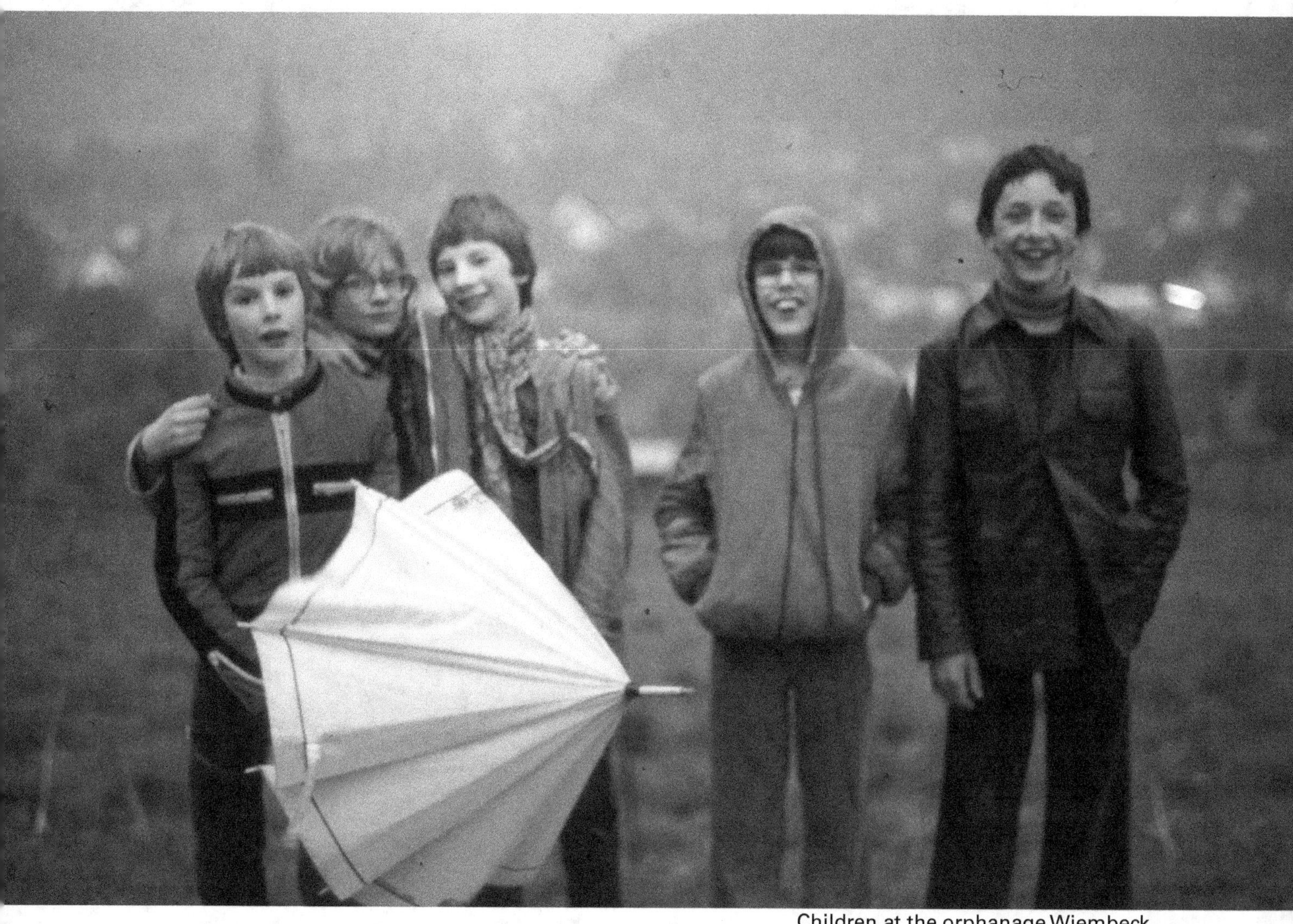

Children at the orphanage Wiembeck

In the early spring we travelled to Paris and Versailles
(next page) interior of mirror hall, Versailles >

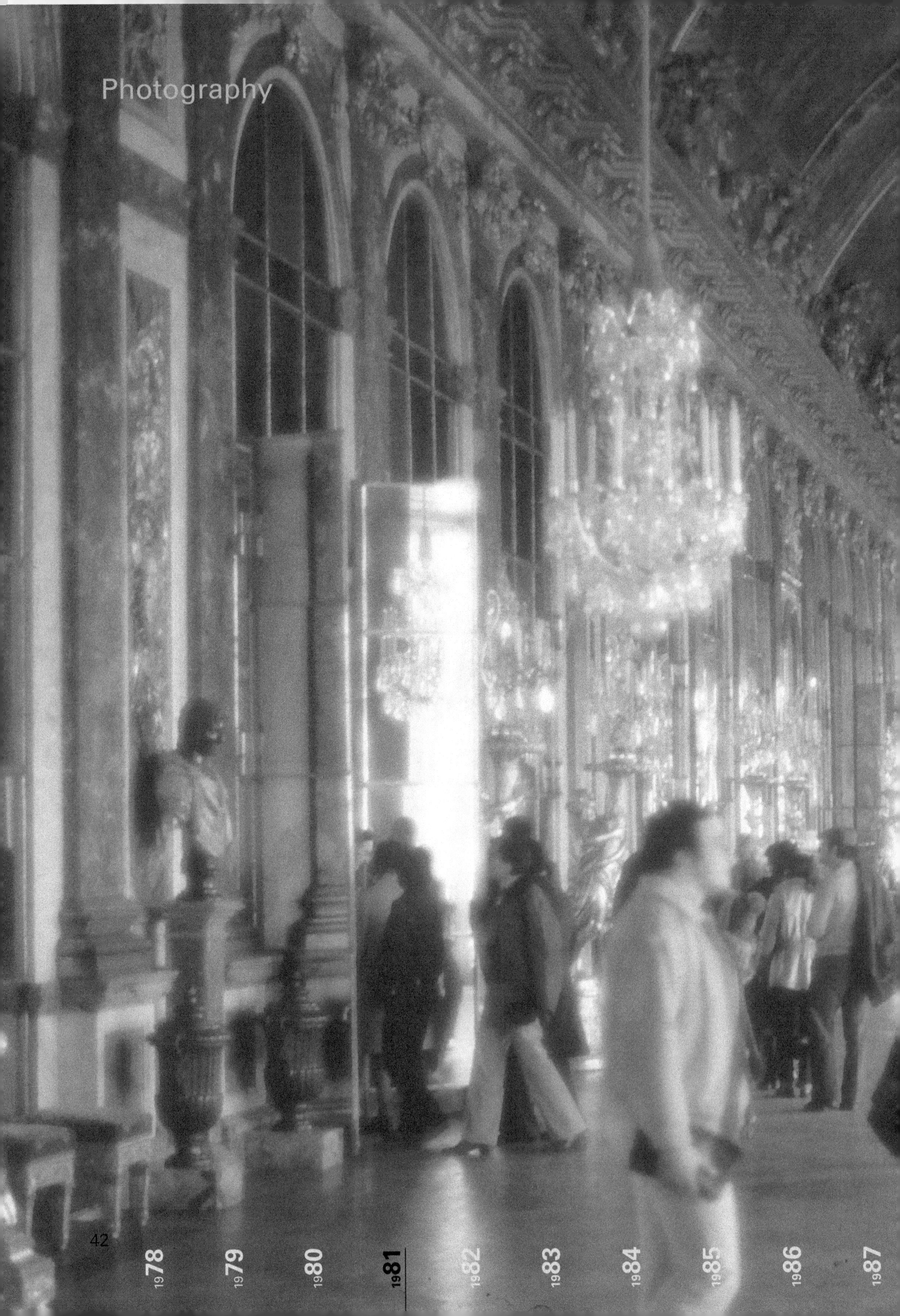

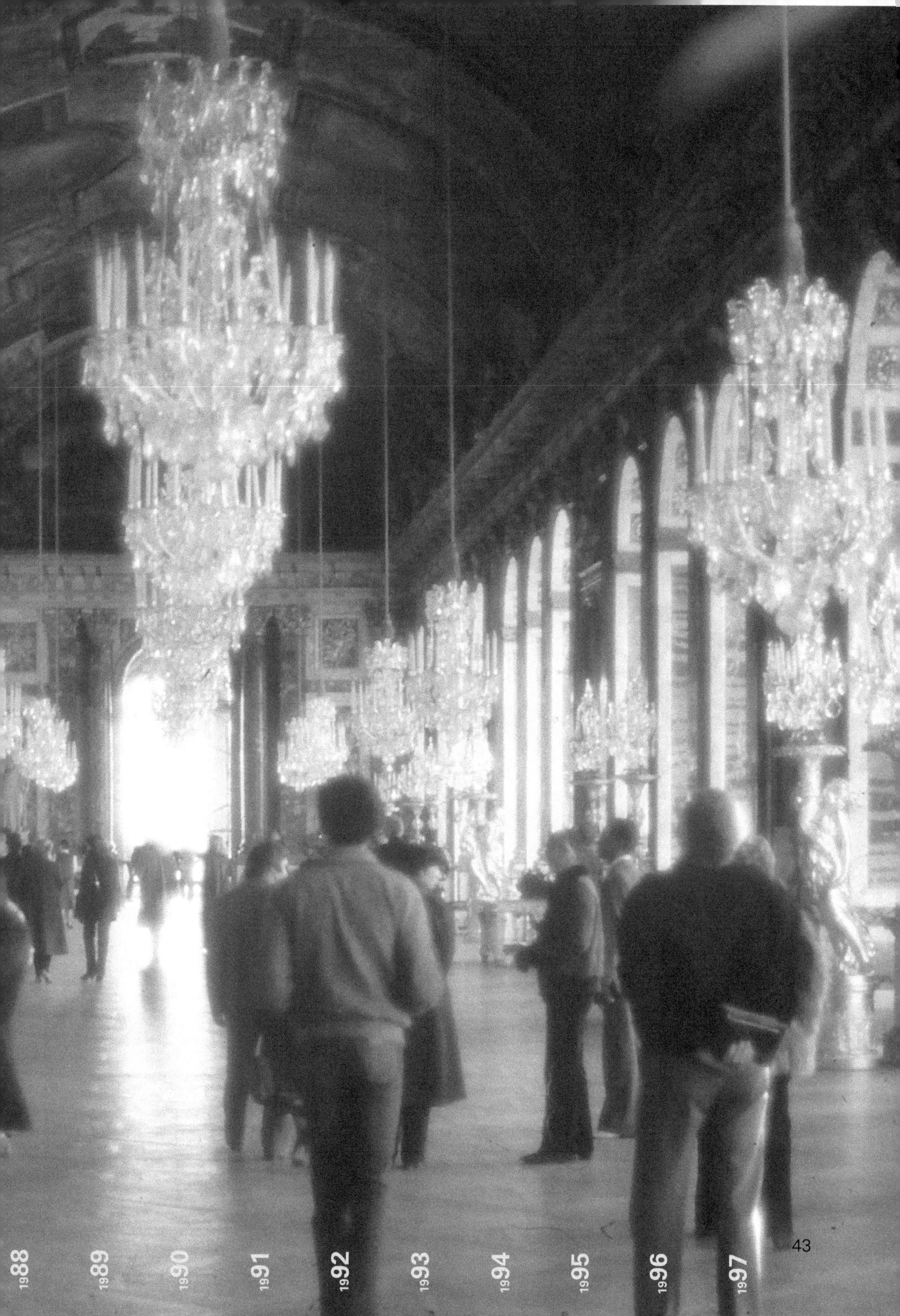

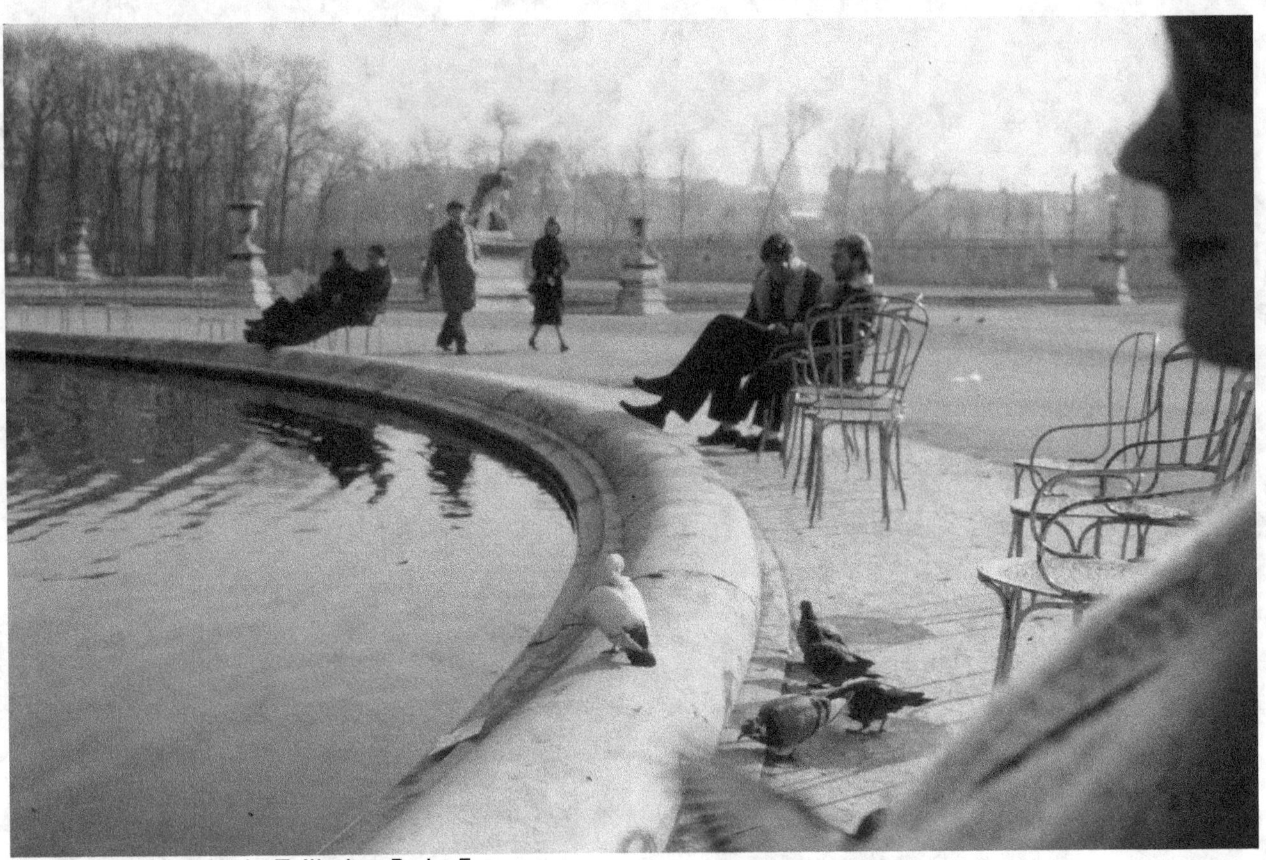

Sunday morning in the Tuilleries, Paris, France

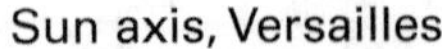

Sun axis, Versailles

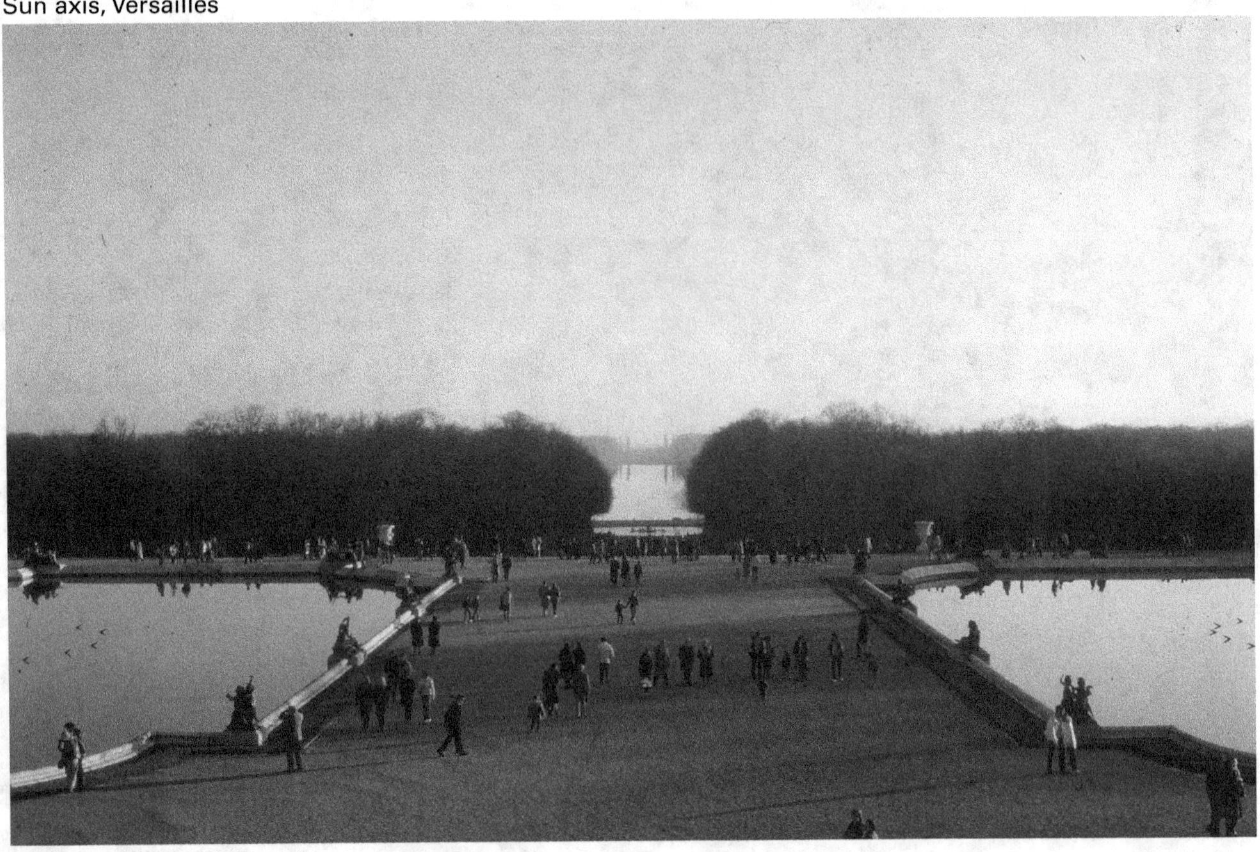

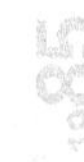
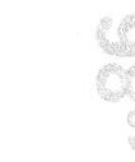

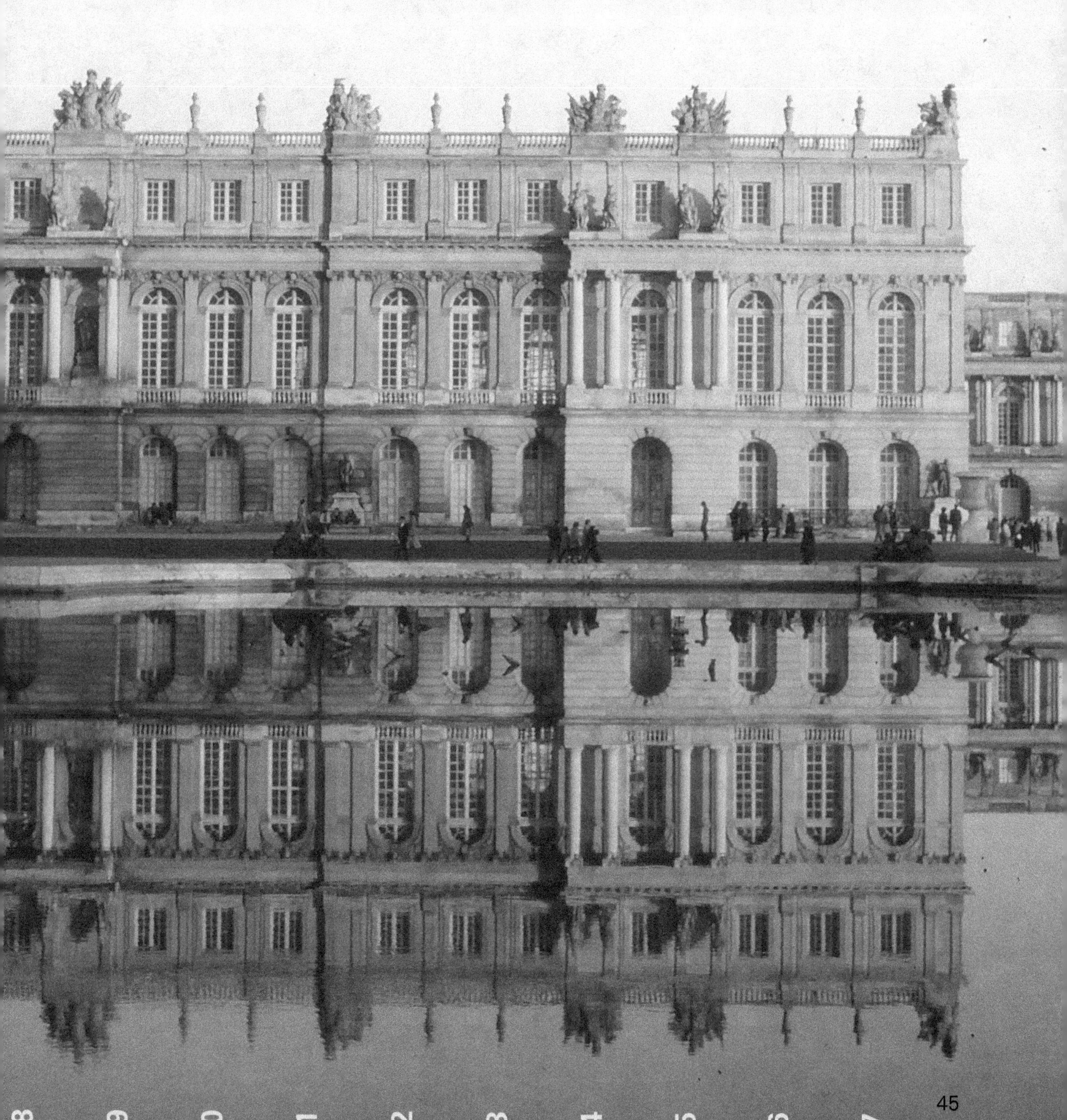

1988

1989

1990

1991

1992

1993

1994

1995

1996

1997

Versailles in December

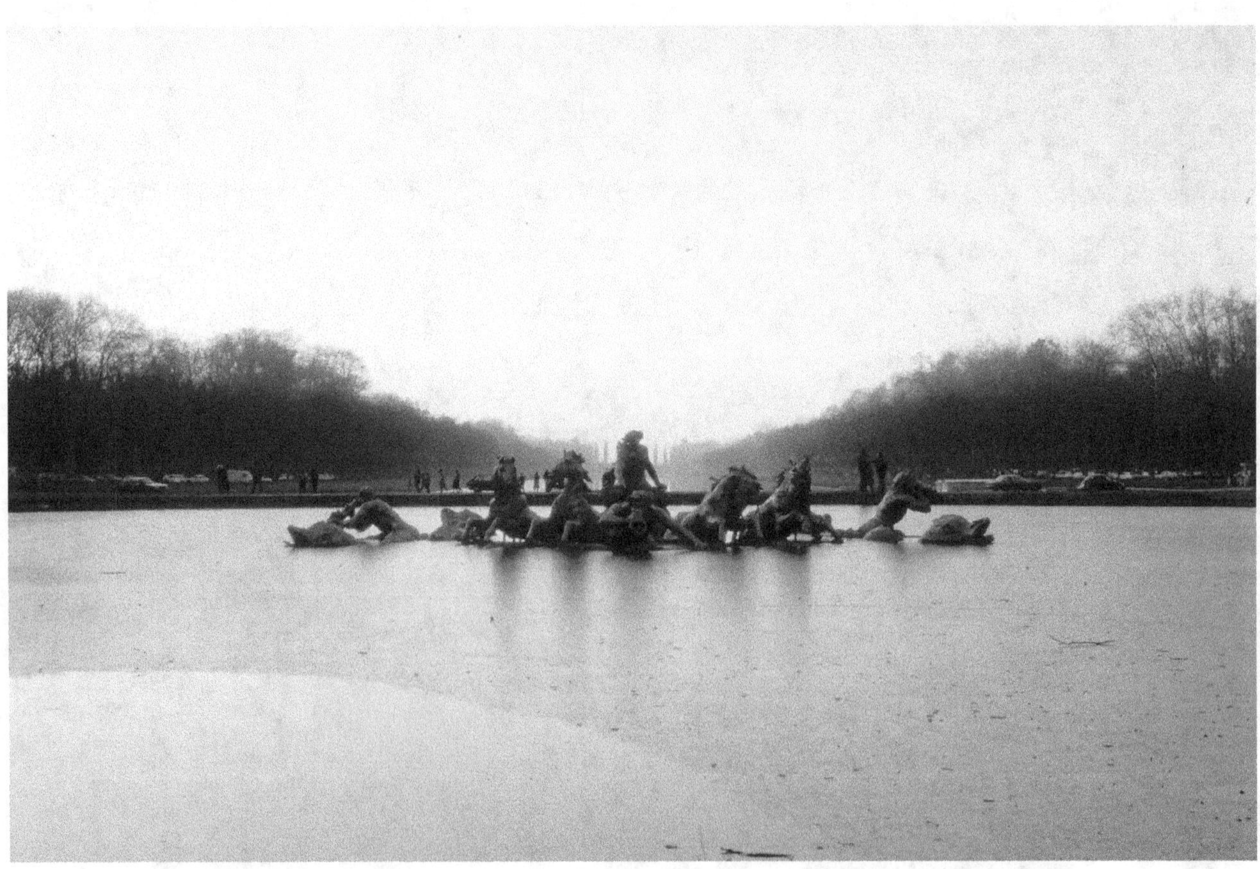

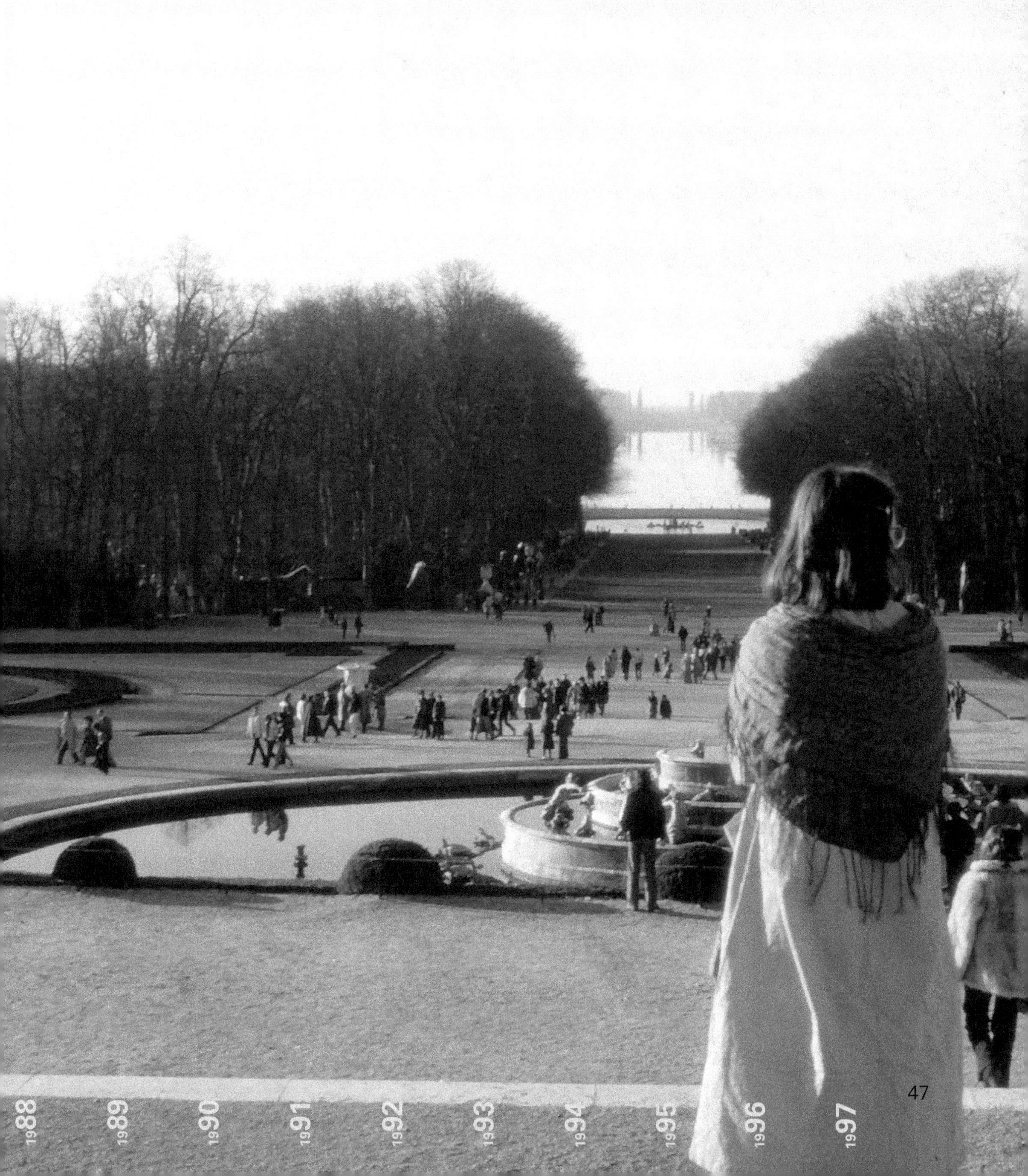

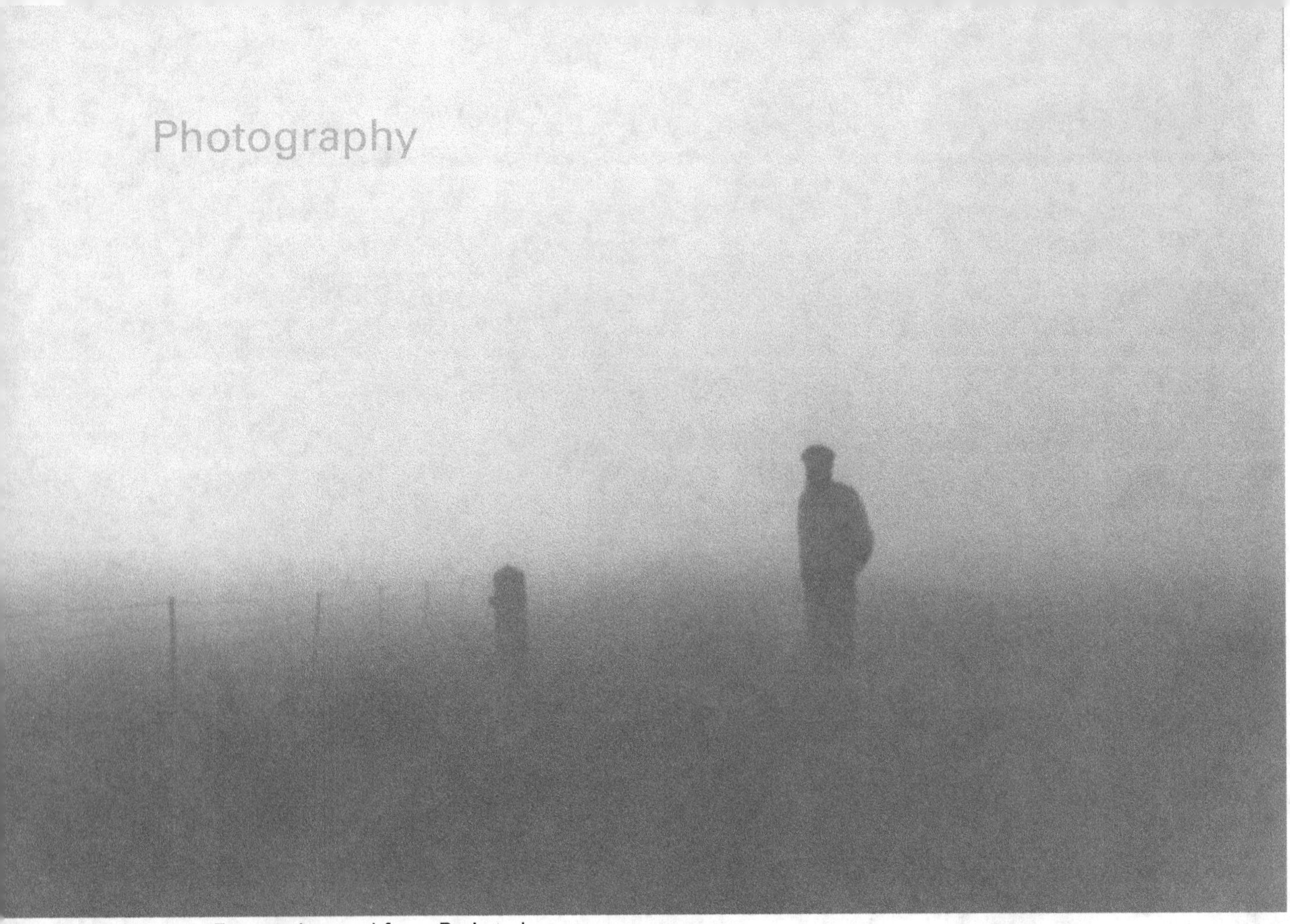

Fog on the road from Paris to Lemgo

My brother and I somewhere in France on our way to pick up Miriam at the Luxembourg airport. We took the doors off of the Citroën to increase the airflow inside the car

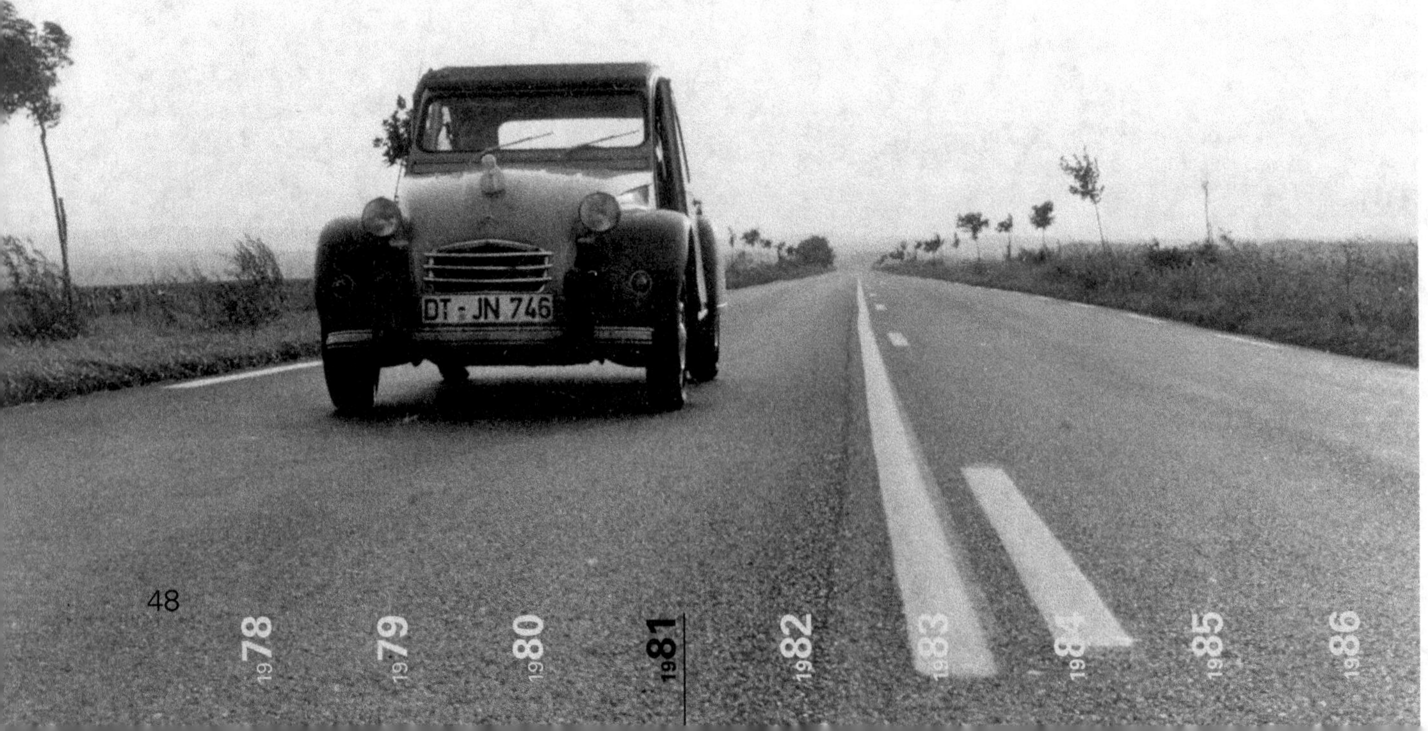

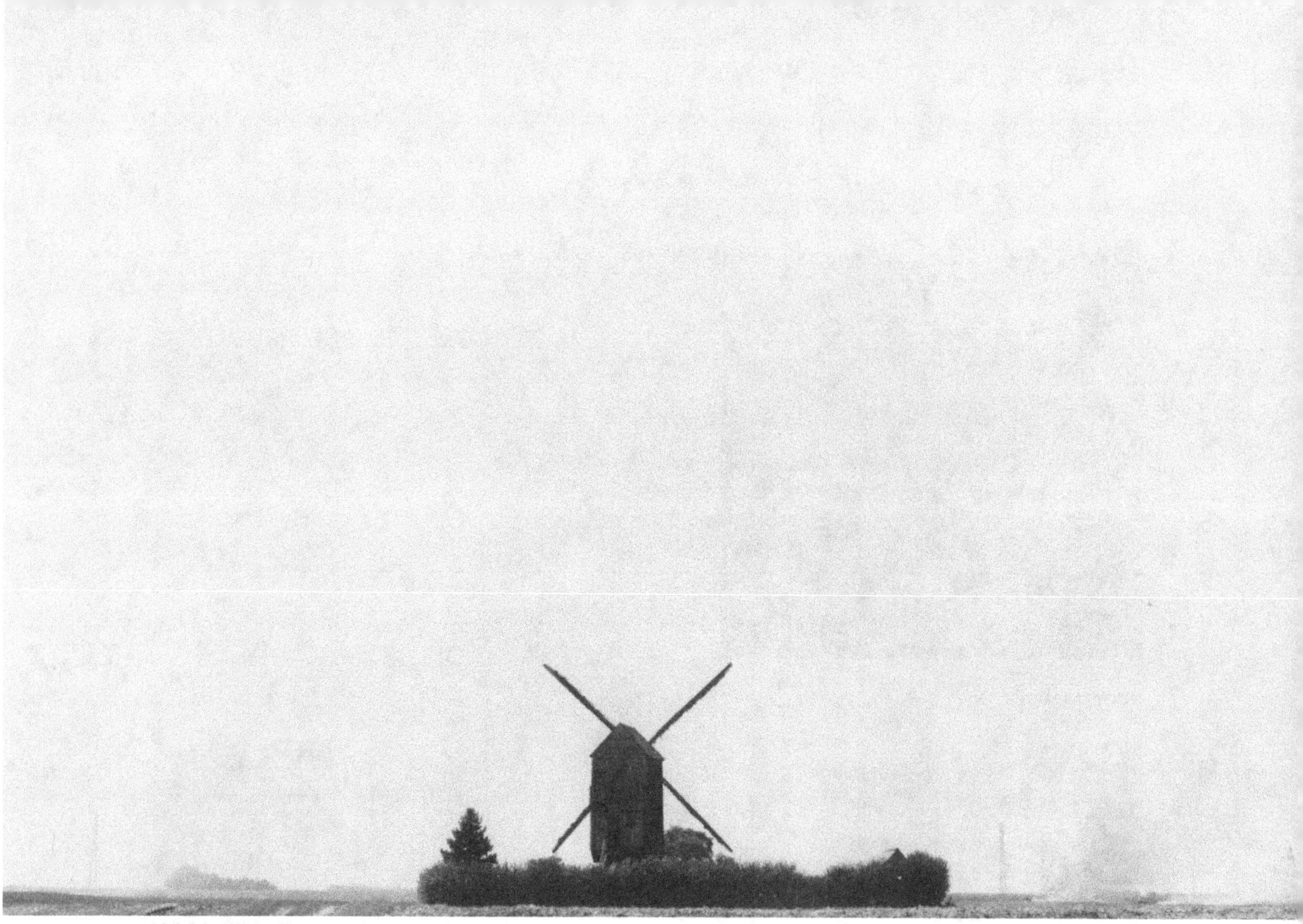

Windmill in France. It was a hot summer day with a strong wind from the south, blowing the freshly cut grain stalks across the golden yellow fields

Woman feeding two cats in Venezia, Italia

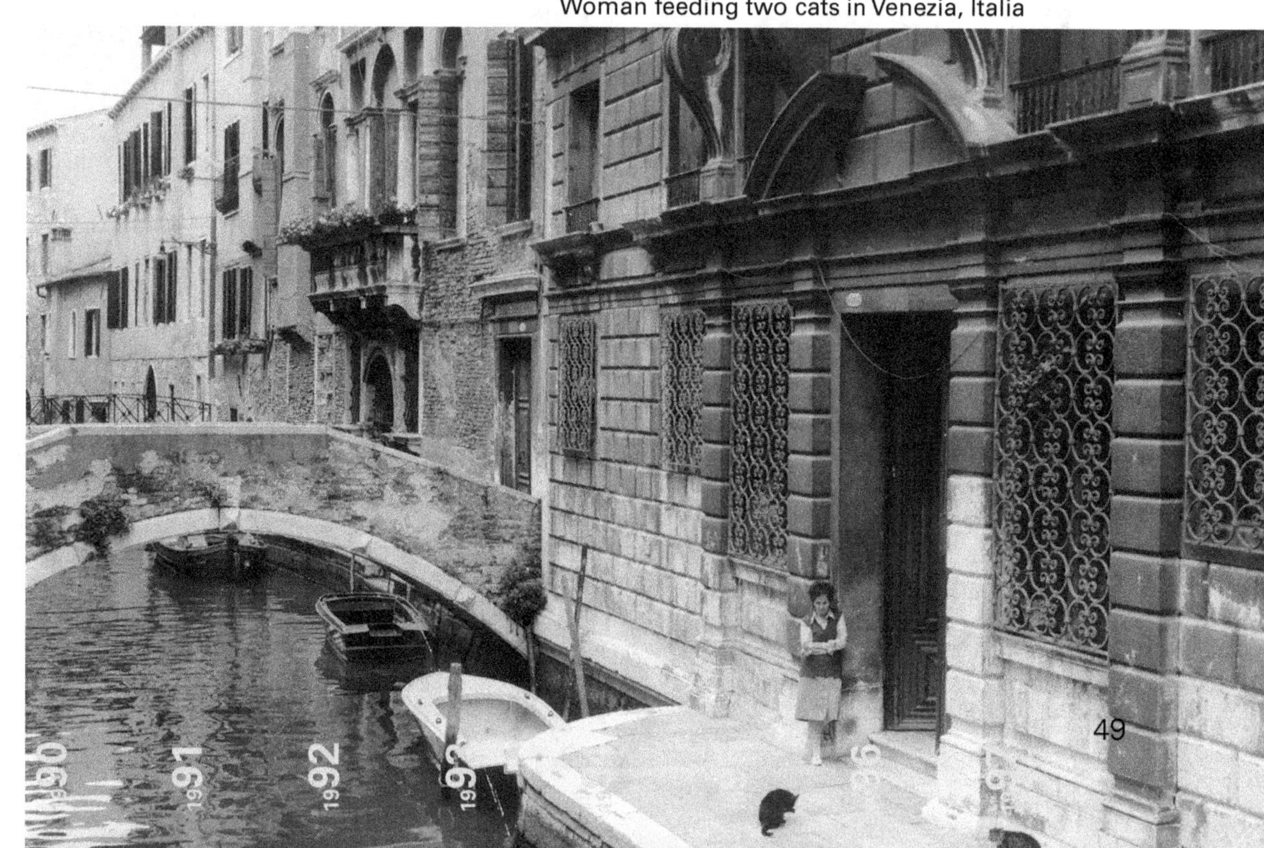

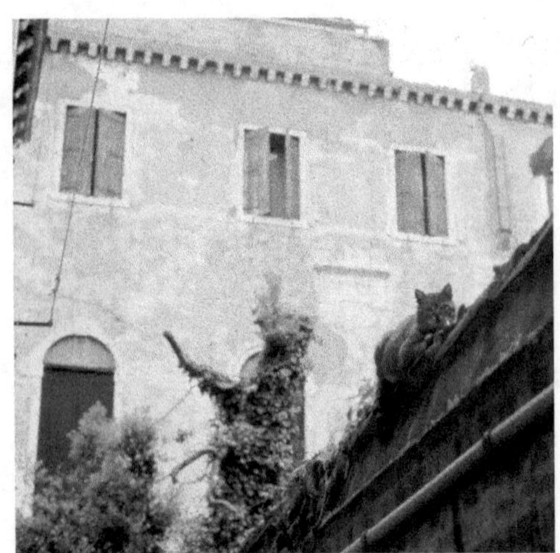

Venezia, Italia

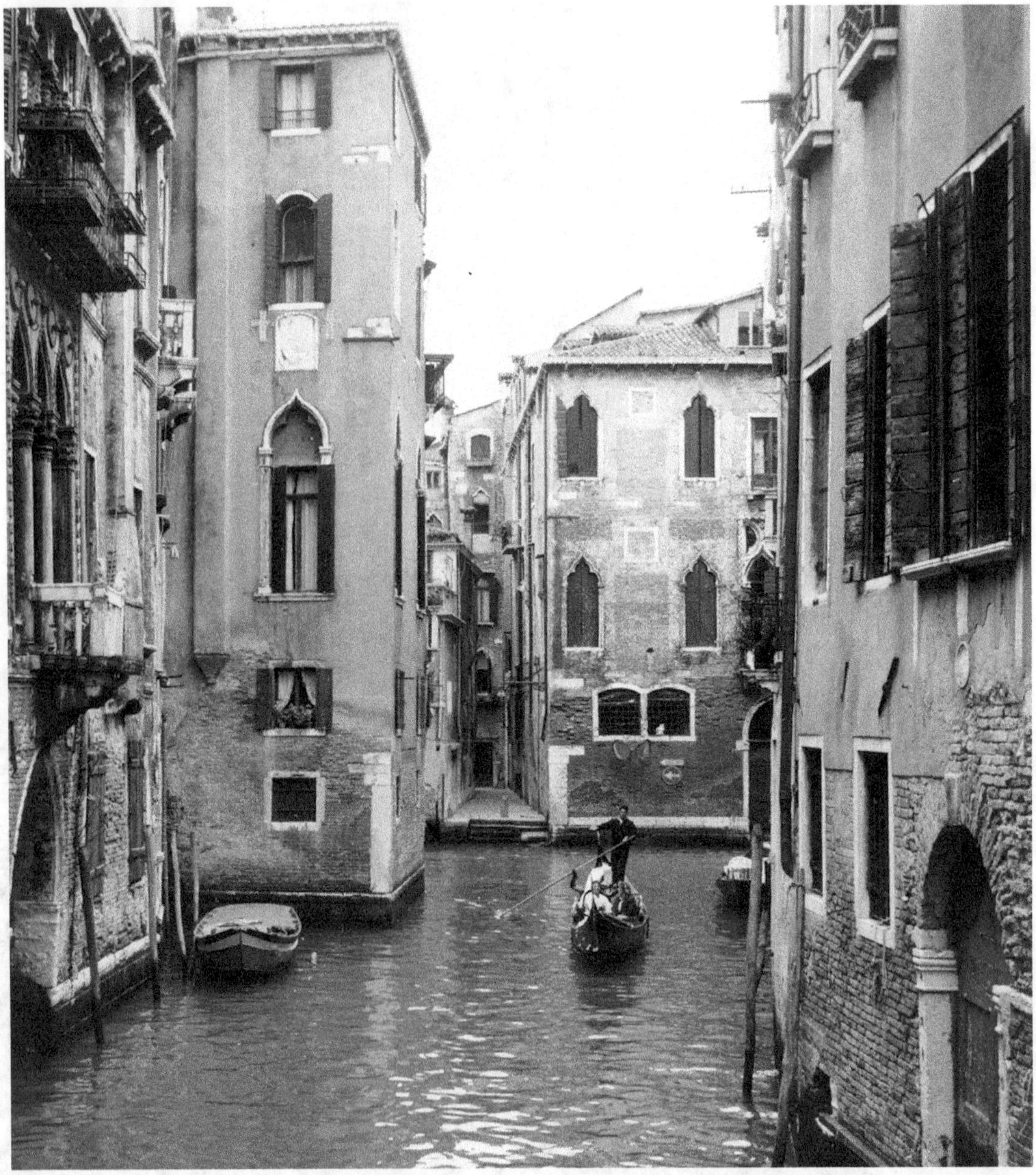

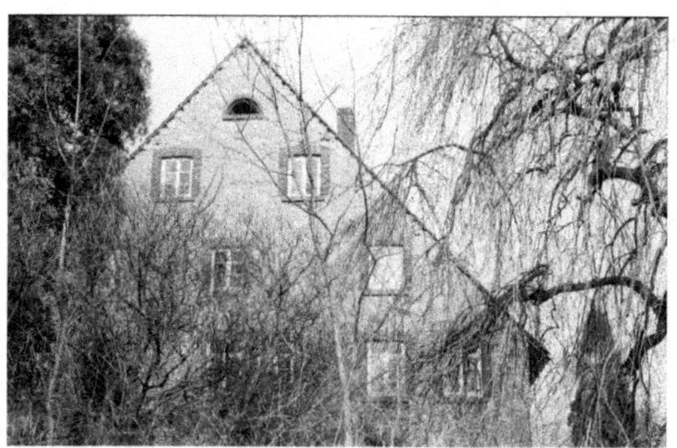

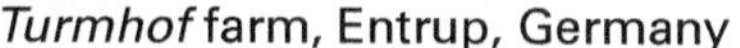
Turmhof farm, Entrup, Germany

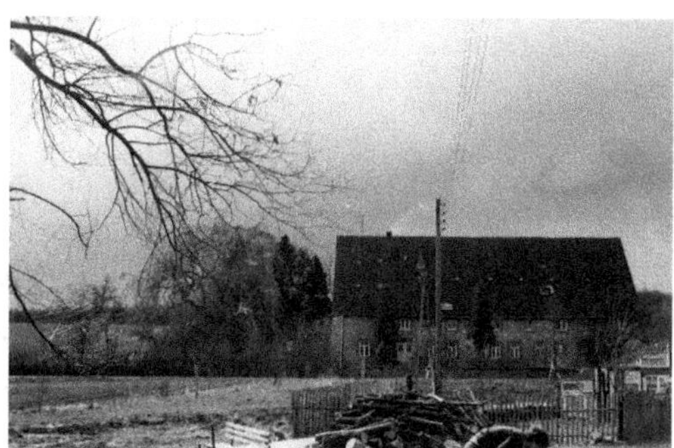
Turmhof farm as seen from watermill

While I was still working at the orphanage, and Miriam had established her music school, we decided to move out of the staff house and try our hands at communal living with eight other idealists on the outskirts of Lemgo. Early on, when there still existed a seemingly perpetual hope for a communal future, or at least the tolerance of a communal moment, the kitchen at the *Turmhof* farm seemed like a romantic French café

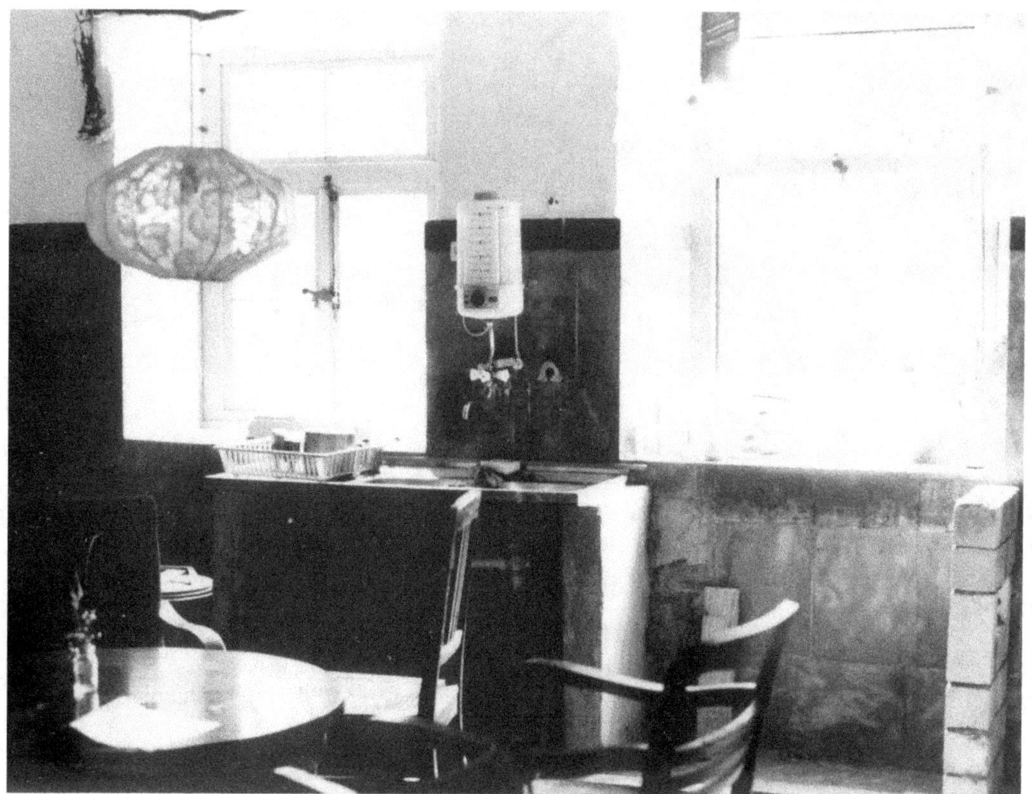

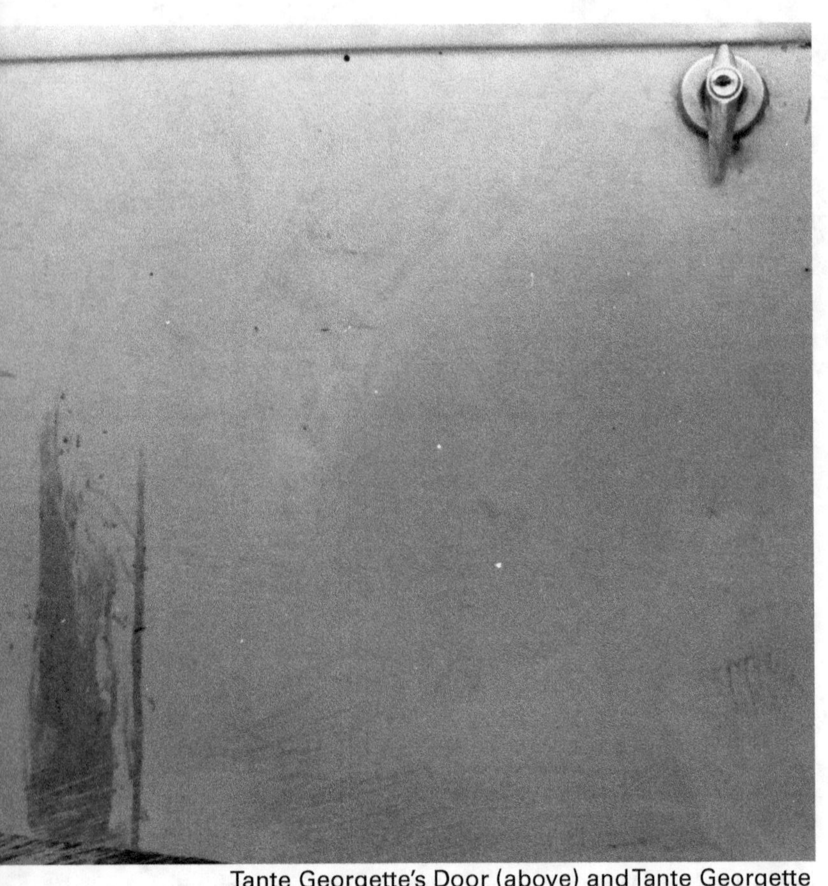

Tante Georgette's Door (above) and Tante Georgette and Miriam (below) somewhere in southern France

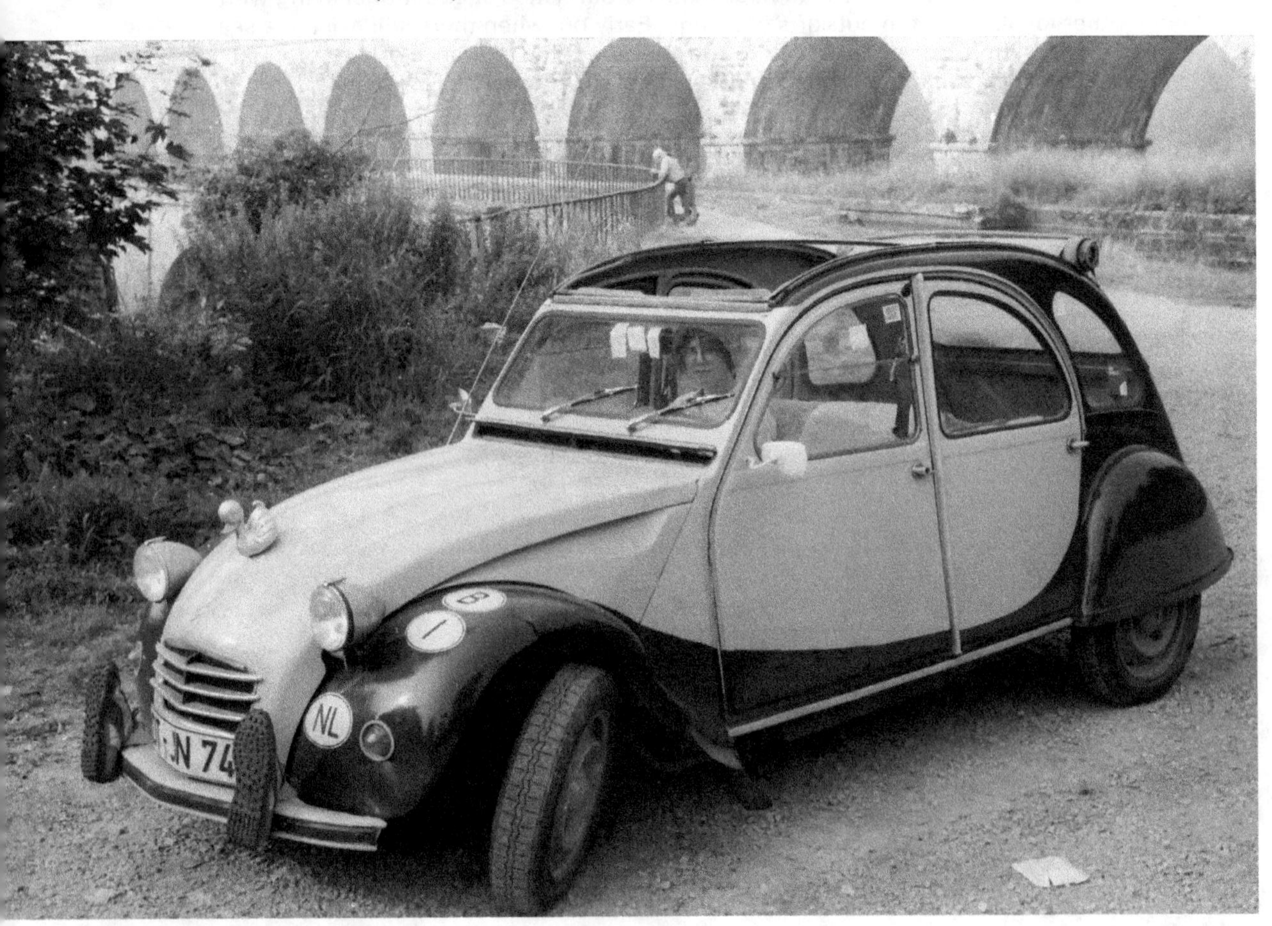

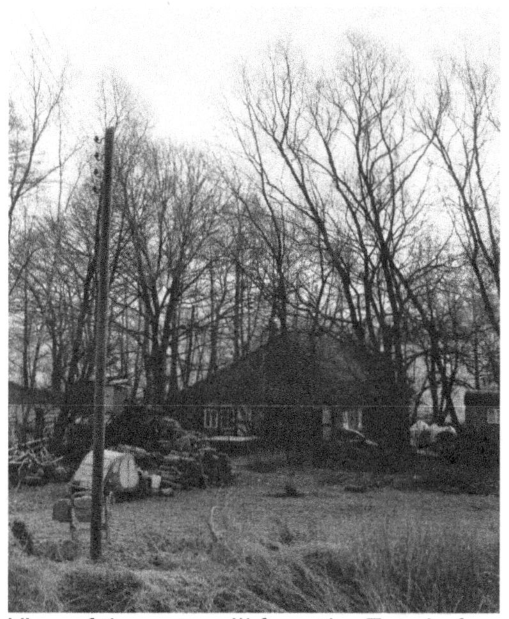

View of the watermill from the *Turmhof* farm

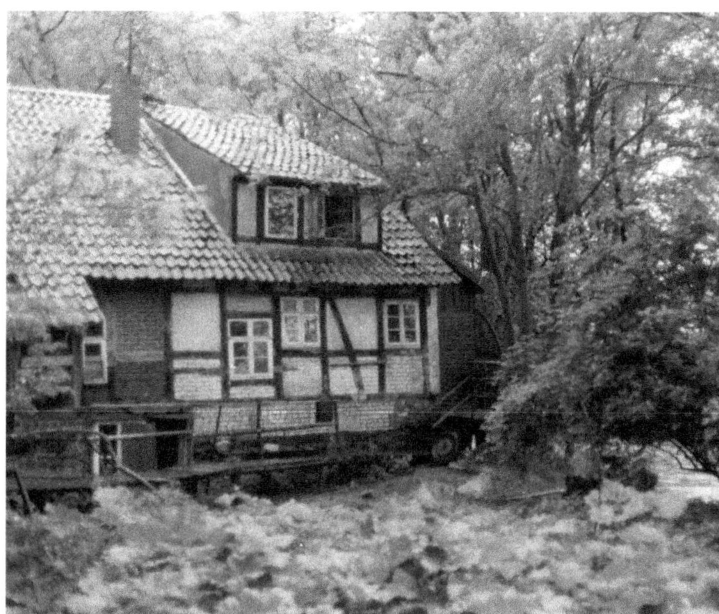

View of the watermill

From the northwest, early on a cold winter morning, the watermill looks like a mother hen with chicks under her outspread wings/roof

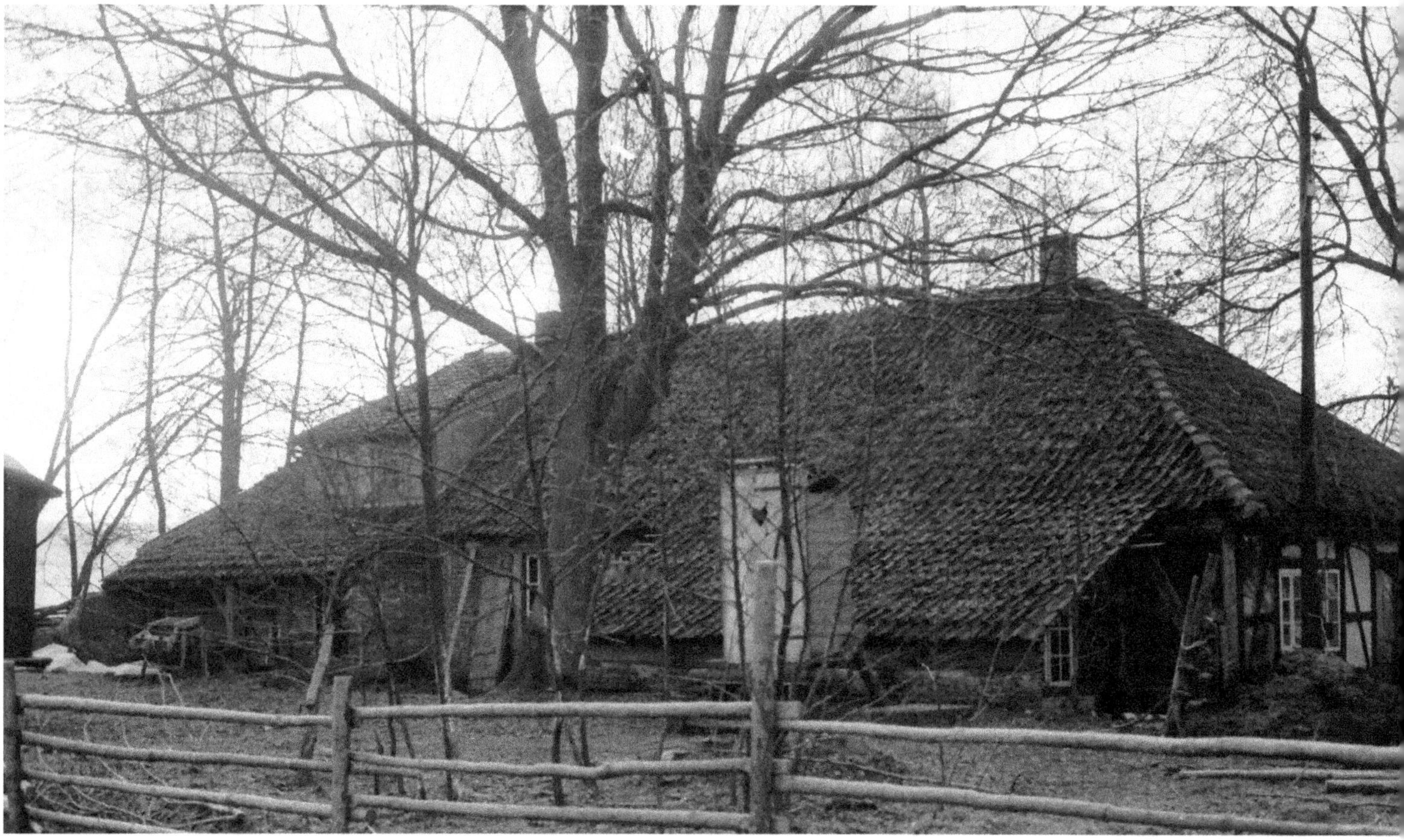

Gerda, the tractor, in the meadow behind the *Turmhof* farm

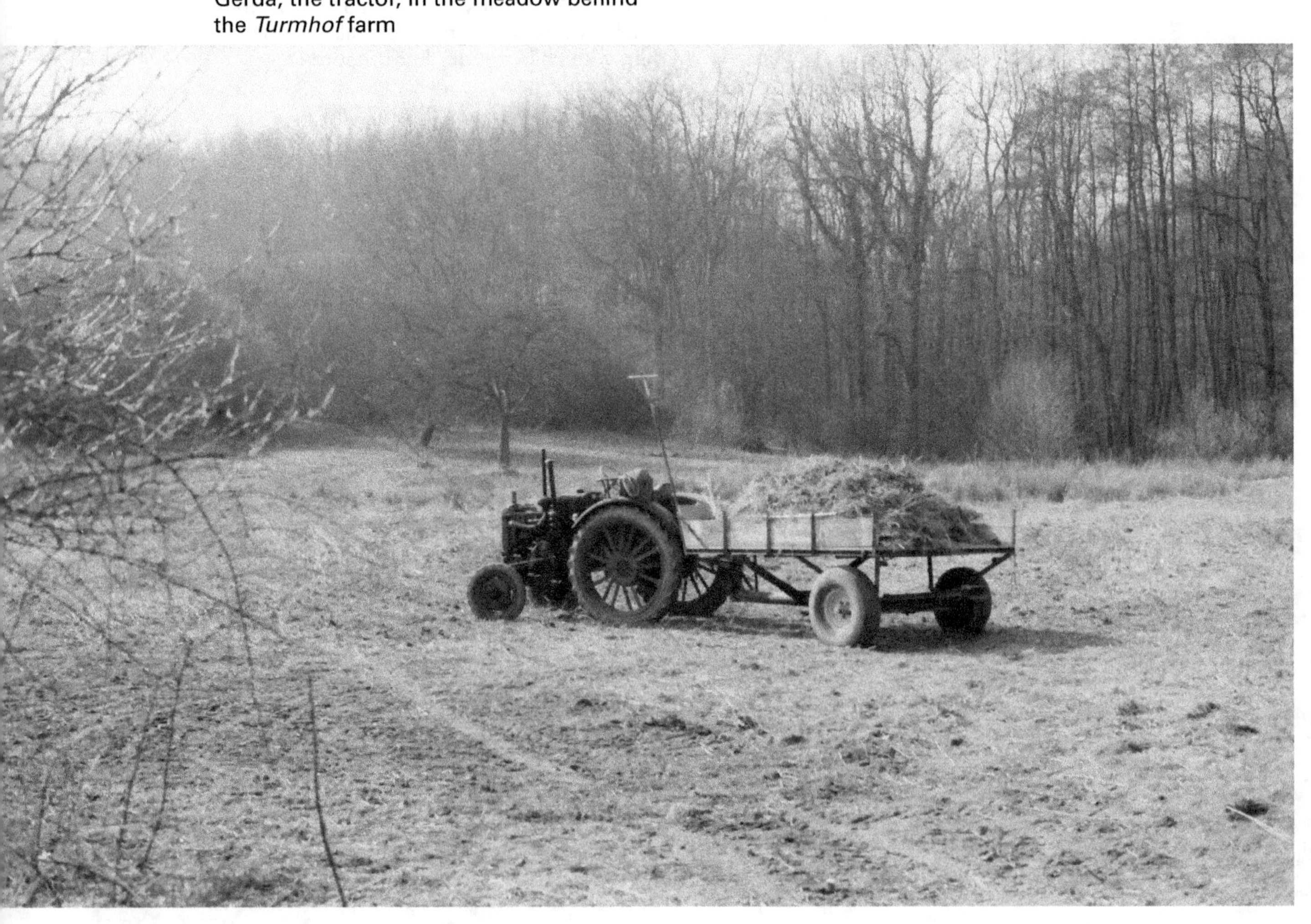

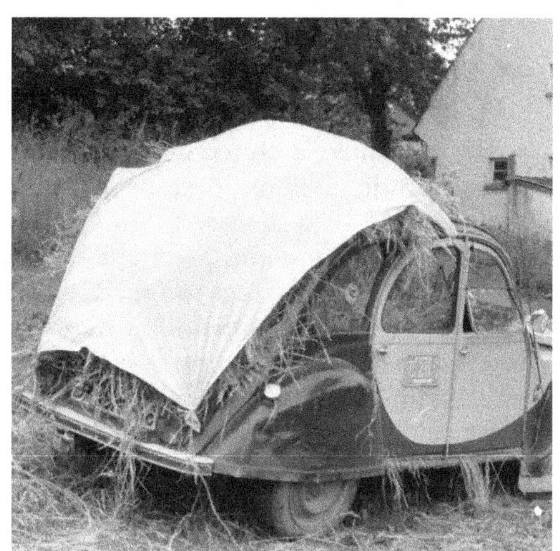

Bringing in a harvest of dry straw before the rain...

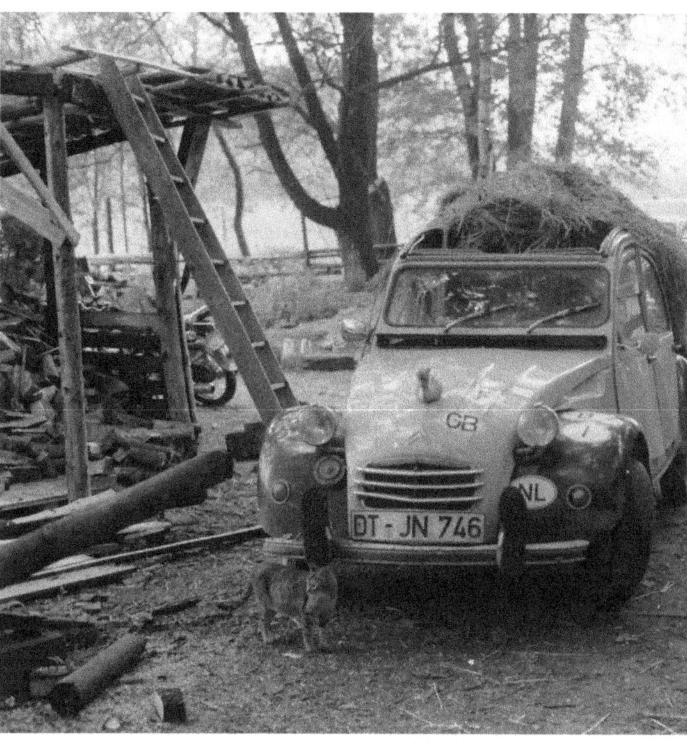

...and enjoying the view out from the watermill, with a good beer and the chickens, after the rain started (photo by Miriam Zach)

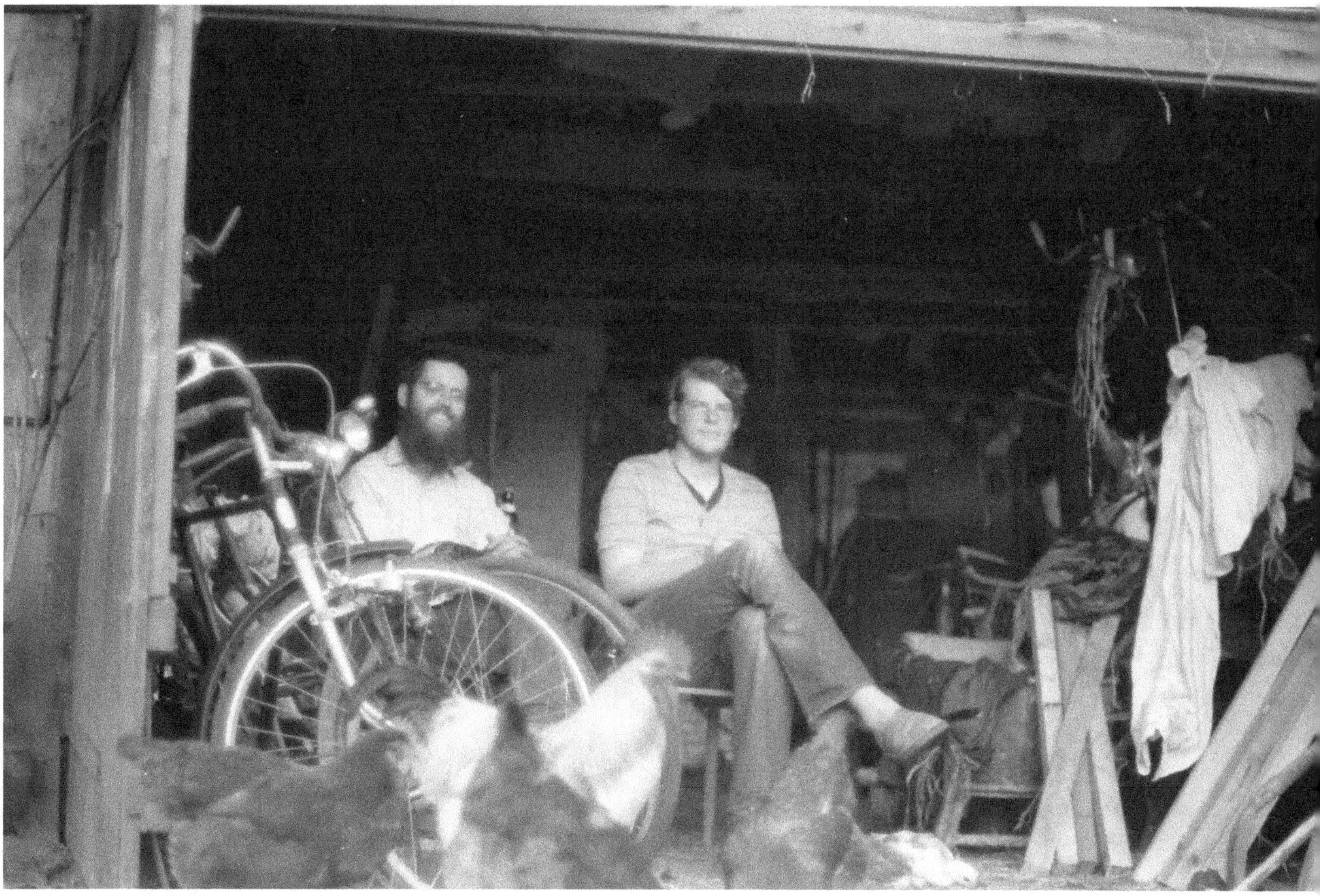

Circus Trailer Living Quarters
Da Capo Conversion

In the summer of 1981 we thought about creating an inexpensive living space that would not require monthly rental payments to a landlord. Our solution for this problem was to invest some saved money, 1200 DM to be exact, in a retired circus trailer, about 32 feet in length, nine feet wide, and with a maximum inside height of eight feet (see Plan #1 on the next page).

The trailer, named Da Capo, was completely empty when we bought it, and in no way thermally ready for the cold winters in Germany. The first step was to analyze what kind of space we had available, and then compare that with our ideas for a living space. Our first solution was realized over the first two years of living in the trailer (see Plan #2 on page 70). This is a relatively conventional design with a strict separation of living, eating, and sleeping.

Some time during the summer of 1983 we felt the need to expand the space, if not physically then visually, as well as change the concept of the rooms. We were interested in Japanese architecture and decided after long discussions to convert the living room and the bedroom into a Japanese-style environment. We built a raised platform in the living room, insulated the space between new and old floor, and covered the new floor surface in a typical four-tatami pattern with self-made straw mats (see Plan #3 on page 98).

We designed a collapsible table for the center half mat so that the living room fulfilled the multi-purpose approach of traditional Japanese architecture. The main space could be used as a second bedroom, a reading room, or a dining room.

We achieved another goal of Japanese architecture—the proximity of a structure to nature—by installing a tree trunk on the polished wood surface of the raised platform, or tokonoma. This log served at the same time as a divider for the niche, a recess in the wall that was used in traditional Japanese houses to hang scrolls with a poem (see image on page 99).

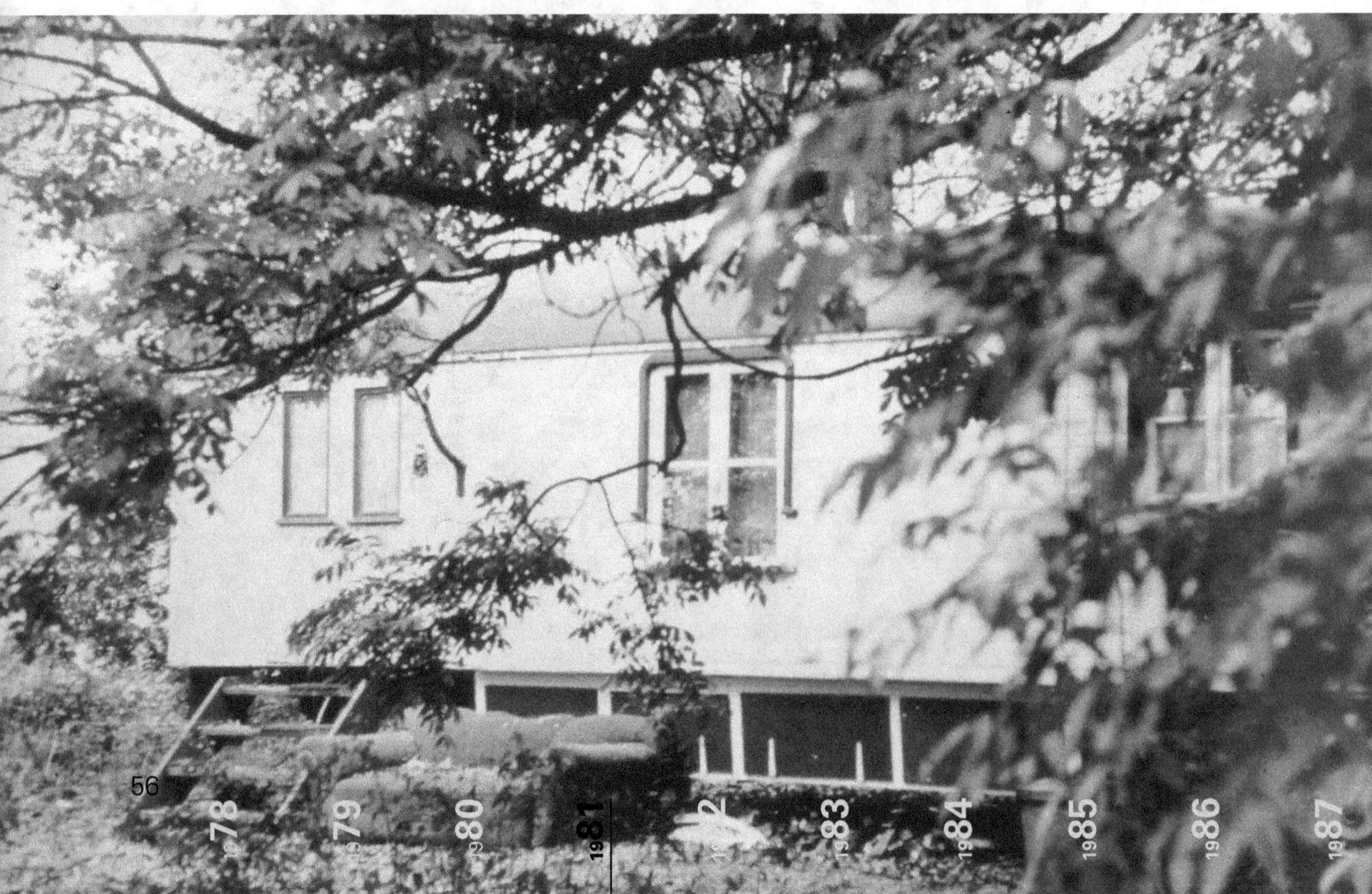

Plan #1: Layout of Trailer, Summer 1981

The trailer is built on a chassis that consists of two steel I-beams running the whole 32′ along the bottom of the superstructure. These two I-beams support steel cross members which in turn carry the wooden floor. The walls are made of 2x2 uprights, spaced about 16″ apart, with tongue-and-groove redwood pine boards screwed horizontally along the outside of the assembly. The trailer had been used as a temporary shelter and storage space for a circus family.

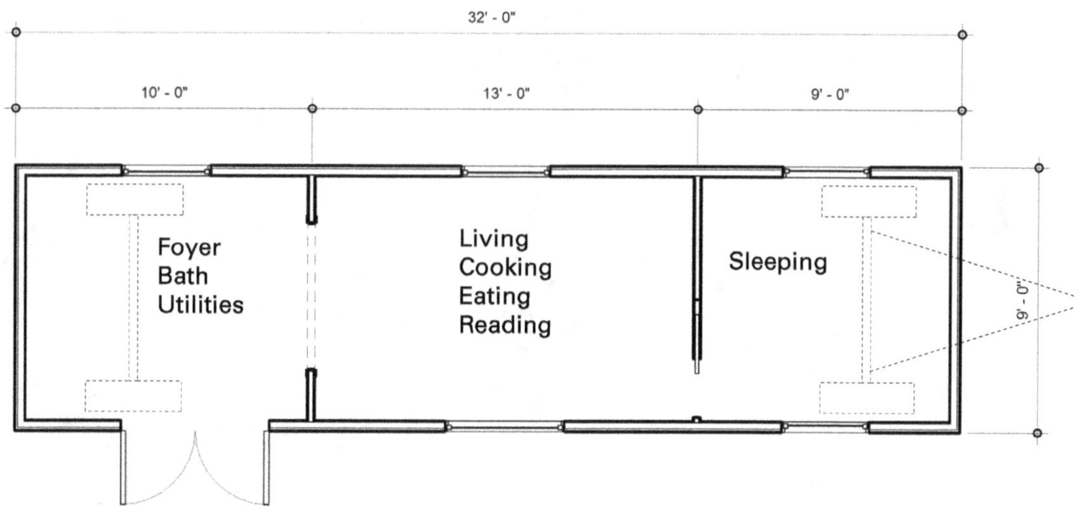

German/American Gothic in front of Da Capo at the watermill (photo by Manfred Frohloff)

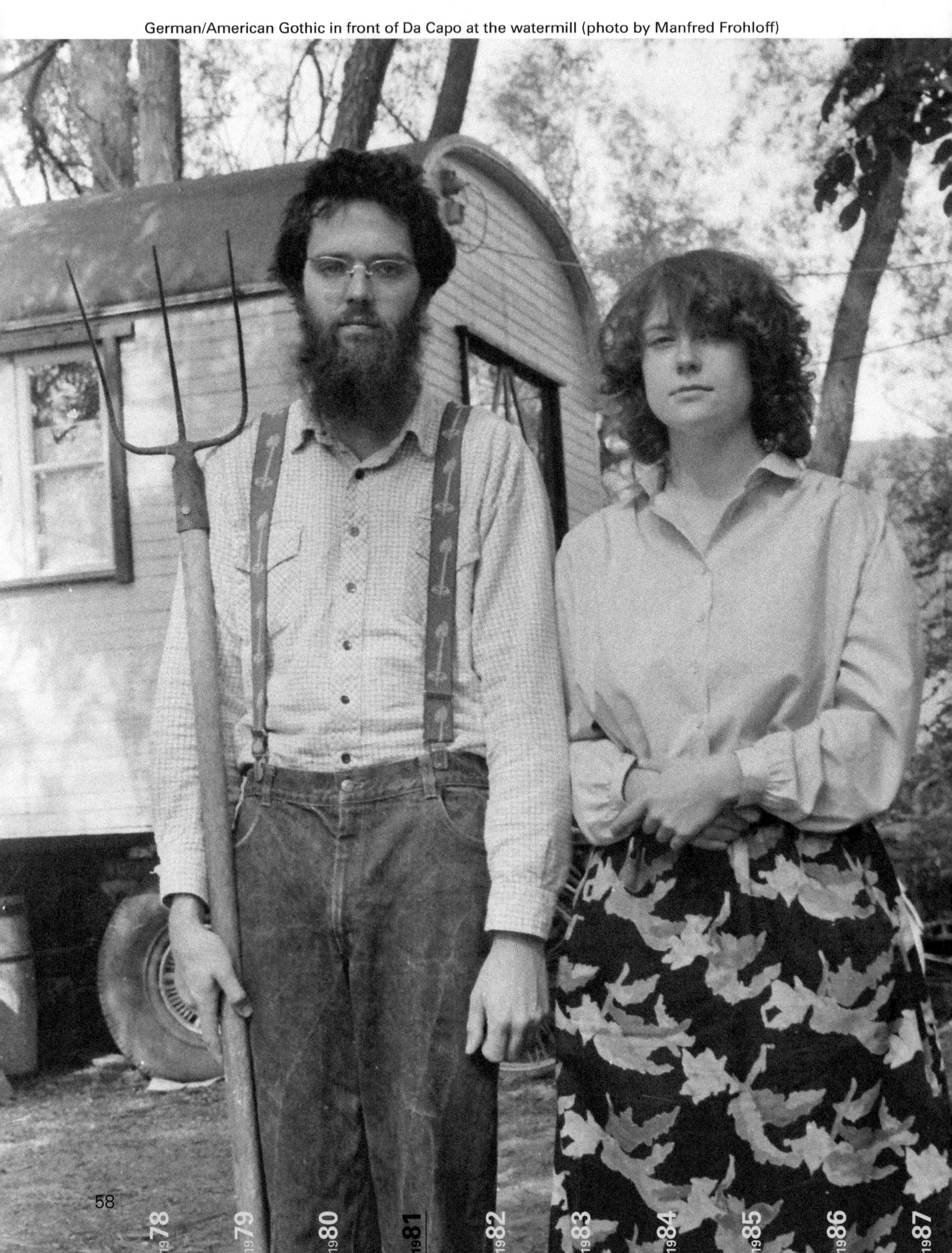

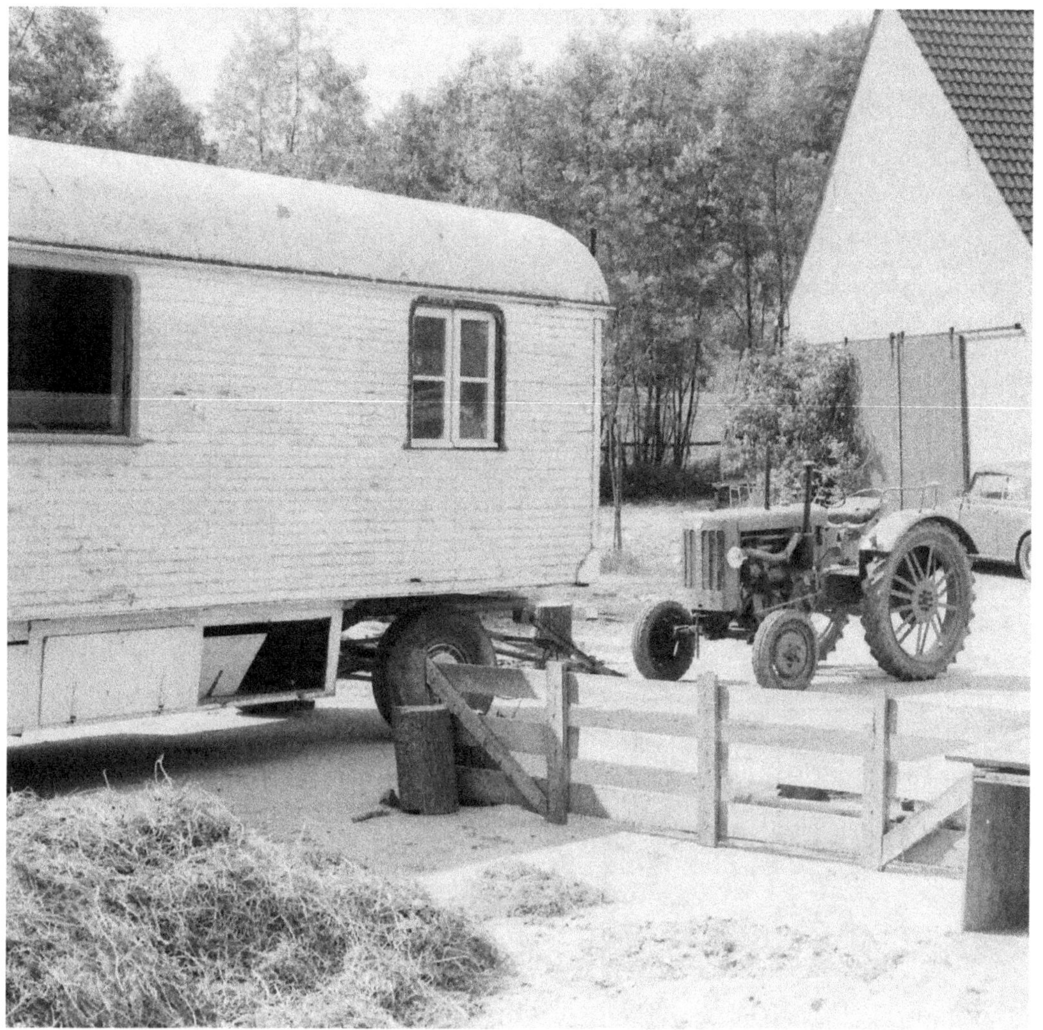

Da Capo, just after we moved the trailer from Hörstmar to the *Turmhof* yard, with Gerda as a moving tractor.

The way Da Capo looked when we first worked on it.

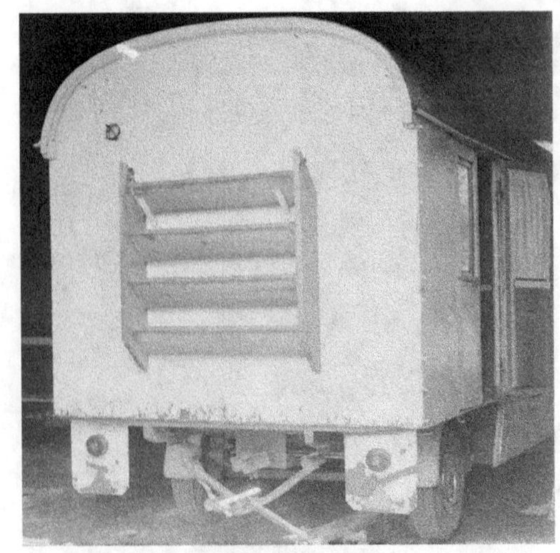

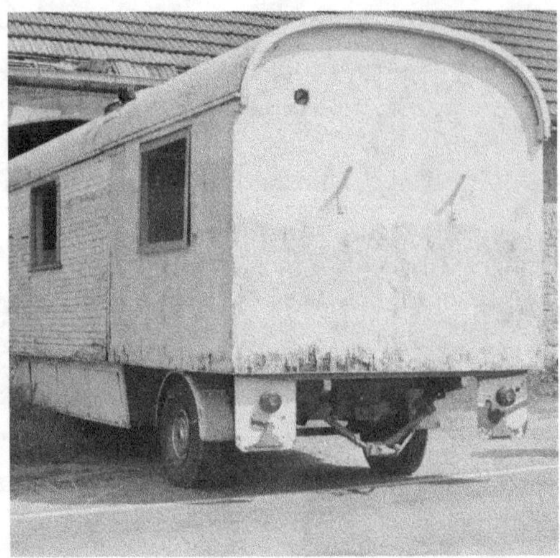

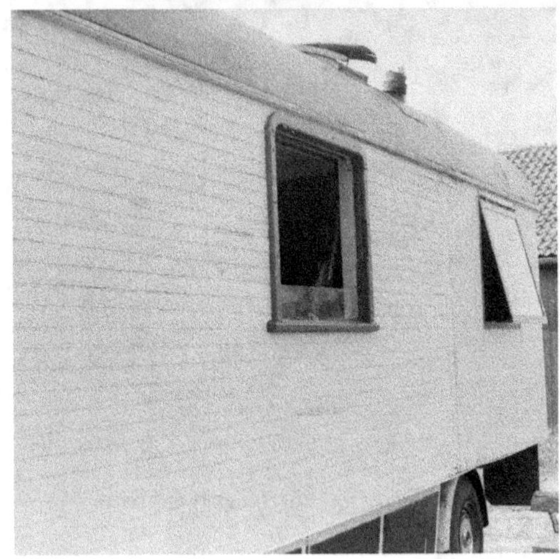

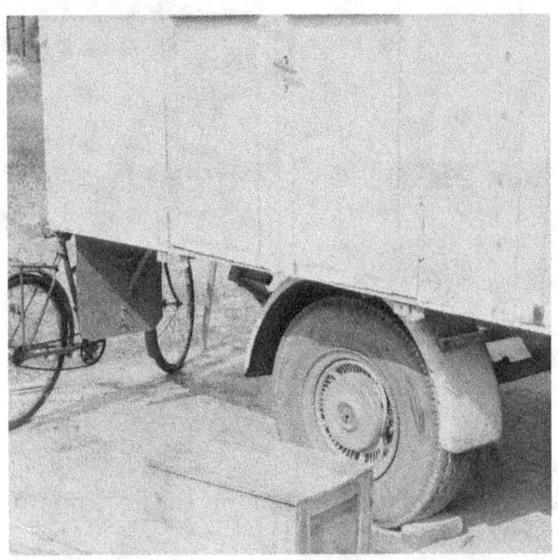

Front axle and spring assembly

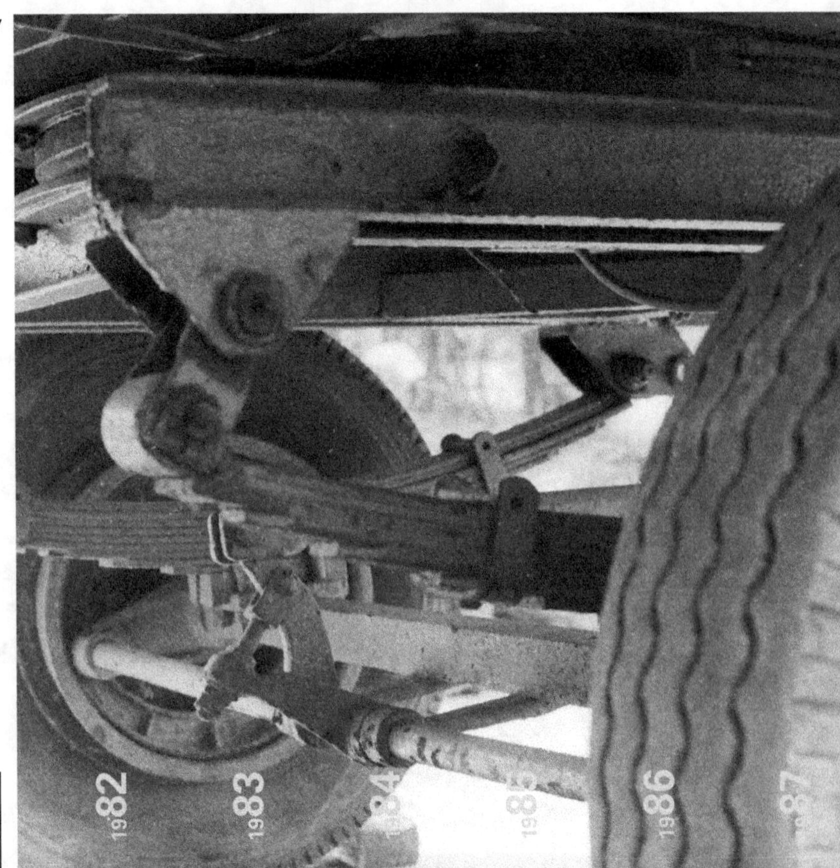

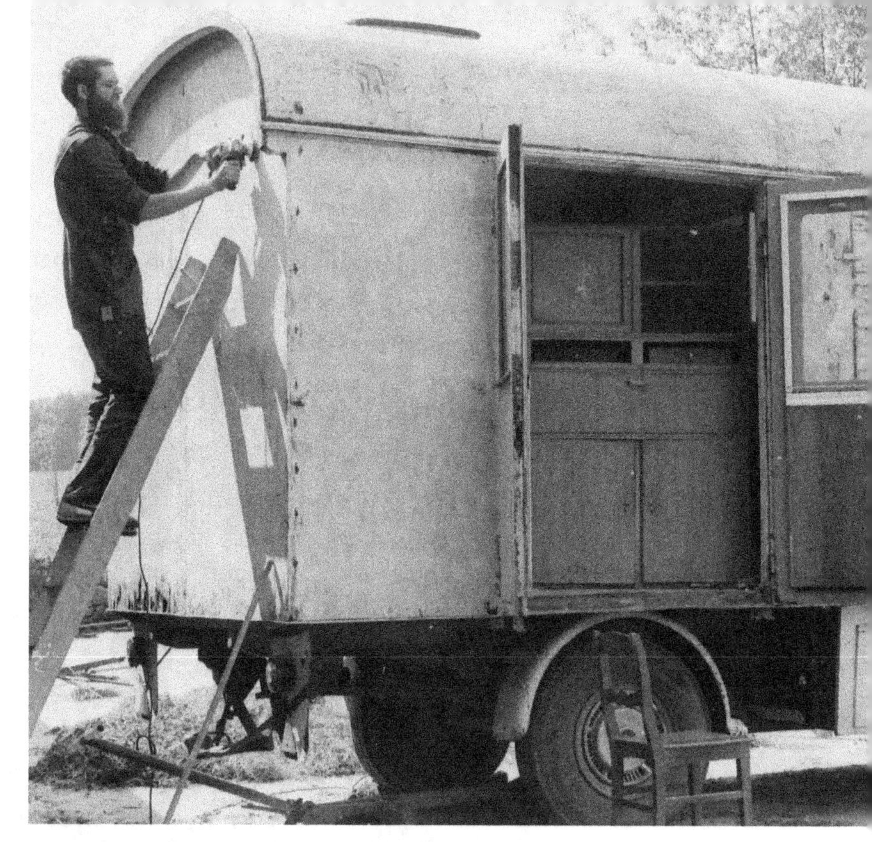

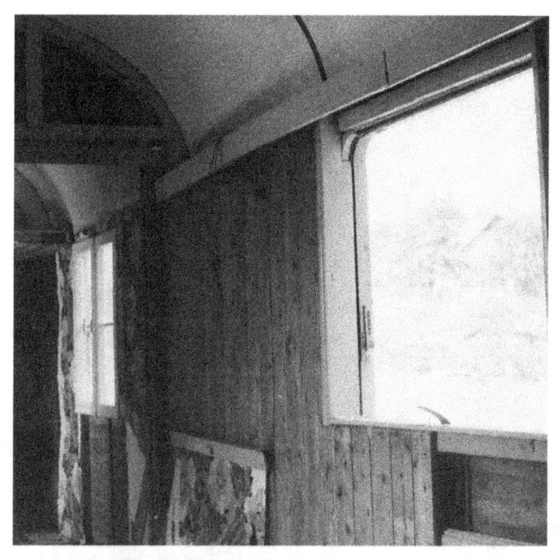

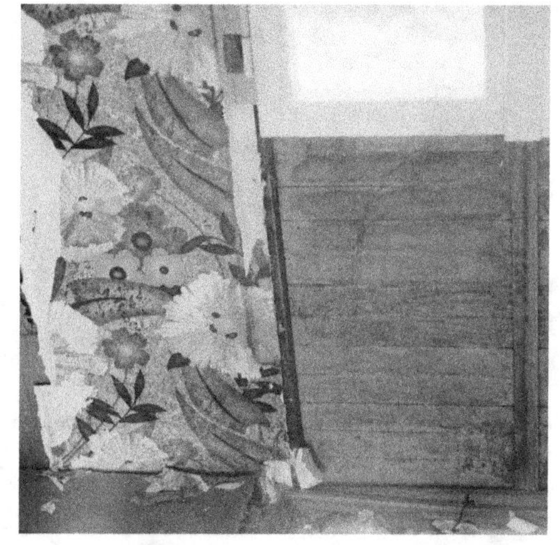

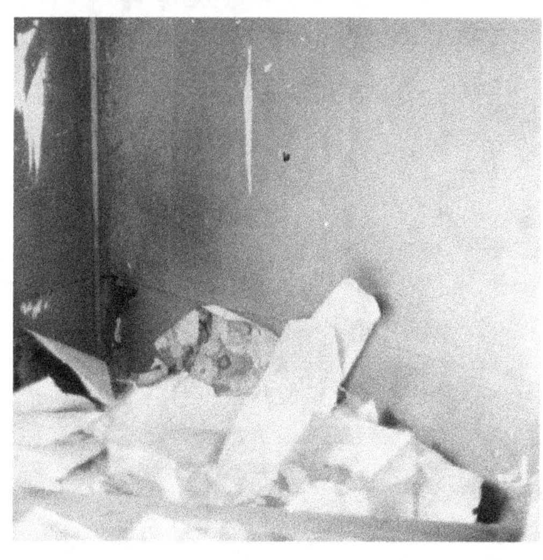

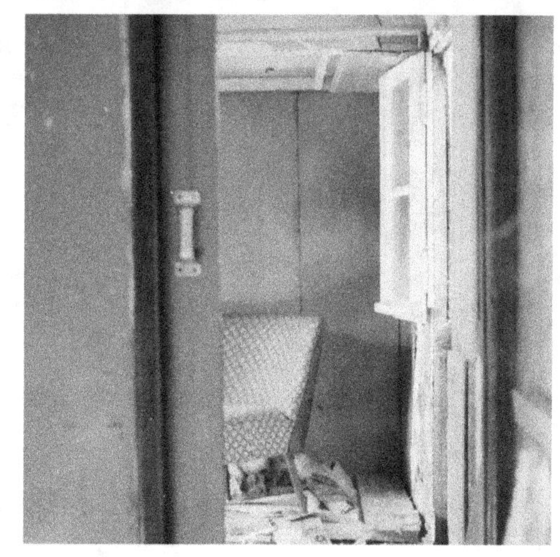

Interior views of Da Capo under construction, and exterior entry stair with chicken

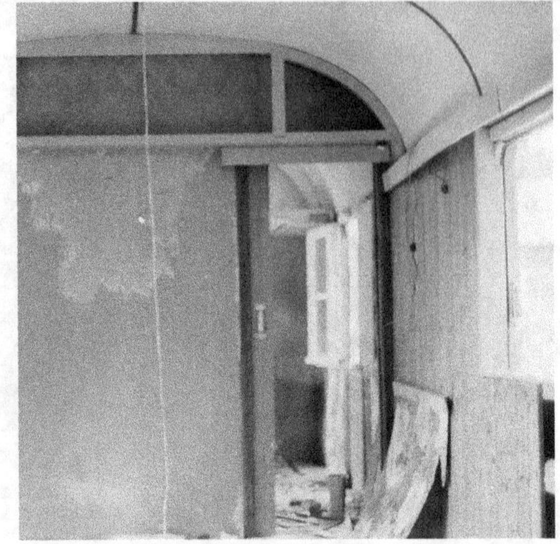

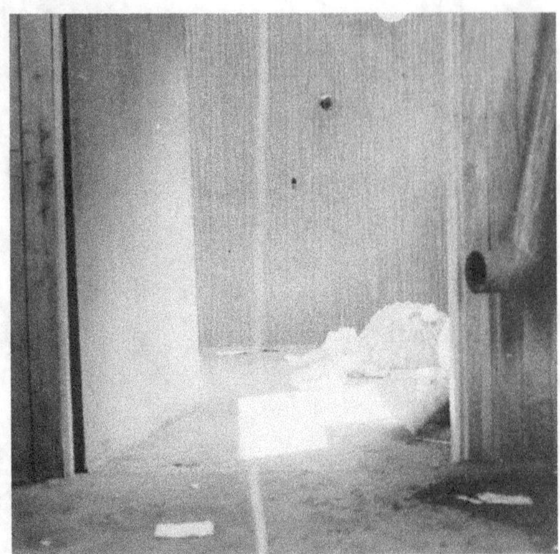

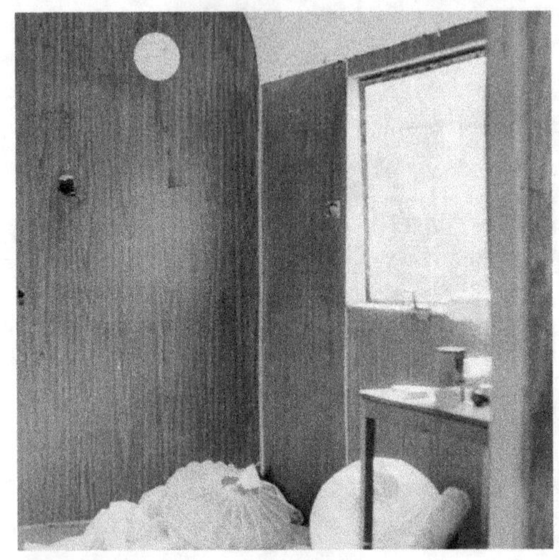

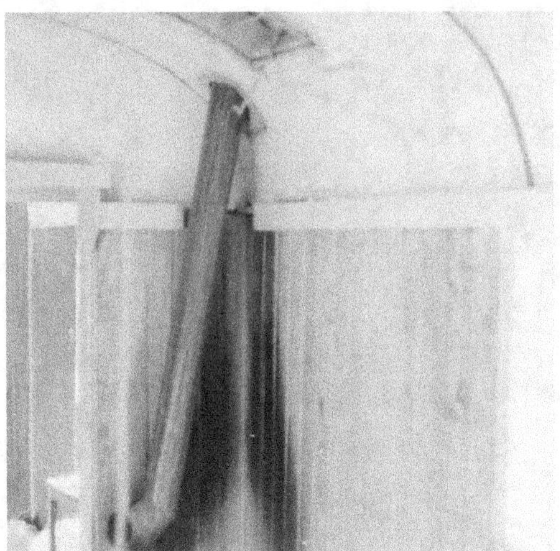

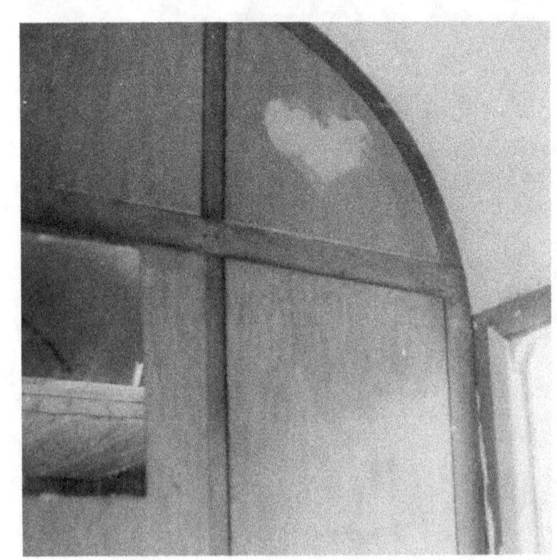

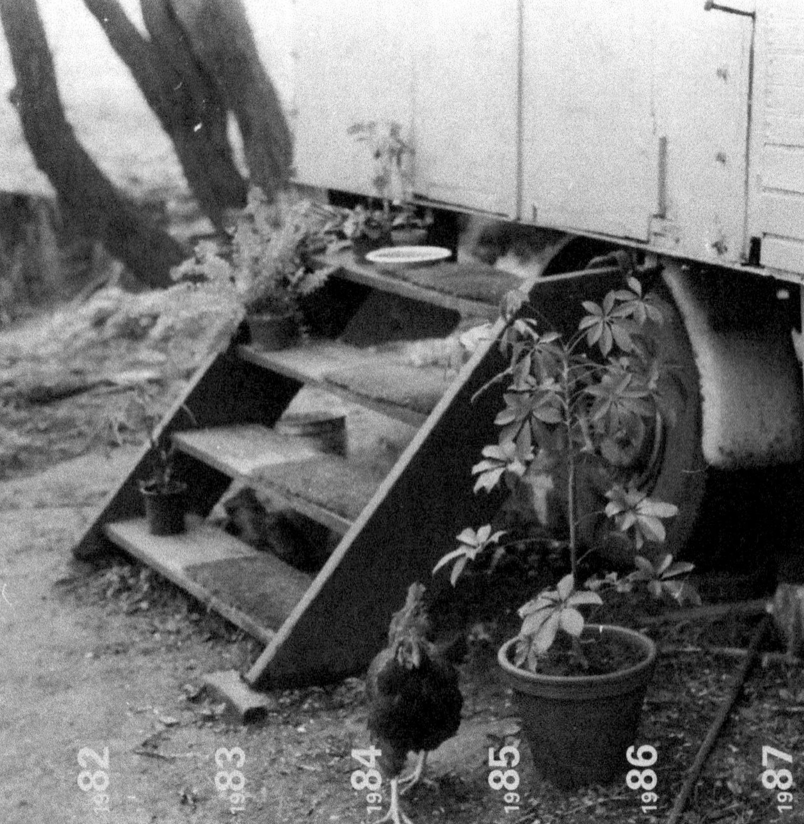

Construction of shower and toilet stall in Da Capo

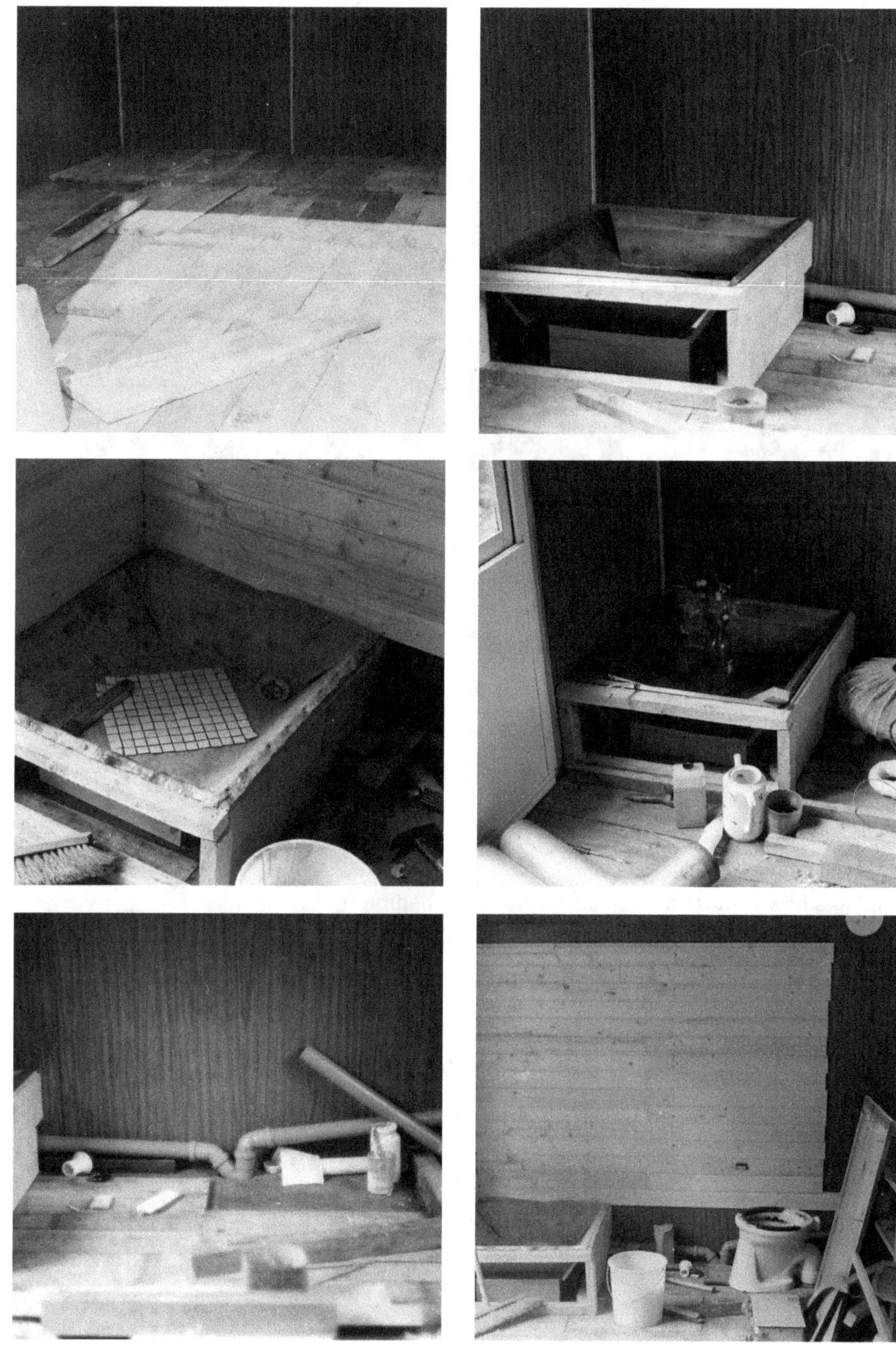

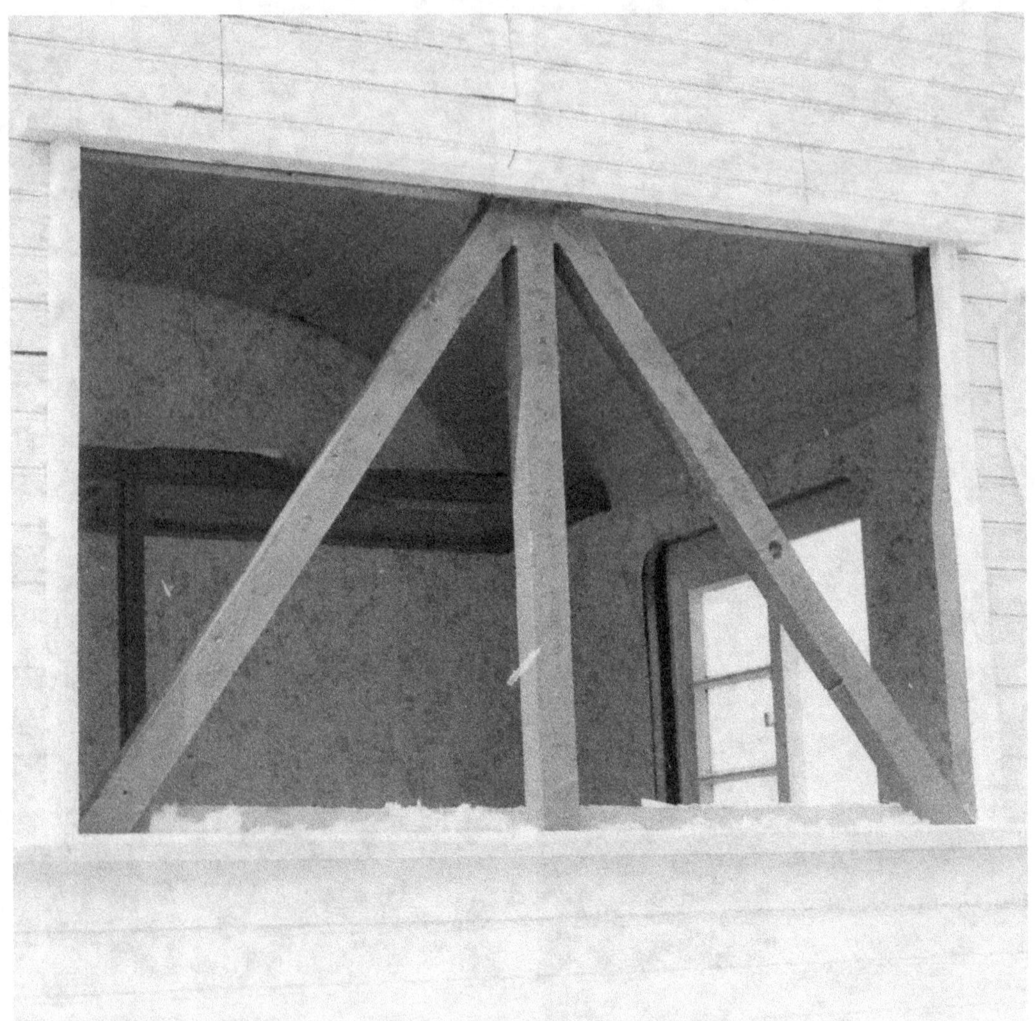

Fitting a new window into Da Capo's front end bedroom.

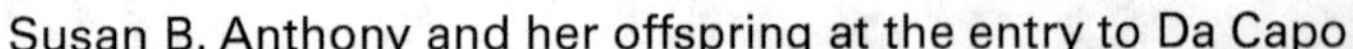

Susan B. Anthony and her offspring at the entry to Da Capo

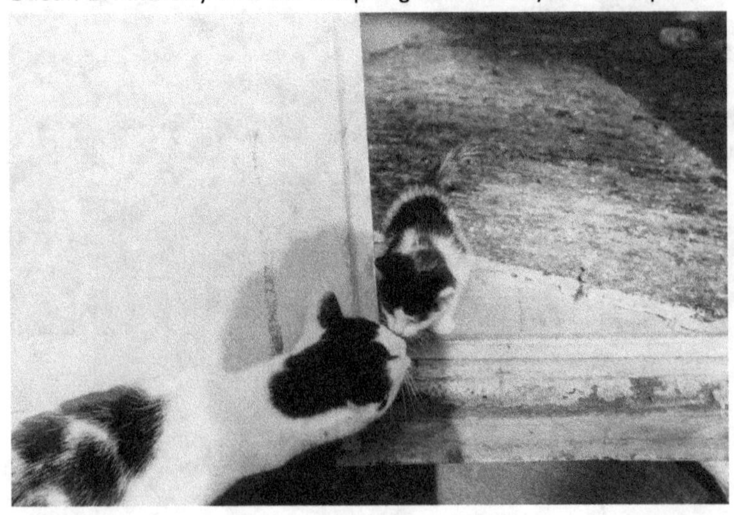

Interior views of first renovation stage

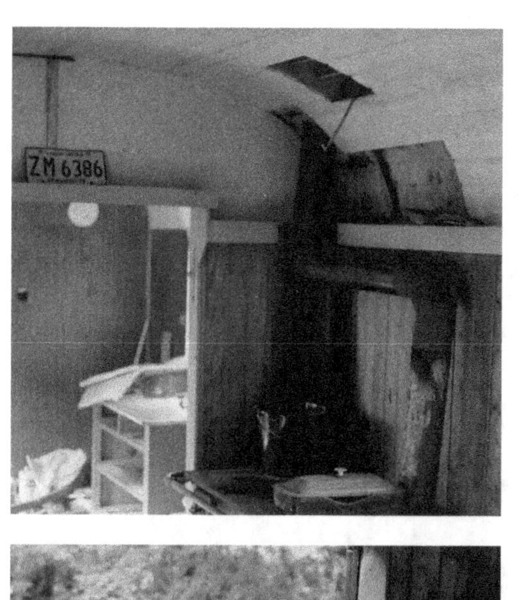

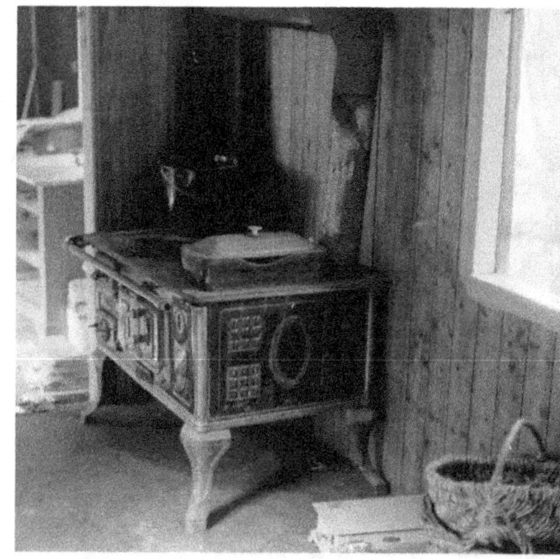

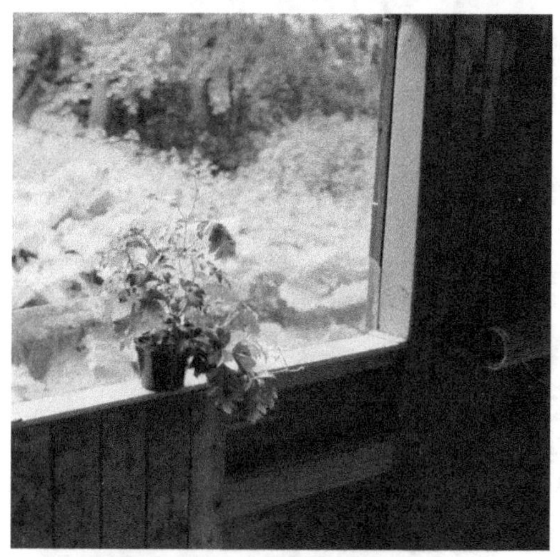

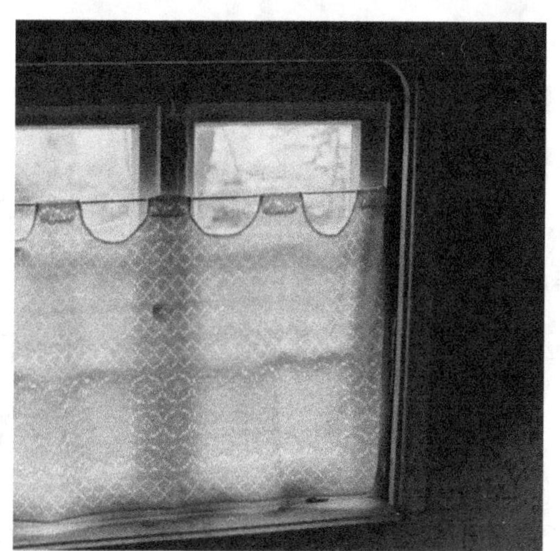

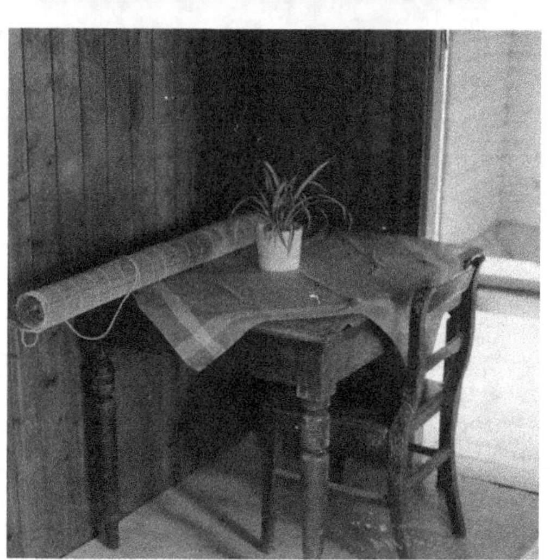

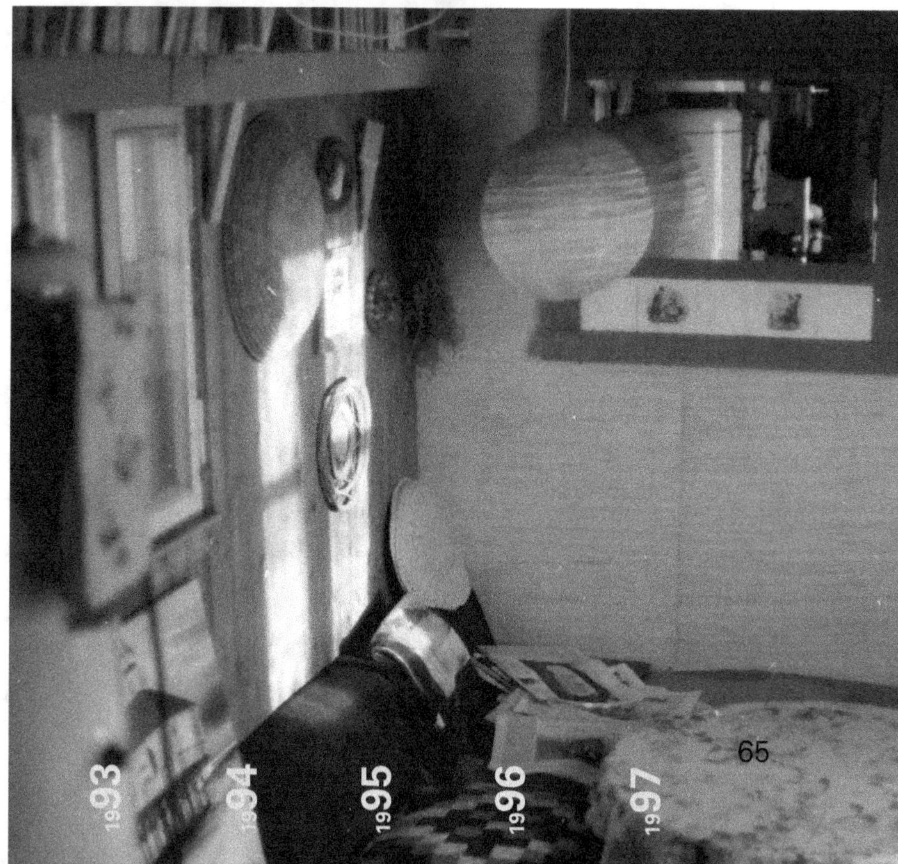

Construction of bed (from recycled bed parts) and views of living room

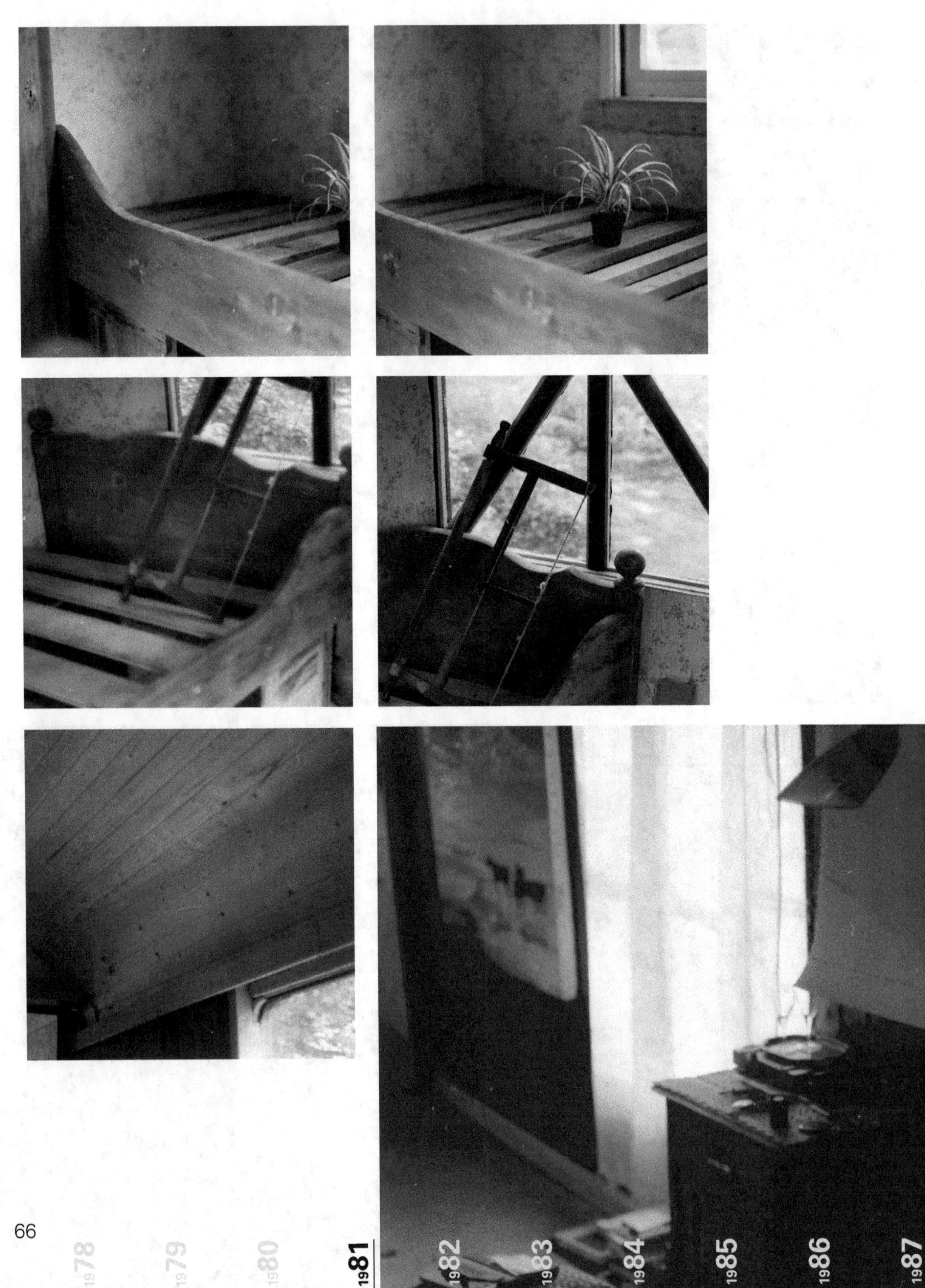

Interior views of Da Capo

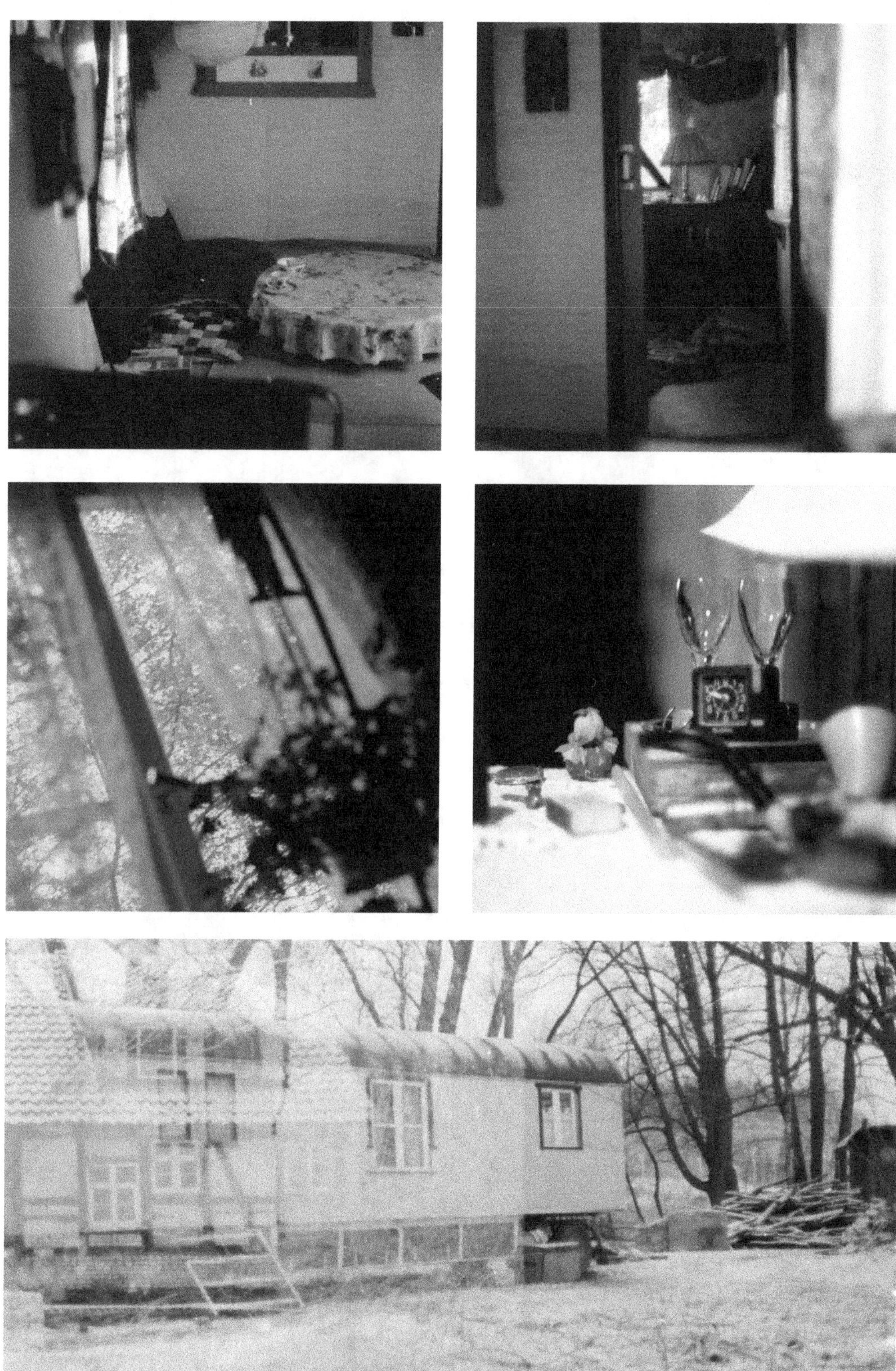

Accidental double exposure of watermill on Da Capo

1982

Circus Trailer Living Quarters
Da Capo Conversion (continued)

Plan #2

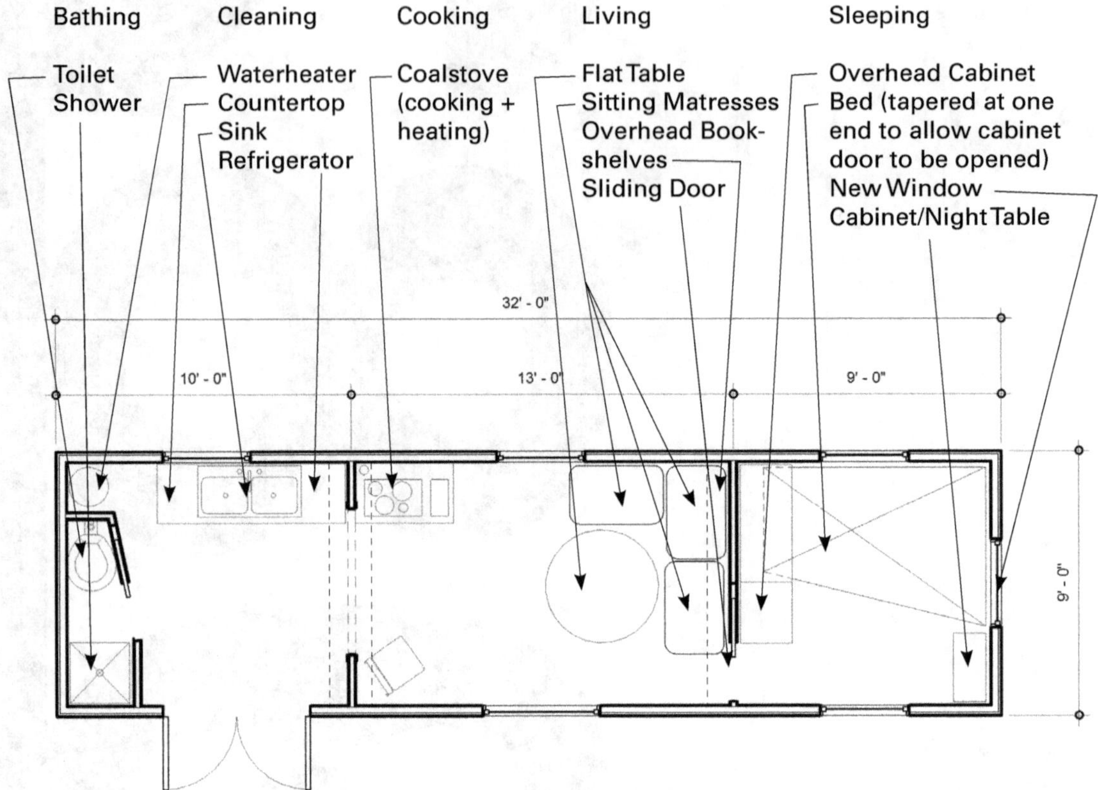

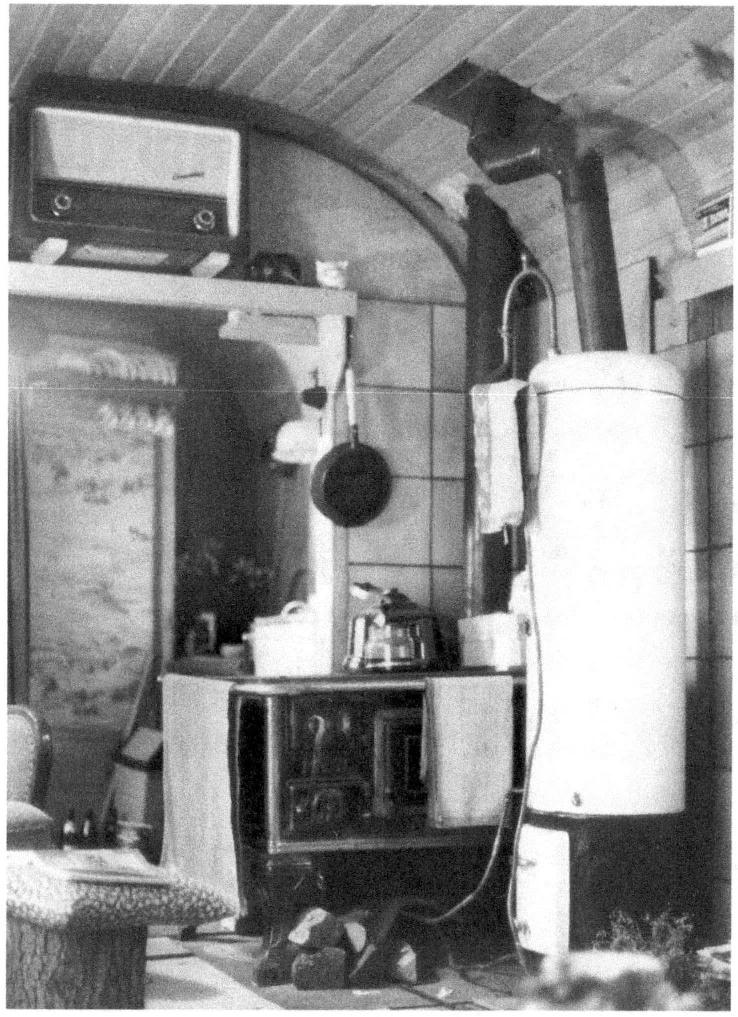

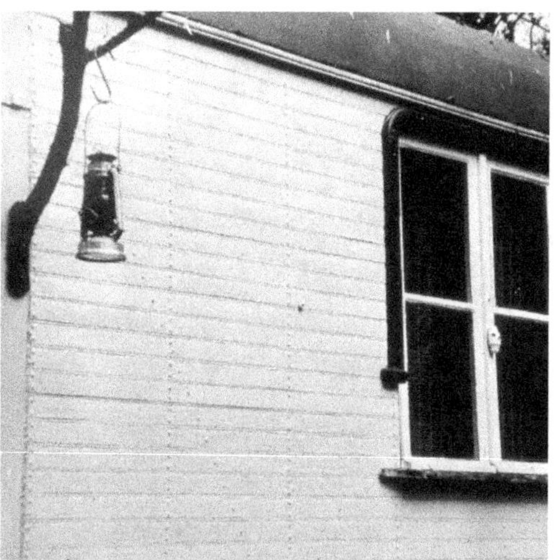

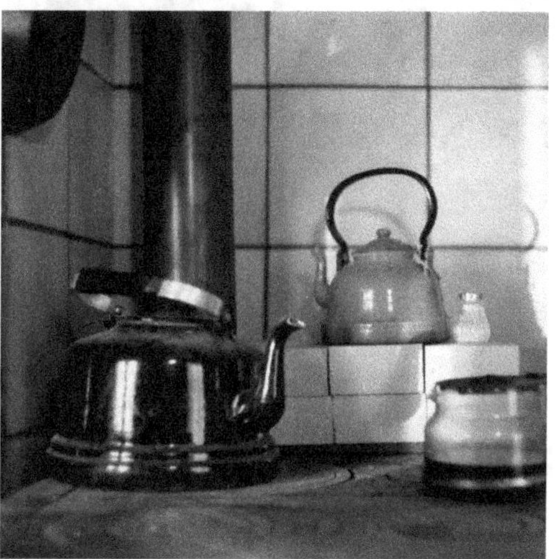

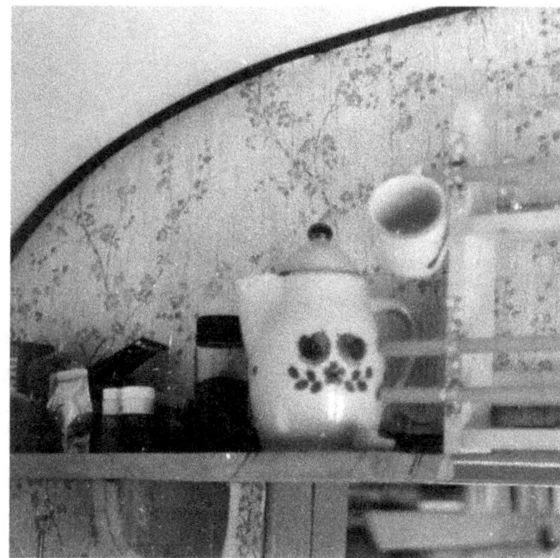

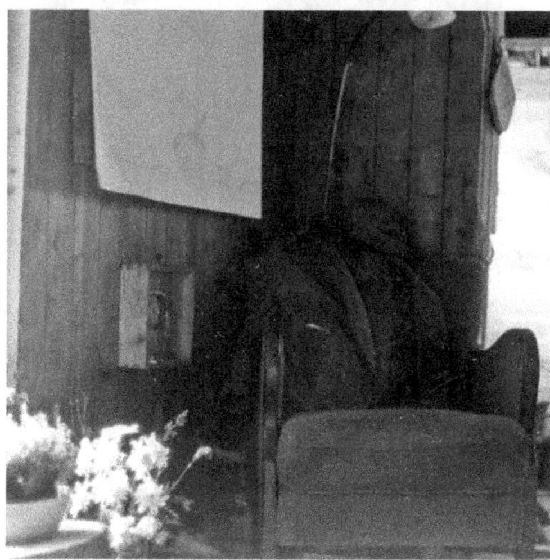

Second iteration of the conversion. Views of interior and exterior.

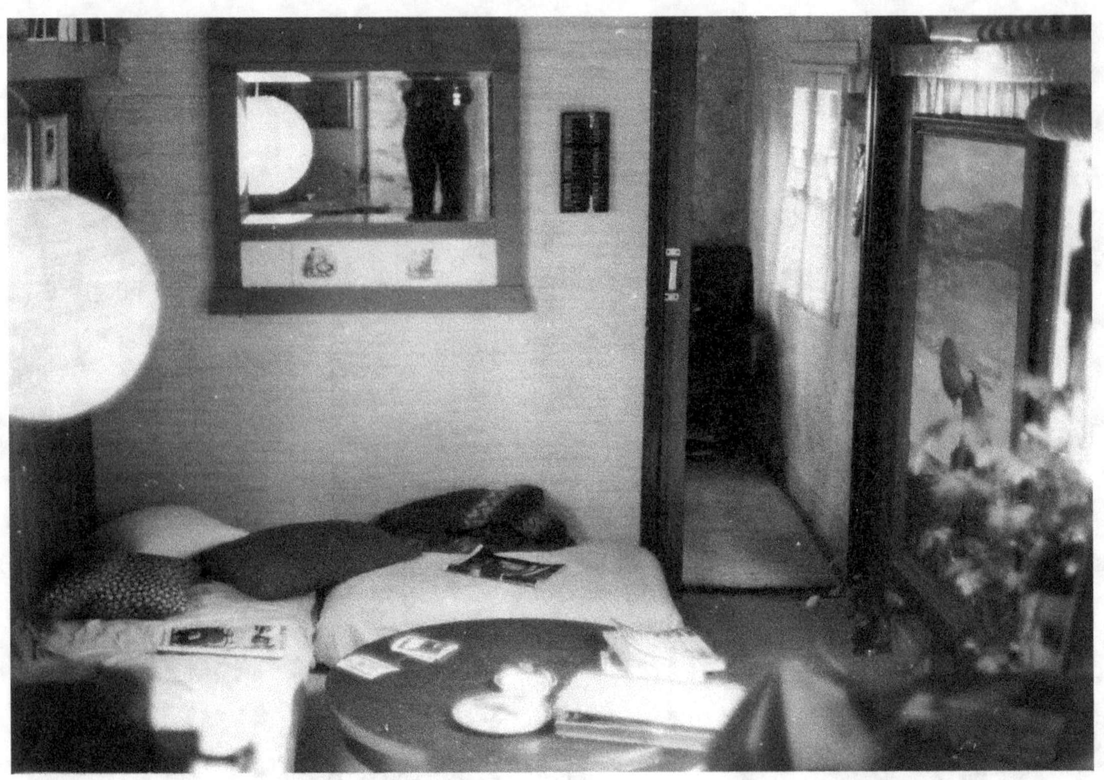

Second iteration of the conversion. Views of interior.

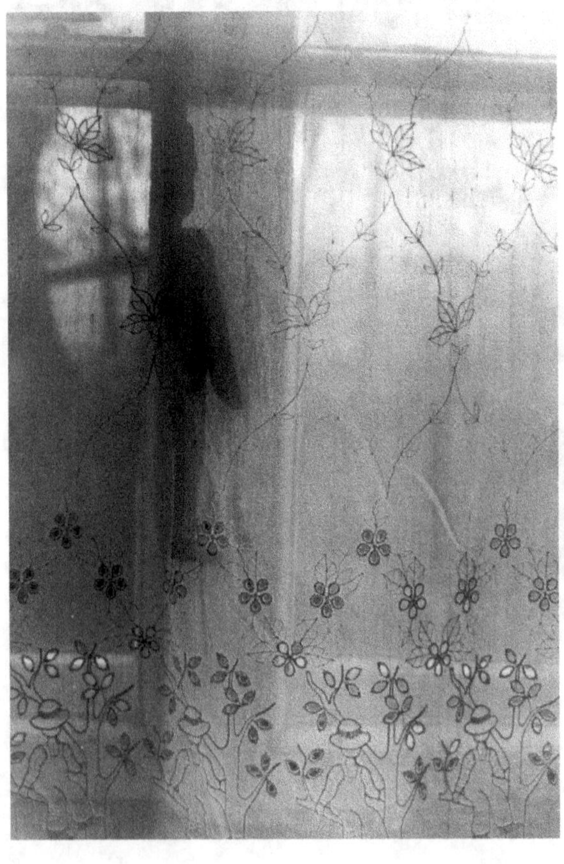

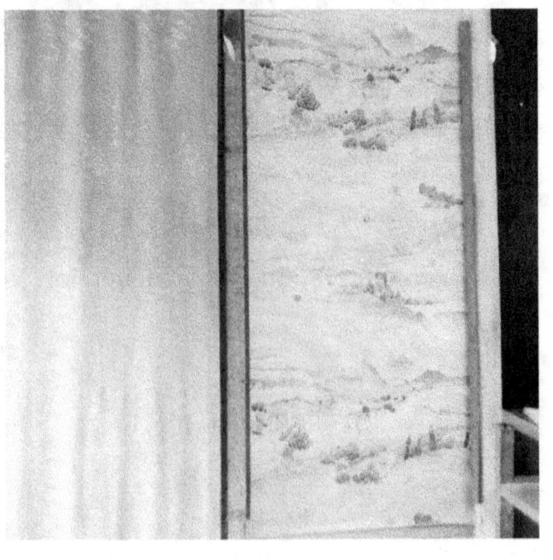

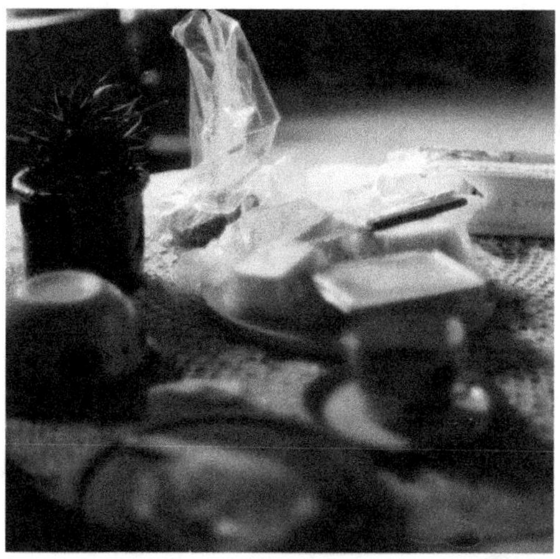

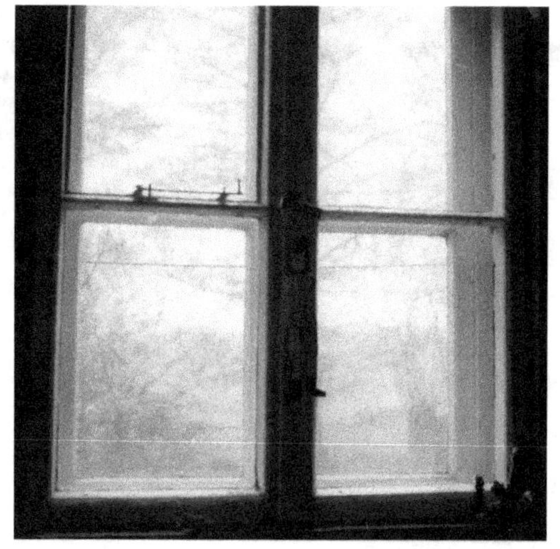

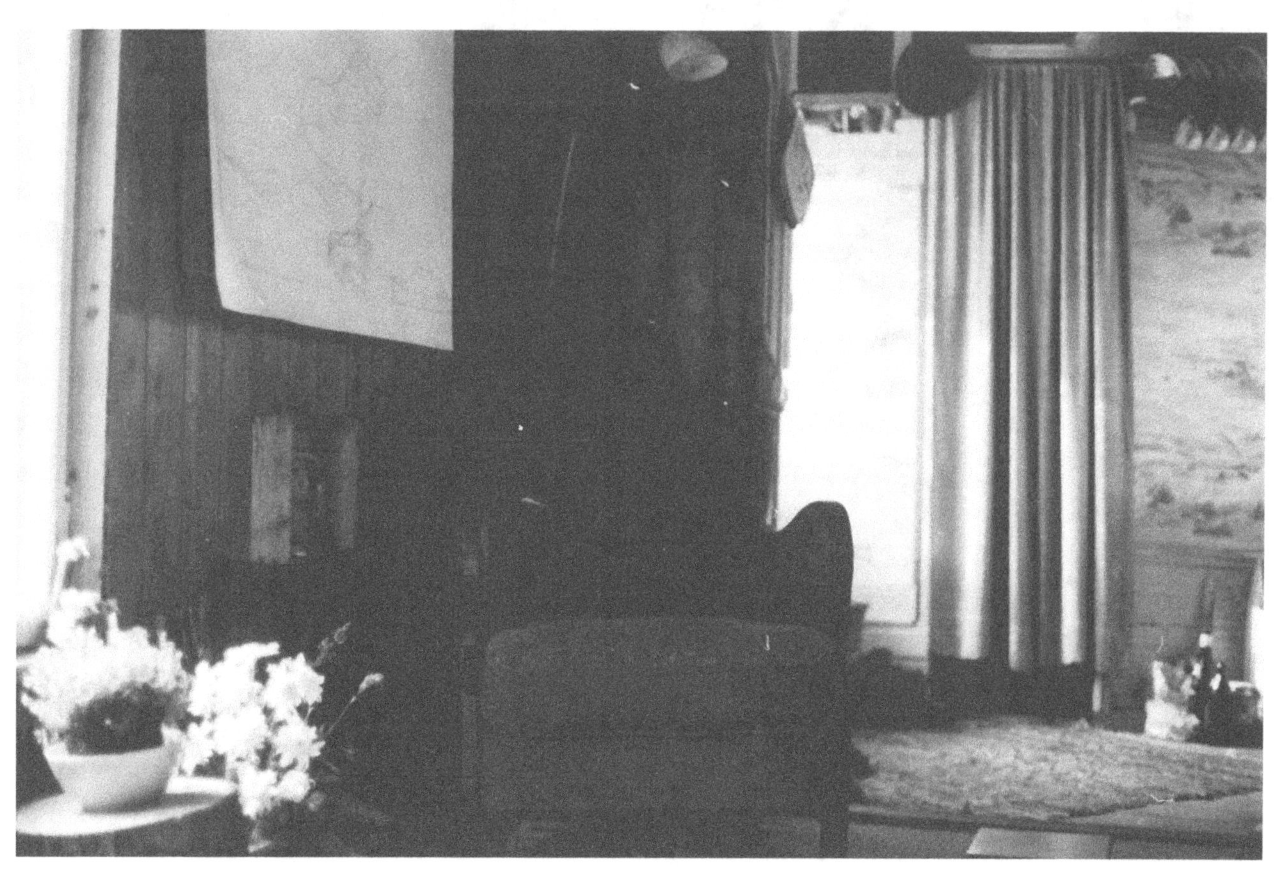

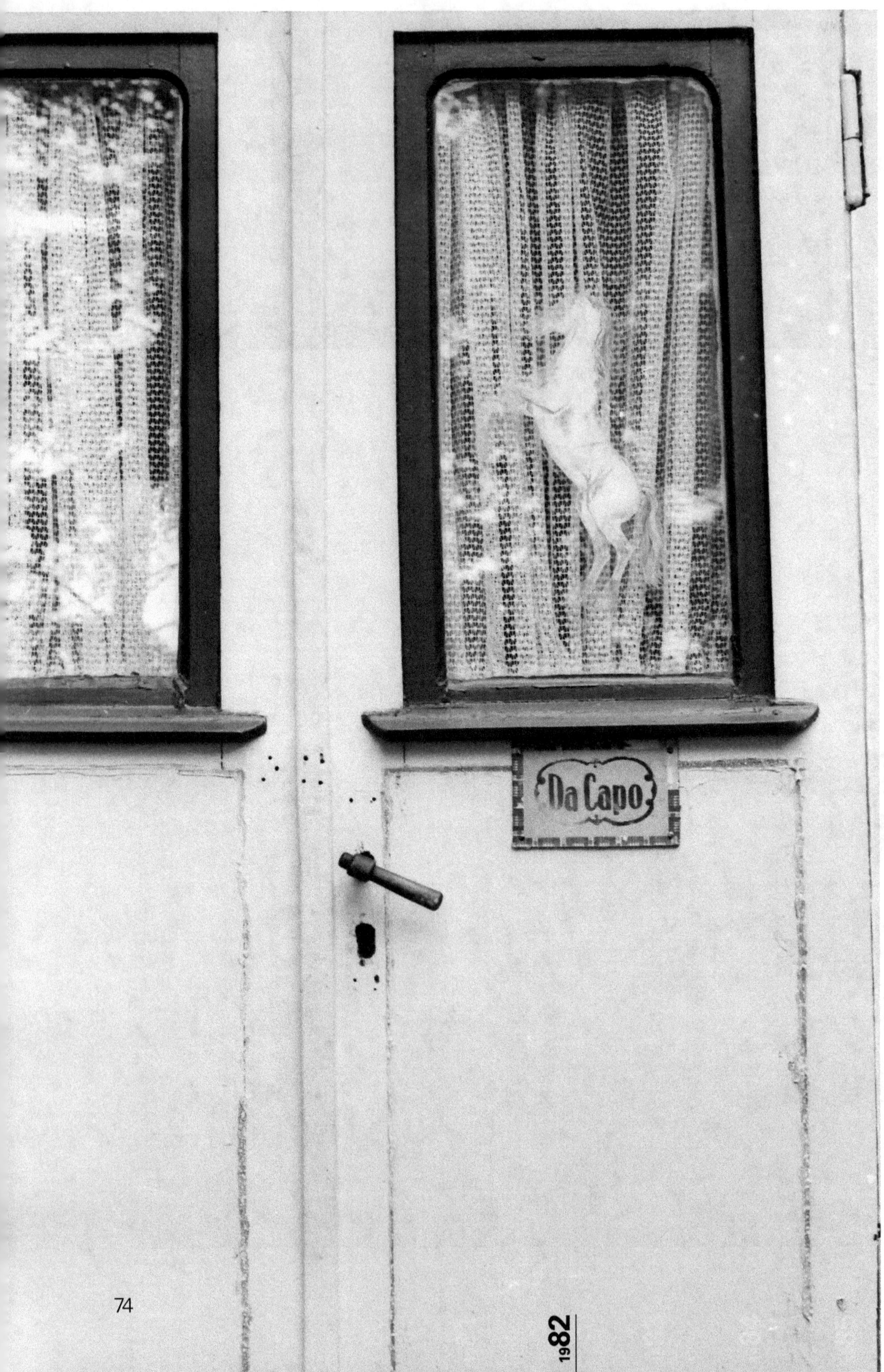
Da Capo

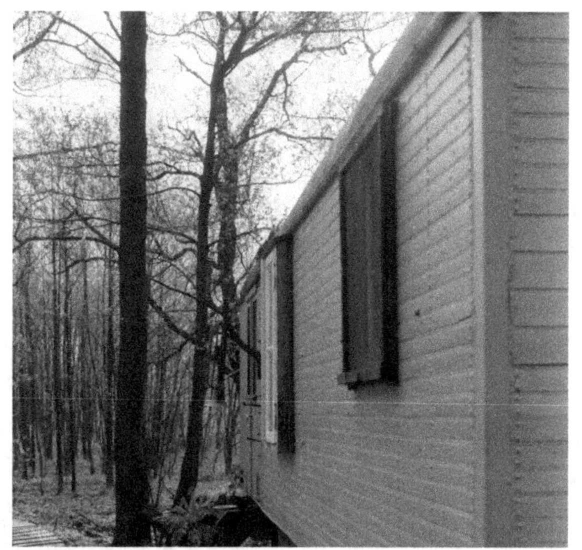

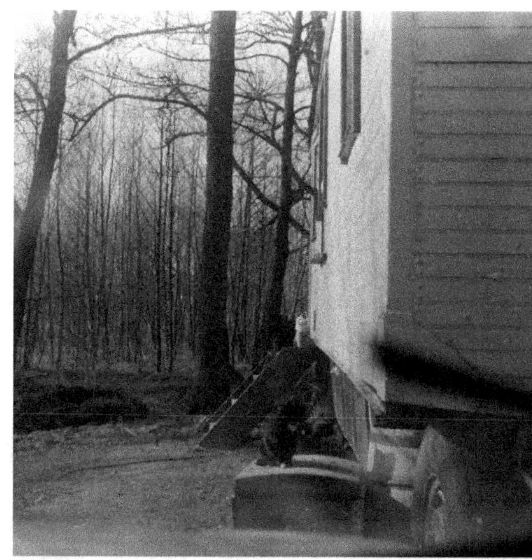

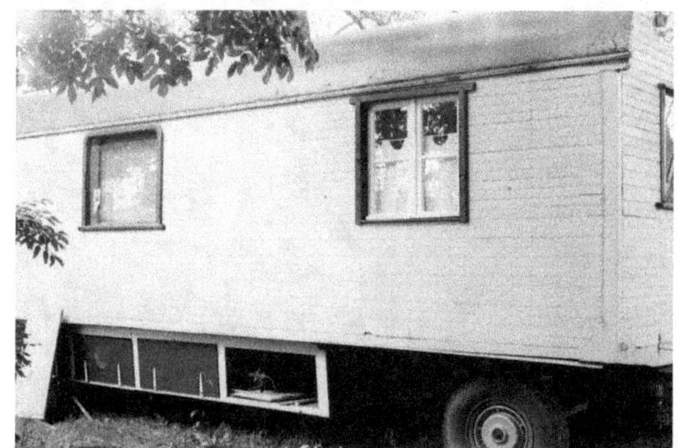

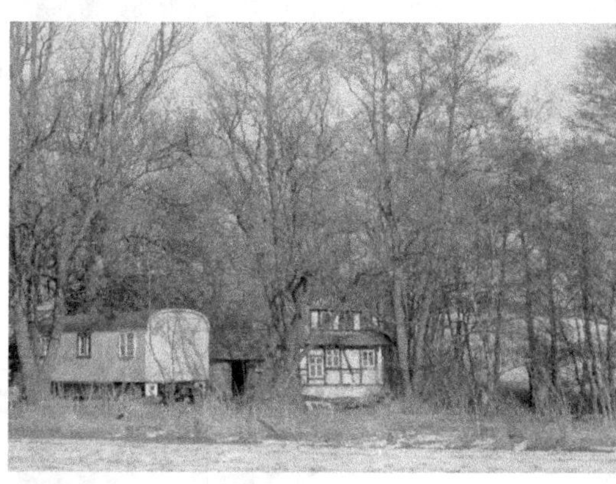

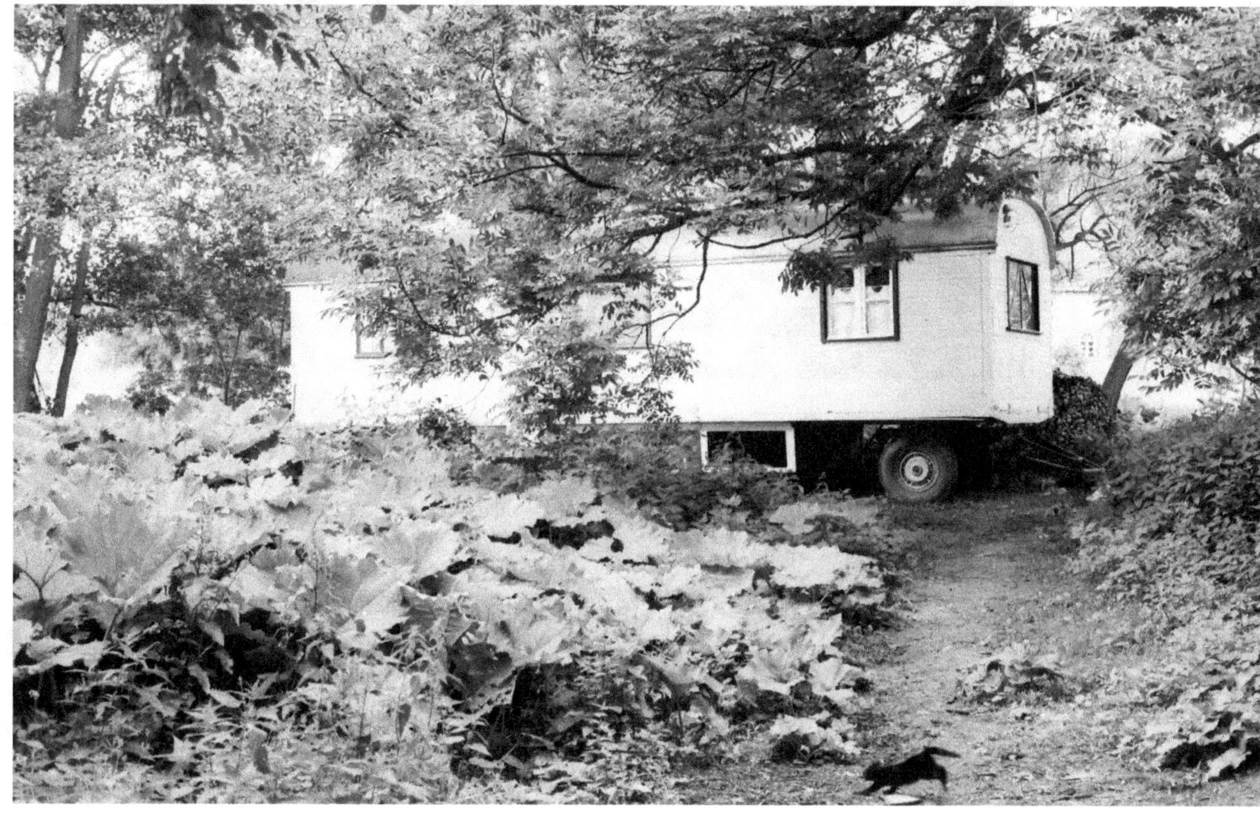

Outthouse

We needed a new outhouse on the watermill grounds. Manni and I decided to start with a frame of rough logs that would give us a three-dimensional skeleton for cladding. We recycled most of the wood. Setting the box up high on a plinth allows for easy cleaning of the tub containing the sewage. A heart, traditionally cut into the door, plus a rustic handle complete the design.

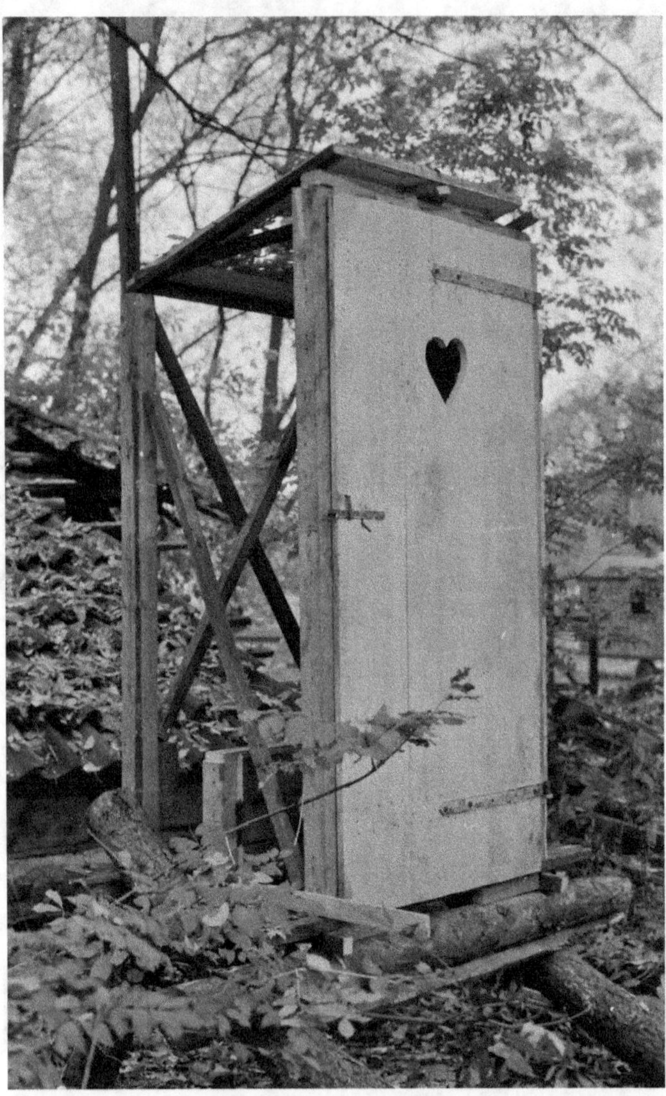

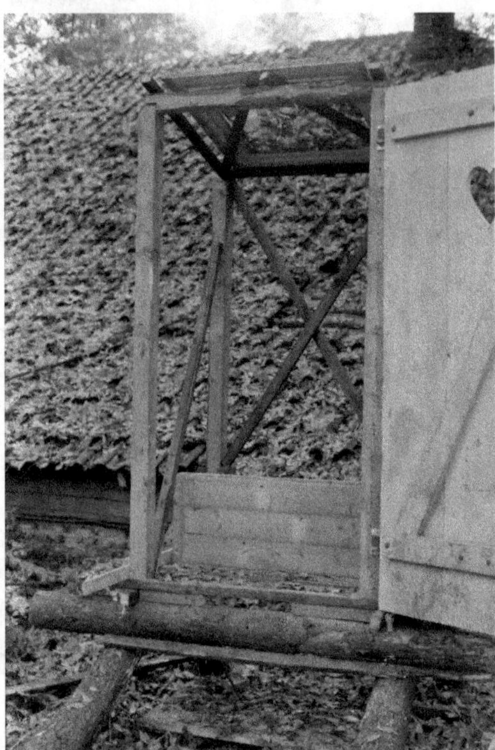

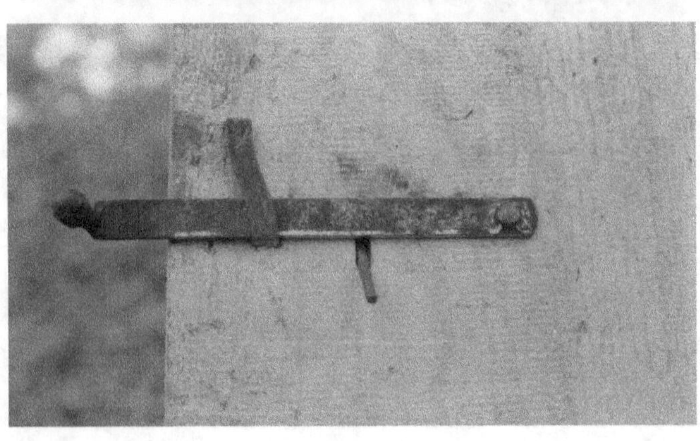

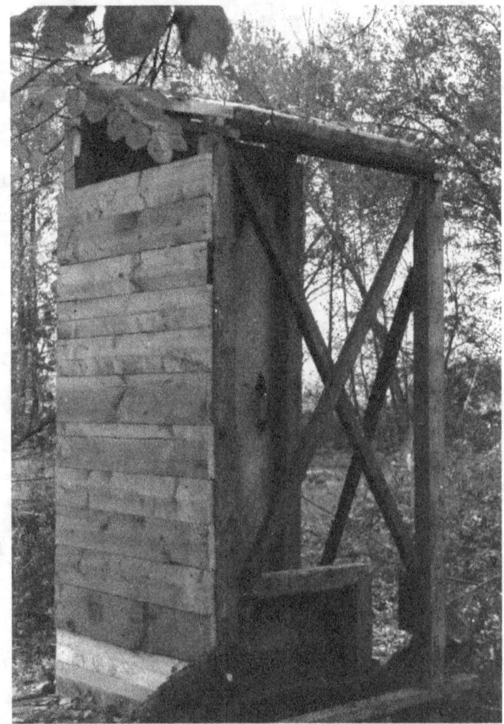

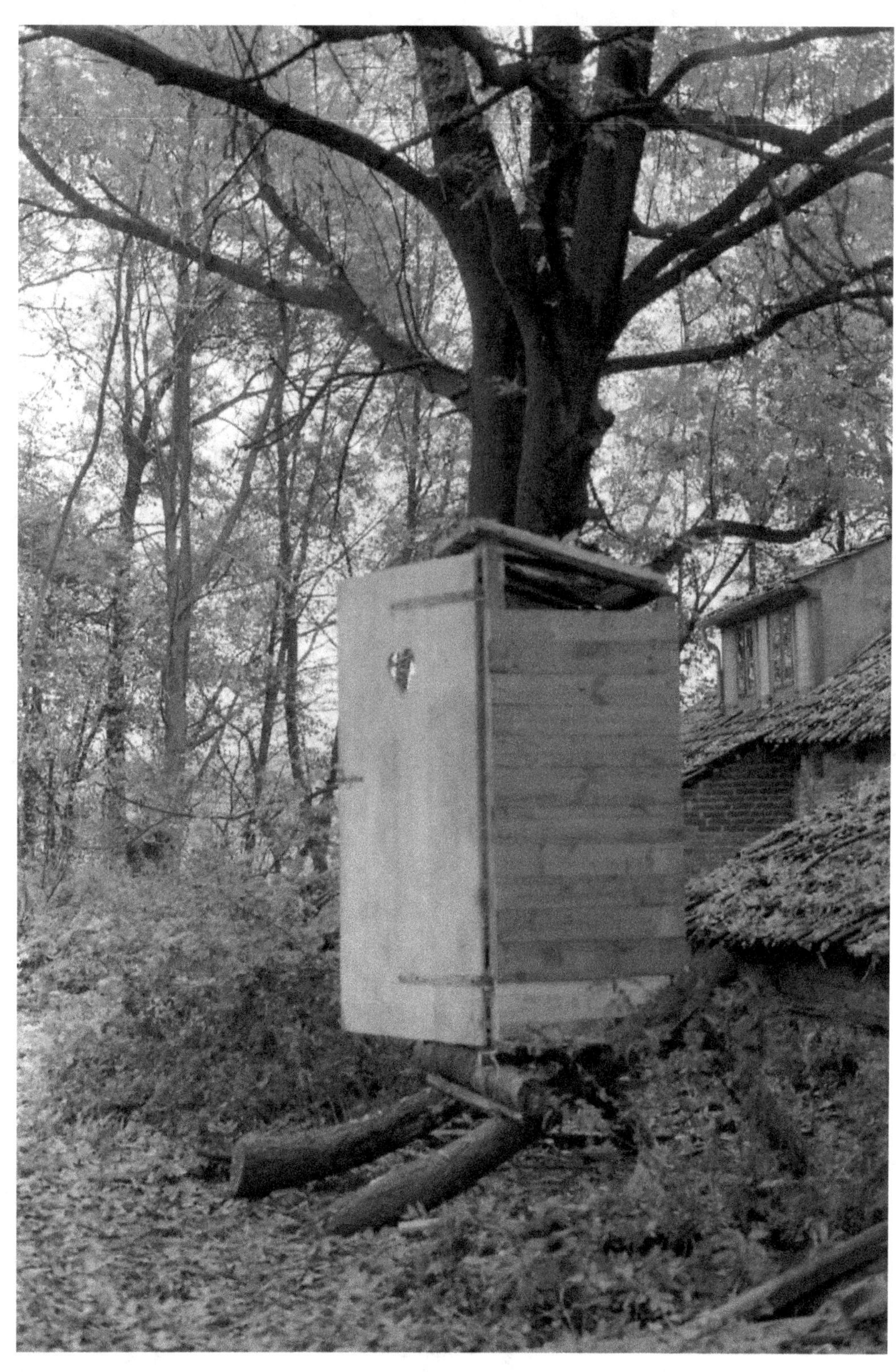

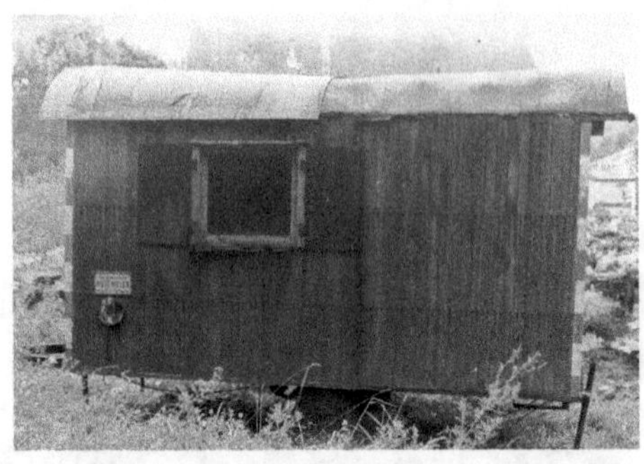

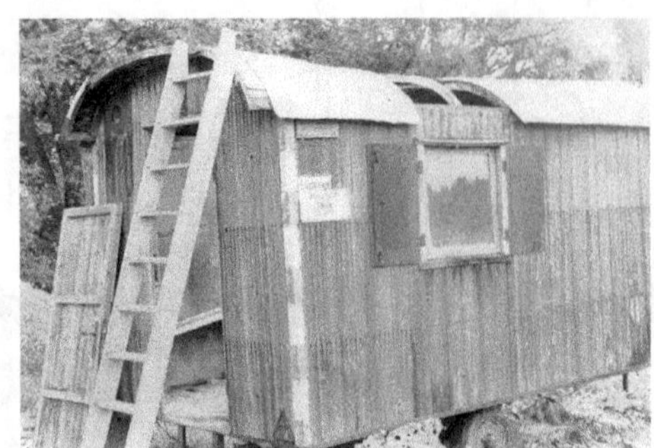

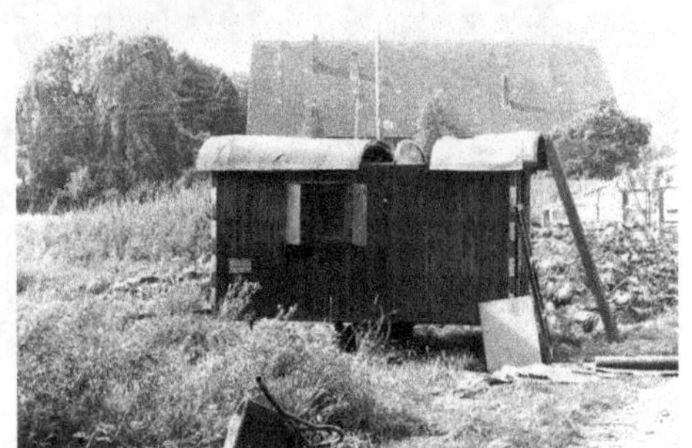

Music Room Trailer

Miriam needed a place to practice piano and teach music. Da Capo was too small, so the next best ideas was to expand our compound with another trailer. I had been scoping out the villages around Entrup and had come across several small construction trailers that might be able to work as a music room. I bought one of the trailers for about $25 from the company Rosemeier Construction in Vlotho and Uffeln, pulled it with our tractor Gerda to our compound, and started to pull it apart so we could add insulation, new interior siding (tongue and groove pine), and a round window in the entry door with a lacy doily.

I also replaced the worn-out single window in the side wall with a found/recycled window of more recent vintage, installed a wood stove, and fixed the leaky roof with a new layer of gritted tar paper.

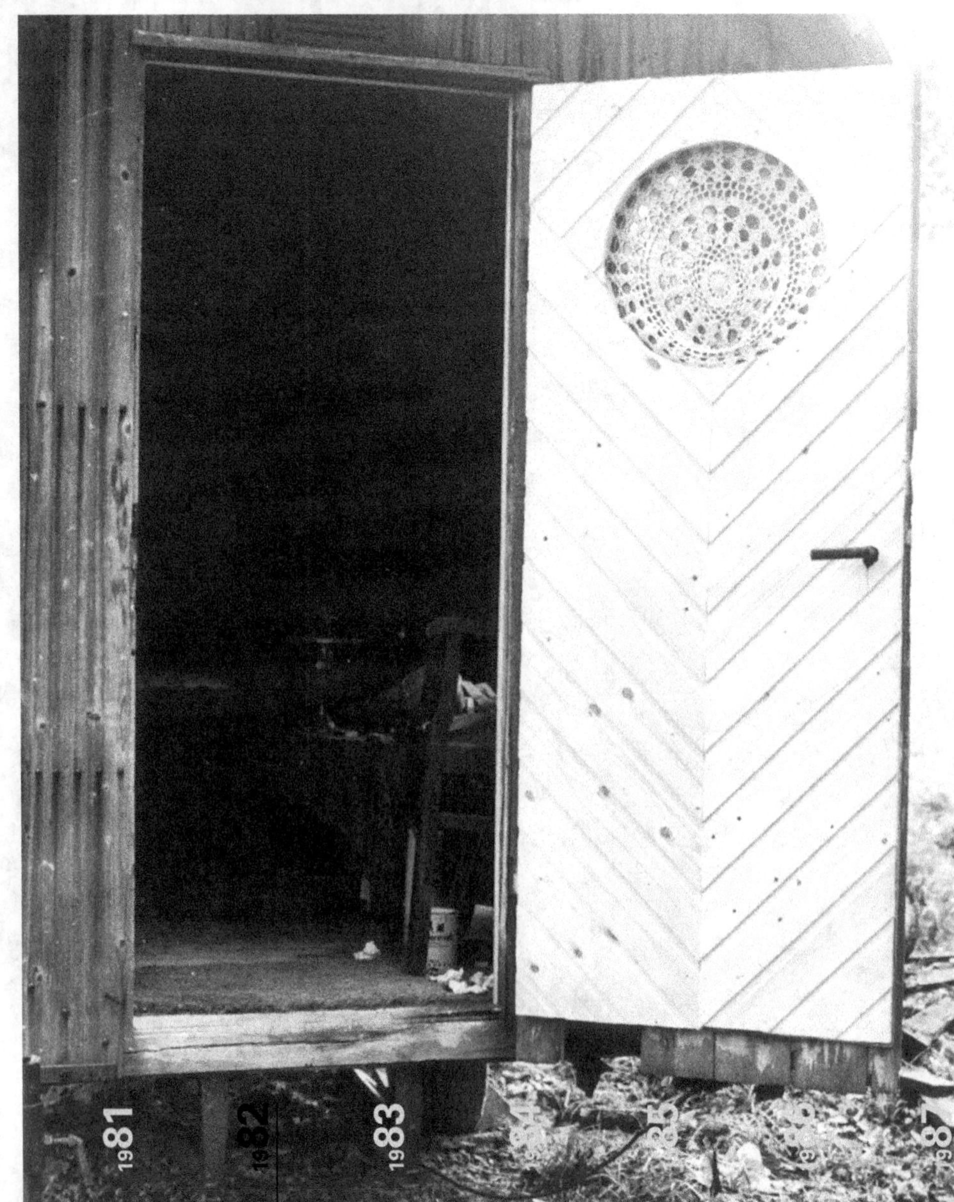

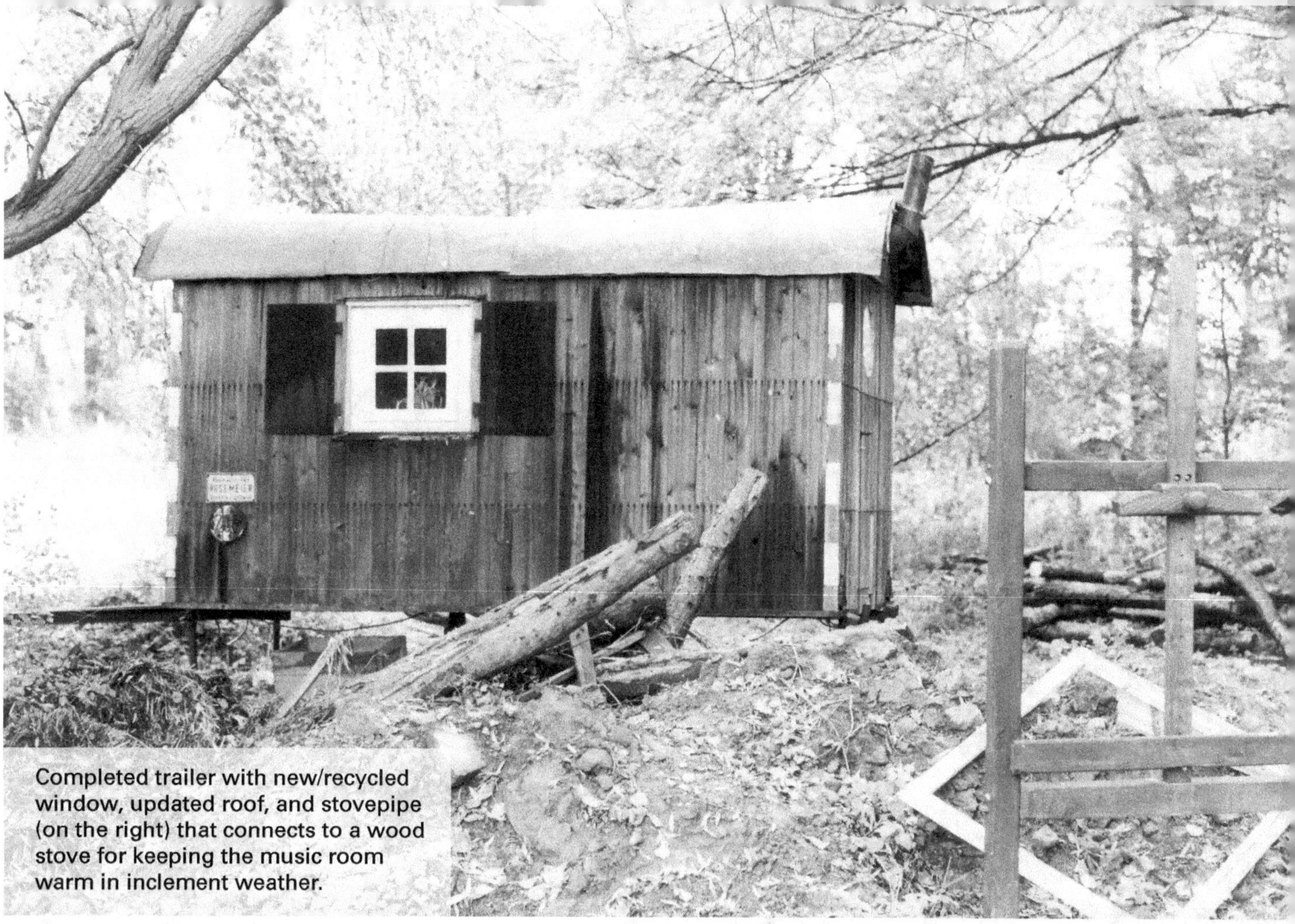

Completed trailer with new/recycled window, updated roof, and stovepipe (on the right) that connects to a wood stove for keeping the music room warm in inclement weather.

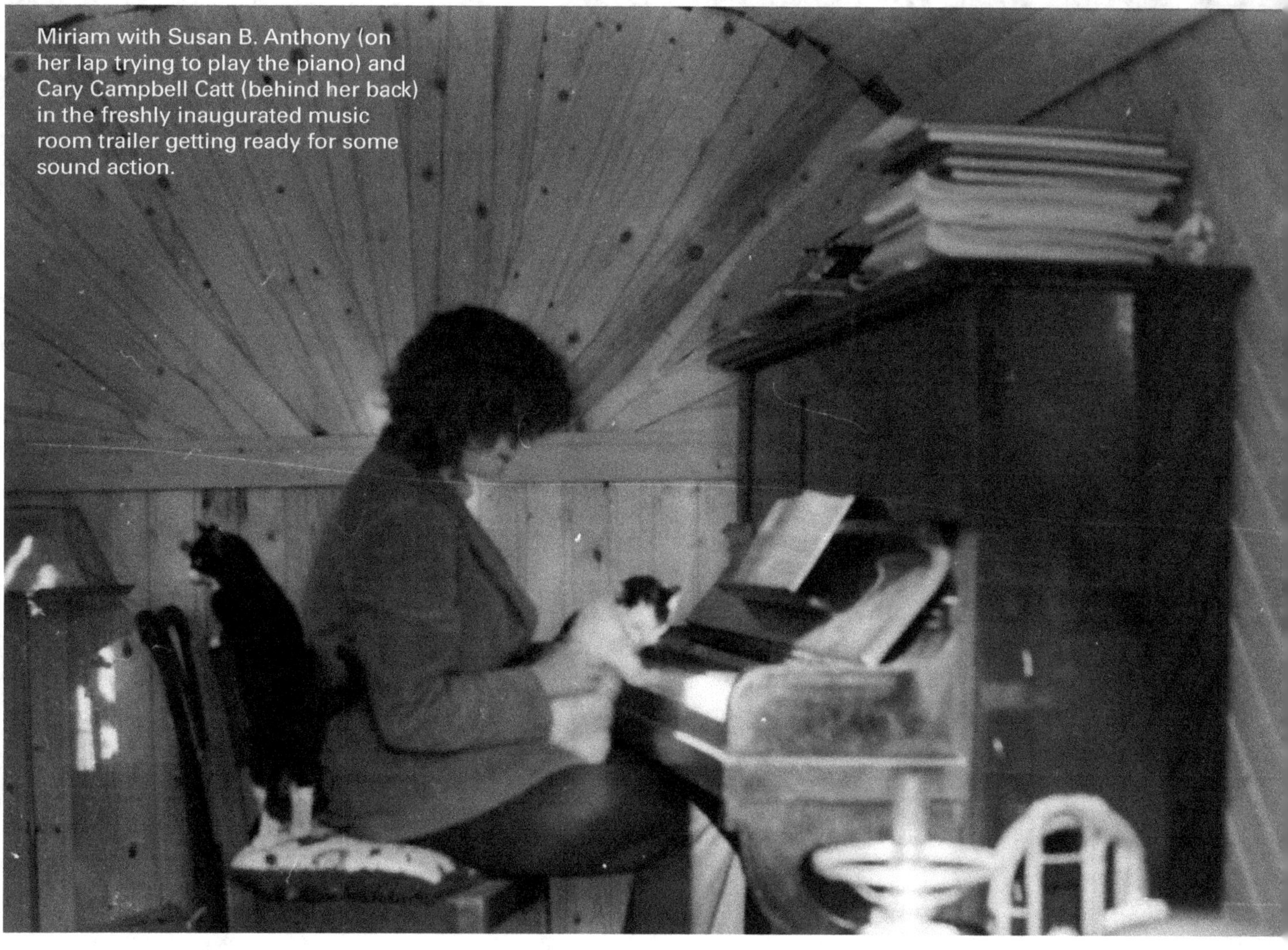

Miriam with Susan B. Anthony (on her lap trying to play the piano) and Cary Campbell Catt (behind her back) in the freshly inaugurated music room trailer getting ready for some sound action.

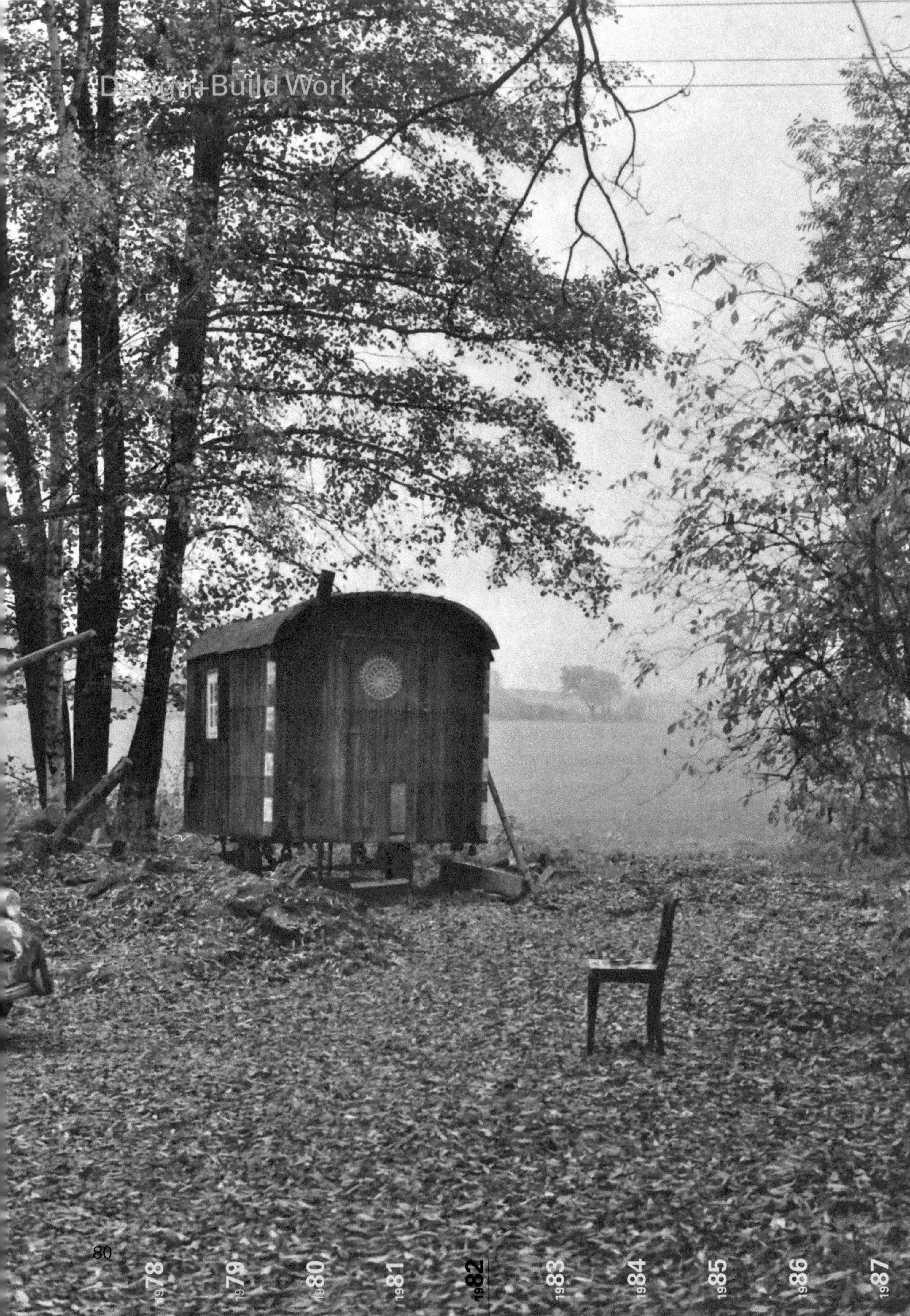

Studio Trailer

After the successfull conversion of one construction trailer into Miriam's music room I decided to make space for my art as well. This time I opted for another 15'-long single-axle trailer but rather than just renovate the interior I wanted

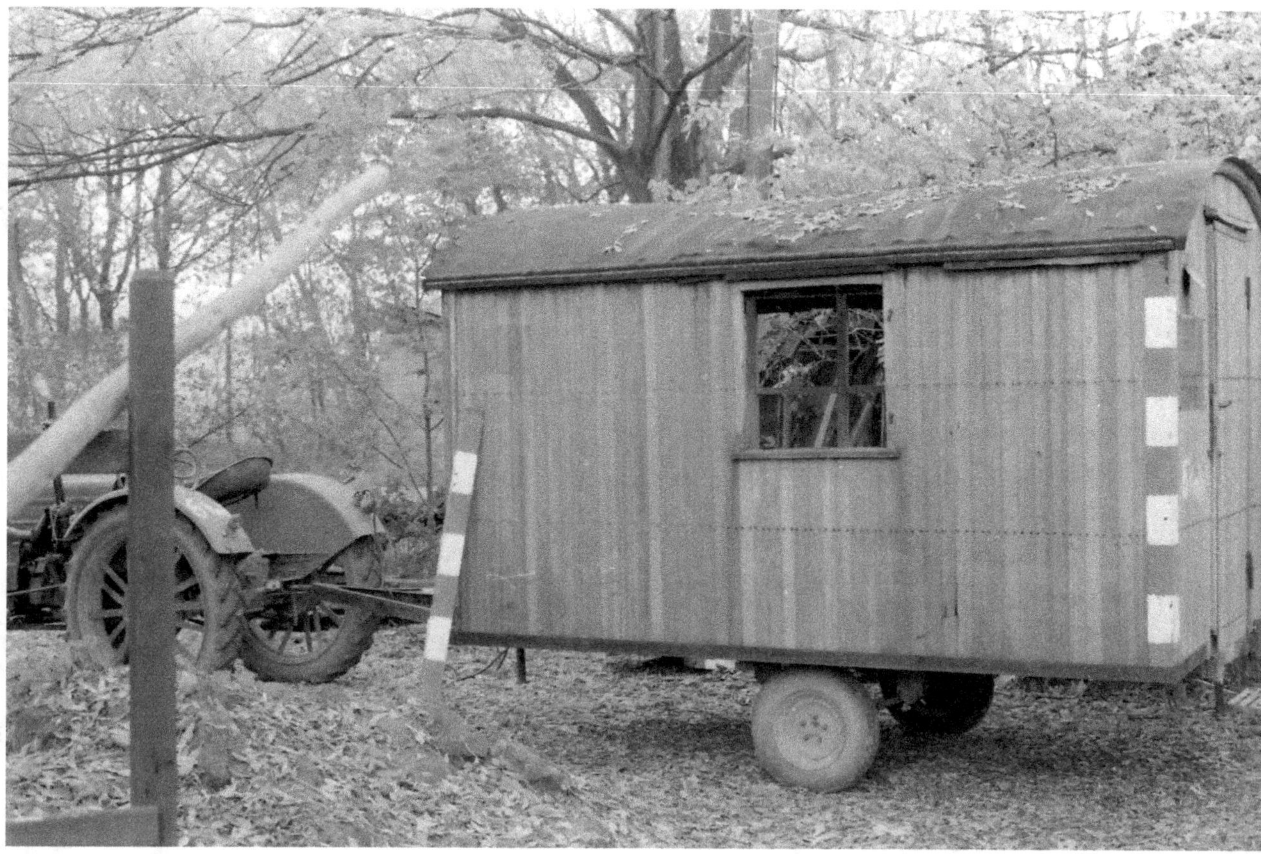

Raw material

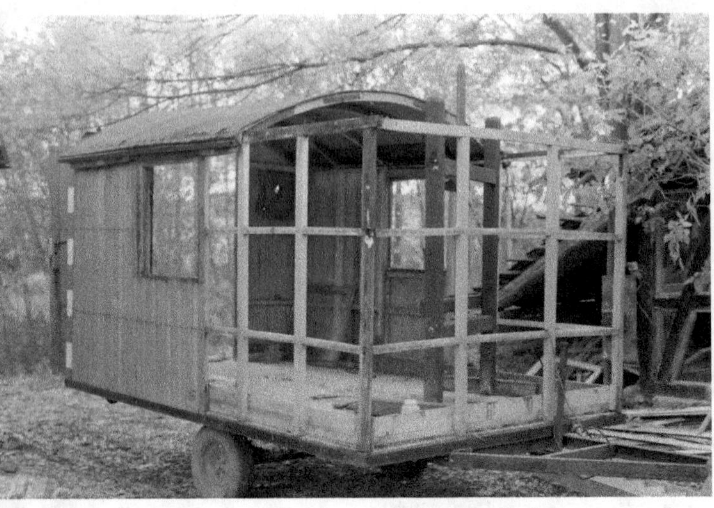

Gradual conversion of trailer with demontage of walls, insertion of a home-made easel, and addition of recycled windows.

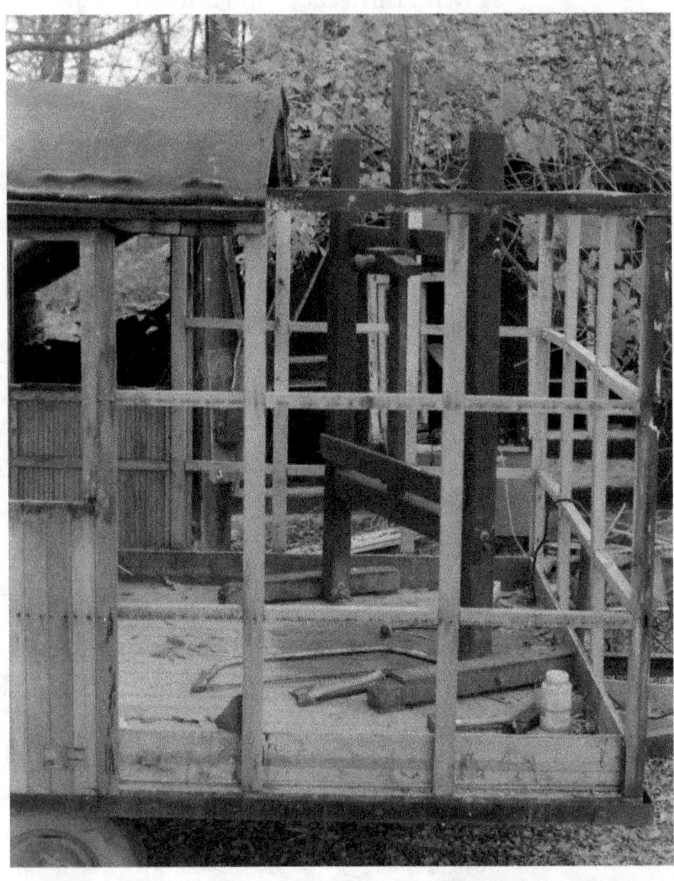

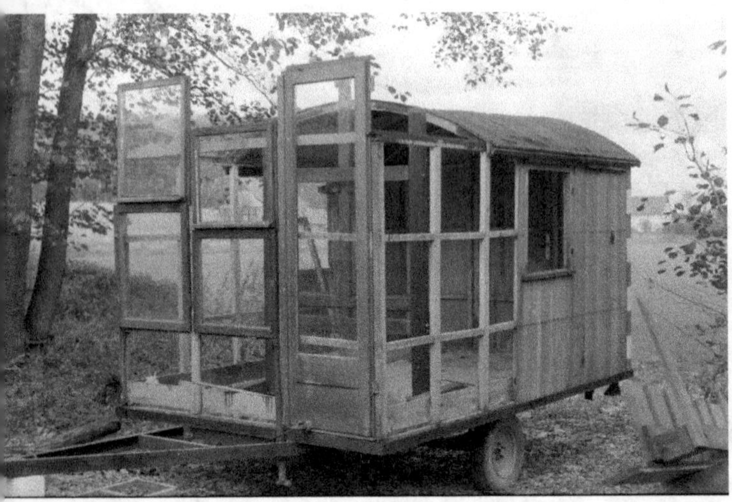

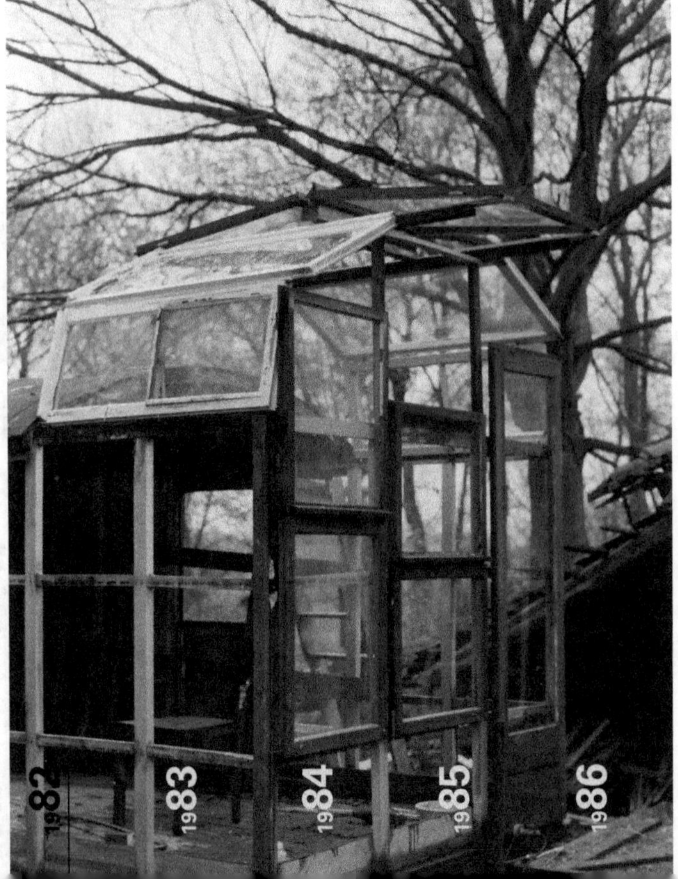

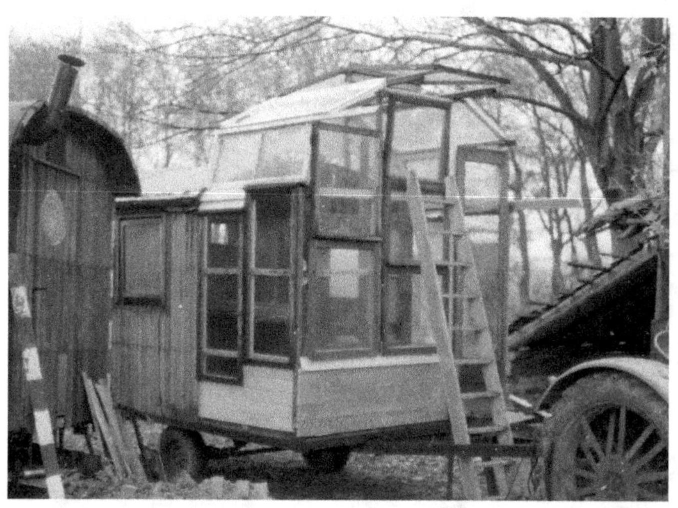

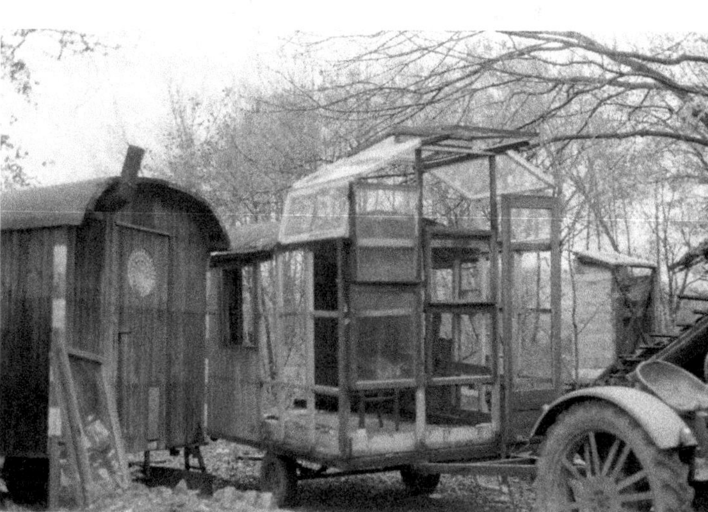

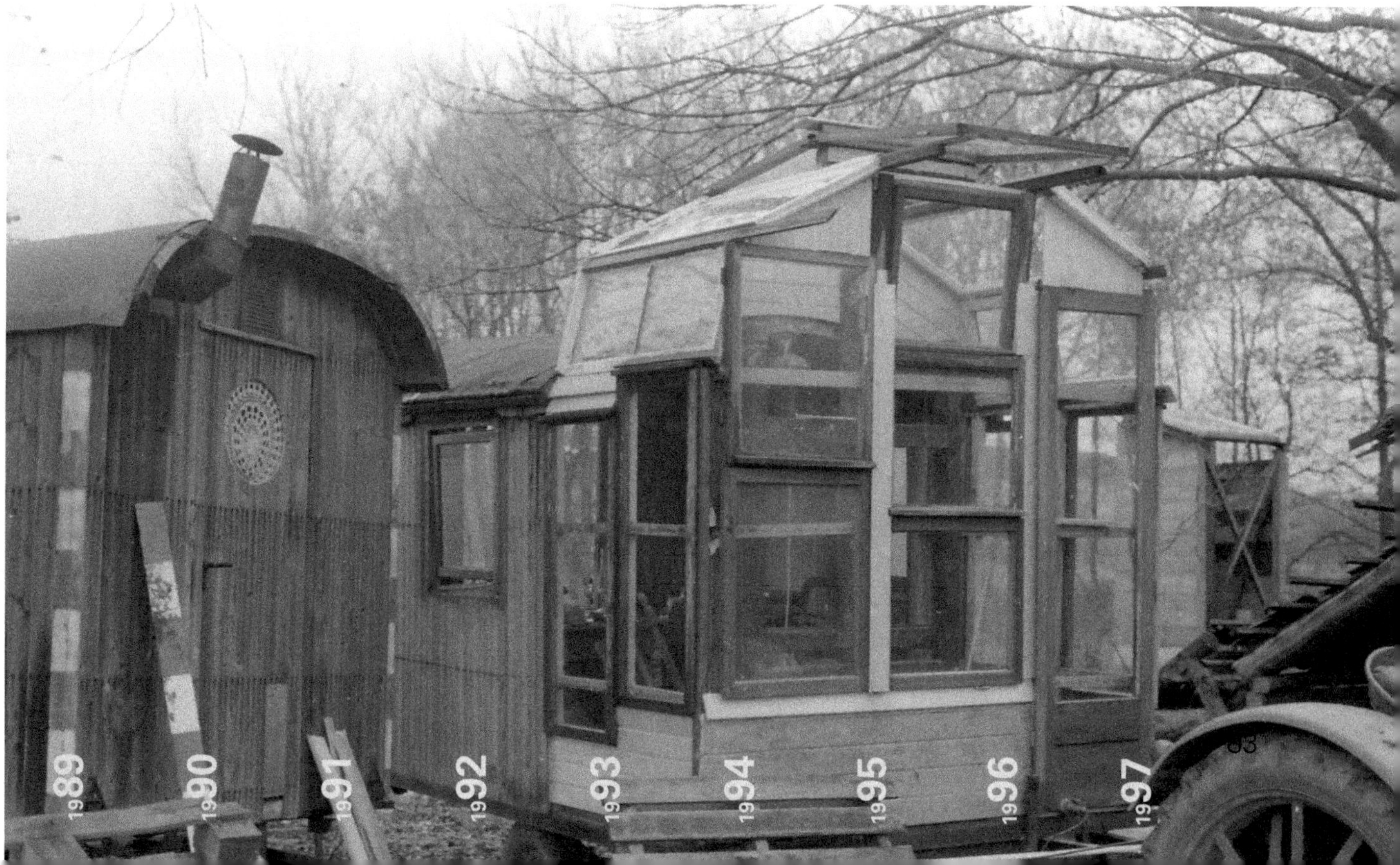

1988 1989 1990 1991 1992 1993 1994 1995 1996 1997

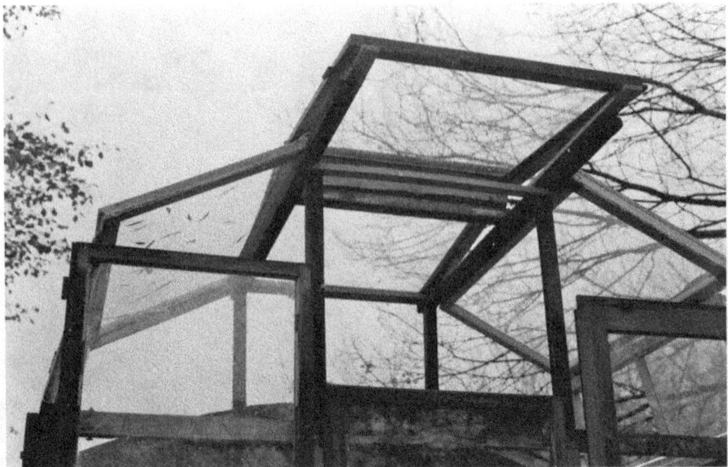

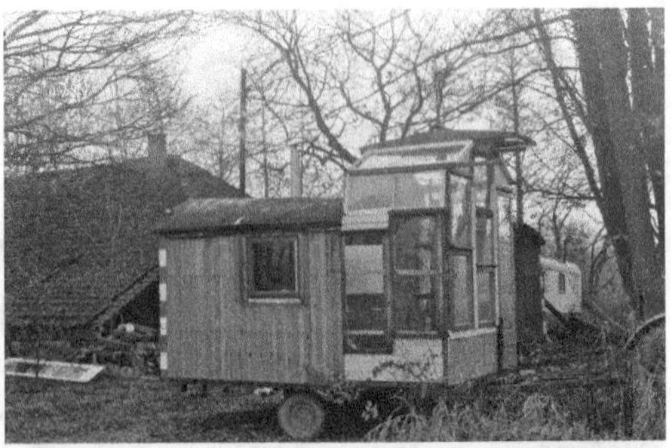

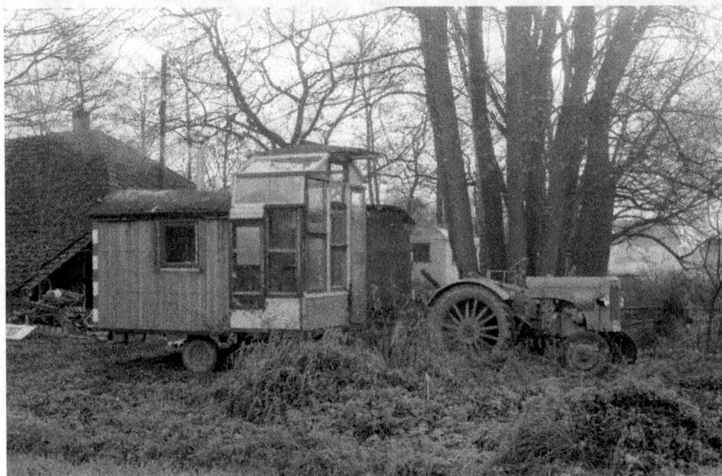

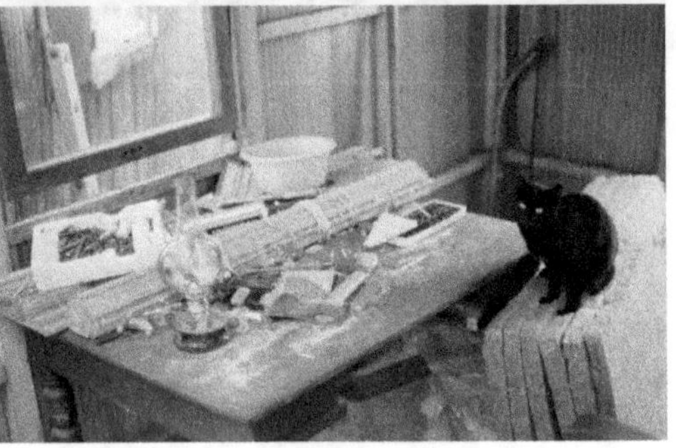

The finished studio trailer.

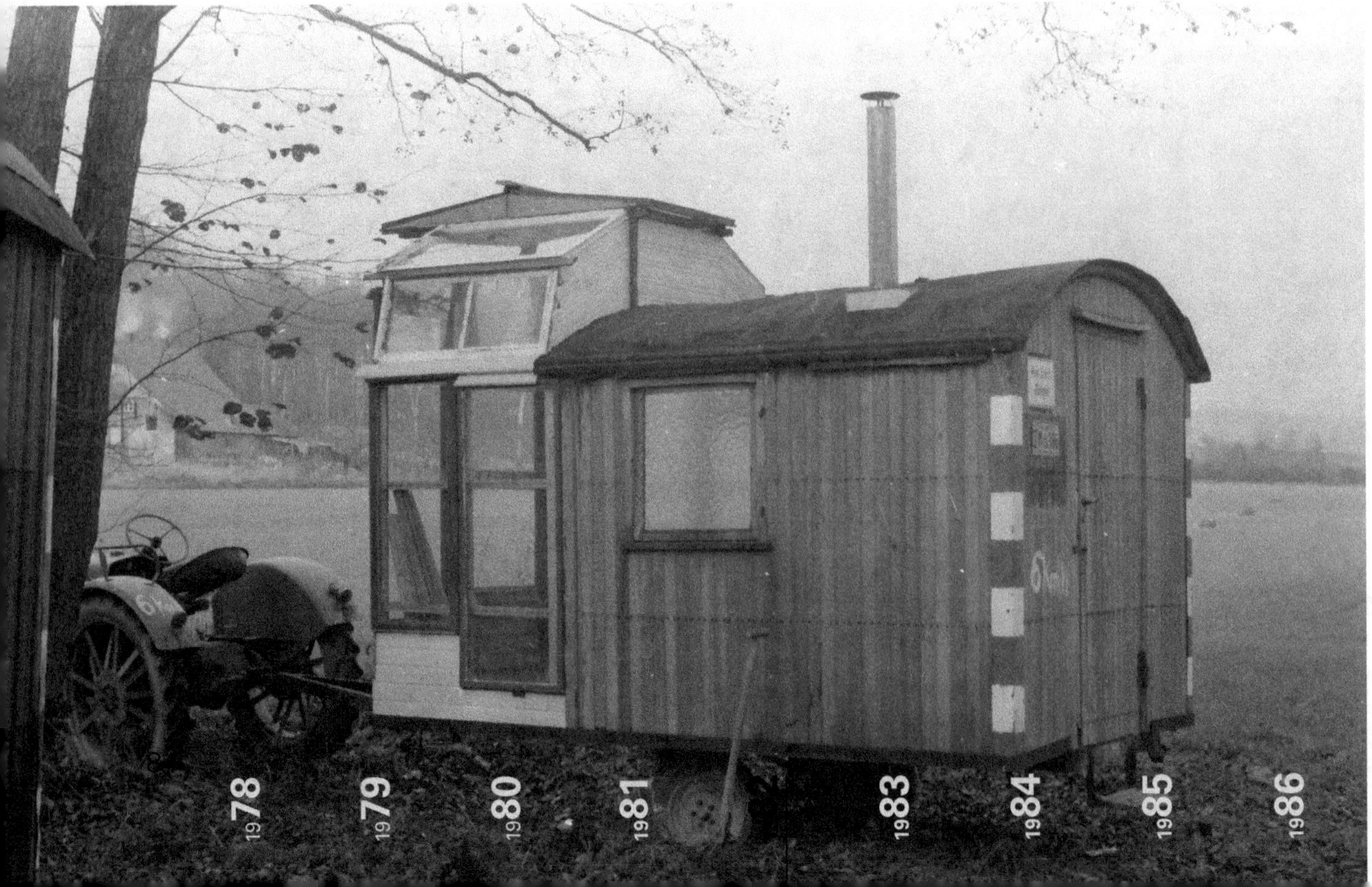

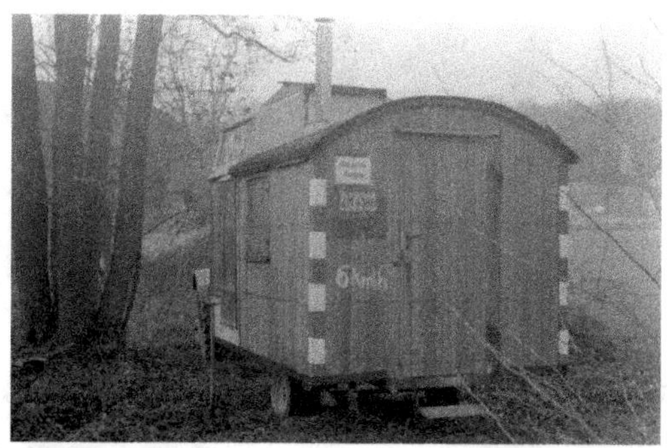

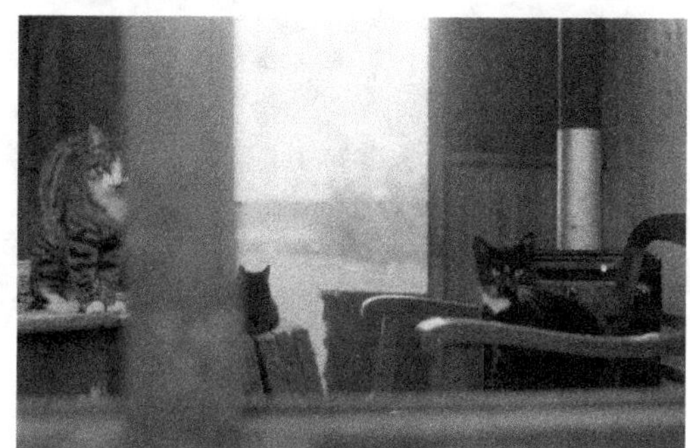

Three cats

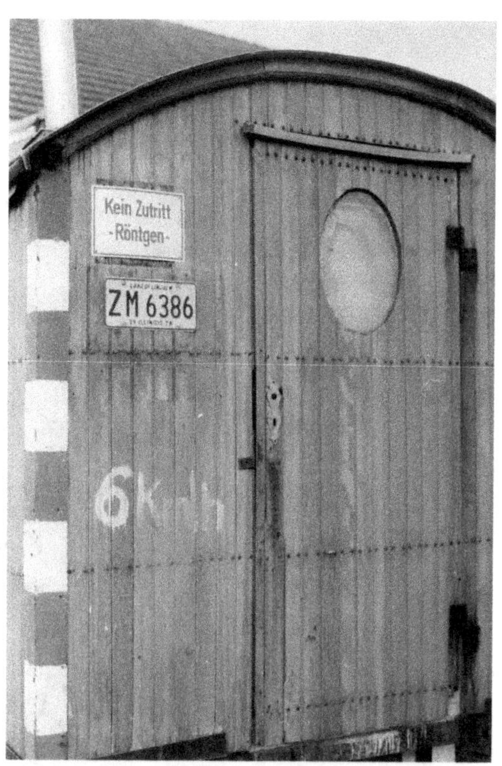

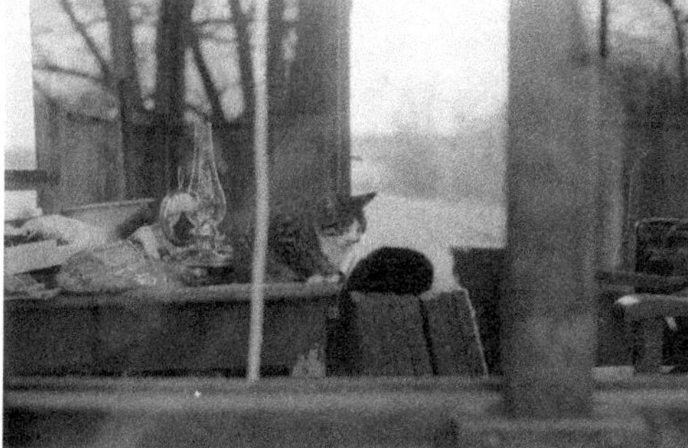

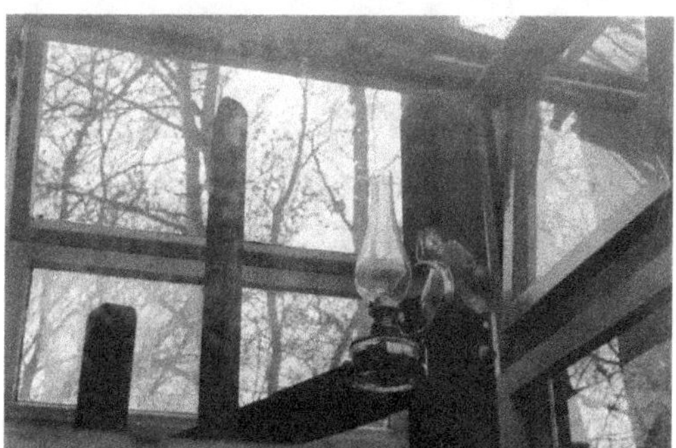

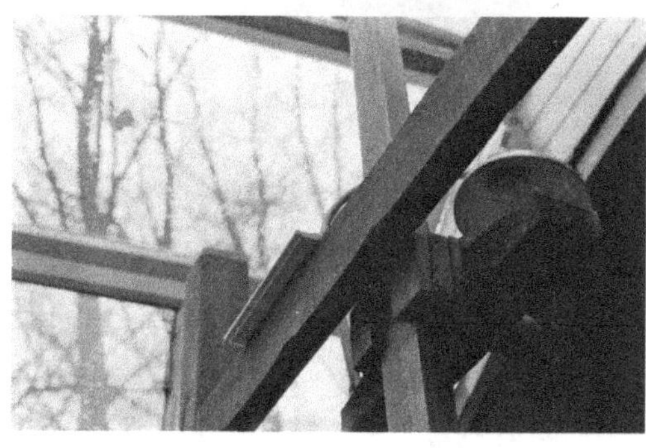

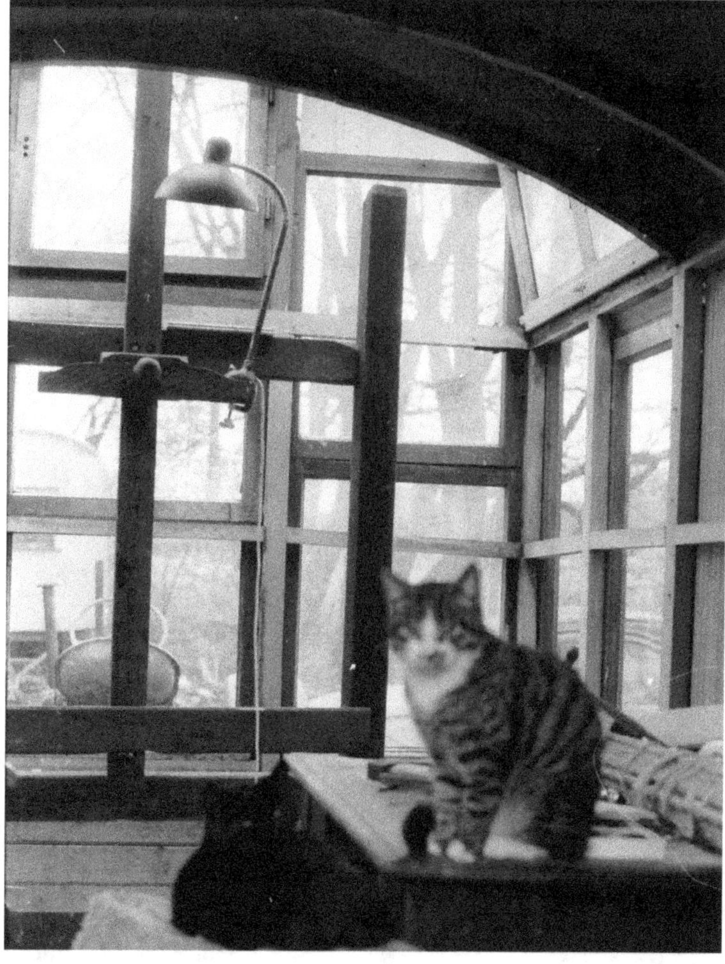

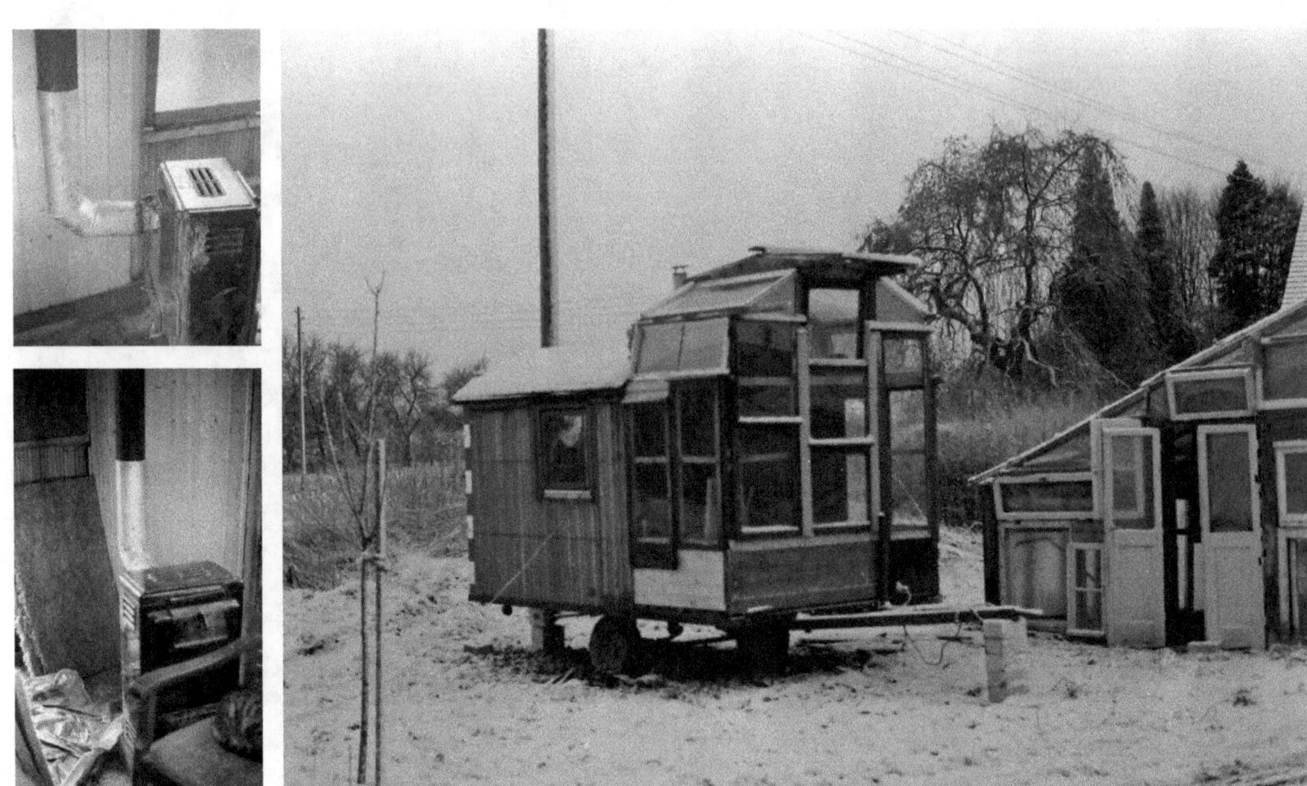

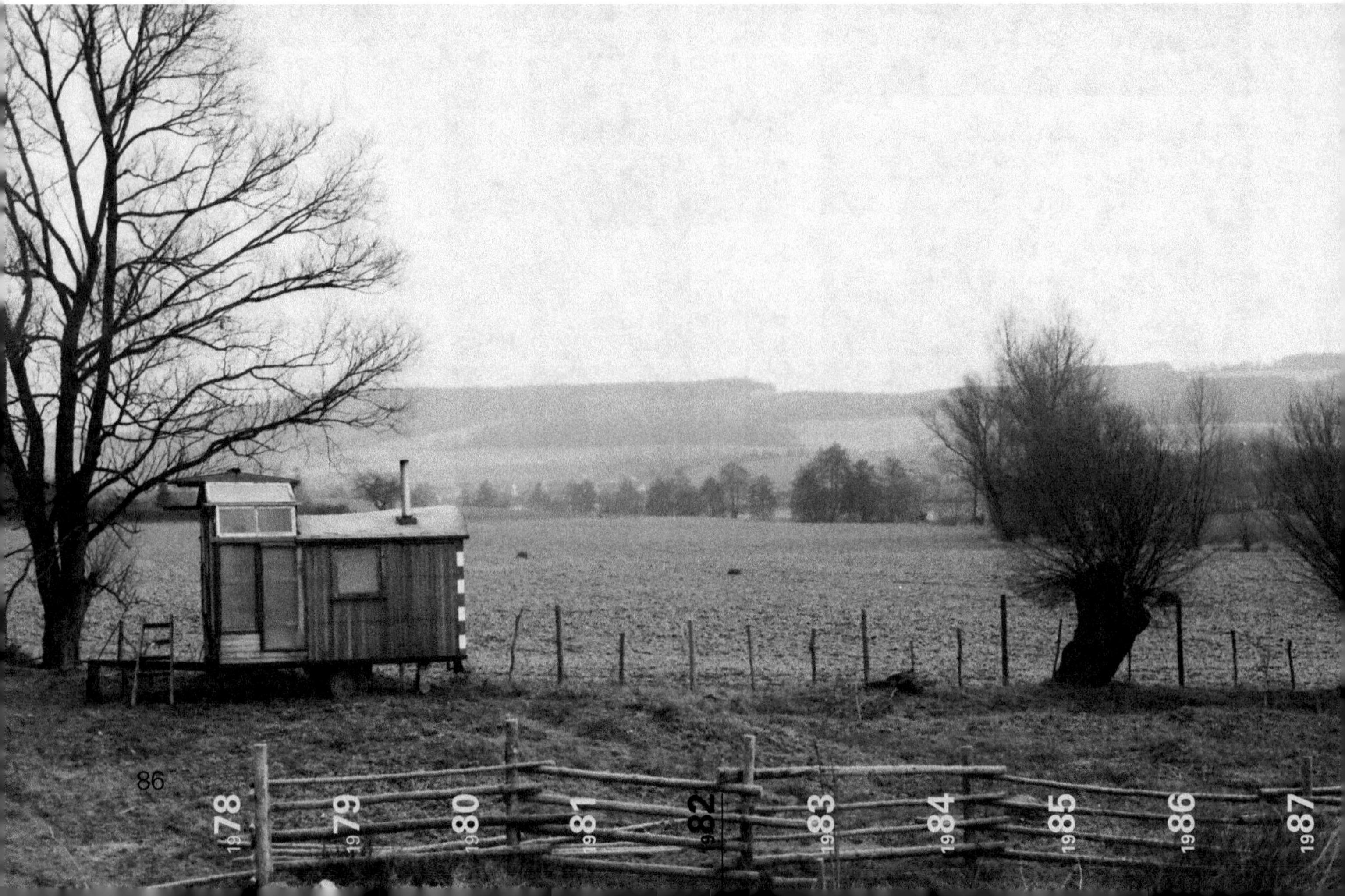

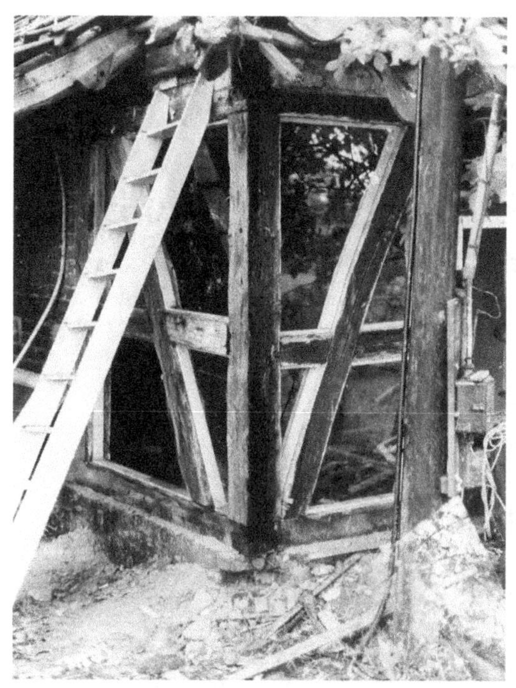

Corner Design

At some point we realized that the corners in the mill rooms were rather dark, and we set out to improve the room's natural lighting. The task was to increase the amount of daylight in a room in which the windows face north and thus let in only a limited amount of light and almost no direct sunlight. I had to be aware of several suppositions prior to starting this project. To begin with, I did not want to change the outer facade of the *Fachwerk* too much, i.e. putting larger windows into the facade was out of the question. Secondly, the new window area had to be insulated as much as possible because the only heating source for that room was a small coal stove. Thirdly, the areas that were destined to be glazed were irregularly shaped which meant that the glass panes had be custom-cut. My solution for these problems was to go to a local glass shop that had specialized in vinyl windows, and ask for permission to salvage all the old window panes that would be otherwise discarded in a dumpster. Permission granted I taught myself how to cut the glass panes out of the salvaged window frames and then cut them down to the shape and size that I needed for the *Fachwerk* spaces. To achieve a higher rate of insulation I used two-inch spacers, nailed on the *Fachwerk* beams, between two glass panes per field, thus creating an air pocket. The glass panes were glued on the spacers with silicon, allowing for the settiling of the *Fachwerk* beams without causing tension in the glass. After completion of the project I used the room as a secondary studio space.

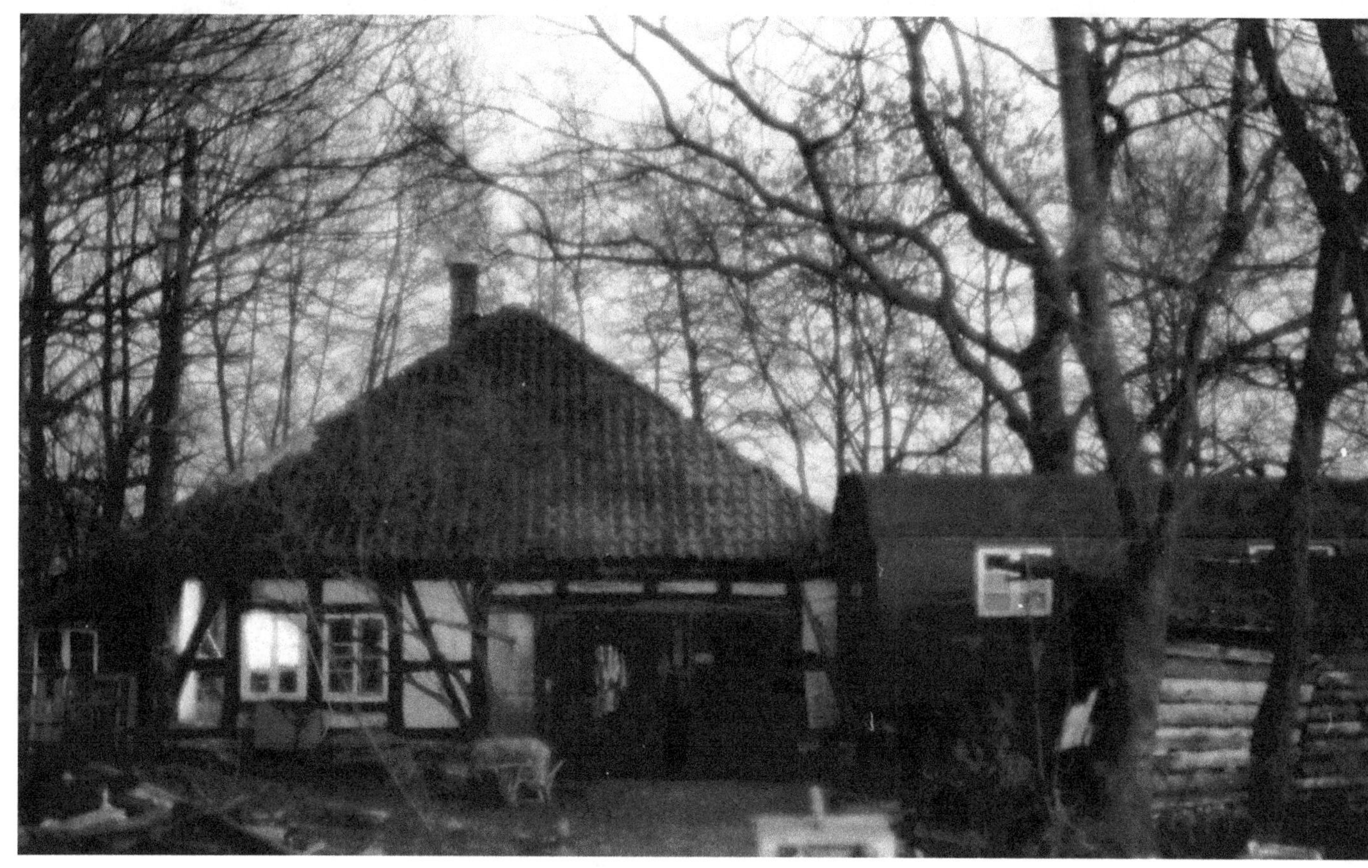

Firewood Storage Shed, Watermill
Design/Build

In the fall Manni and I decided to design-build a wood storage structure to the west of the watermill. The idea was to keep the freshly cut firewood dry, and to camouflage Da Capo who was always more visible from the road in the winter.

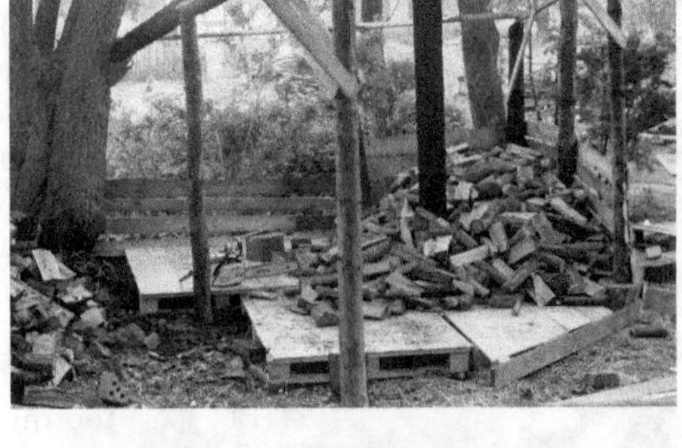

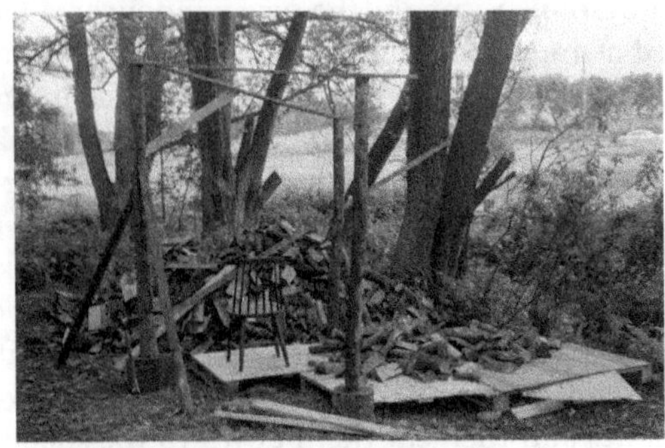

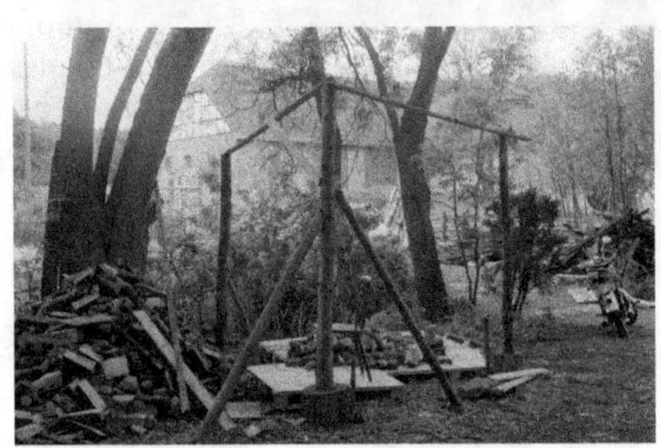

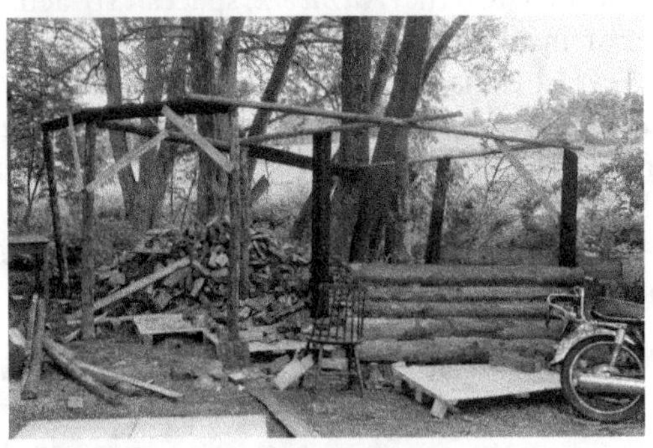

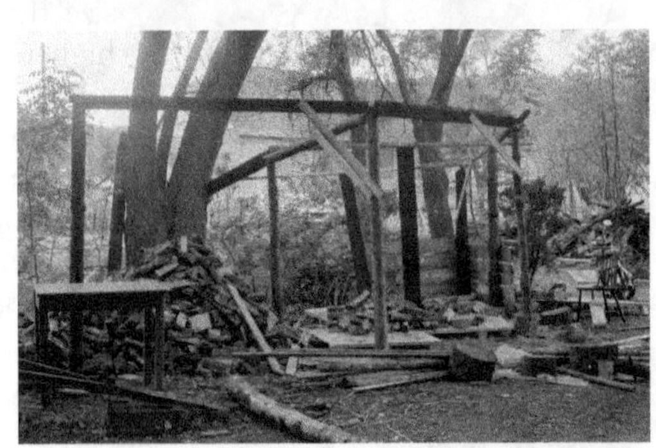

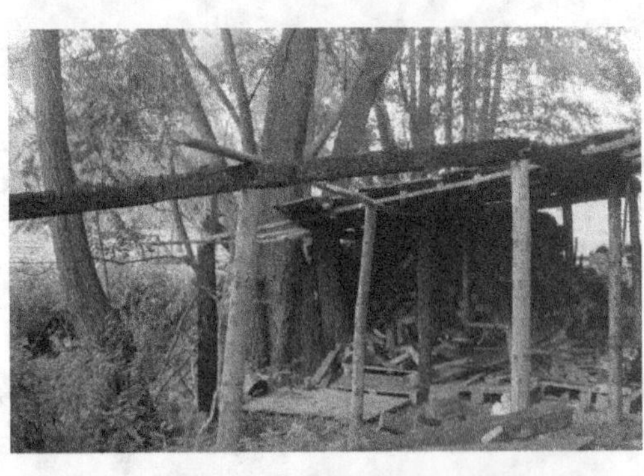

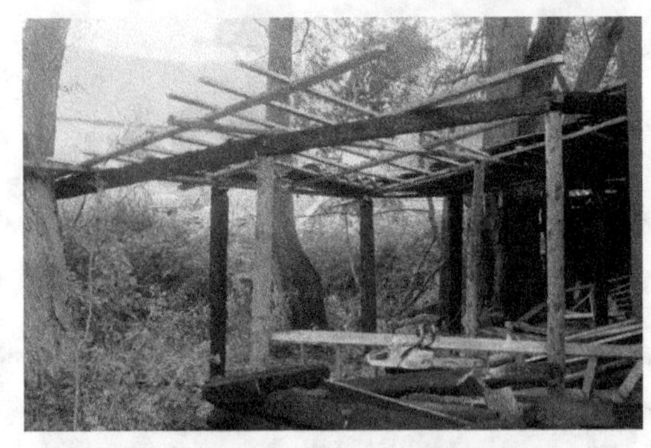

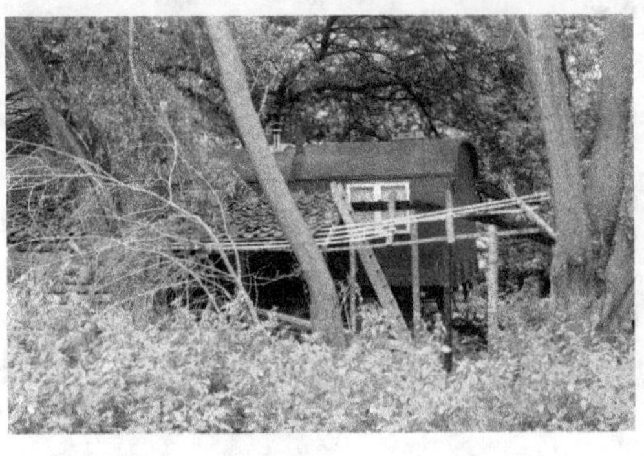

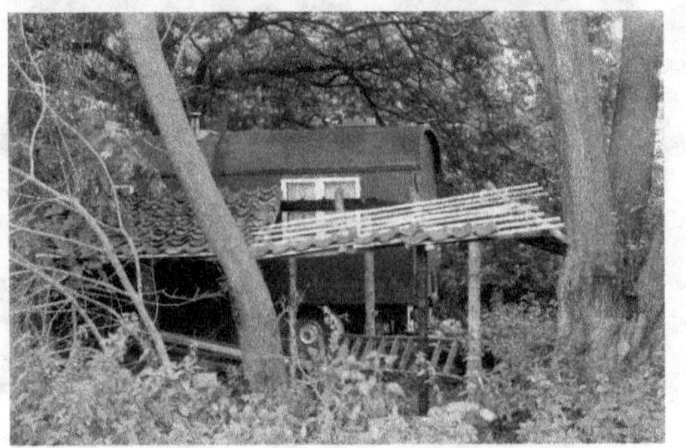

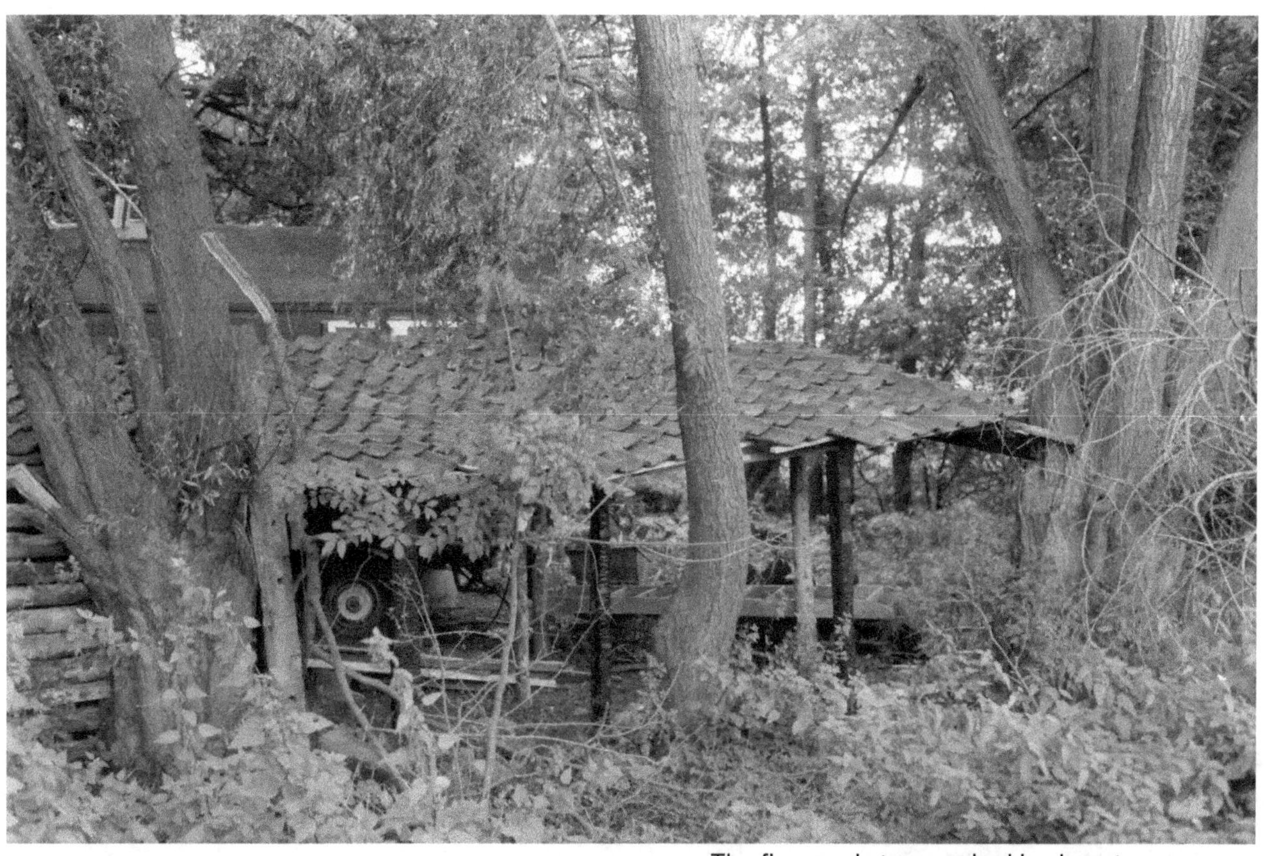

The firewood storage shed is almost complete, and hides Da Capo behind a scaly scrim of recycled wood columns and clay roof tiles

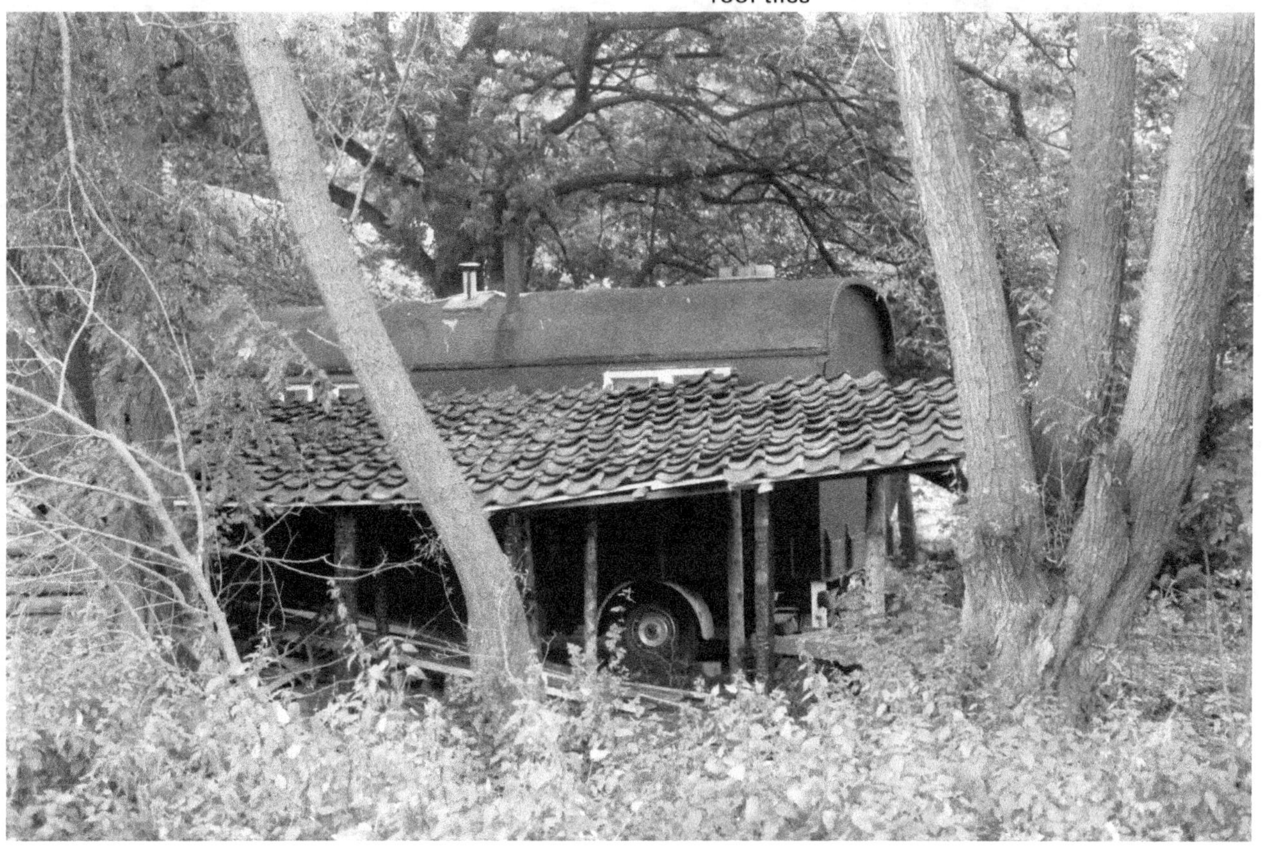

A goose (lower right corner) flying in from the fields adjacent to the watermill, early in a summer morning...

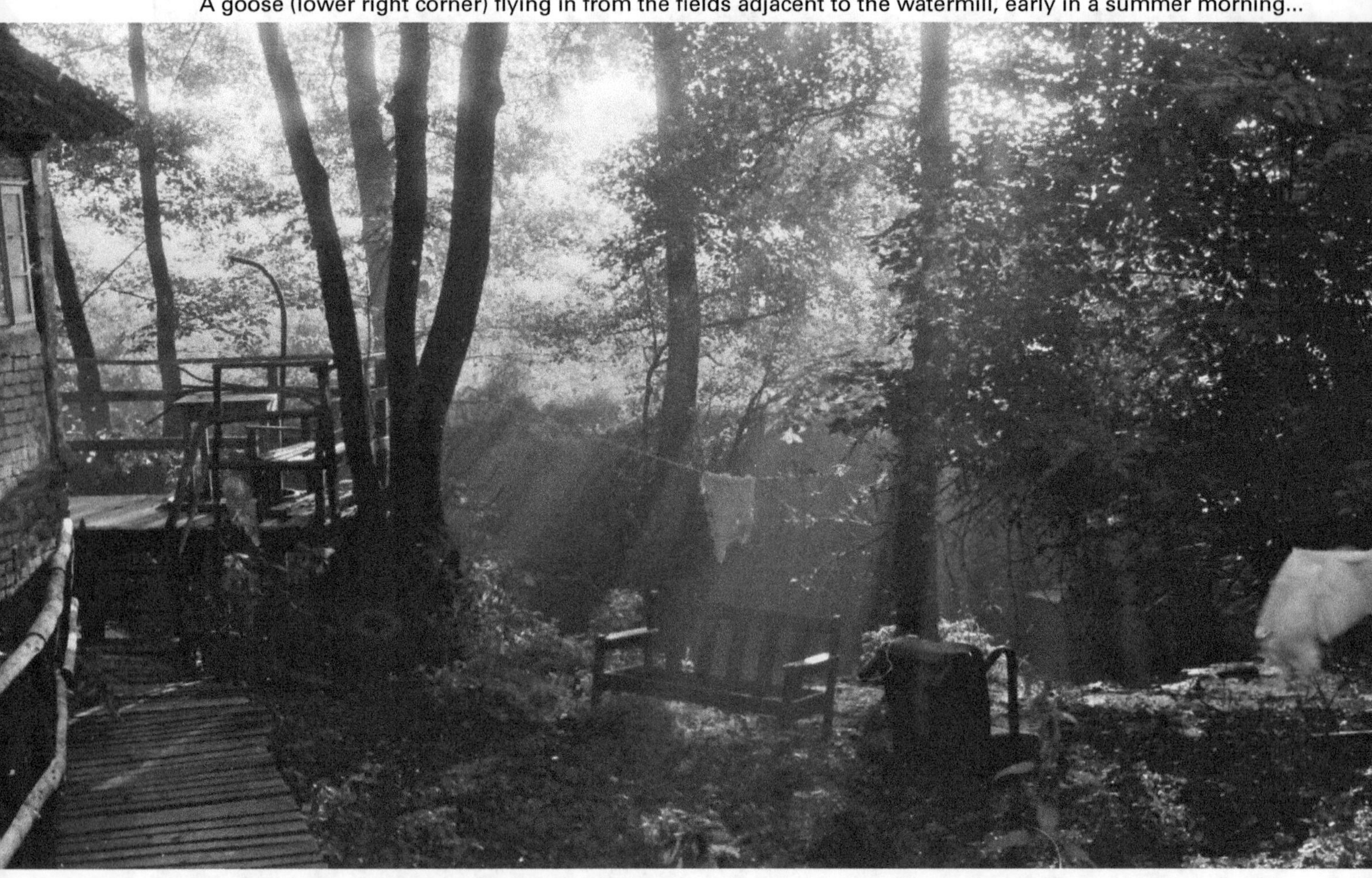

...and the watermill, all overgrown with vegetation in mid summer

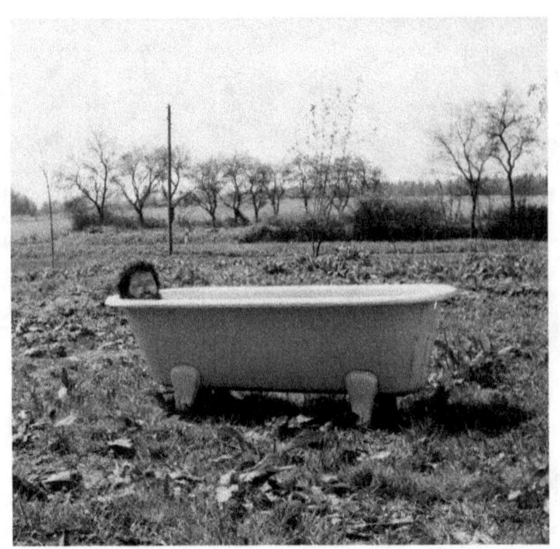

Too much time at the watermill in combination with a found bathtub and a tenor horn can lead to strangeness in the middle of Germany (photos by Tom Zimmermann, and no, he's not Bob's cousin)

Rowing

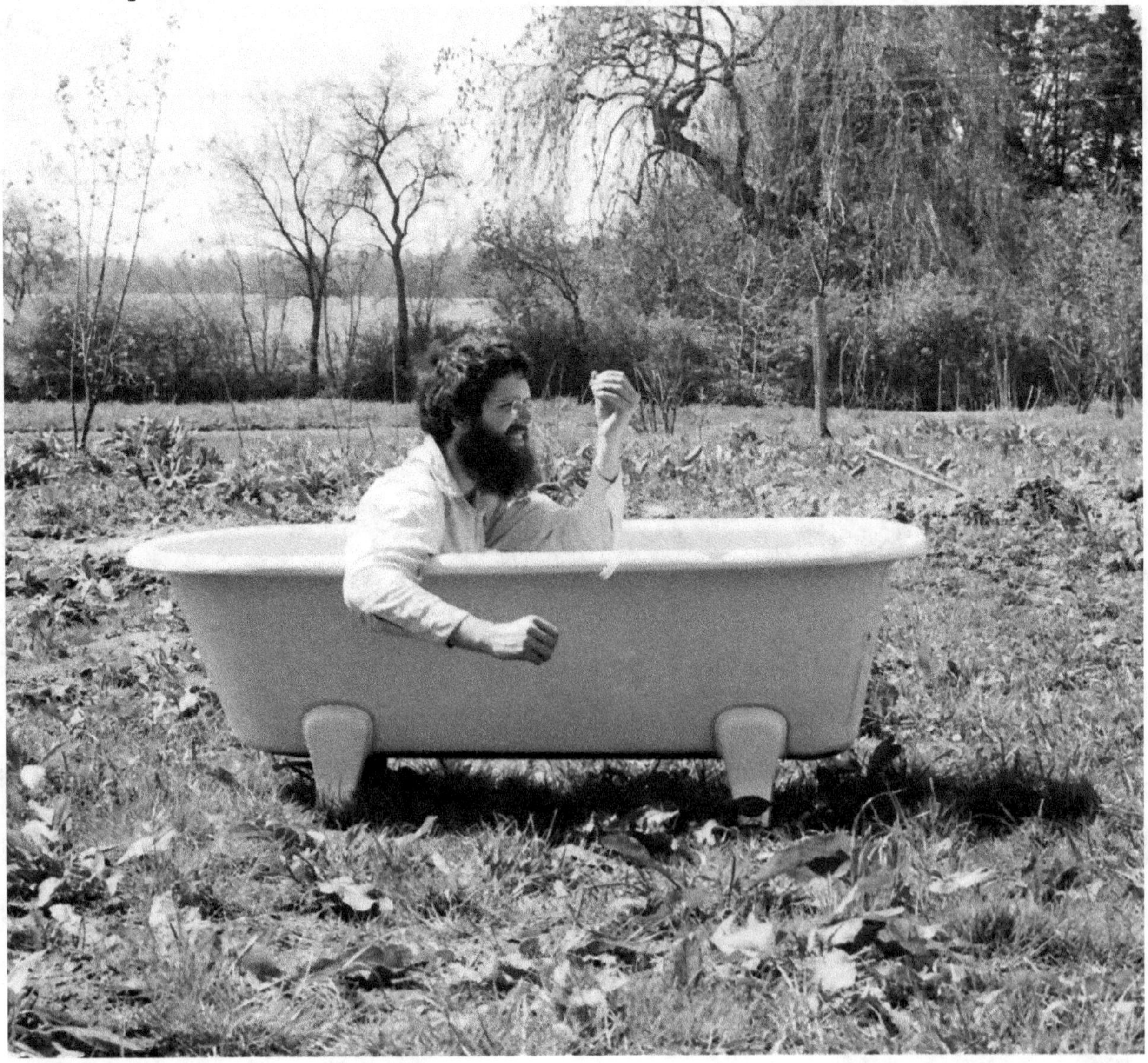

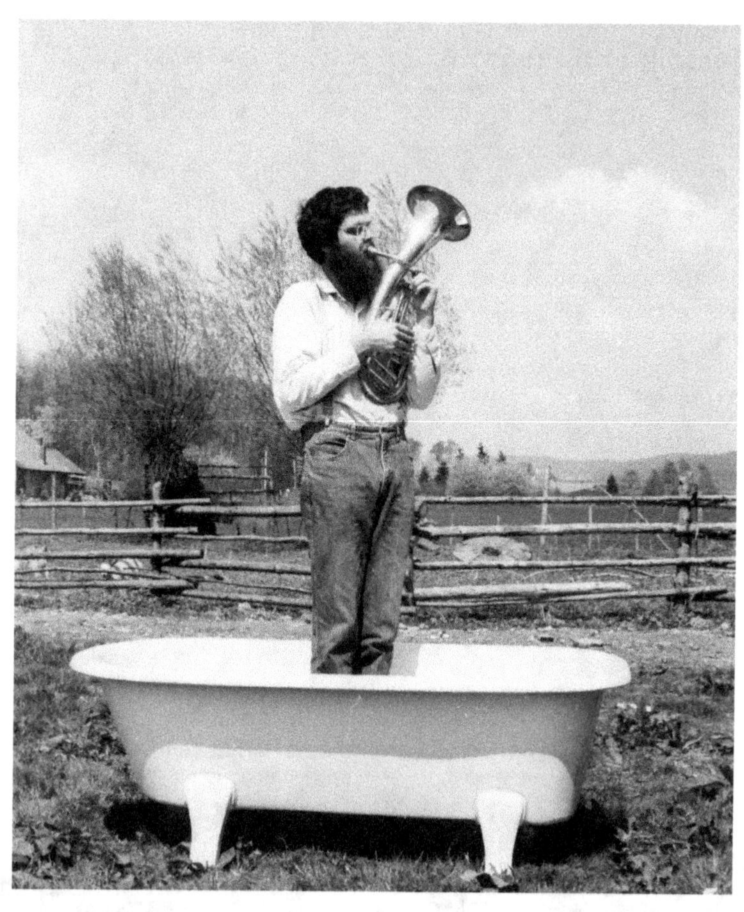

Master of my domain

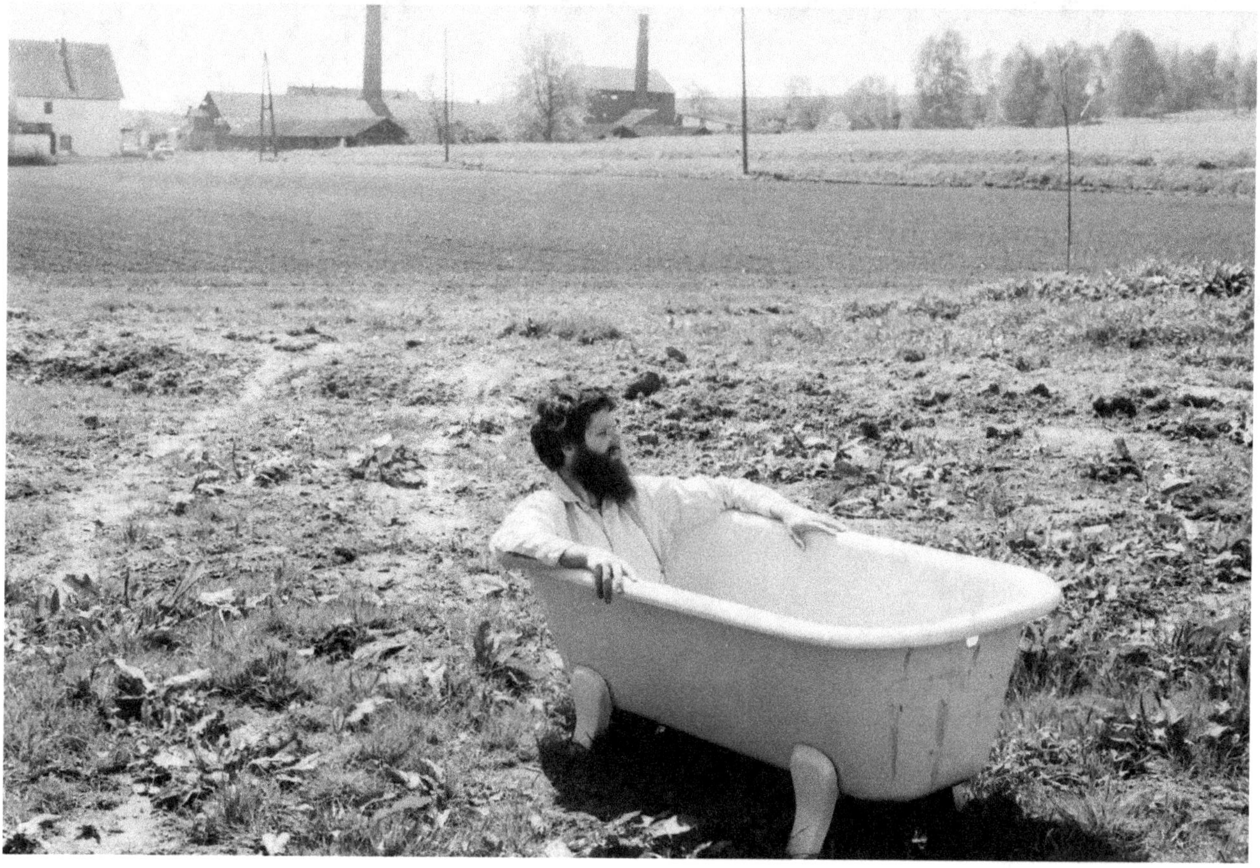

Photography

Italy
Pistoia and Environs

In the ralm of music, as in the other arts, it's important o be curious (photo by Miriam Zach)

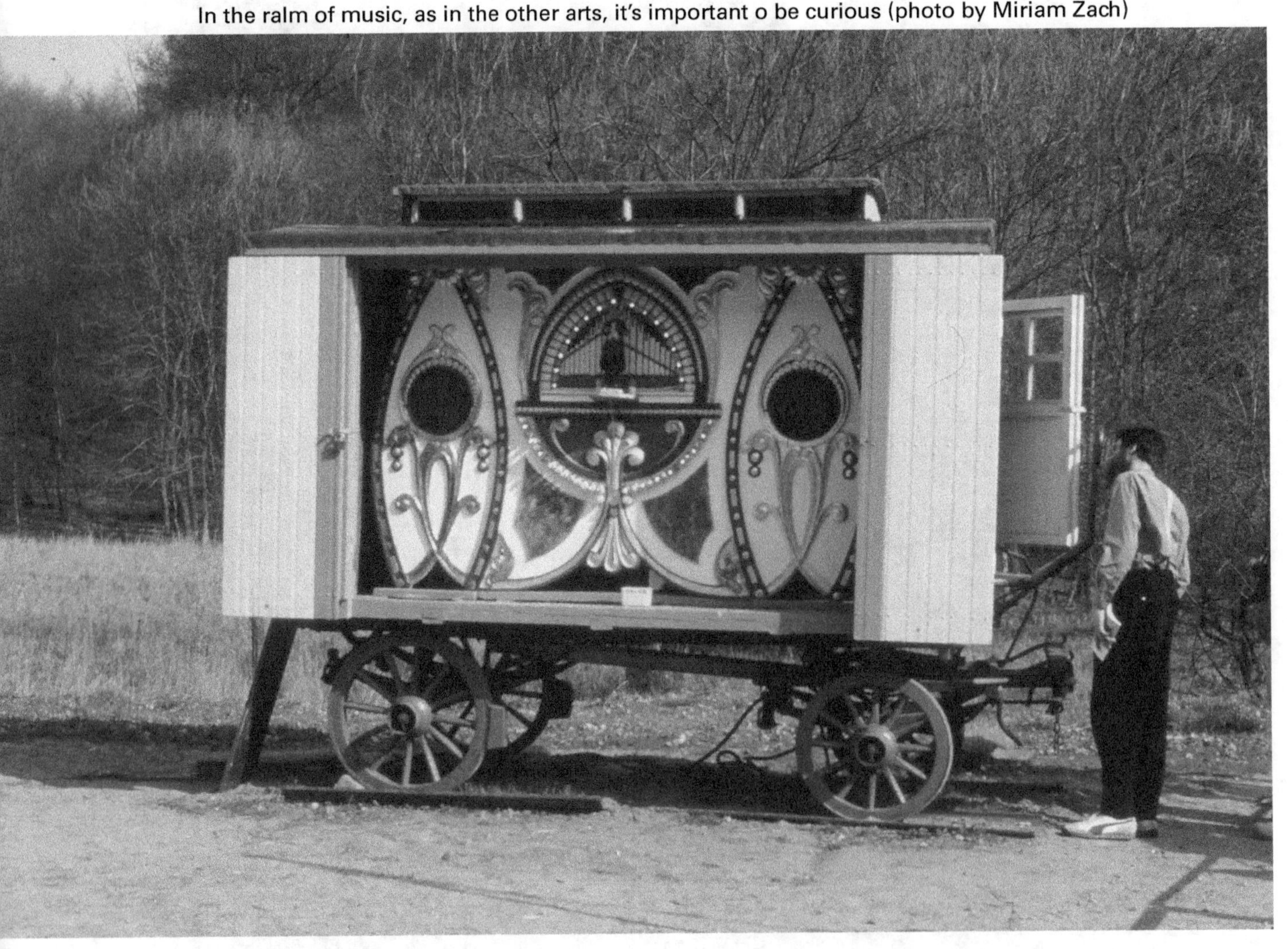

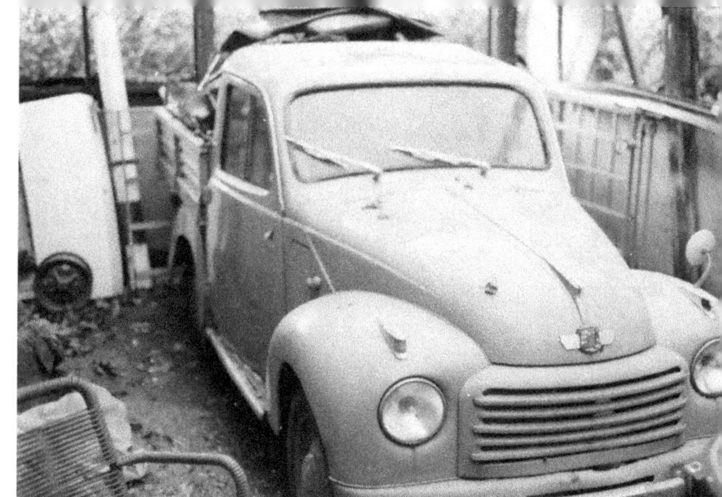

A Fiat Topolino. I've always been fascinated by the relations between names and objects. This must be a German affliction, given how we name everything through compound words. A refrigerator is a 'cool wardrobe', a glove is a 'hand shoe', and a small, mouselike car in Italy is a topolino.

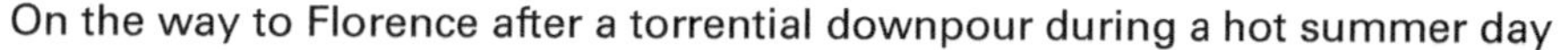

On the way to Florence after a torrential downpour during a hot summer day

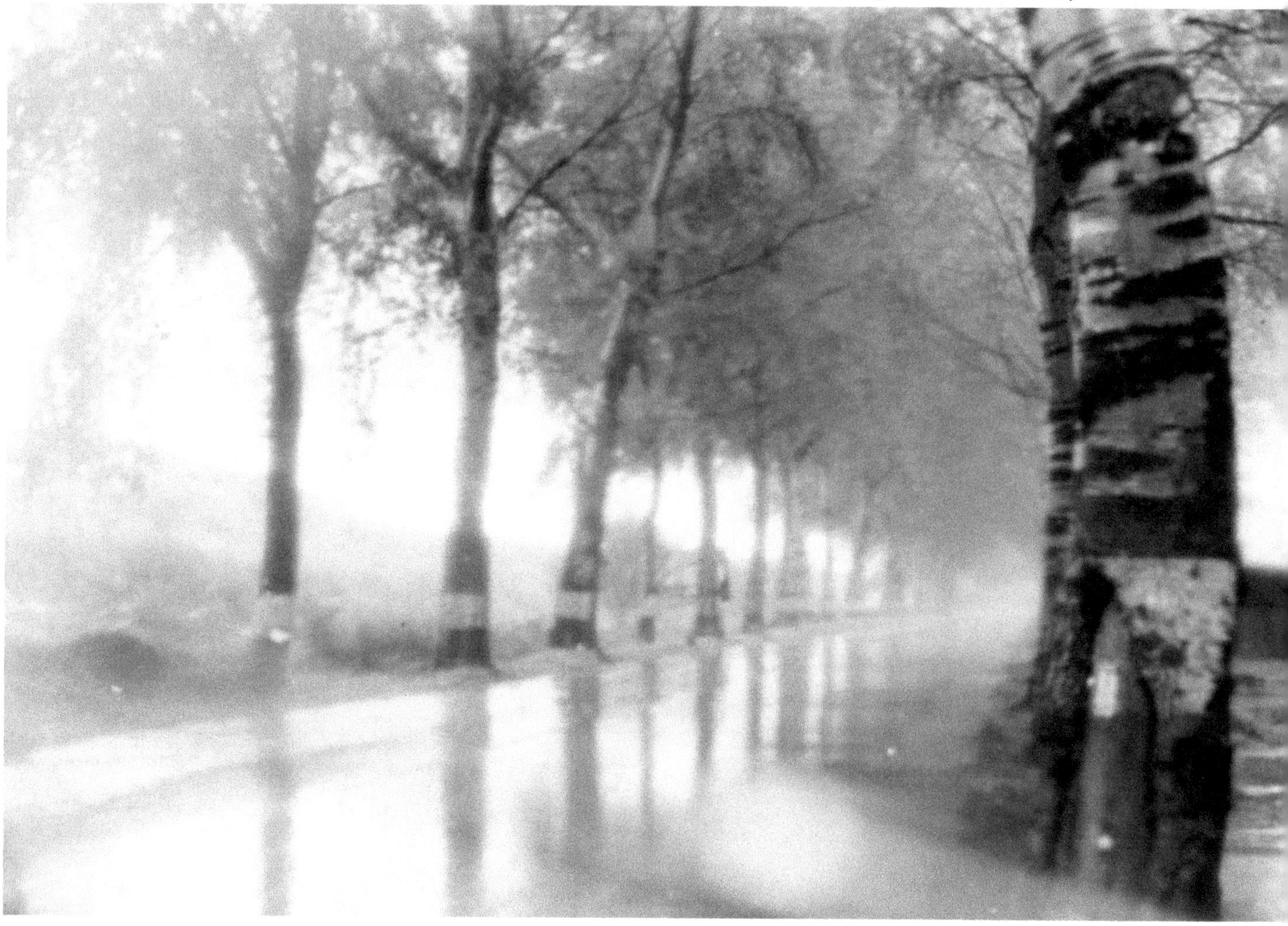

1983

Circus Trailer Living Quarters
Da Capo Conversion (continued)

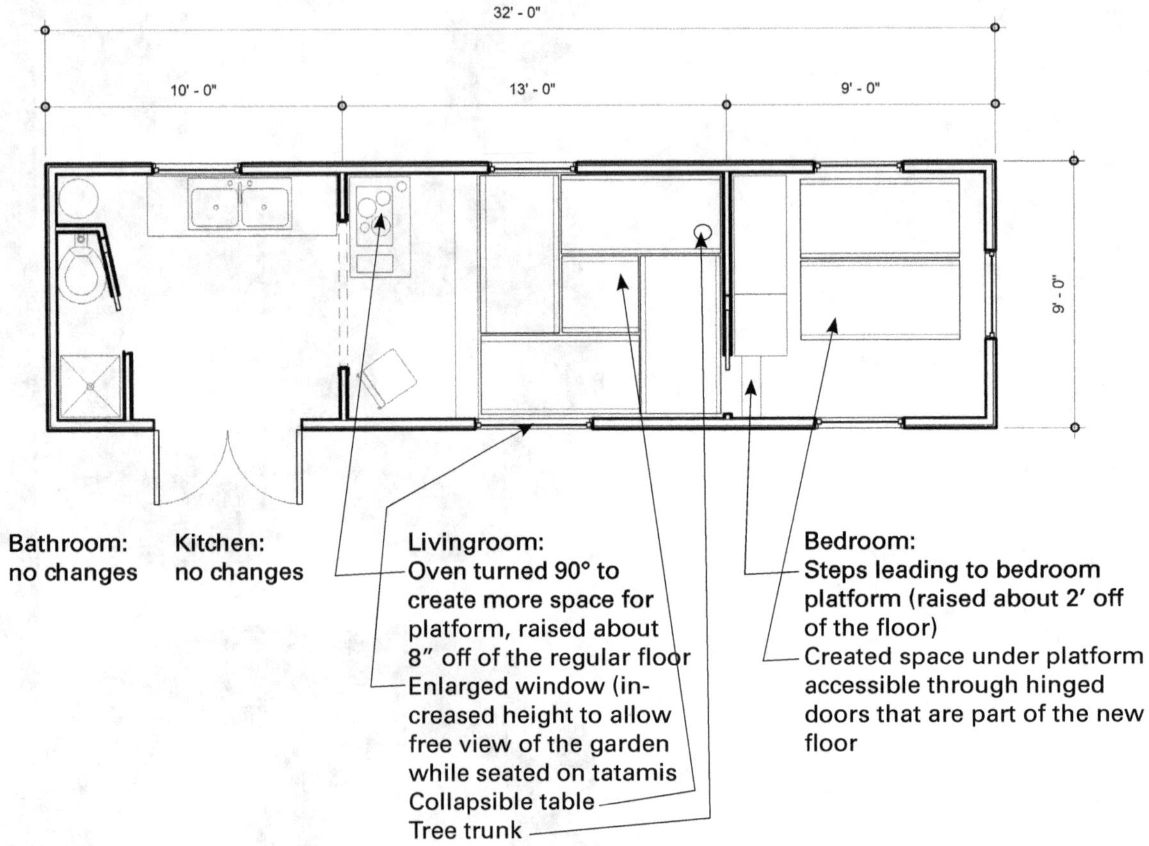

Plan #3

Layout of Trailer, Summer 1983
The table in the living room is flush with the surface of the tatamis, when lowered, thus allowing the use of livingroom as bedroom. Tree trunk forms tokonoma and simultaneously supports the overhead book shelf.

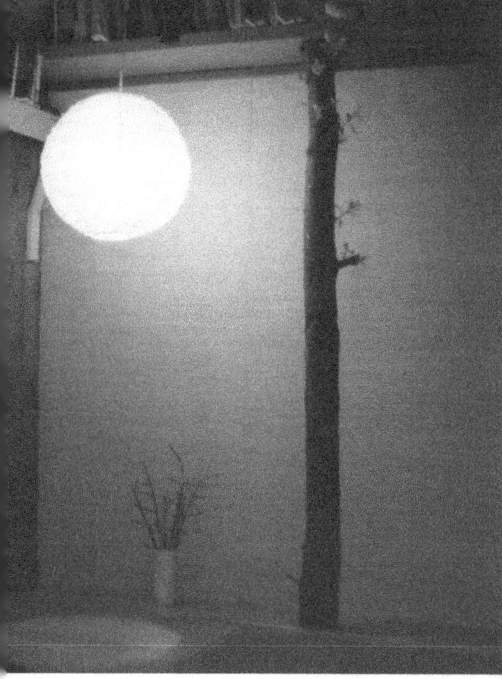

Tokonoma with tree trunk (and budding leaves)

Livingroom wall with screened window to soften light

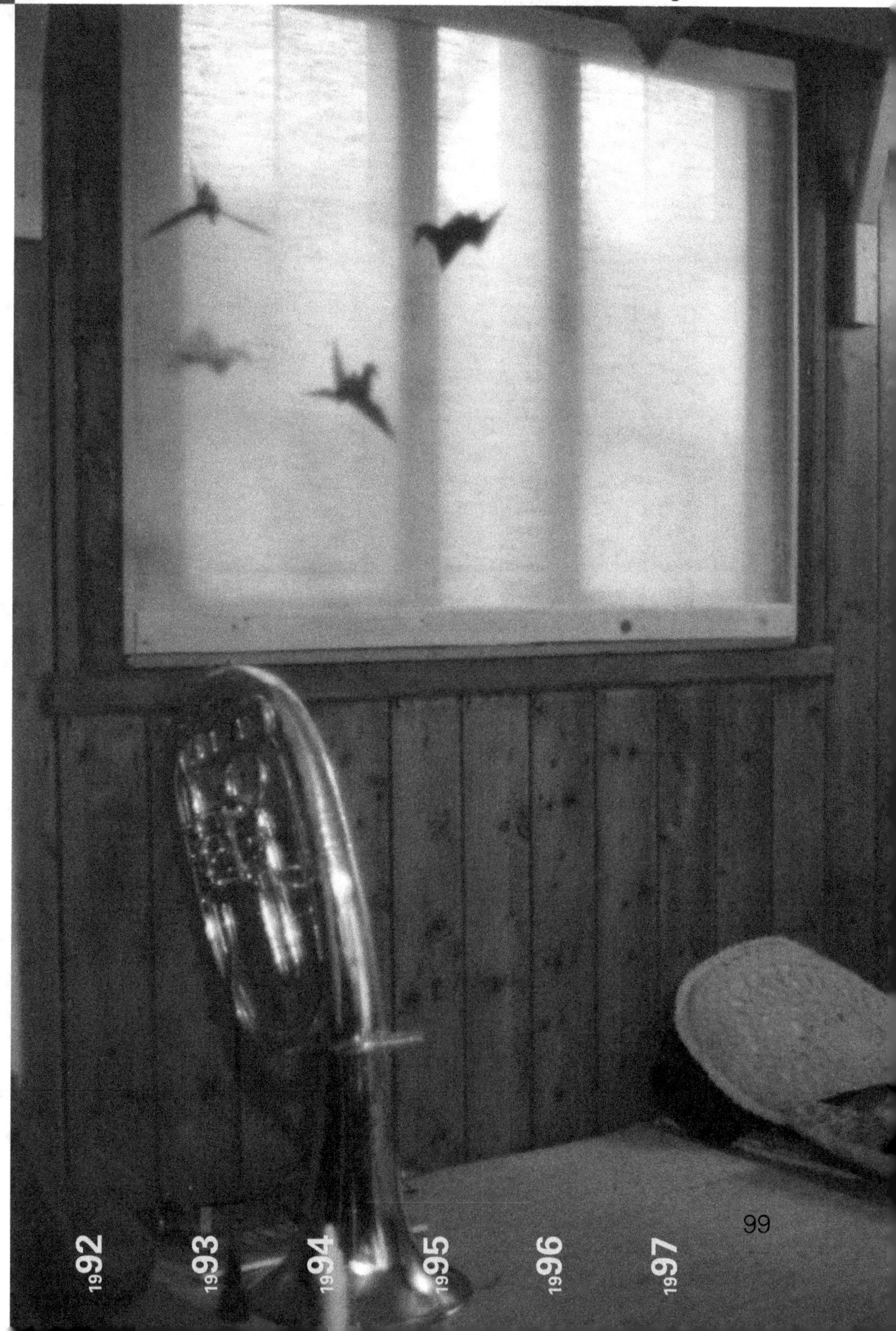

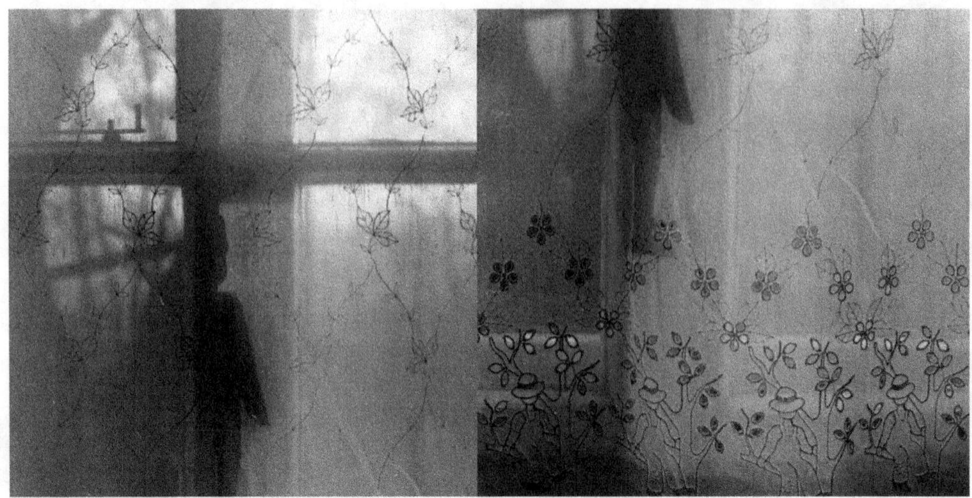

Window and curtain in livingroom

Tokonoma

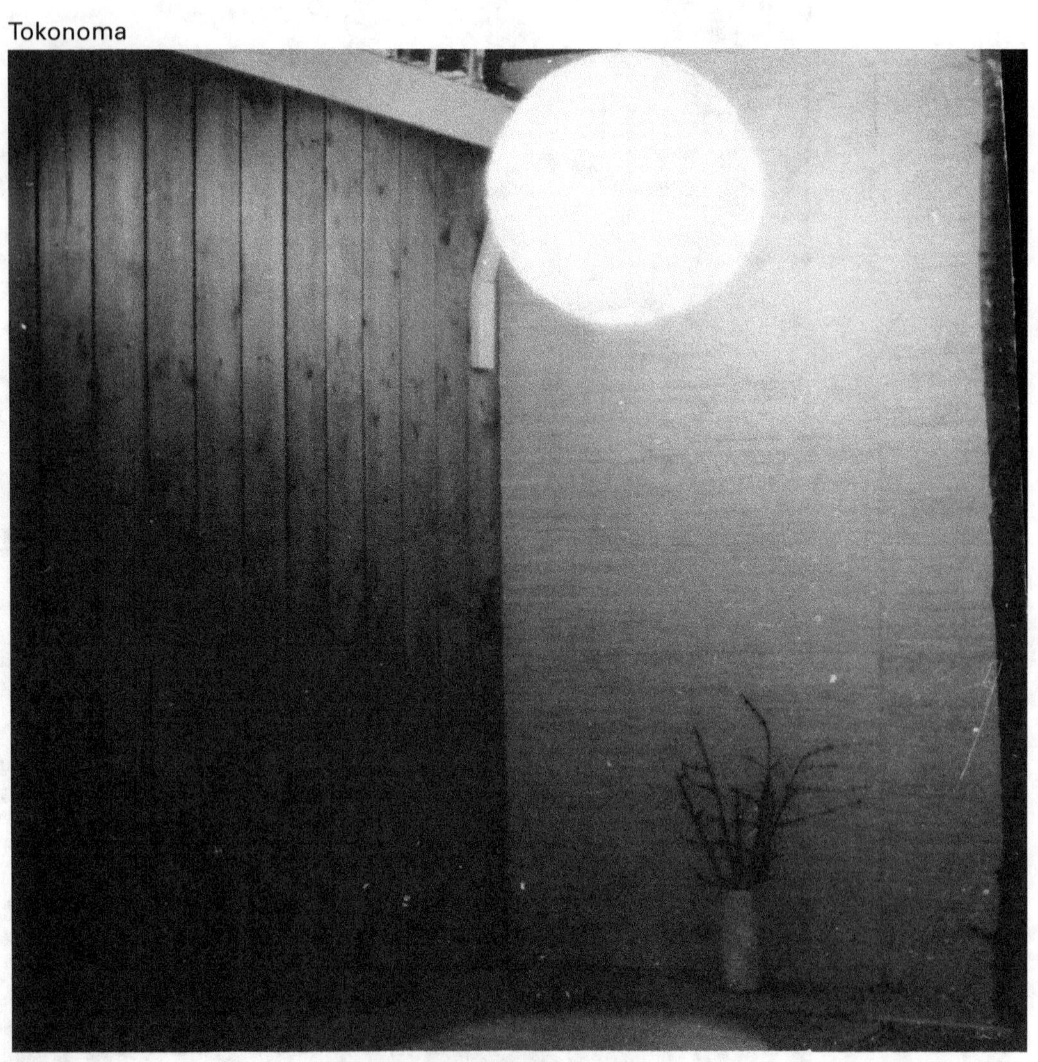

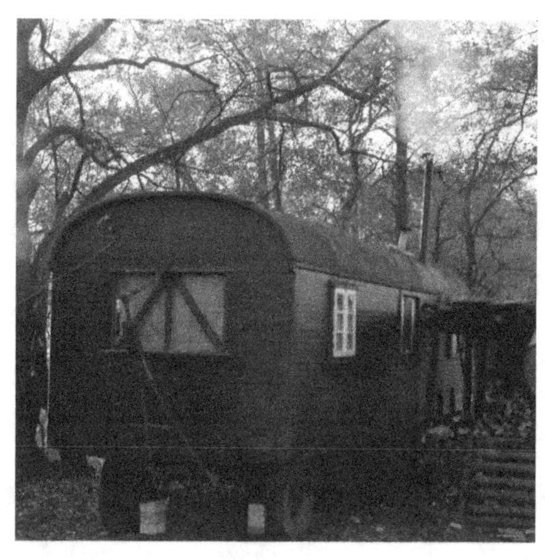

On a cold morning

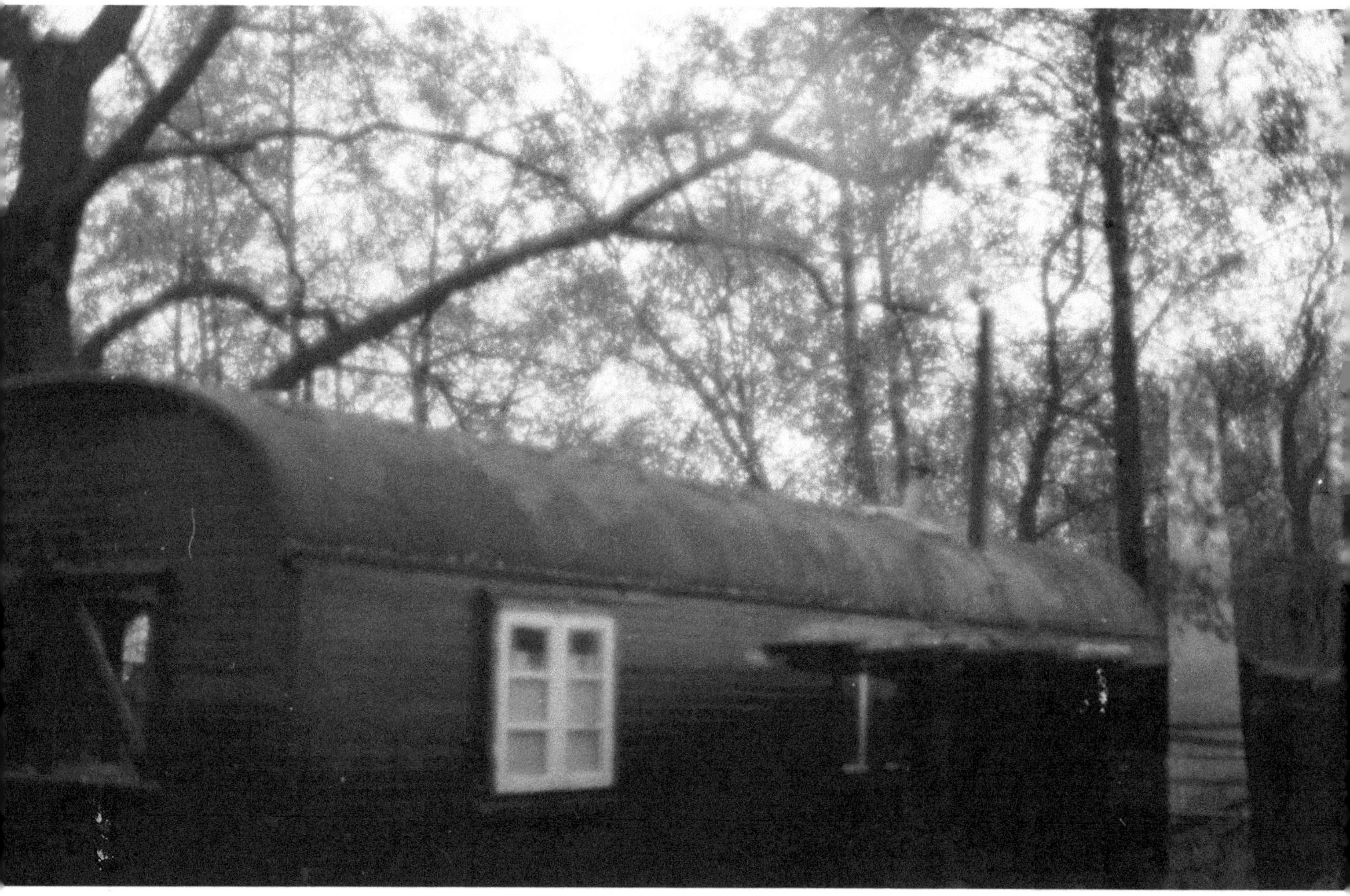

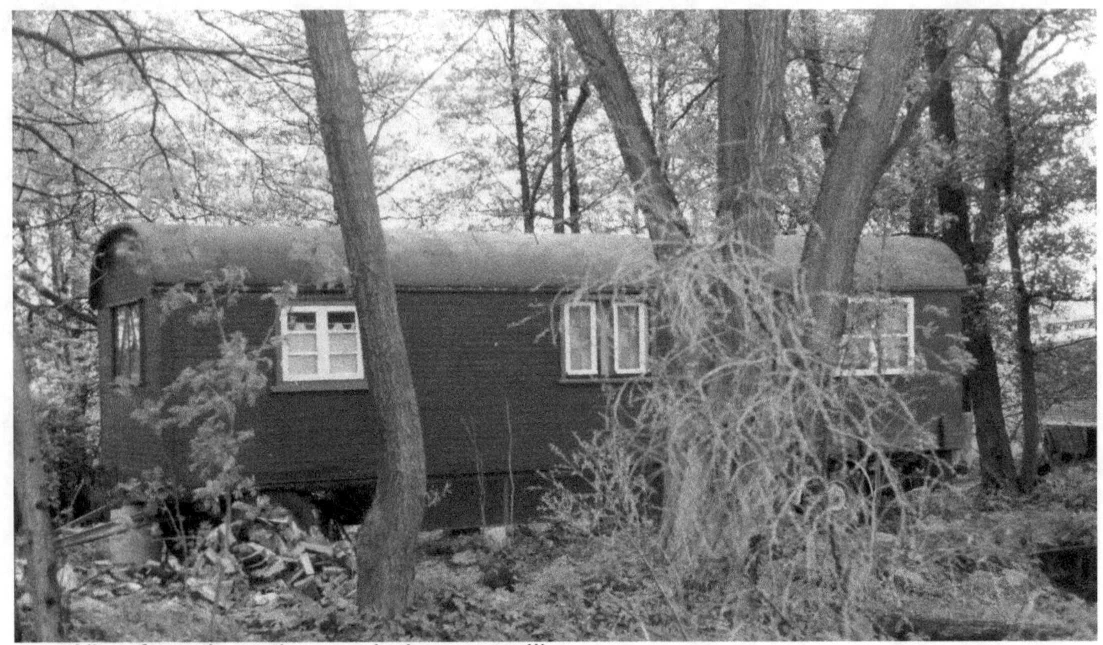
View from the path towards the watermill

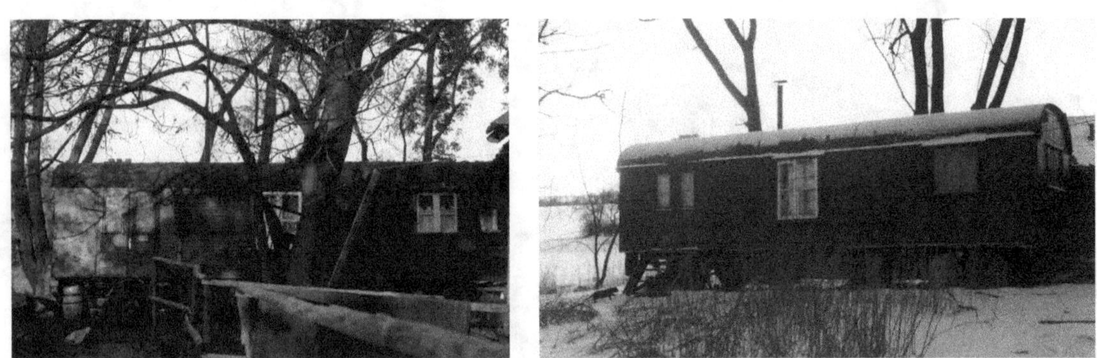
Two views from the watermill, one in the fall and one in winter

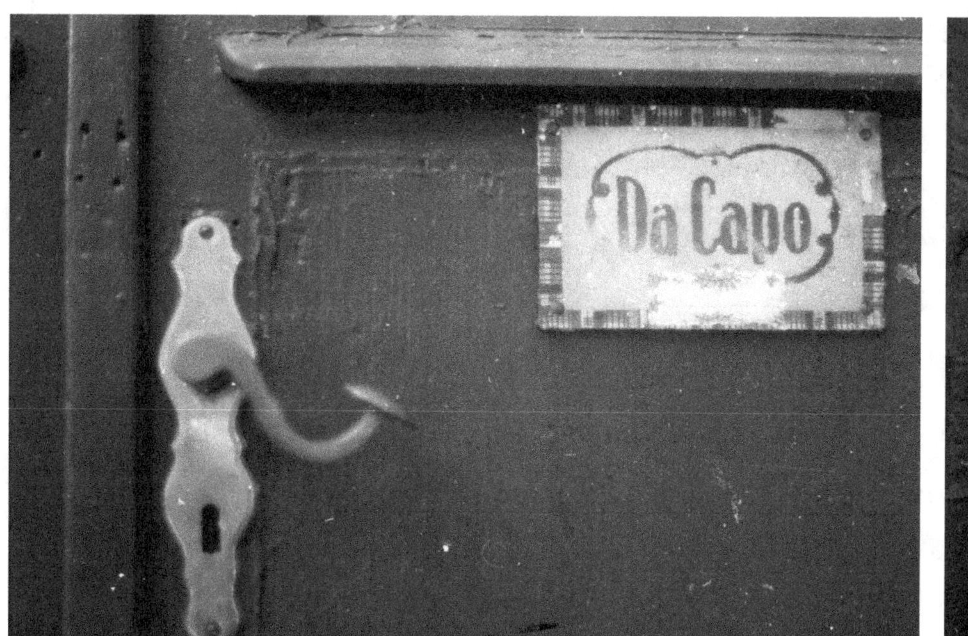

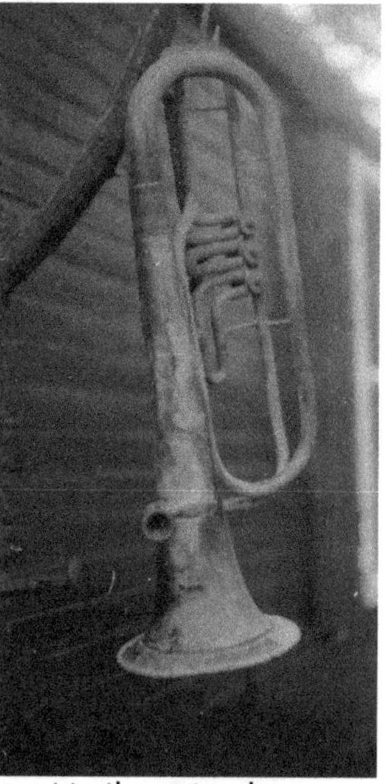

The entry door after we had painted Da Capo a dark brown, and the tenor horn next to the entry door

View of Da Capo at night from the watermill

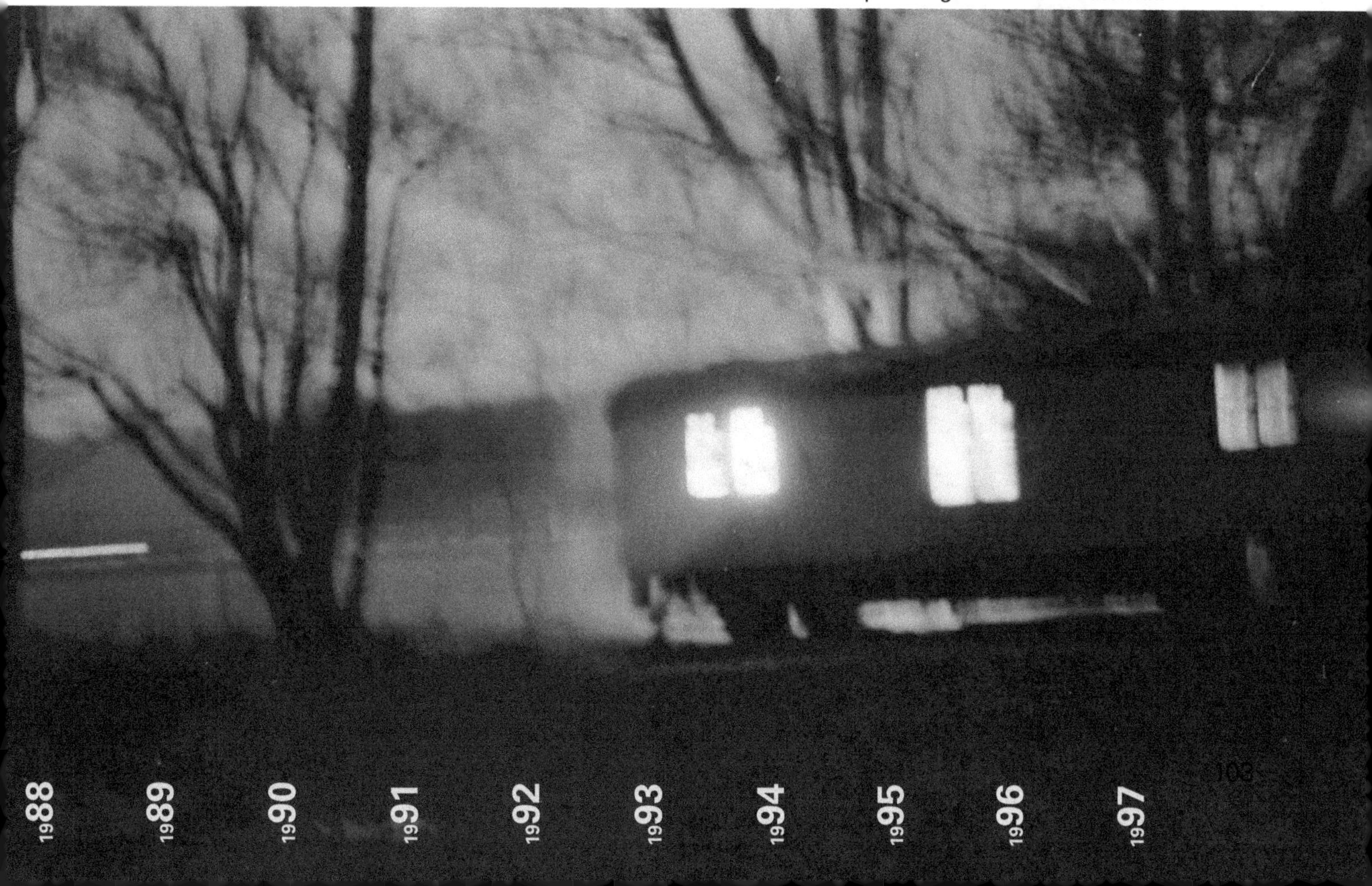

1988 1989 1990 1991 1992 1993 1994 1995 1996 1997

Travel in the United States
Waukegan and Chicago

What I noticed during my return trip to the United States as a European was the infrastructure in the form of electric lines, overhead traffic lights, and the size of the vehicles. All of them were hard to miss when I was heading north on US 441/13th Street in Gainesville at the intersection with NW 16th Avenue on a hot winter day in Florida

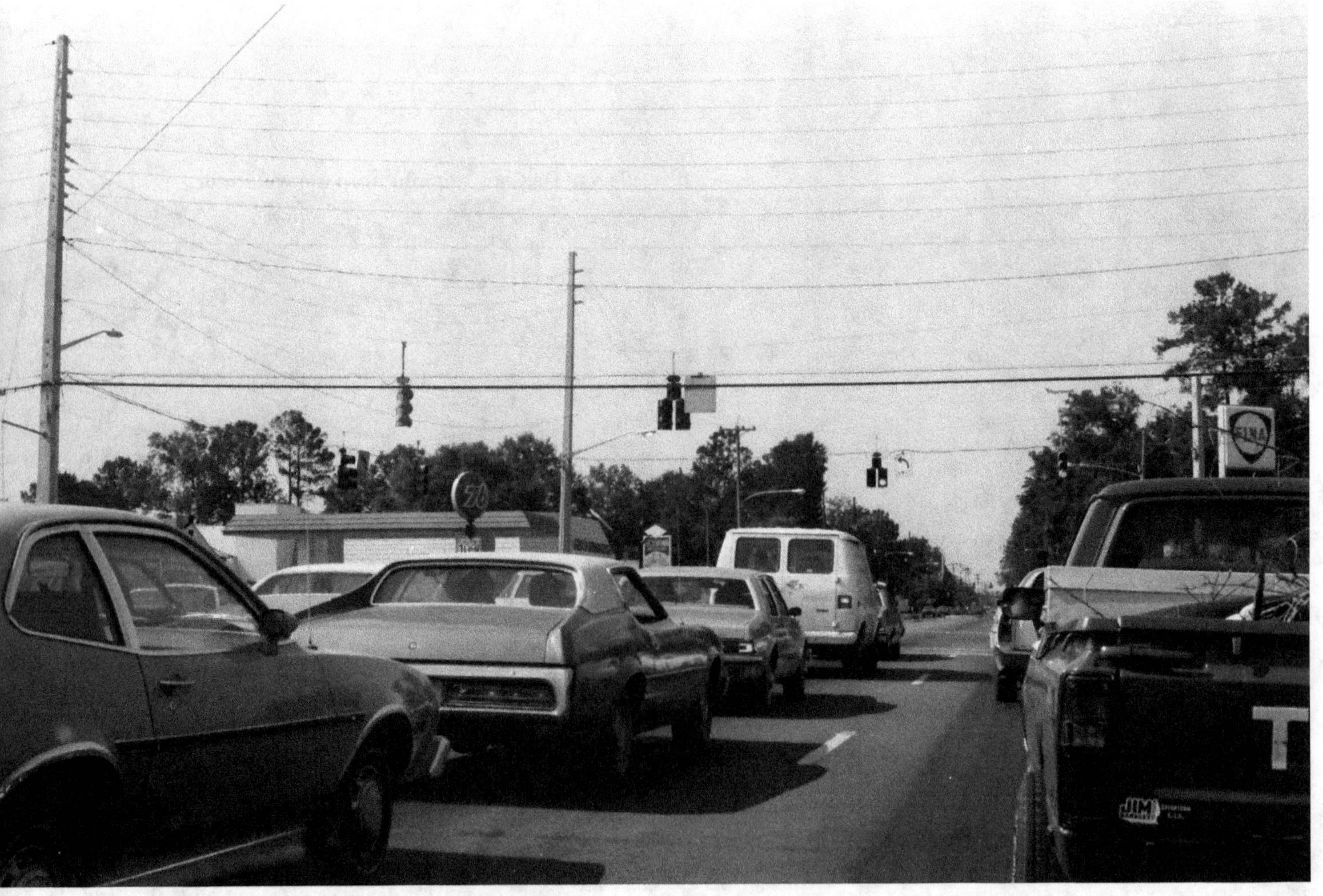

In 1983 I flew back to the United States to drive my future in-laws from their northern hometown of Waukegan, Illinois to their winter residence in Port Charlotte, Florida. I spent a few days in Chicago visiting friends on the southside before we headed to Florida. To the right is a view toward Lake Michigan at the intersection of Sheridan Road and Water Street in Waukegan taken out of the Chevy Van that I would soon point south towards the land of oranges.

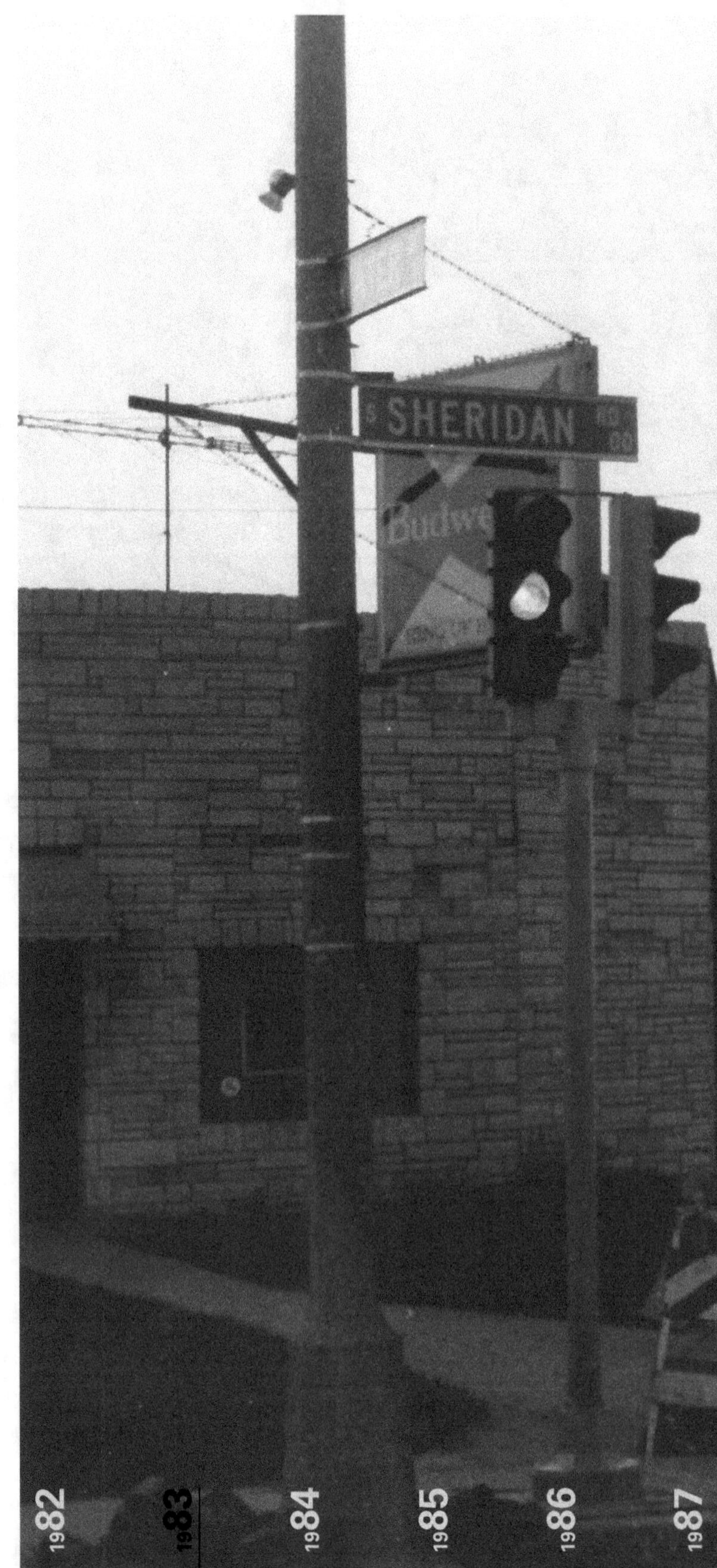

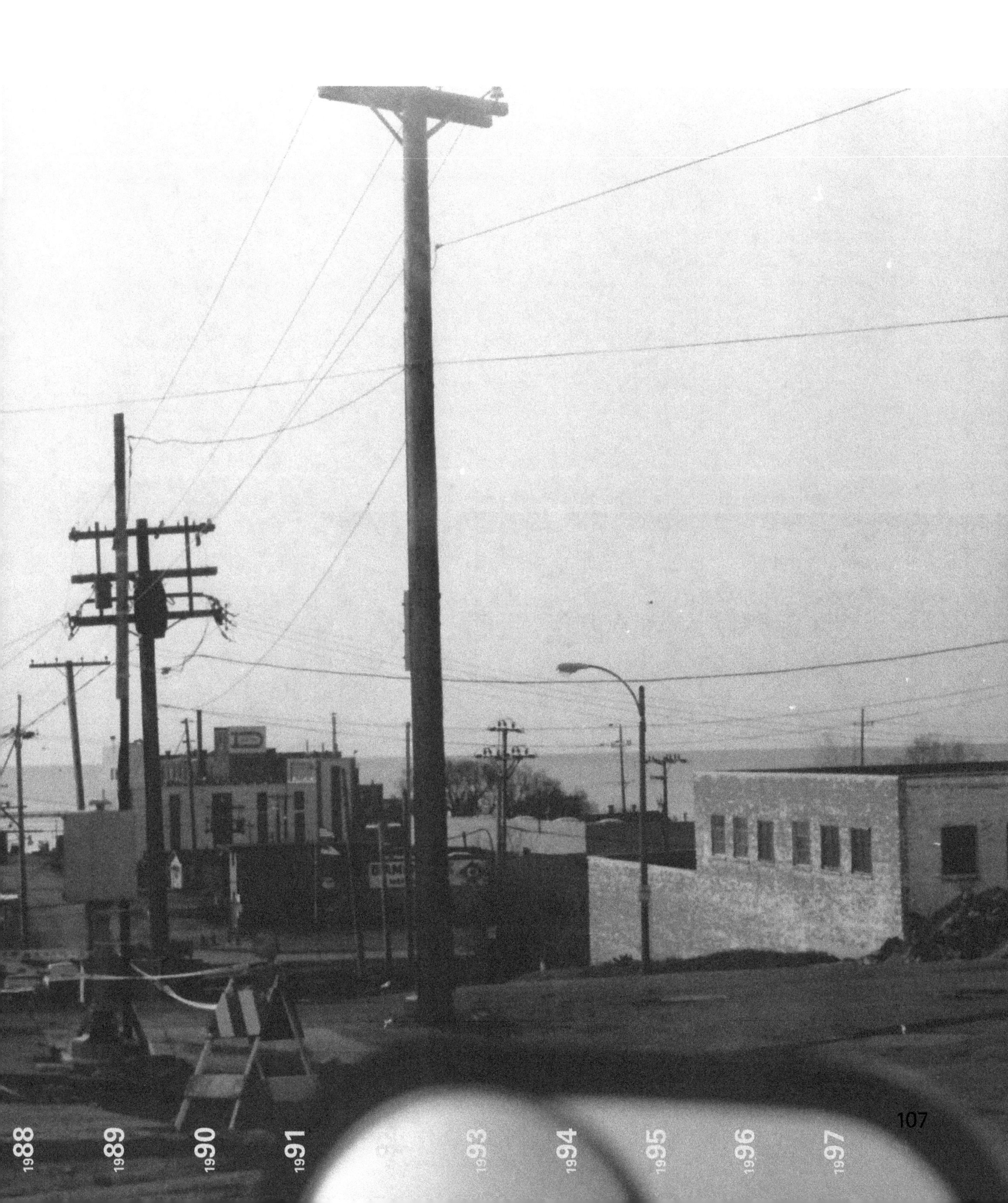
1988
1989
1990
1991
1993
1994
1995
1996
1997

Margaret in the driver's seat of her !976 Chevy van.

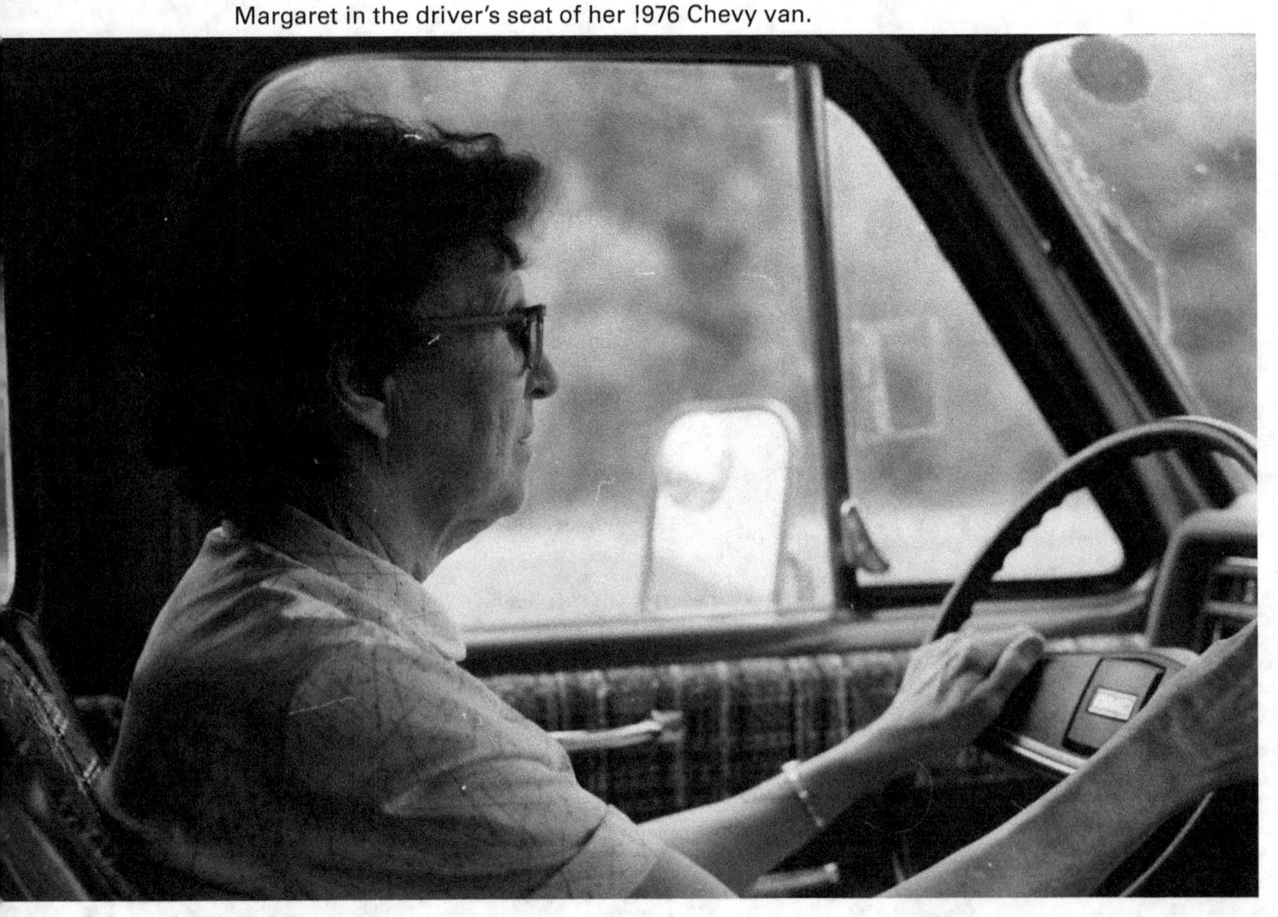

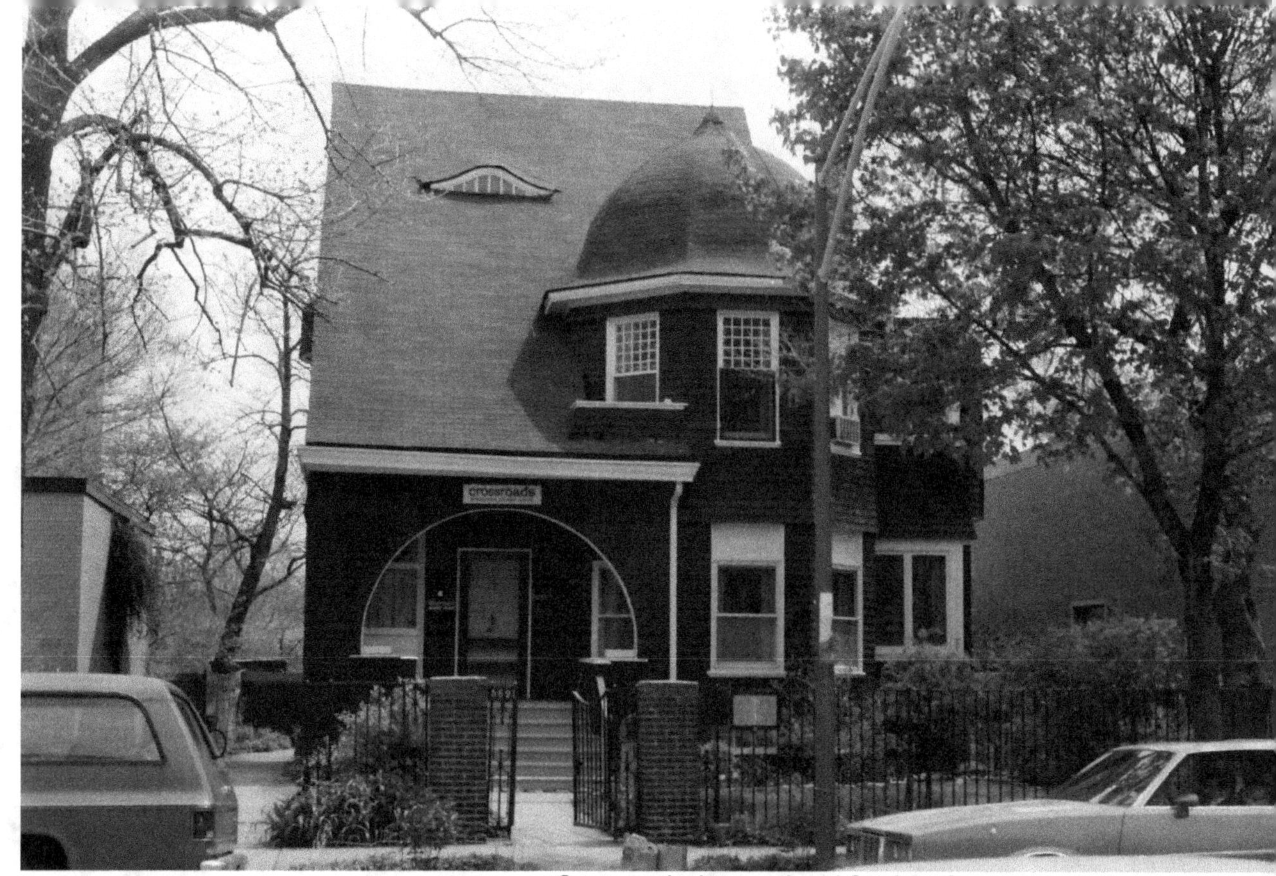

Crossroads: International Student Center on South Blackstone Avenue in Hyde Park, IL, the place where Miriam and I met in January of 1980 for the first time.

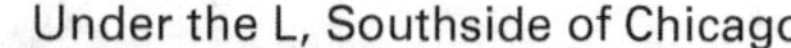

Under the L, Southside of Chicago

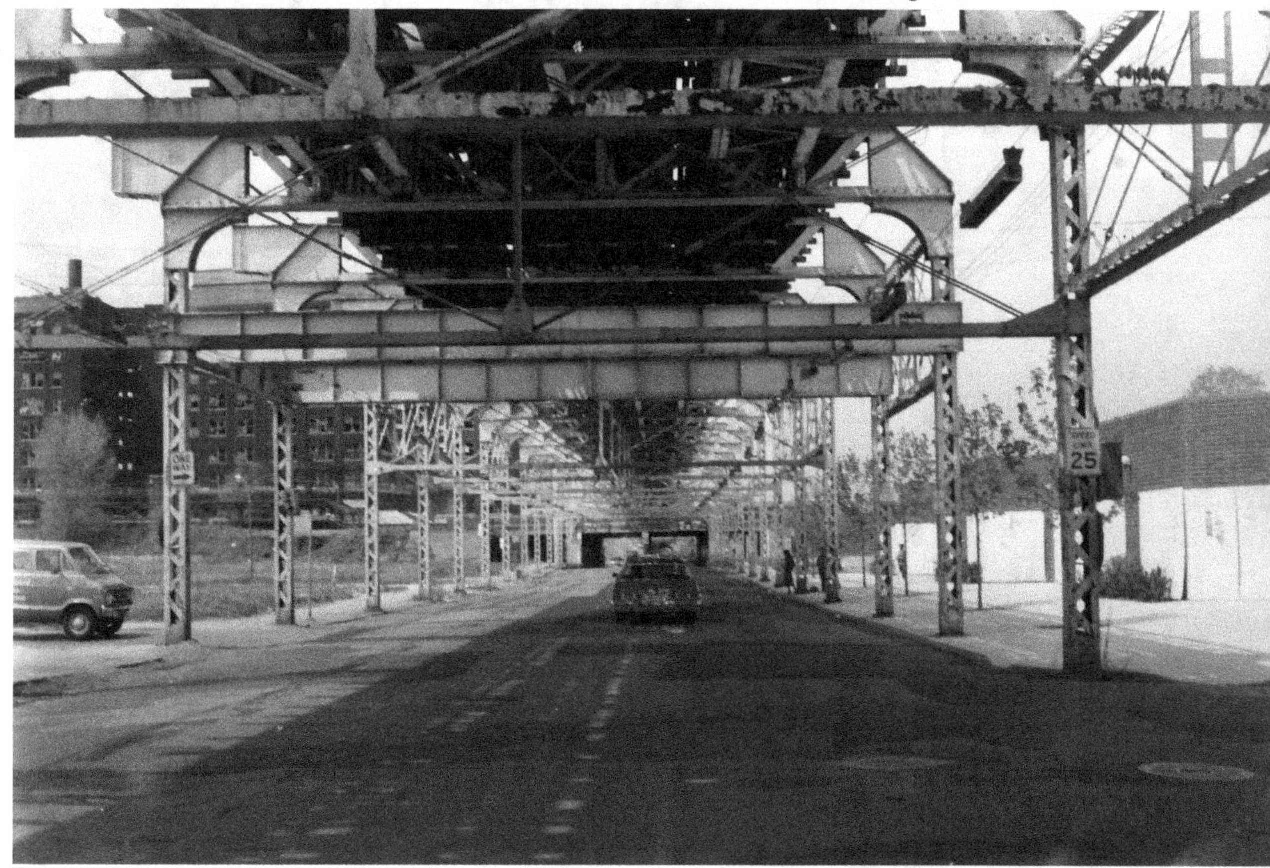

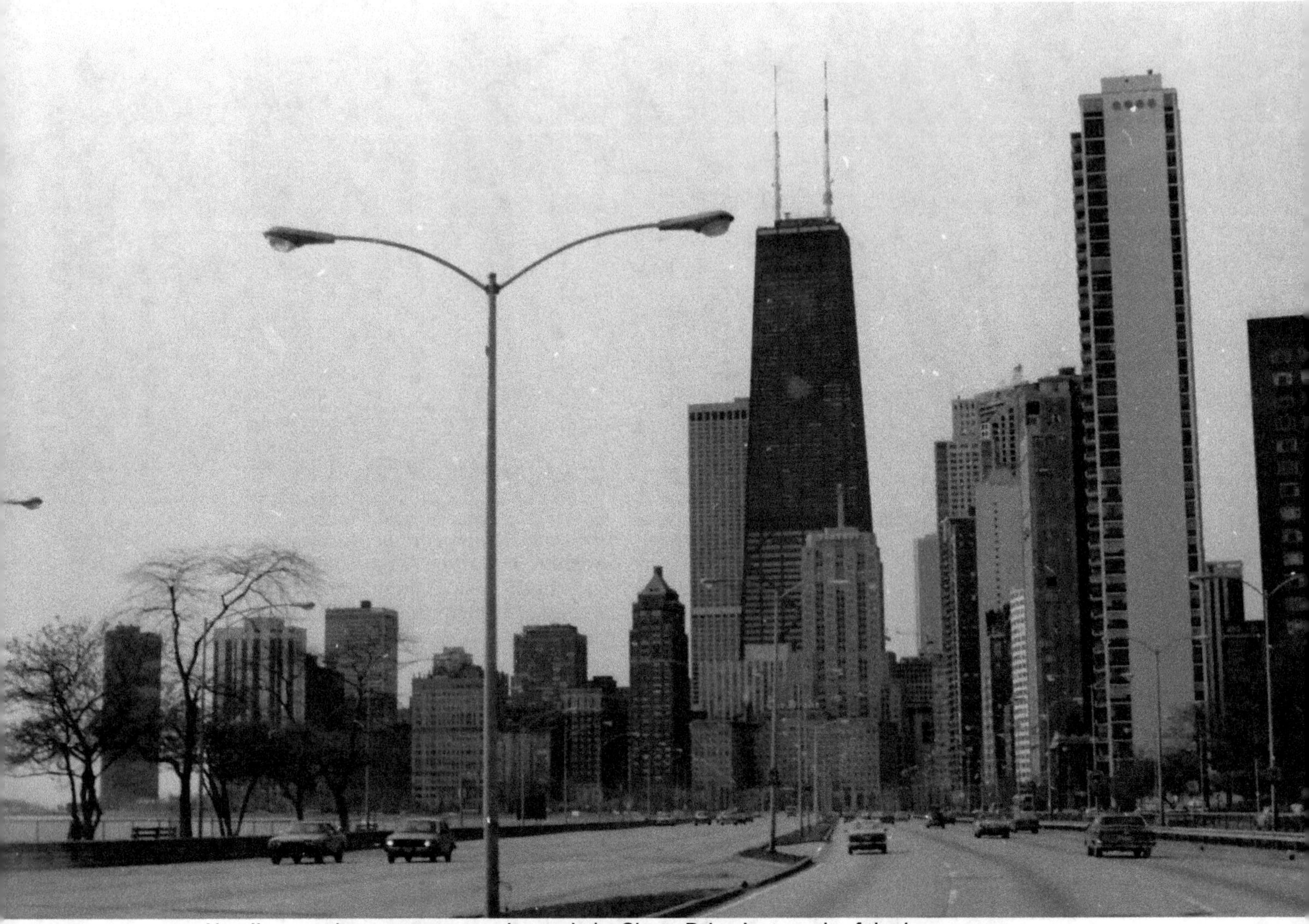

Heading south on an overcast day on Lake Shore Drive just north of the Loop

Incomplete painting of the same view from further north

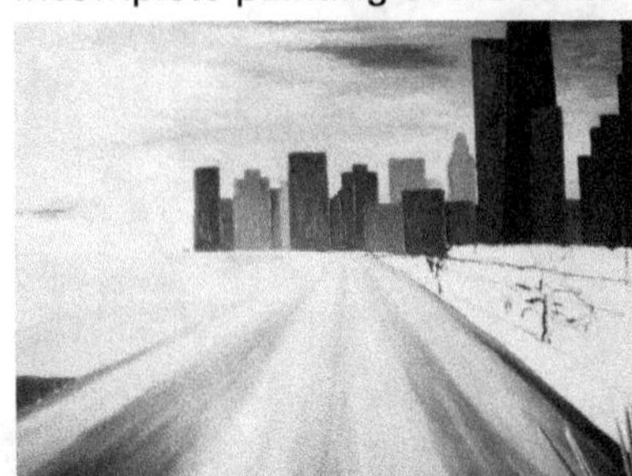

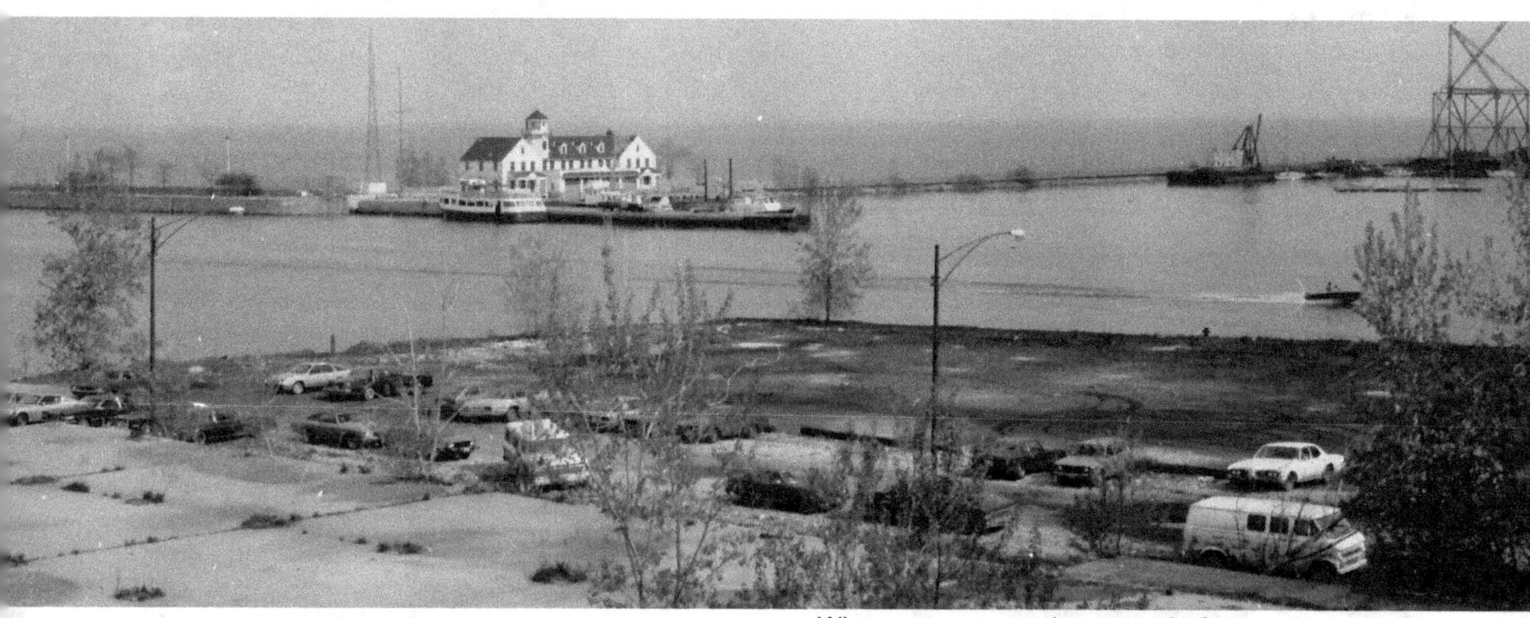

Whenever we went downtown I often dreamed of living in that house out in Lake Michigan. I think it was an old customs station and to my naive and overly creative mind it seemed perfect for a private residence from which to view downtown Chicago. It was a sweet intersection of privacy and publicness, remoteness and access, day dream and reality...

In the early 1980s Navy Pier was mostly deserted with large spaces full of industrial detritus.

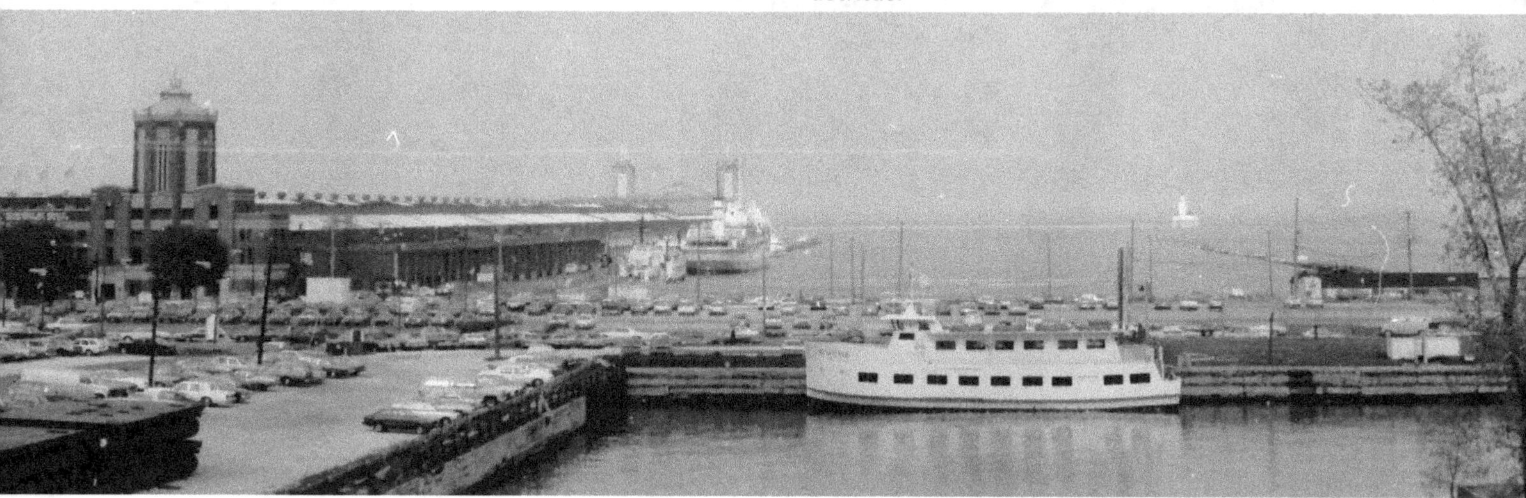

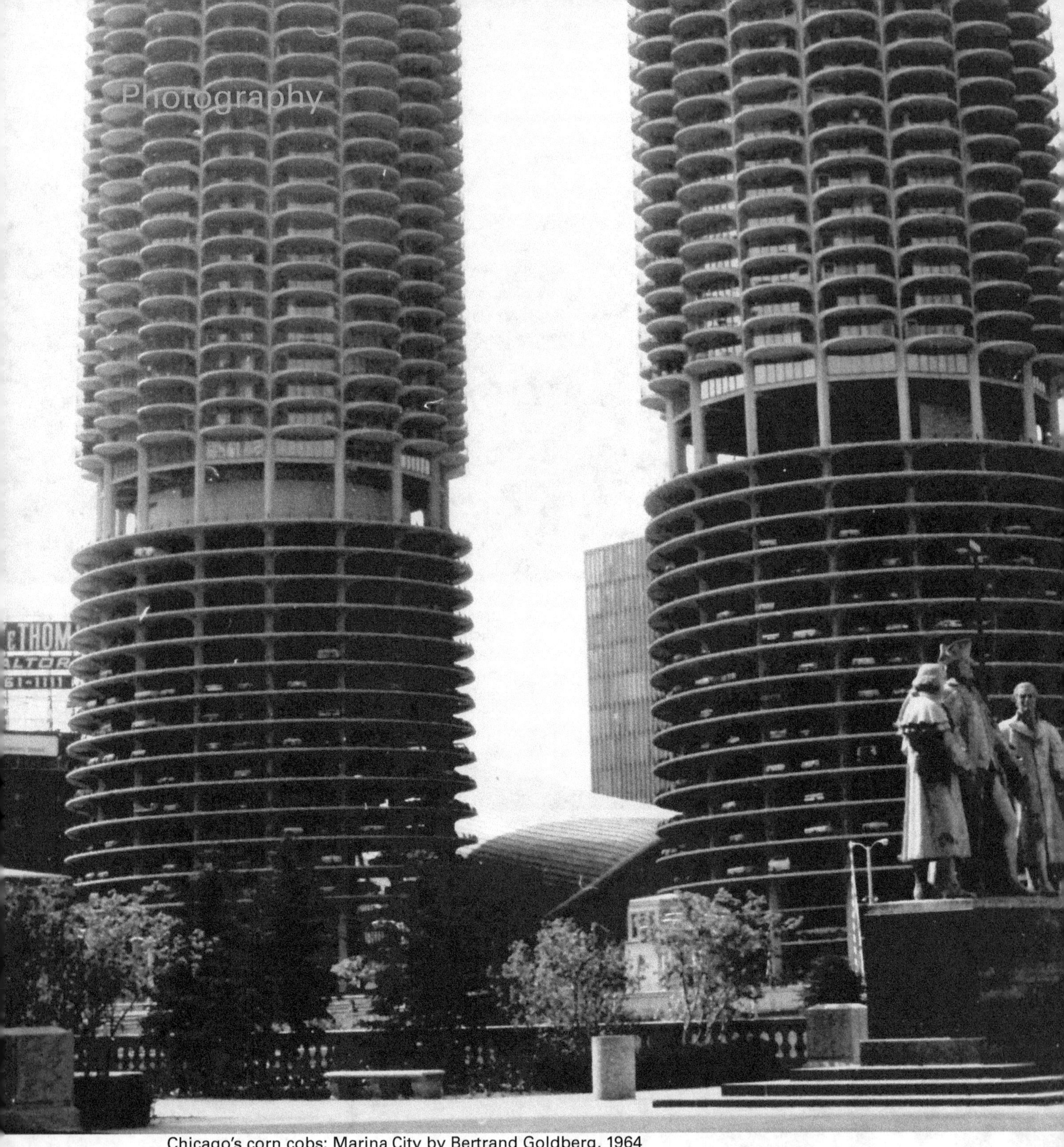

Chicago's corn cobs: Marina City by Bertrand Goldberg, 1964

John Hancock tower and the Old Water Tower, old + new, pre- and post-fire in close proximity >

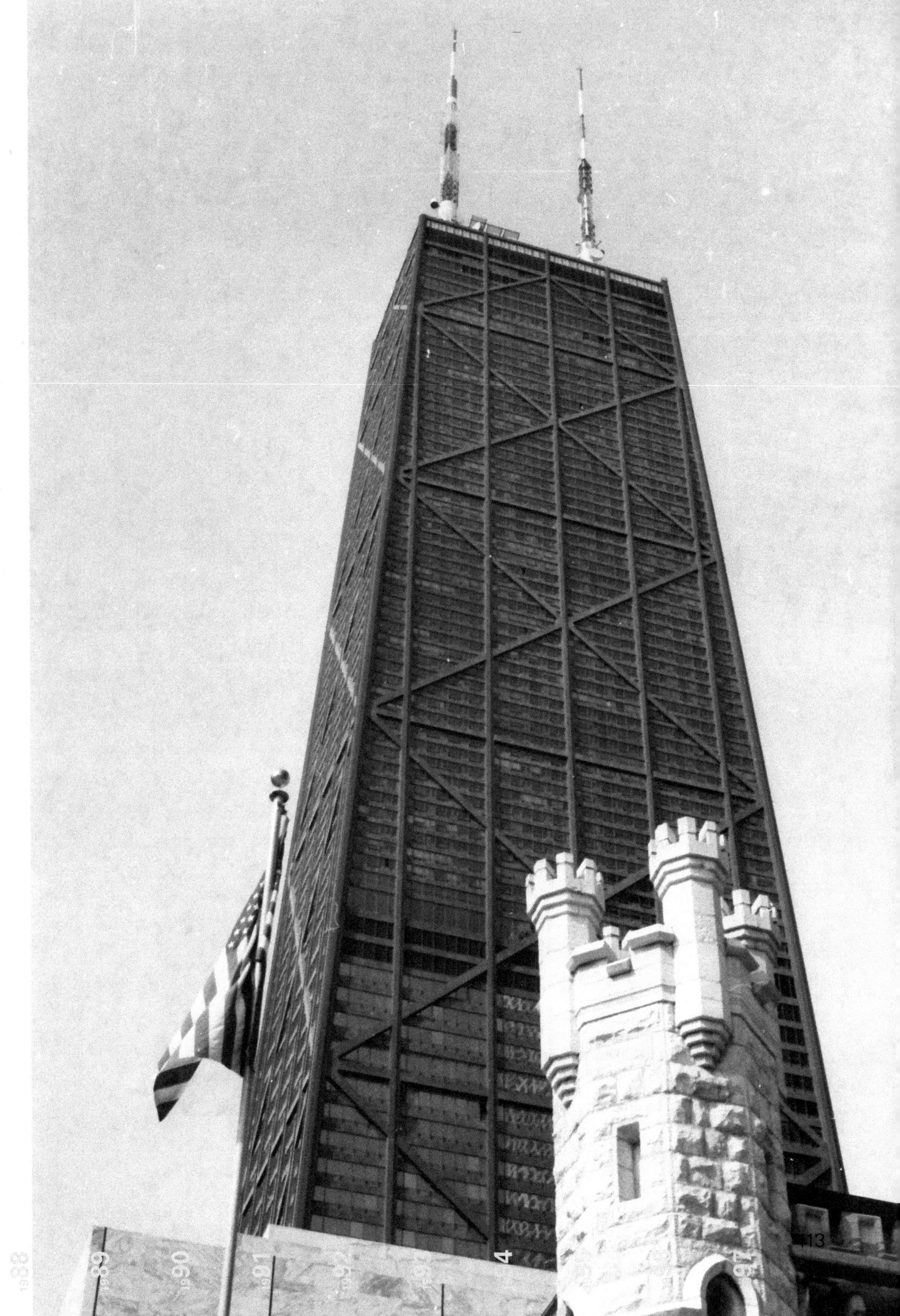

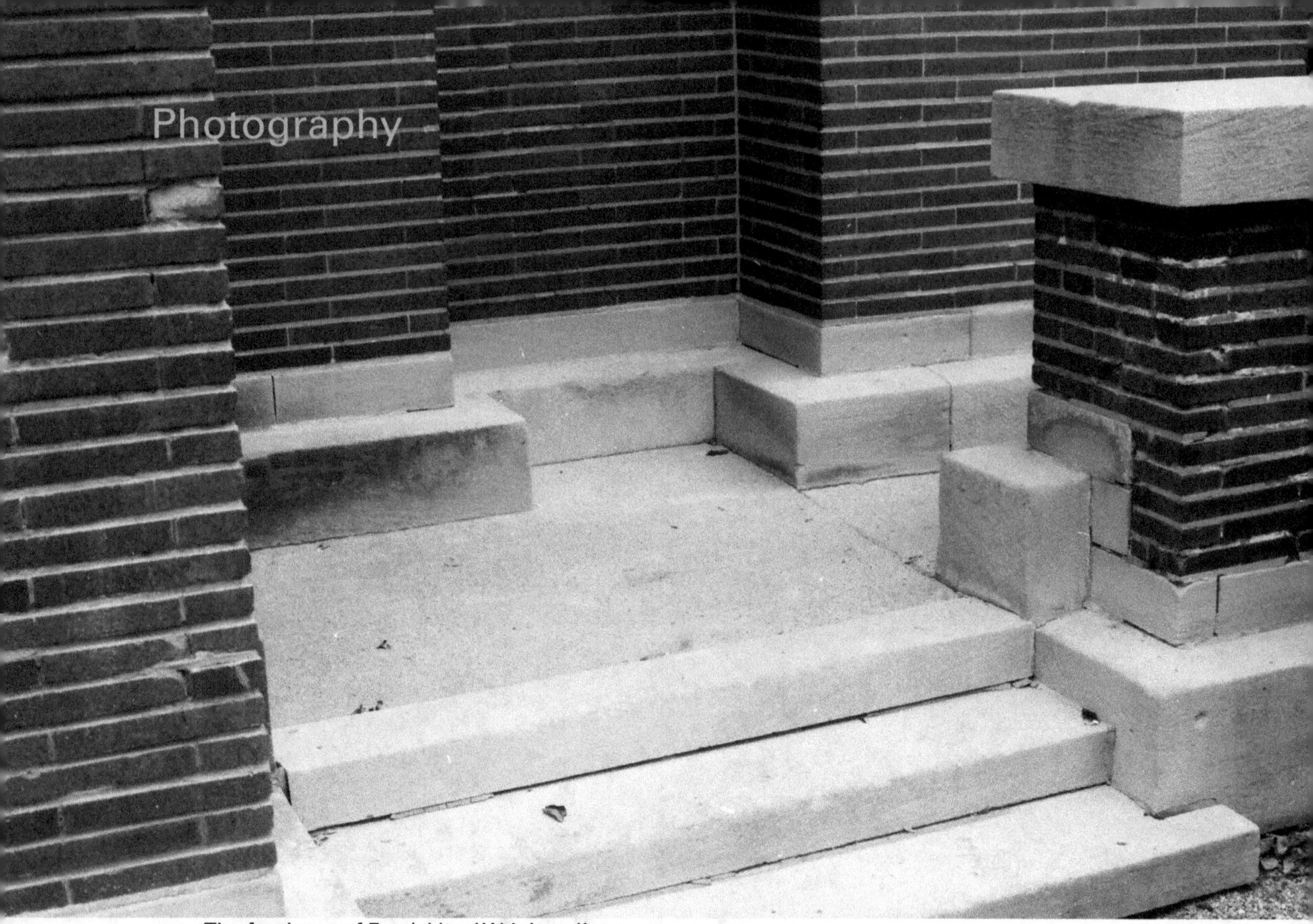

The fussiness of Frank Lloyd Wright.... I've visited Frank's Robie House in Hyde Park many times over the years. At some point I noticed on the exterior the awkwardness of the marble wall base, as it snakes around the corners, following blindly every turn the wall makes above. It is either the sign of a control freak (who can't see the opportunity of a built-in exterior bench) or a careless architect (who lets others make decisions without supervision).
The rest of the house is of course just marvelous, and an opportunity for taking pictures of oneself in the reflective stained-glass windows that were, as usual, completely inadequate in the cold Illinois winters.

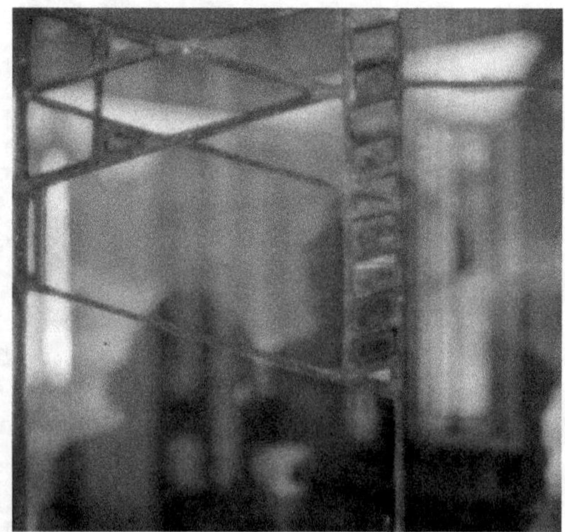

Miriam (left) and Mikesch (right) reflected in one of the living room windows of the Robie House, as seen from the exterior. I took the image some time in the spring of 1980 >

The Marquette building, from 1895, site of another project six years later (see 1989) >

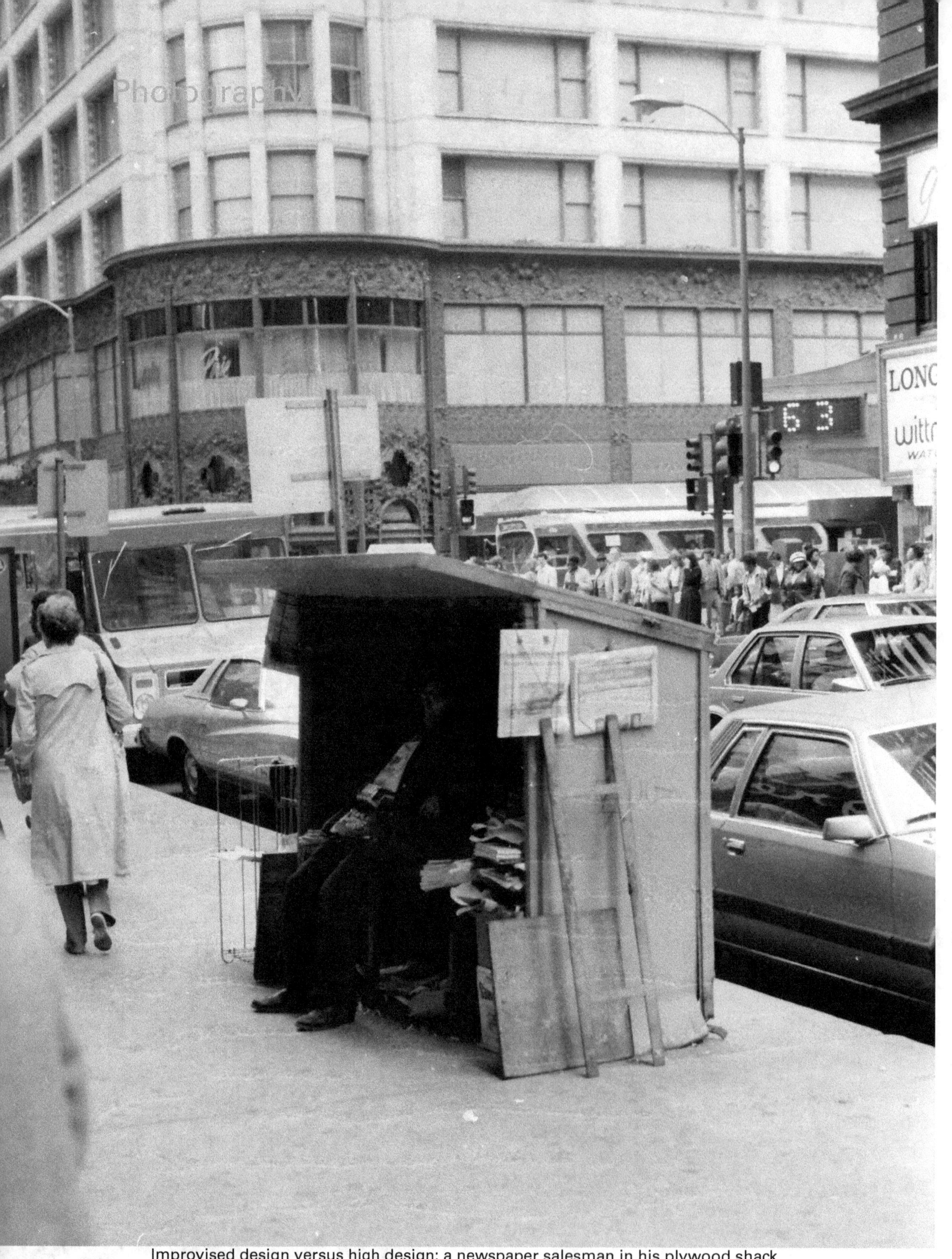

Improvised design versus high design: a newspaper salesman in his plywood shack across from the Louis Sullivan-designed Carson-Pierie-Scott department store is waiting for customers on West Madison Street.

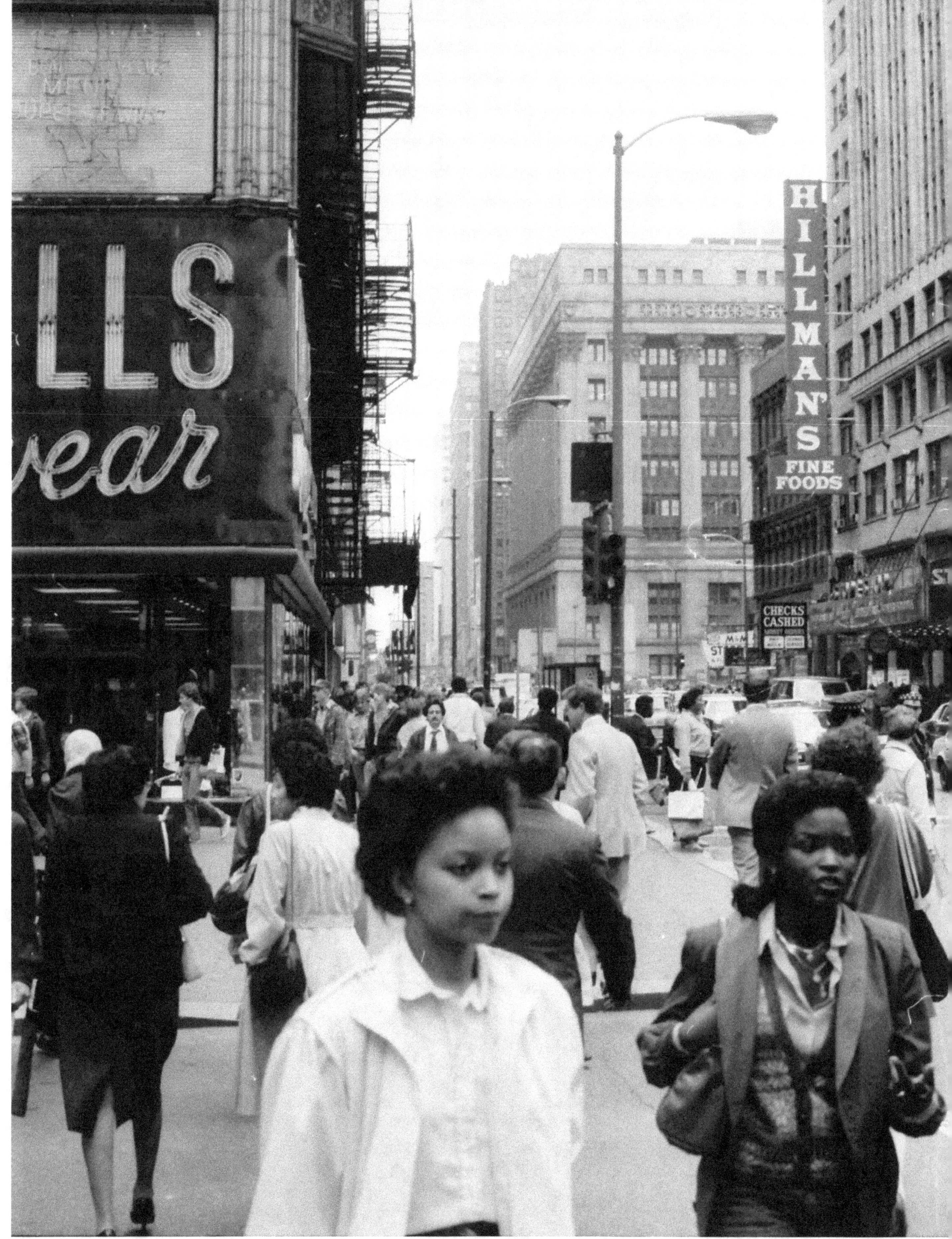

The Loop on an overcast and muggy summer day.

Standing in Grant Park I was keenly aware of the contrast between the upward reaching trees and their stony equivalents along Michigan Avenue. At times I would wonder what they might converse about if they were not leading parallel lives.

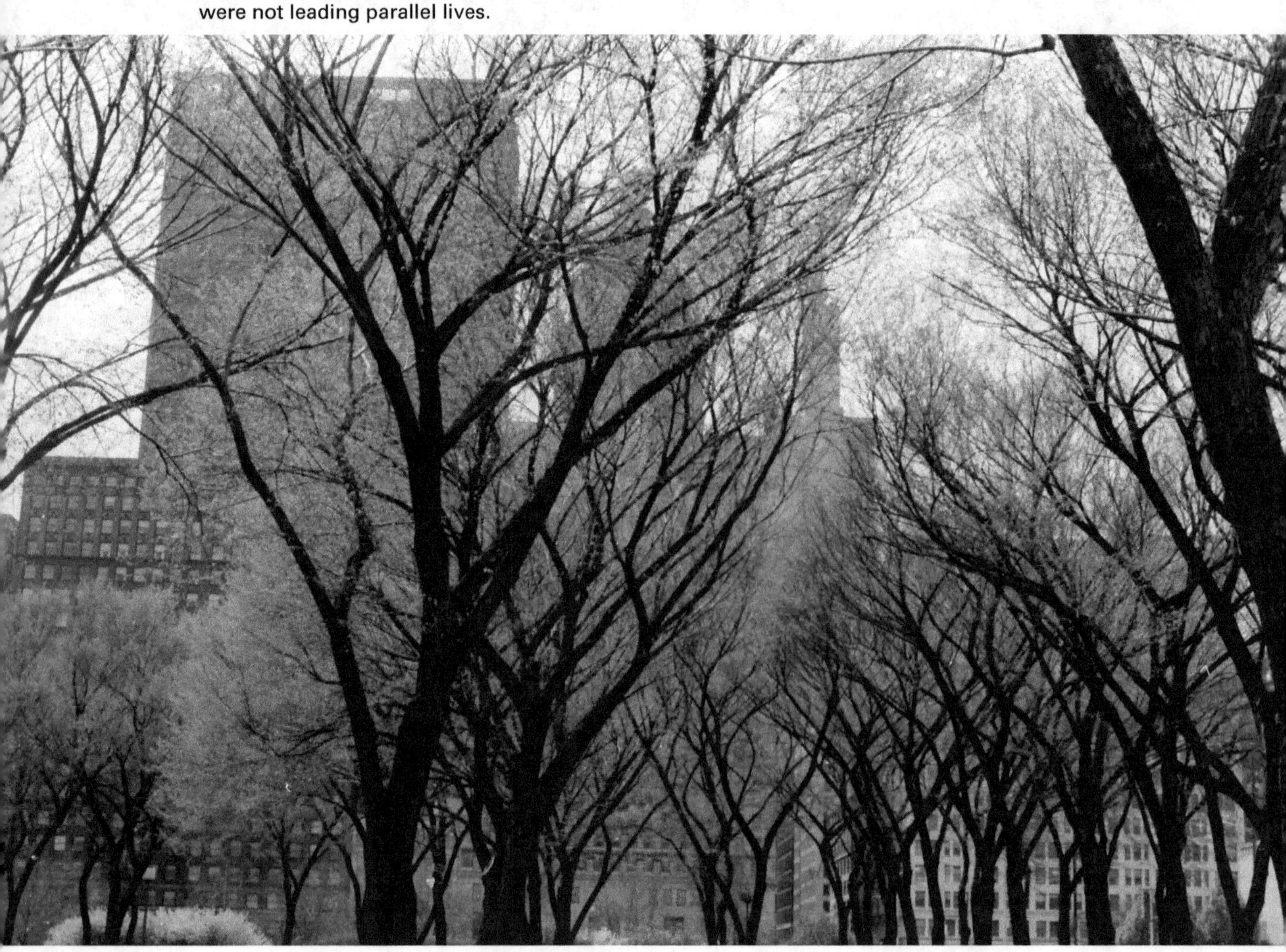

In the early spring we were walking by the lake on a cloudy day when the sun decided to make a temporary appearance way out on the water. Just for a moment there was this bright spot announcing the coming summer.

View from Navy Pier

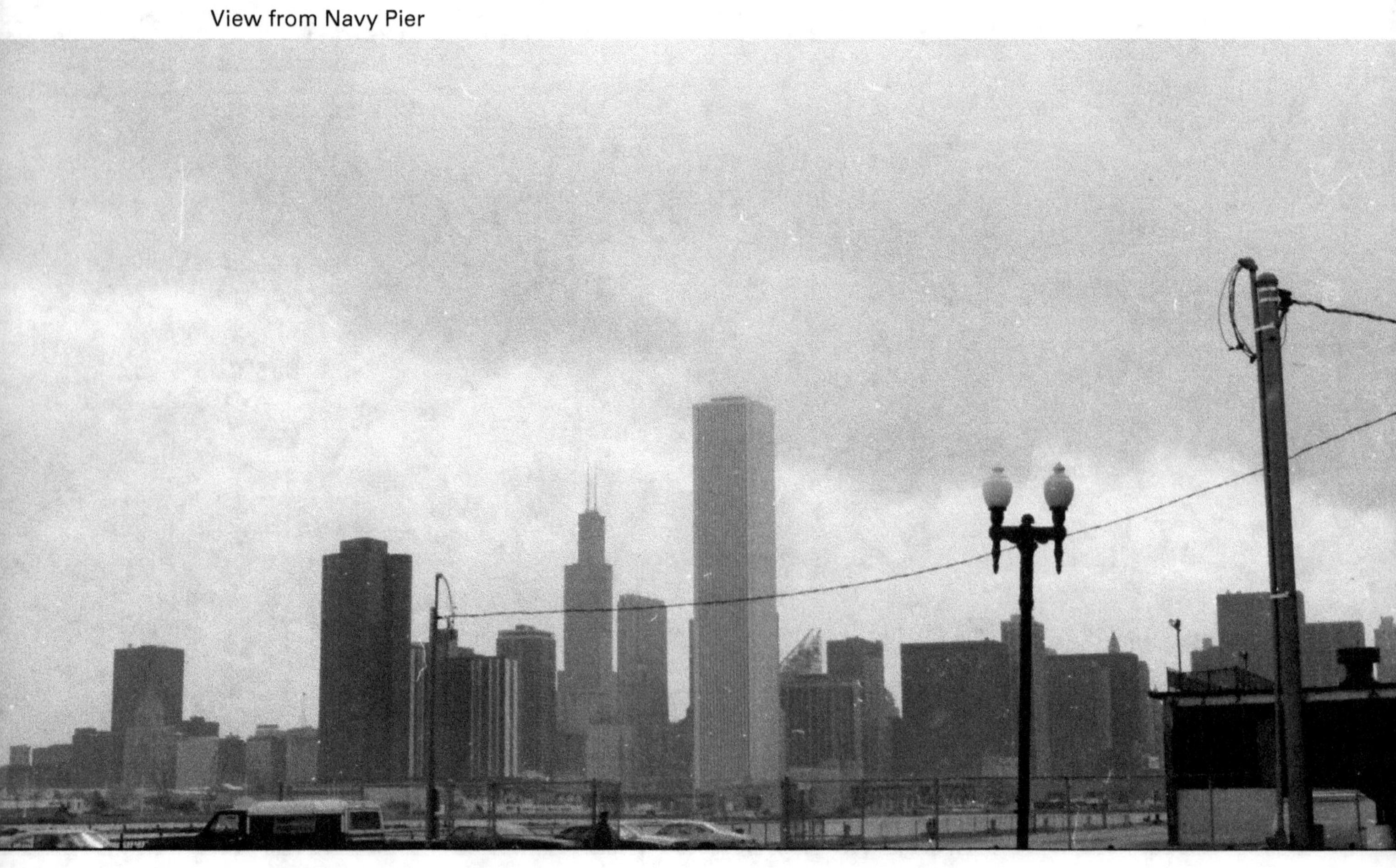

Plane behind the Standard Oil building

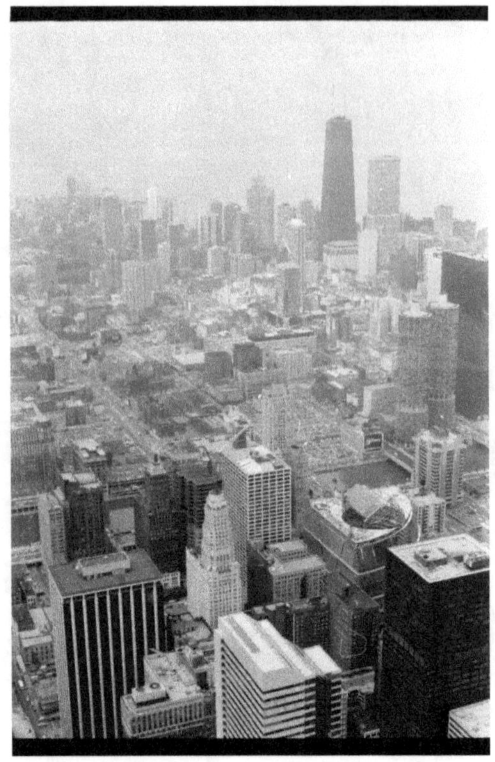

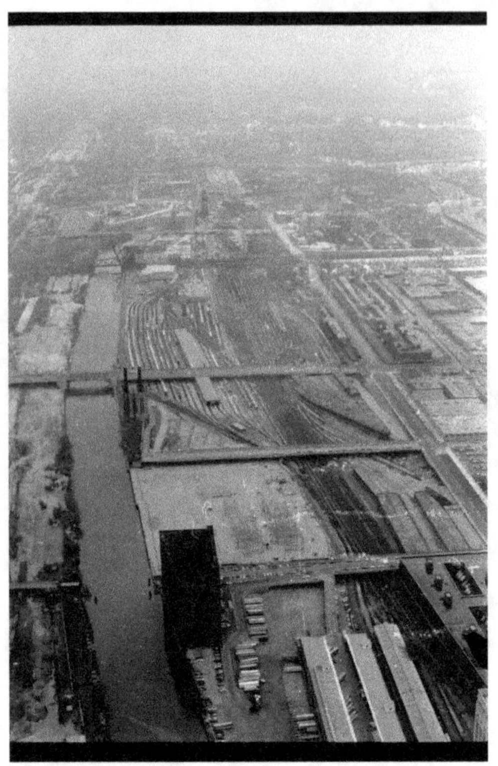

Views from the Sears Tower

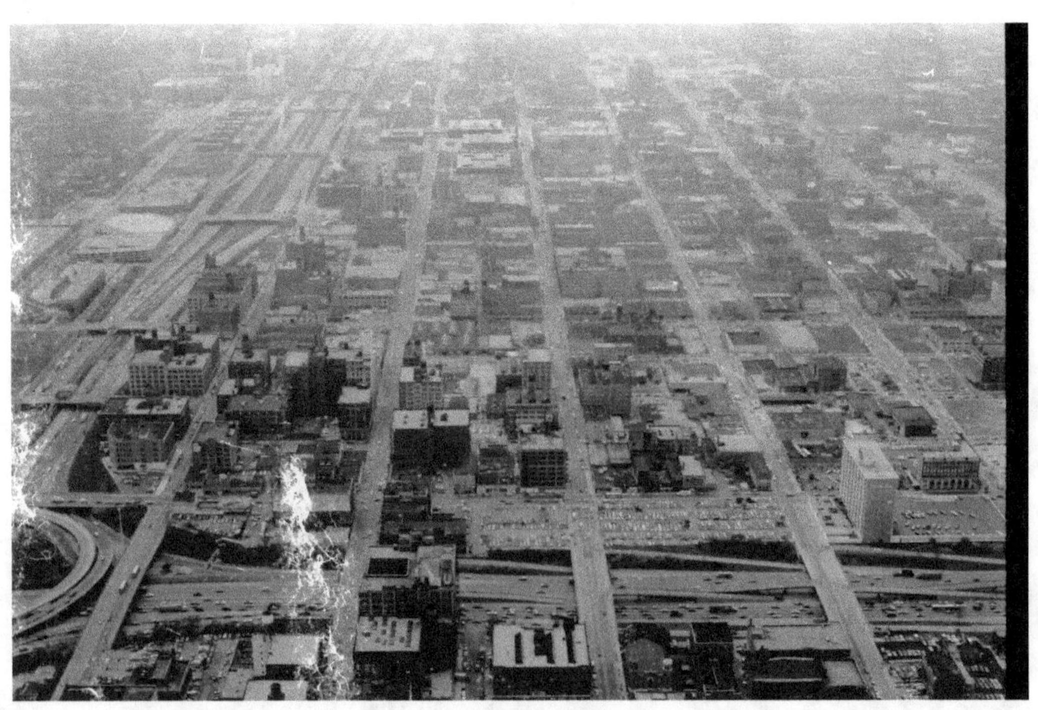

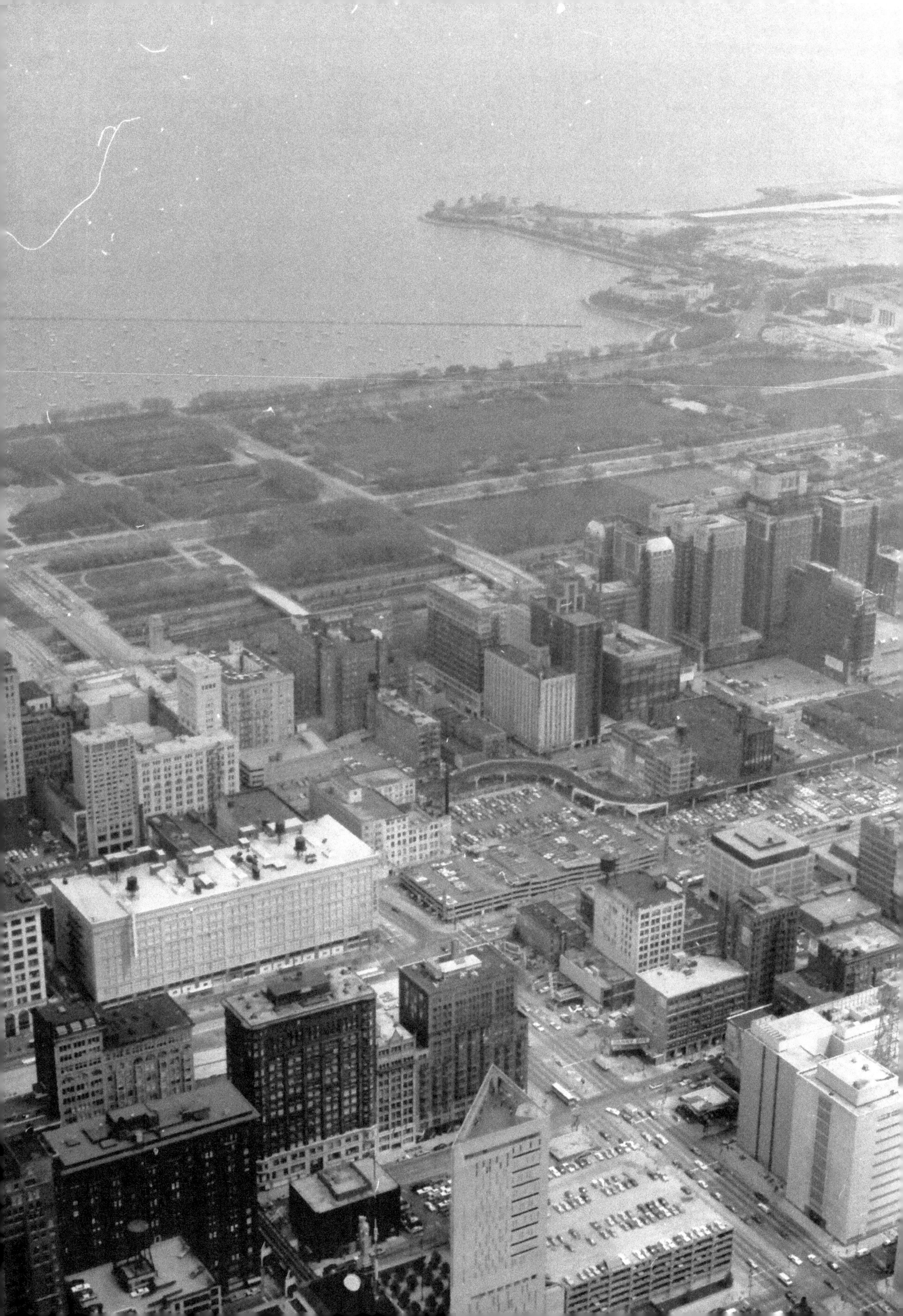

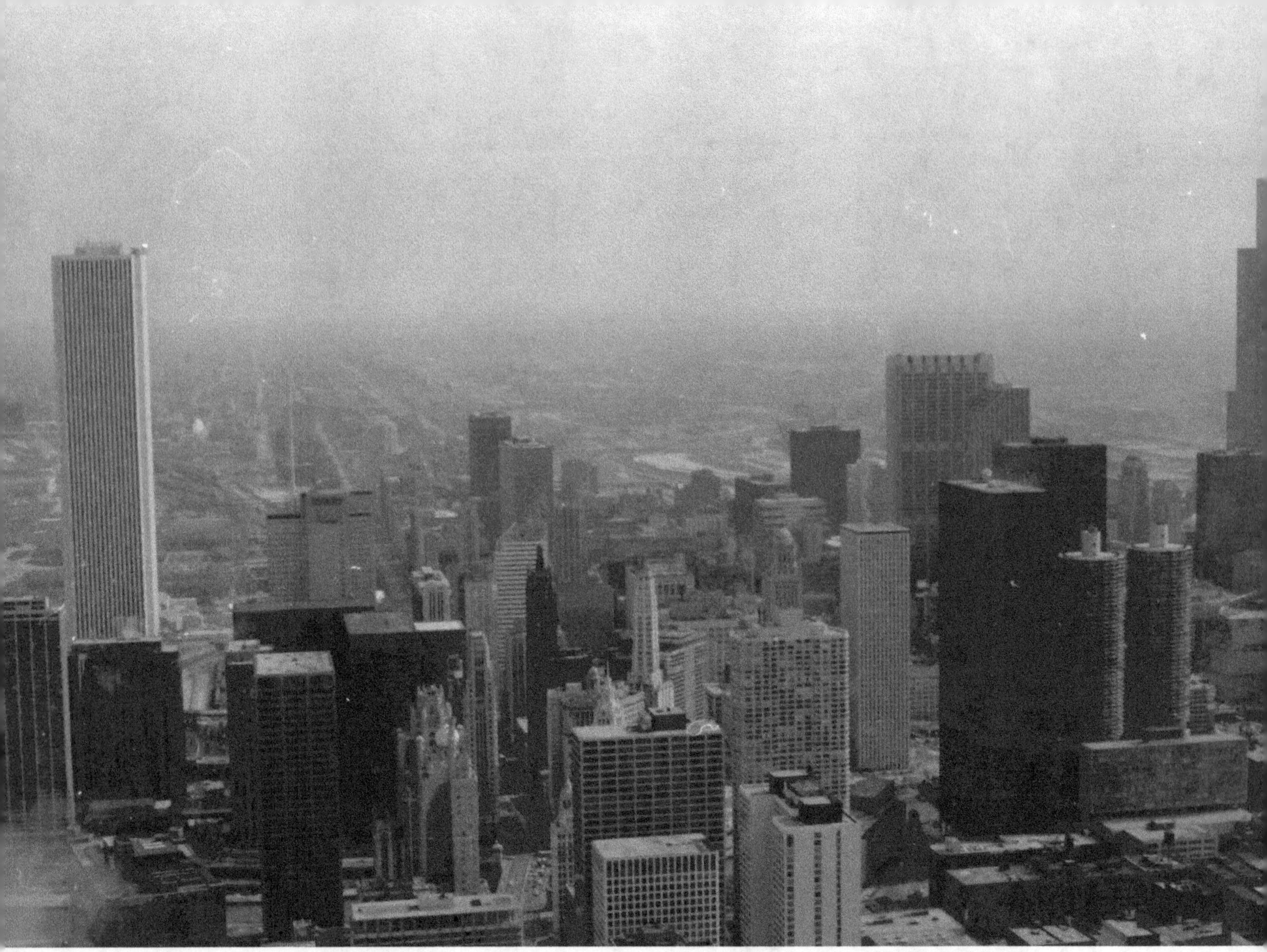

Views from the McCormick Tower

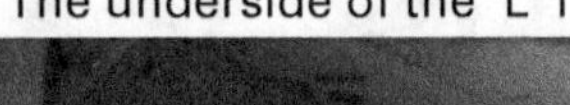

The underside of the 'L' 1

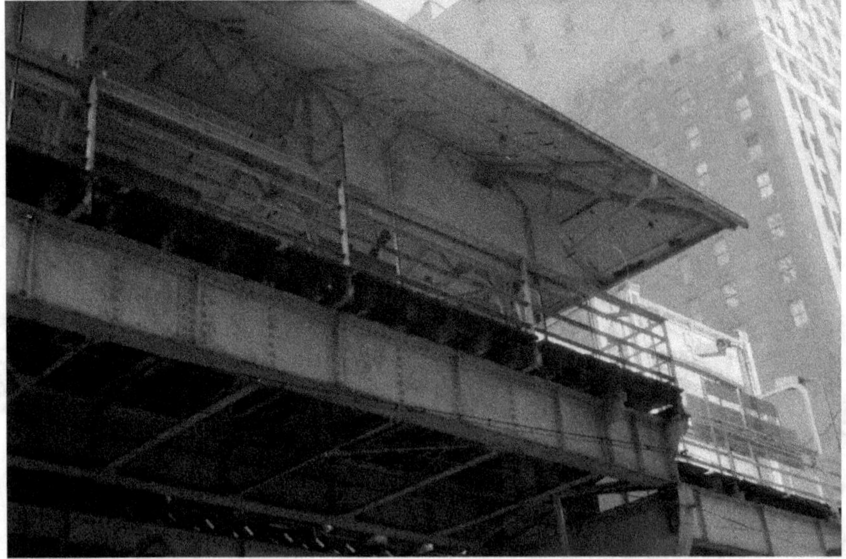

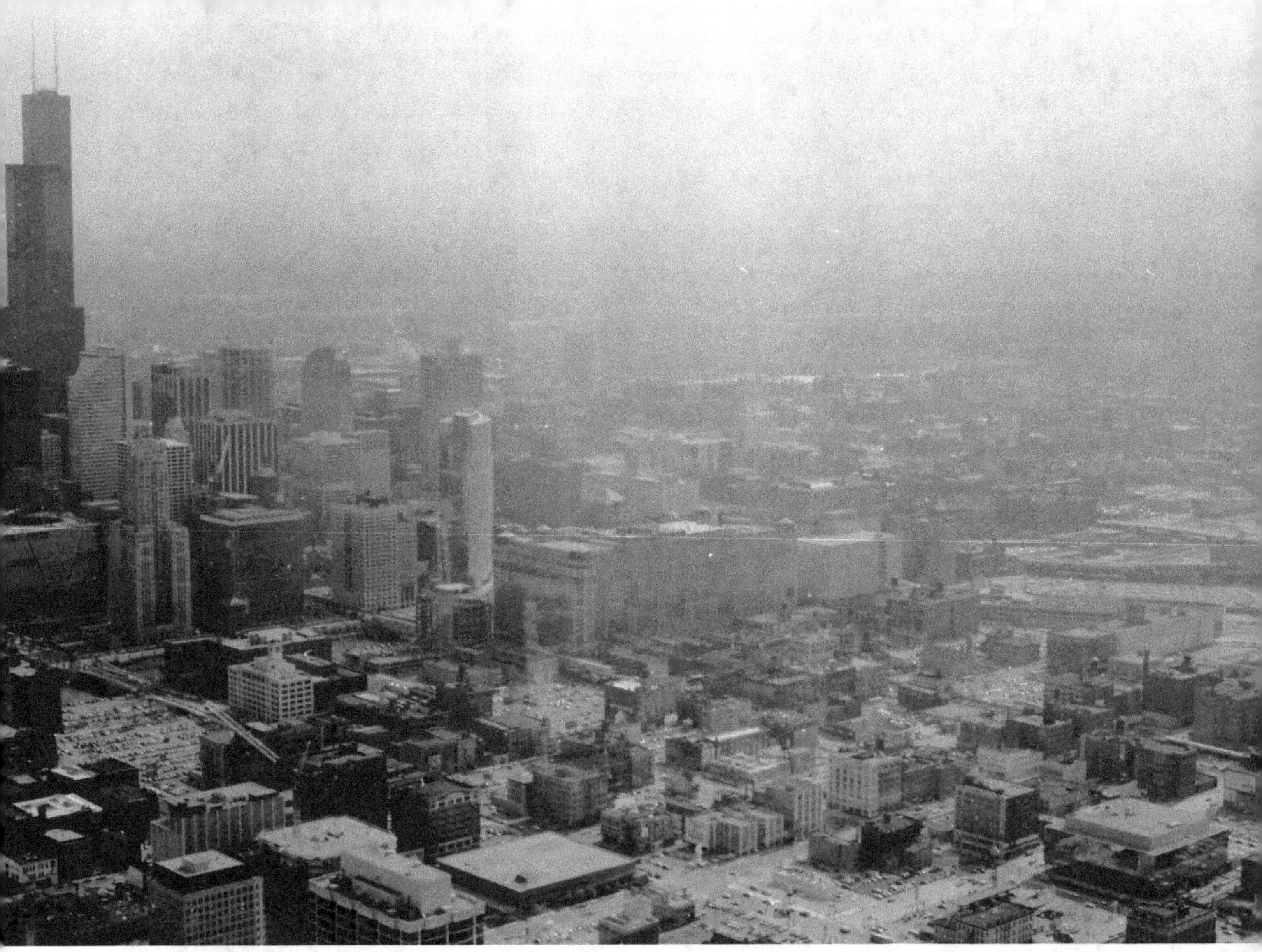

The underside of the 'L' 2

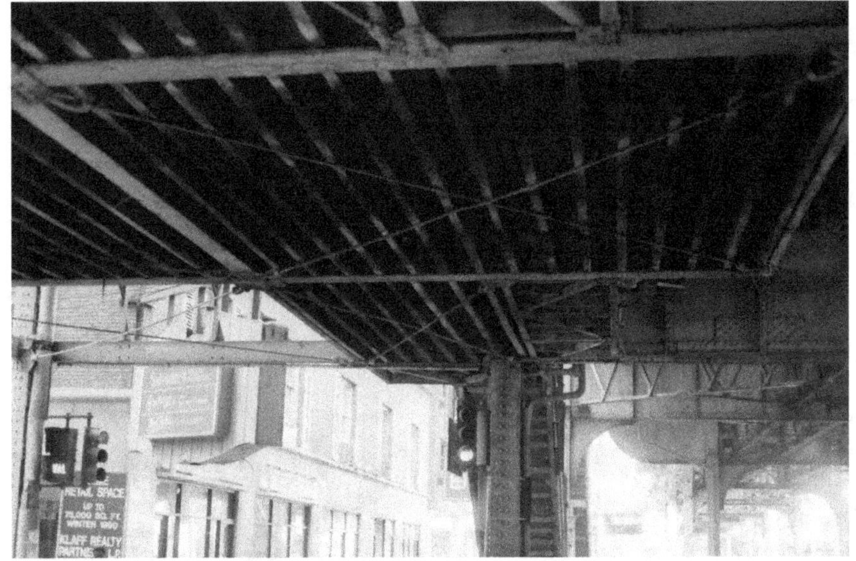

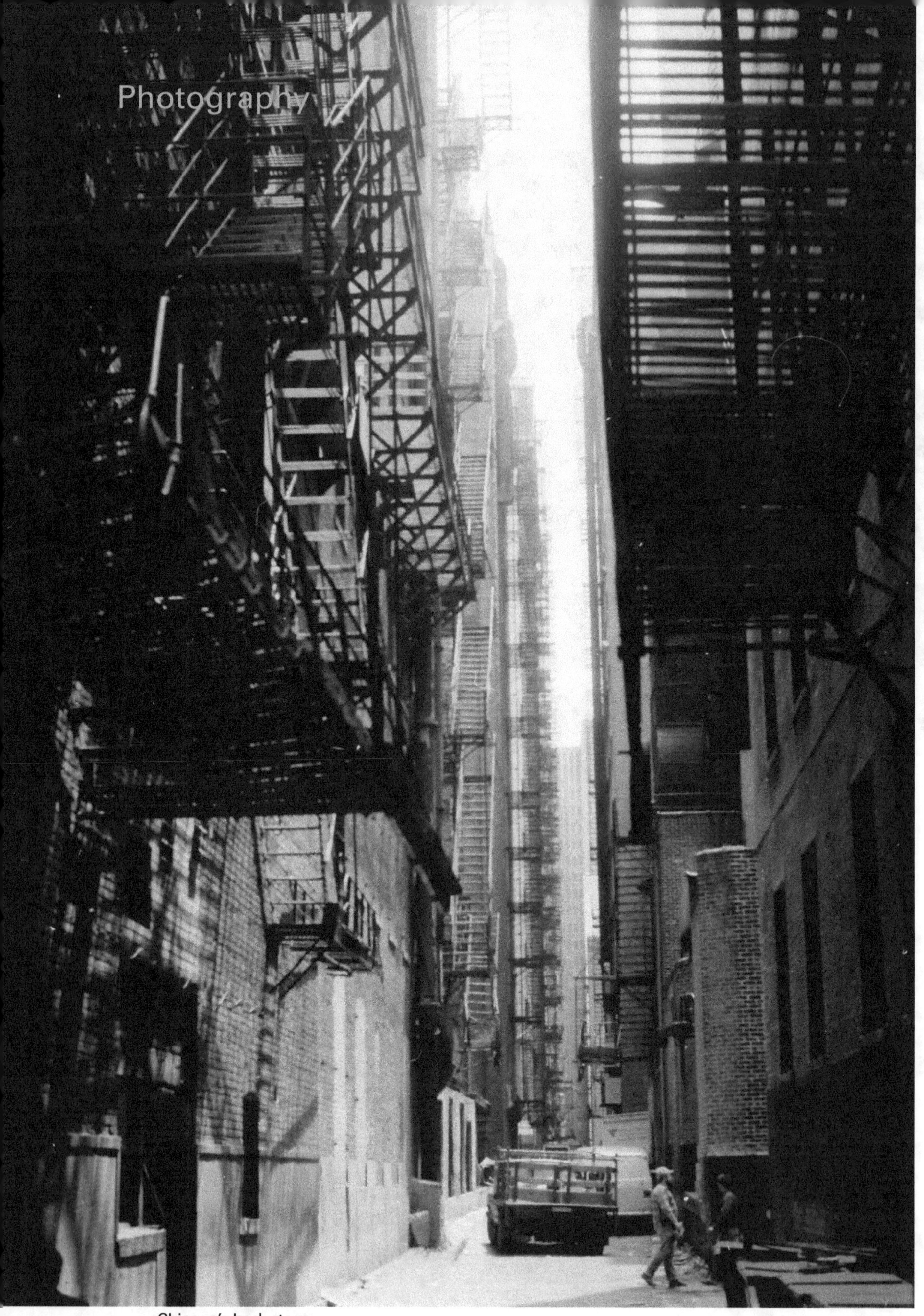

Chicago's back stage

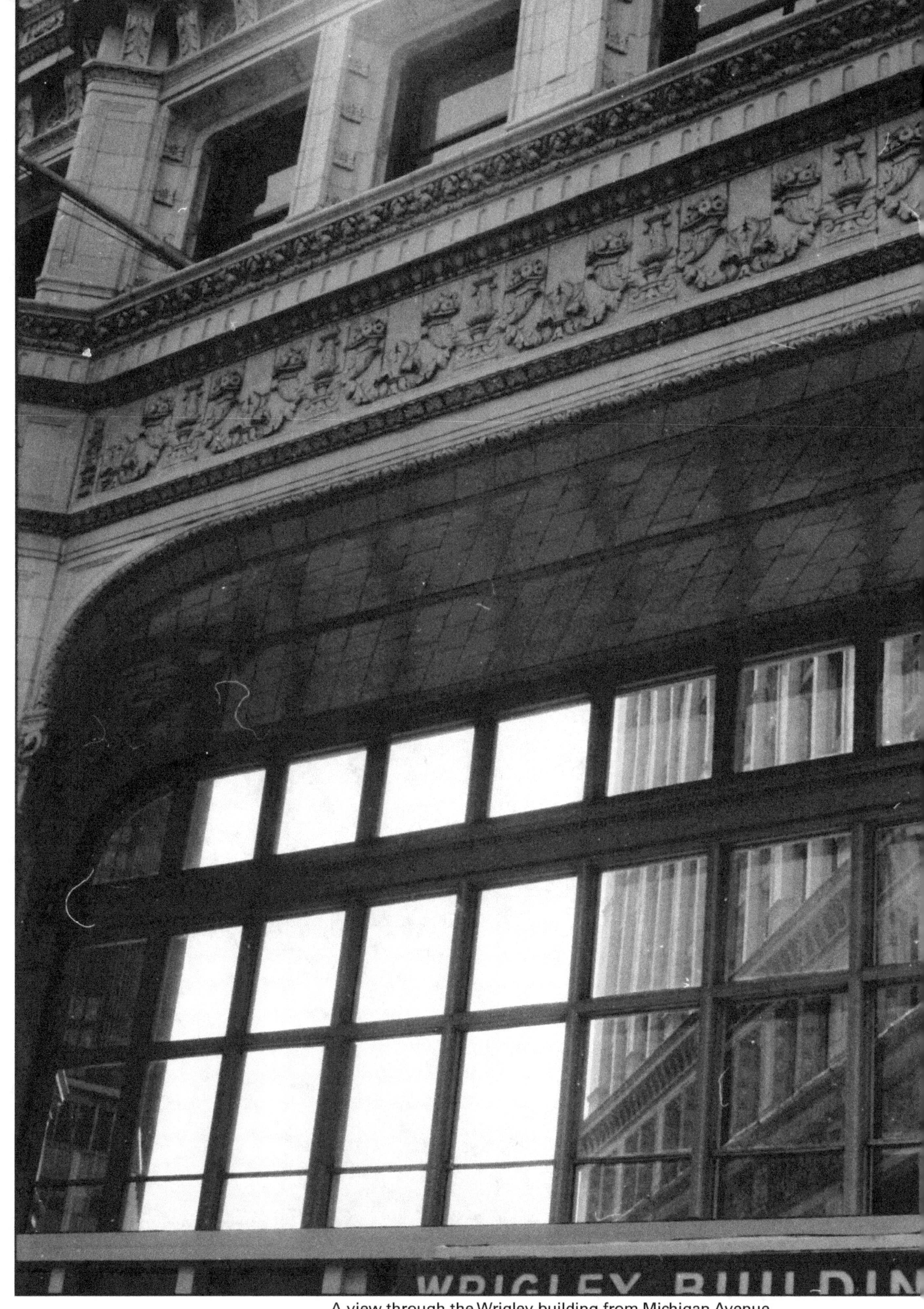

A view through the Wrigley building from Michigan Avenue

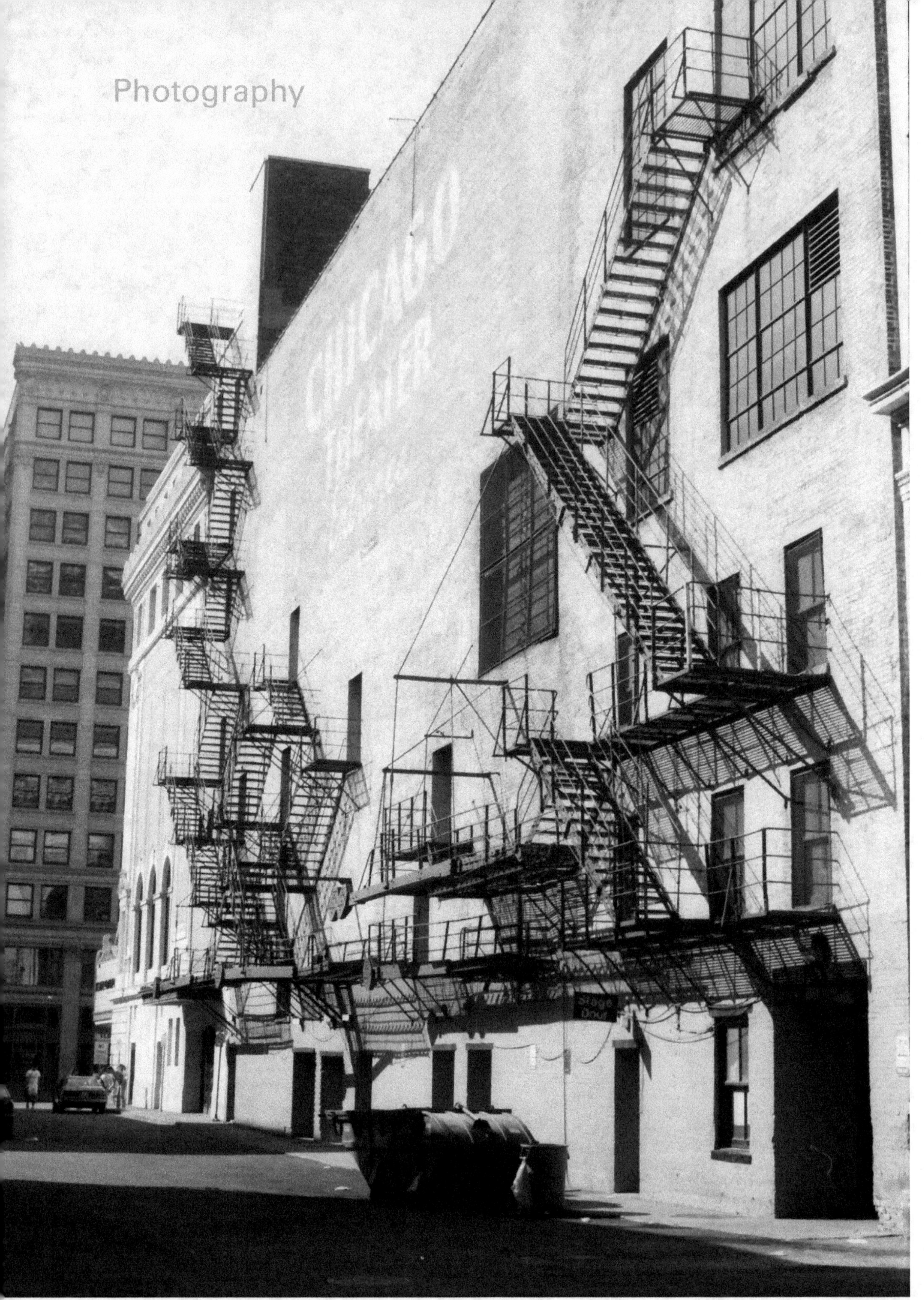

The city's back stage, where the mask is off

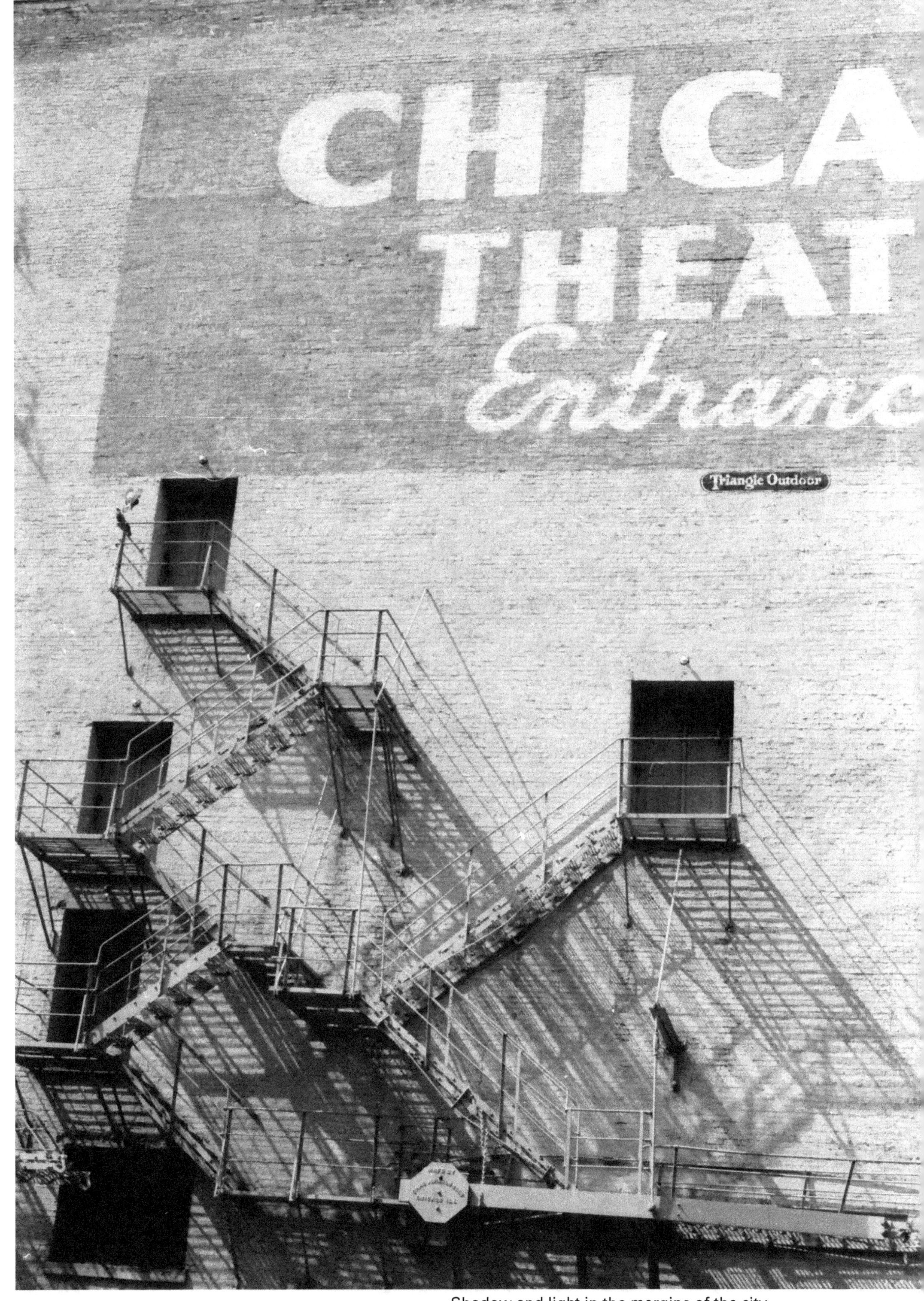

Shadow and light in the margins of the city

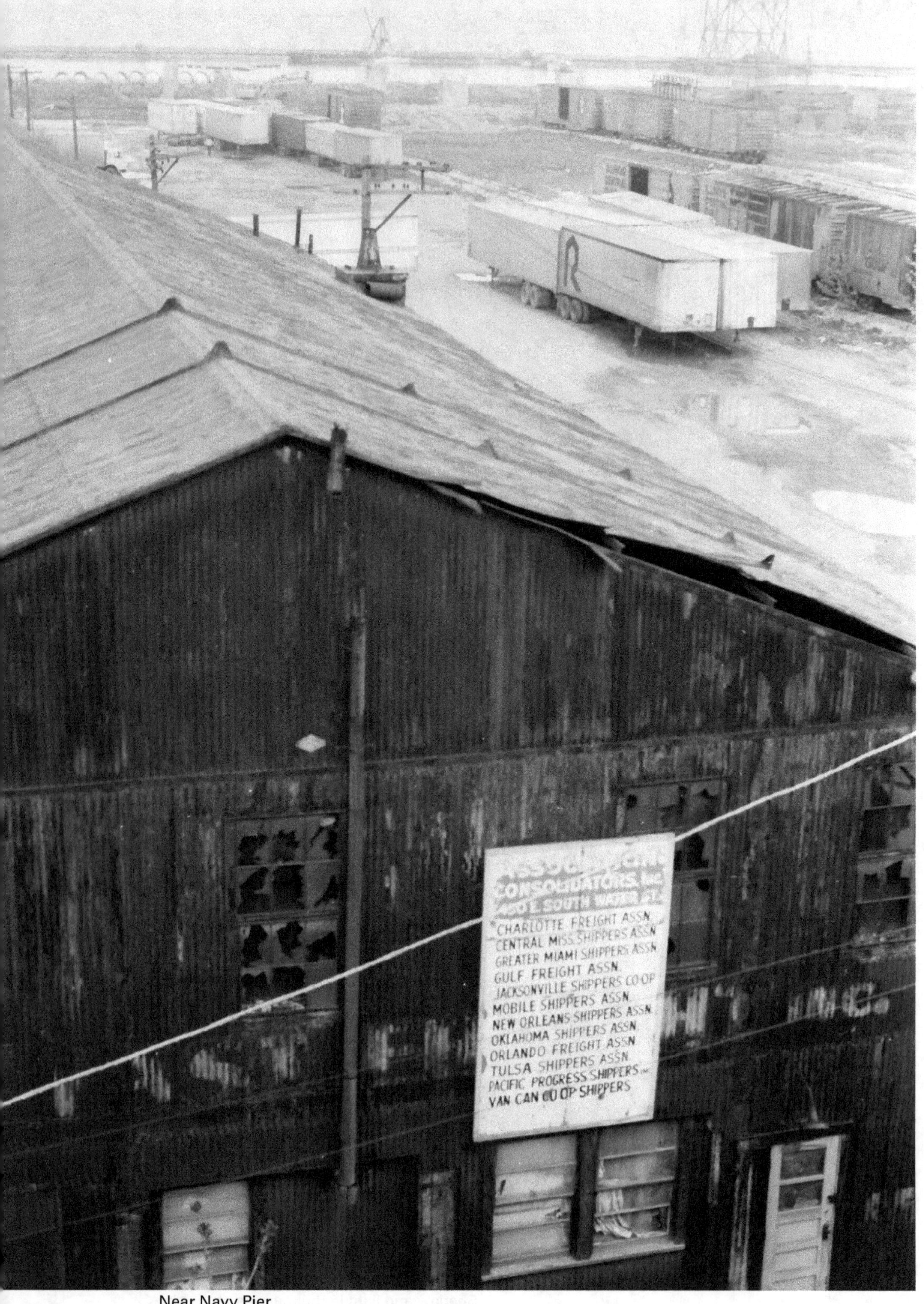

Near Navy Pier

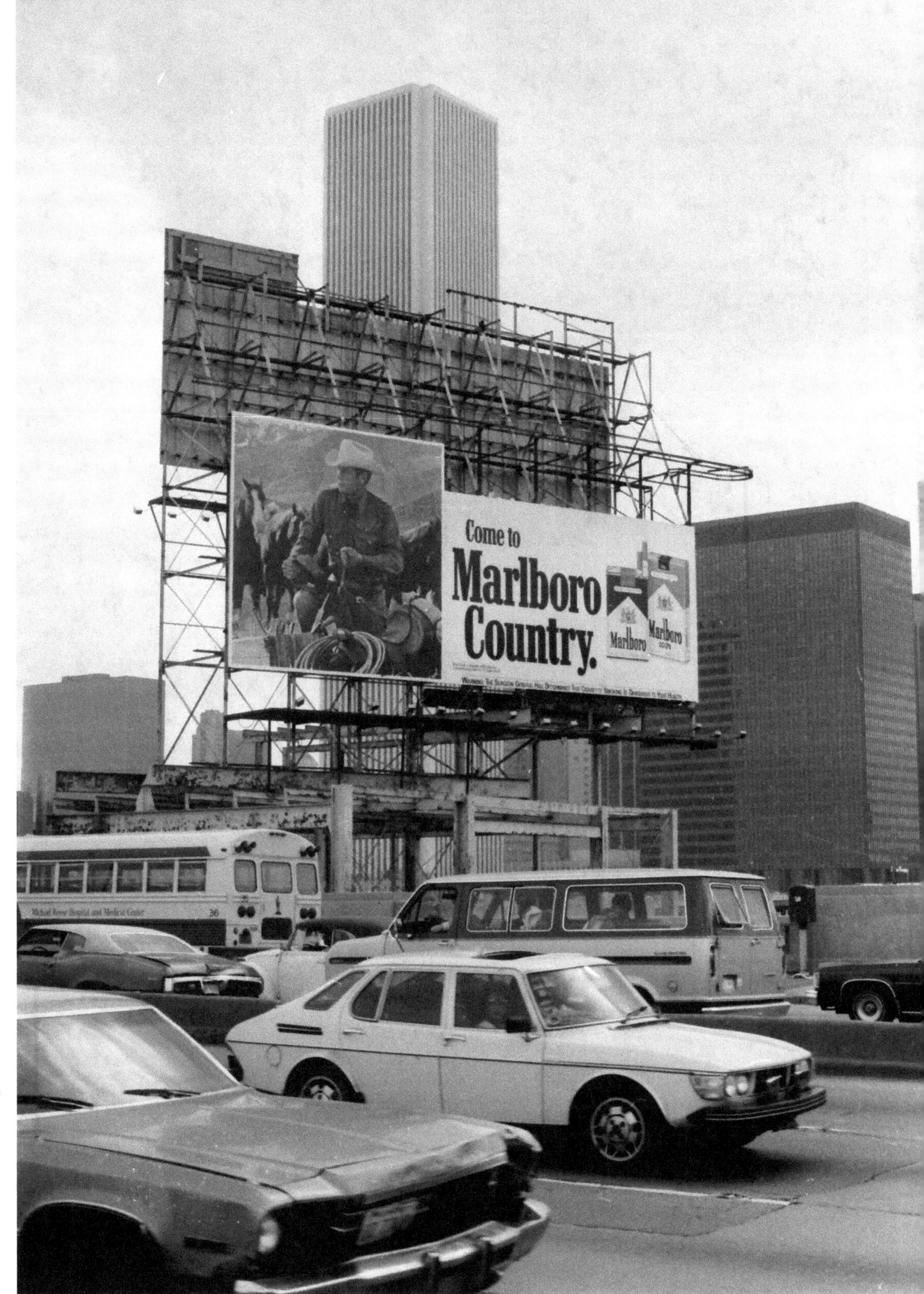

Lake Shore Drive at rush hour

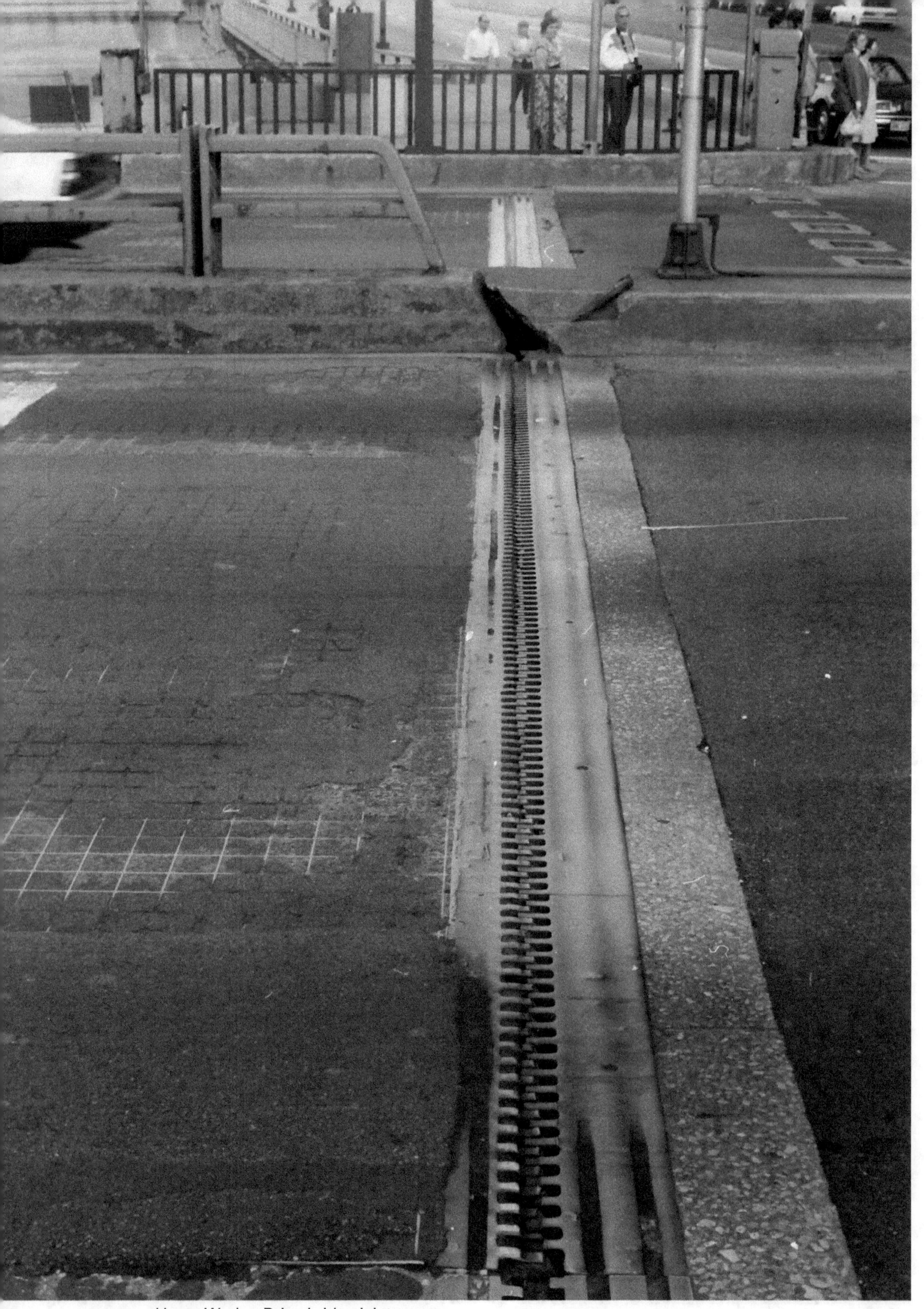

Upper Wacker Drive bridge joint

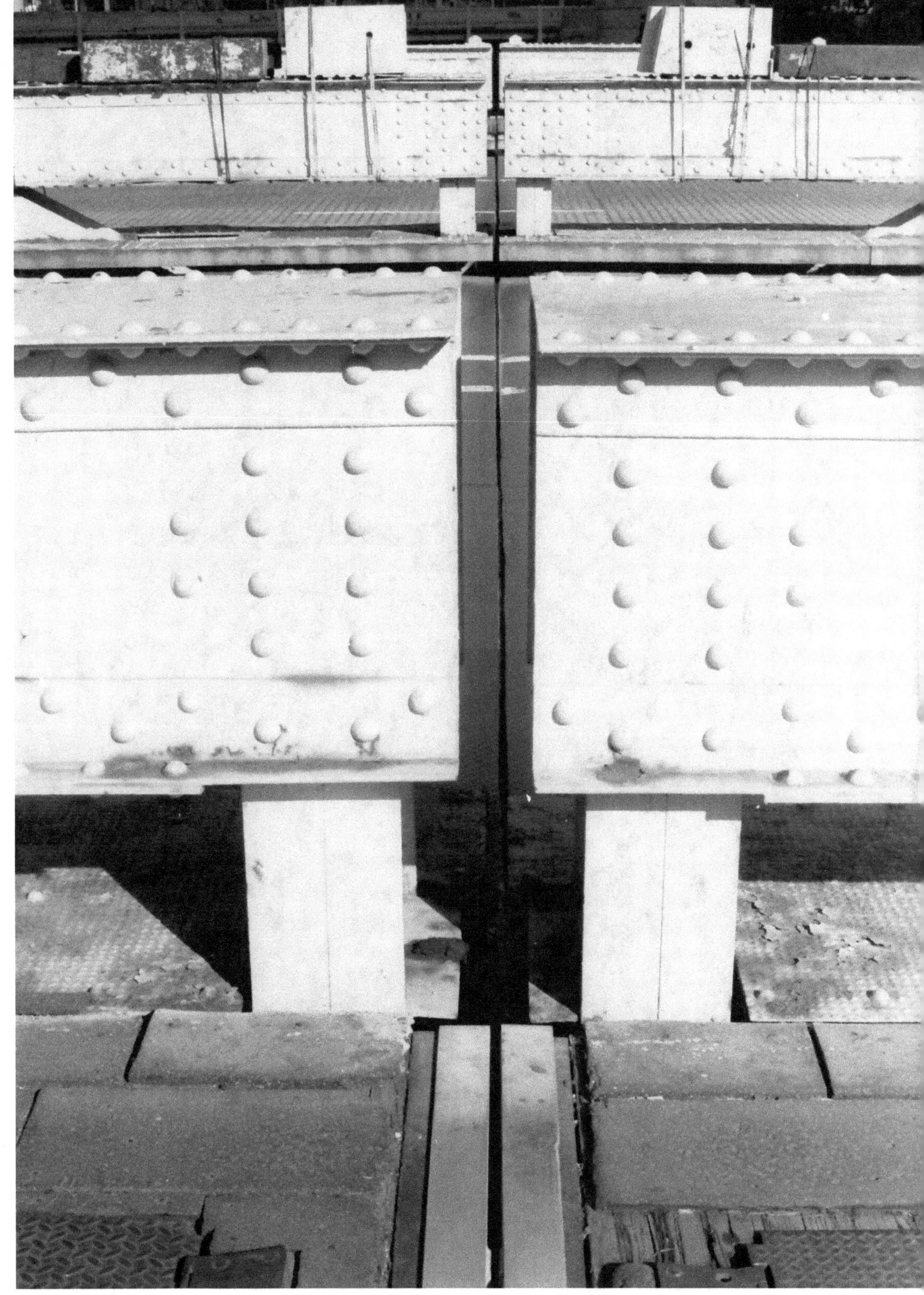

Gap at the middle of a Chicago bridge

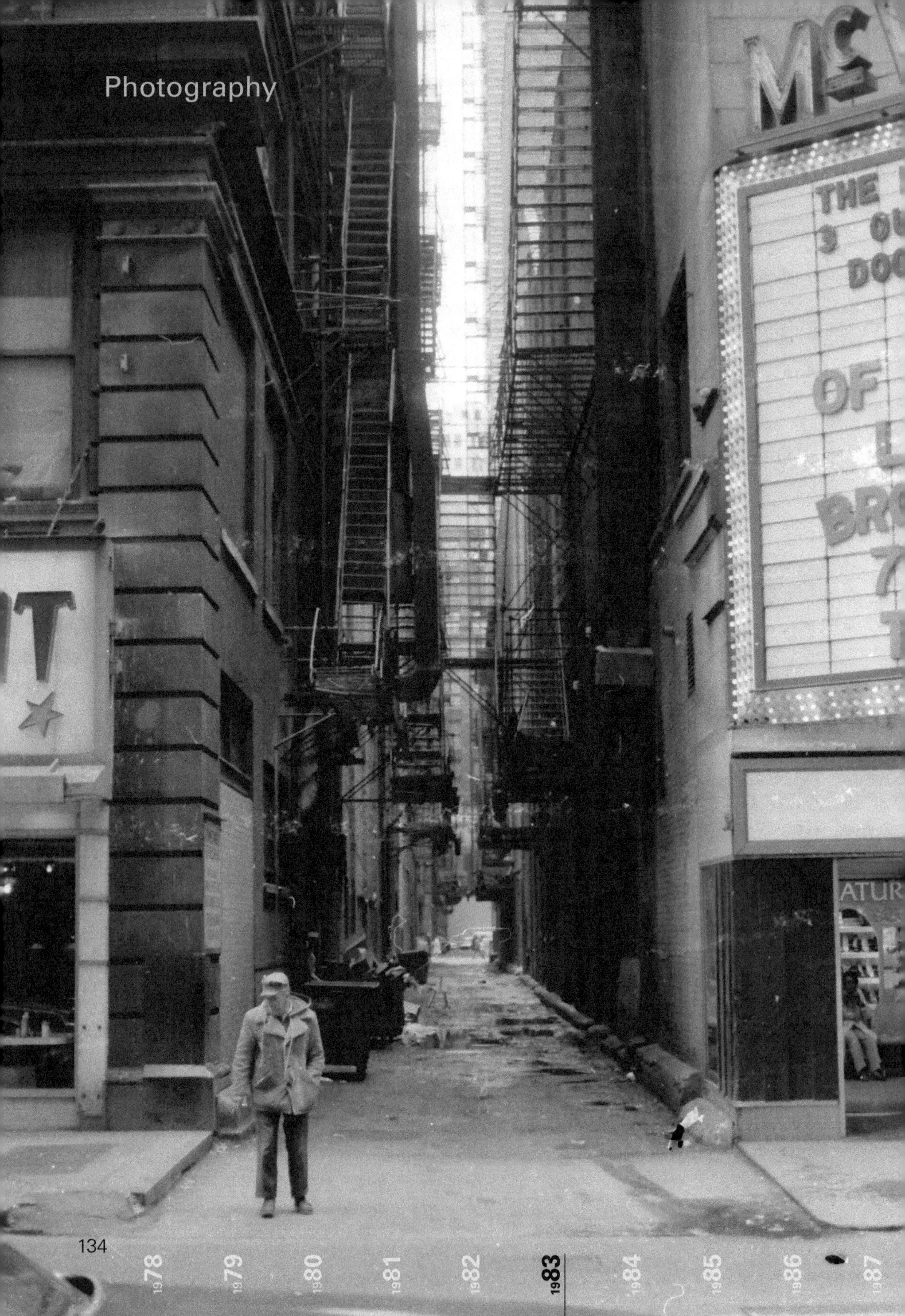

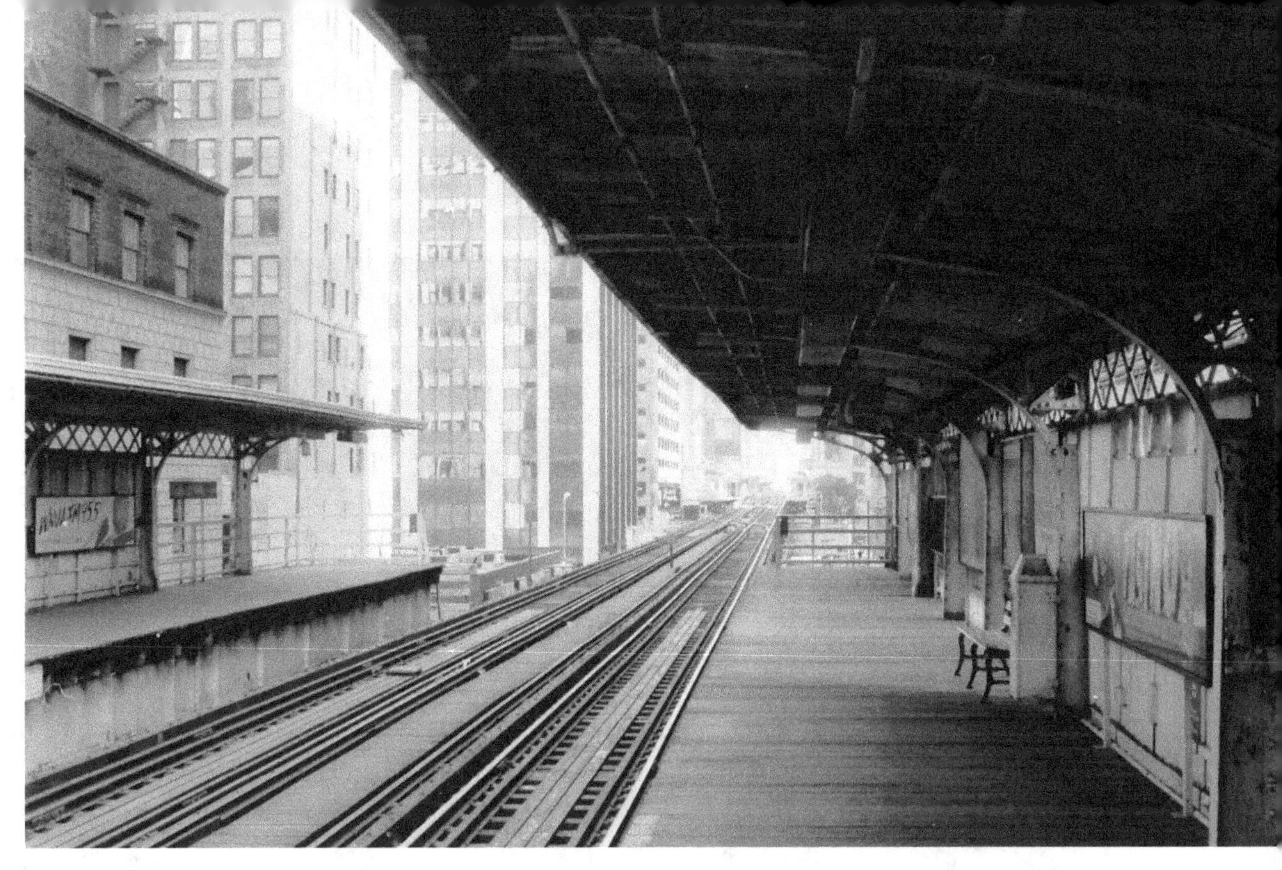

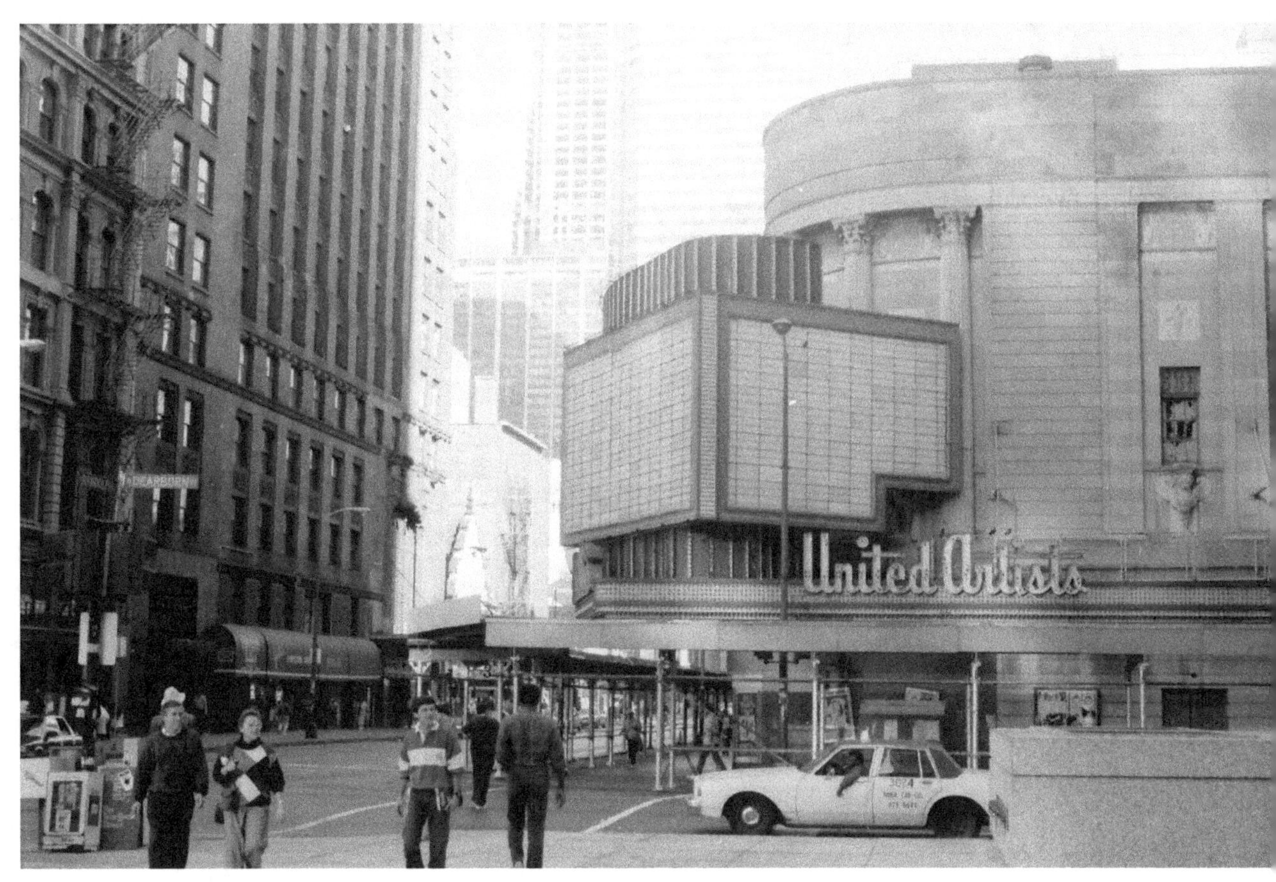
United Artists

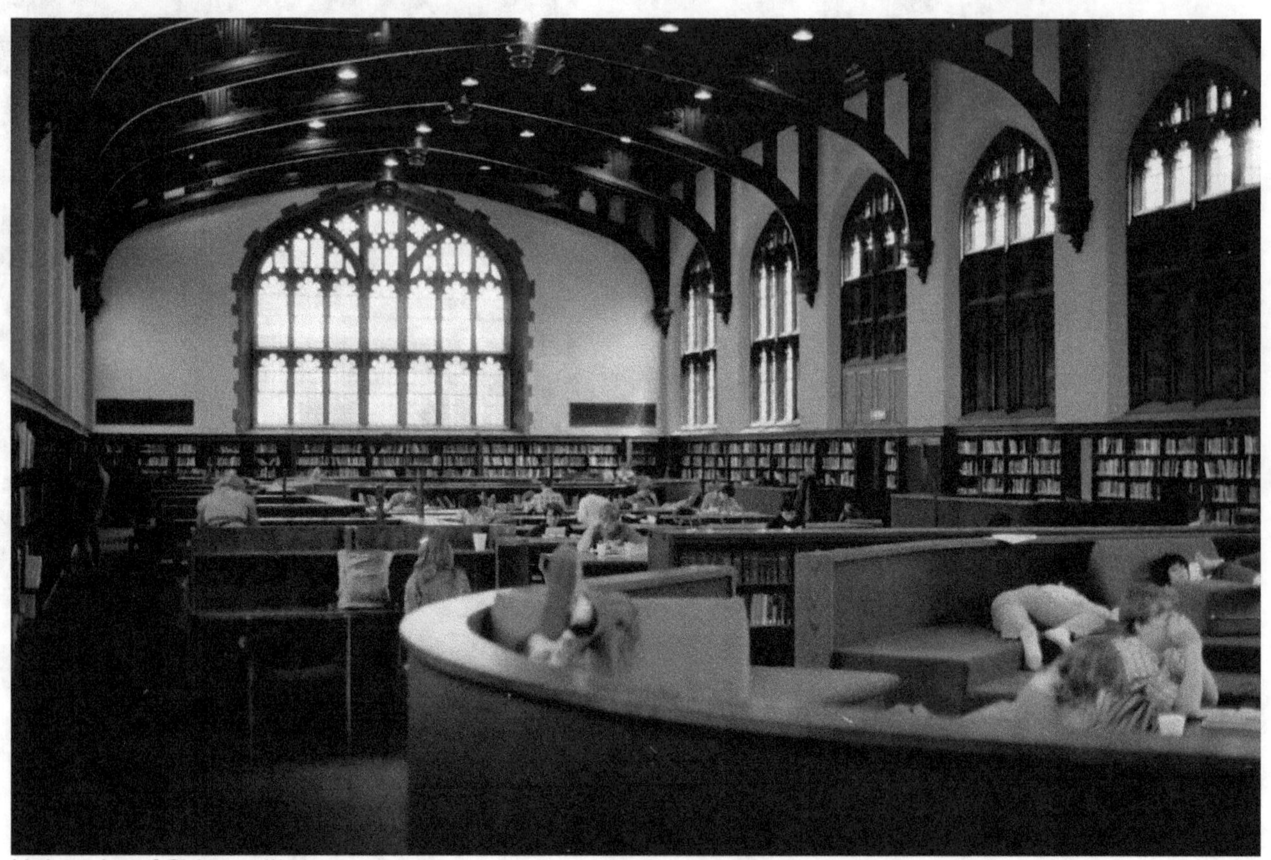
University of Chicago library

Hyde Park

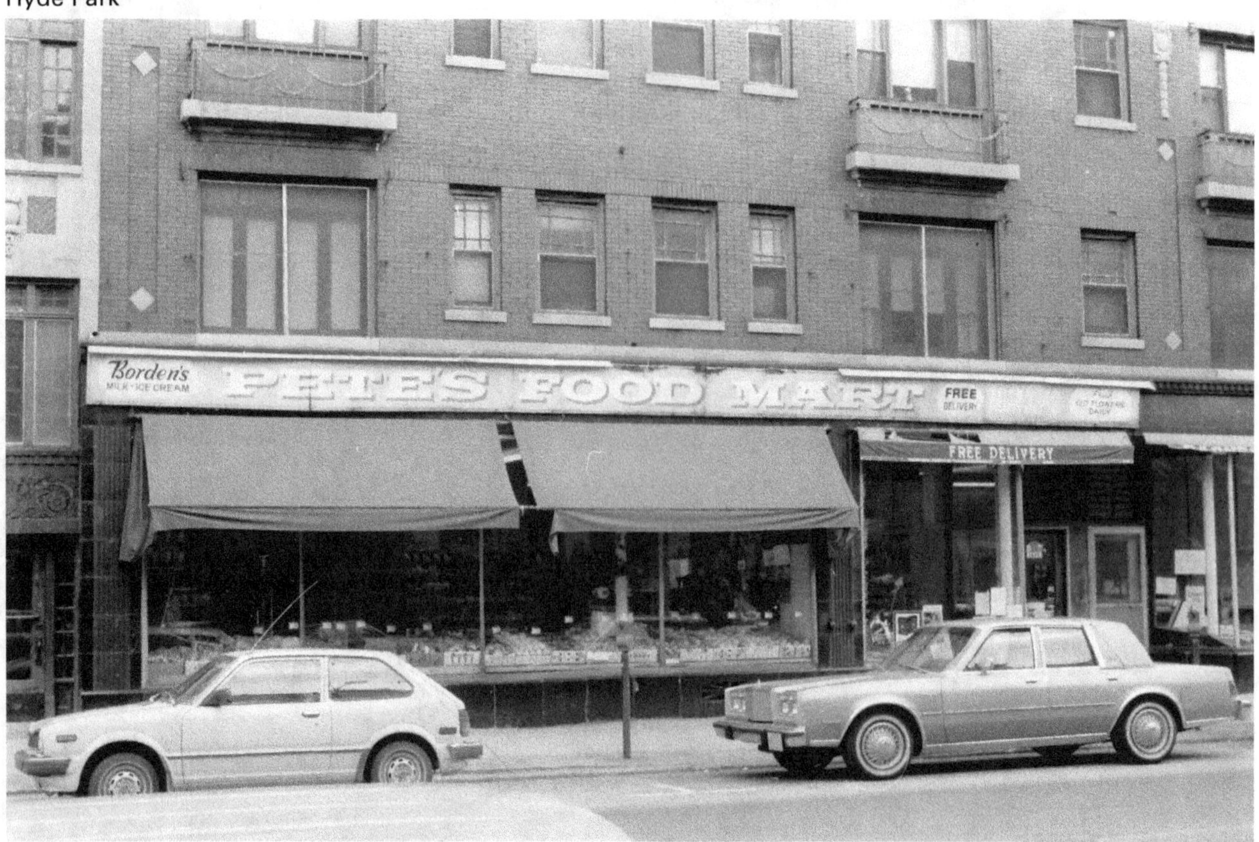

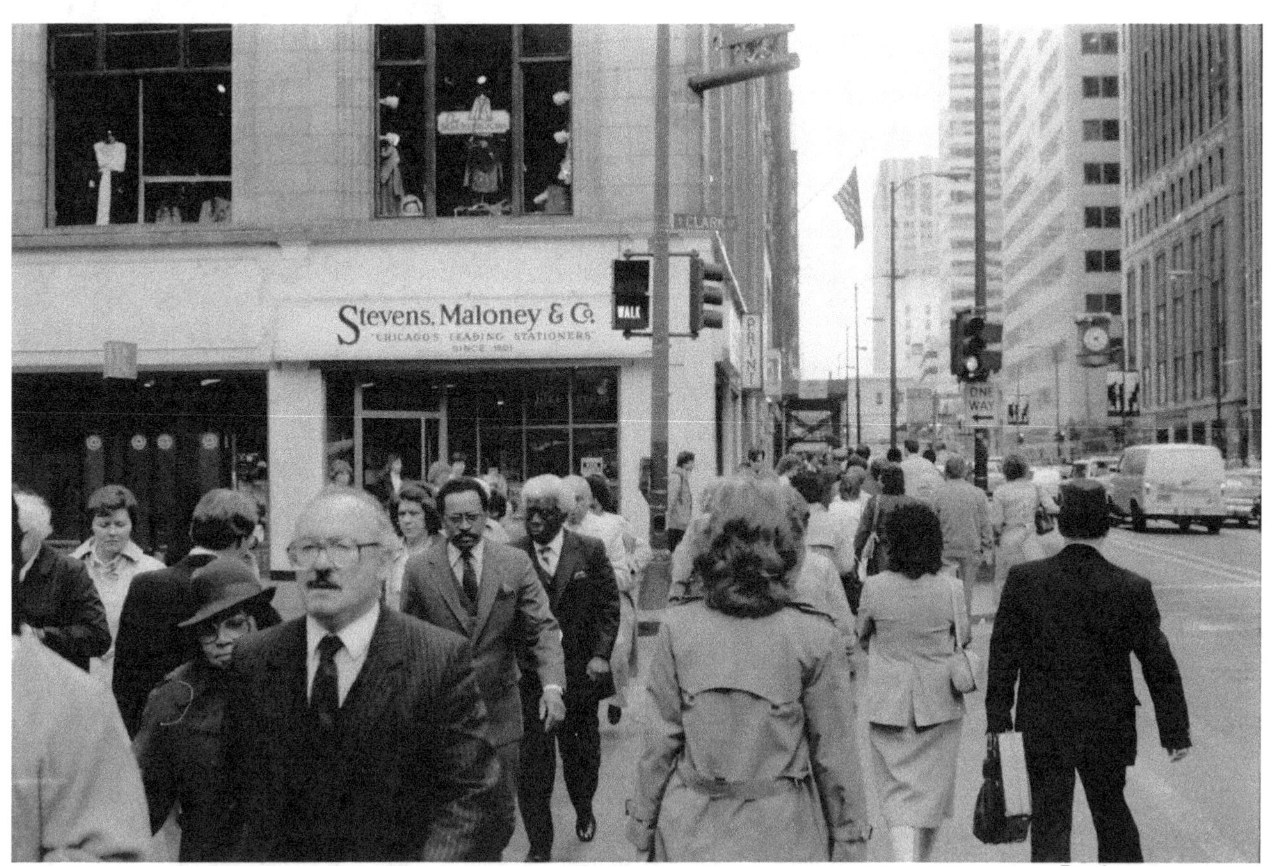

Business as usual

Lucky Strikes Again...

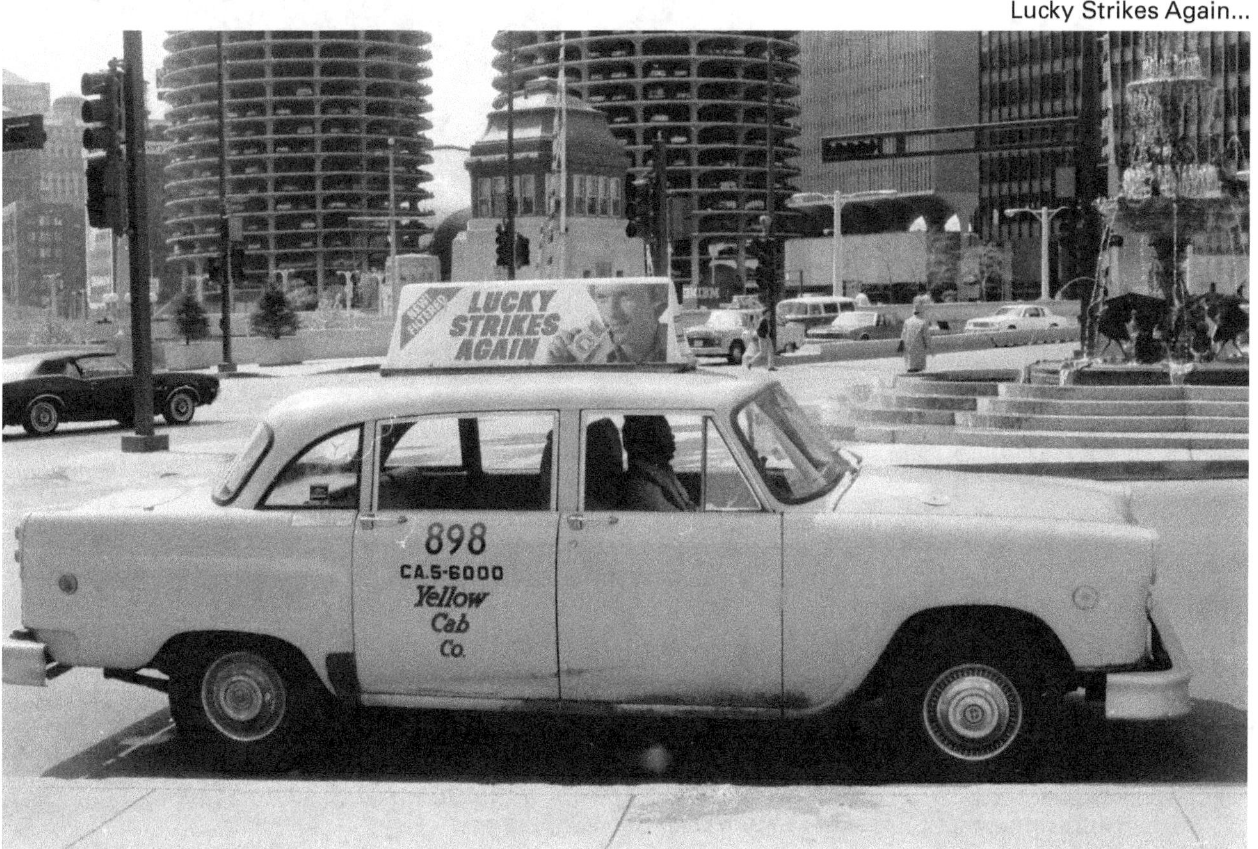

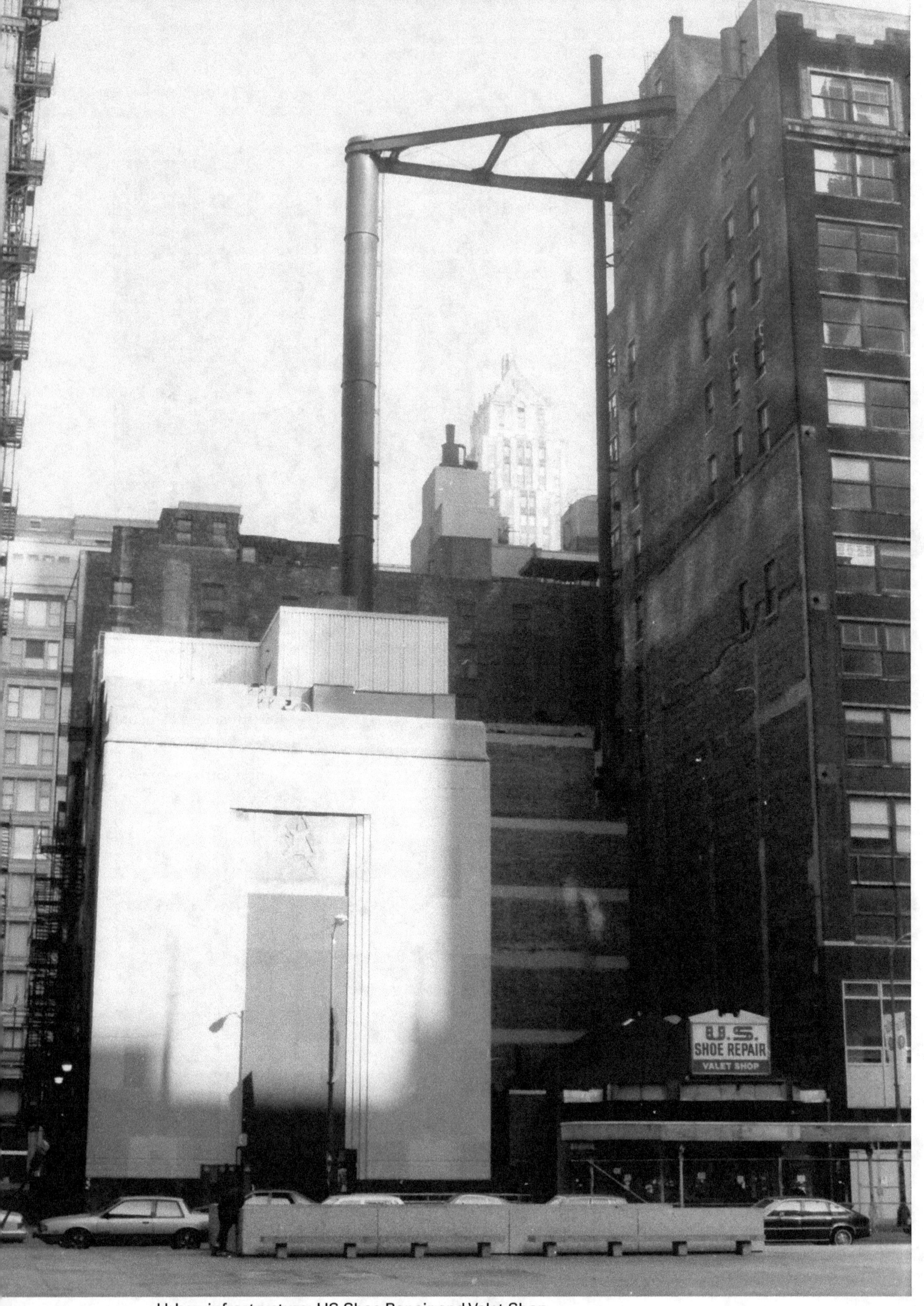

Urban infrastructure: US Shoe Repair and Valet Shop

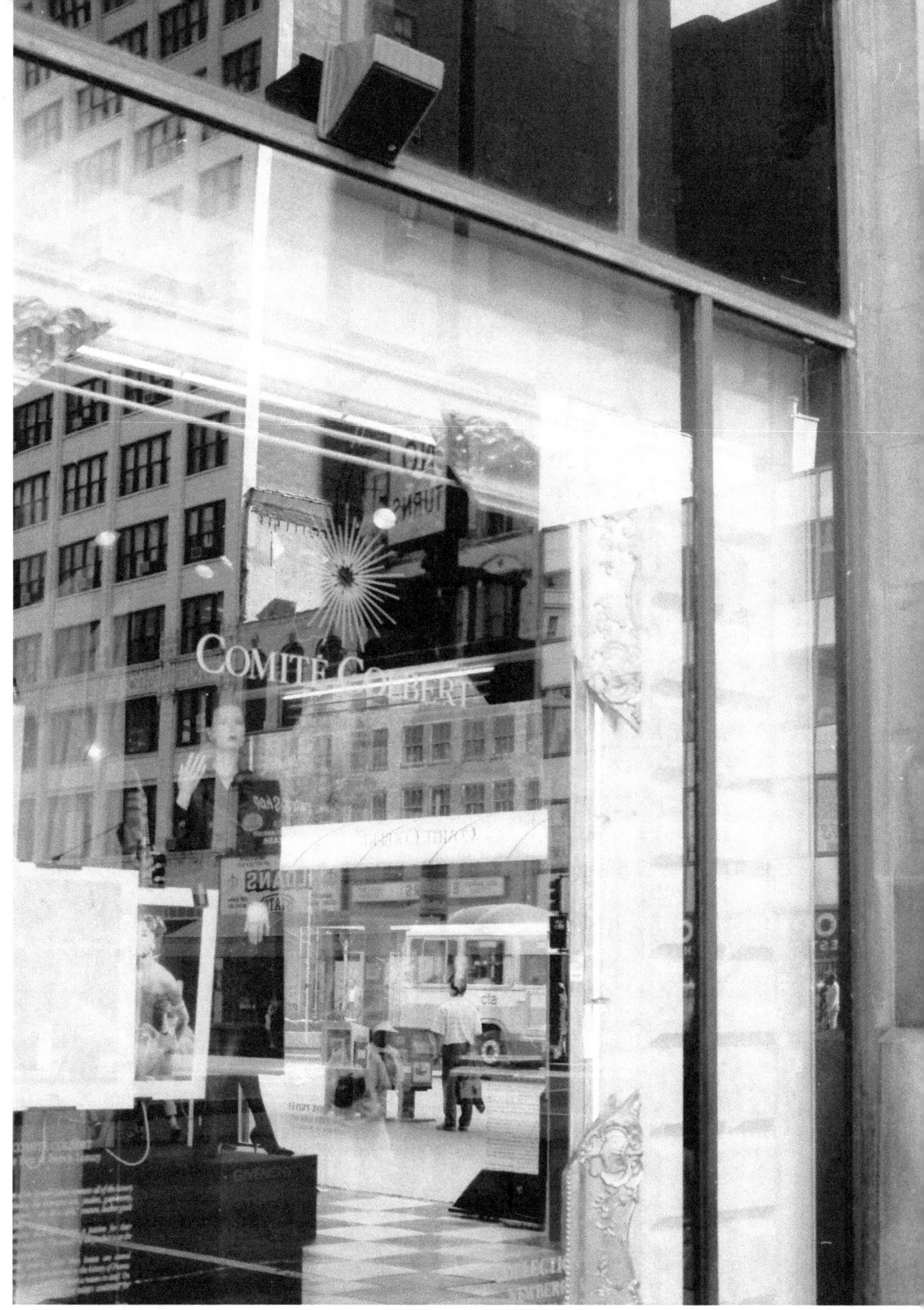

Window shopping on State Street

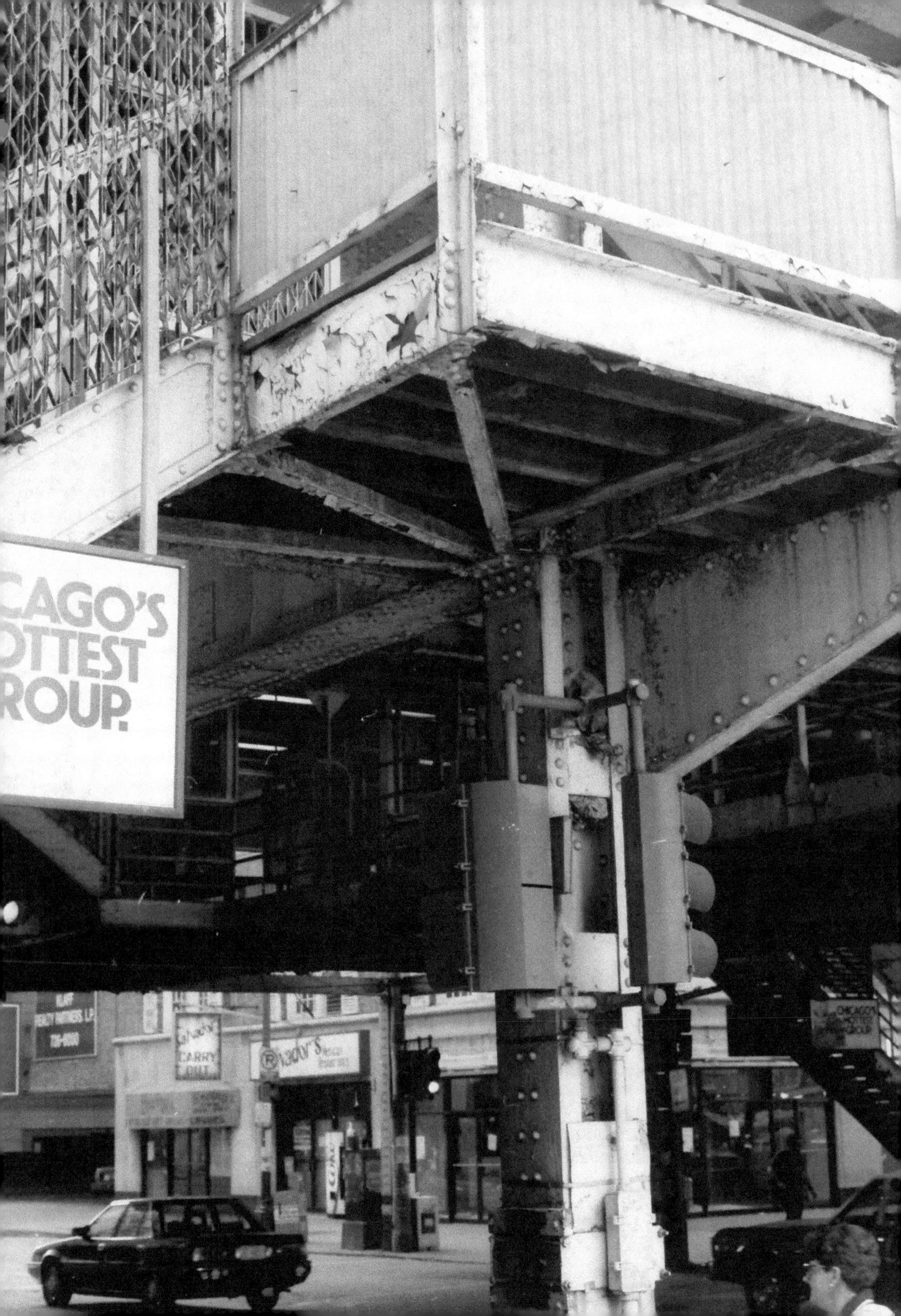
CAGO'S
OTTEST
ROUP.

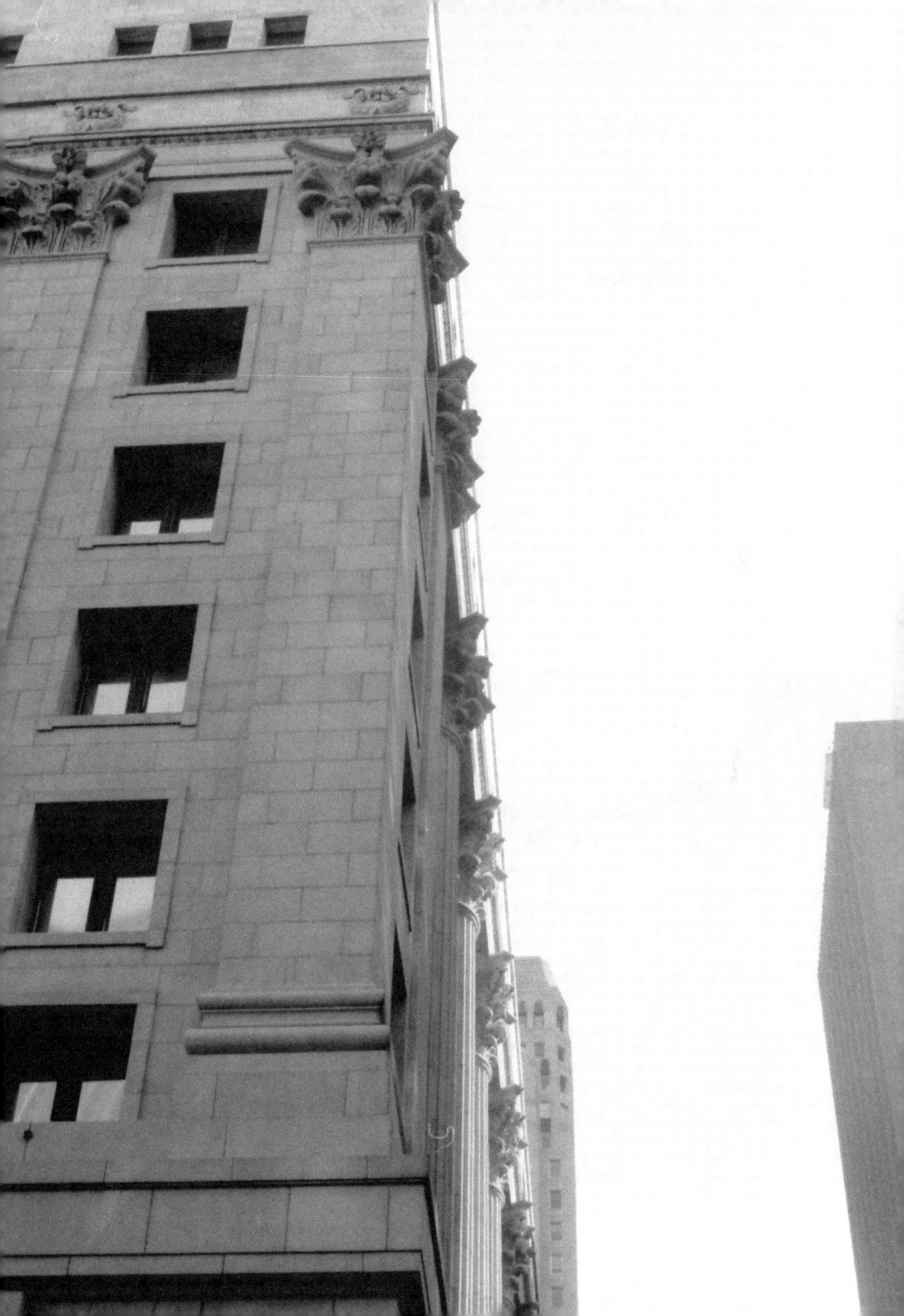

Driving east on a street in Chicago right after a downpour

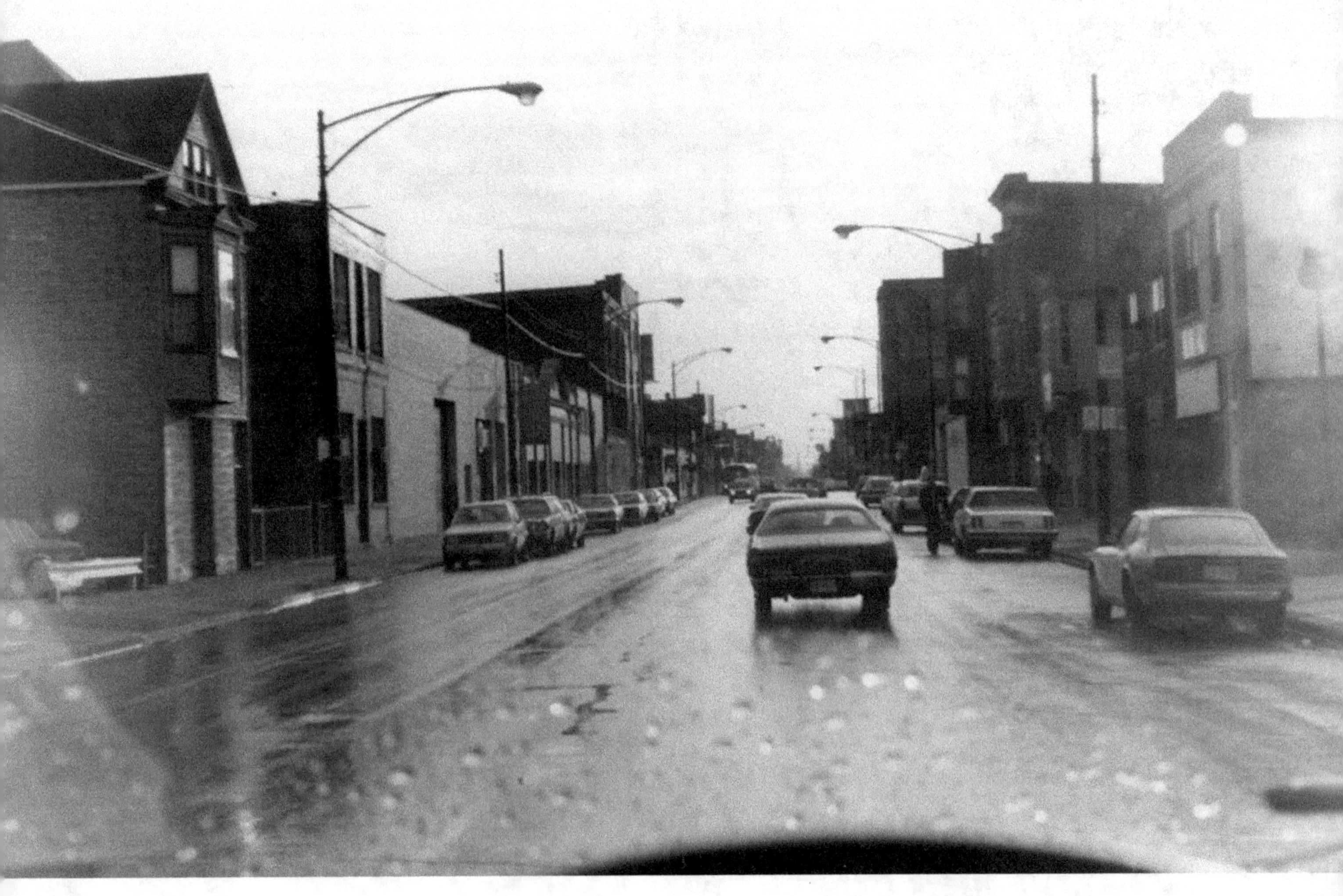

1988 1989 1990 1991 1992 1993 1994 1995 1996 1997

Travel in Great Britain

In the summer we took our Citroën 2CV via ferry over to the UK, and spent three weeks touring the countryside. On the first day we encountered this village early in the morning when everyone was just getting up to a foggy dawn

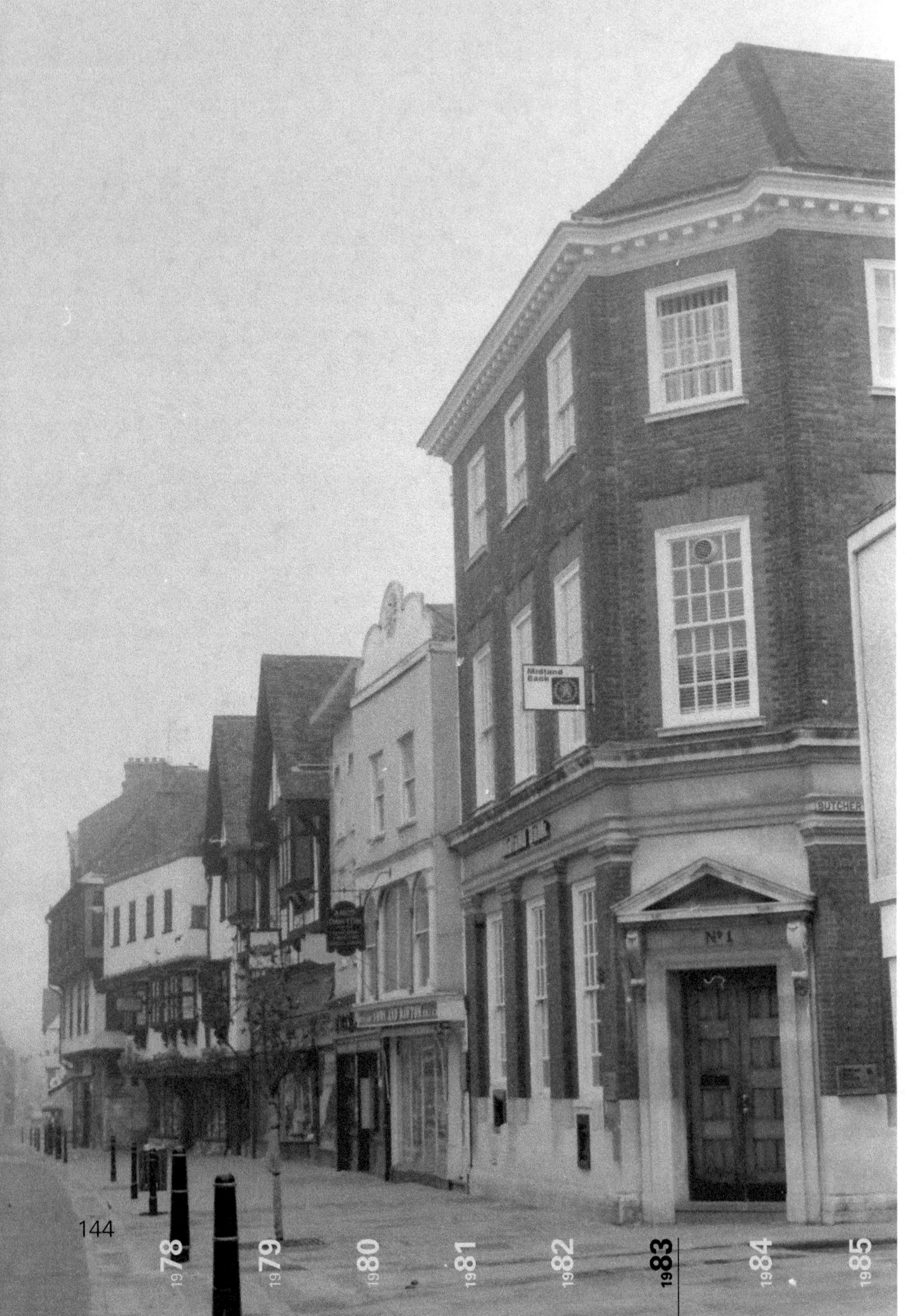

Wales

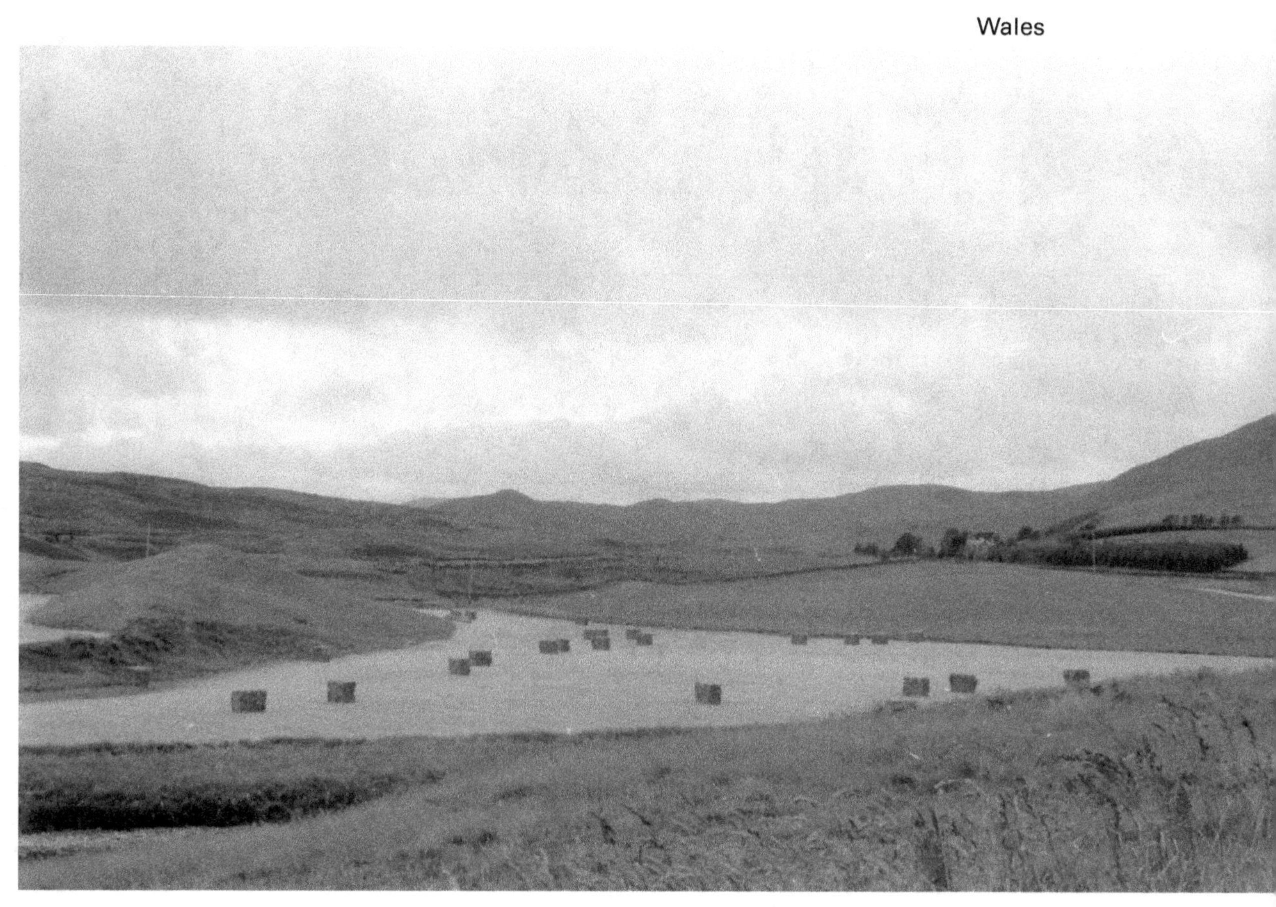

England

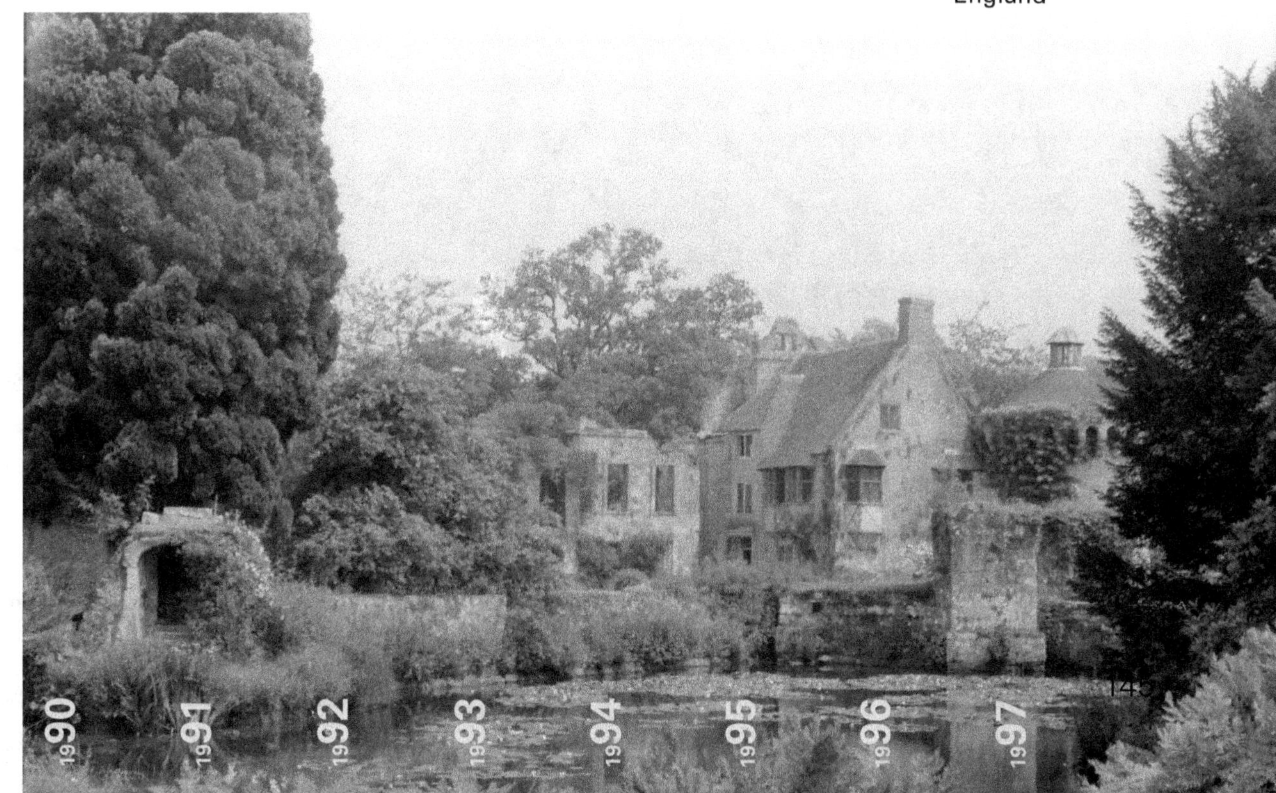

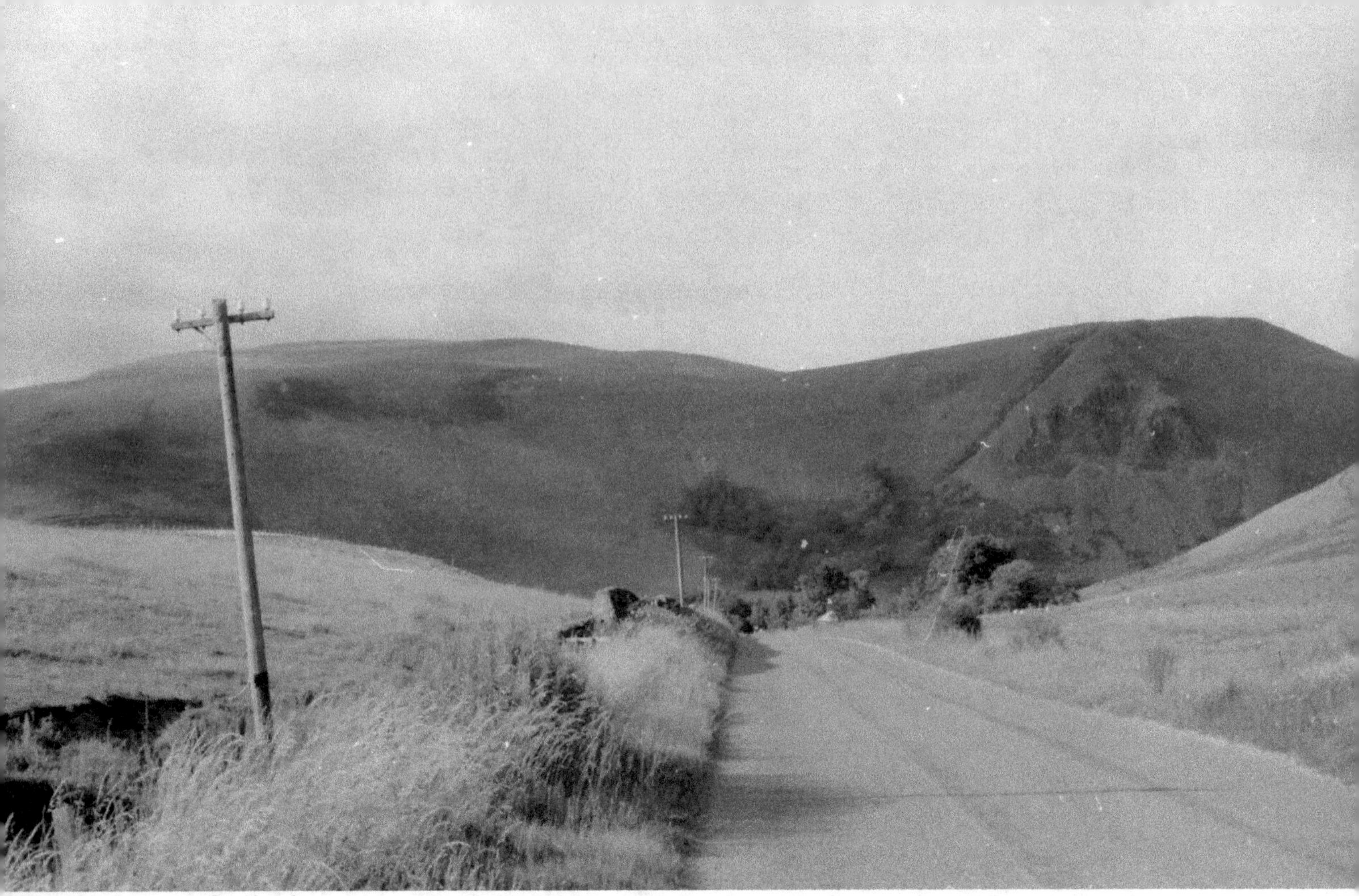

Scotland

Brighton Beach and Pier >

Some loch

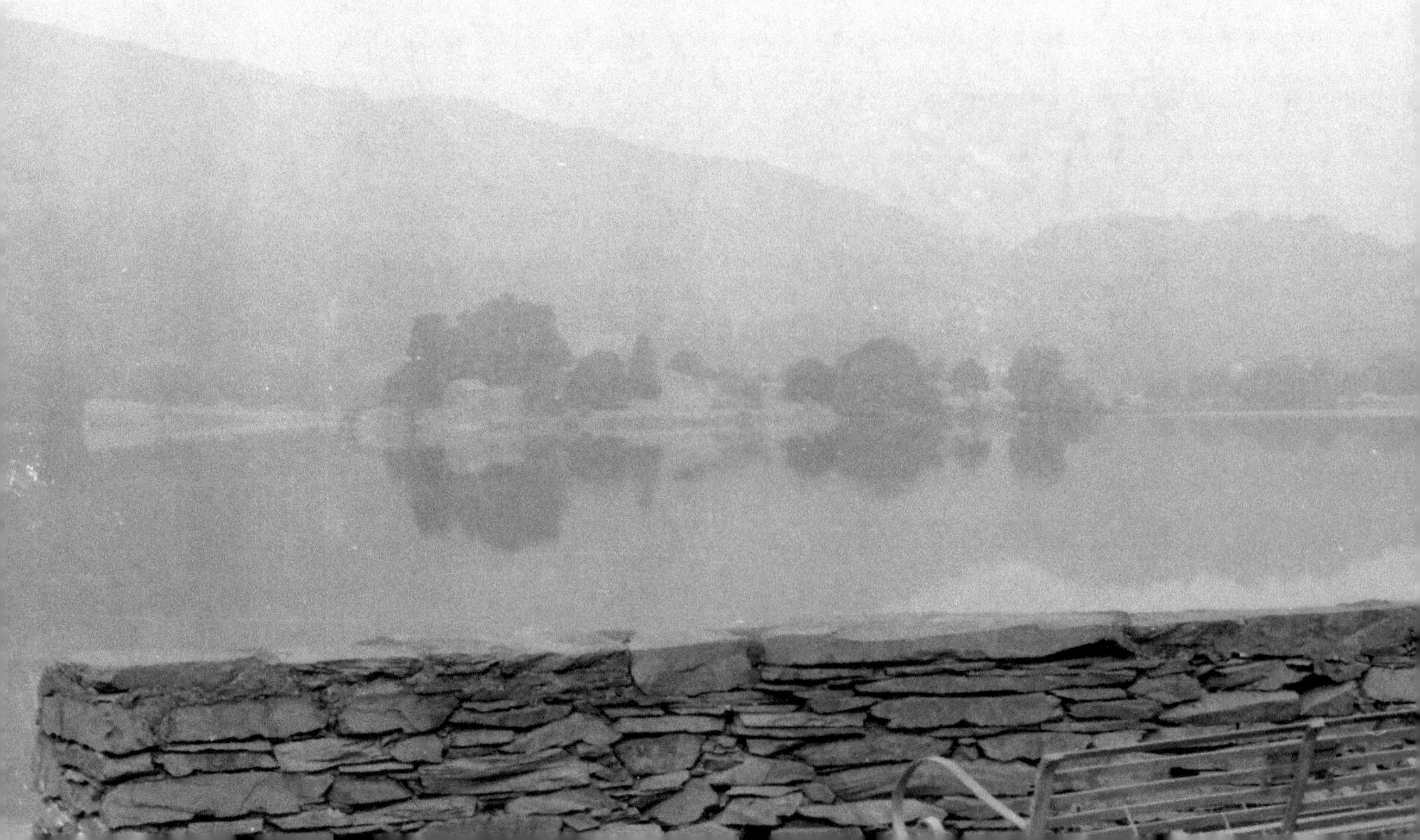

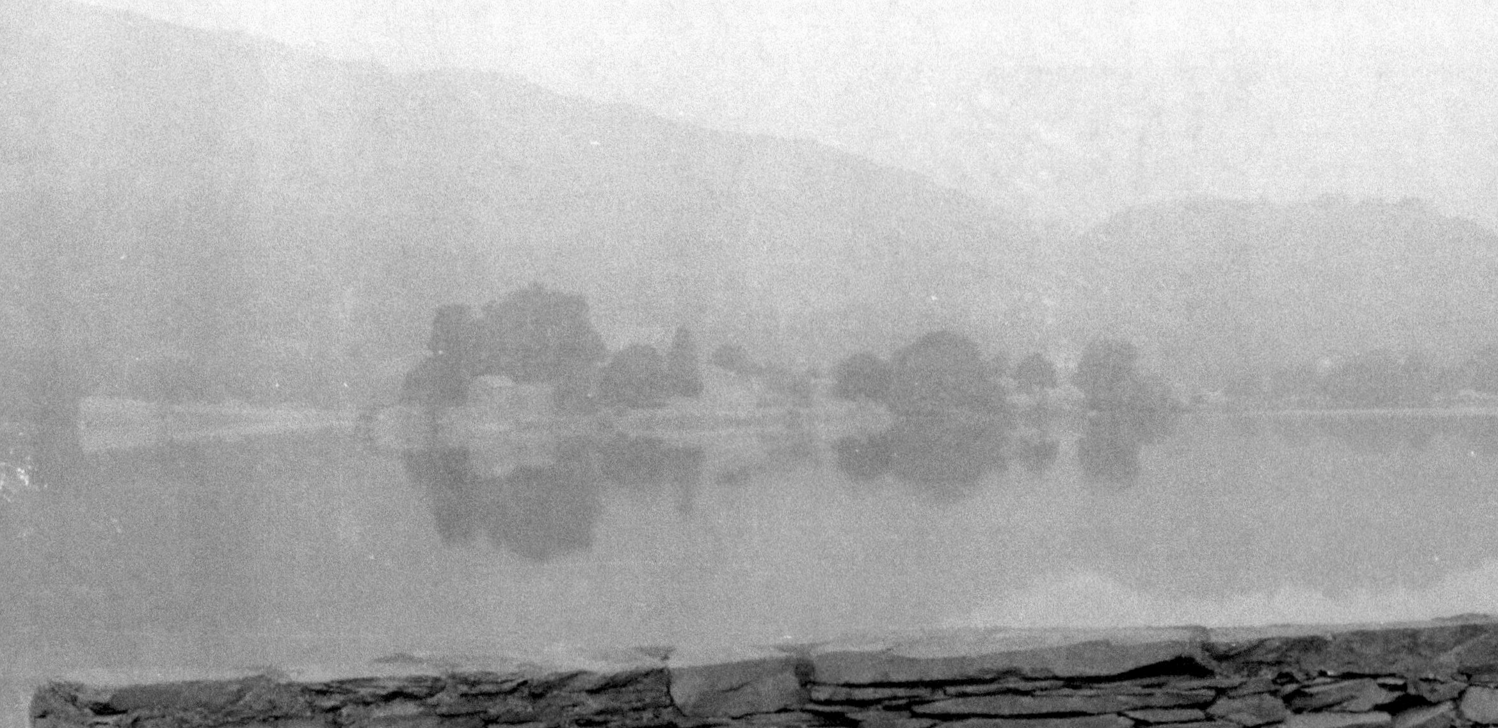

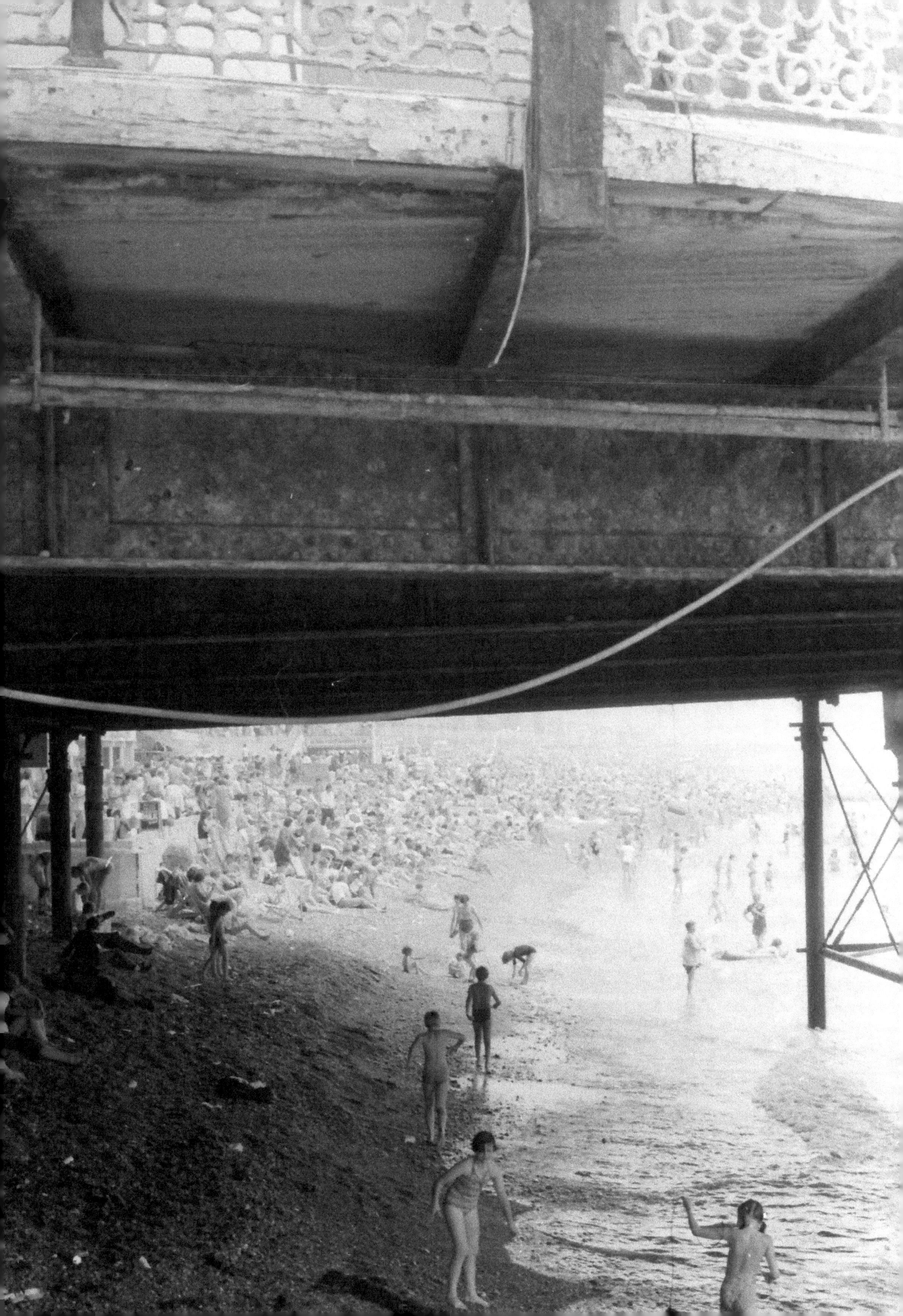

Dignified donkeys at Sidmouth beach

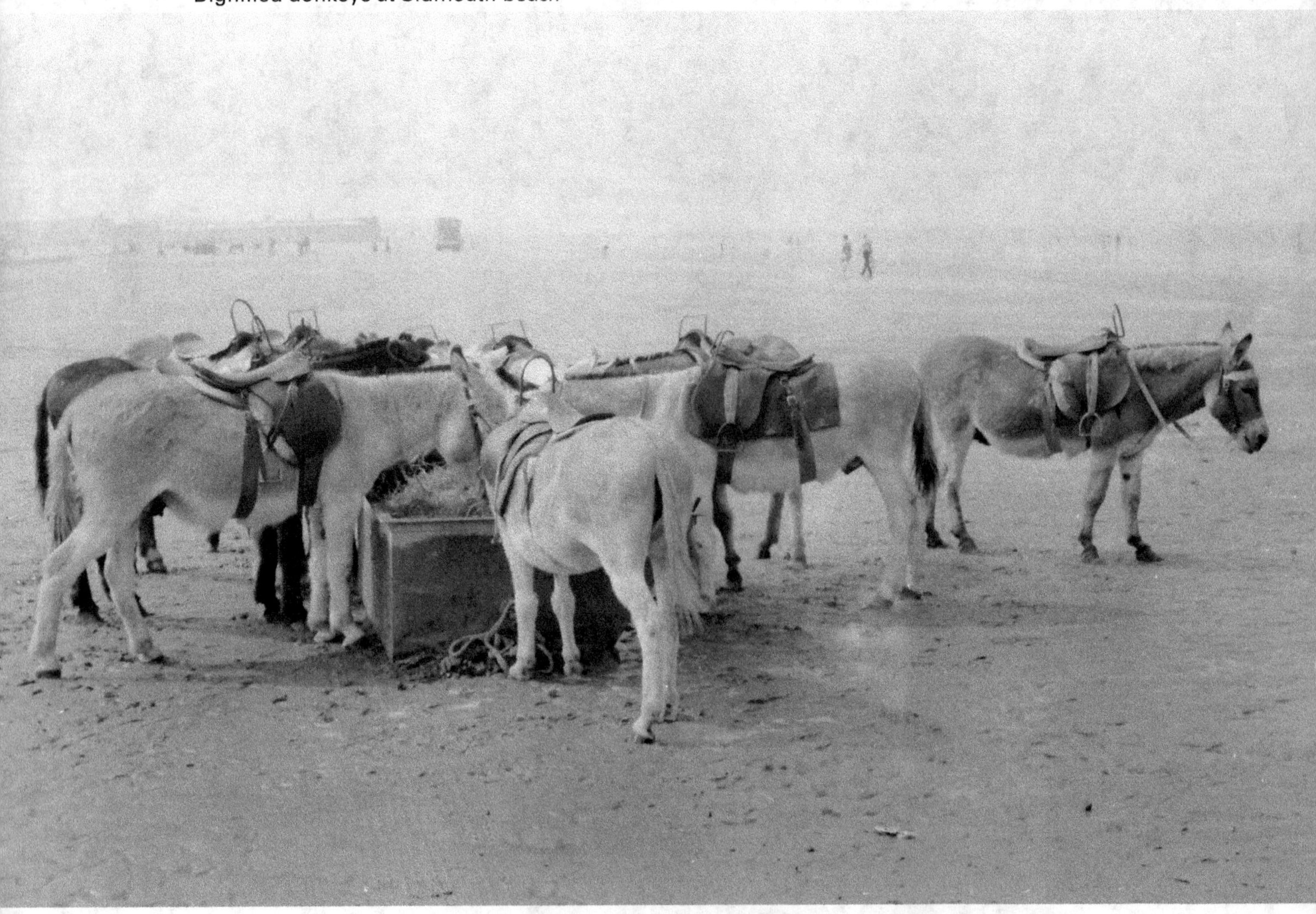

Painting

oil on canvas

Man on buggy with horse moving through the tidal flats of the Northsea >

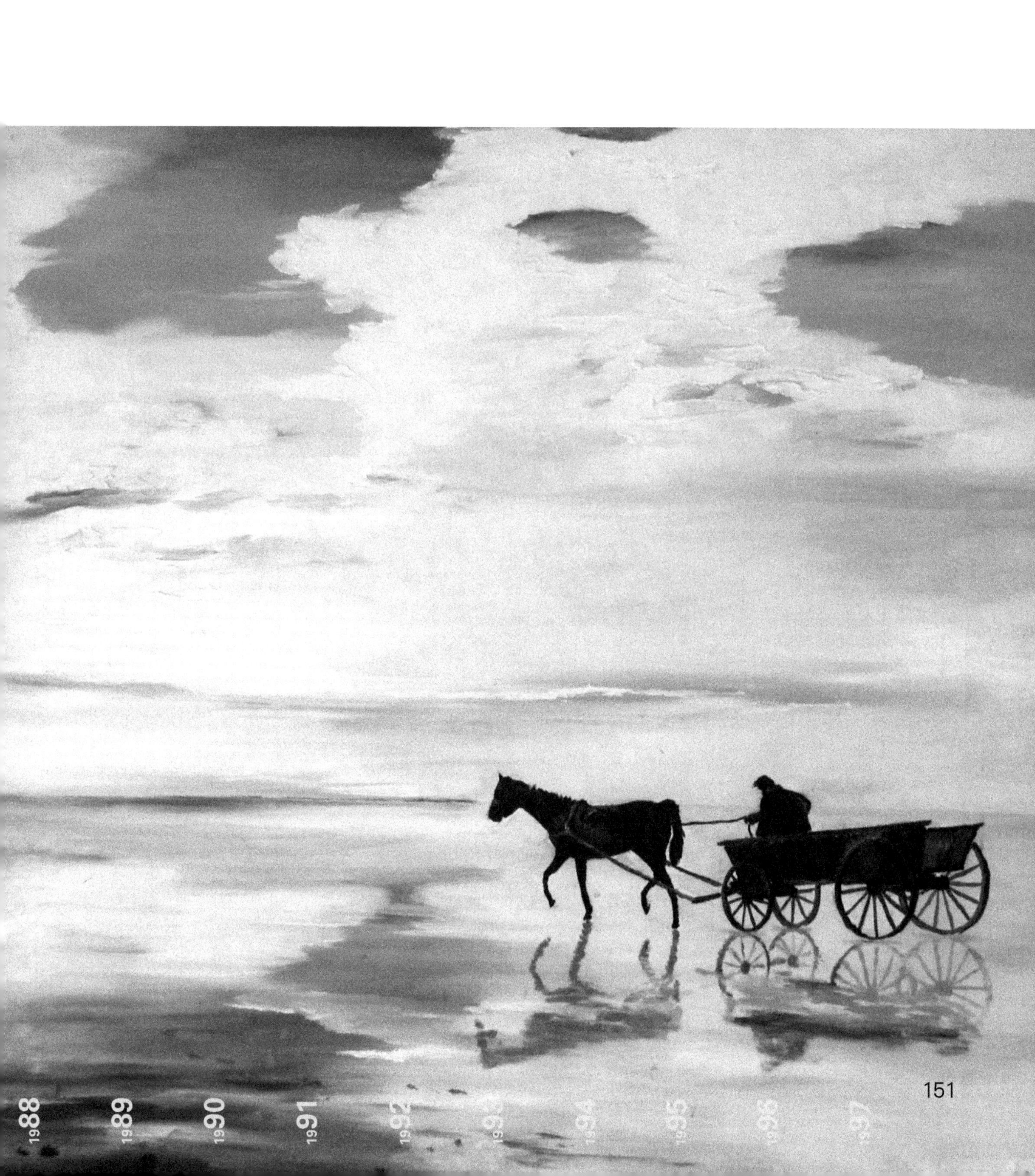

1984

Drawing

pencil and ink on paper

Piano House

One of my early attempts to translate ideas into a building, during my formalist phase when I was concerned more with shapes than acoustics. The building is a sign, not an instrument.

preliminary sketches

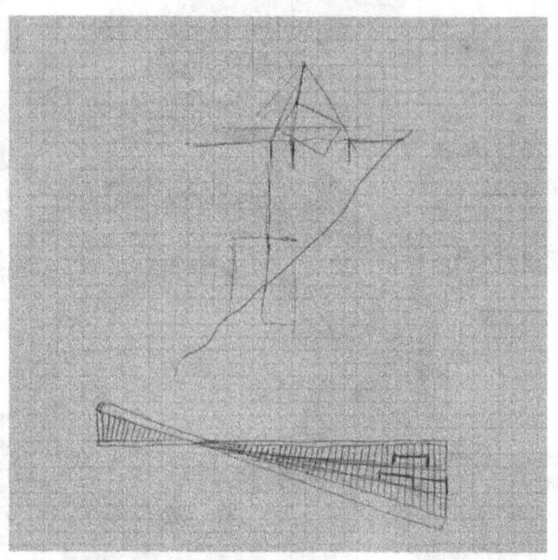

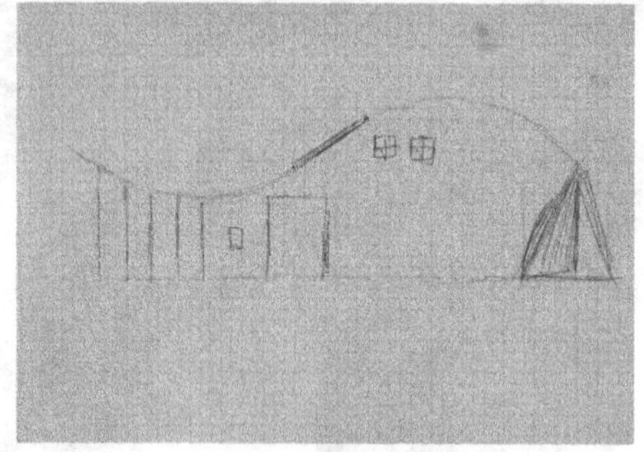

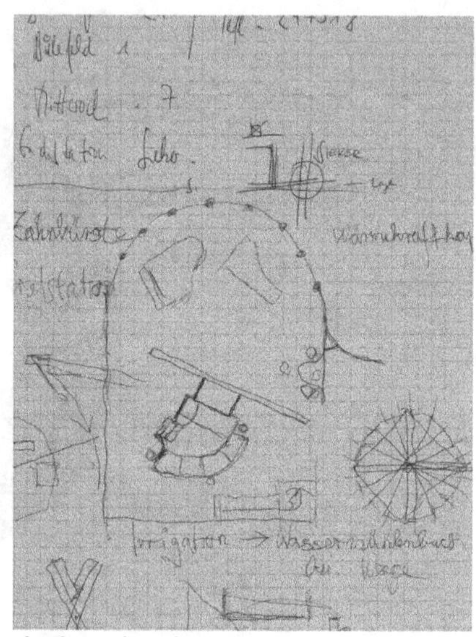

design sketches

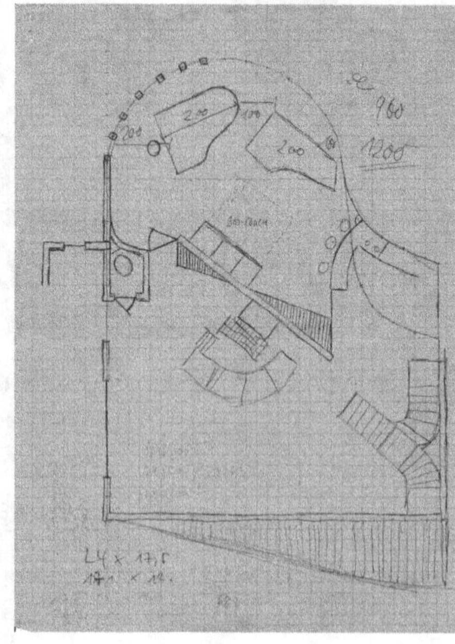

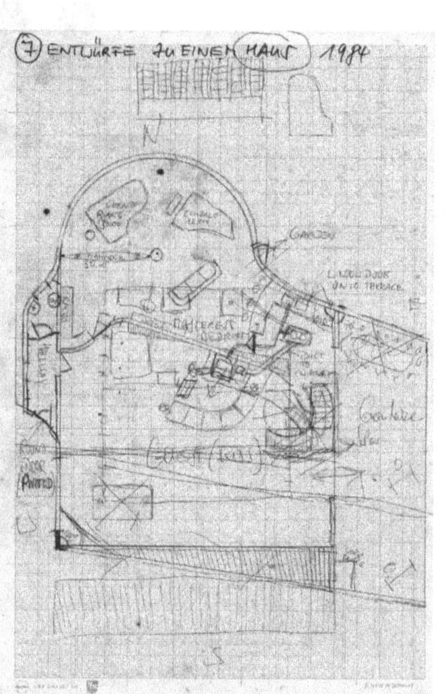

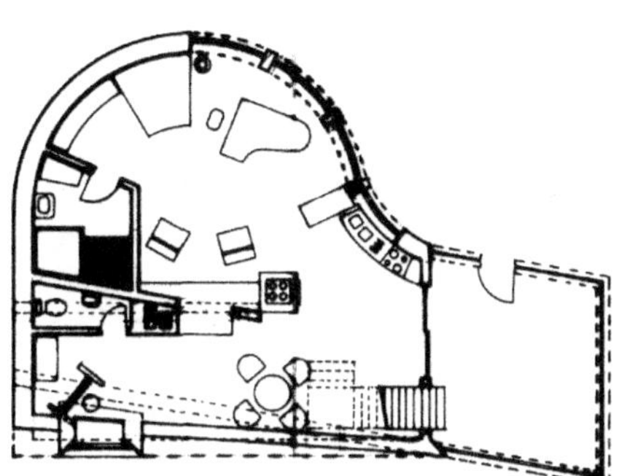

Plan drawing of house, ink on mylar

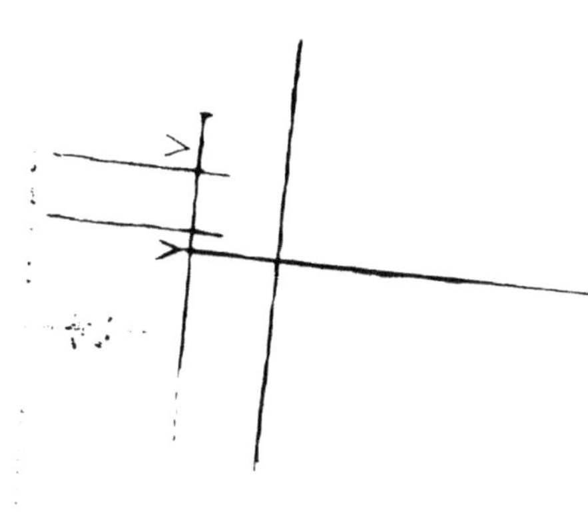

...mistaking the form for the function...

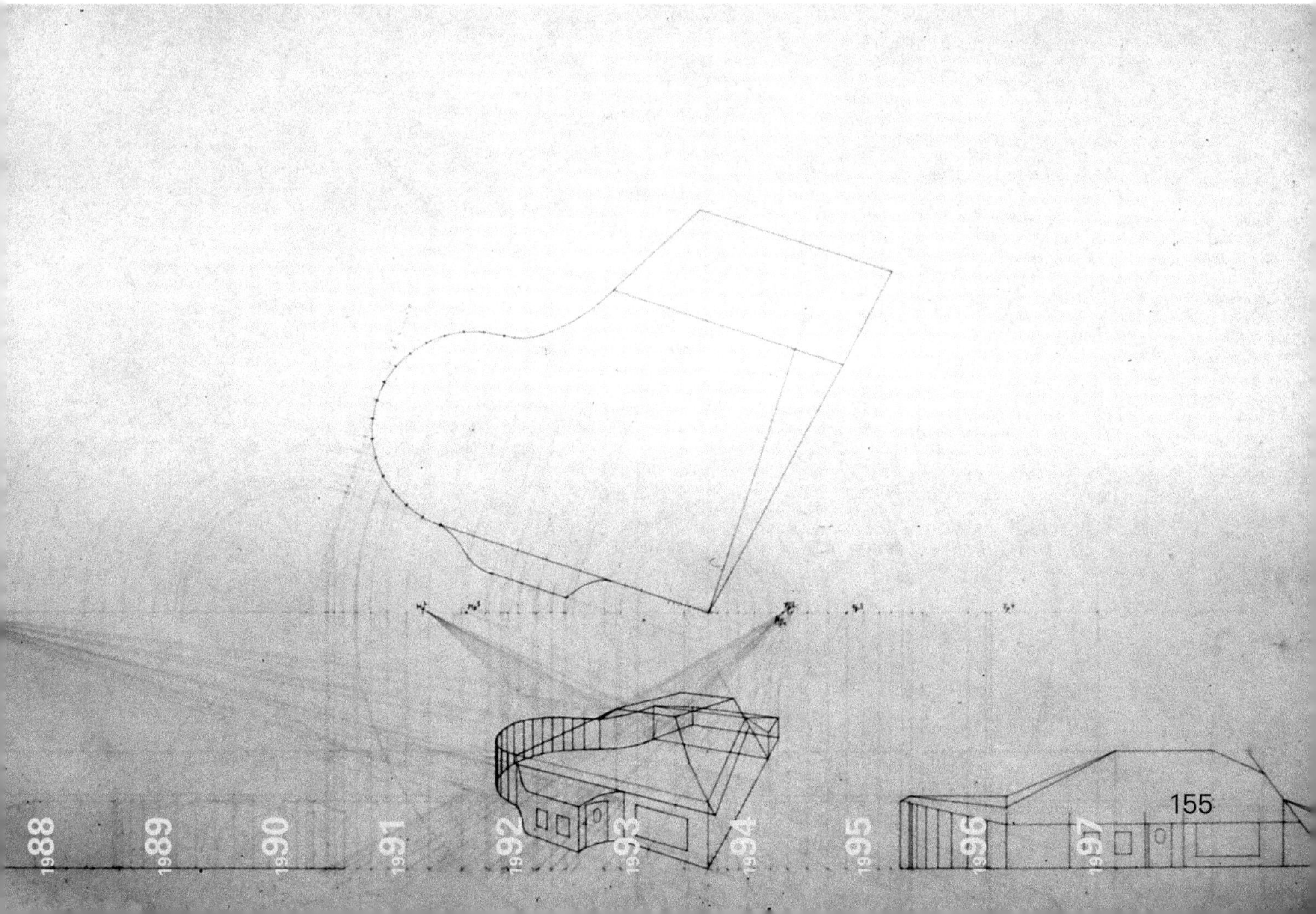

1988 1989 1990 1991 1992 1993 1994 1995 1996 1997

Drawing

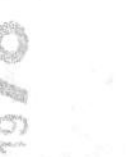
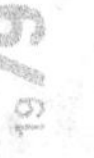

pencil on paper

Lemgo marketplace with city hall and St. Nicolai church
(a present to Margaret and Herbert Zach)

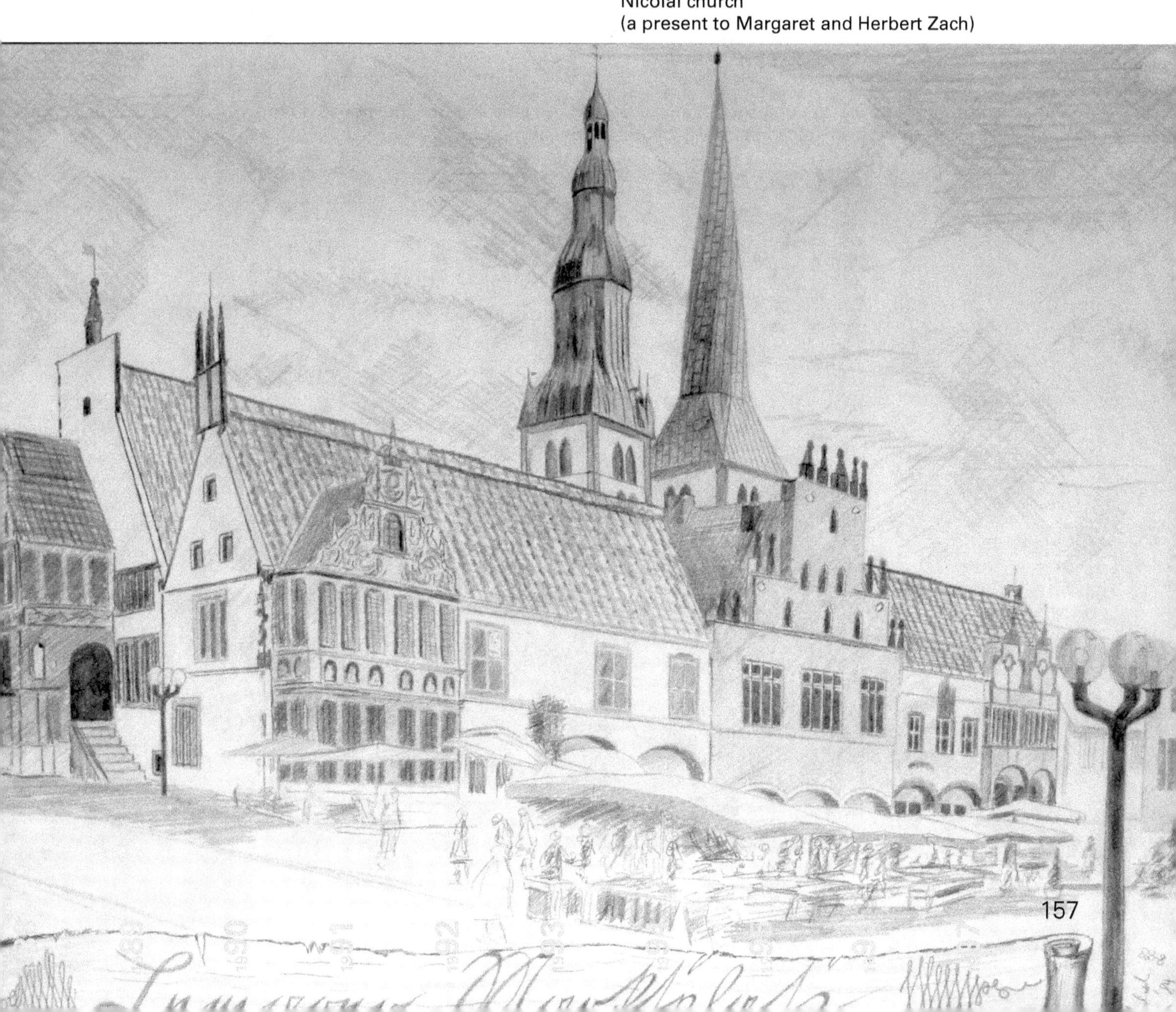

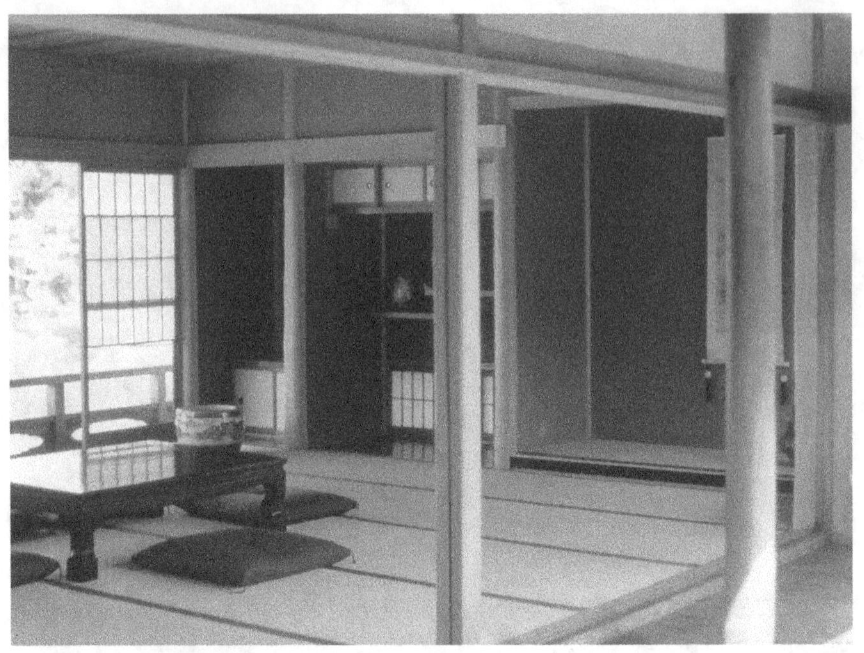

Japanese House at the Chicago Botanical Garden. An amazing feat, the house is constructed without any metal parts. All joinery is done in wood.

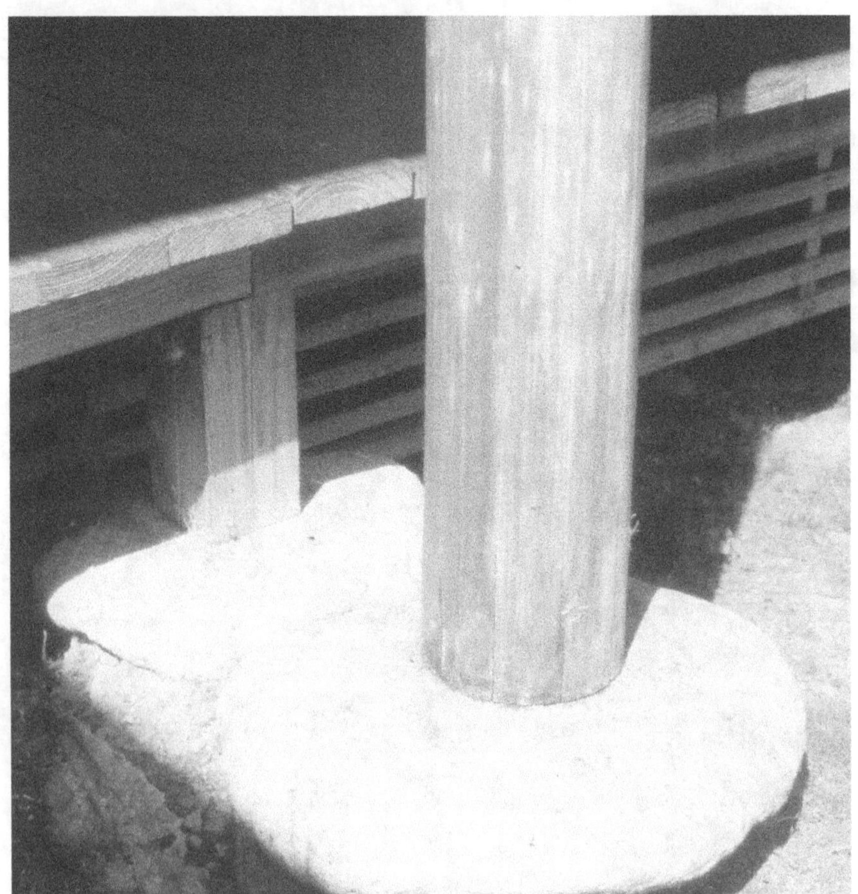

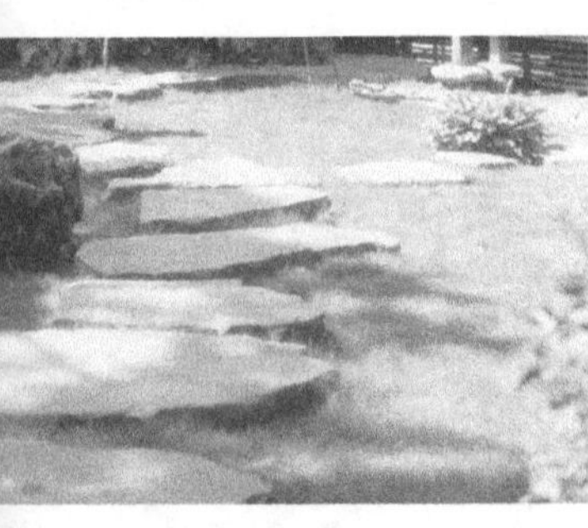

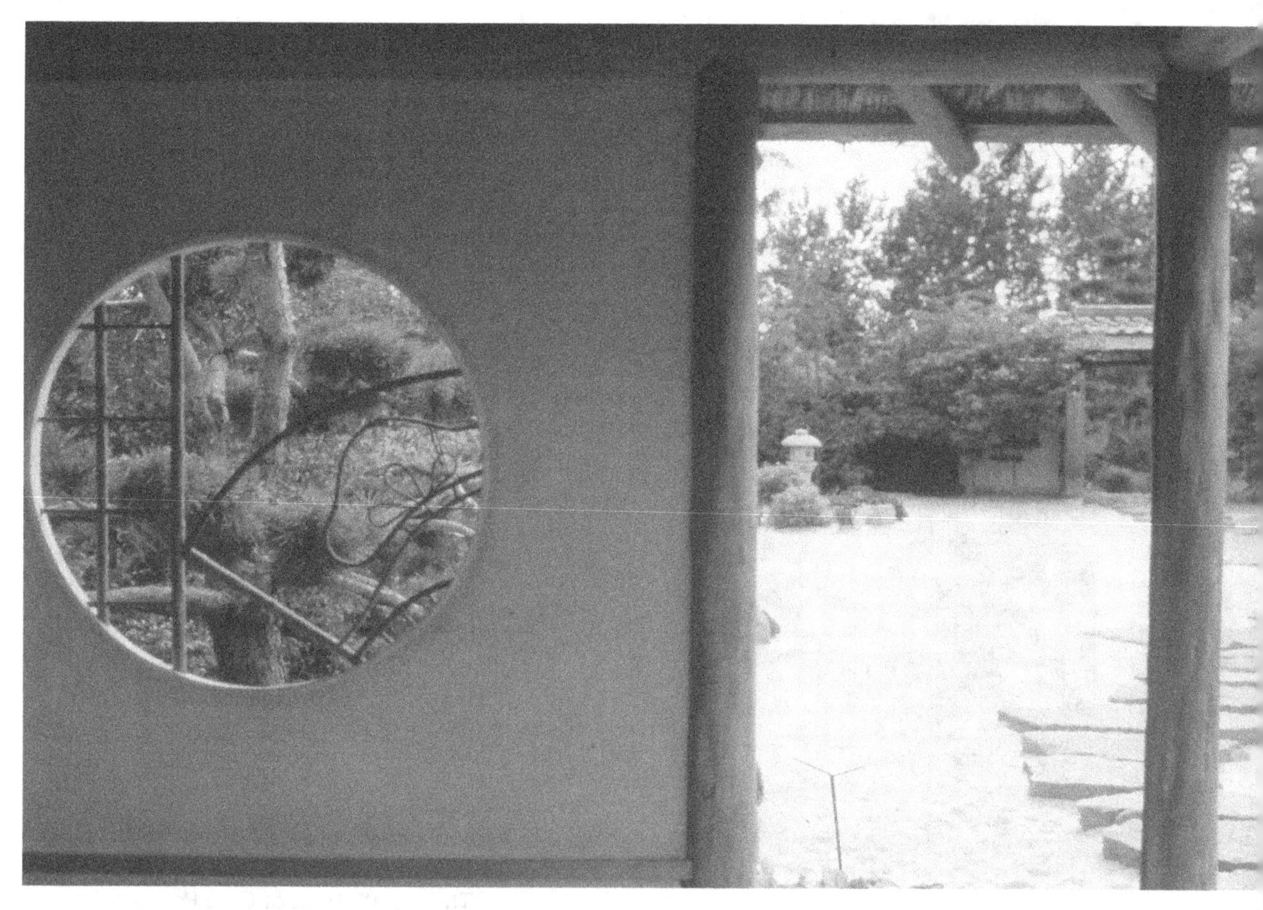

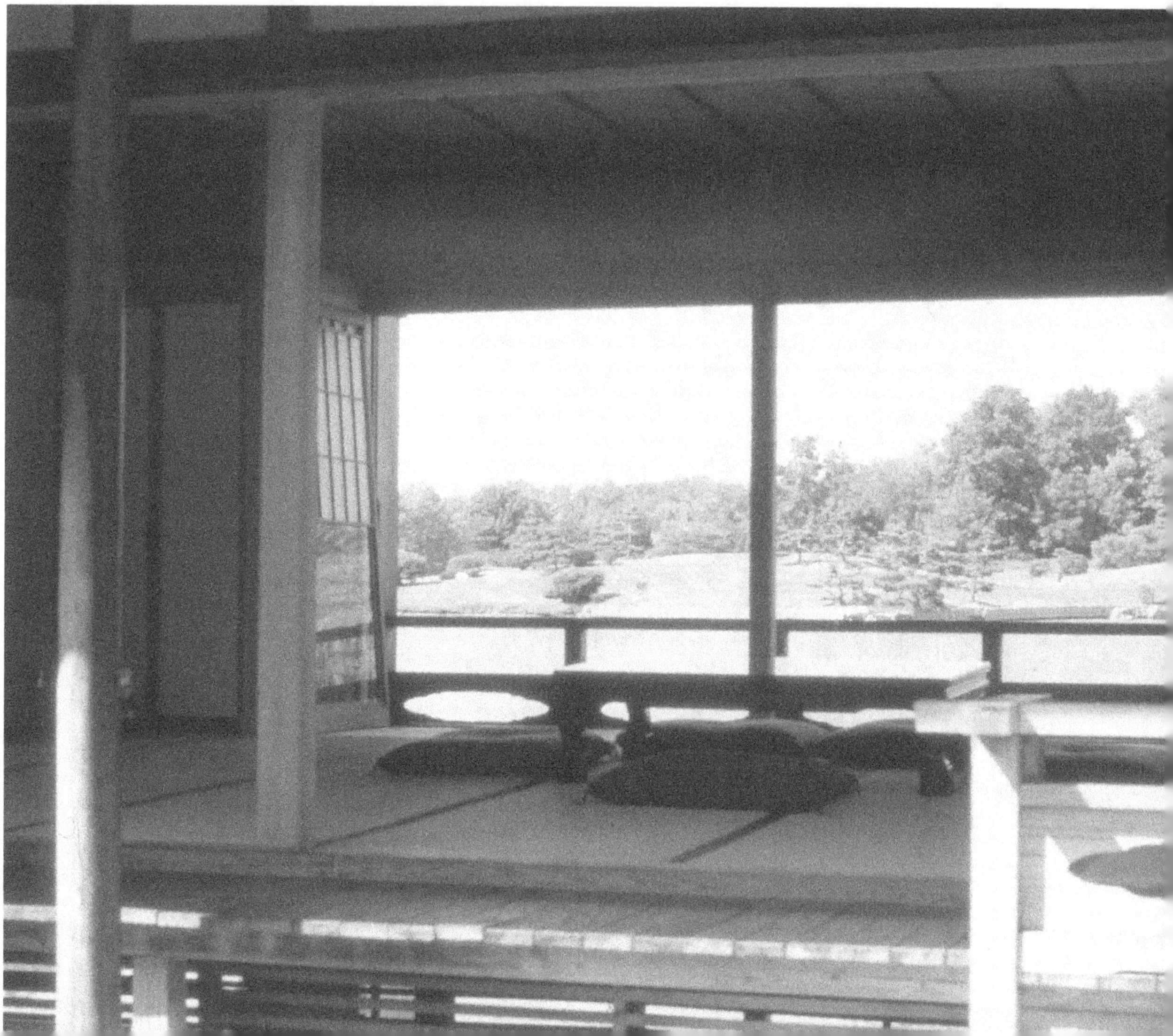

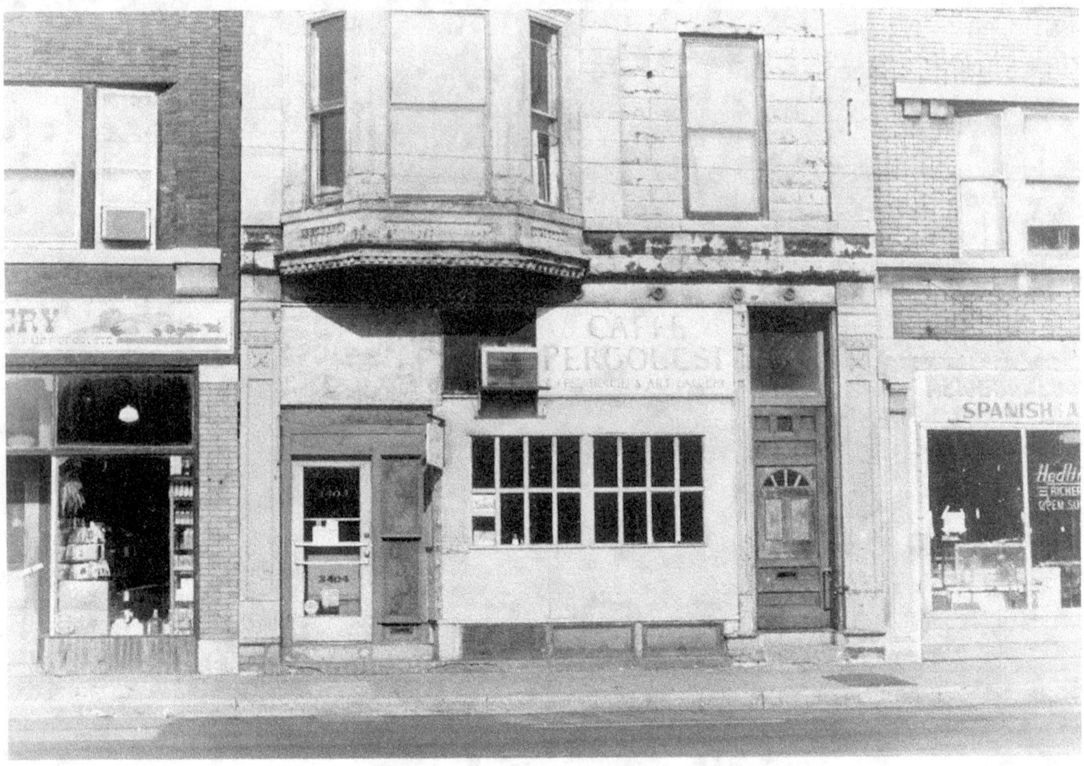

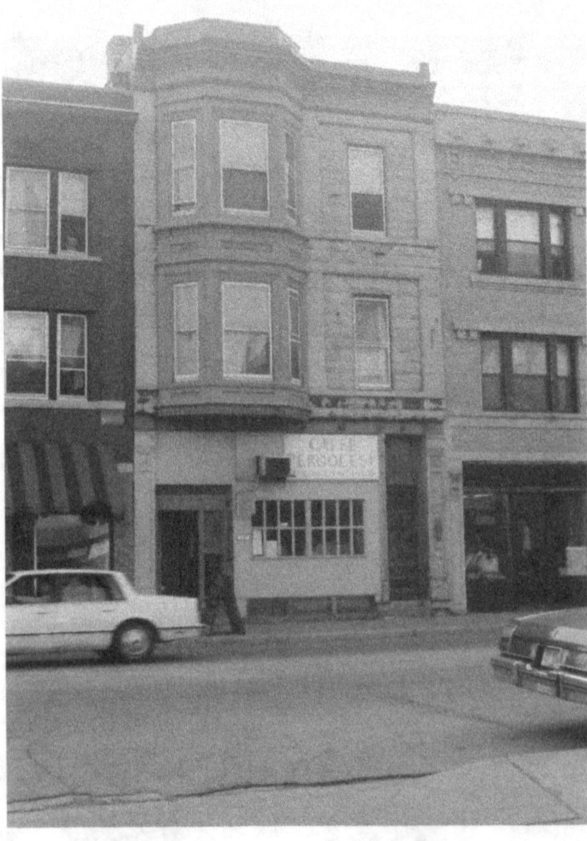

The great ghost of Café Pergolesi on Halstead Street in Chicago. The real thing is no longer there.
In the winter of 1980 I remember a zen-like calmness in a music-filled space on a bitter-cold Chicago winter night in February with a fresh bouquet of bright yellow daffodils sitting in a small vase on the tiny round table between us.

And I realized that nothing mattered...

Progress (in Walter Benjamin's sense) >

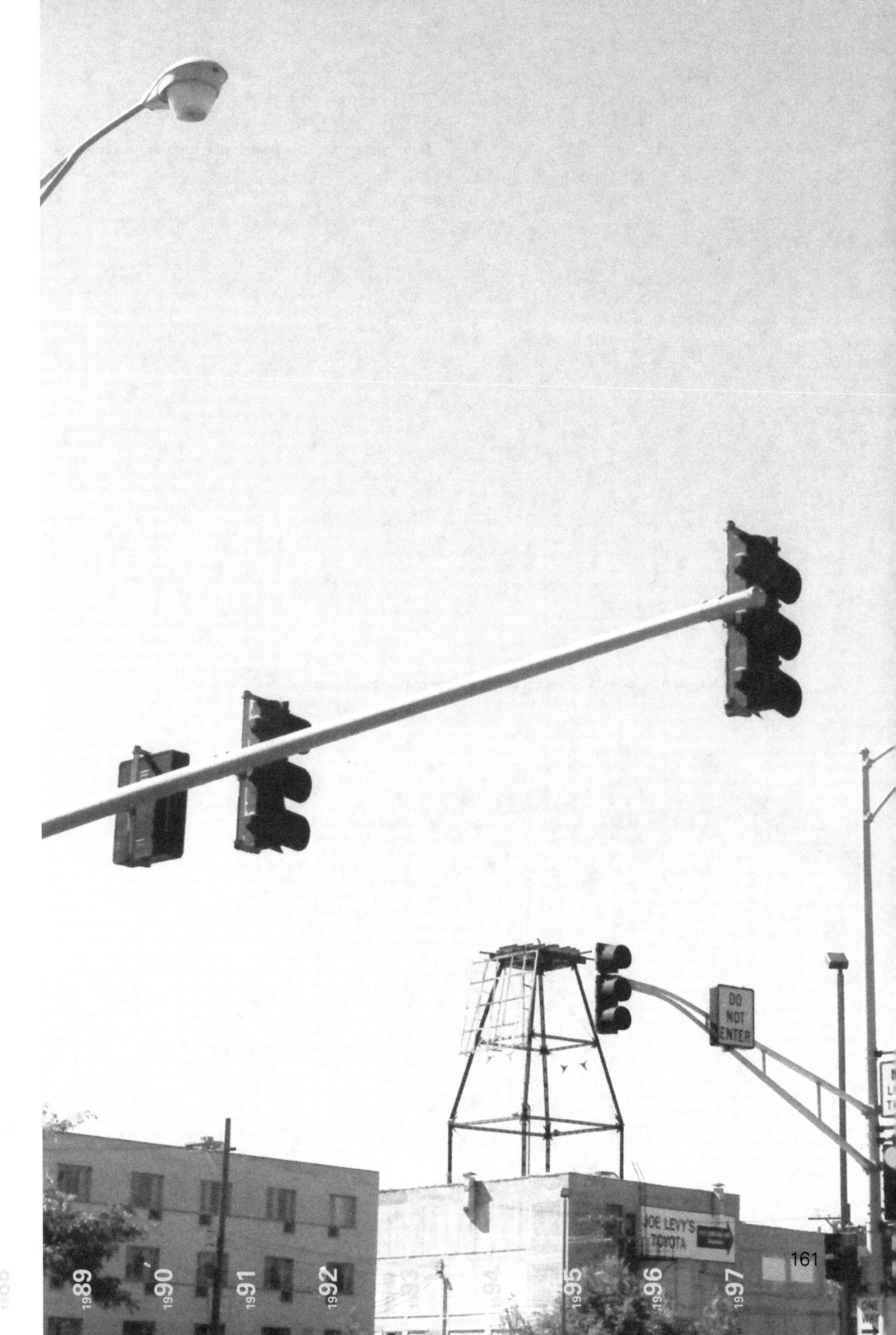
DO
NOT
ENTER
JOE LEVY'S
TOYOTA
ONE
WAY

Construction site: the beauty of temporary scaffoldings >

Near Newberry Library, Chicago, a convergence of ruin and history

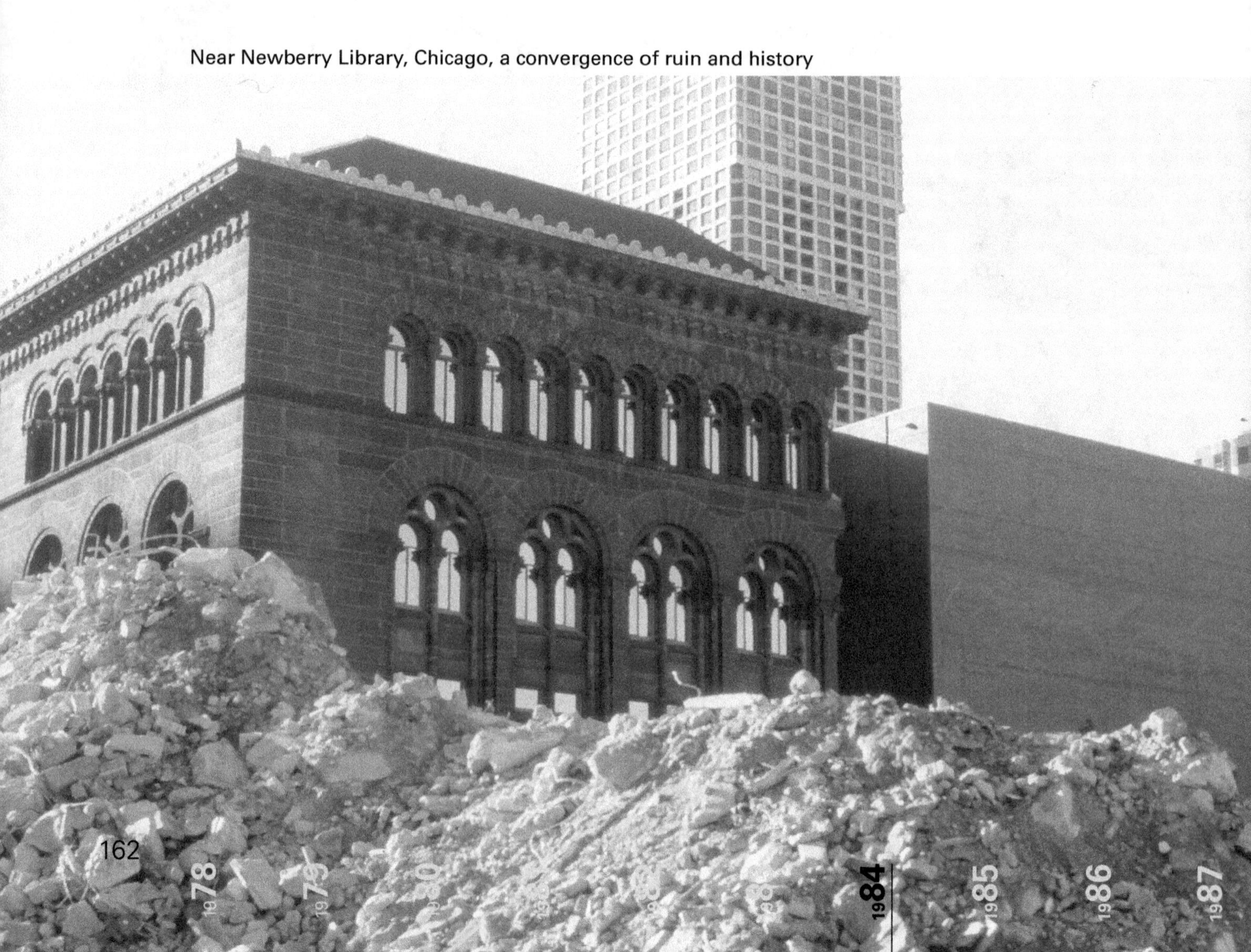

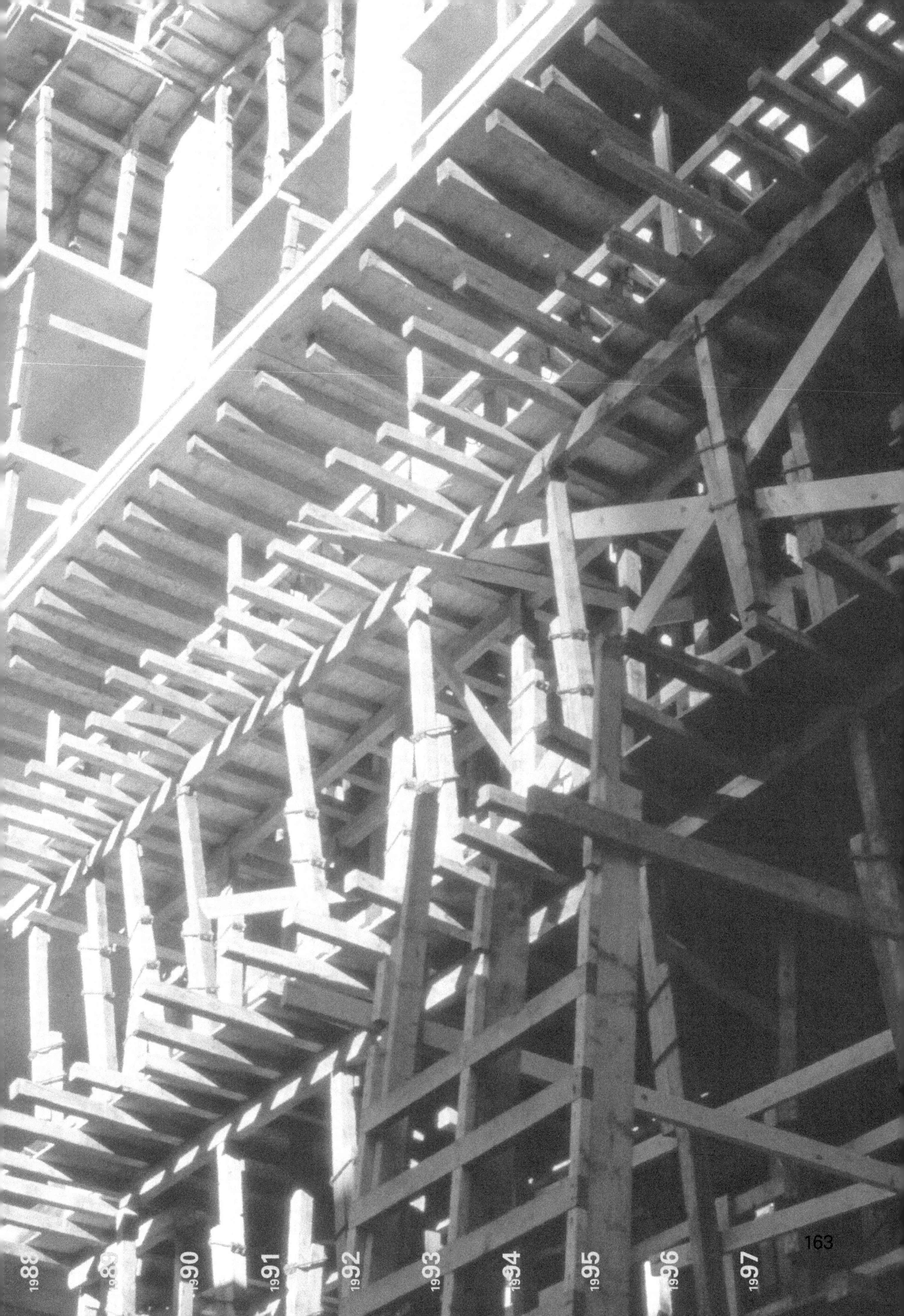
1988
1989
1990
1991
1992
1993
1994
1995
1996
1997

Chicago Fire Escapes

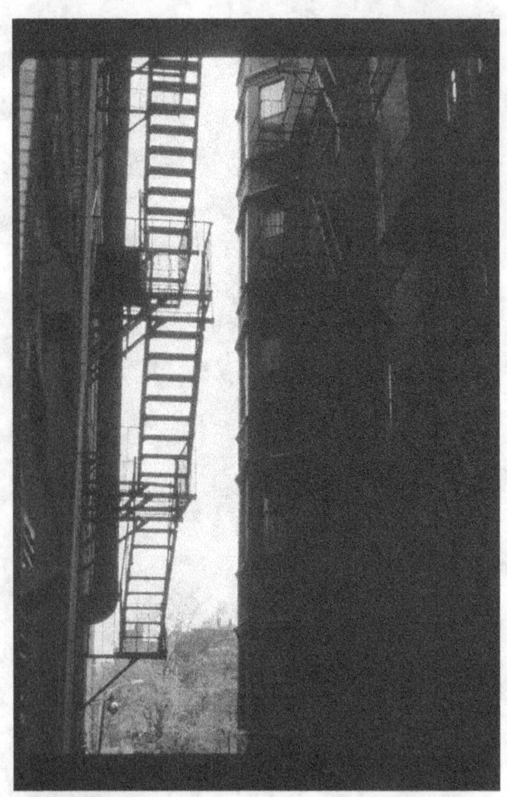

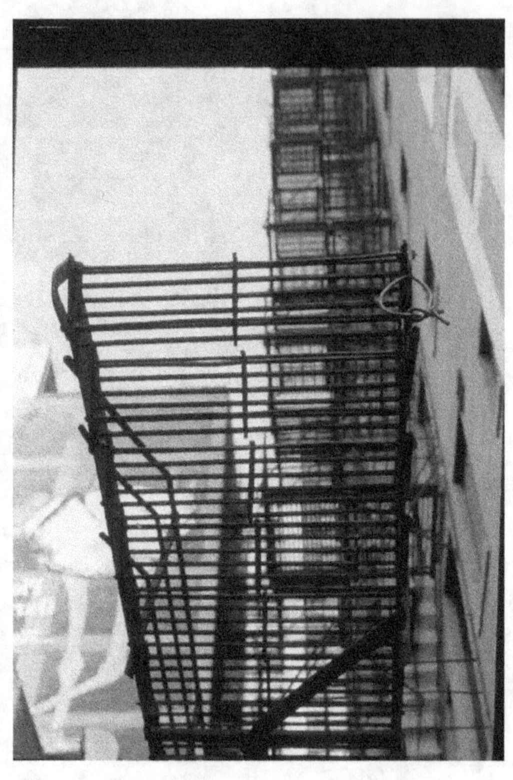

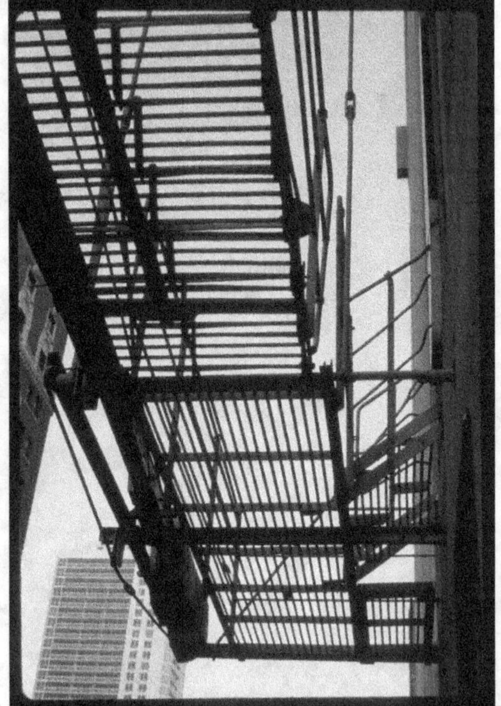

Walking the city I was always fascinated by the external fire escapes that combine potential catastrophy and the possibility of being saved in one parasitic device that hangs off of the buildings in downtown Chicago. And, of course, the play of light and shadow in the street and on the facades is nothing short of divine.

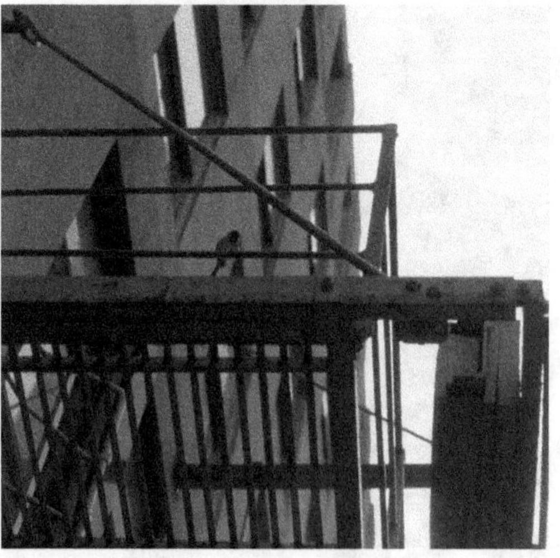

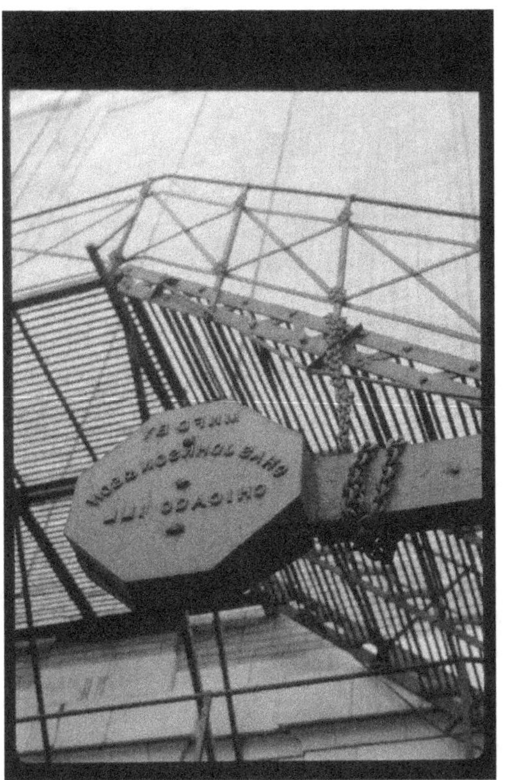

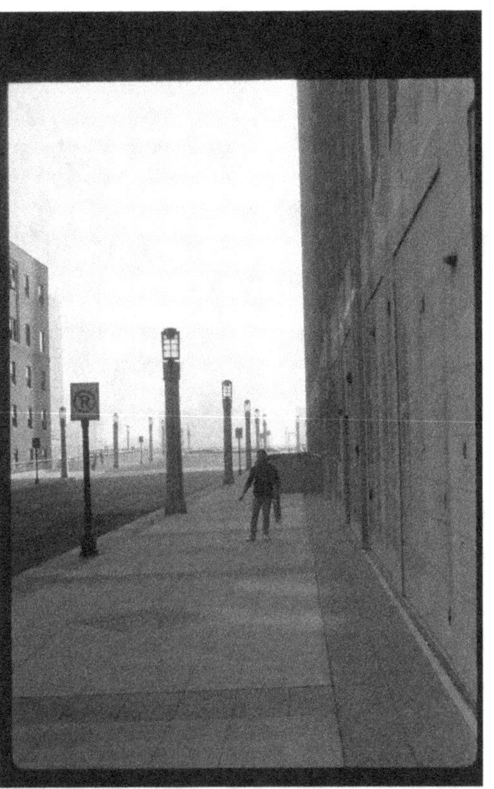

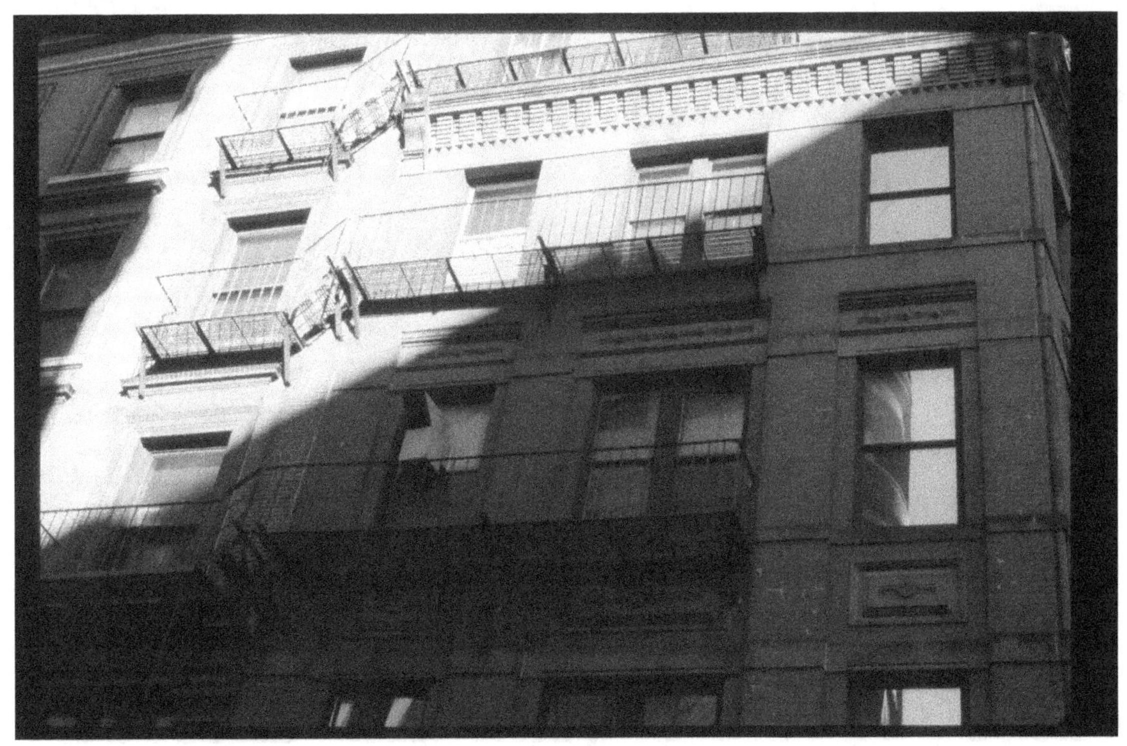

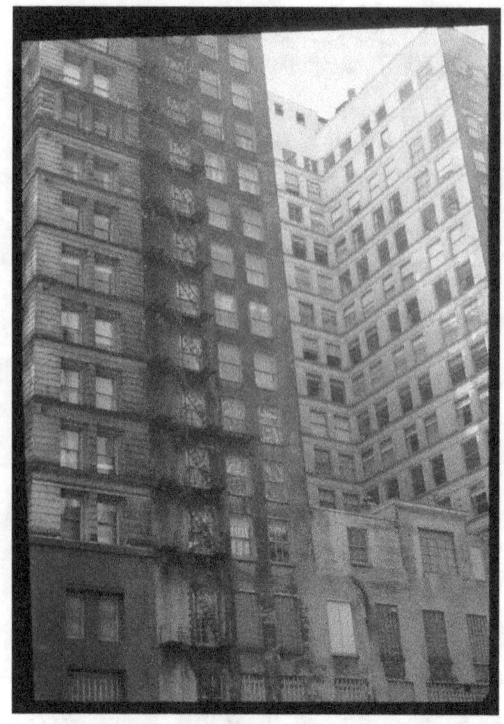

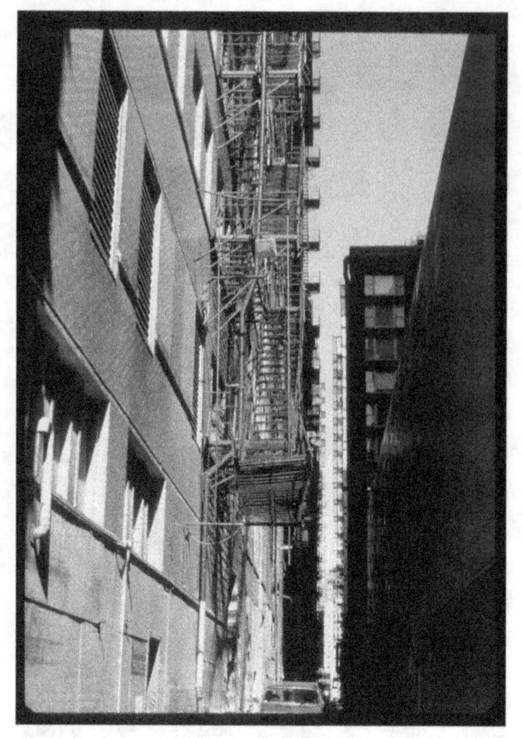

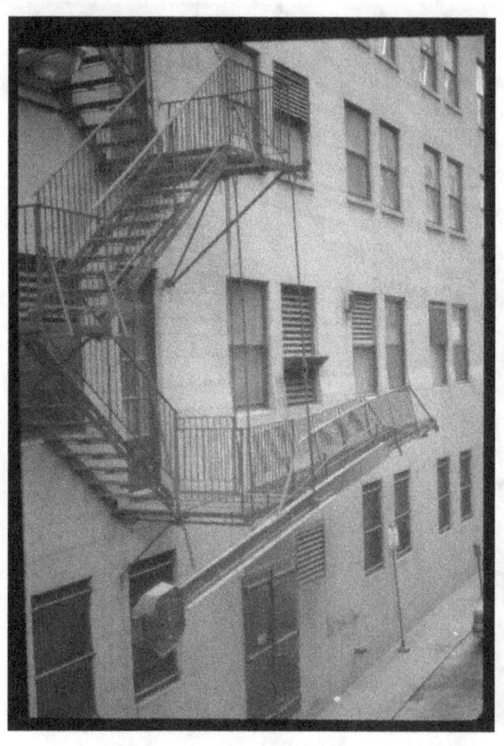

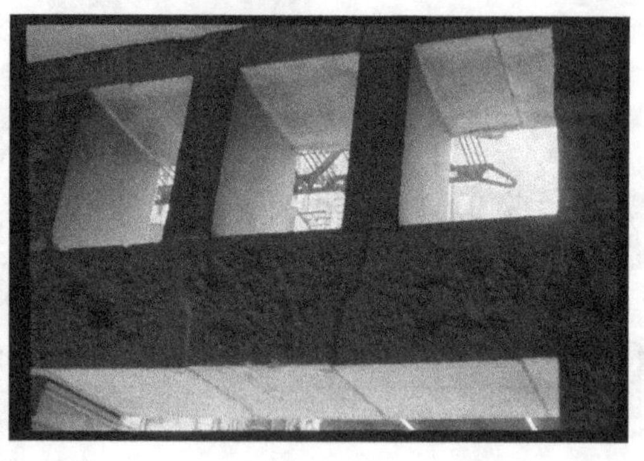

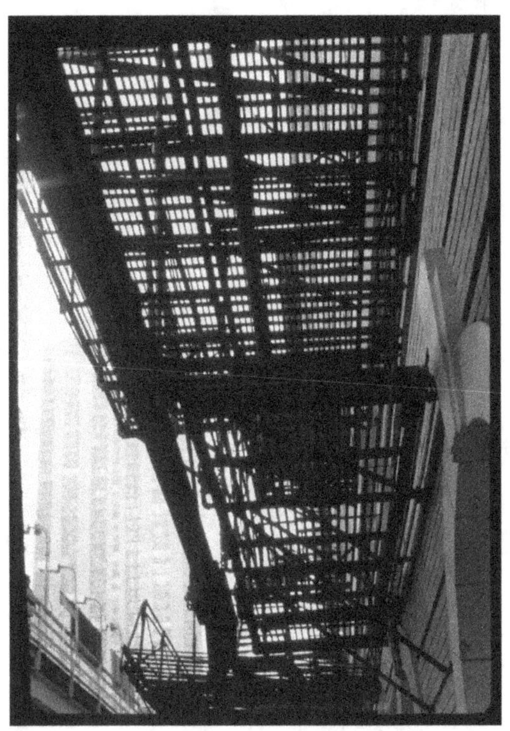

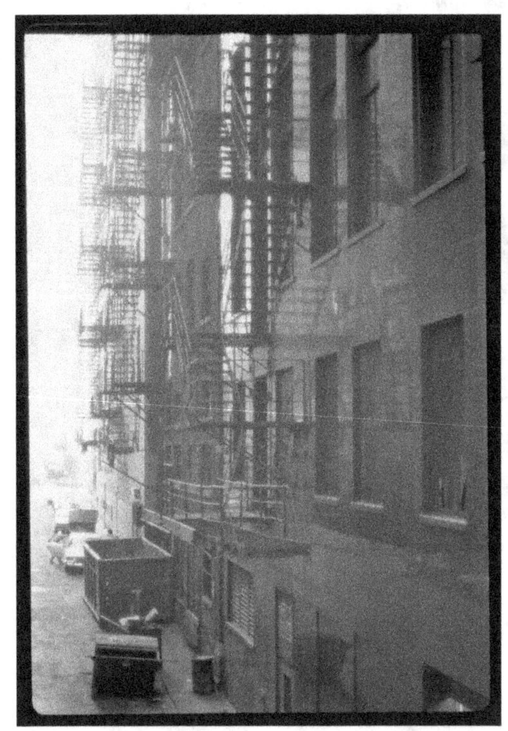

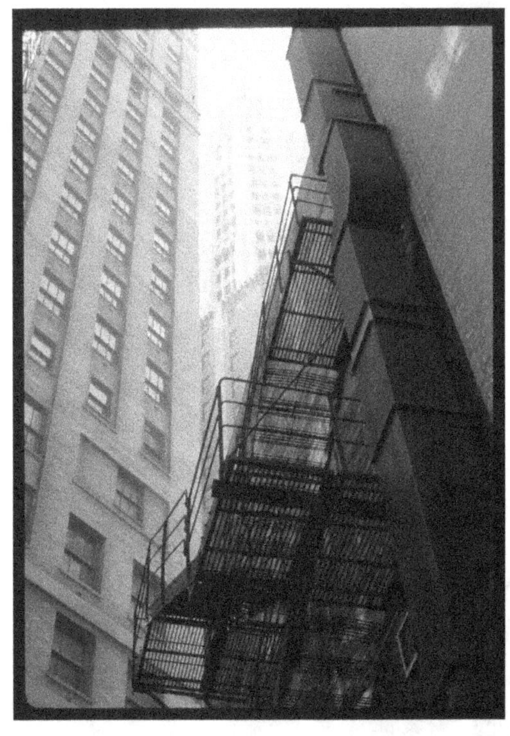

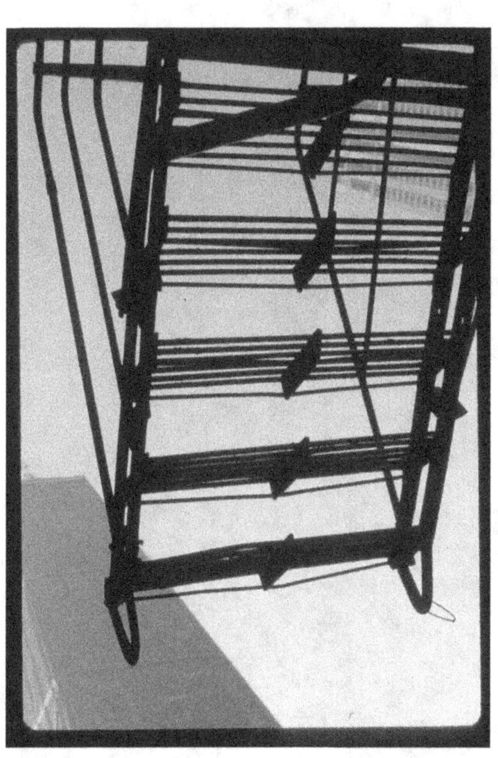

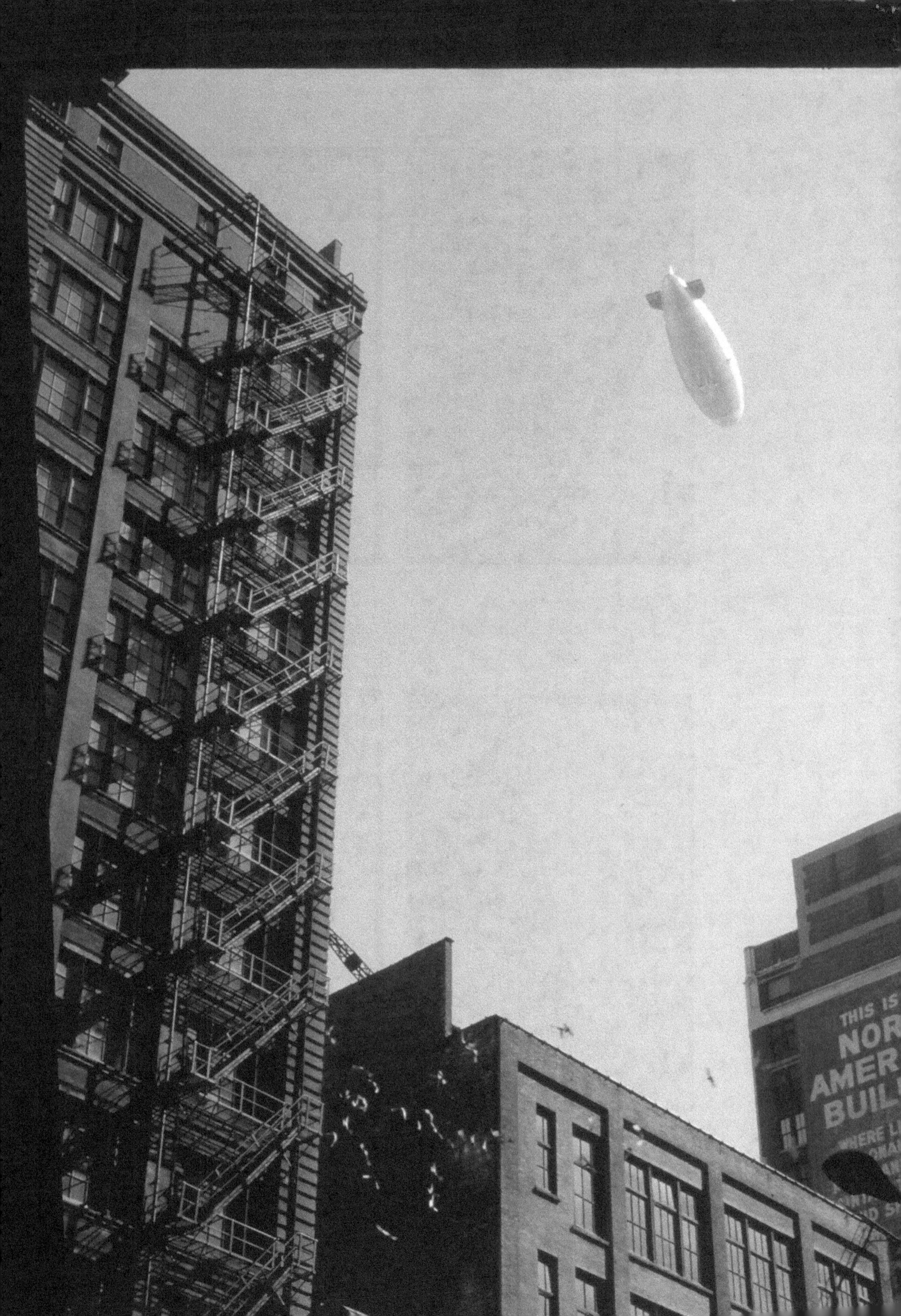
THIS IS
NOR
AMER
BUIL

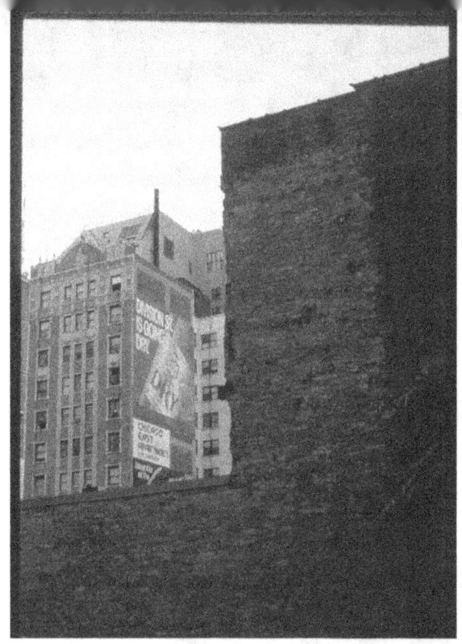

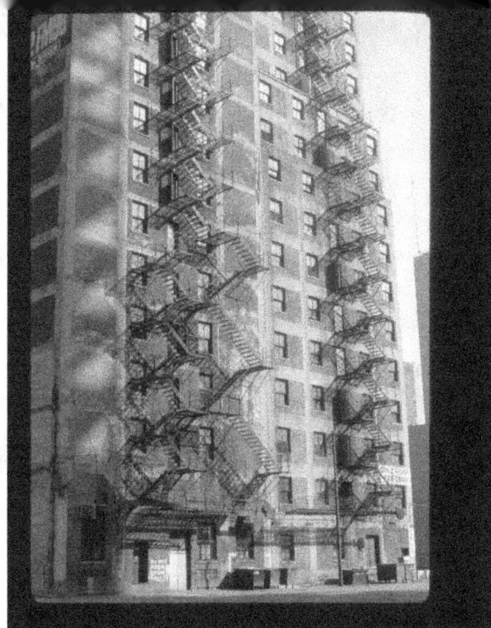

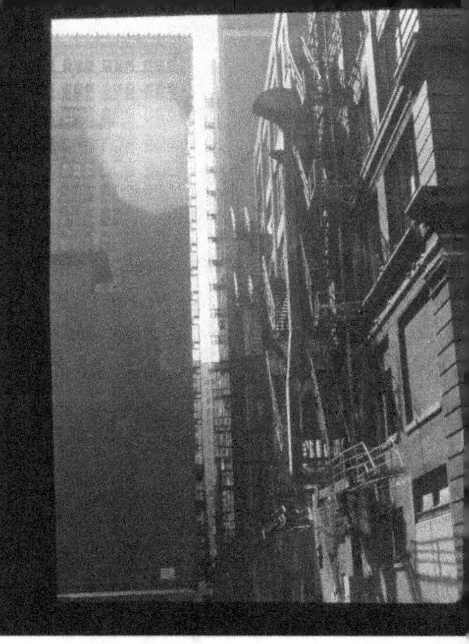

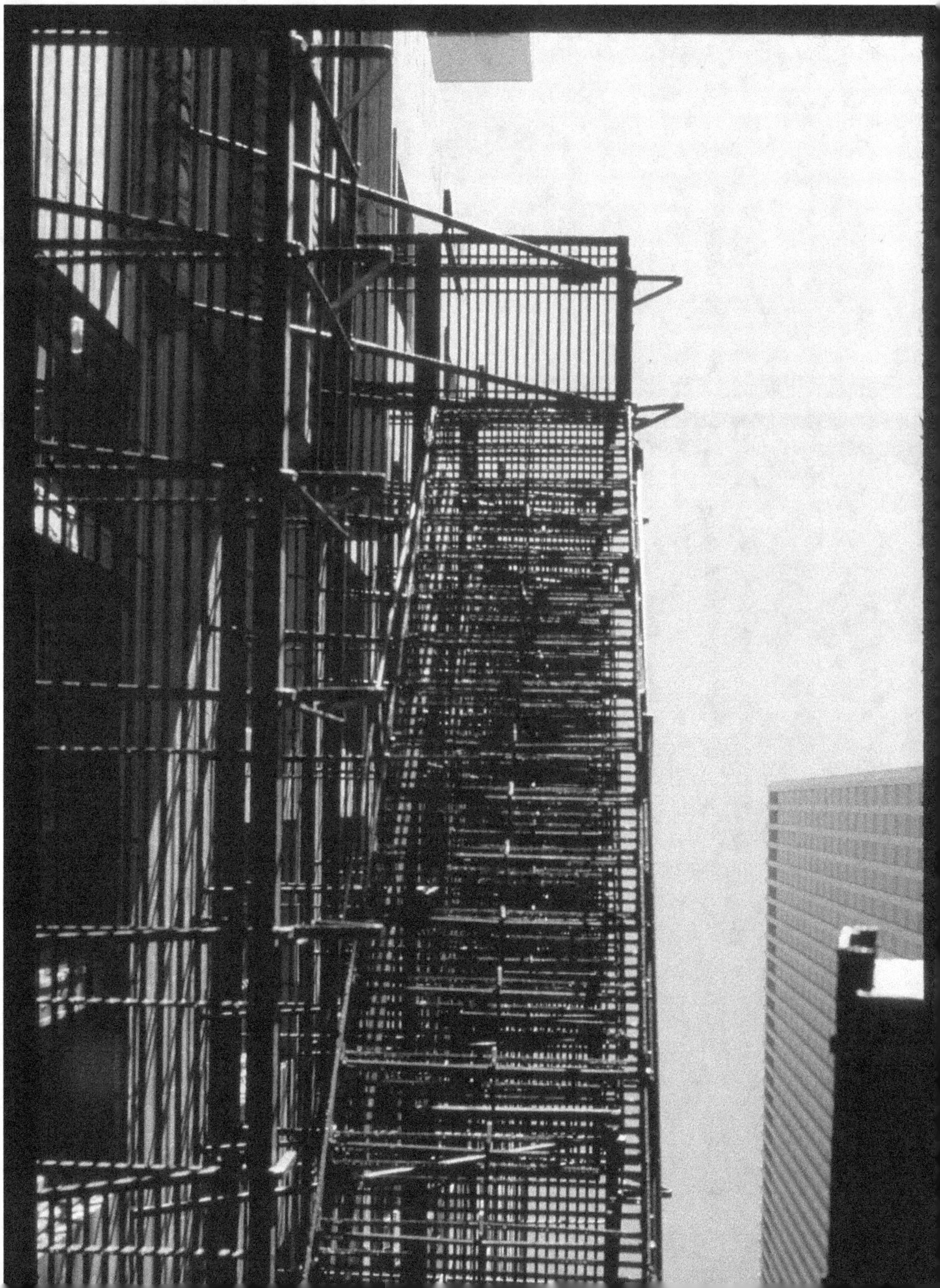

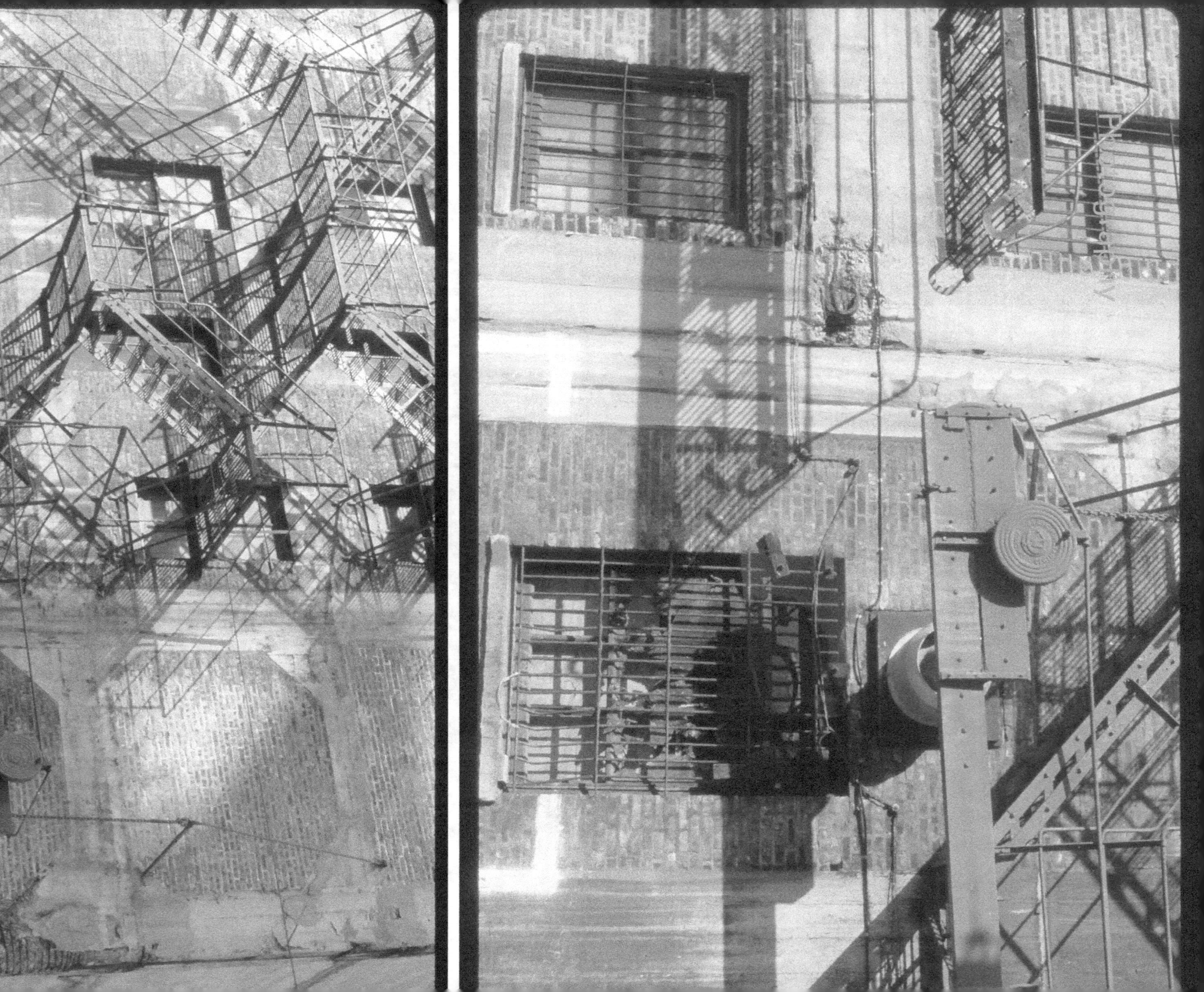

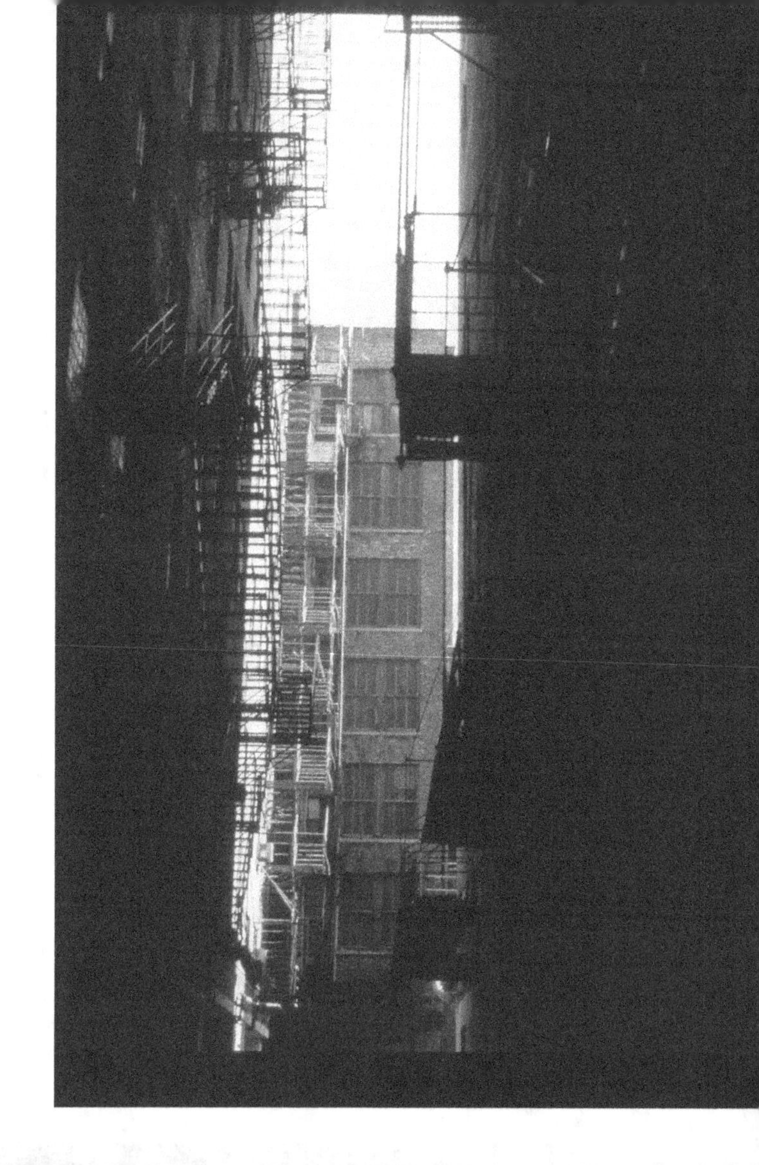

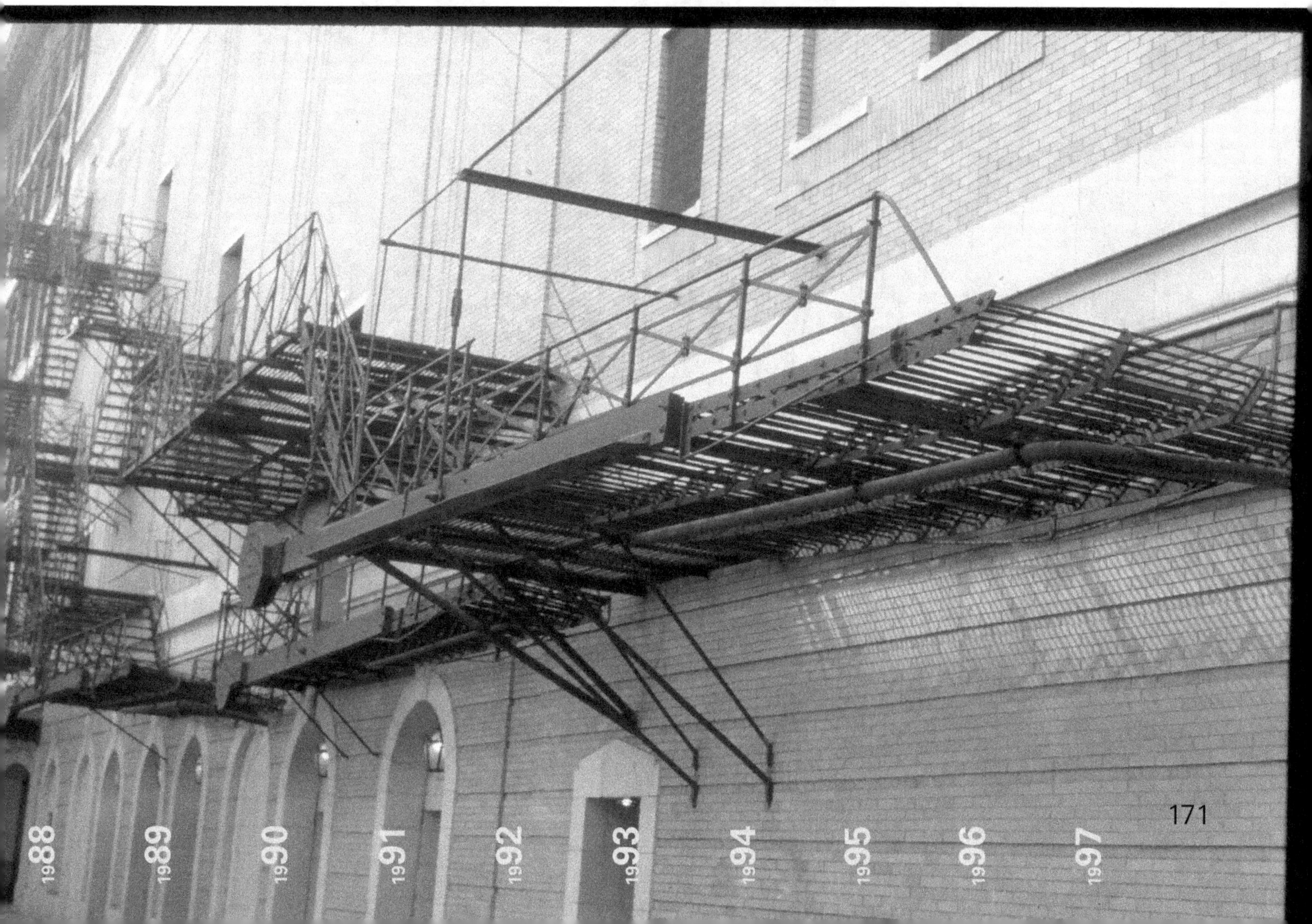

1988 1989 1990 1991 1992 1993 1994 1995 1996 1997

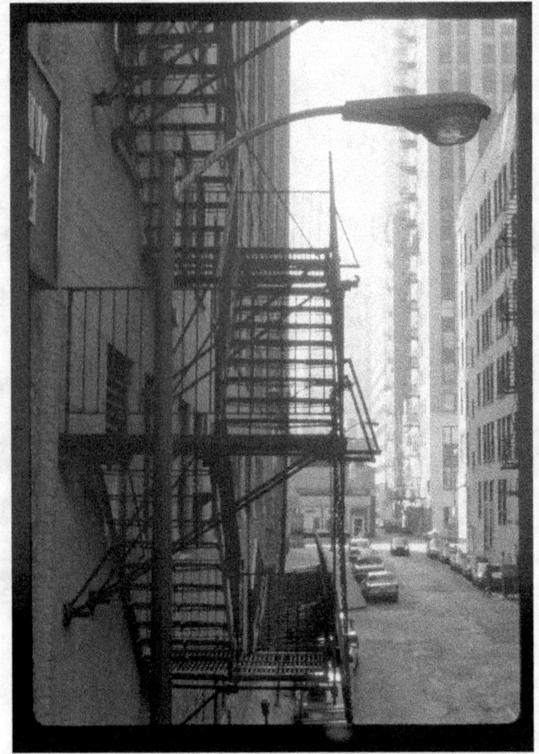

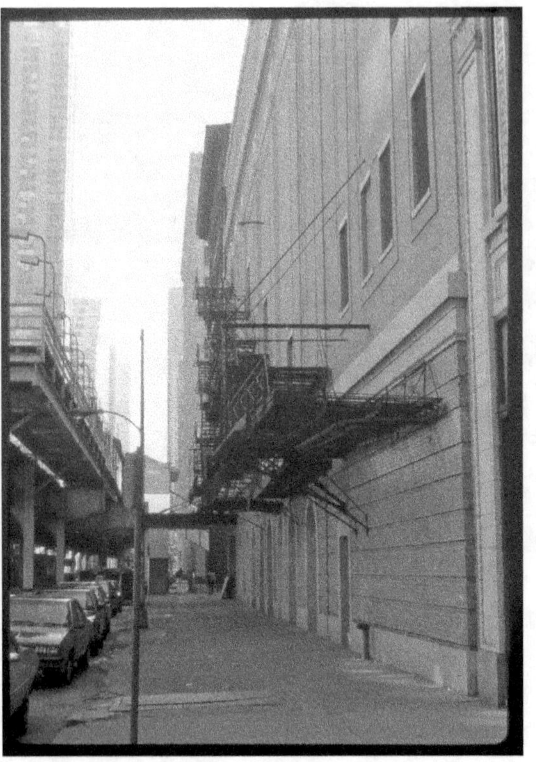

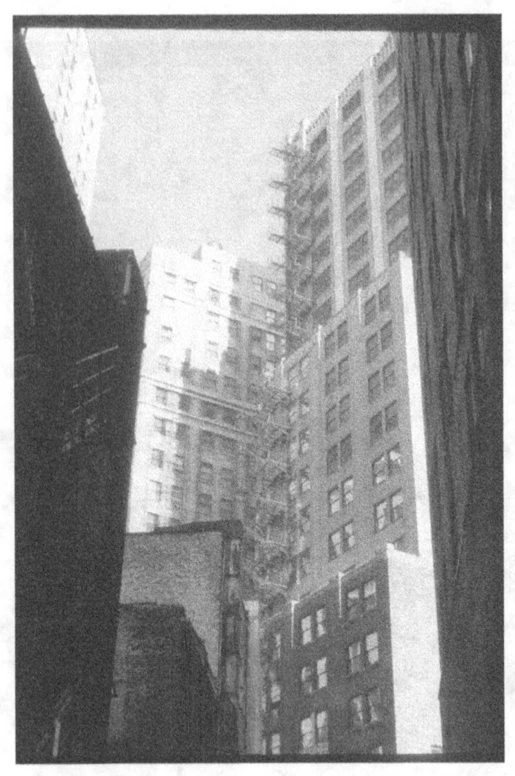

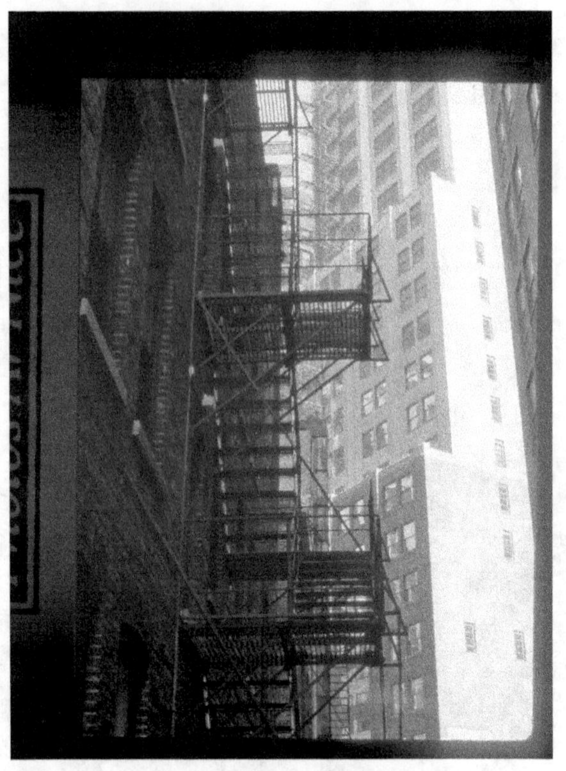

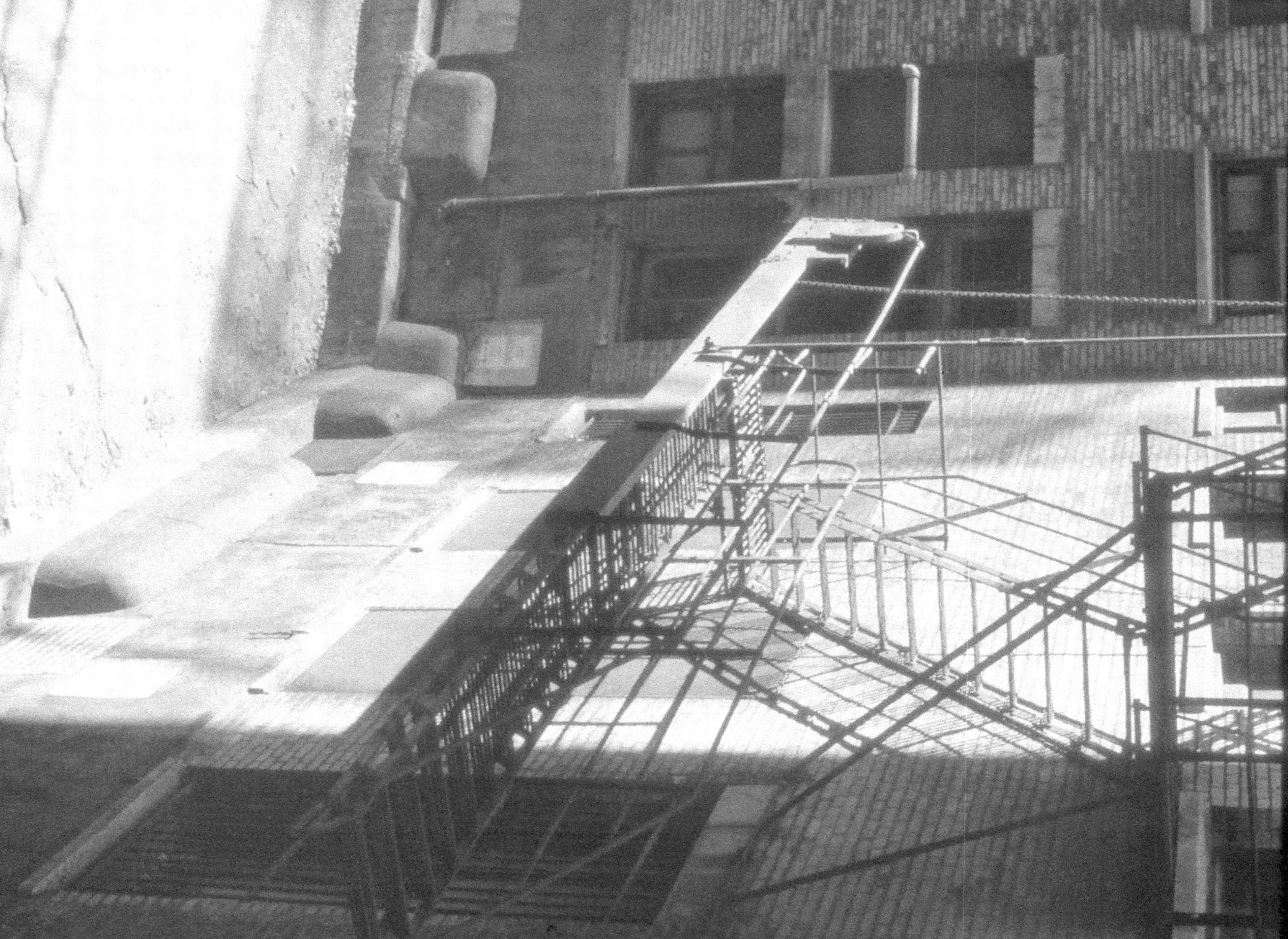

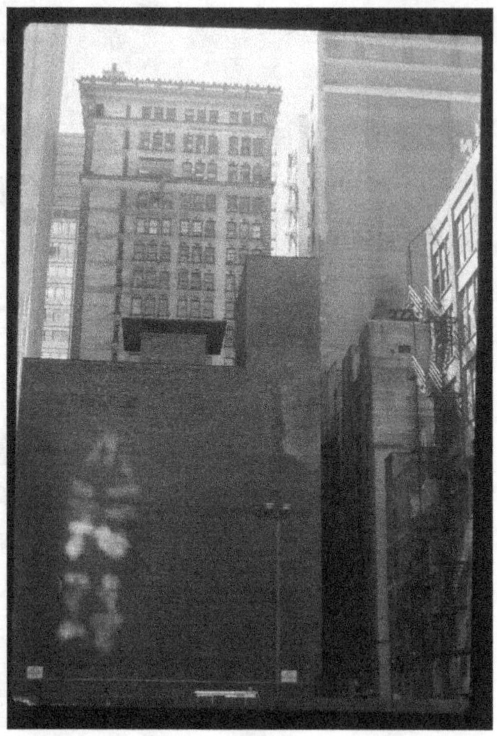

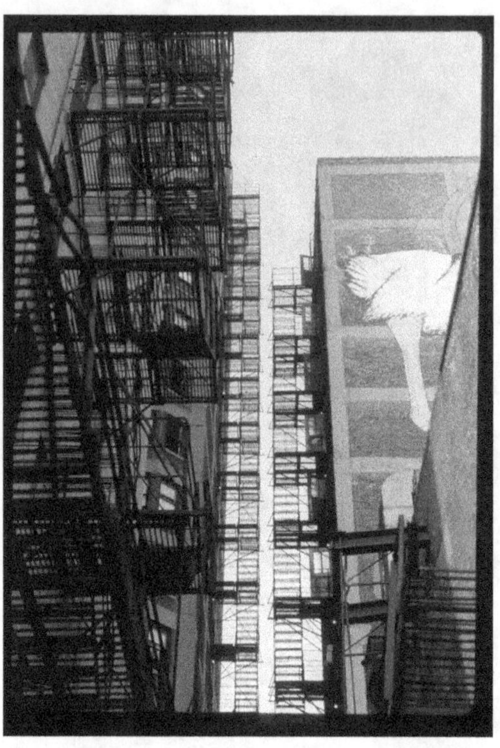

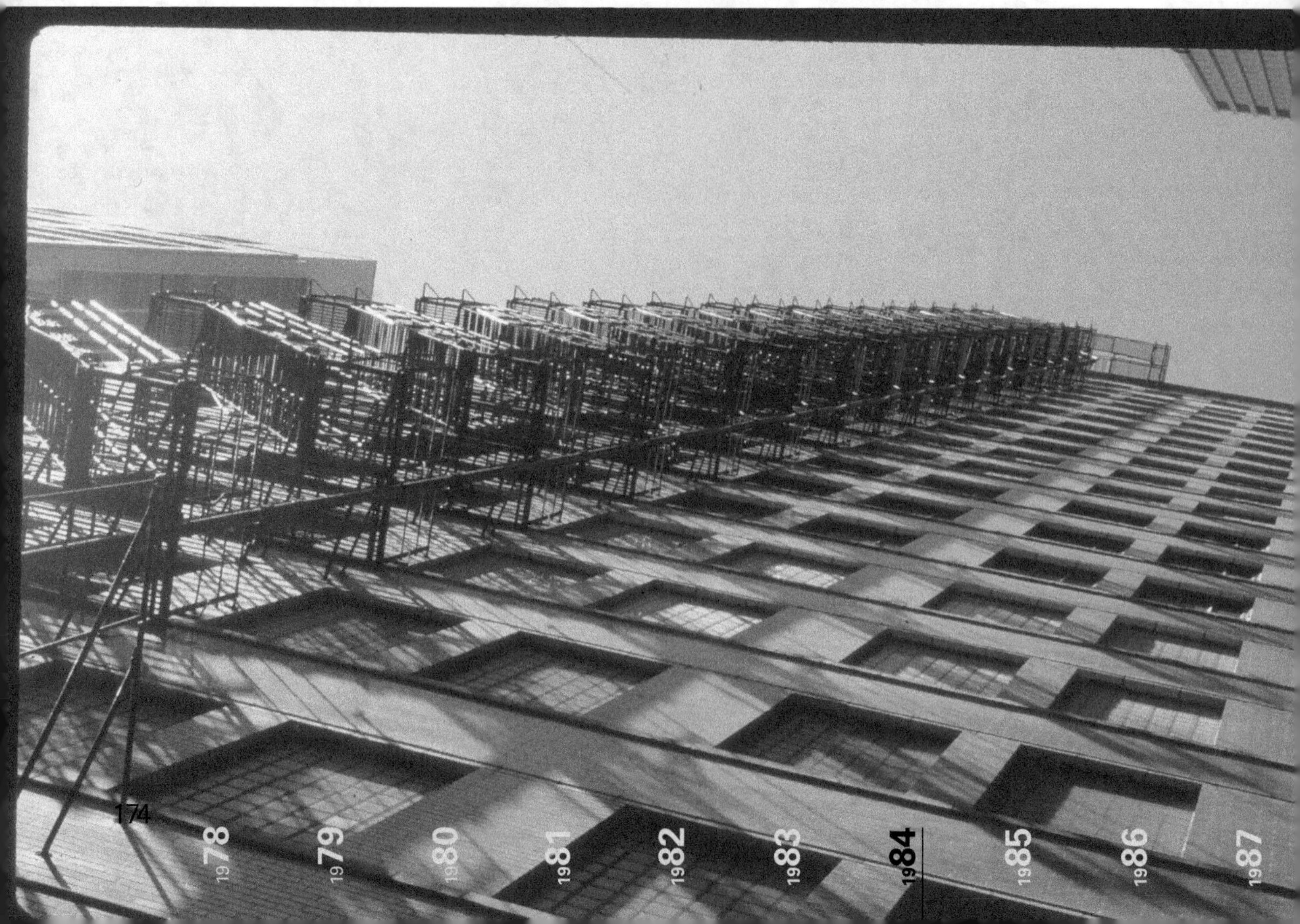

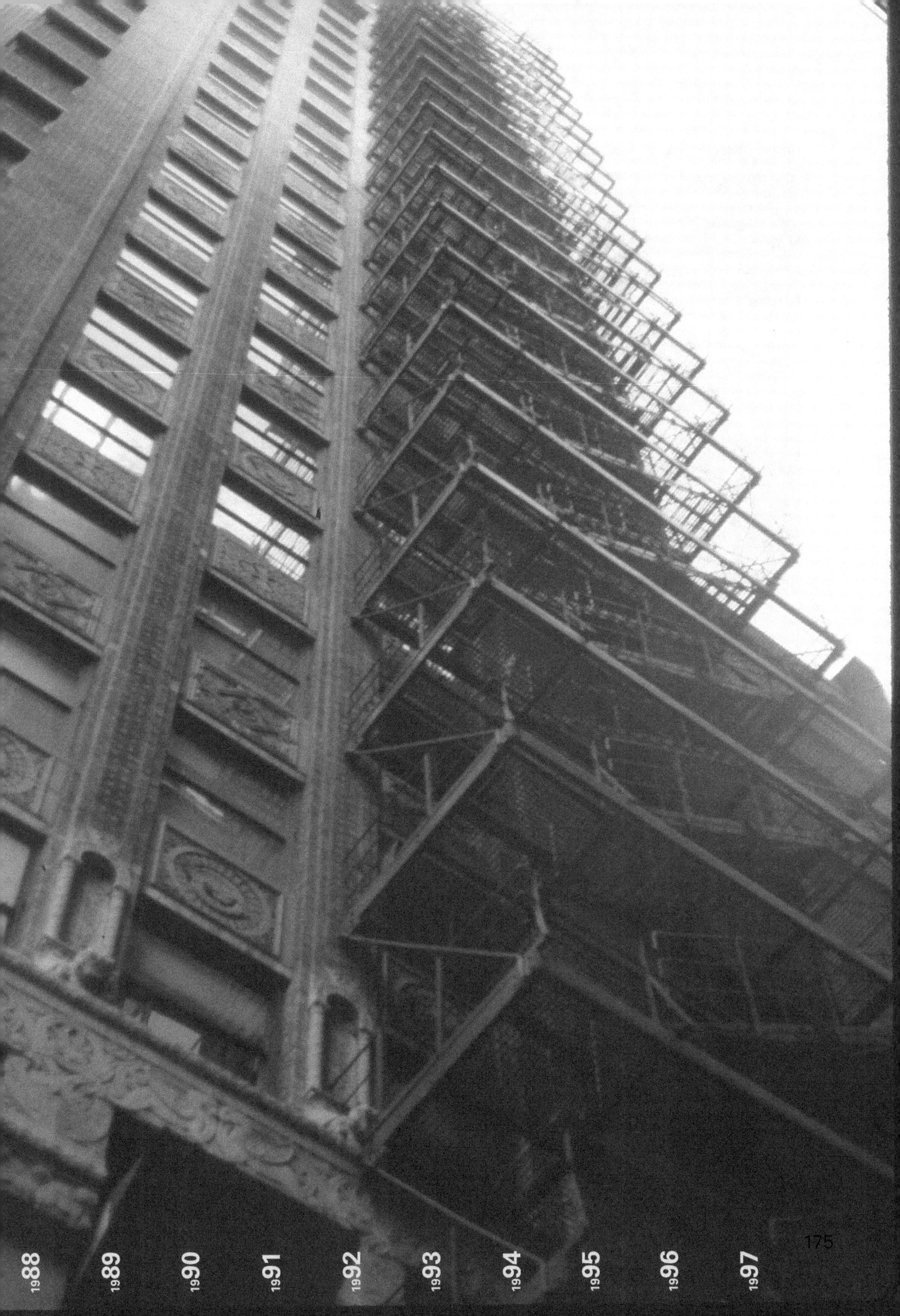

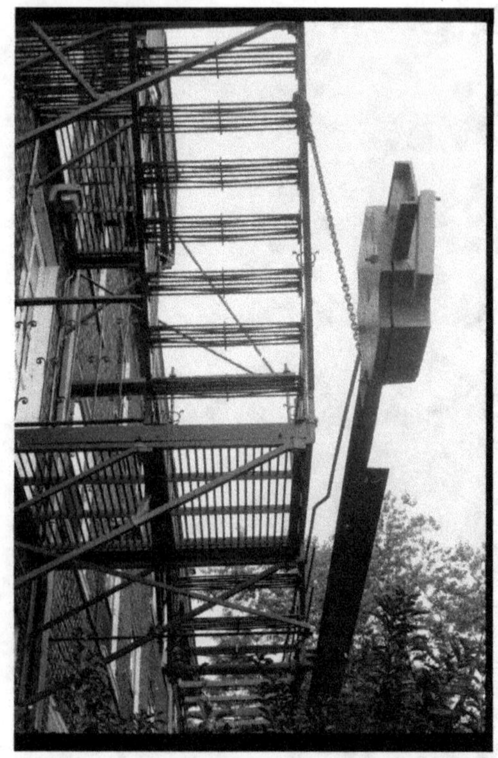

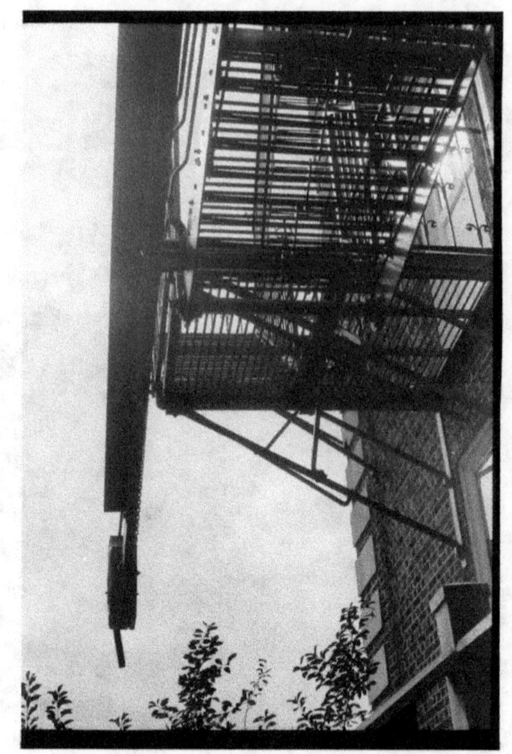

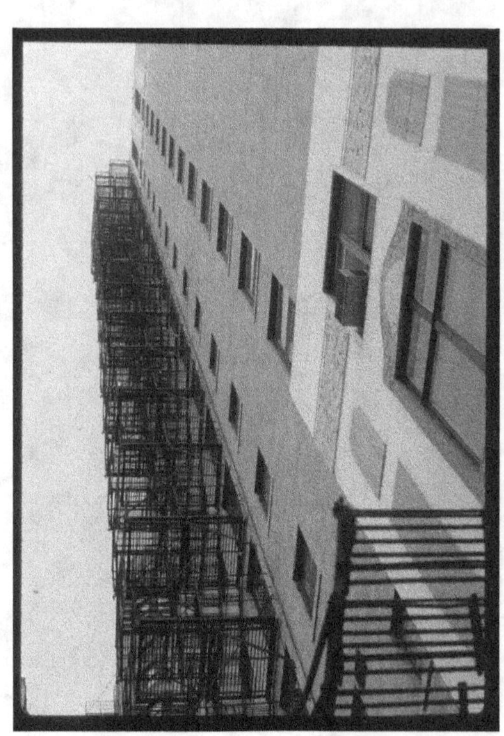

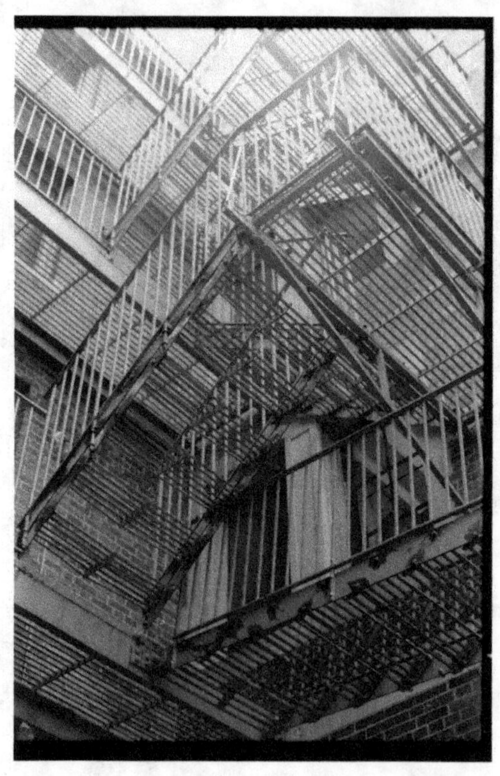

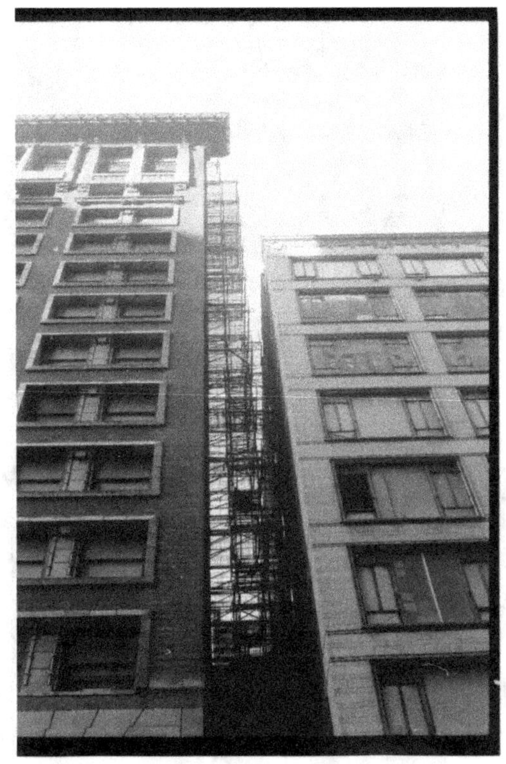

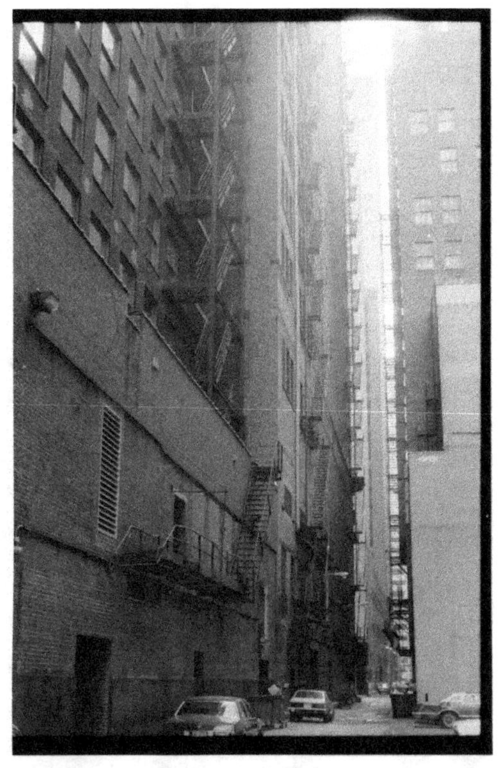

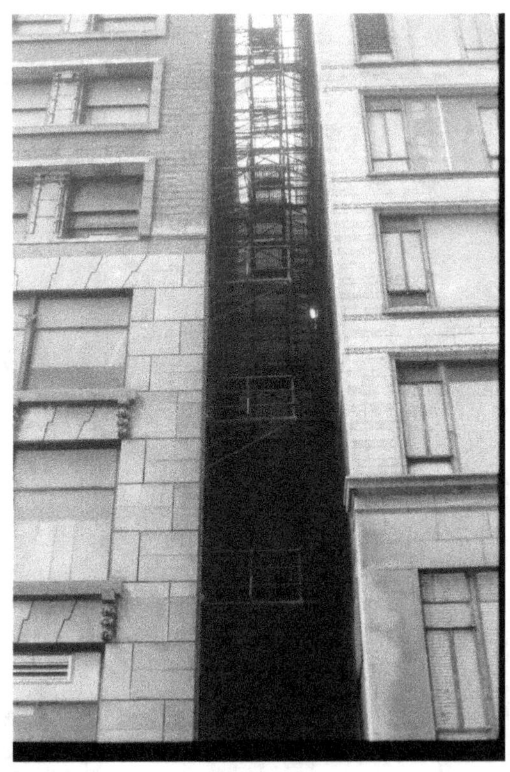

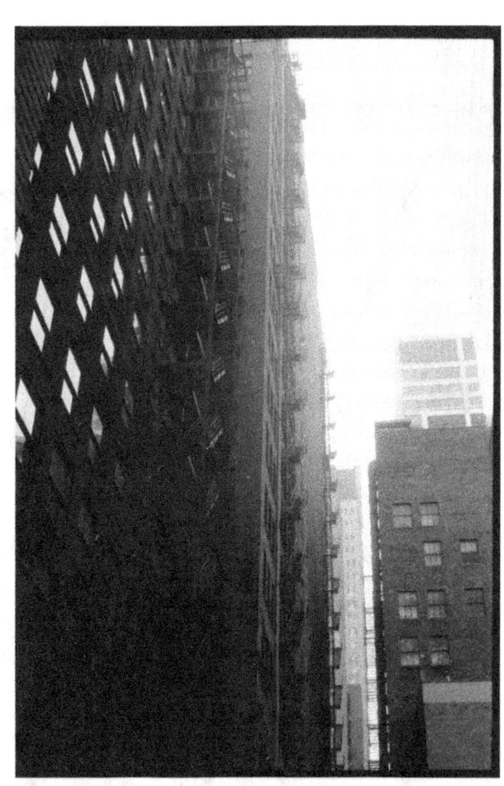

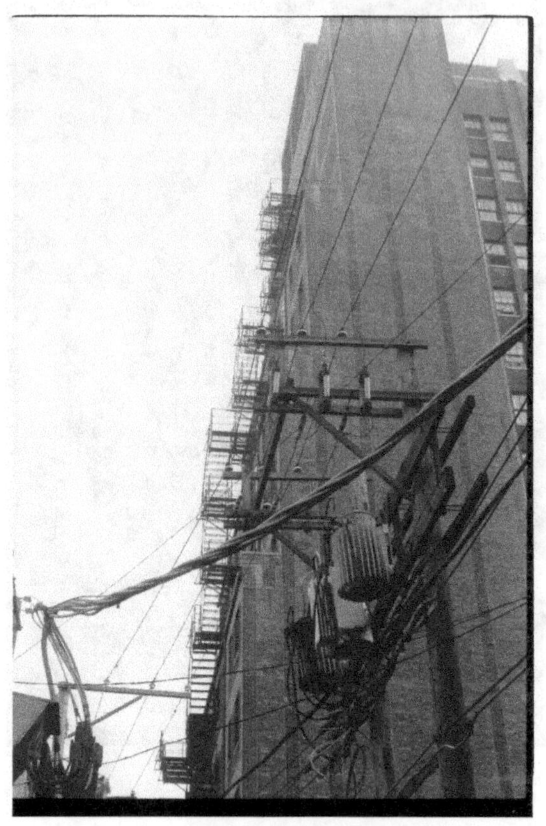

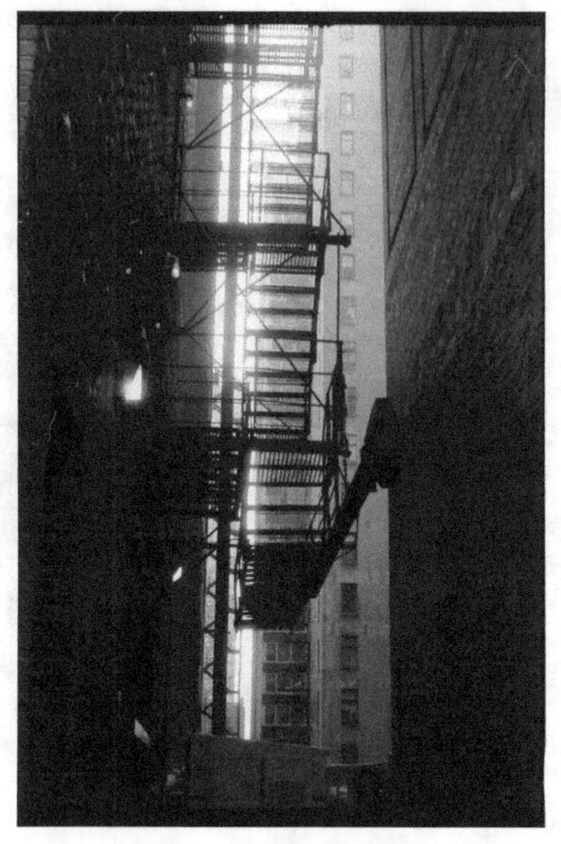

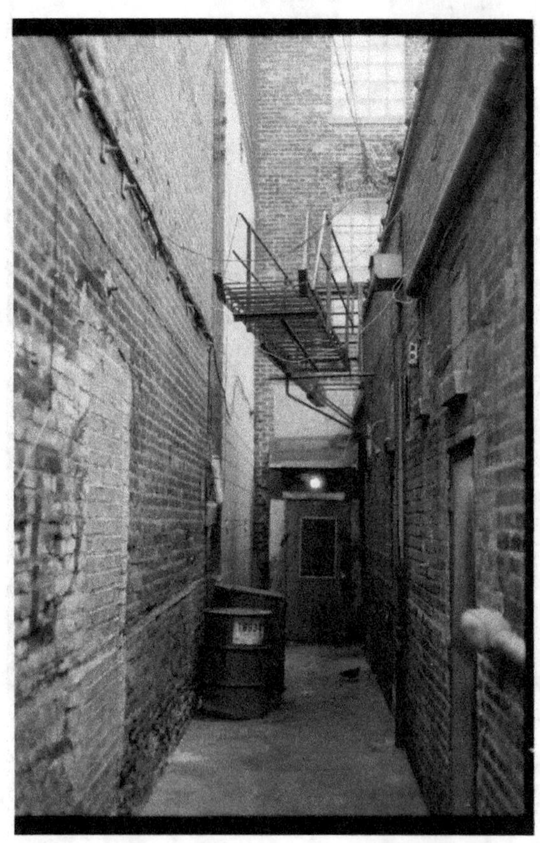

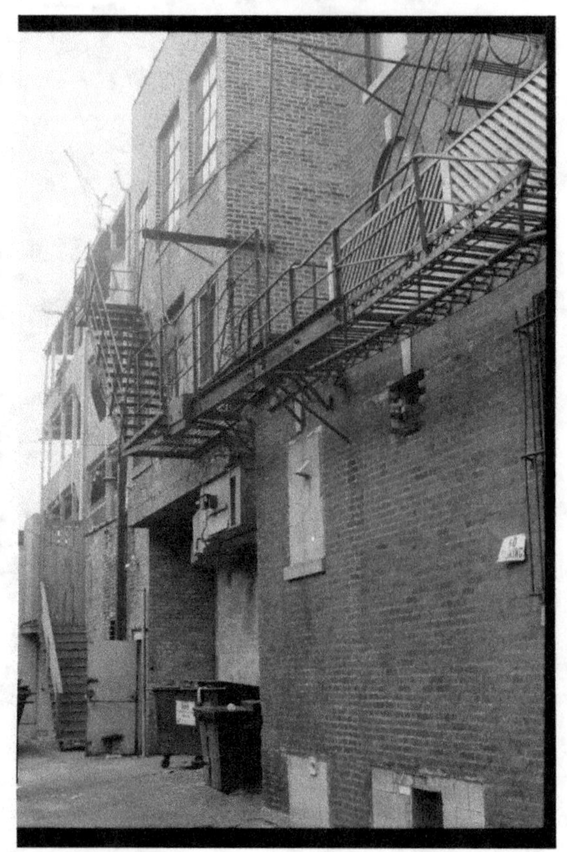

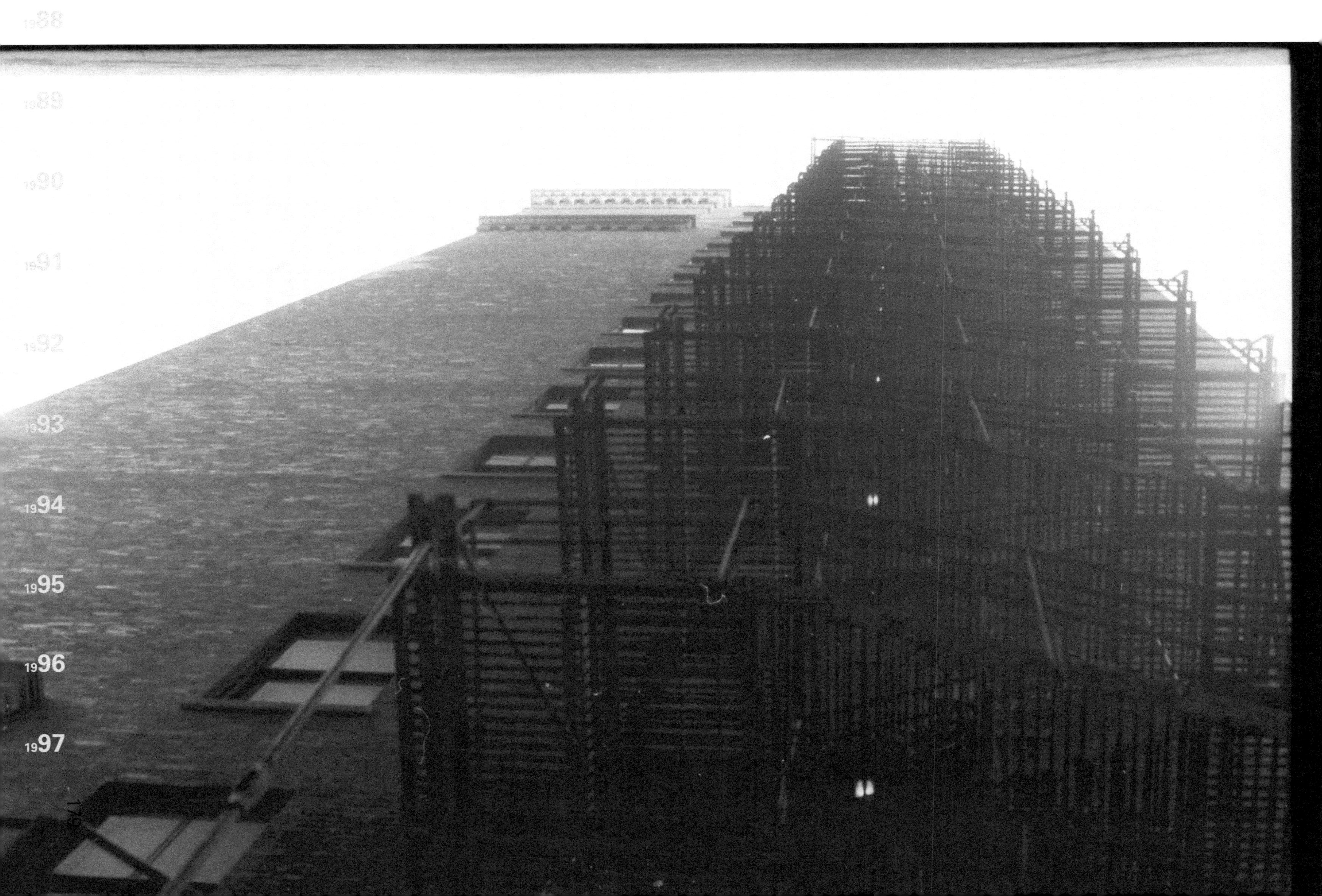

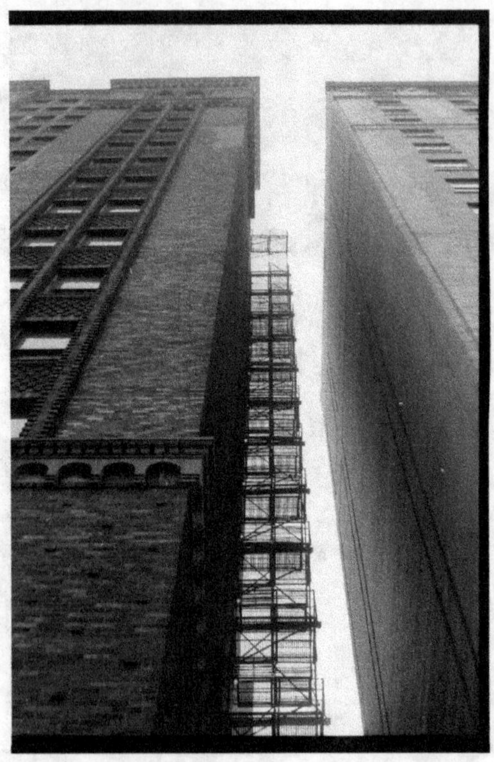

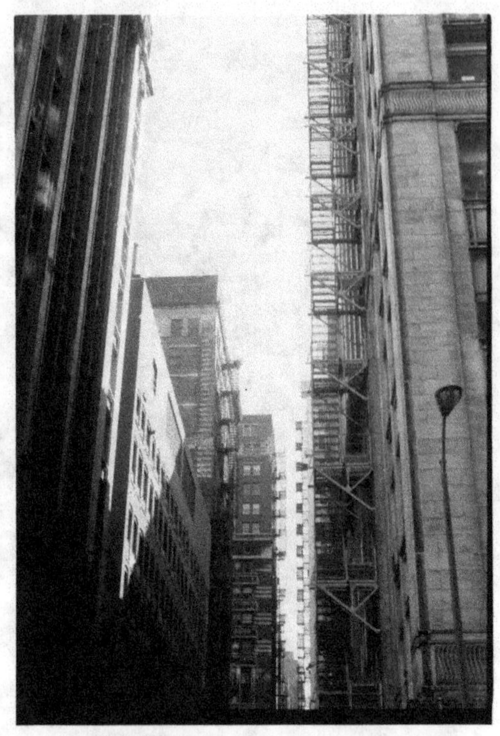

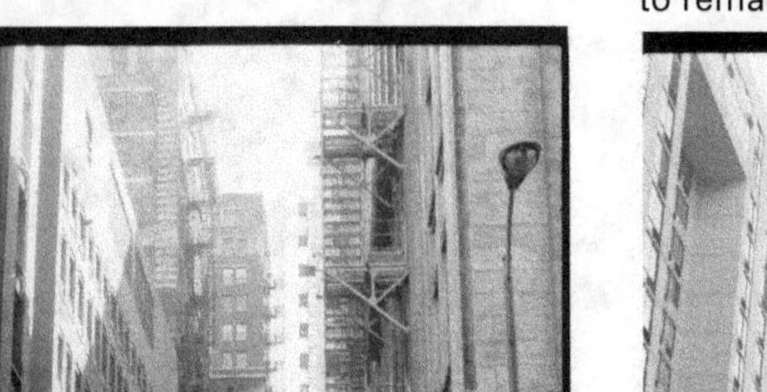

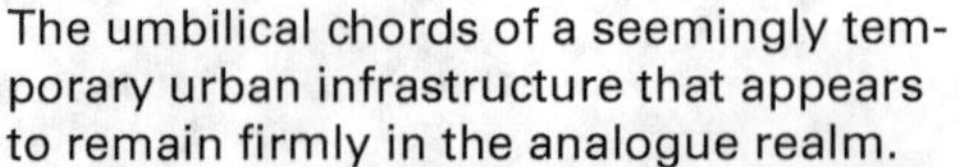

The umbilical chords of a seemingly temporary urban infrastructure that appears to remain firmly in the analogue realm.

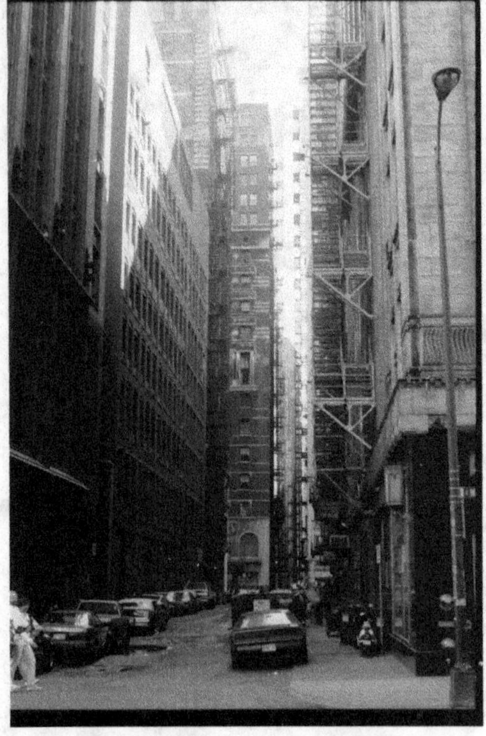

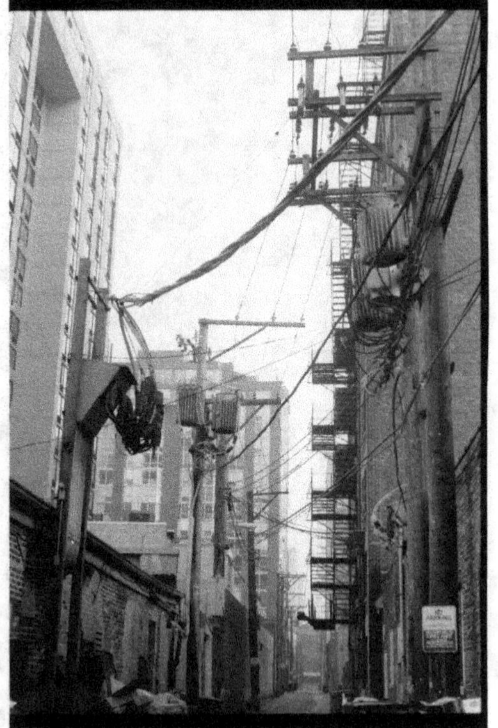

Travel in Belgium and France

Near the small town of Stavelot in Belgium a bridge leads over a stream that shows the rest of the town underneath the roadway arch, far below the water surface in the foreground; it's a geographical oddity, not unlike the one in the movie *O'Brother*

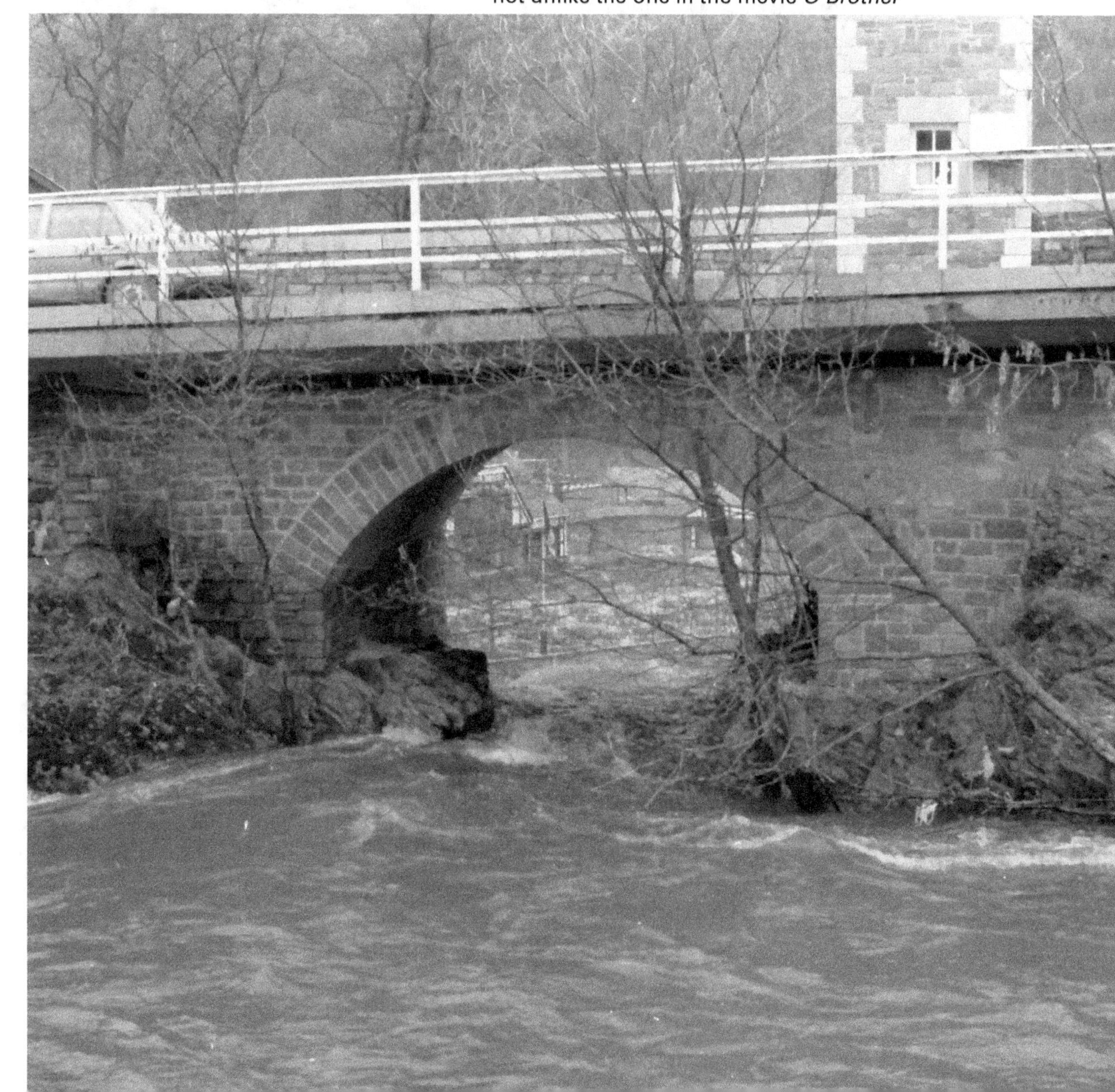

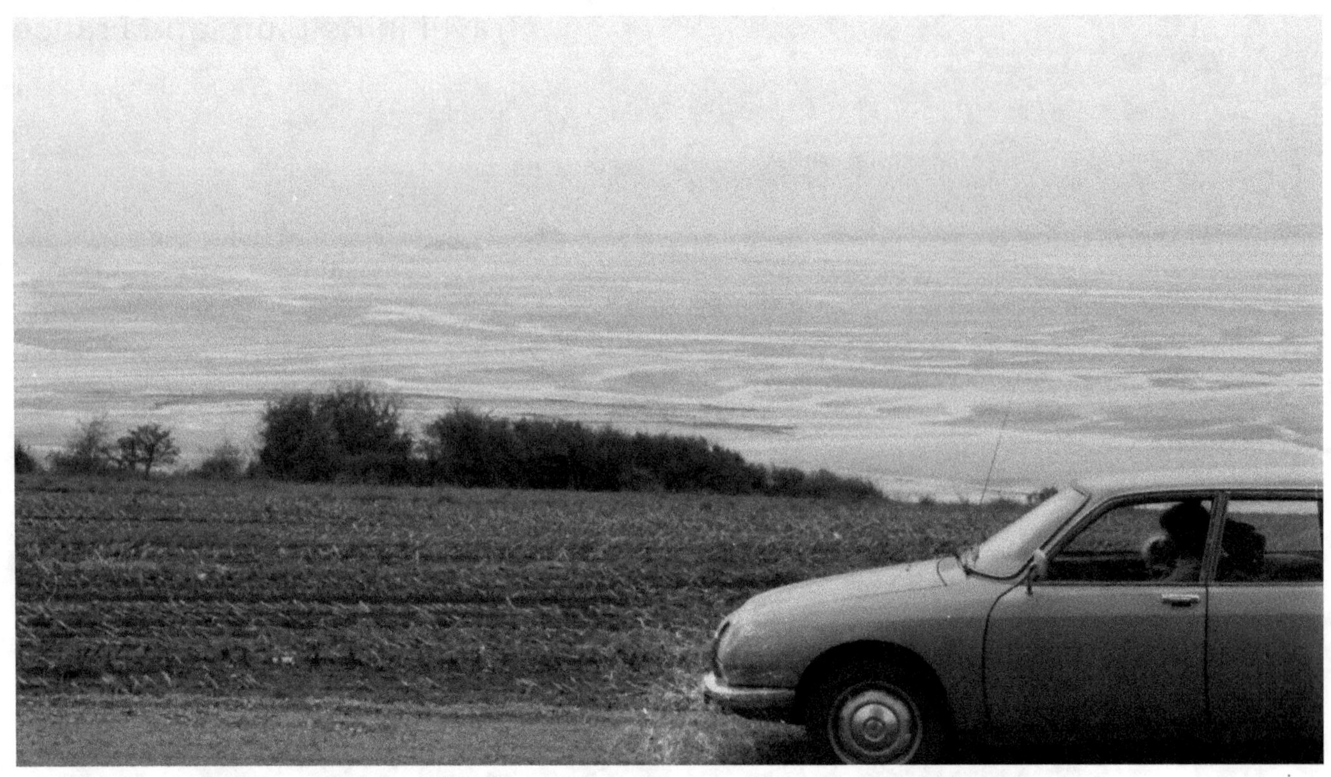

Approaching Mont St. Michel (visible in the distance, above) and viewing the landscape-with-Miriam from the Mont terrace (below).

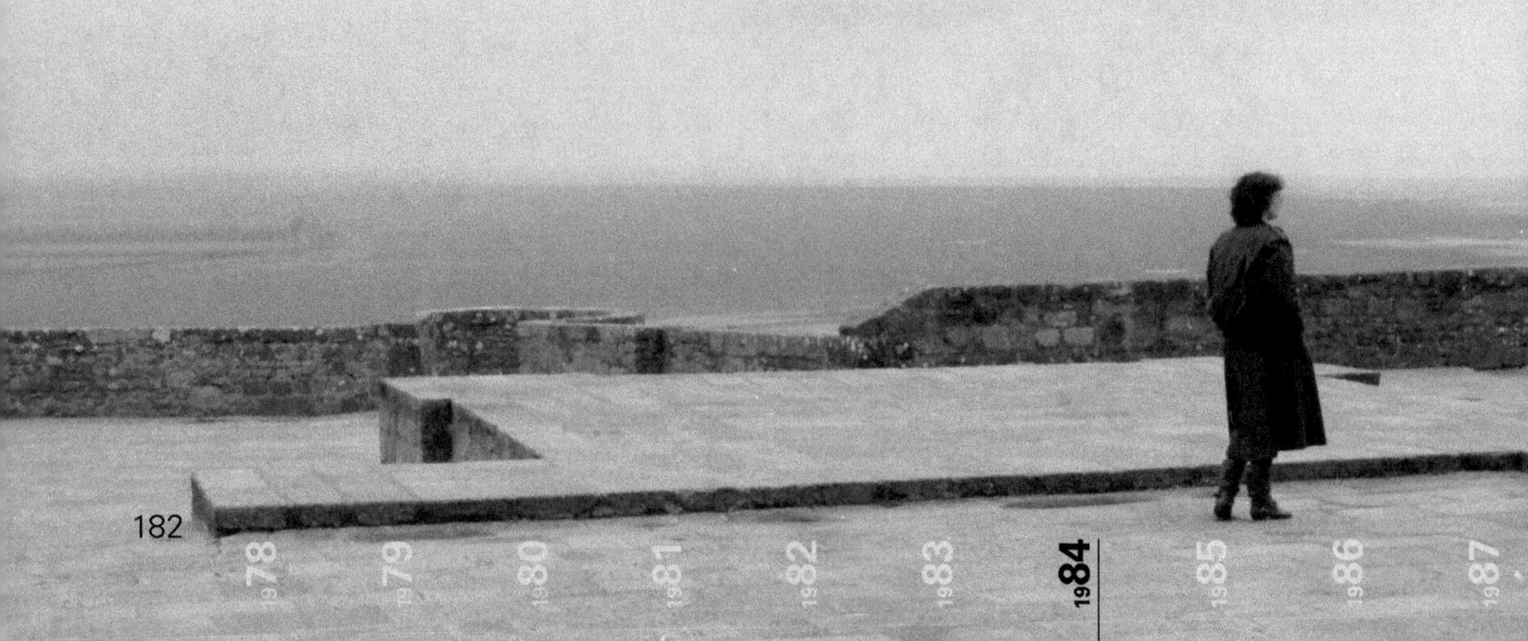

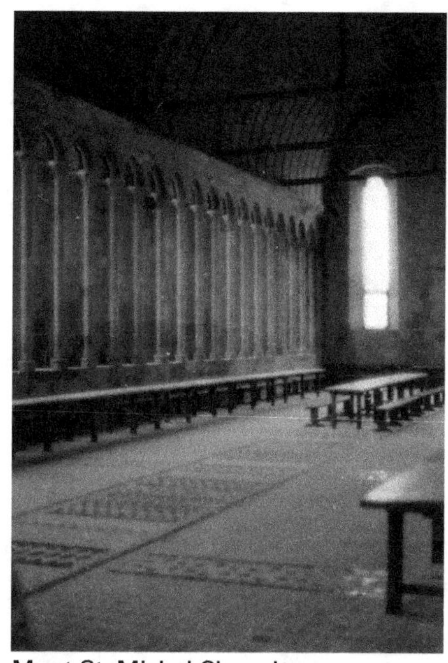

Mont St. Michel Chapel

View from Mont St. Michel: Miriam's reluctance to be photographed does little to reduce the perception of the landscape as a painting demonstrating the power of perspective.

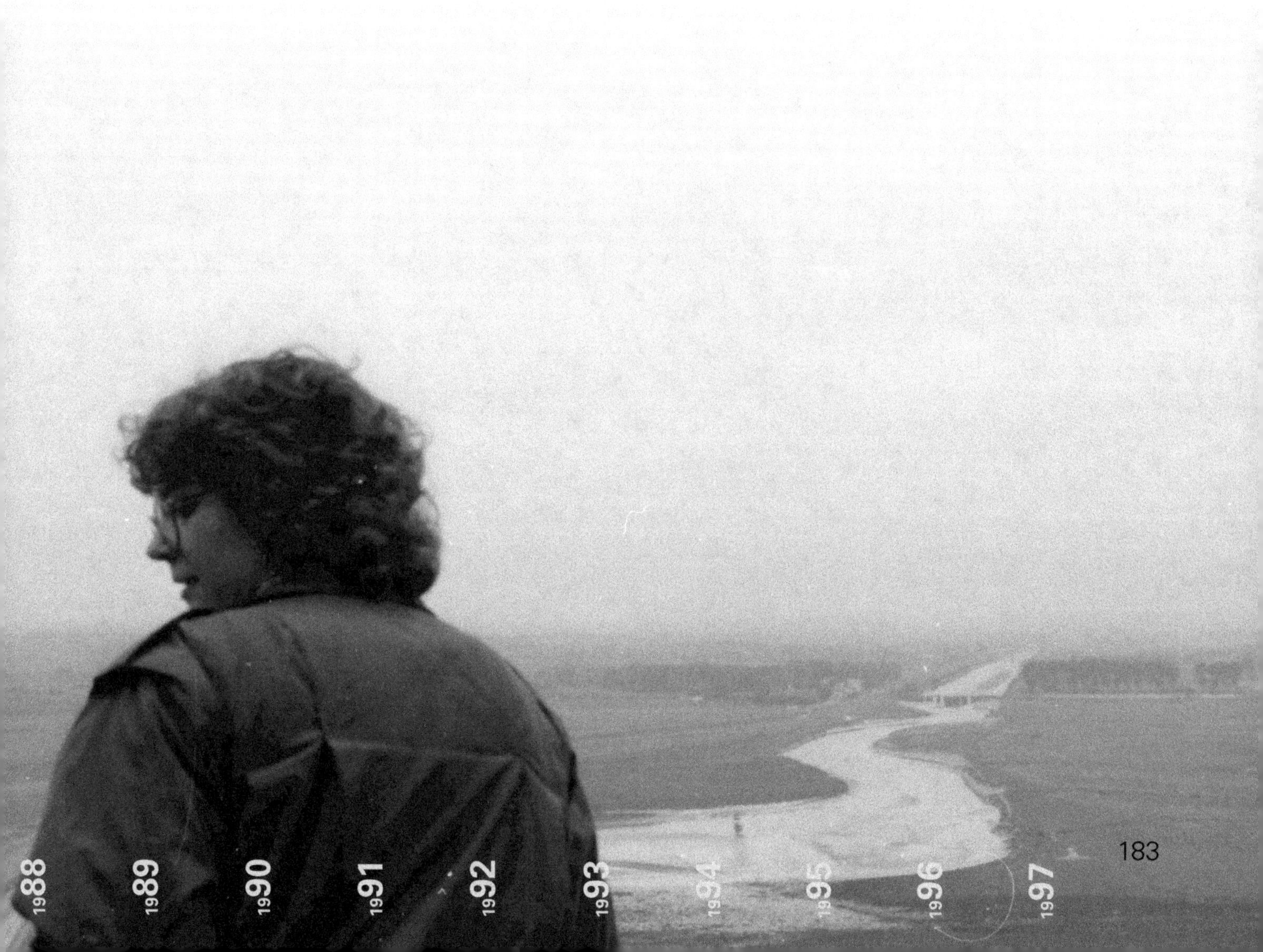

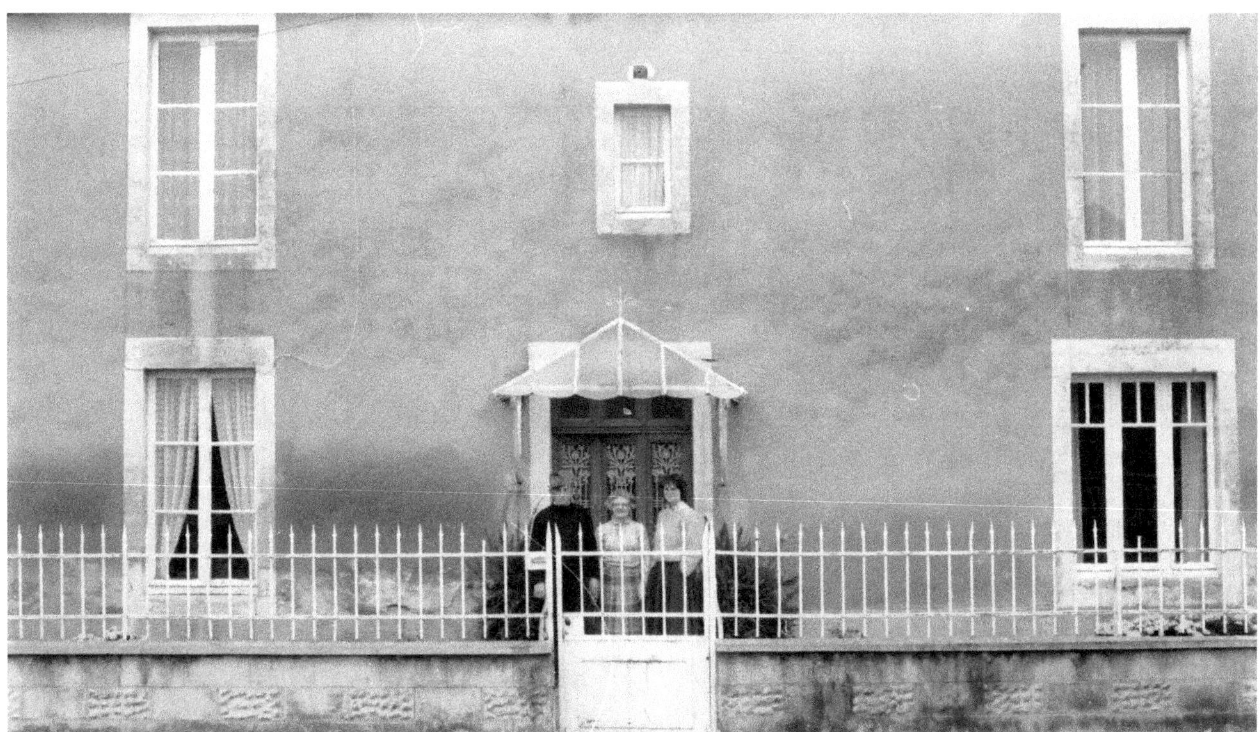

While traveling in northern France we had the odd but funny realization that every family we stayed with was named Hue. It became a running joke between us that the next night's B&B would happen in another Hue residence.

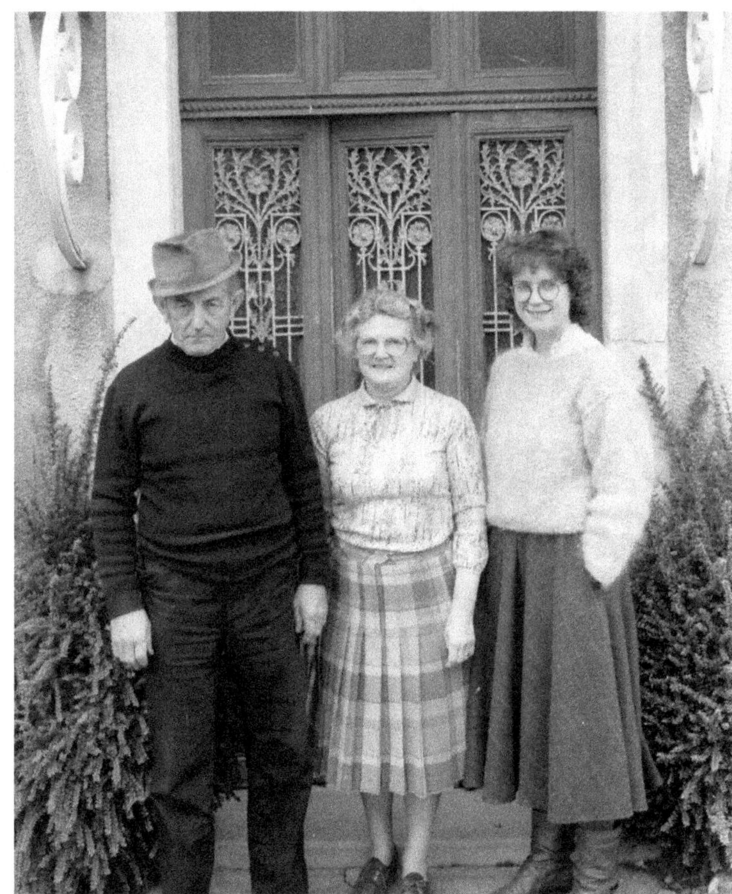

Portrait of a tense Franco (Mr. and Mrs. Hue)-American-German encounter. Mr. Hue doesn't look too happy about our tri-national proximity.

< View from Mont St. Michel to one of the village houses below.

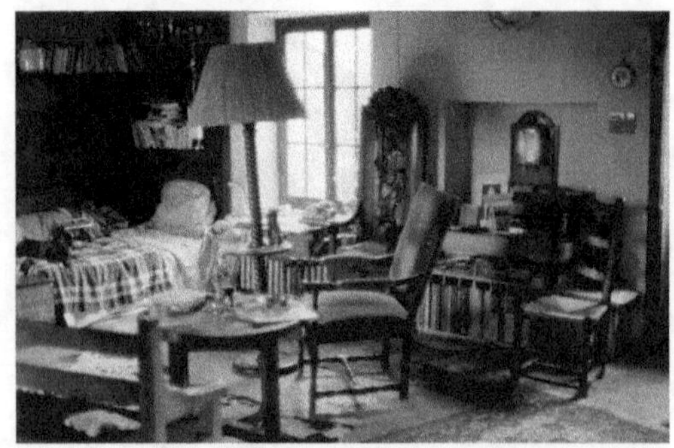

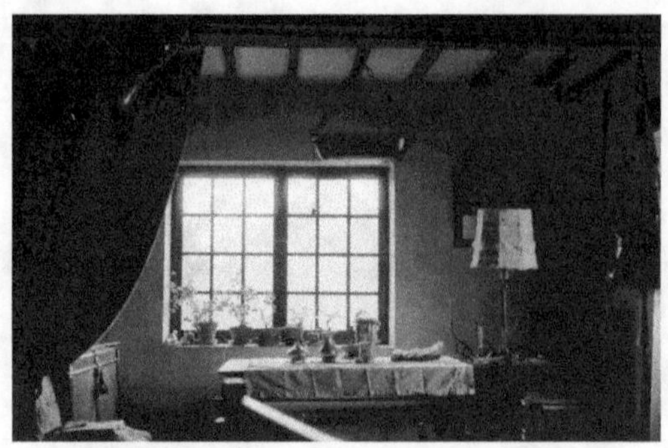

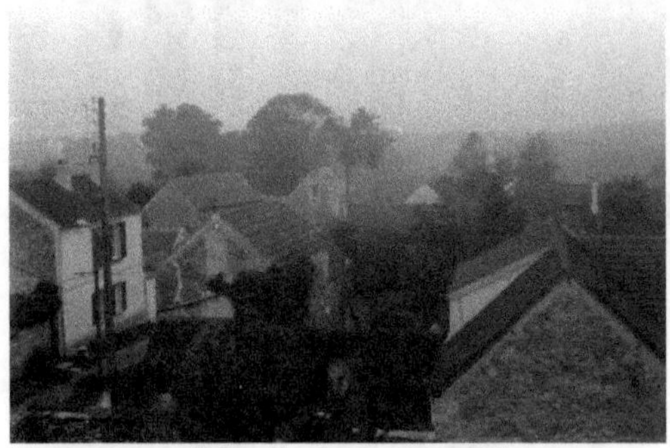

View toward Senlis from our attic room

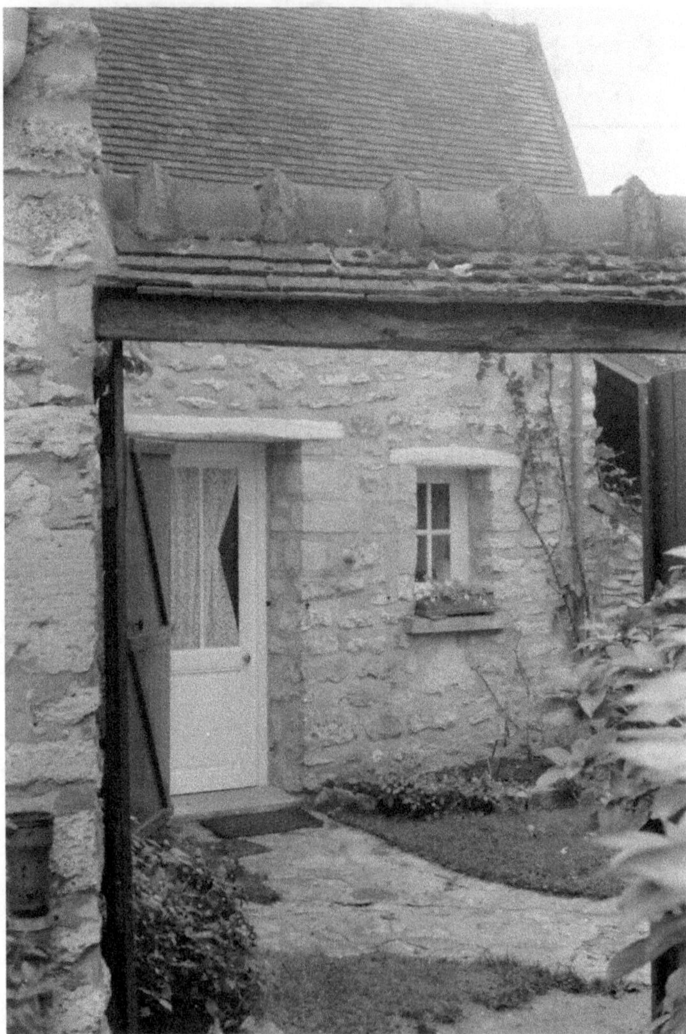

We stopped in Senlis, north of Paris, knowing that the town had served as the stageset for the movie *King of Hearts*. Arriving late in the afternoon we stayed outside the town in a rustic B&B with another family named Hue whose great-grandmother was the button maker for Marie Antoinette. Our room was located in the attic with a great view of the medival town center in the distance. Anticipating the same clear view we had encountered the night before, we found next morning a beautiful foggy soup surrounding our house, and no Senlis in sight....

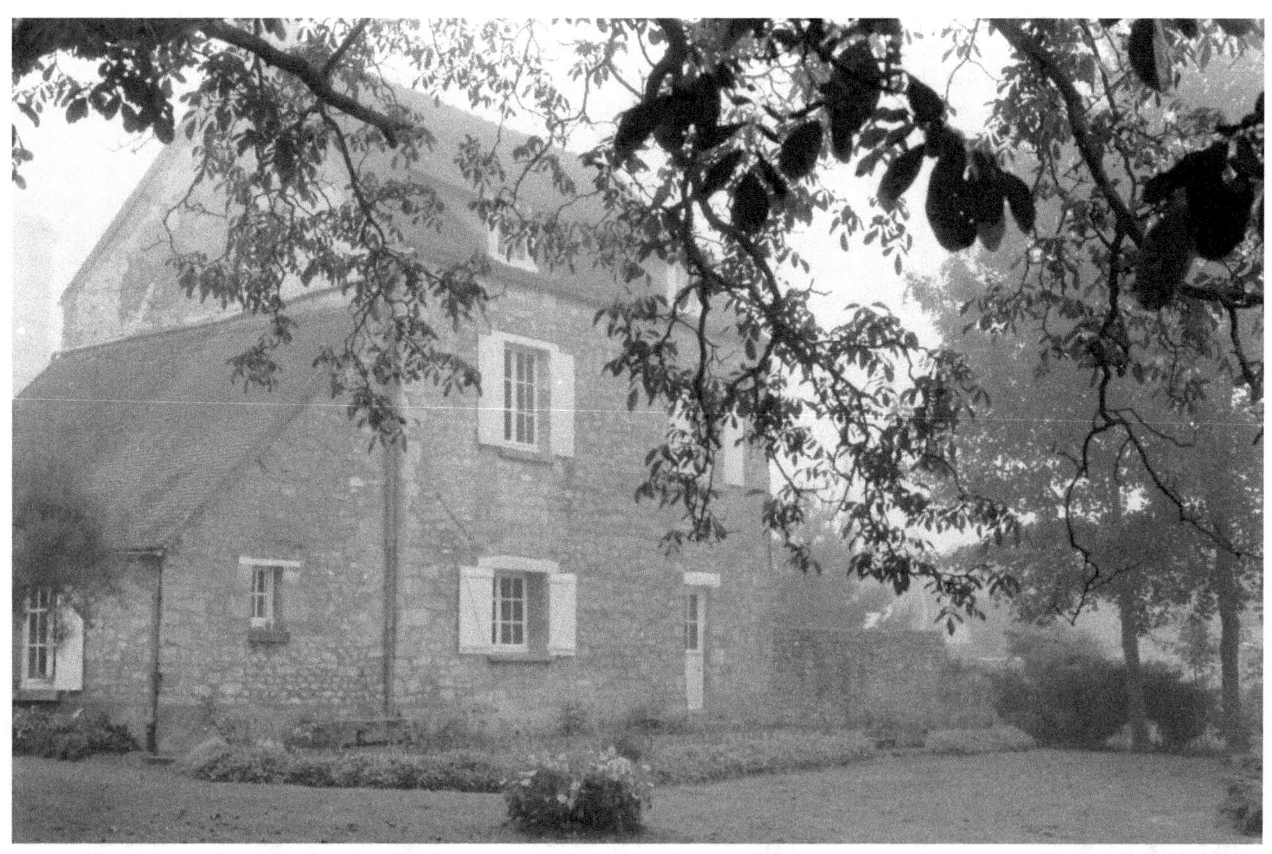

A bucolic scene outside our B&B early in the morning before we headed into Senlis to find the asylum from *King of Hearts*.

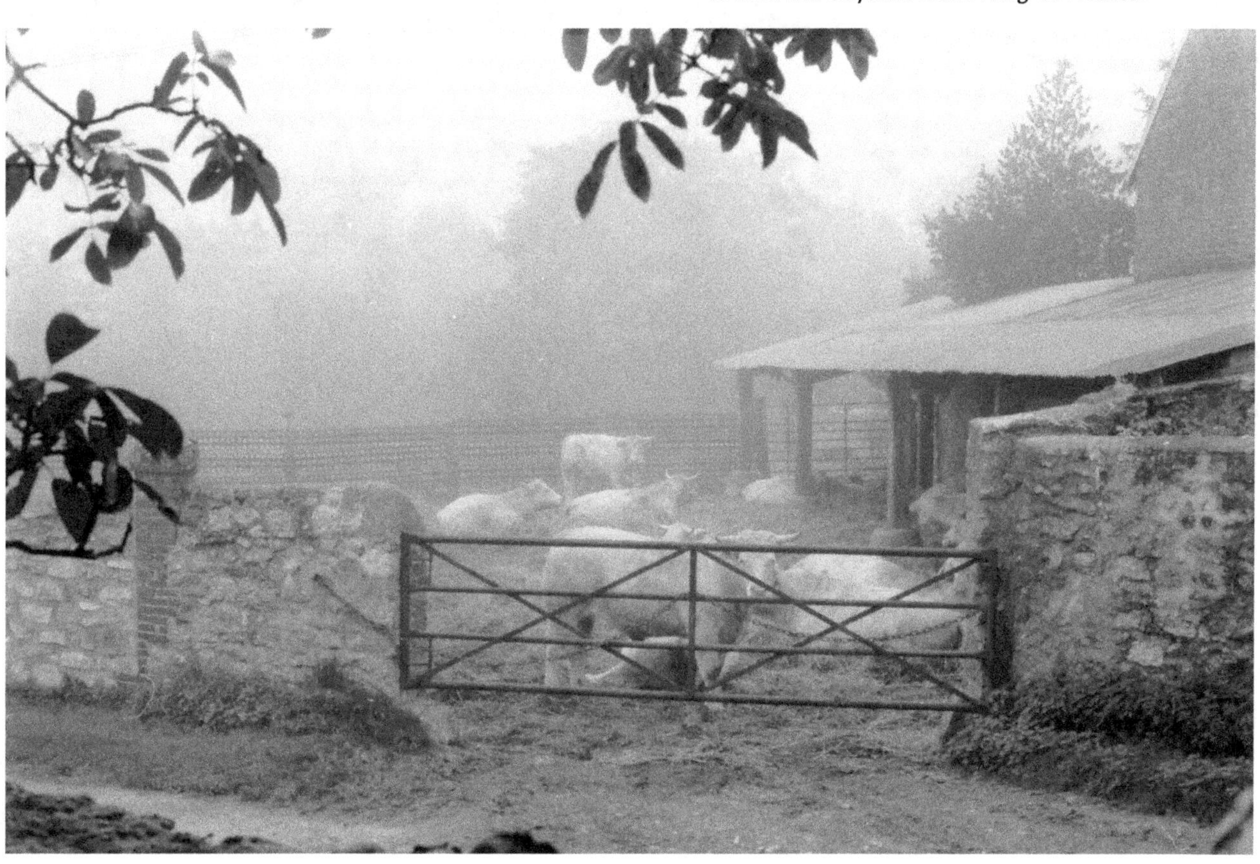

There was a sign on the side of the road that said 'hotel' in handwritten letters. We were tired of driving and decided to take a chance. Coasting down the country lane we arrived soon at the Hotel Doux Repos (Haute-Bodeux 34, 4983 Basse-Bodeux, Trois-Ponts, Belgium). The place is surrounded by fields and forests. We were carefree, named the dancing tree in the meadow (image to the right) and played the way children play—with abandon (below).

Dancing tree on the meadow as seen from Doux Repos >

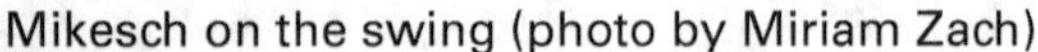

Mikesch on the swing (photo by Miriam Zach)

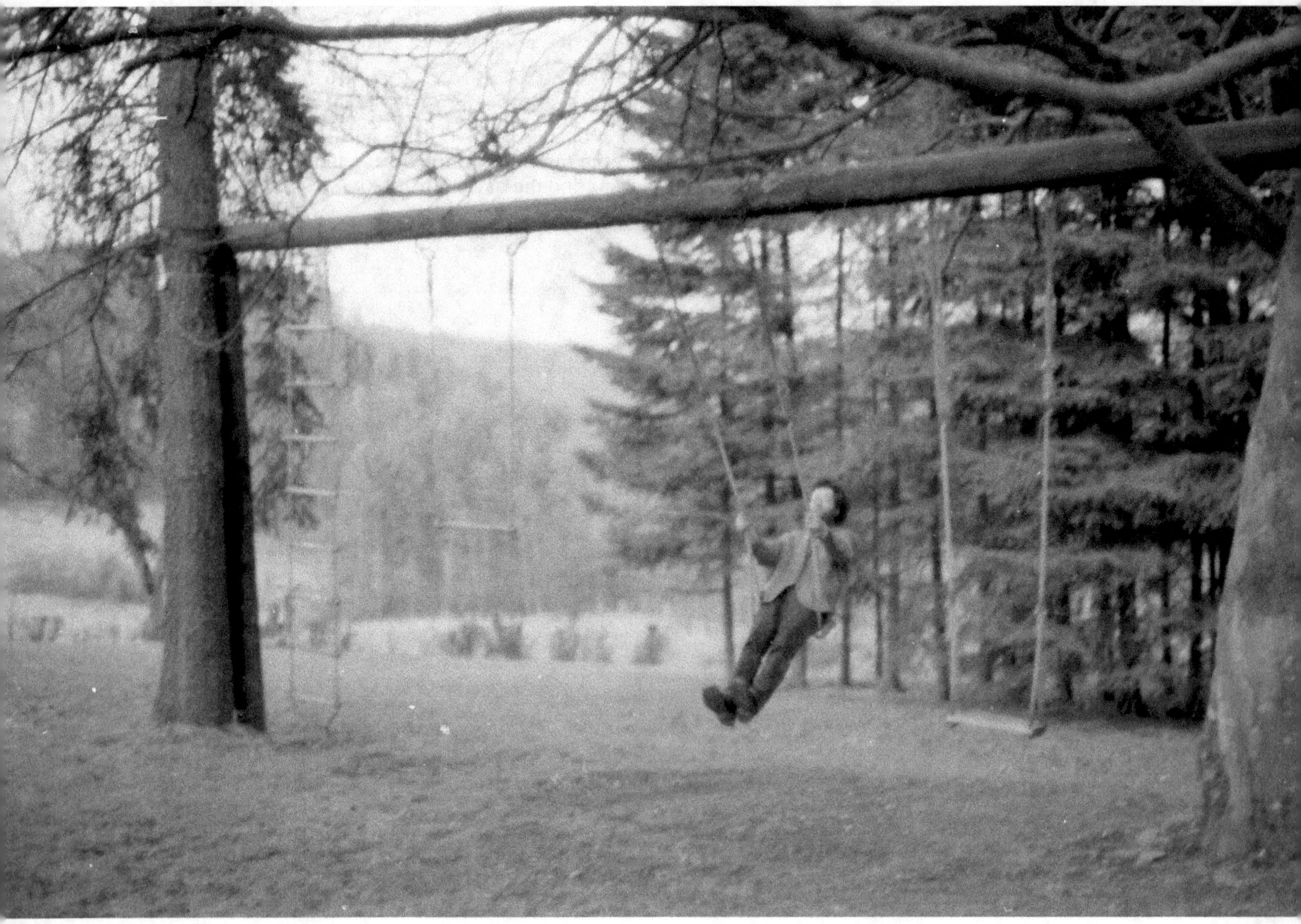

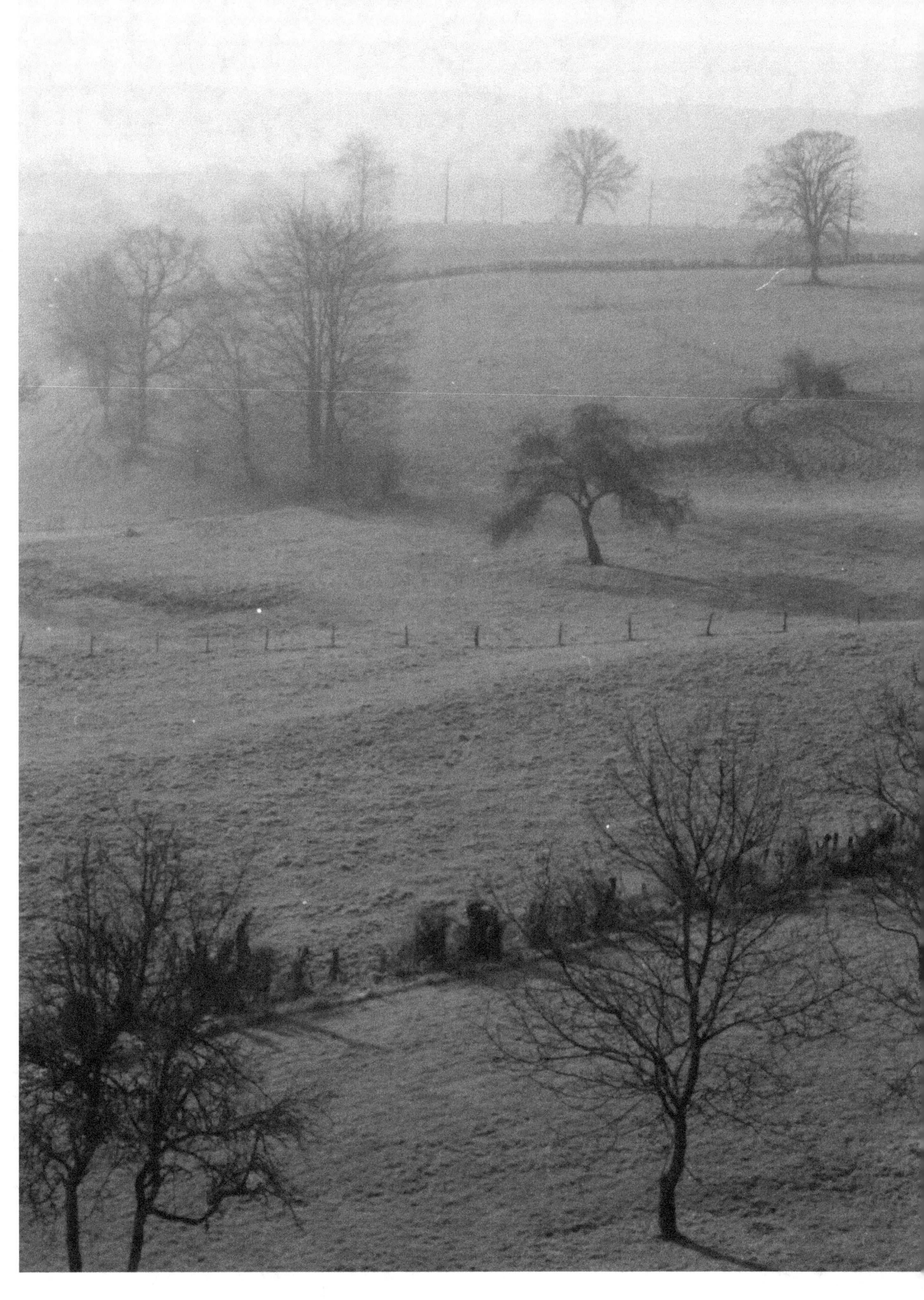

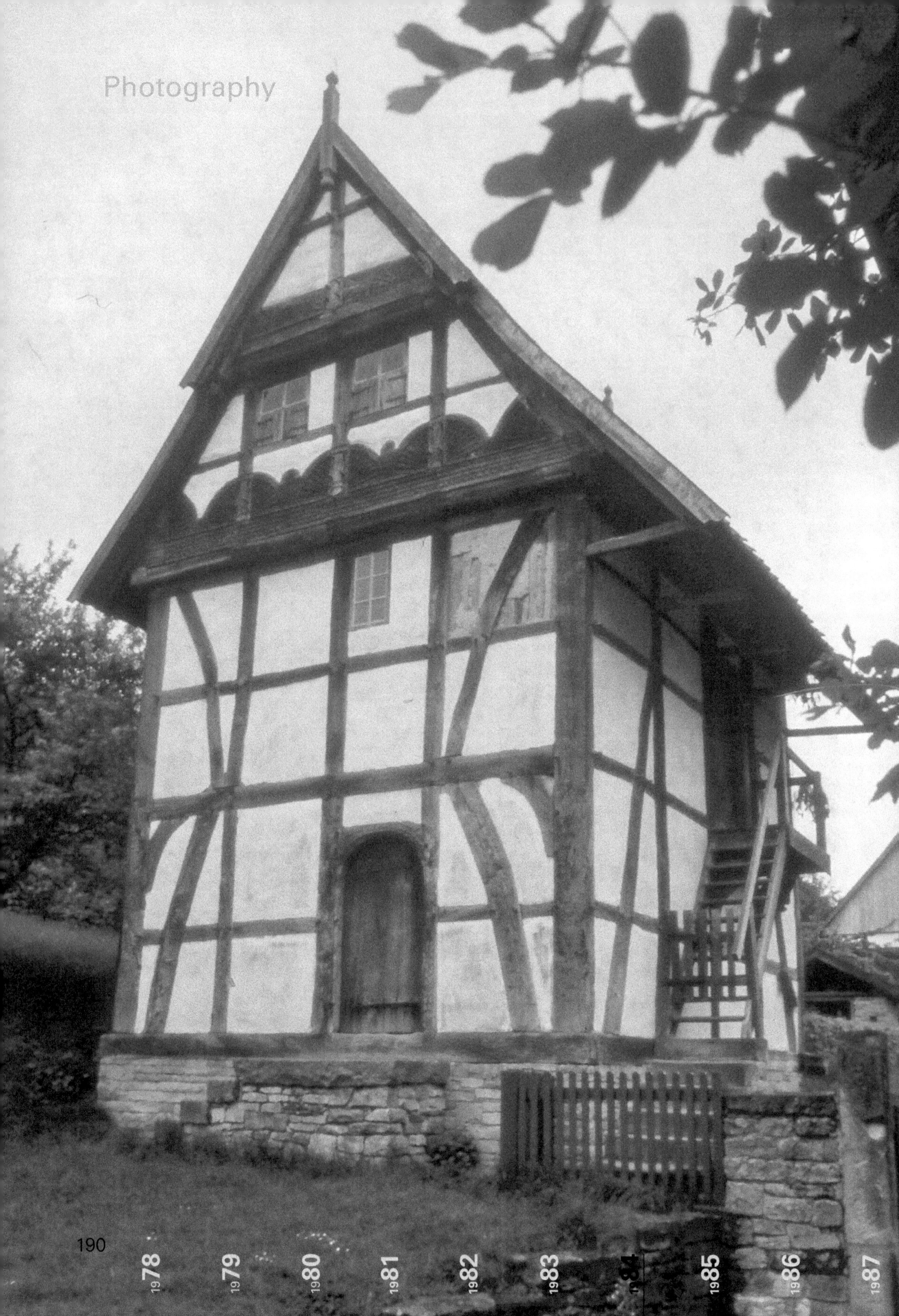

Westfälisches Freilichtmuseum Detmold

Open-Air Museum in Detmold, Germany

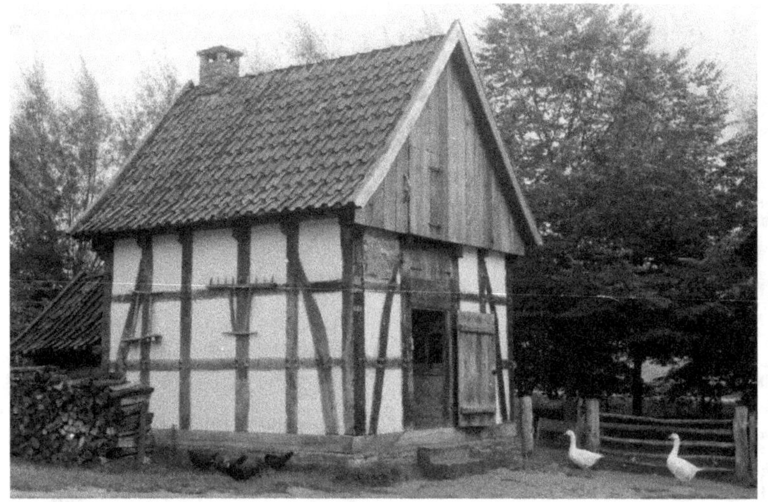

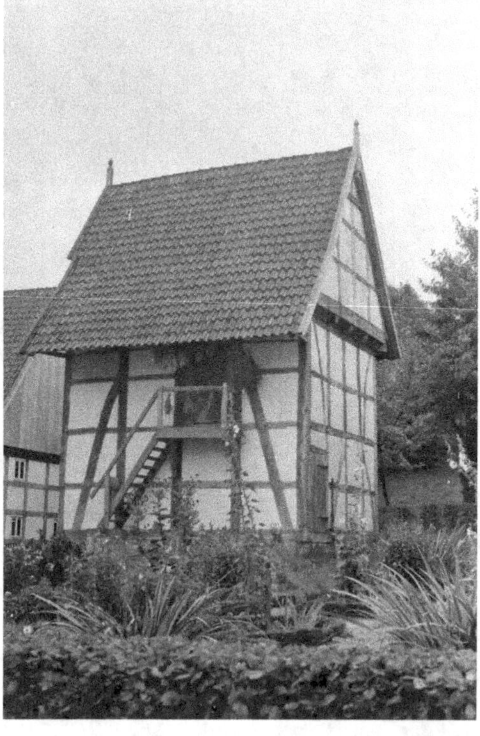

Some of the Fachwerk-style buildings have anthropomorphic gestures, like the farmstead below that looks like a one-eyed ogre with big teeth (the two entry gates).

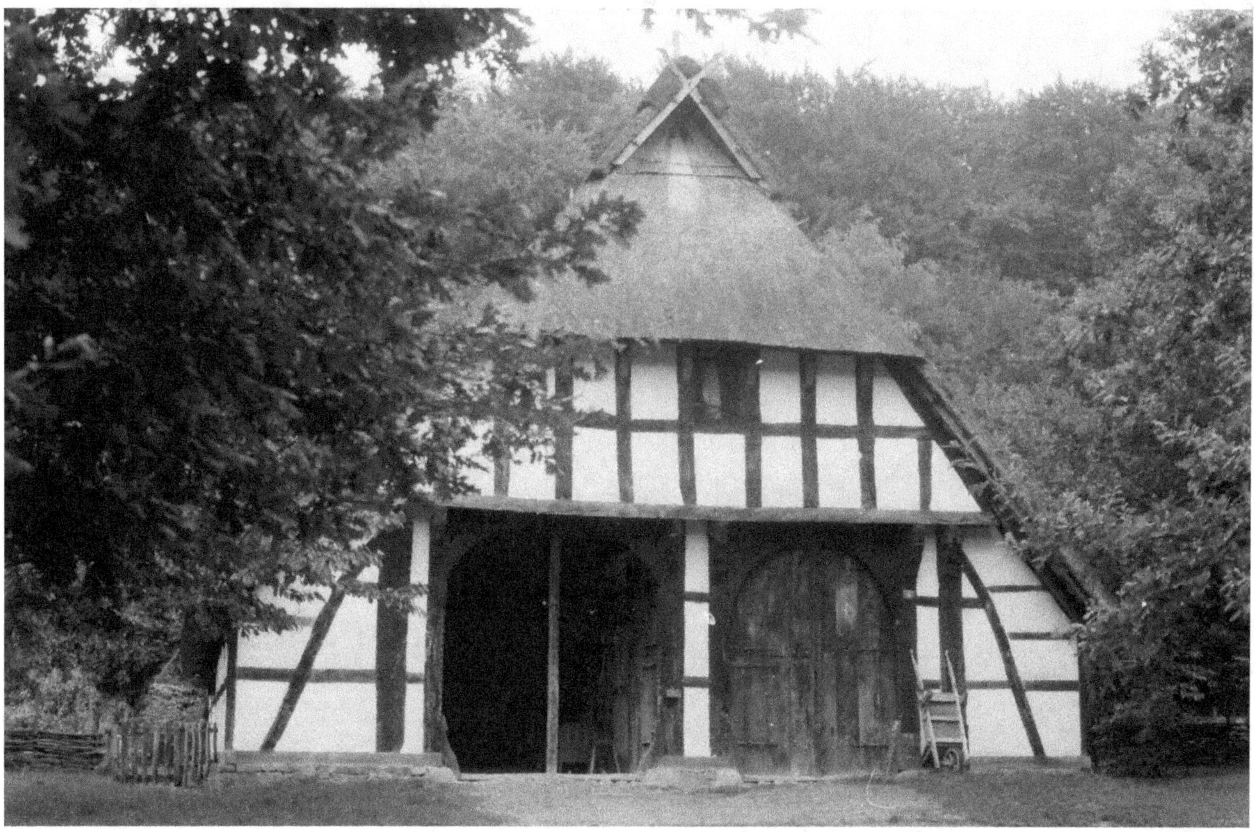

< Storage shed in the Paderborner Dorf, Westfälisches Freilichtmuseum, Detmold, Germany.

Photography

< outside + inside >

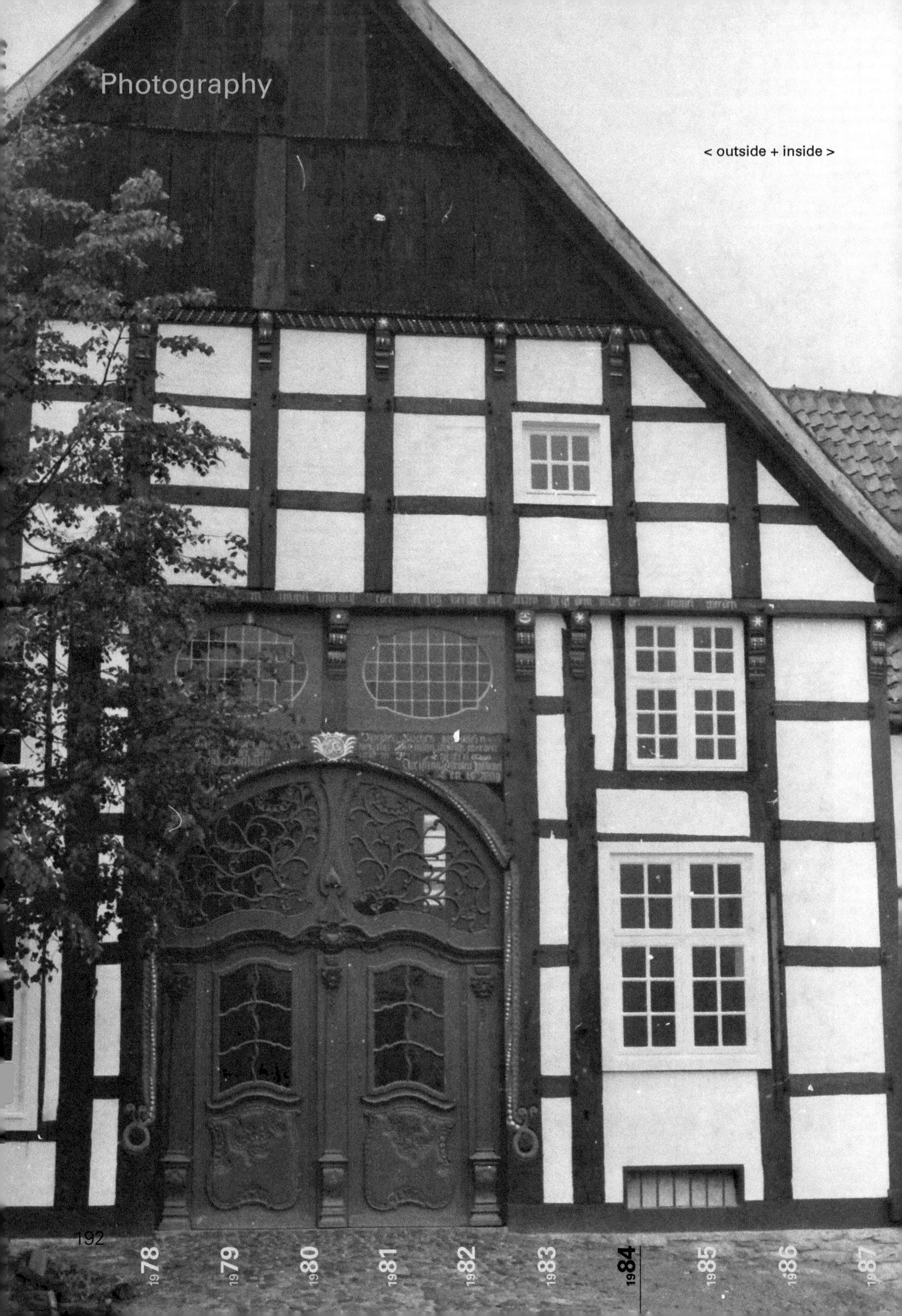

1978 1979 1980 1981 1982 1983 **1984** 1985 1986 1987

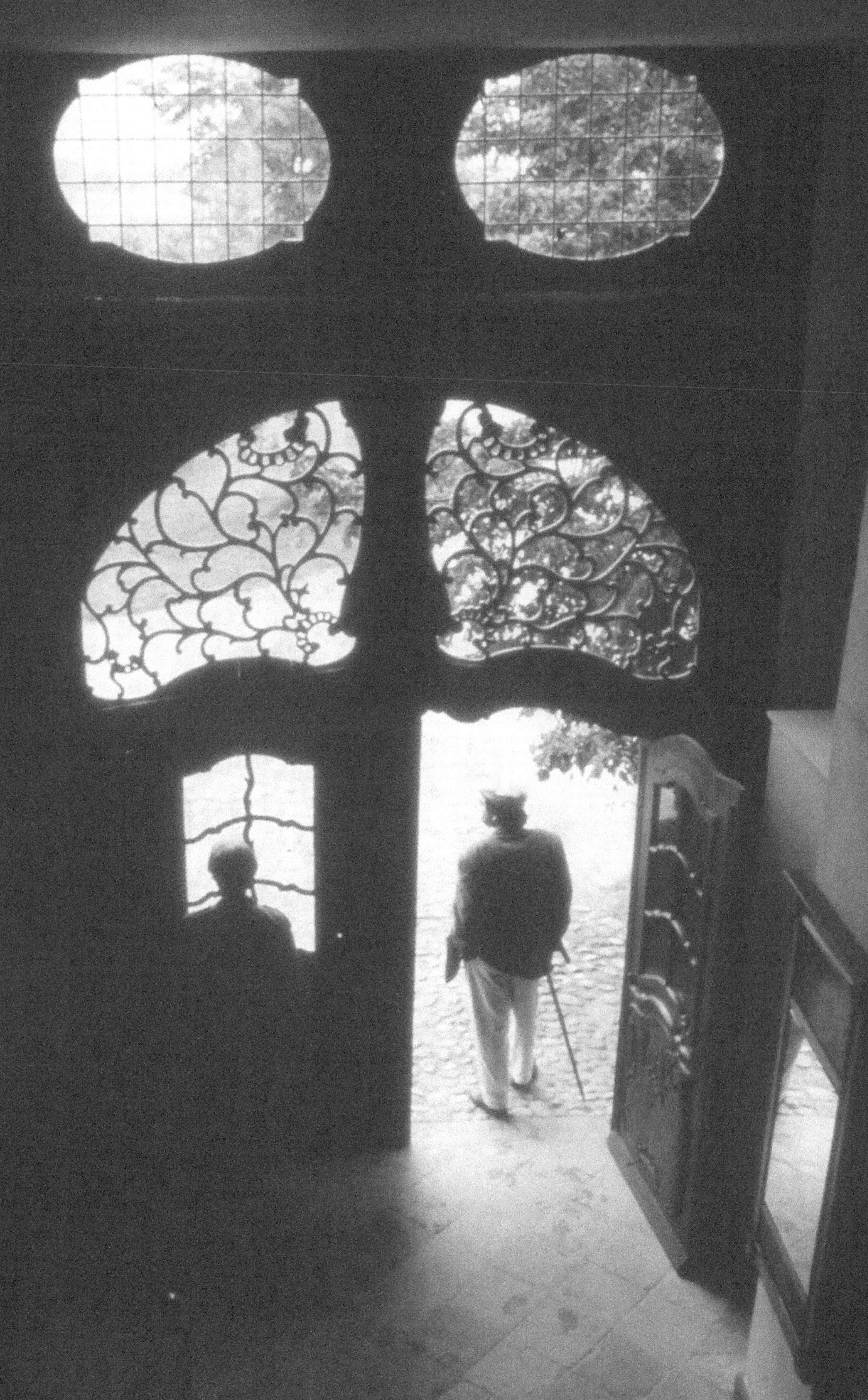

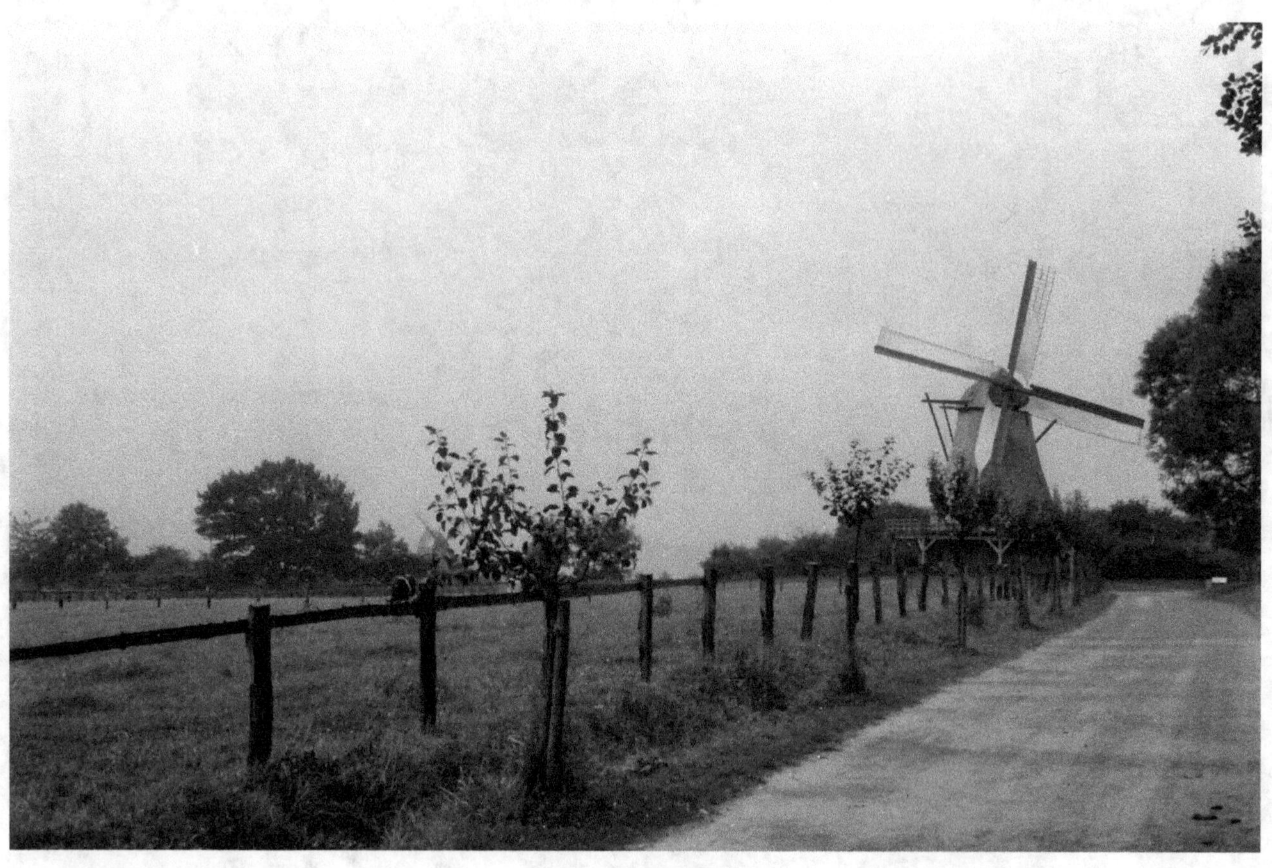

I had an early affinity for windmills....such as these in the open-air museum in Detmold, Germany

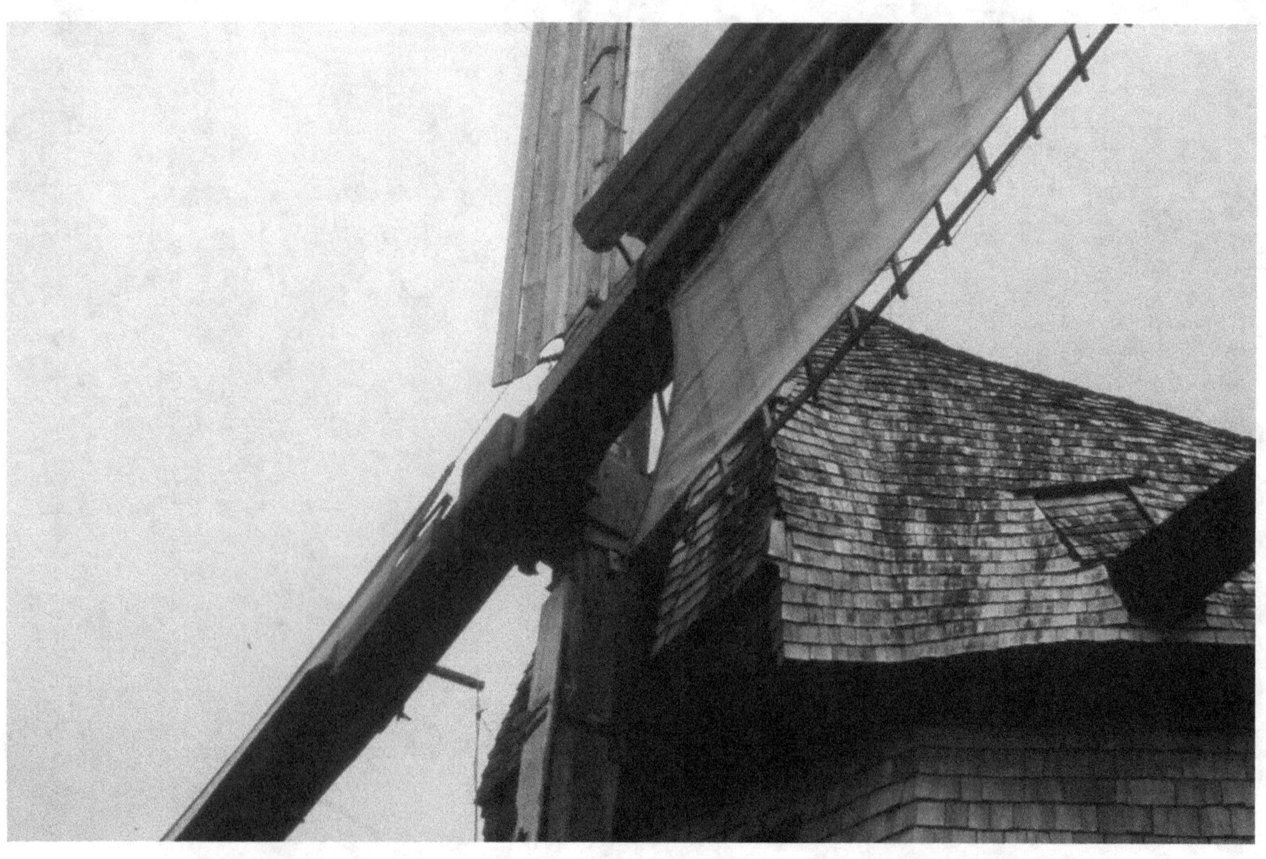

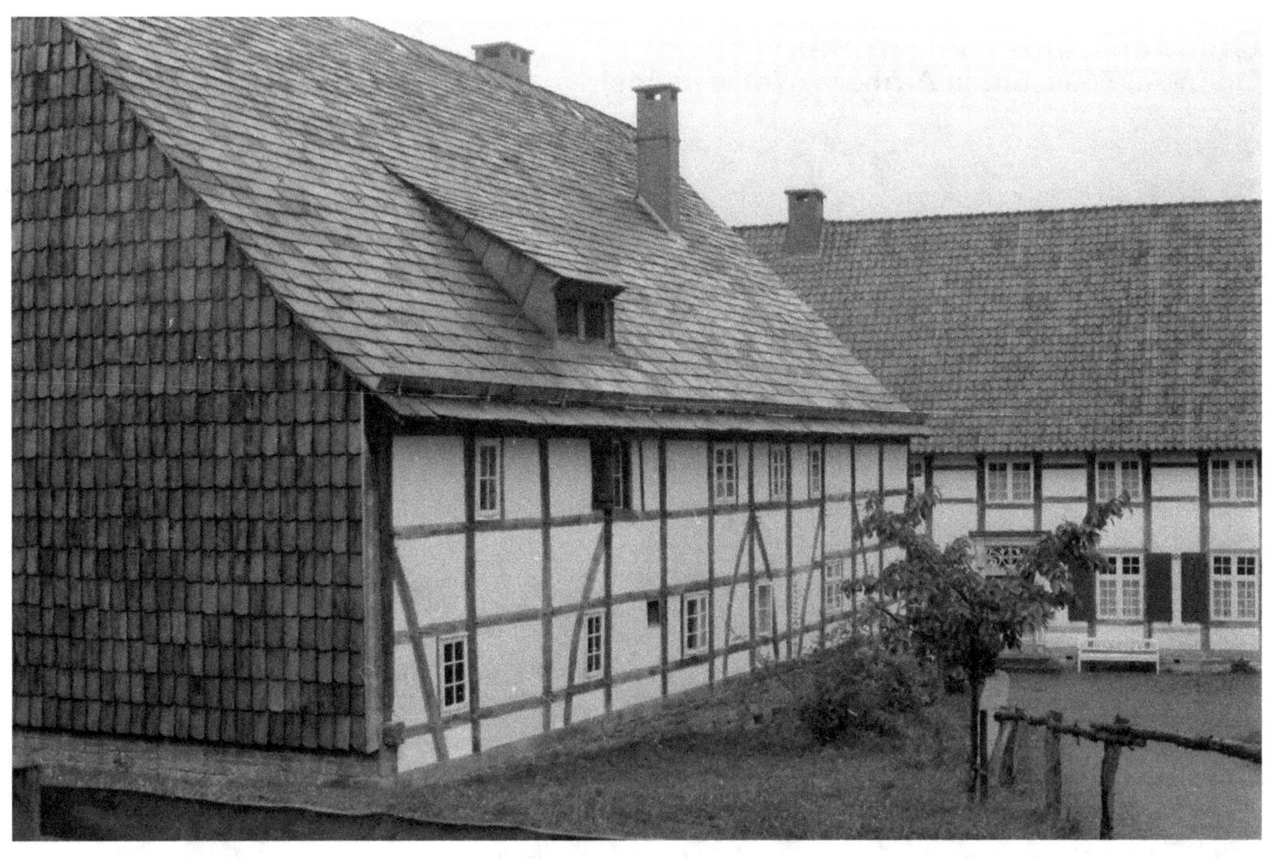

Paderborner village in the open-air museum in Detmold, Germany

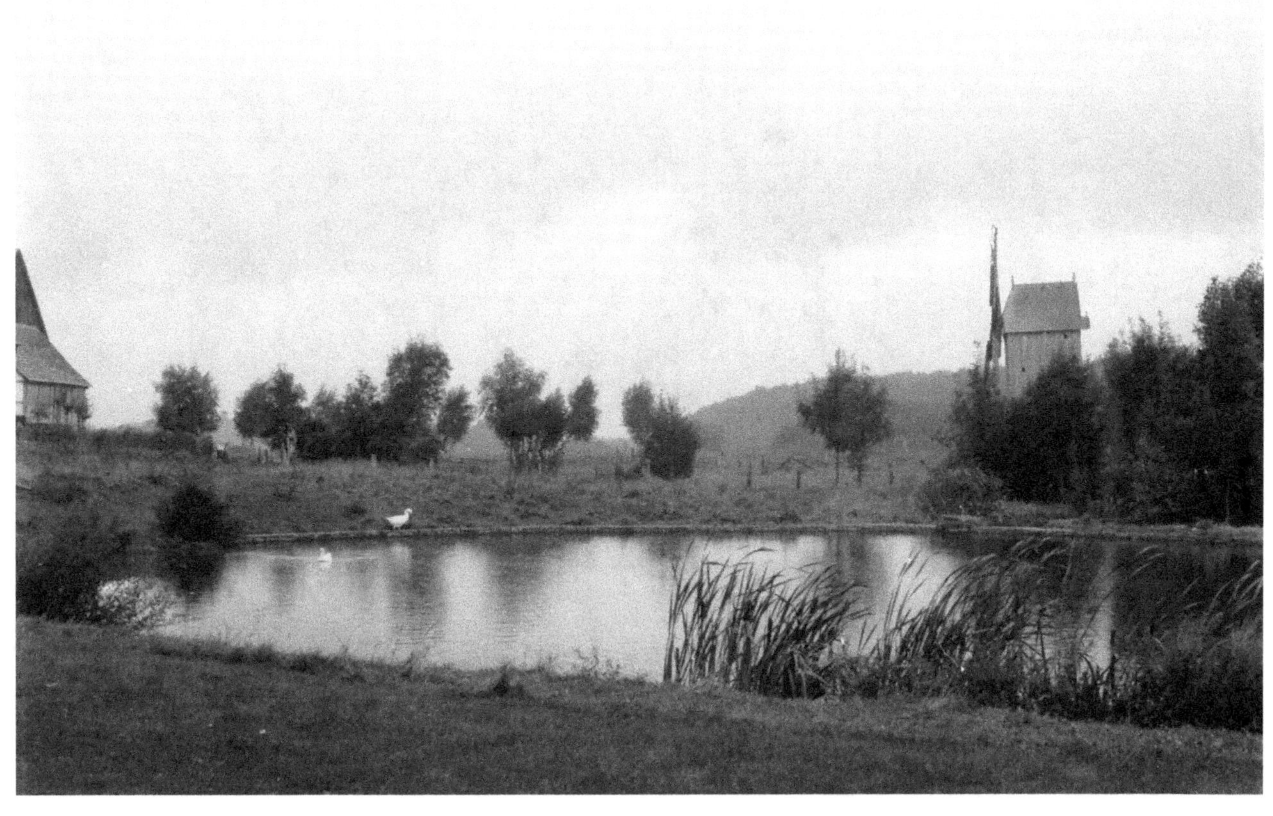

Openluchtmuseum Arnhem
Open-Air Museum in Arnhem, Netherlands

How to make an entry >

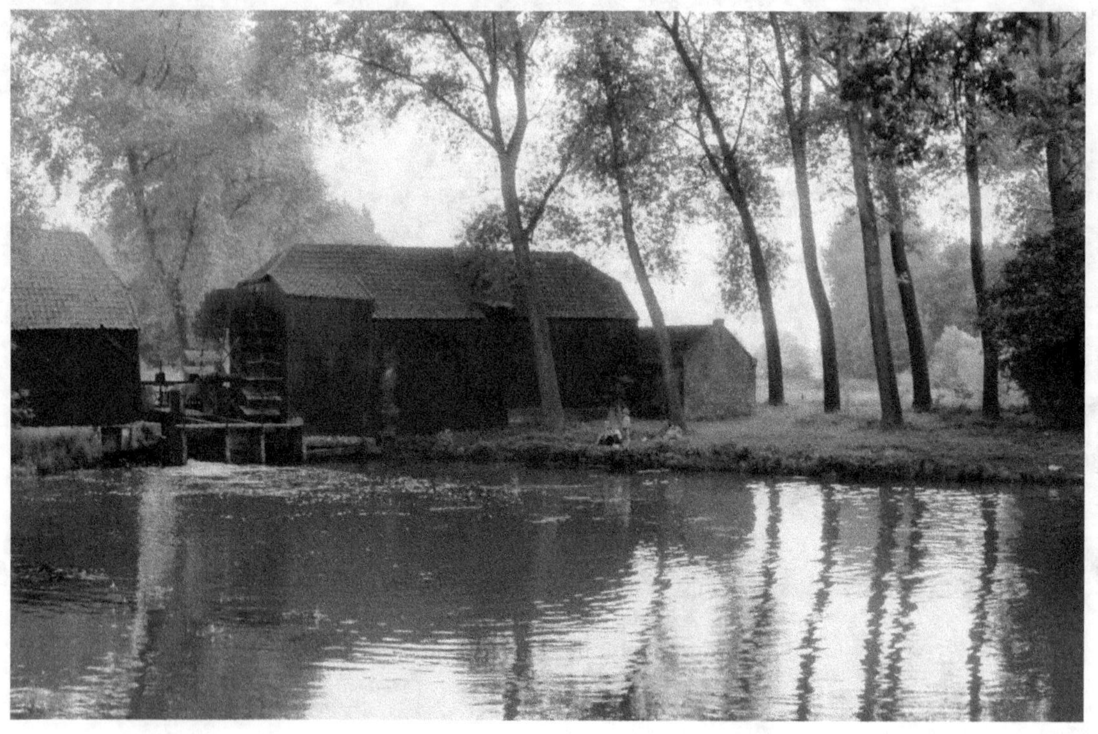

Water mills

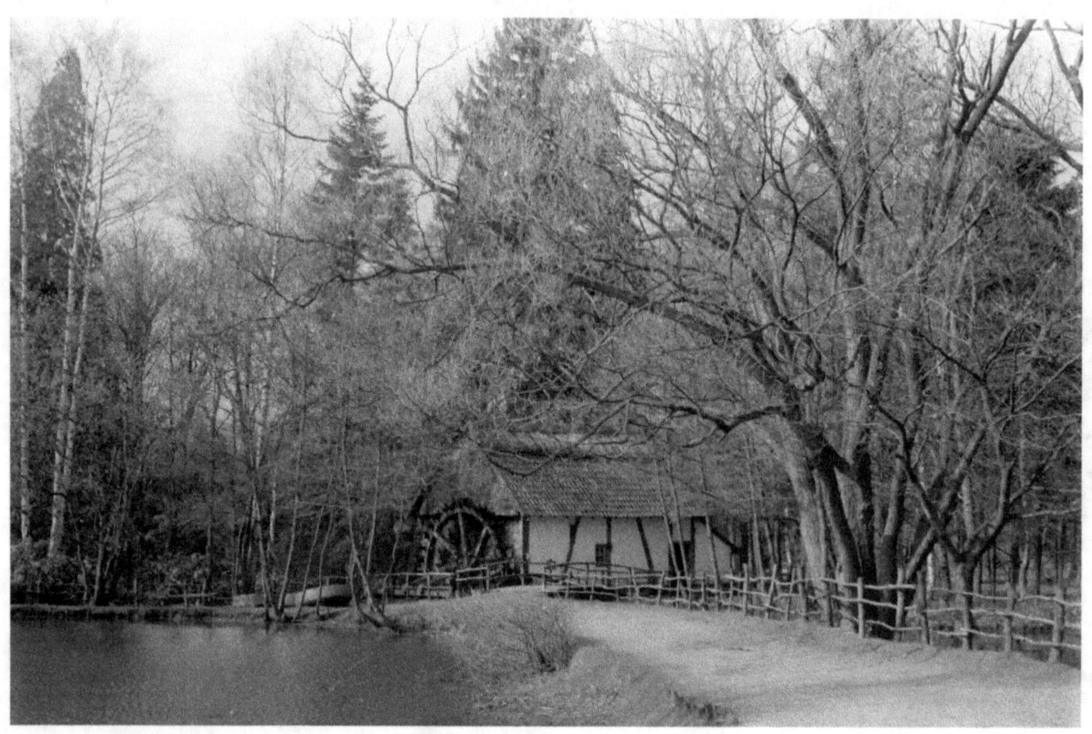

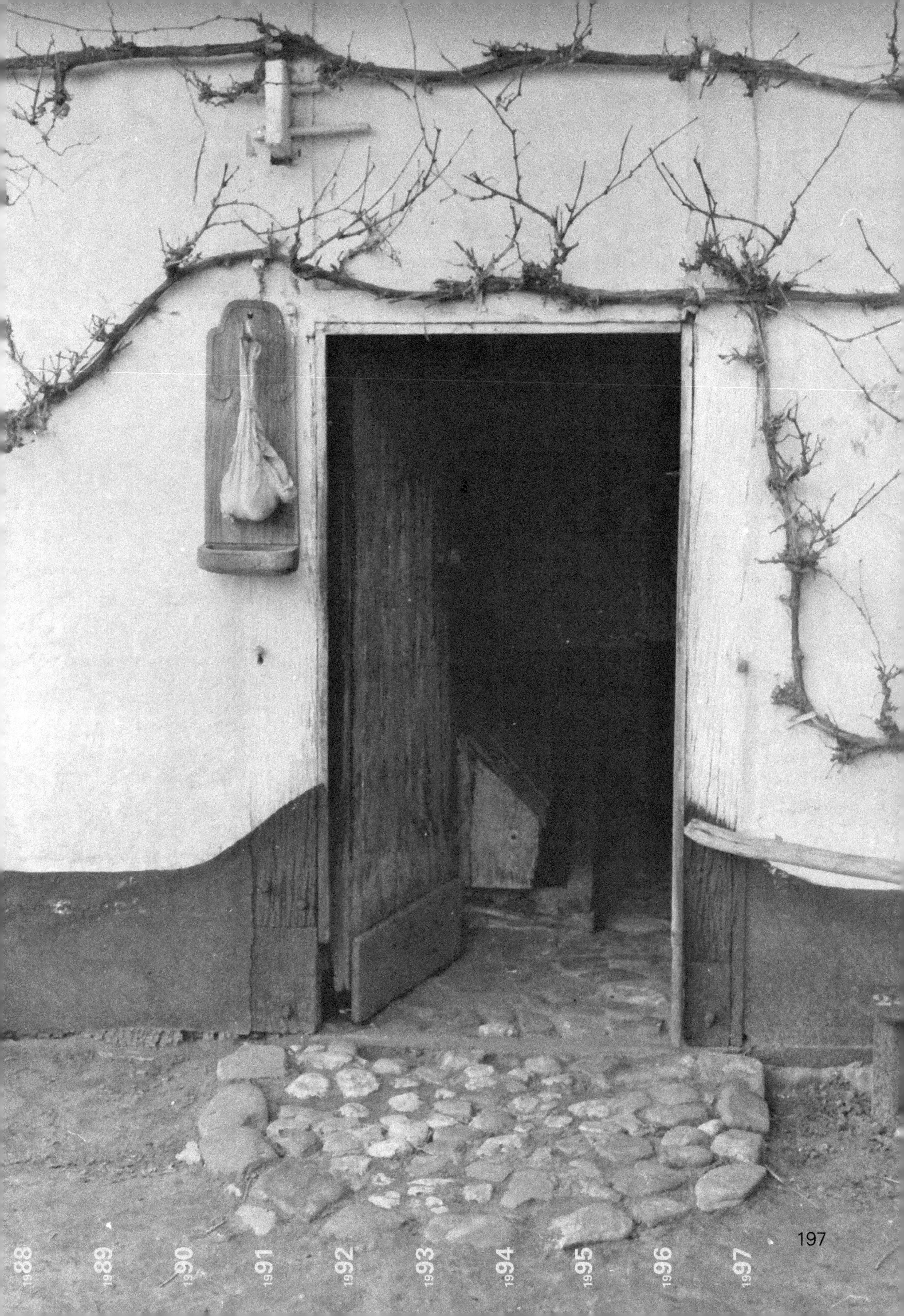
1988
1989
1990
1991
1992
1993
1994
1995
1996
1997

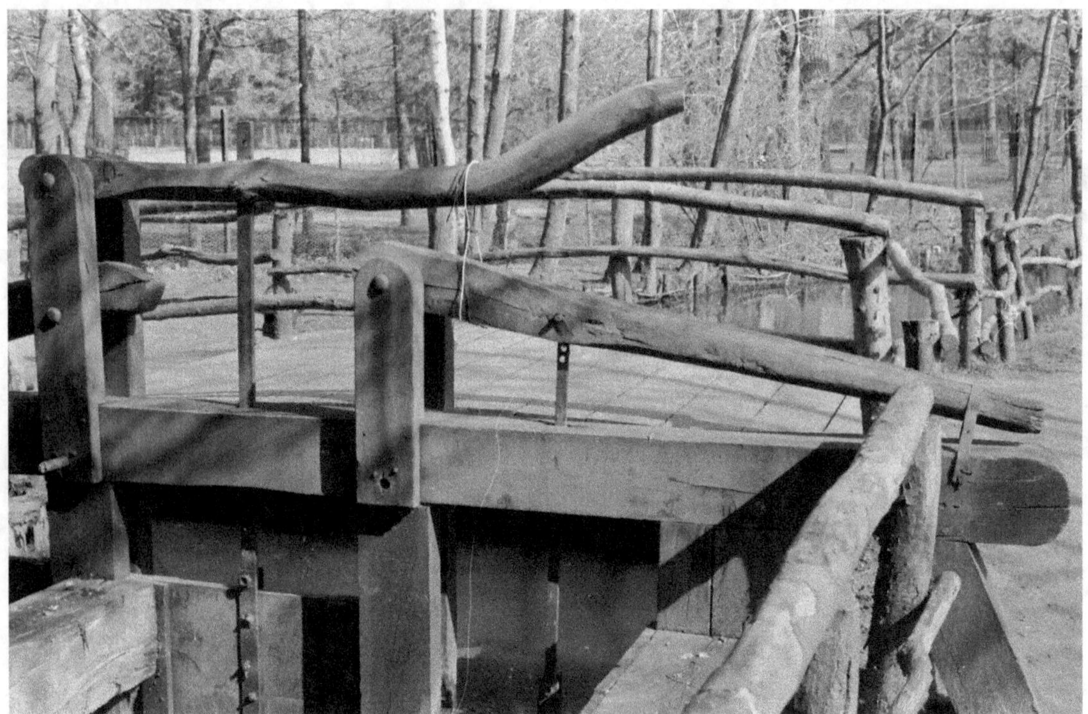

Sluice gate

Water mill

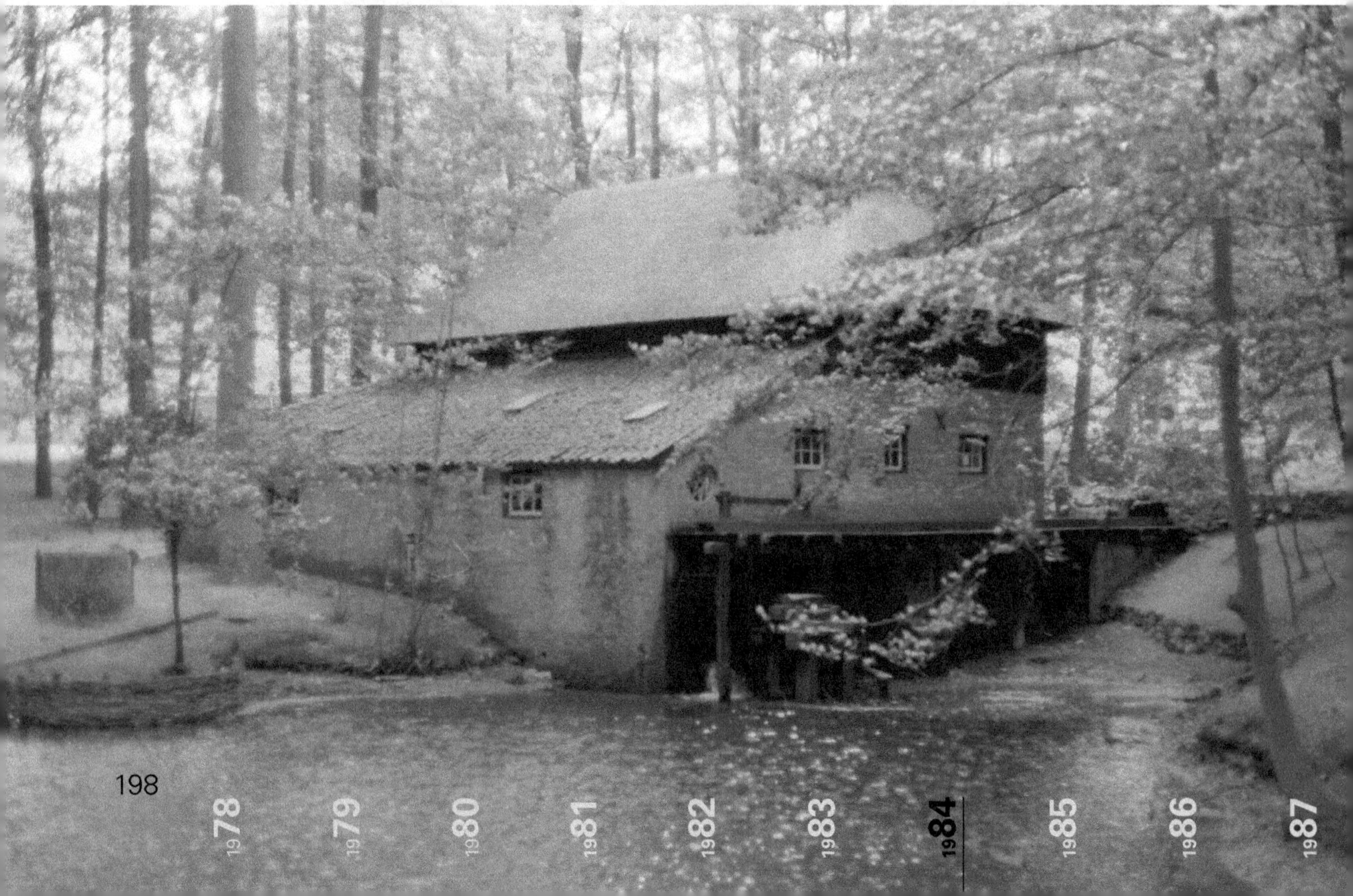

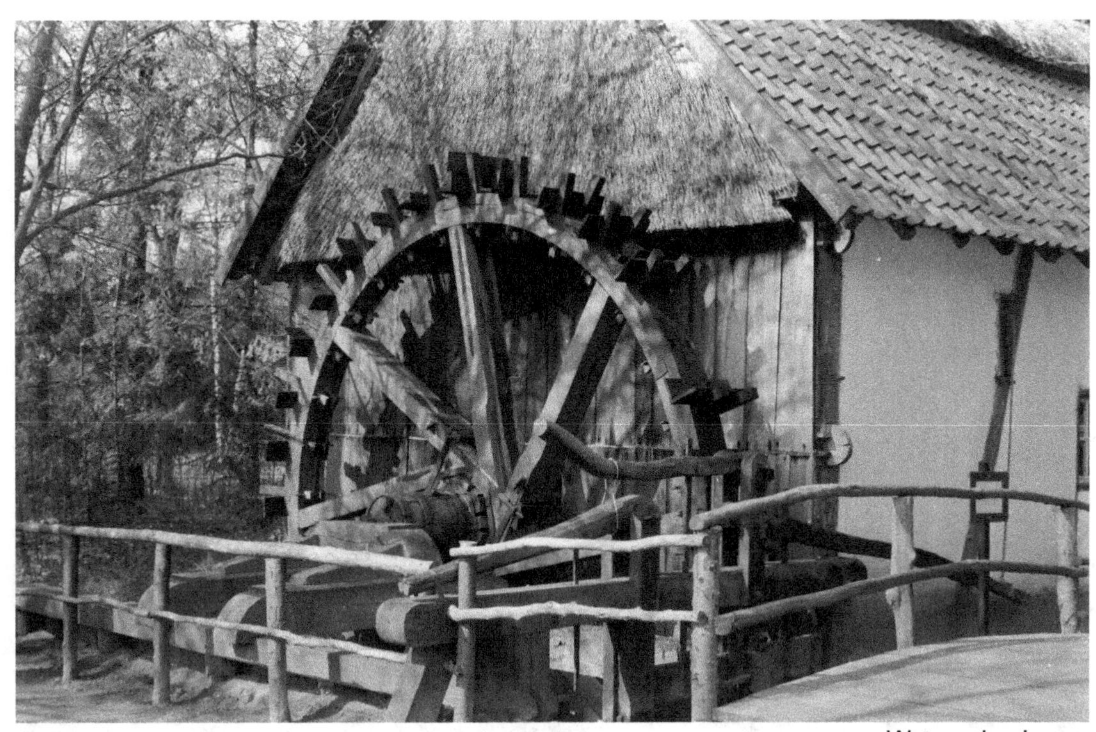

Water wheel

Detail of water wheel

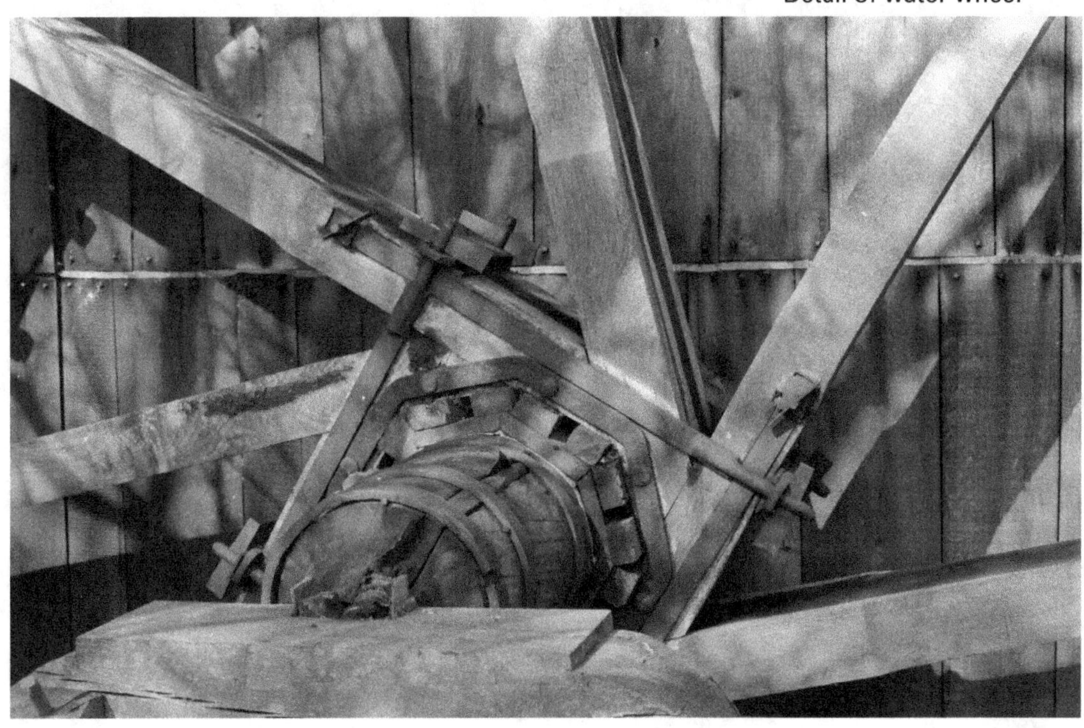

Miriam walking through the woods that are part of the Openlucht Museum

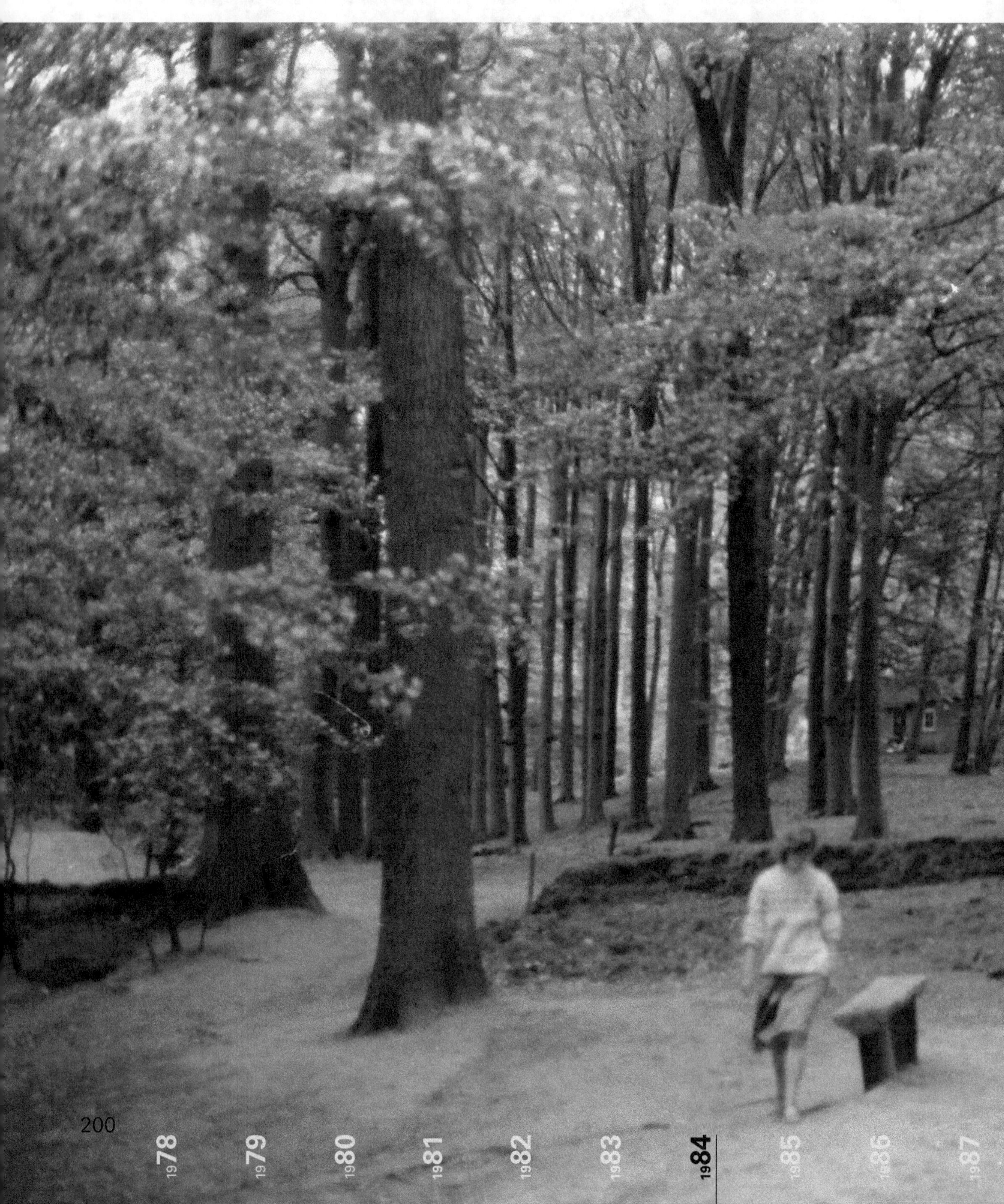

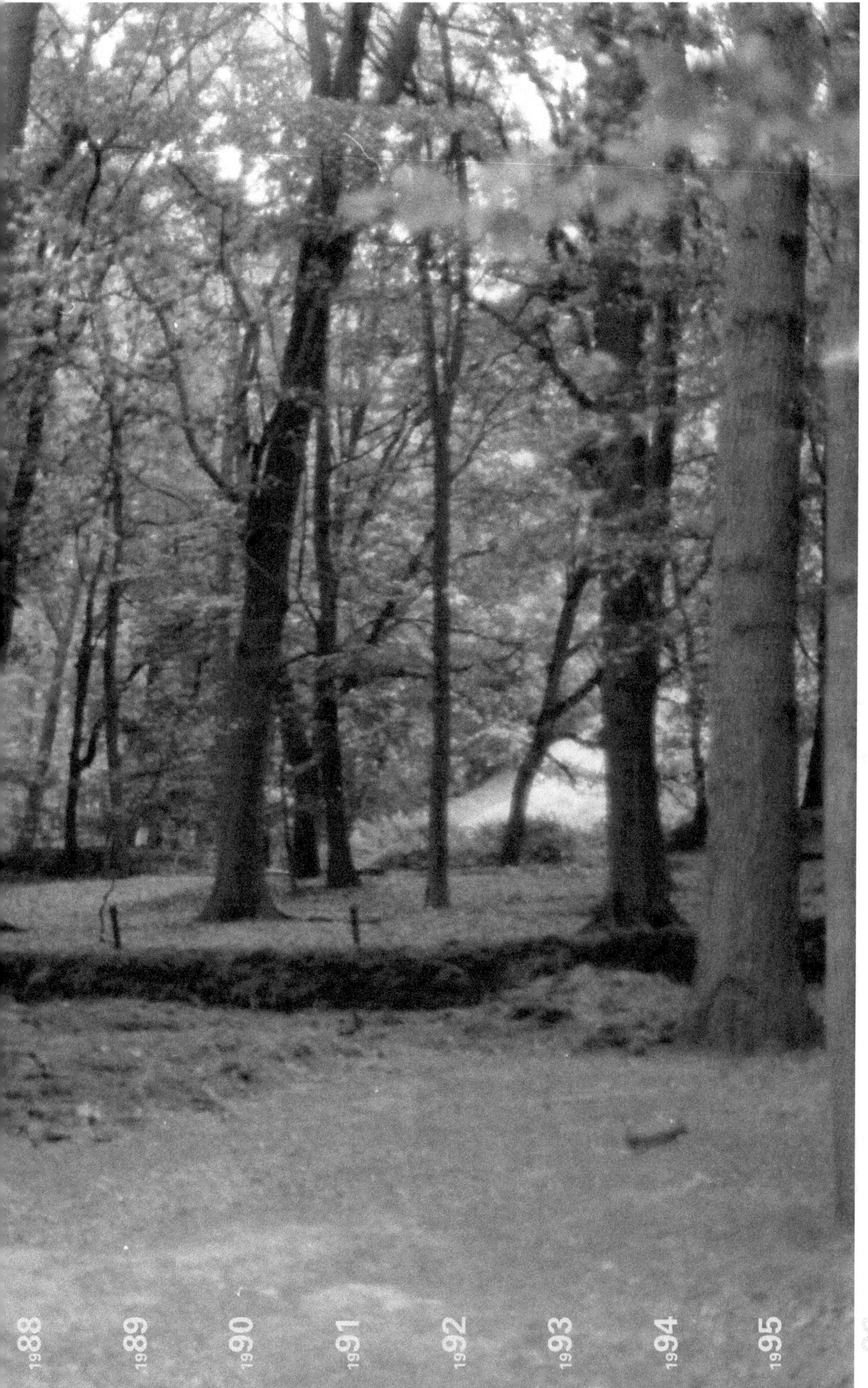

Photography

London, England

In the summer of 1984 we accompanied a group of Martin Cutzé's music students to London, England, ostensibly to assist as chaperones. However, we also did some sightseeing along the way.

The Garrick Theatre on Charing-Cross Road near Leicester Square, London, England, showing "No Sex Please, We're British."

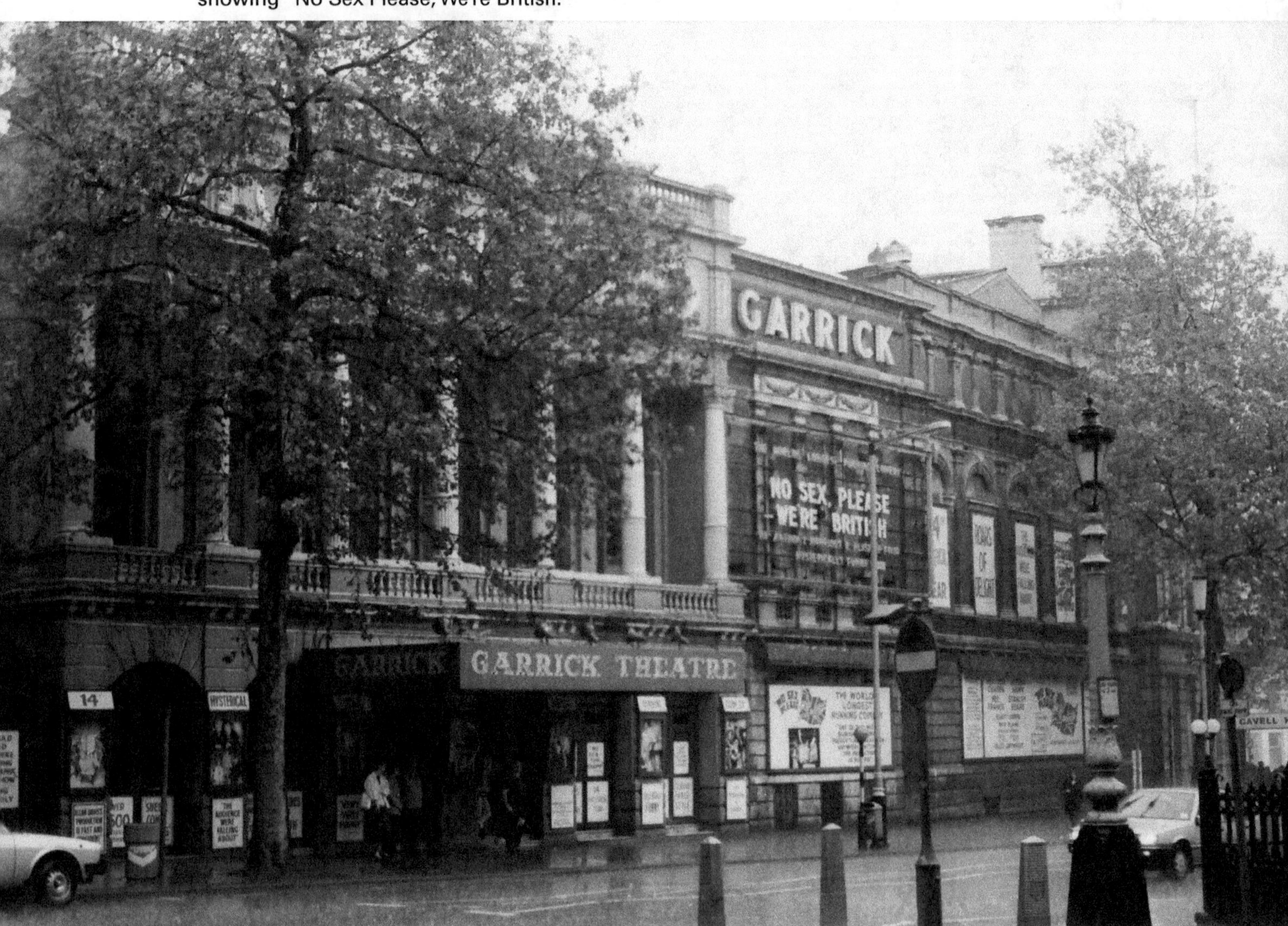

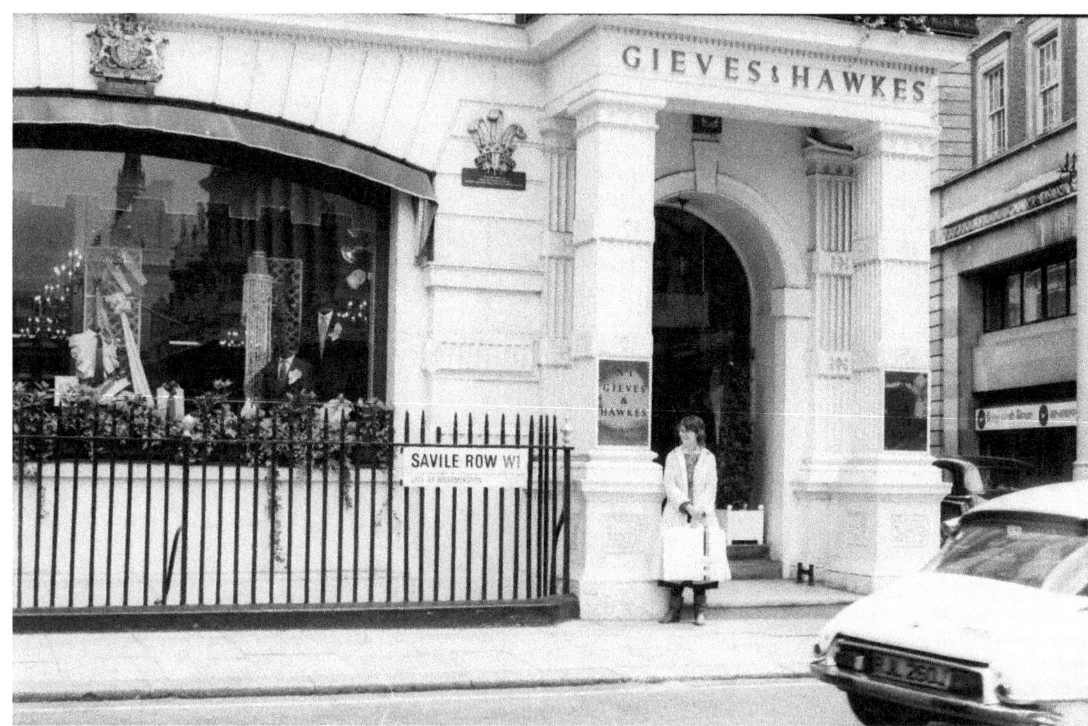

Miriam in front of Gieves & Hawkes on Savile Row. I made a serious gaffe while we were buying a rain coat for Miriam's dad, telling the clerk that we wanted to "purchase a trench coat." I felt stupid pretending to be someone I was not in these haughty premises.

I'm sporting the Gieves & Hawkes trench coat and a bird's nest of a beard in London (photograph by Miriam Zach).

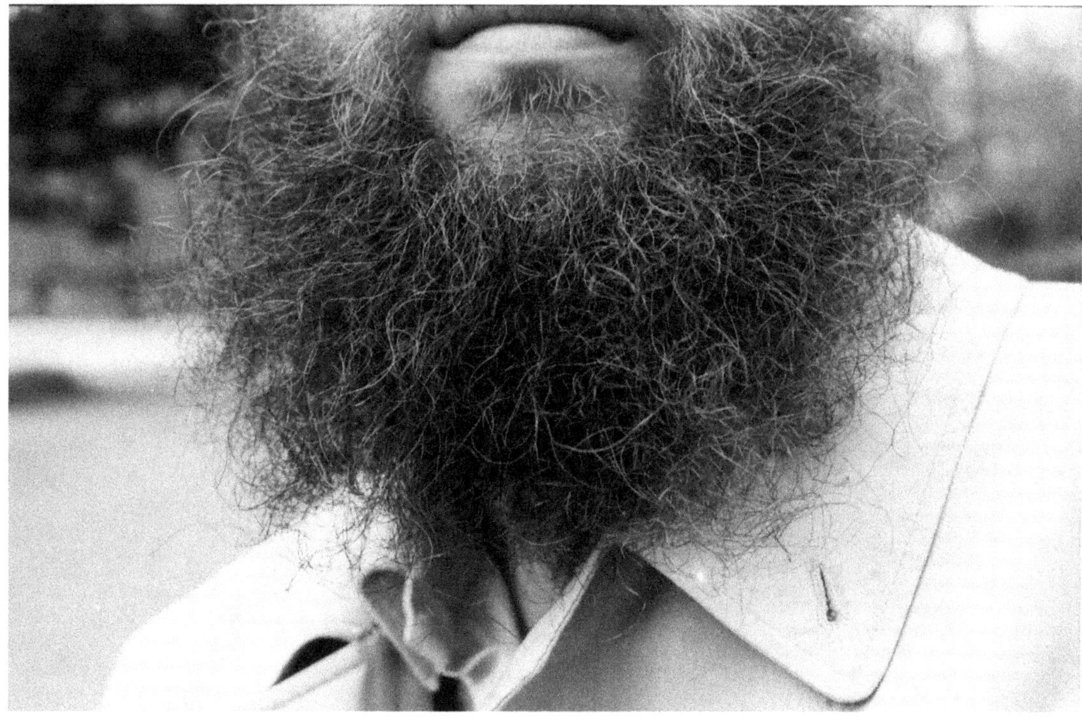

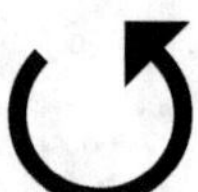

Notting Hill Gate subway station >

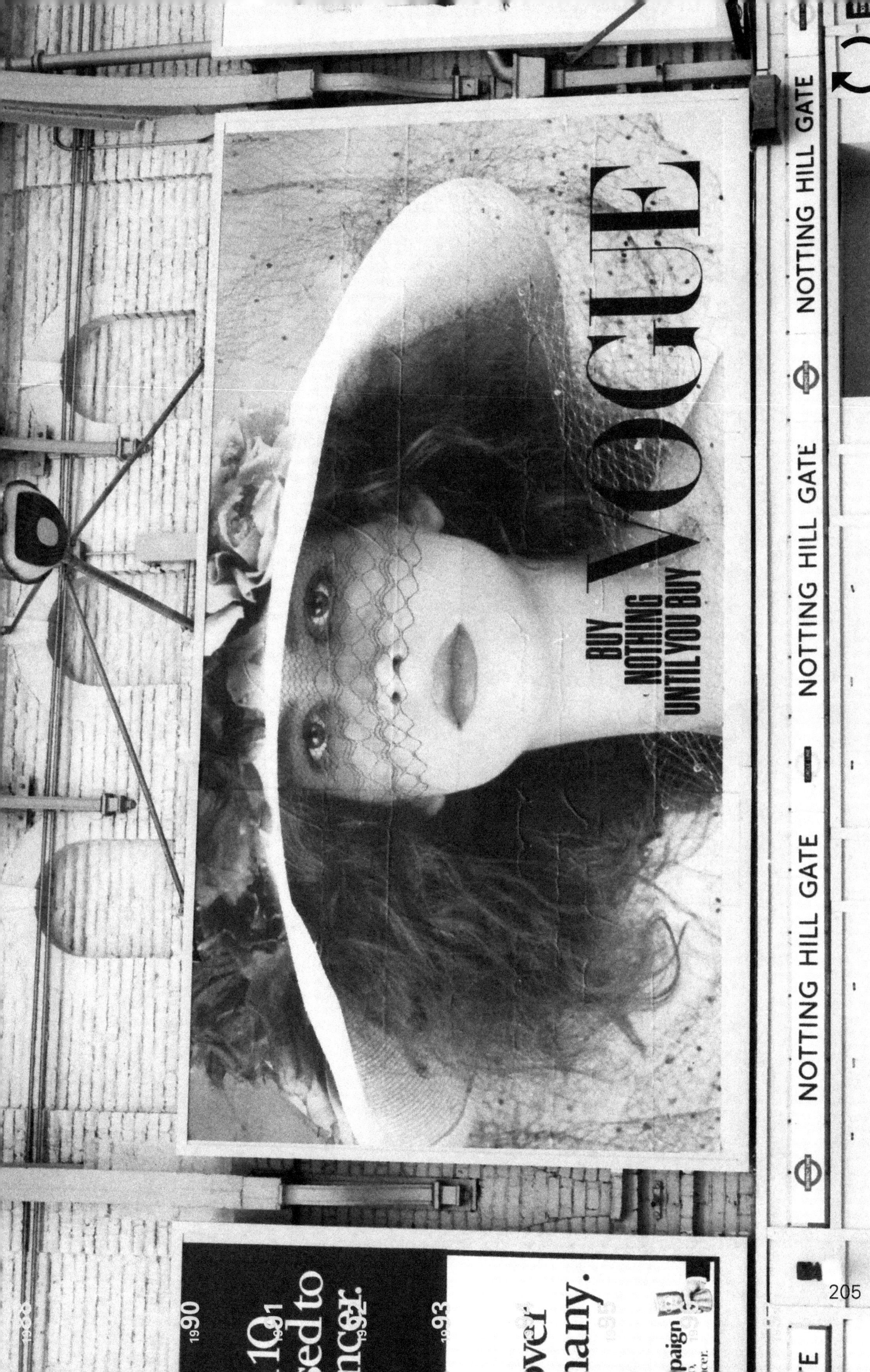
BUY
NOTHING
UNTIL YOU BUY
VOGUE
NOTTING HILL GATE
NOTTING HILL GATE
NOTTING HILL GATE
NOTTING HILL GATE

oil on canvas

Copy and Translation of Art: Oil Painting

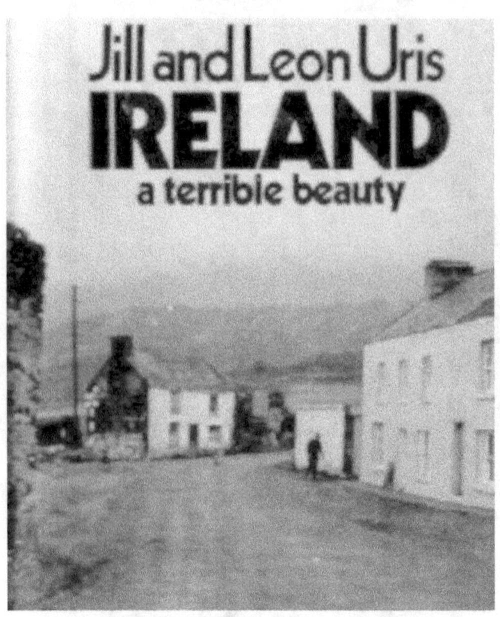

My dad would bring home long and skinny newspaper print rolls, discarded from the enormous printing press at the end of a print run before a new fat roll was put in place. For me the five-feet wide by fifty-feet long blank, creamy white paper was an invitation to redraw what I saw, which was, at that point, mostly images that detained me: TV stars and comic images, preferably from the Asterix series, written by René Goscinny and illustrated by Albert Uderzo. I recall drawing, in color pencil and water color the scene of Cleopatra's arrival by galleon from the Asterix and Cleopatra book as a 10′ x 6′ illustration, and the mug of the TV personality Rudi Carrell from a cover page of HörZu. Later I broadened my pallette and started to use oil paint, mostly because I love the smell of the paint.

Origin (above) and Copy (below)

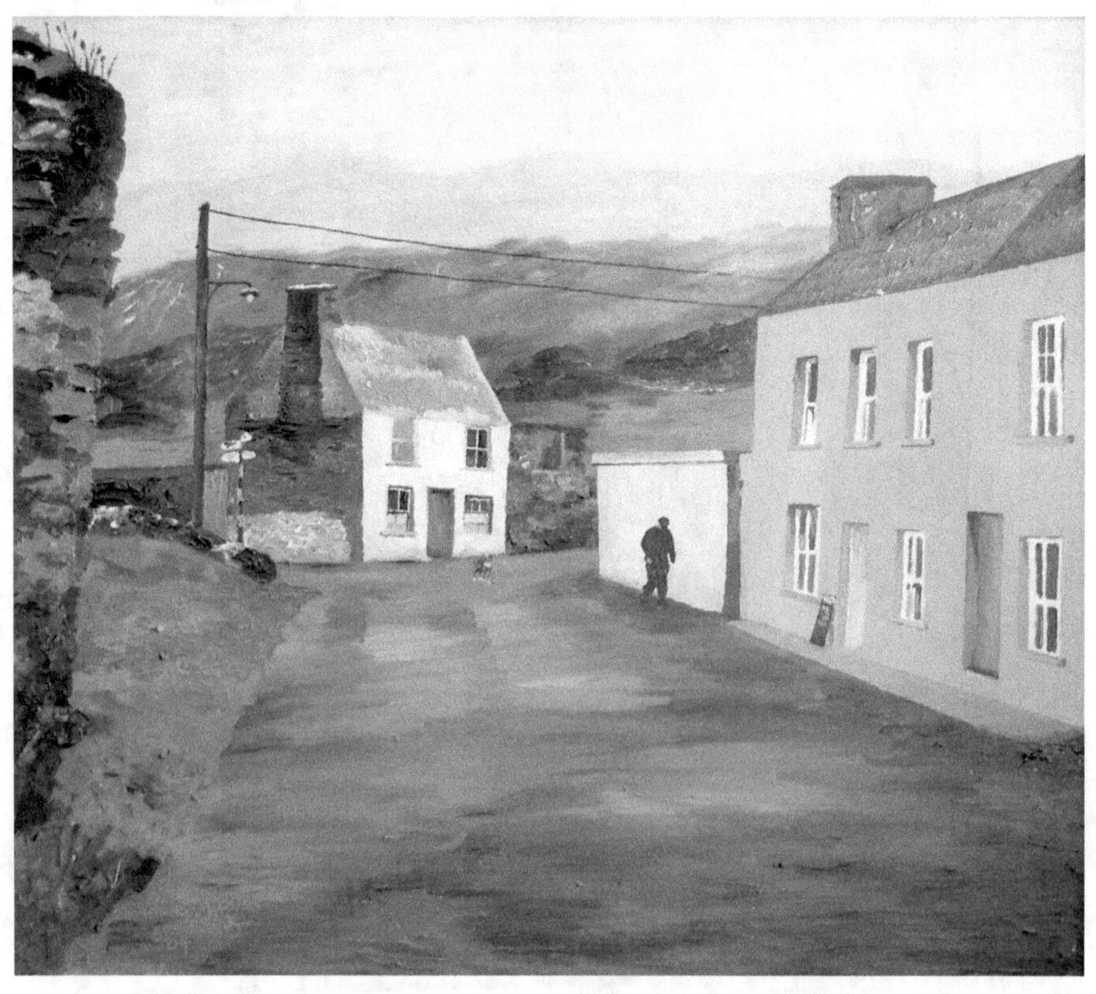

"The original is unfaithful to the translation."
Jorge Lois Borges

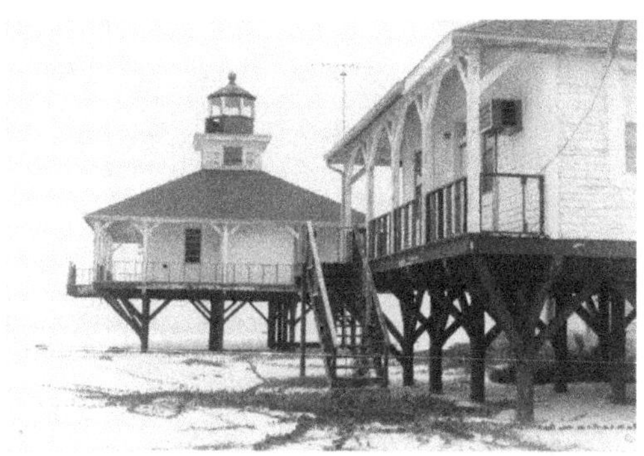

Origin: the old light houses on Sanibel Island, Florida (above)...

...and my translation with Miriam before a rising storm (below)

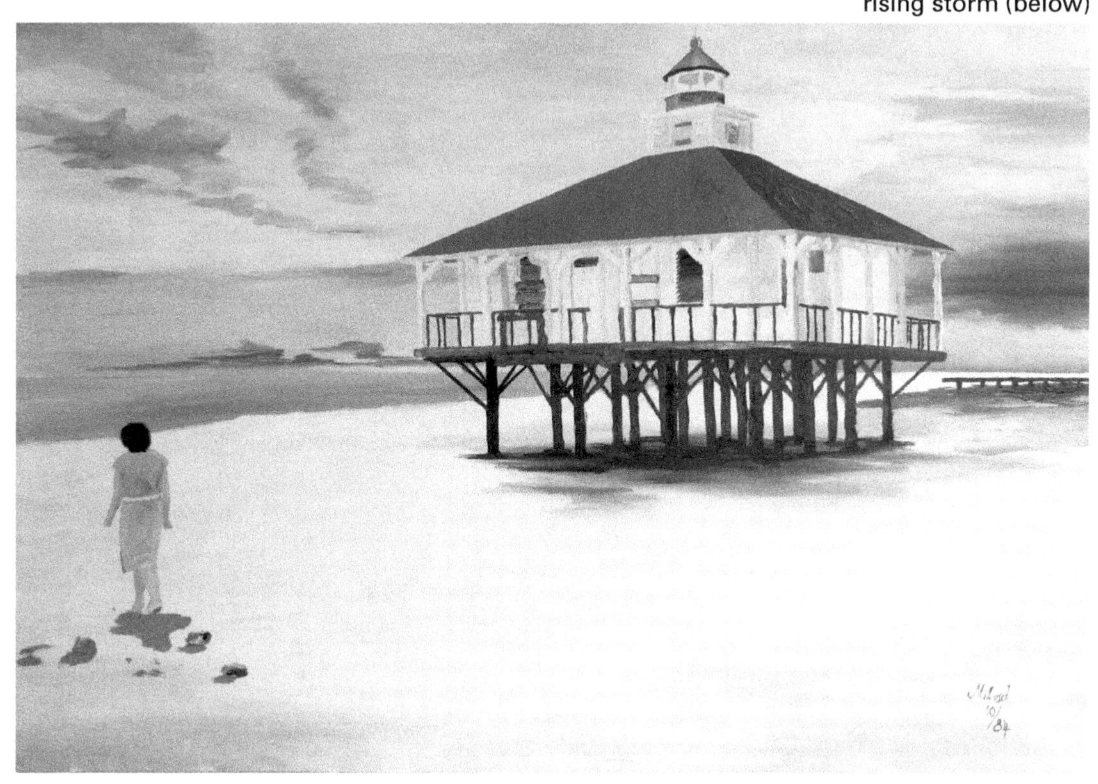

1985

Drawing

pencil on paper

Chicken or Egg? >
after René Magritte

Self portrait as *Der Souffleur* (The Prompter)
based on a piece by André Heller

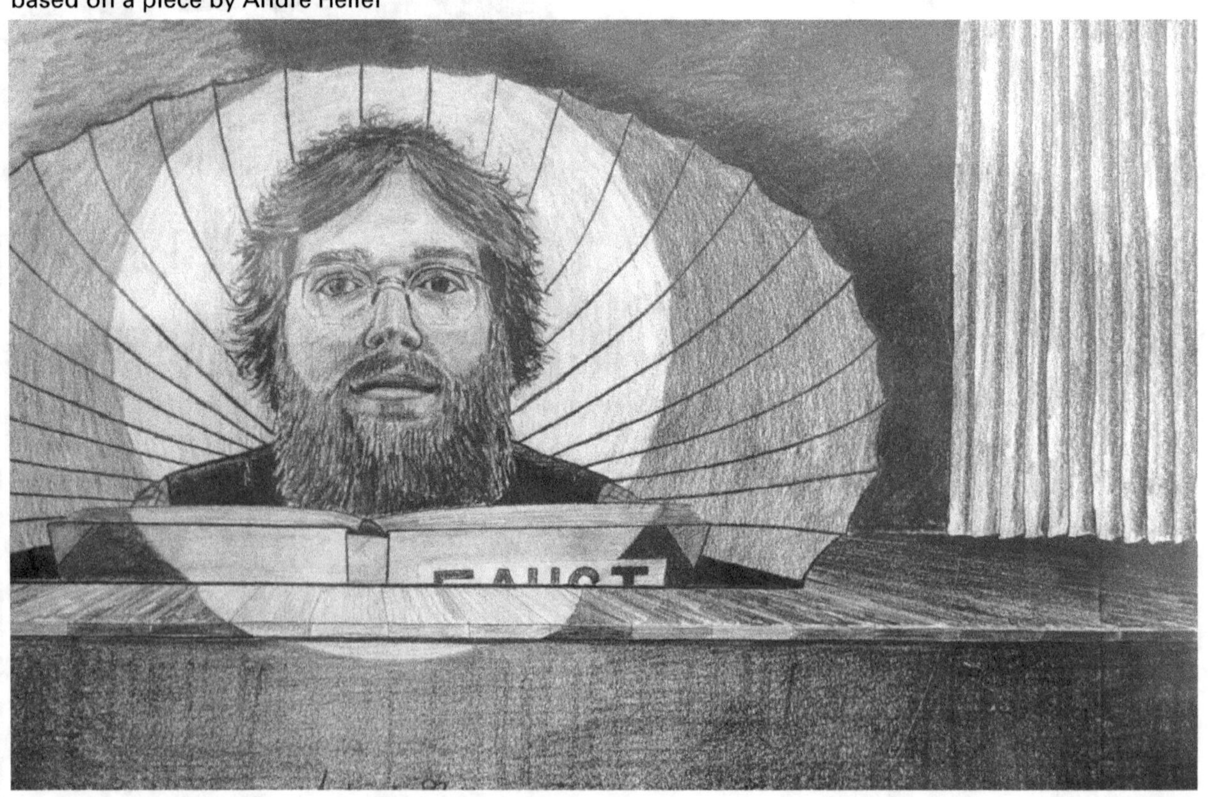

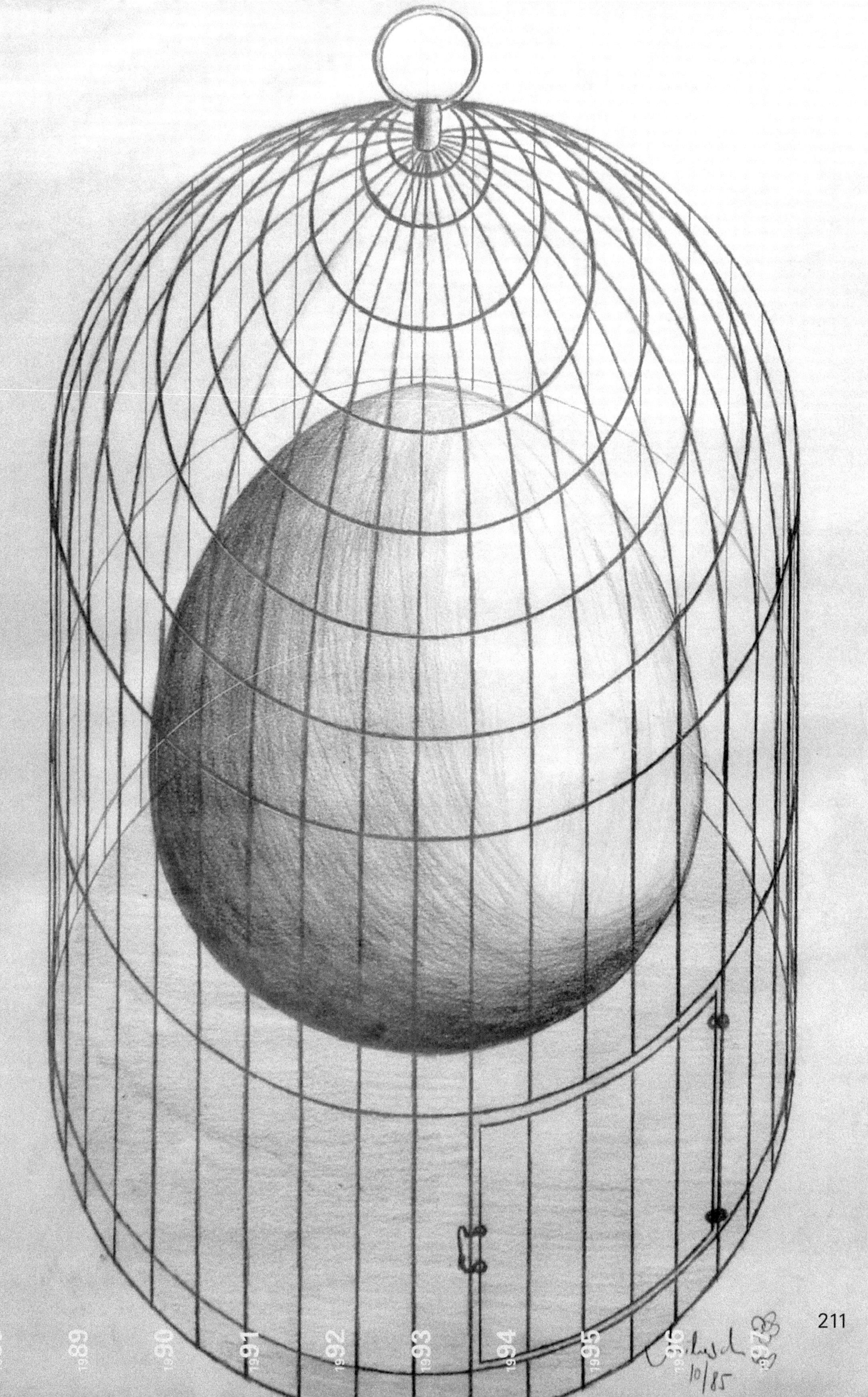

Photography

Chauffeur
Travel from Illinois to Florida

In the fall of 1985 I drove Miriam's parents from Waukegan to their winter place in Port Charlotte, FL in a Chevy Van with a, for my experience, big V8 engine. Along the way I took photographs.

American vernacular: somewhere between Waukegan, IL, and Port Charlotte, FL

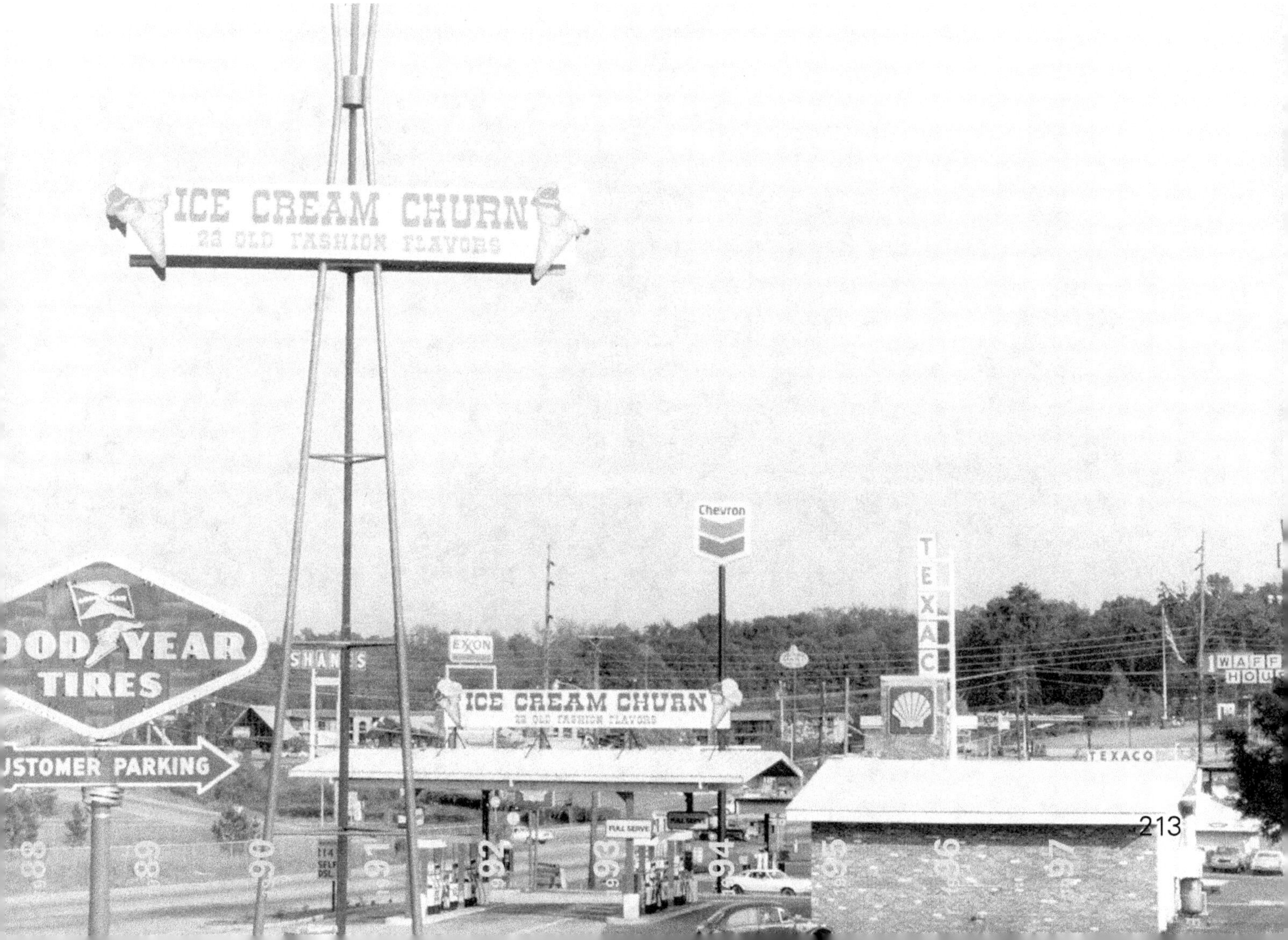

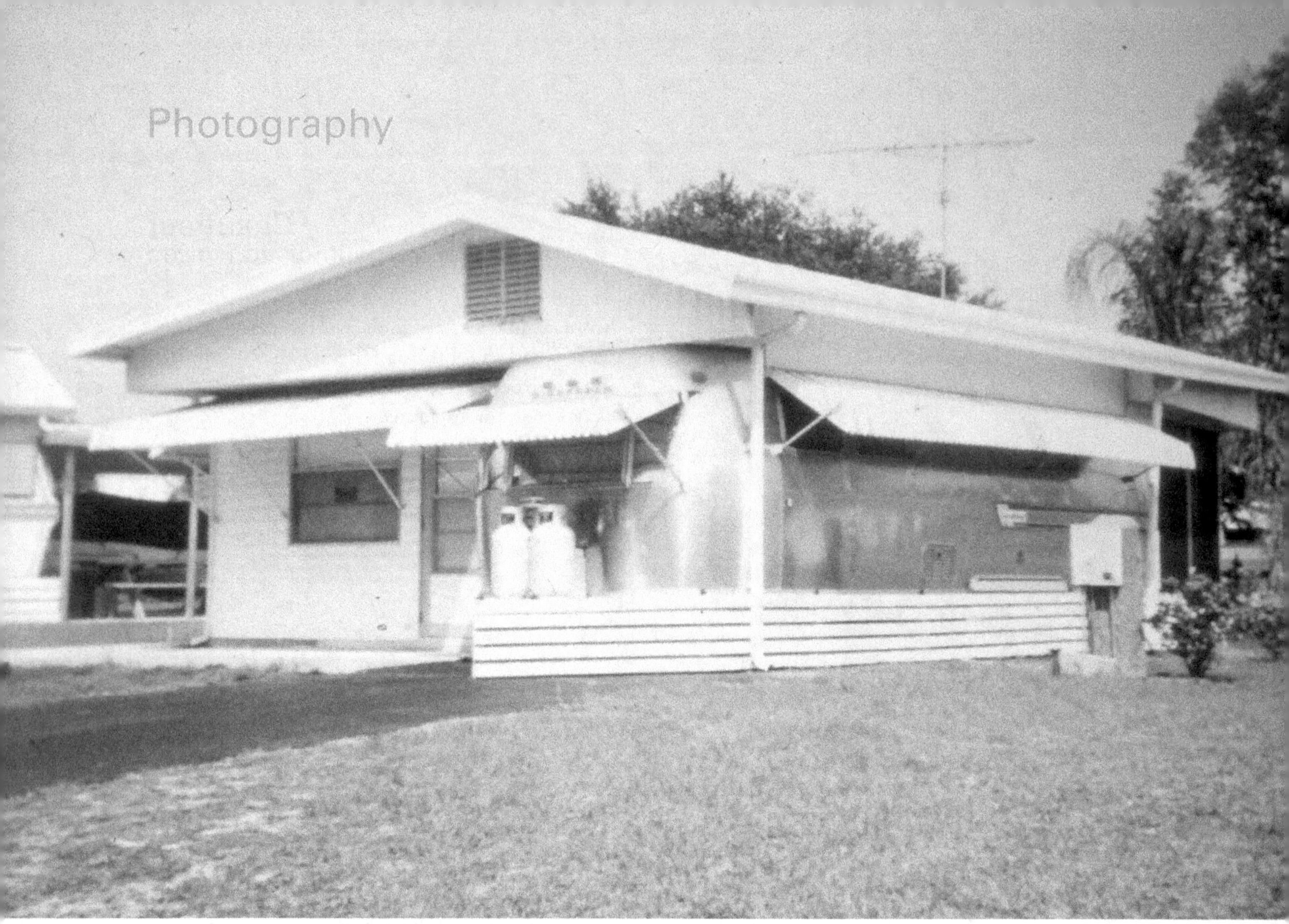

Hybrid housing: Airstream trailers and Florida park-models in Saddlebag, Lake Wales, Florida

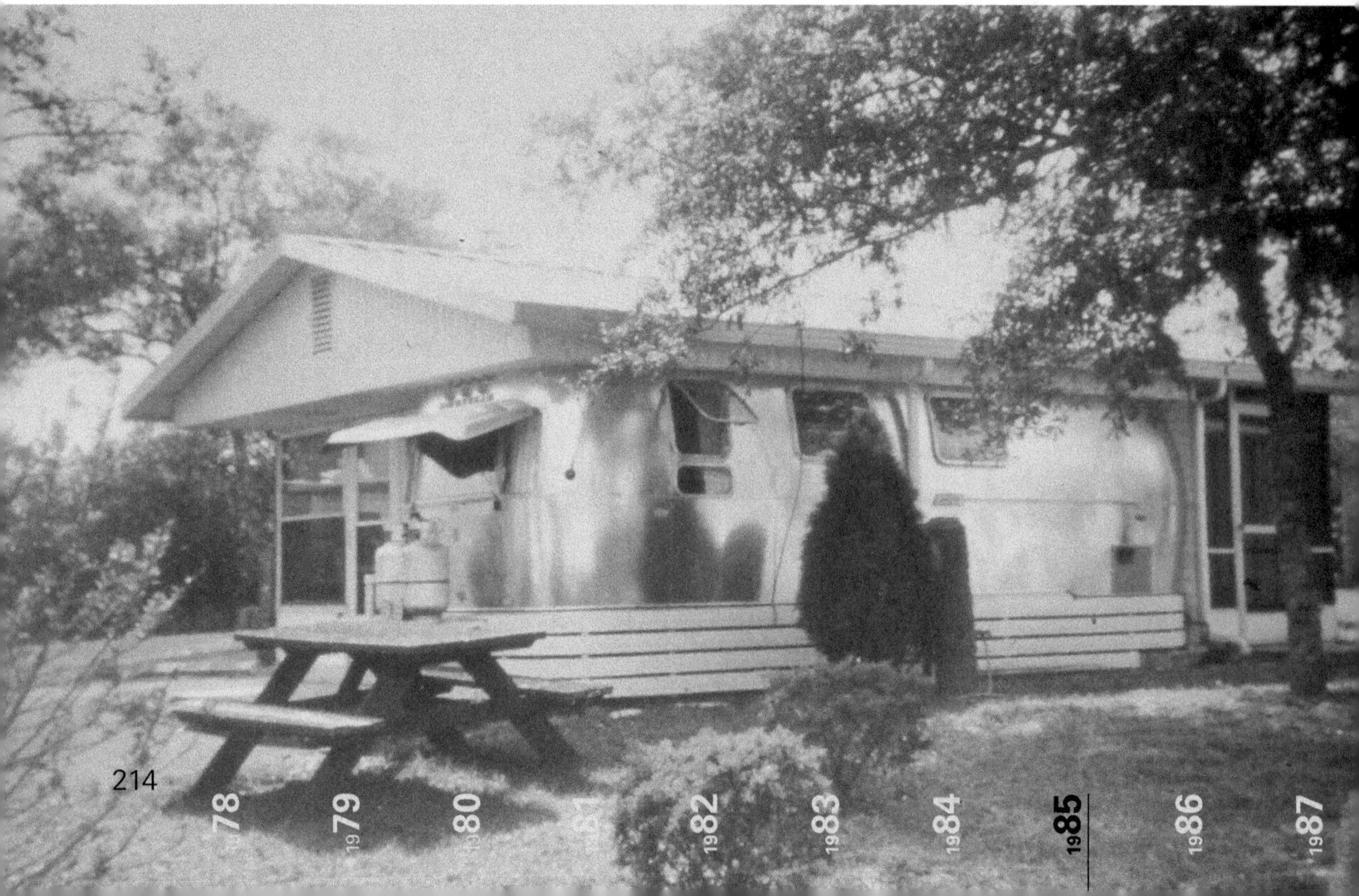

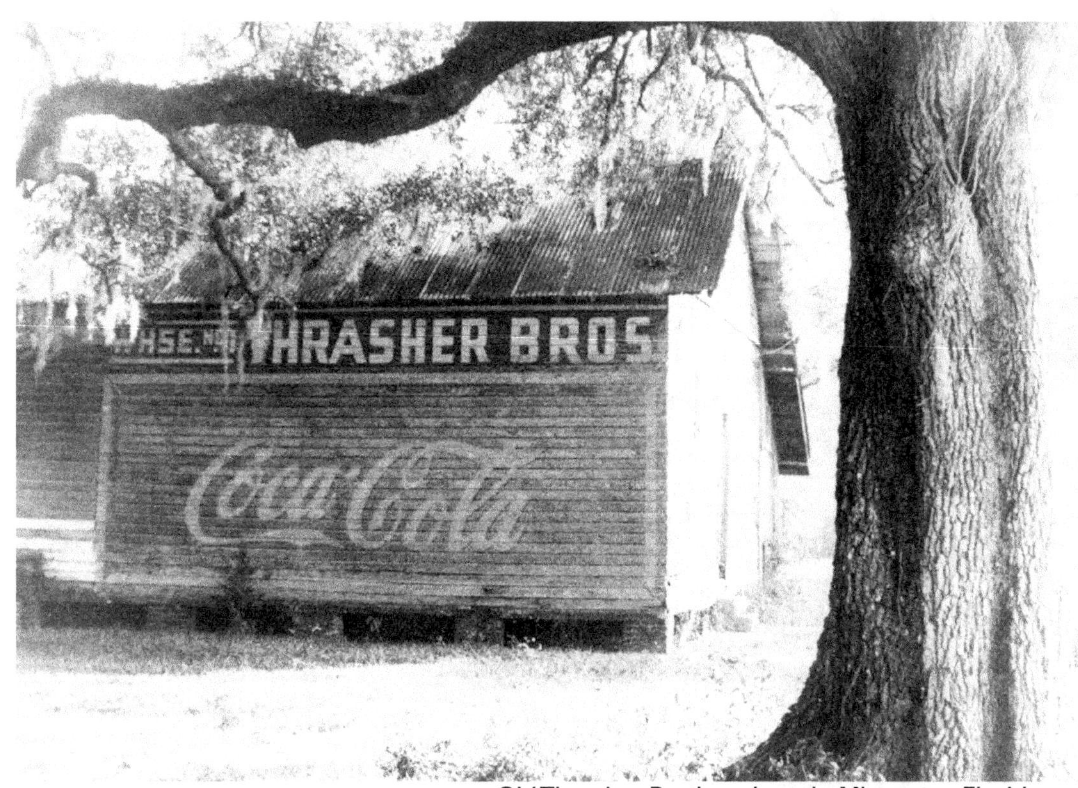

Old Thrasher Brothers barn in Micanopy, Florida

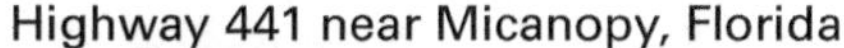
Highway 441 near Micanopy, Florida

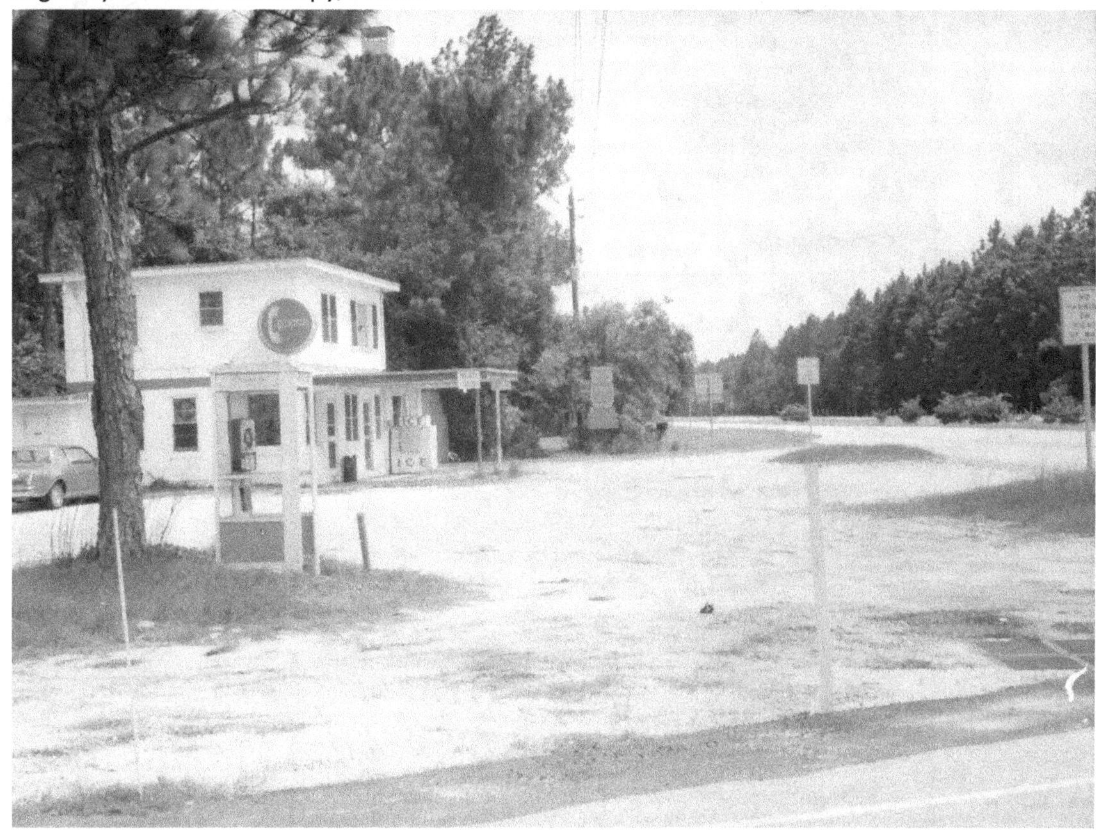

On the road to Hawthorne, Florida, during a typical torrential rain storm

1988
1989
1990
1991
1992
1993
1994
1995
1996
1997

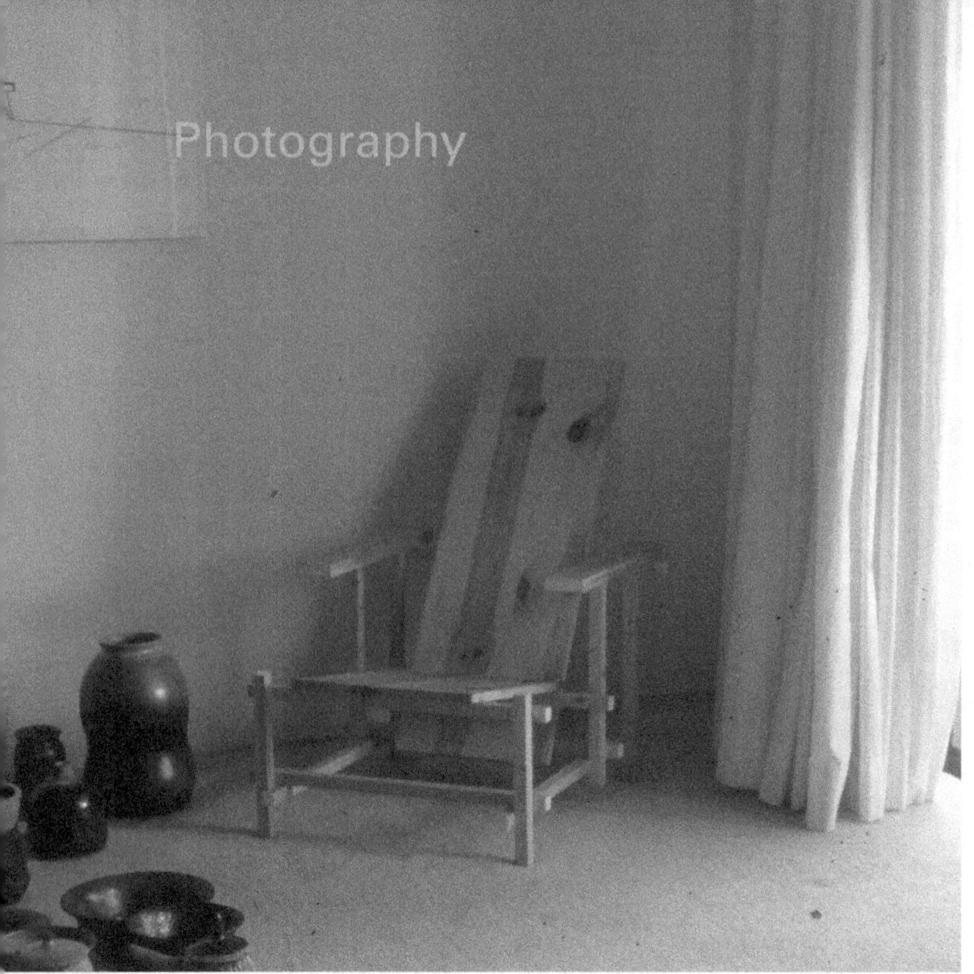

Gaineswood Apartments, Unit 2-D with 'green' Rietveld chair

Gaineswood Apartments, Unit 1-F, living room with Mikesch

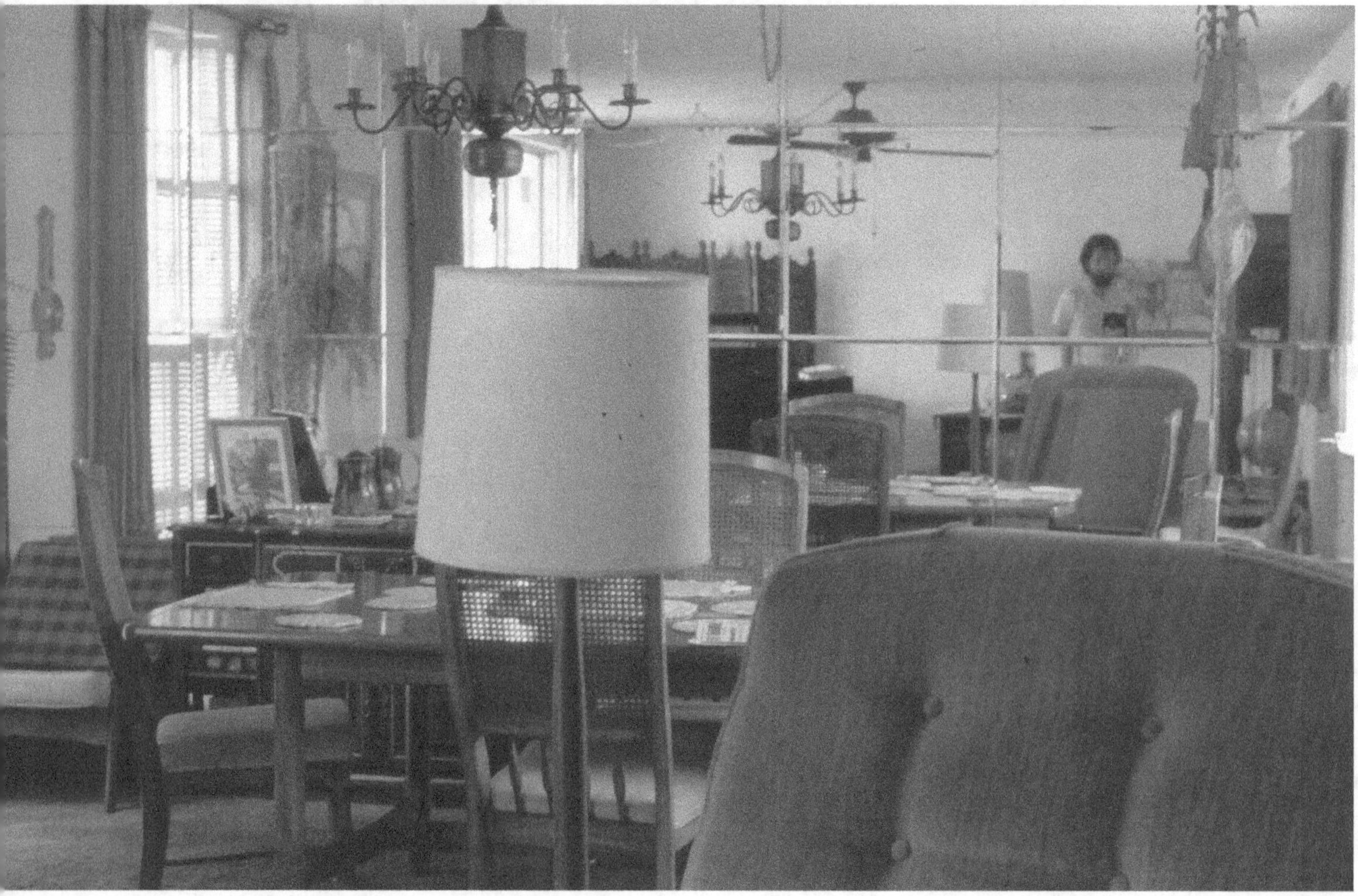

Surreal space: Eucalyptus tree grove near Fort Matanzas, south of Crescent Beach, Florida

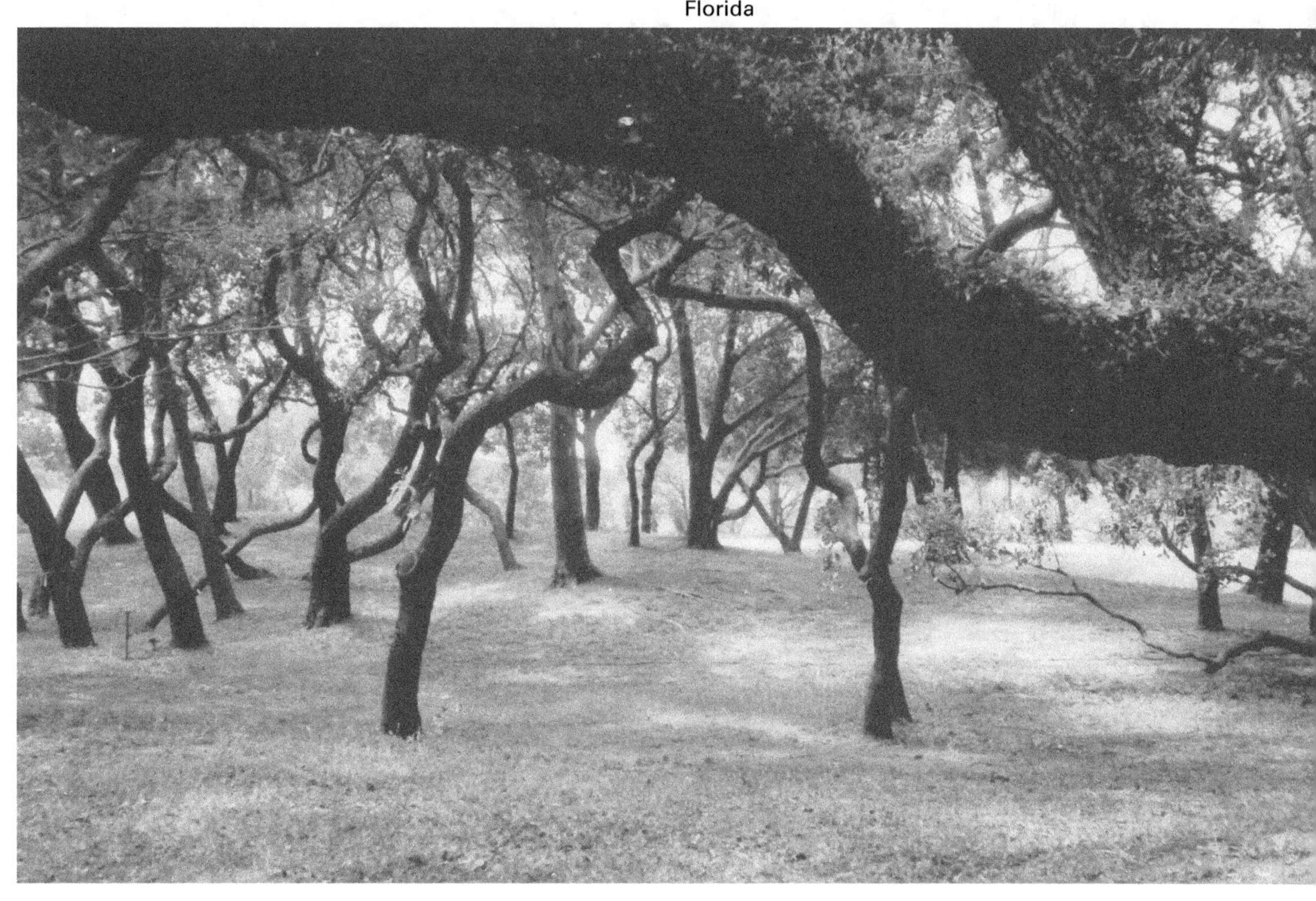

oil on canvas

Copy and Translation of Art: Oil Painting

Sources

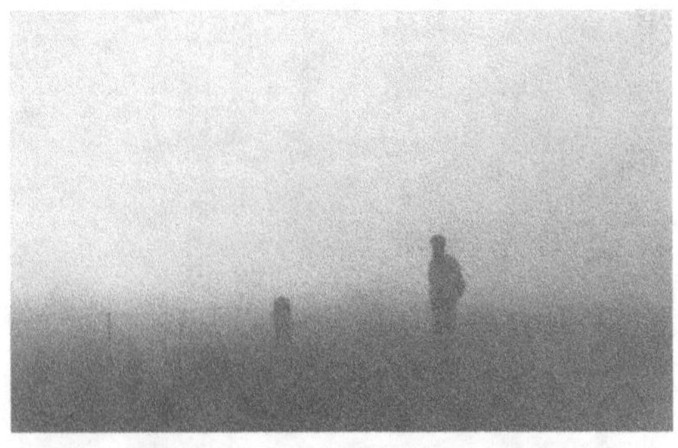

Driving back from Paris to Lemgo we encountered some of the thickest fog I've ever been in. At some point the sun broke through the soup and we took some pictures (photograph by Miriam Zach).

During one of my winter vacations in Wyk auf Föhr I took a few photographs of the almost empty beach. The melancholy was palpable.

The final oilpainting (18″ x 24″)

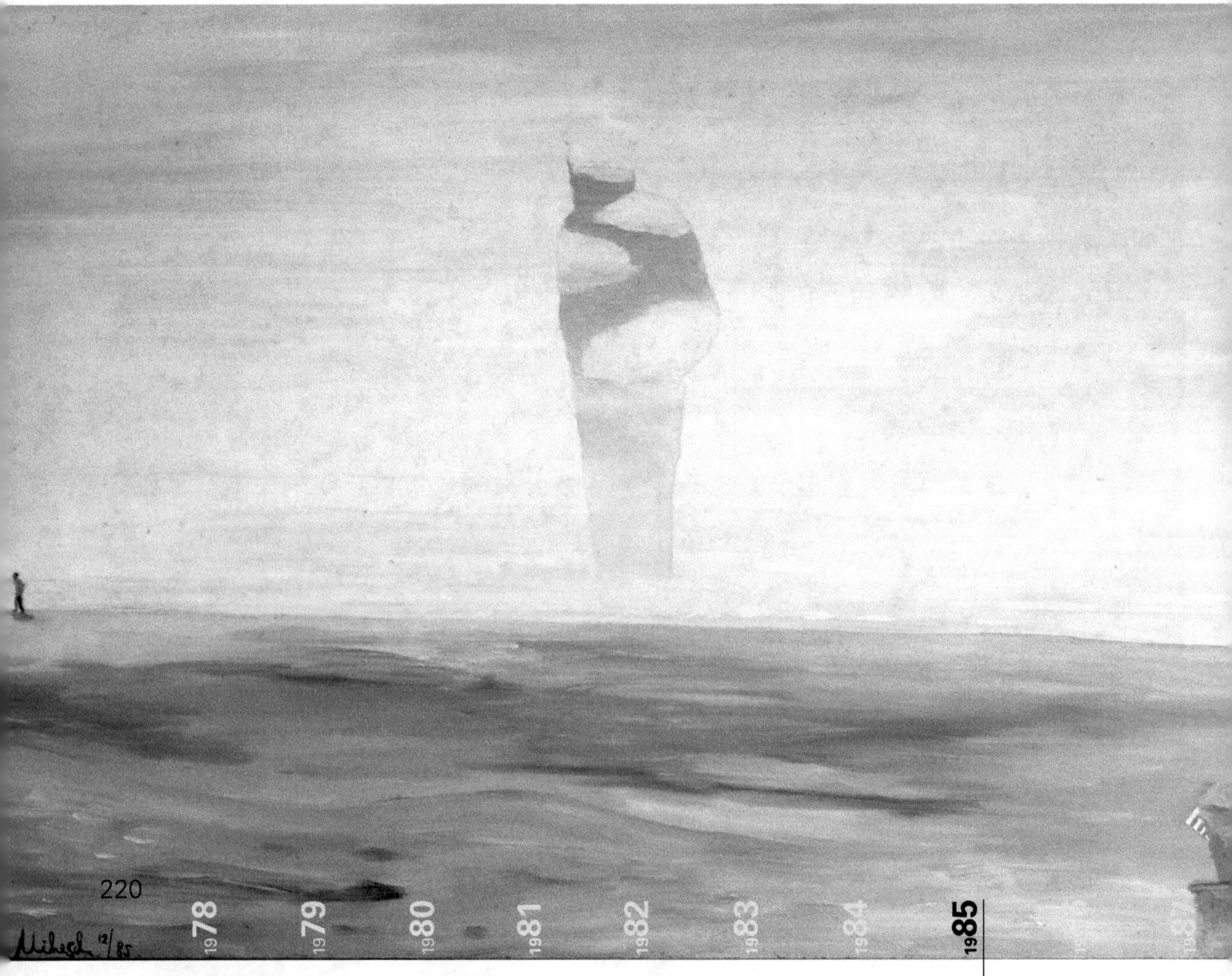

Source

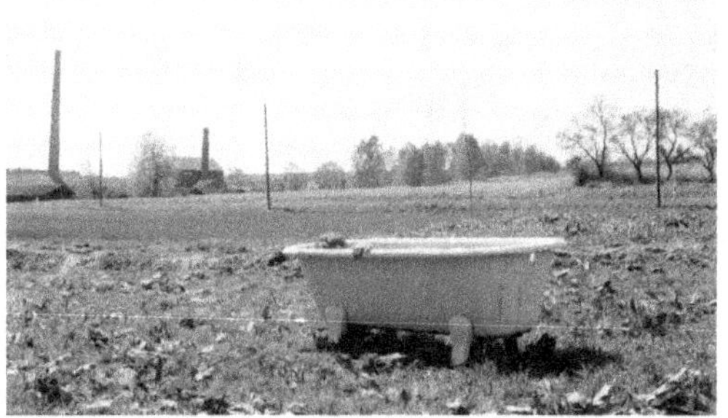

Final painting, inspired by Magritte but without the talent (18″ x 24″)

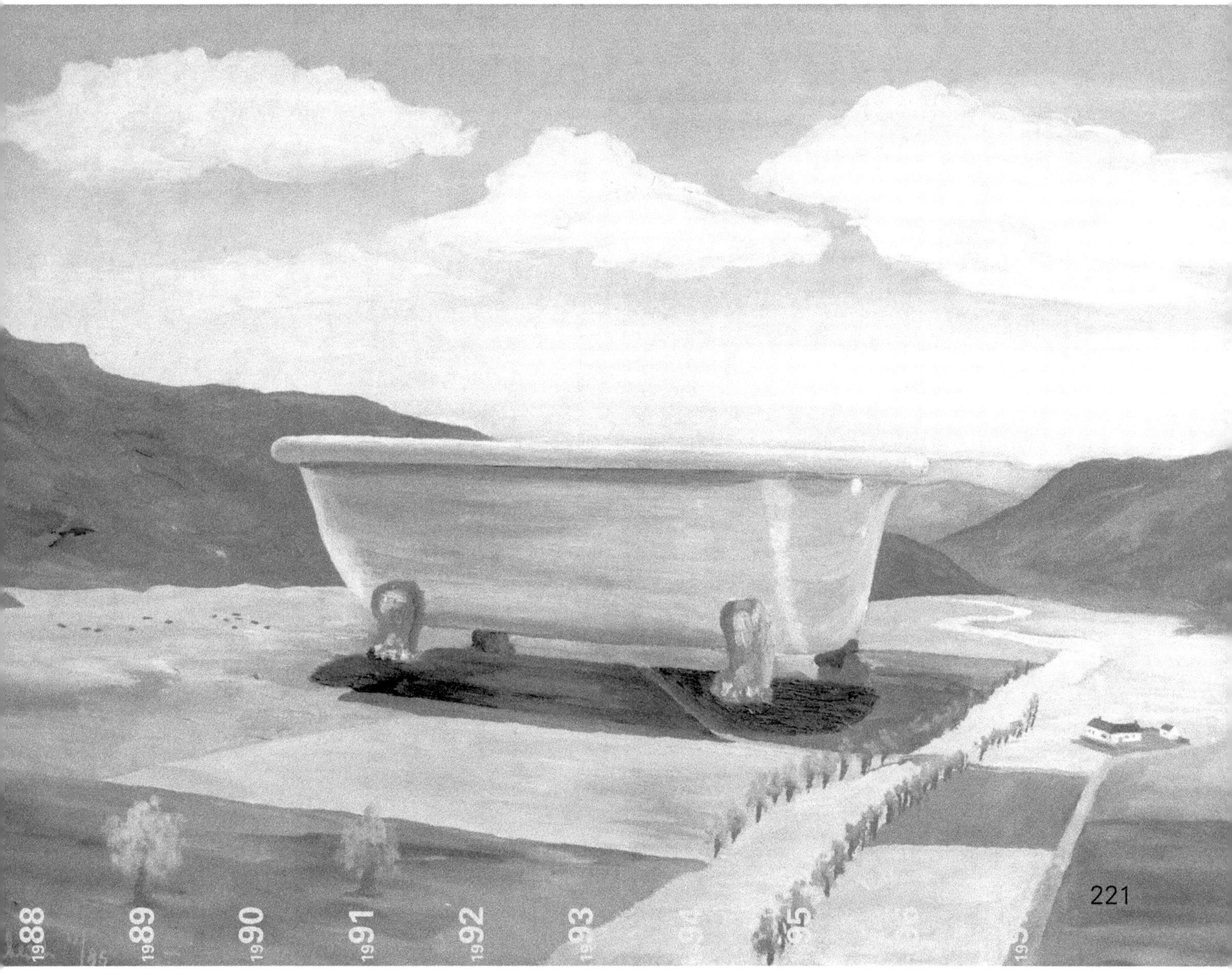

Painting

oil on canvas

Still inspired by Magritte and his word + thing theory (words and things have arbitrary connections), I was tracking German compound words. In this case *Streichinstrument* (literally brush instrument) is a pun on stringed instruments like a violin, and its equivalent in the graphical arts to a brush. *Streichen* can mean both painting and playing a stringed musical instrument, oil painting (24″ x 36″) >

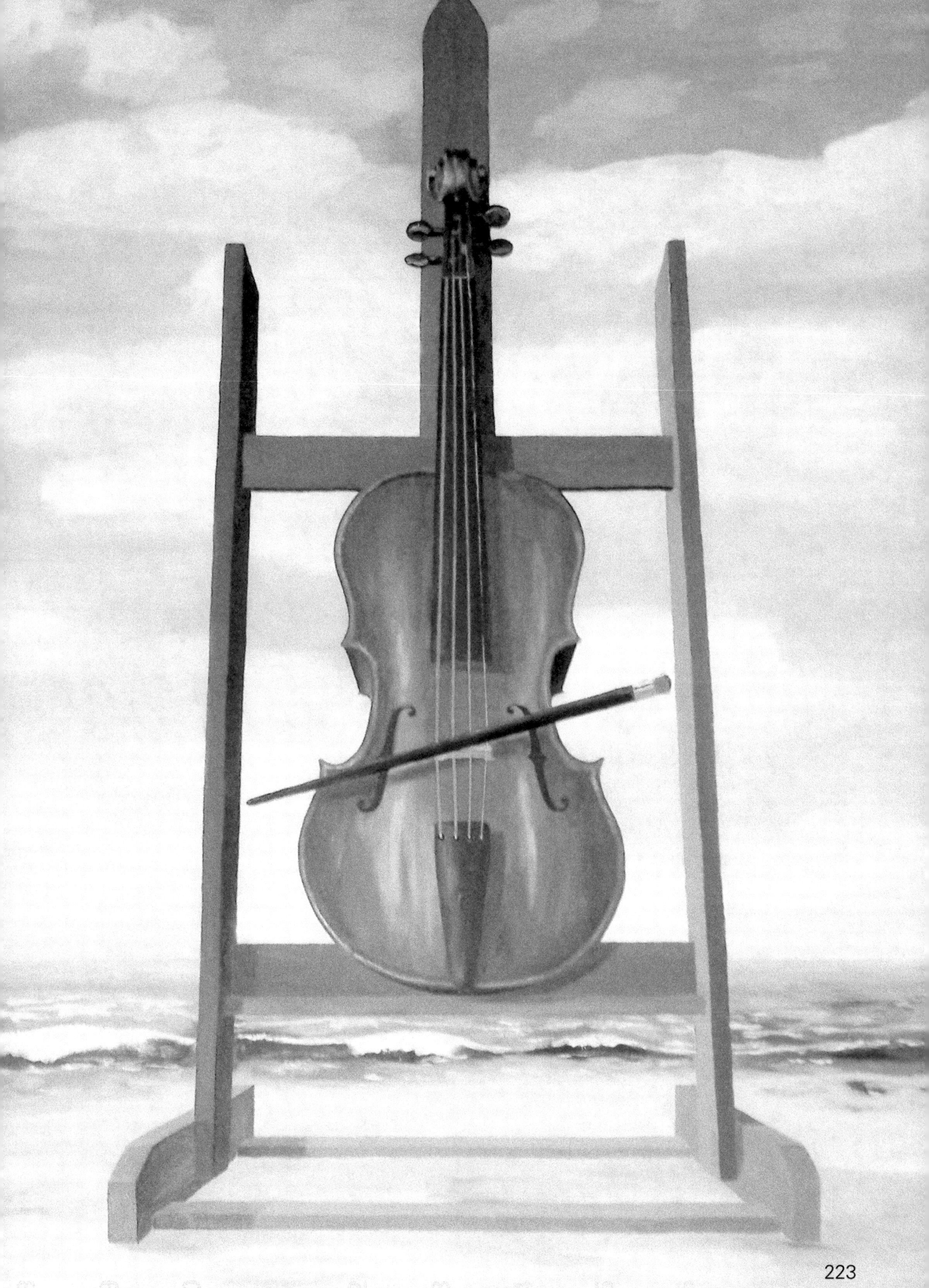

1986

Painting

oil on canvas

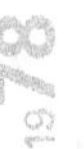

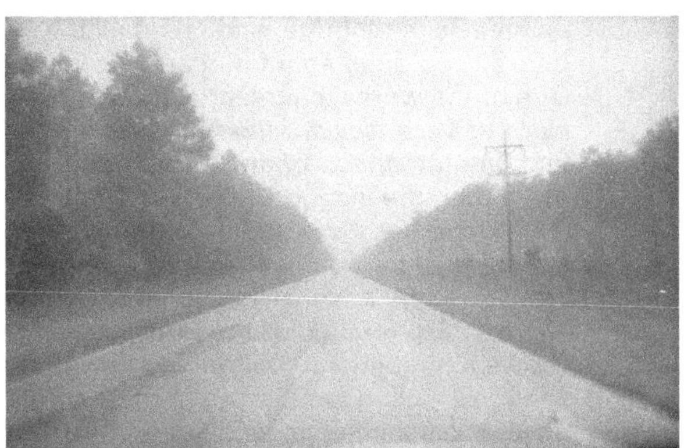

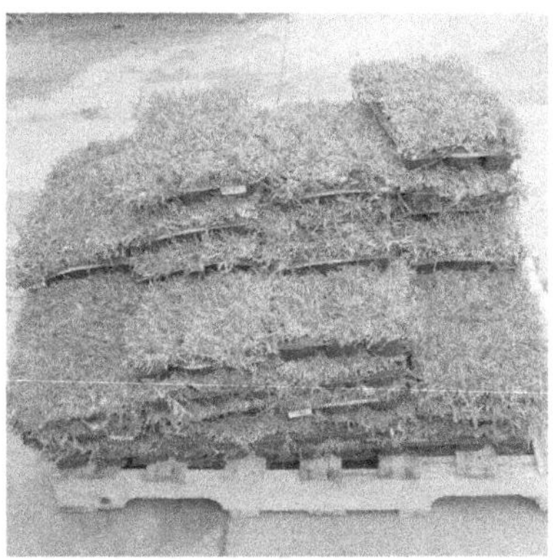

For me Florida has always conjured death. After one of the many days filled with sudden downpours the sweet smell of decay permeates the humid air. Since watching *Stranger than Paradise*, and then moving to the state in 1985, the landscape of Florida has always seemed temporal. During our time in Gainesville we worked as weekend gardeners at Bob and Millie's round house, pulling weeds on Saturday mornings. The plants would grow with astonishing speed, especially the wysteria, which I called 'snake plant' because you could almost see it grow and slither snakelike through the thicket of a hedge above and below ground. I was convinced then that nature in short order would take back what humans had wrested from it. The painting below was based on a photograph I took of the then still two-lane Highway 20 between Gainesville and Hawthorne, shortly after a torrential rain. I imagined the road taken over by plants, and a large sod piece hovering threateningly over the asphalt.

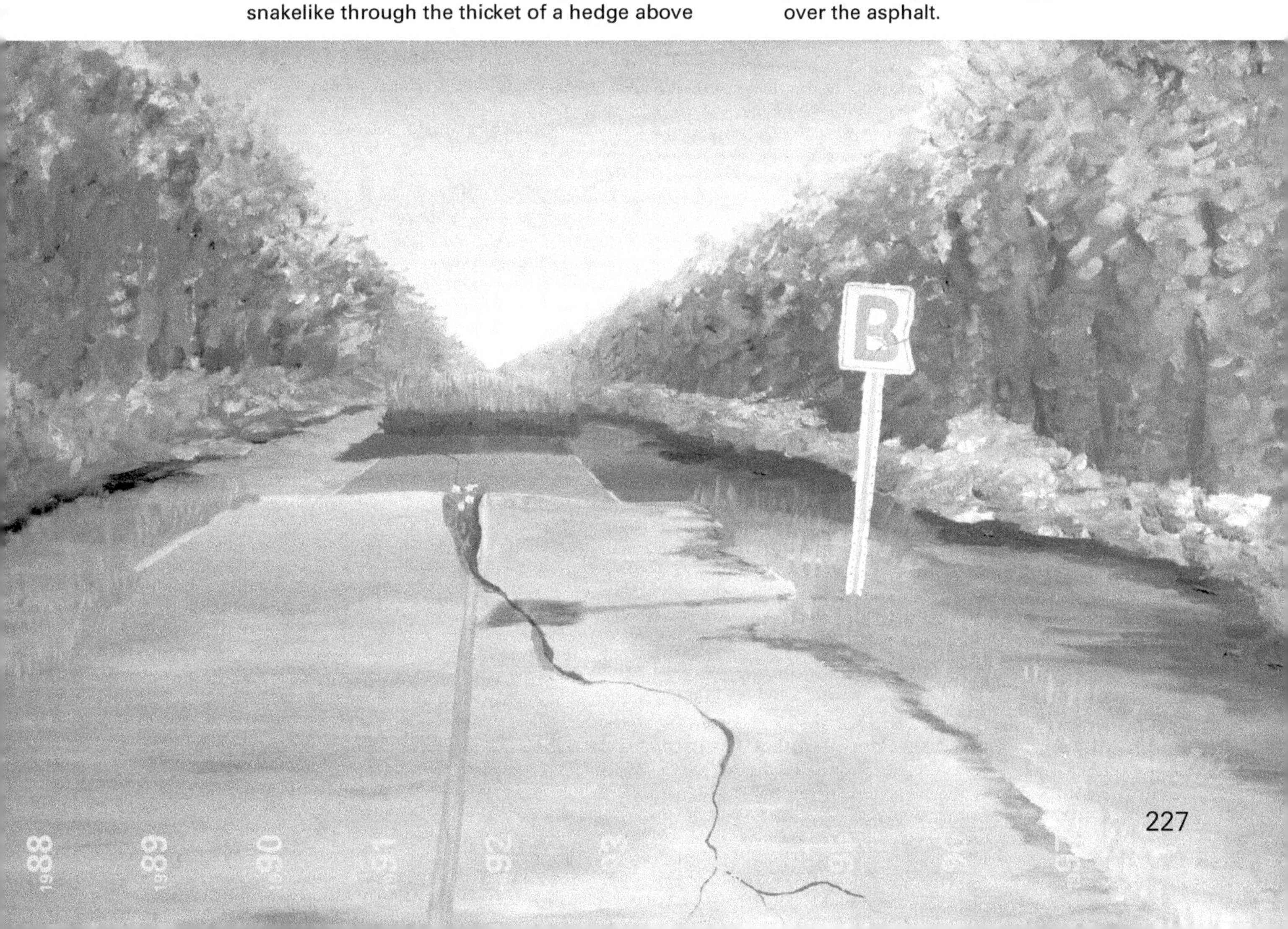

Painting

oil on canvas

In my late teens I had been inspired by the strange imagery of the Belgian surrealist painter René Magritte, and I read all the books I could get about him and his work. One of the works that resonated with me was *Les Vacances de Hegel*, a glass of water standing on top of an open umbrella. More than the incongruent meeting of a 2/3 filled water glass and an umbrella was the salmon-colored background. The color was shocking, and I was inspired to use it in my oil painting *For the Birds*, which shows a hirsuit hand holding a straw that supports a plain temple with a male cardinal bird perched on a cantilevered rod that sticks out to one side.

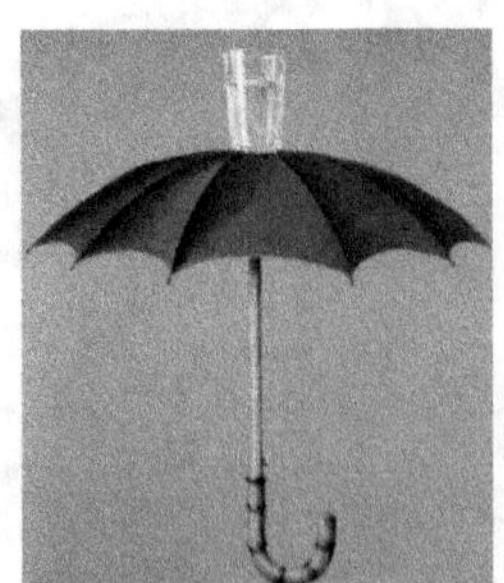

René Margritte, *Les Vacances de Hegel*

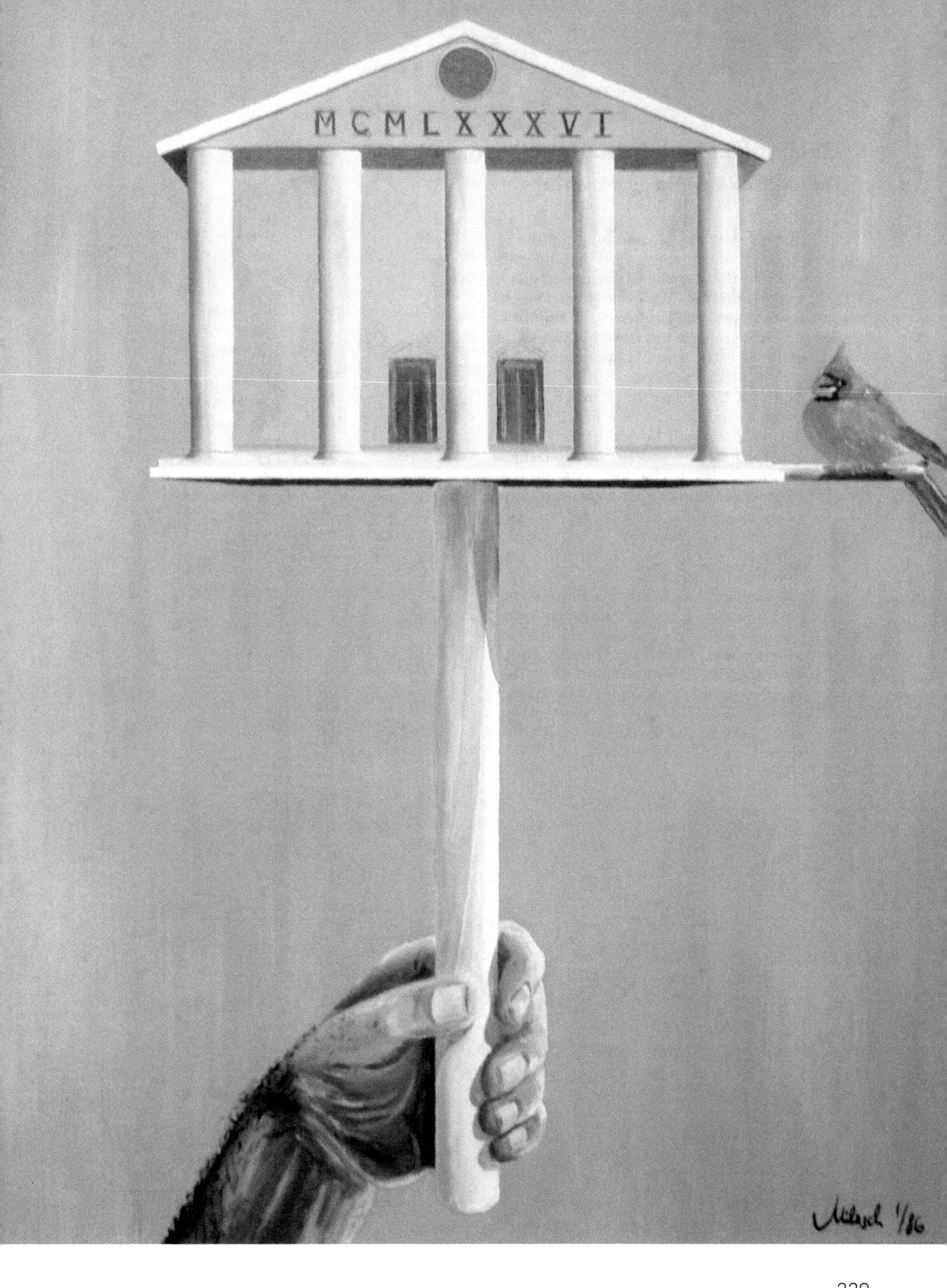
MCMLXXXVI

Gate House for a History Professor

Adirondack Mountains, New York

The following architectural projects represent a selection of work I completed while in the Bachelor of Design program at the University of Florida. Even though is a non-professional degree, the emphasis on architectural learning was intense, with a studio every semester, accompanied by technical and history courses.

The gate house project creates an entry to a villa on the other side of the bridge. This villa was built by Adolf Loos. Thus I appropriated Loos' ideas on architecture for the design of the gate house.. The major characteristics include the following: carved space, design from insided out, and *Raumplan*, a name coined by Loos for his 'space-plan' design, i.e. interrelated but differentiated spaces.

The building itsef is conceived as a frame with a massive central core that marks the turning point of the approach. This shift in direction also indicates a horizontal change from public to private functions. The building displays a closed face towards the public access side (roadway with bridge) and opens up in its more private zone towards nature.

Isometric of Gate House, Ink on mylar (30" x 30") >

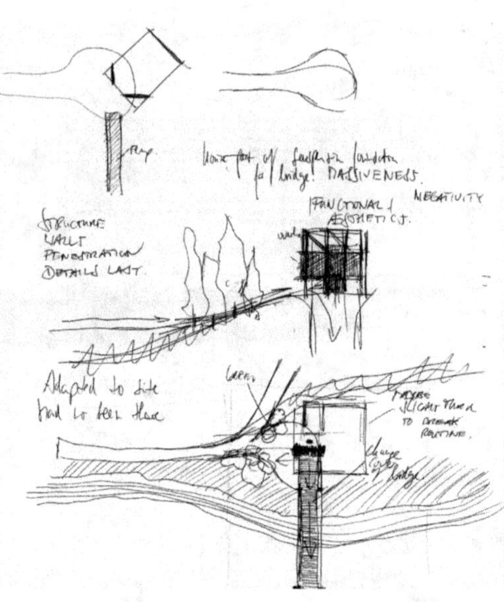

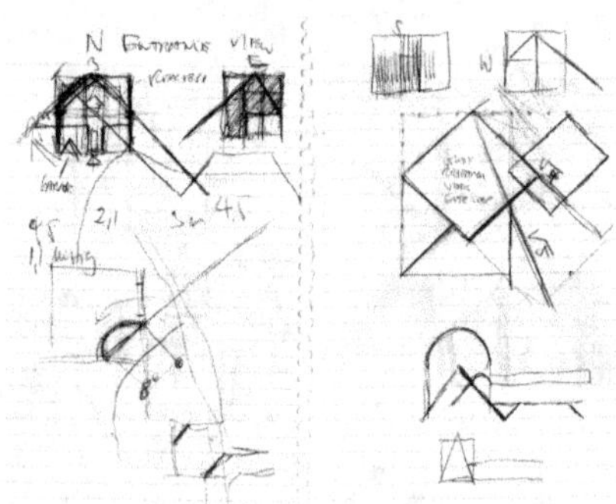

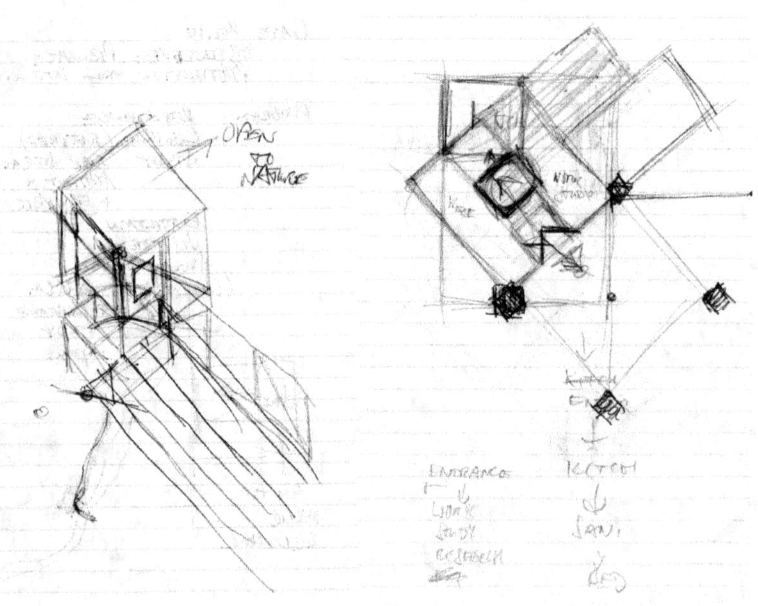

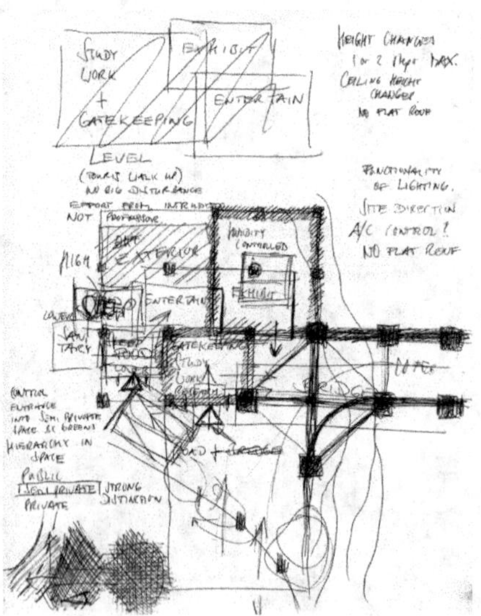

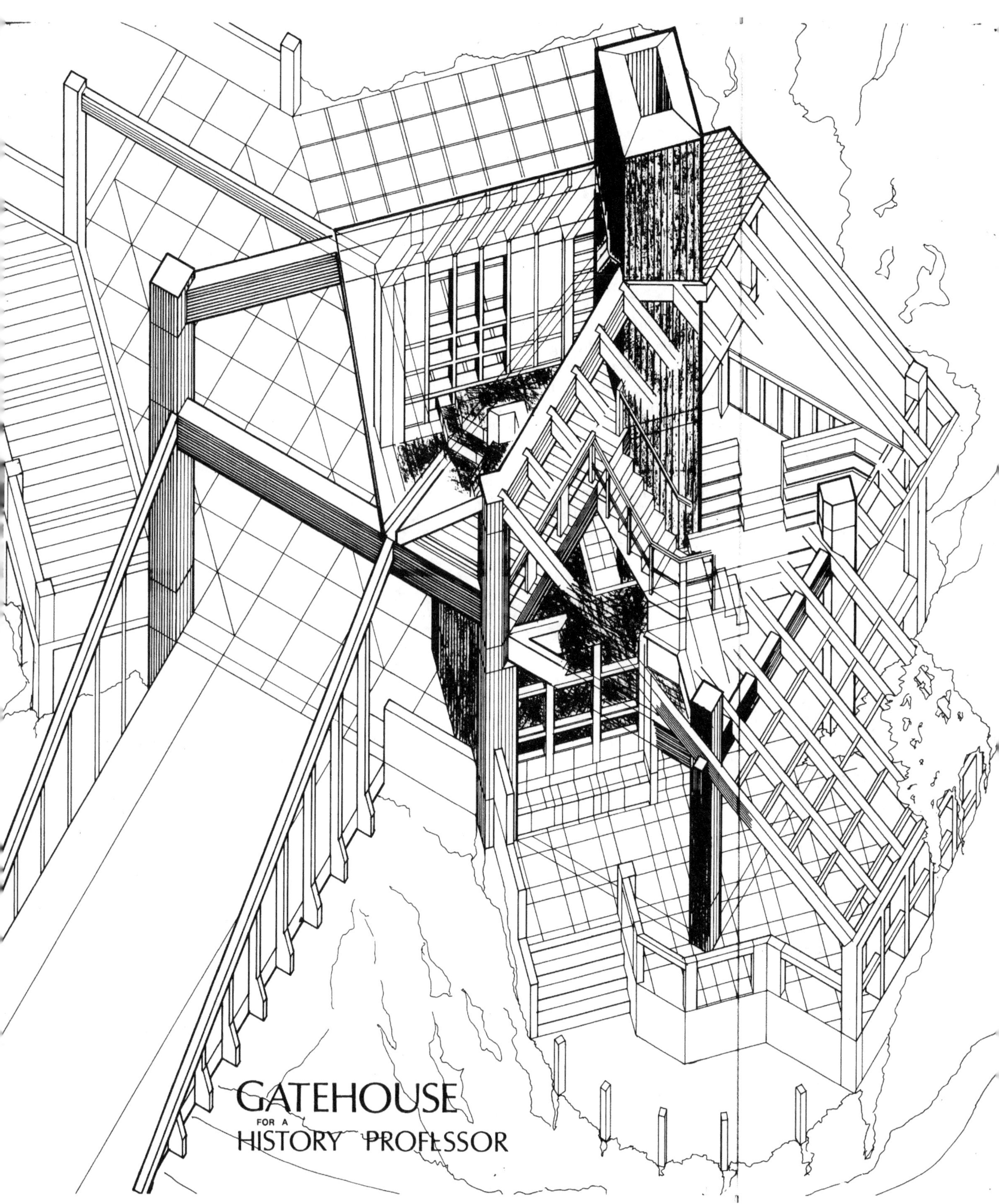
GATEHOUSE
FOR A
HISTORY PROFESSOR

Rug Museum

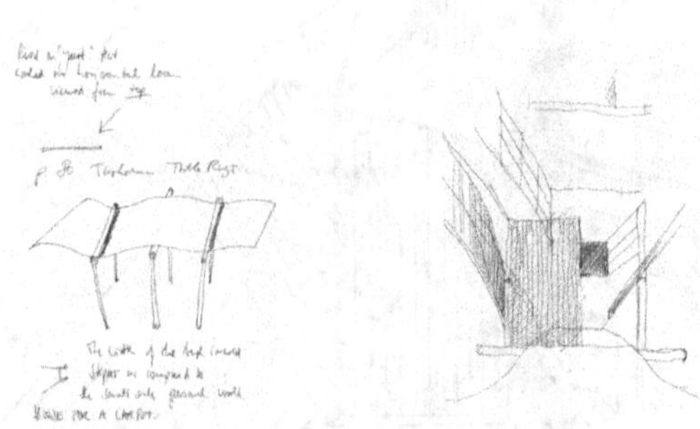

The design of the rug museum evolved out of the act of weaving. The long building is made of sections that change as you pass through the spaces. Just like the rugs tell stories through their weaving, the sequence of spaces, like stories, create a linear spatial narrative along which the visitor can explore the exhibits. The rugs on display hang from the loom-like structure and create various viewpoints as the museum visitor winds her way, shuttle-like, through the space.

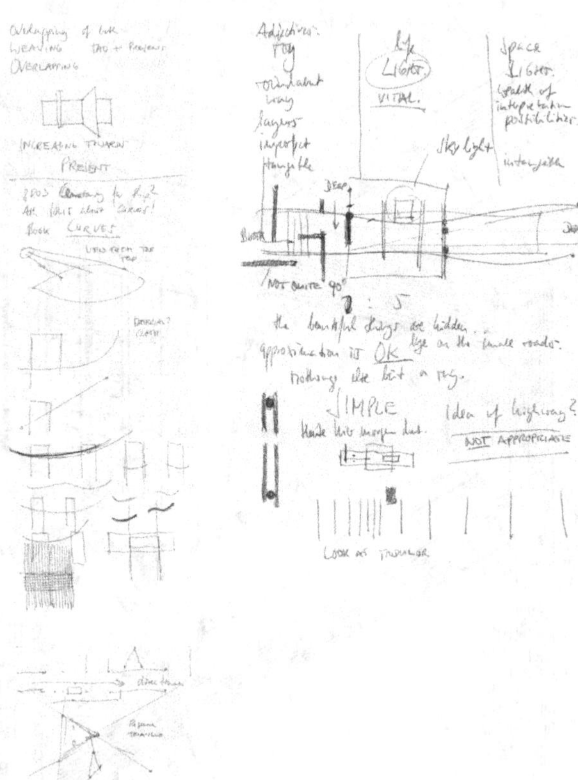

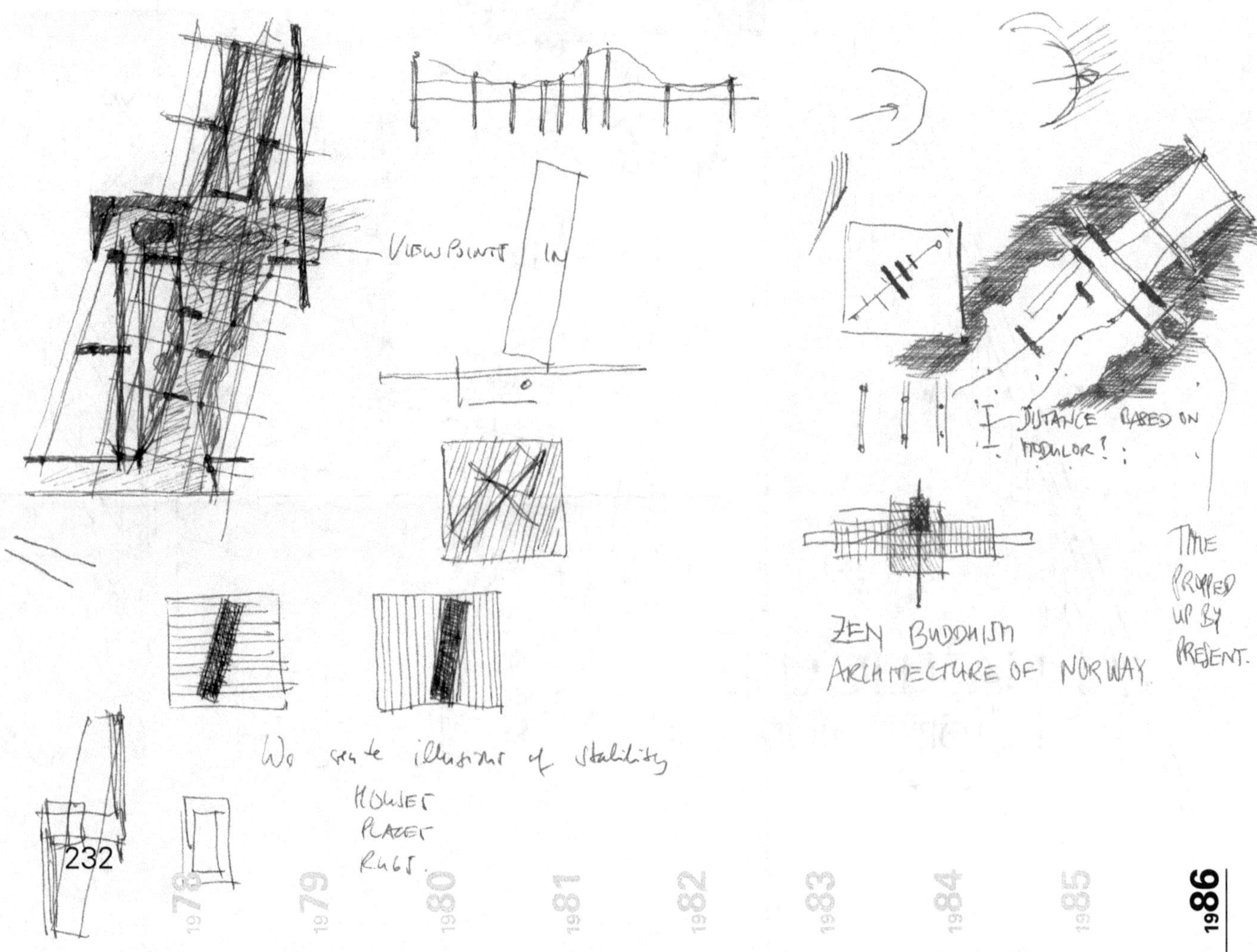

VIEW POINTS IN

DISTANCE BASED ON MODULOR?

ZEN BUDDHISM
ARCHITECTURE OF NORWAY

TIME
PROPPED
UP BY
PRESENT.

We create illusions of stability
HOUSES
PLACES
RUGS.

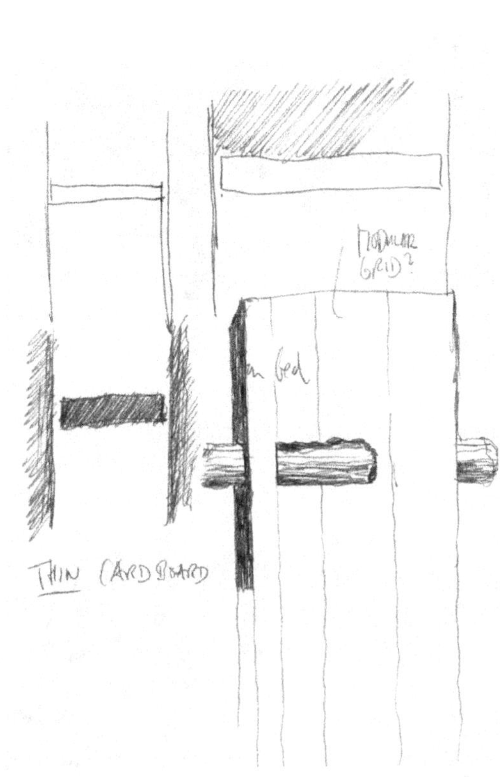
MODULOR GRID?
THIN CARDBOARD

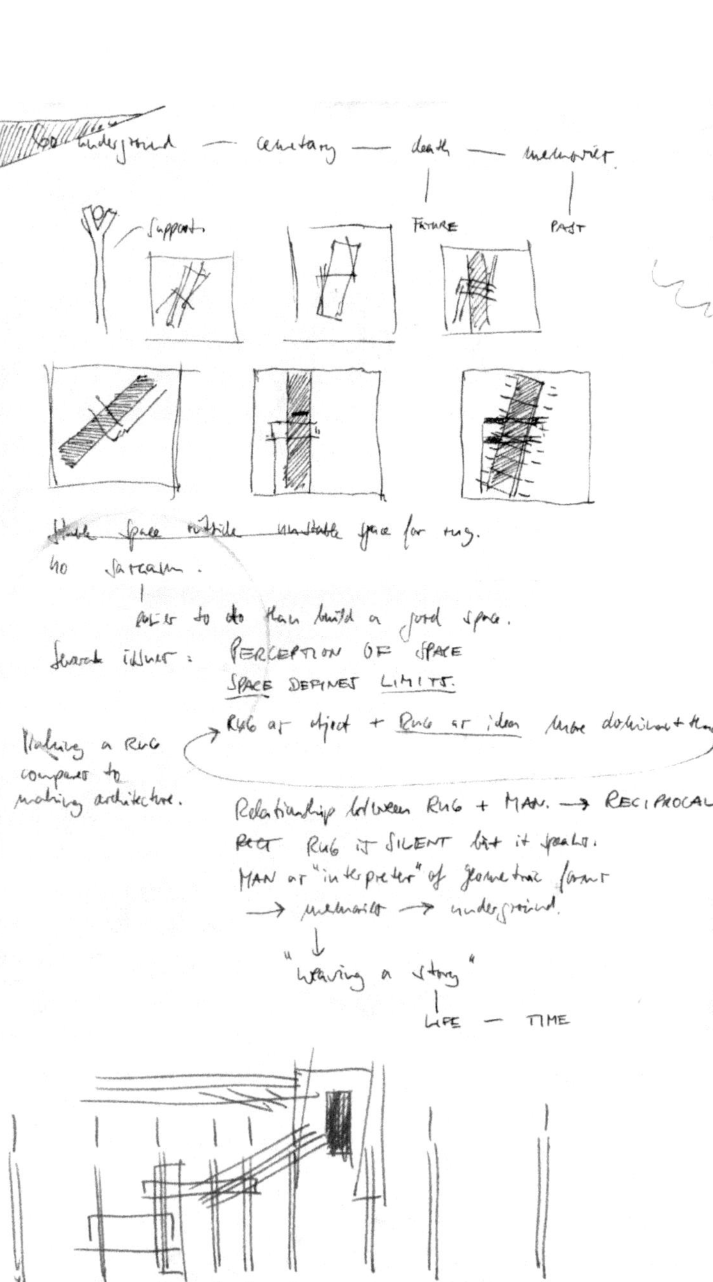
underground — cemetary — death — memories.
support
FUTURE
PAST
PERCEPTION OF SPACE
SPACE DEFINES LIMITS.
Making a RUG compared to making architecture.
RUG as object + RUG as idea
Relationship between RUG + MAN. → RECIPROCAL
RUG is SILENT but it speaks.
MAN as "interpreter" of geometric forms
→ memories → underground.
"weaving a story"
LIFE — TIME

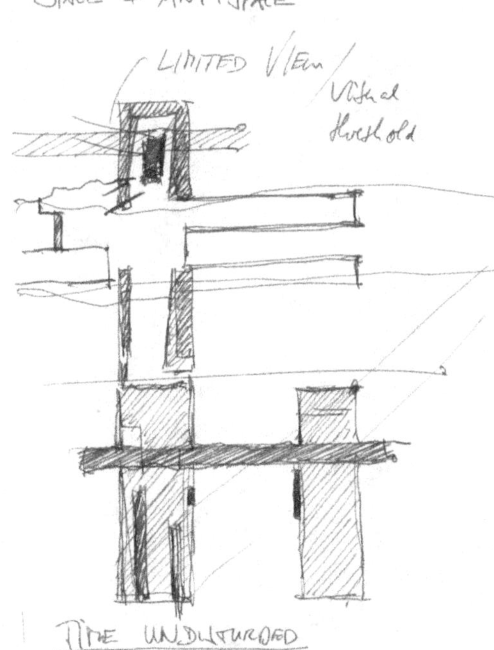
SPACE + ANTI SPACE
LIMITED VIEW
TIME UNDISTURBED
by HUMANS ?

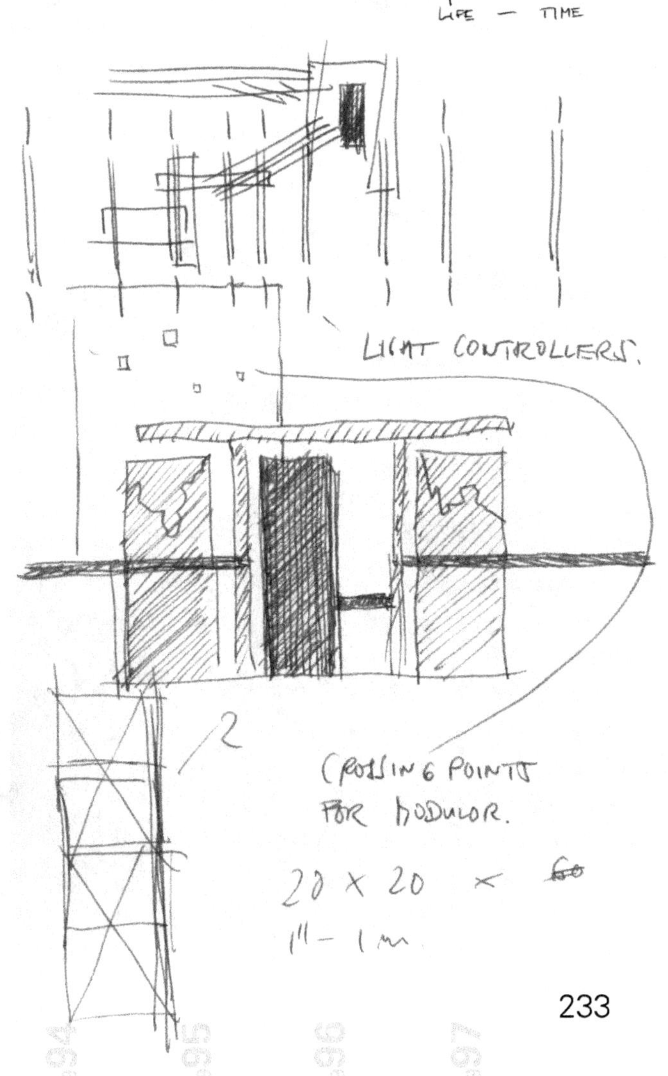
LIGHT CONTROLLERS.
CROSSING POINTS
FOR MODULOR.
20 × 20 ×

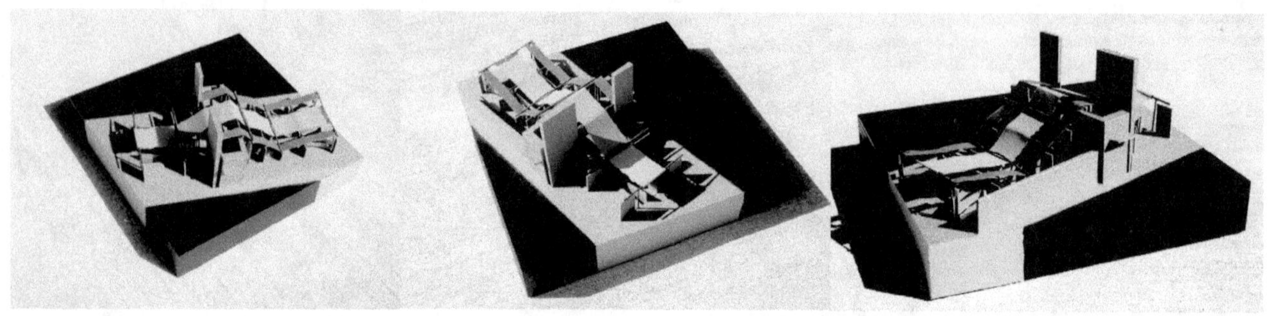

Final model of rug museum made of cardboard, twigs, and colored paper

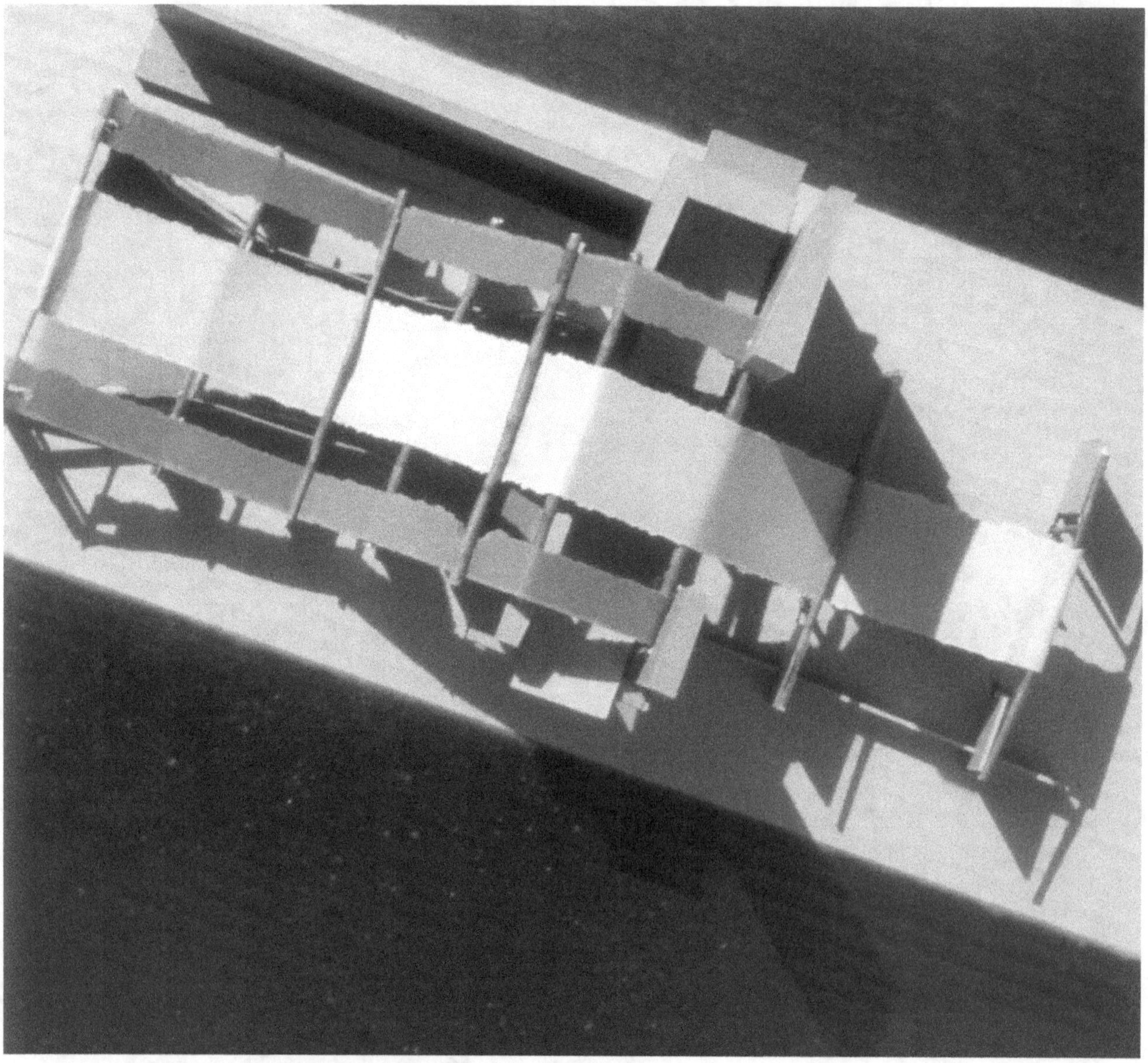

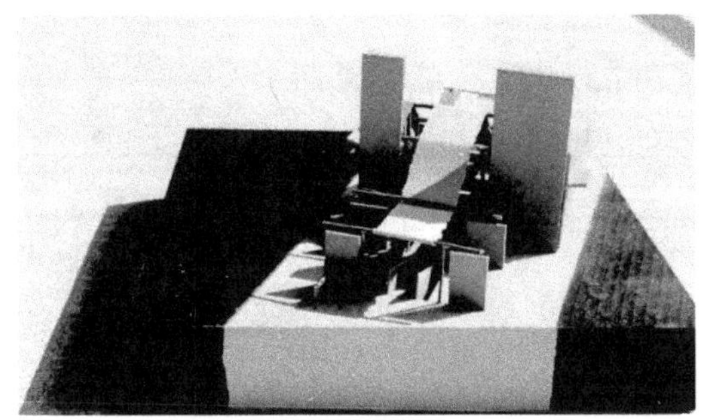

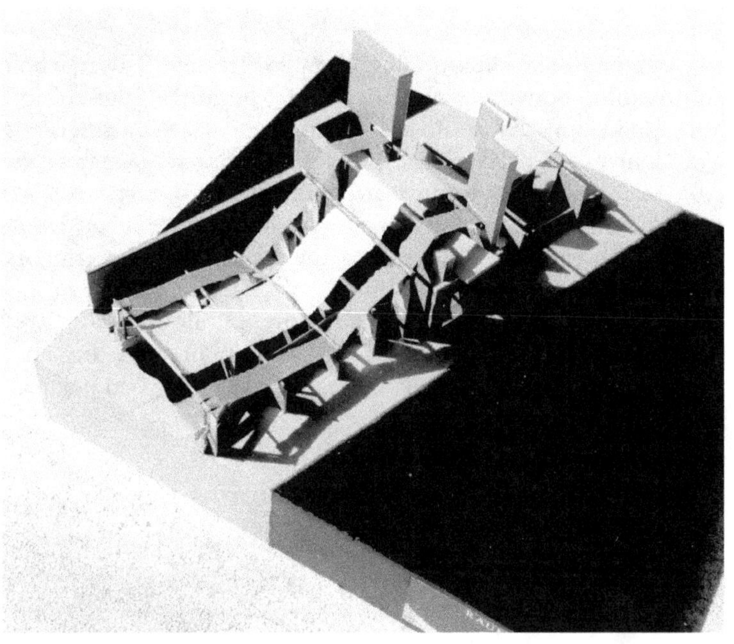

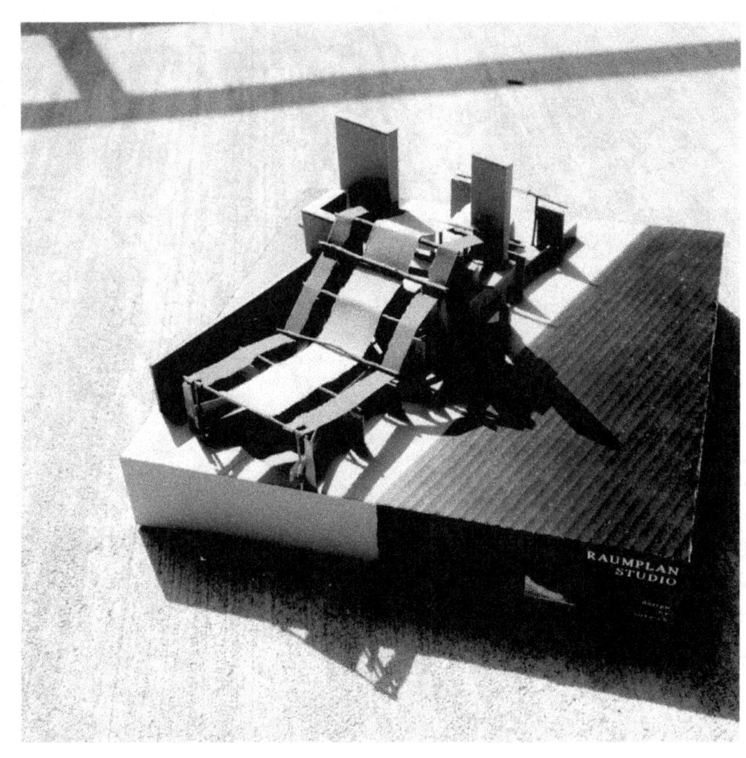
RAUMPLAN
STUDIO

Center for Latin American Studies

Lake Alice, Gainesville

At one scale the building complex creates a joint between Lake Alice and Museum Road, in the south-west corner of the University of Florida campus. At another scale the central courtyard joins the two major programmes: private apartments which grow finger-like into the lake, and public activities (auditorium, offices) that are located adjacent to the more public realm, the street bounding the property on the west and south sides.

The whole building complex becomes the meeting ground between nature and artificial architecture while the courtyard creates a meeting place for different cultures.

Even the layout for the individual apartments reflects on the micro scale the concept of joint and center. Here the stairs create a joint between the different spaces in the apartment (see perspective drawing on page 239).

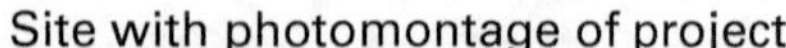
Site with photomontage of project

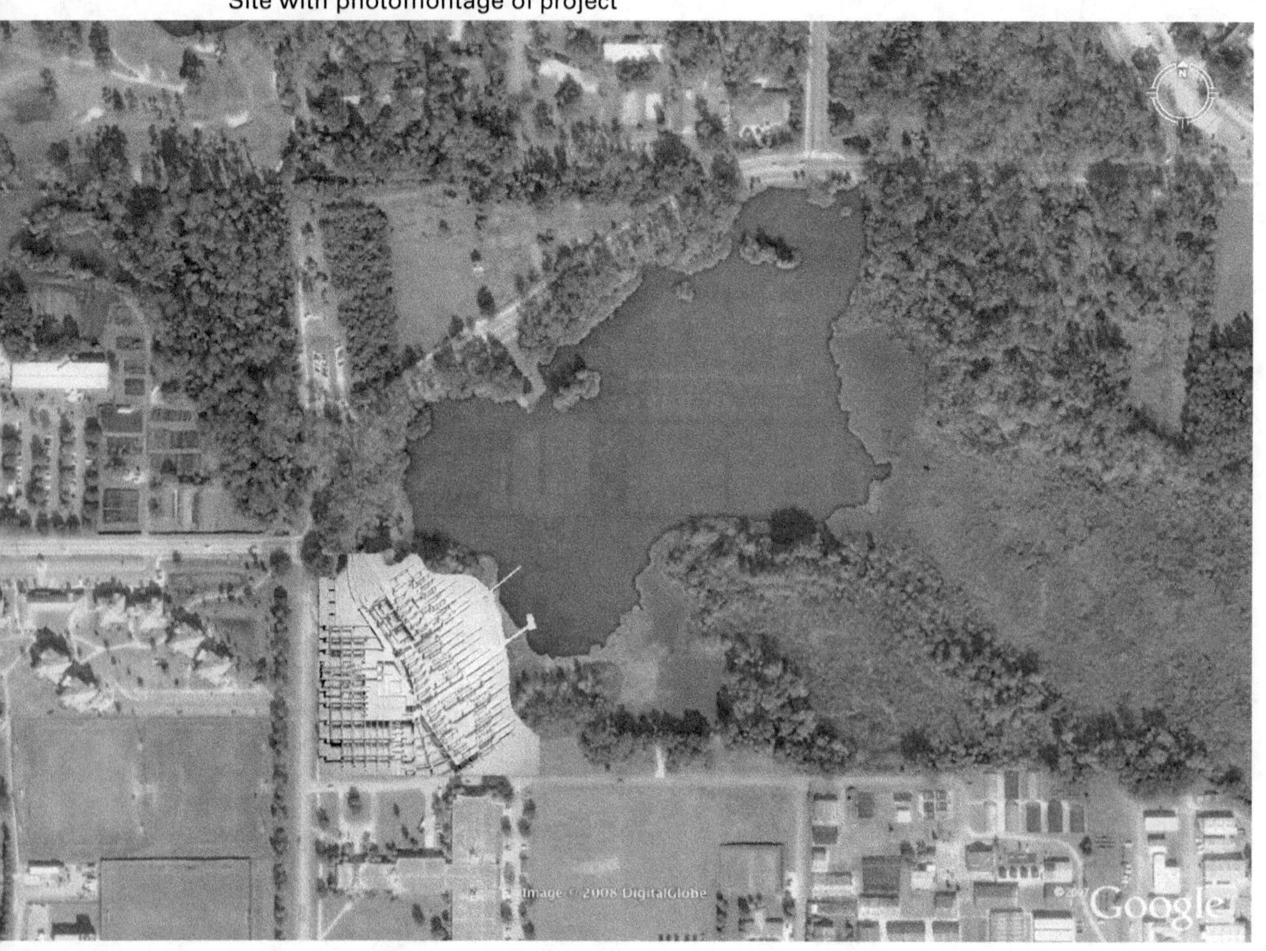

Process Sketches

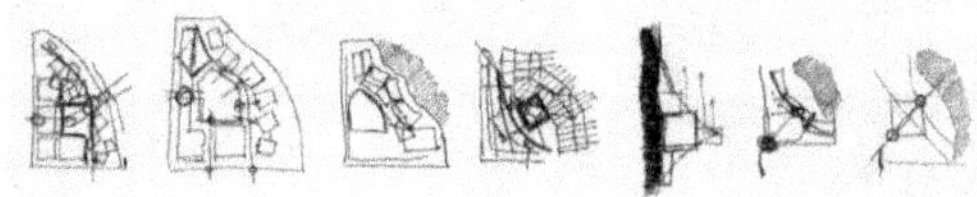

Final diagrammatic model at 1/32″= 1′

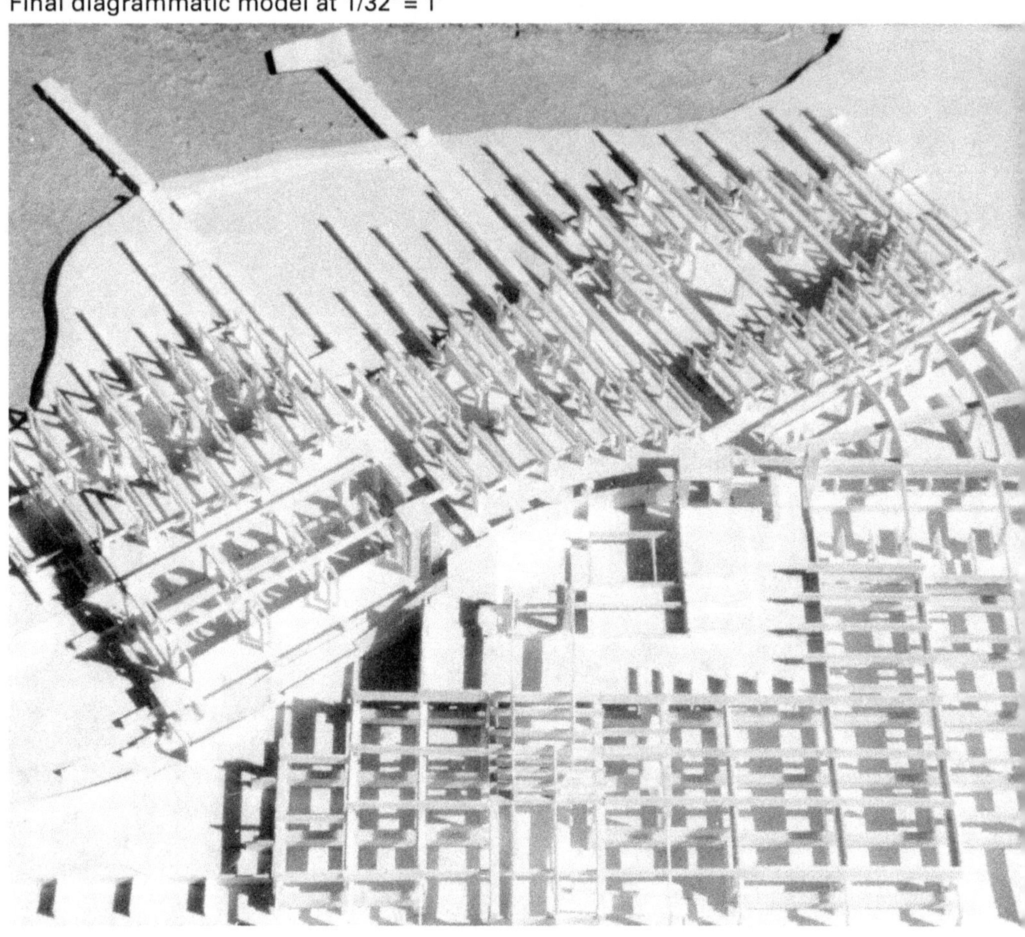

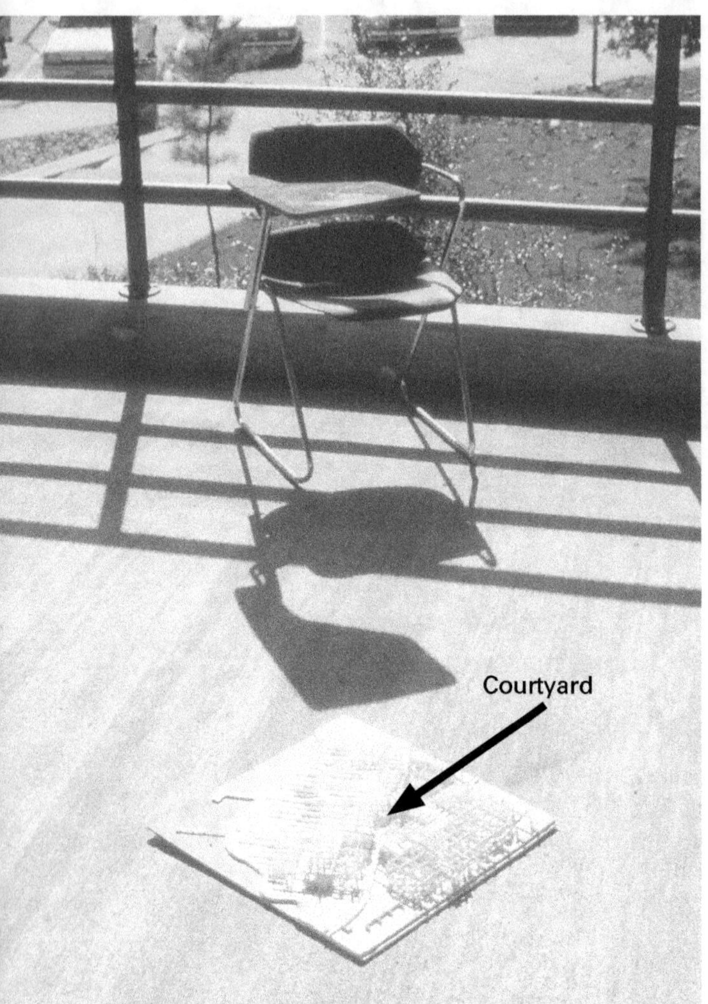

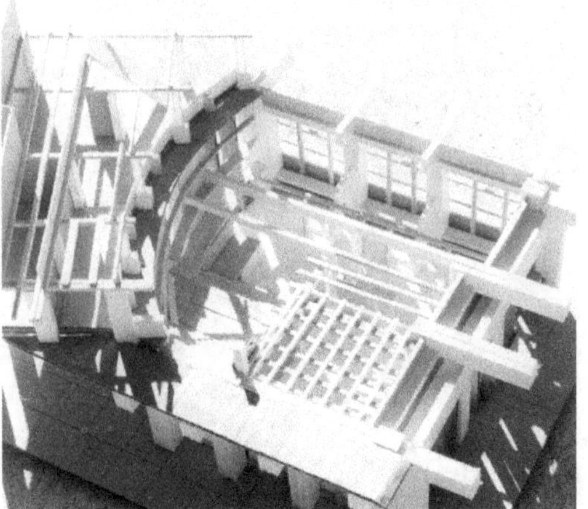

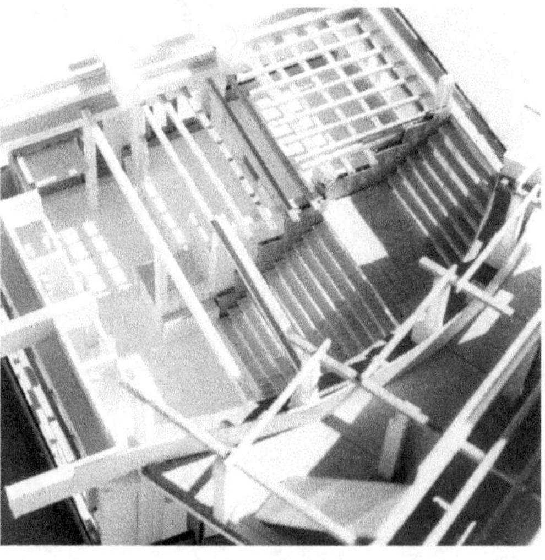

Courtyard Models
(1/4″ = 1 foot),
cardboard, bass wood,
foam core

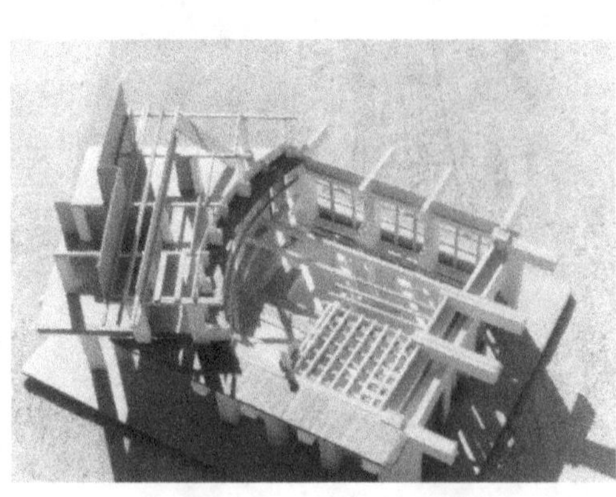

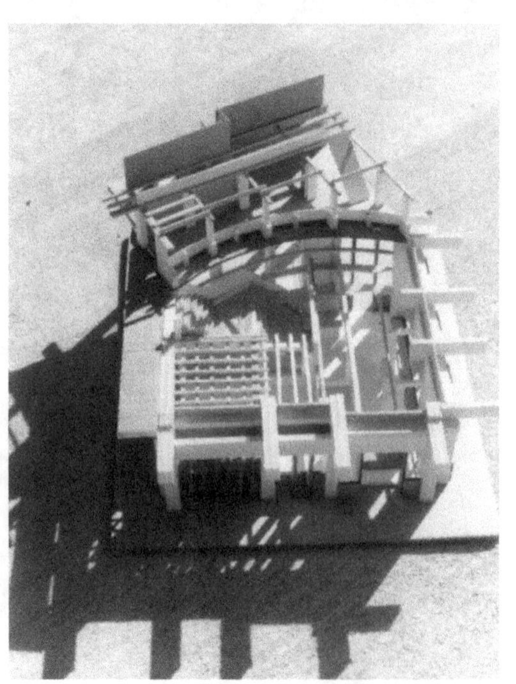

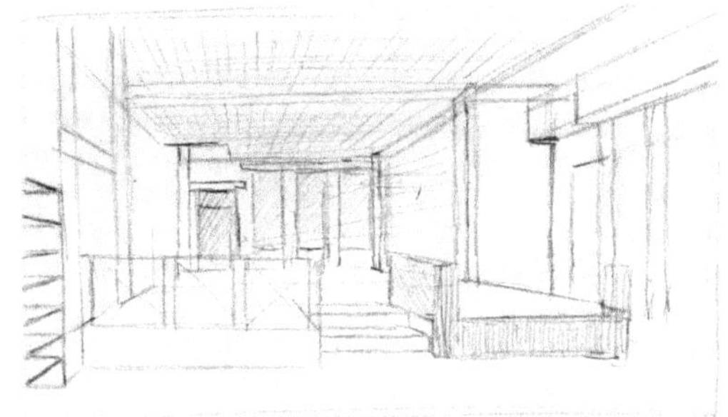

Typical Apartment Interior, design sketch

Typical Apartment Interior, Ink on Mylar

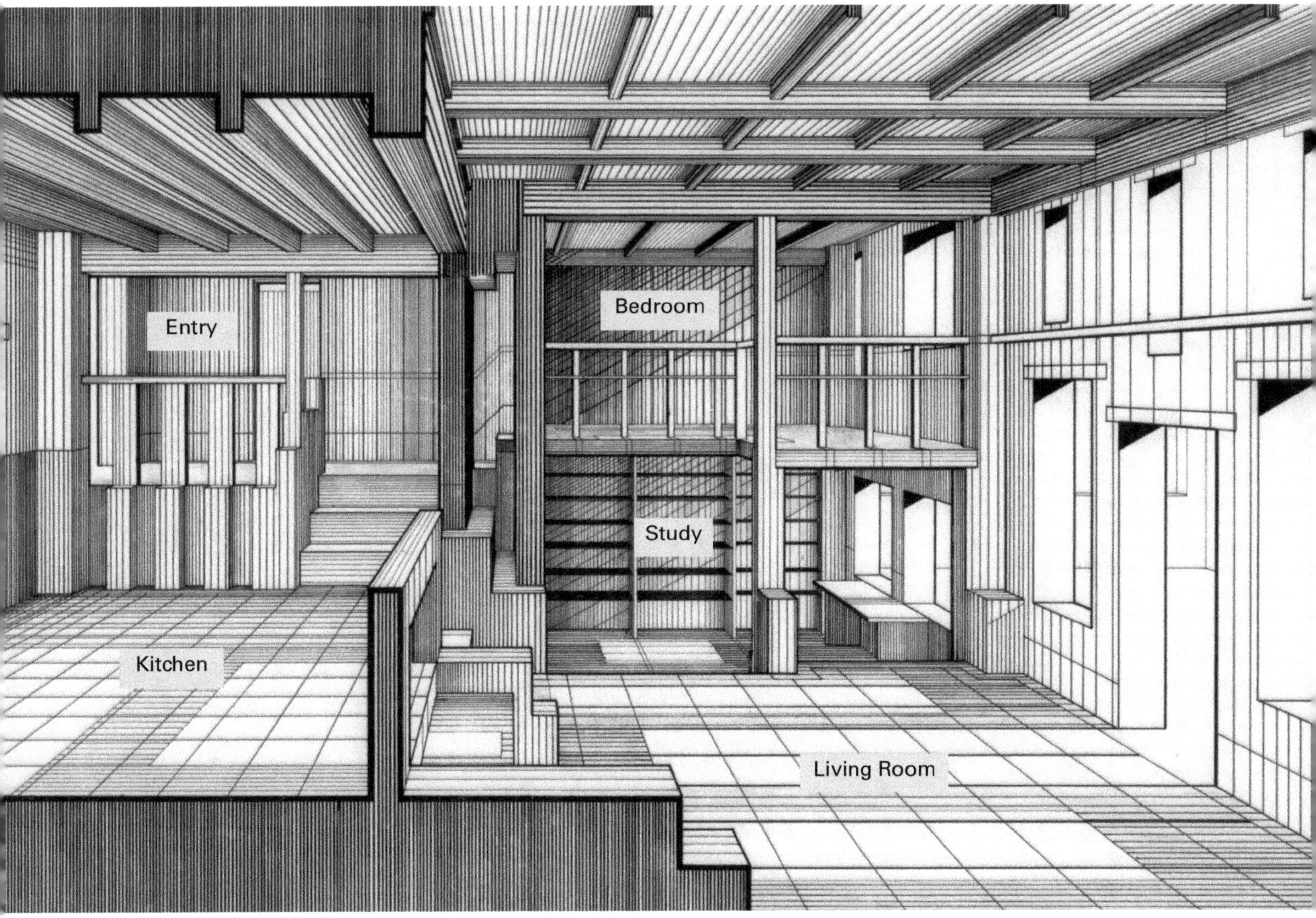

Entry

Bedroom

Study

Kitchen

Living Room

1987

Tower for Observation and Contemplation

Task: Design a tower that has two distinct spaces; one for the act of observing, the other for deep meditation. Connect the spaces with a path.

Problem Statement: the main focus is to establish a theory base for design through the investigation of these architecture/art movements (constructivism, de Stijl, cubism).

Theory Base: De Stijl
...to evolve a plastic idiom that would be equally applicable to painting, architecture, and the decorative arts.
...rejected individualism and all its manifestations, whether impressionist or expressionist.
...led to pure geometrical abstraction... relationship of horizontals and verticals.
...color was limited to three primaries: red, yellow, and blue, and the neutral colors black, grey, and white.
...achieving a universal harmony through the balance of contrasting elements:

the line:
dividing, defining, limiting the second dimension

the plane:
four lines intersecting, creating inside and outside

colored planes in the third dimension defining, limiting space, yet reaching out into space, far beyond their physical dimensions.

Project Parts:
1. Rolling hills
2. Tower with
3. Observation space
4. Meditation space, and
5. Path that connects both spaces.

Ideas:
tower
vertical
to observe
look into outside world
to meditate
look into inside world
duality
expansion of space
light
open
contraction of space
dark
closed

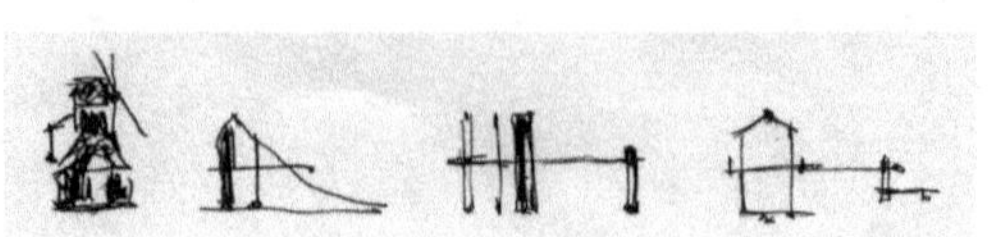

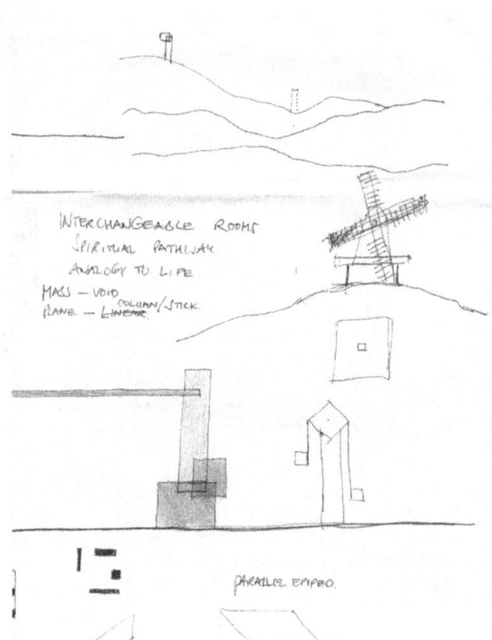

Process Sketches

For this project I studied the theory base of De Stijl which originated in the Netherlands. Subsequently I decided to investigate the idea of tower in terms of the De Stijl theory but also in concrete terms as a windmill.
The two distinct spaces—observation and contemplation—became two elevator boxes connected with a steel cable. If the observation space moves up, the meditation space moves down, and vice versa.
The whole building can be turned to allow for viewing in all directions. In order to escape the dilemma of a purely orthogonal architecture, the exit out of the tower is managed via an s-shaped slide.

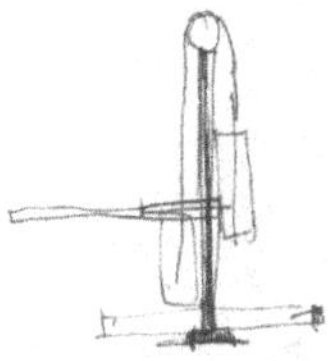

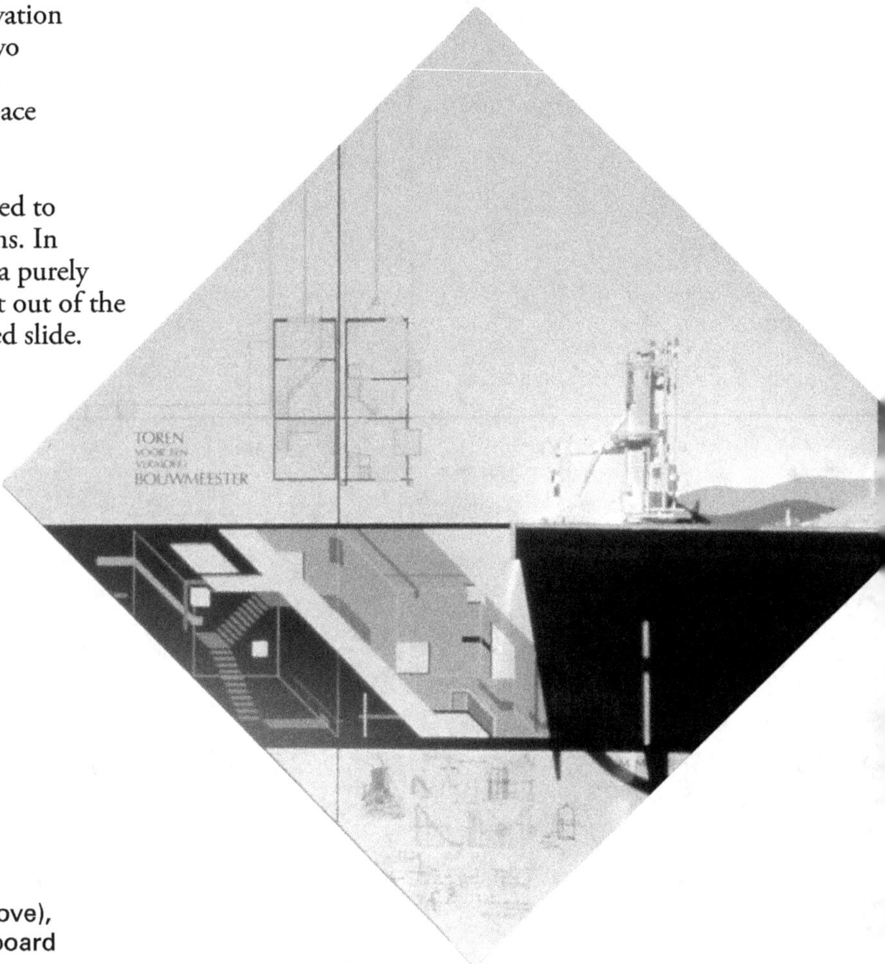

Final Pinup
3′ x 3′

Study Models (as seen from above), white foam core and museum board

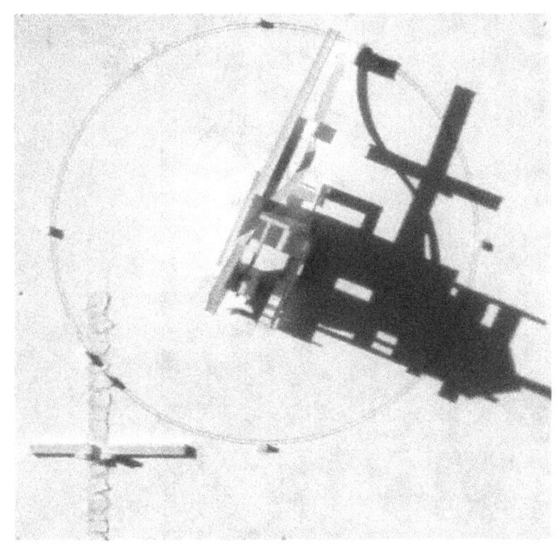

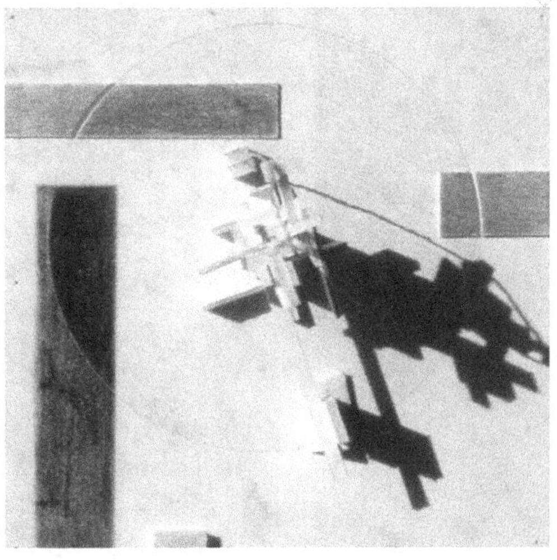

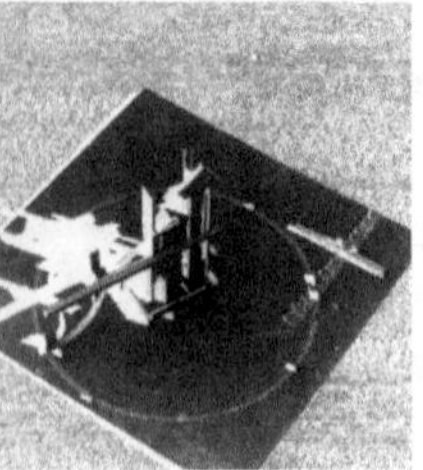

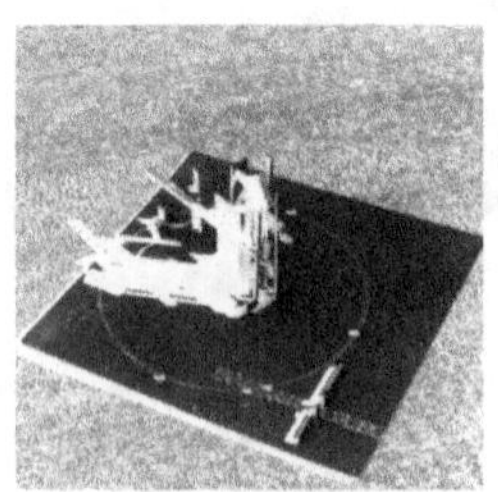

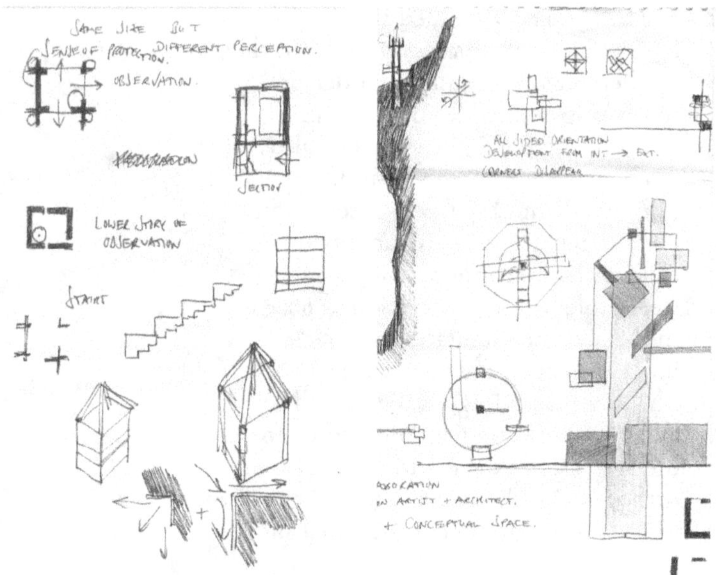

Study Models (inverted negatives),
white foam core

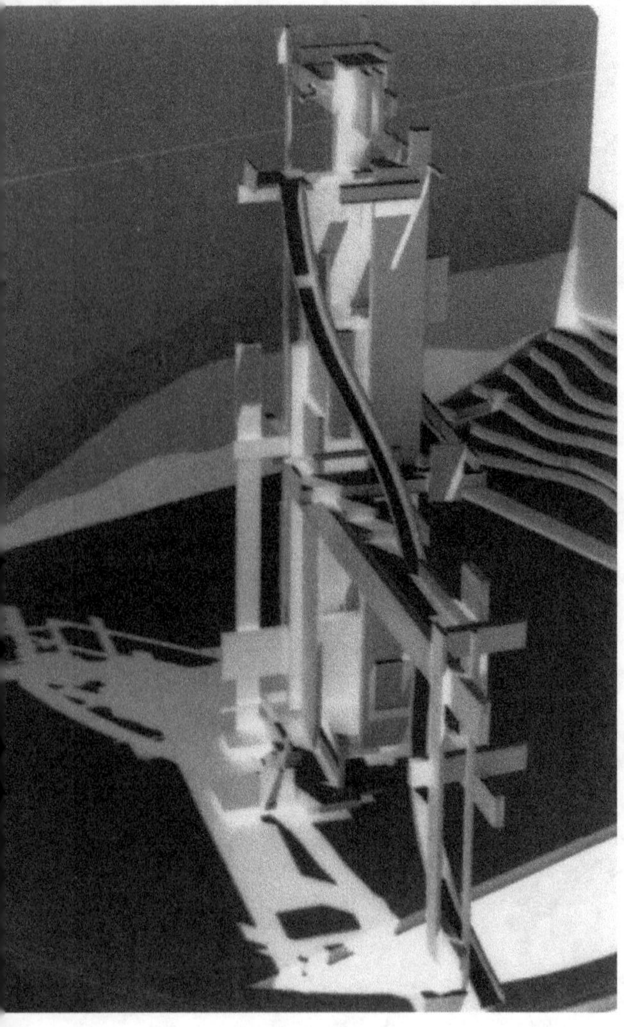

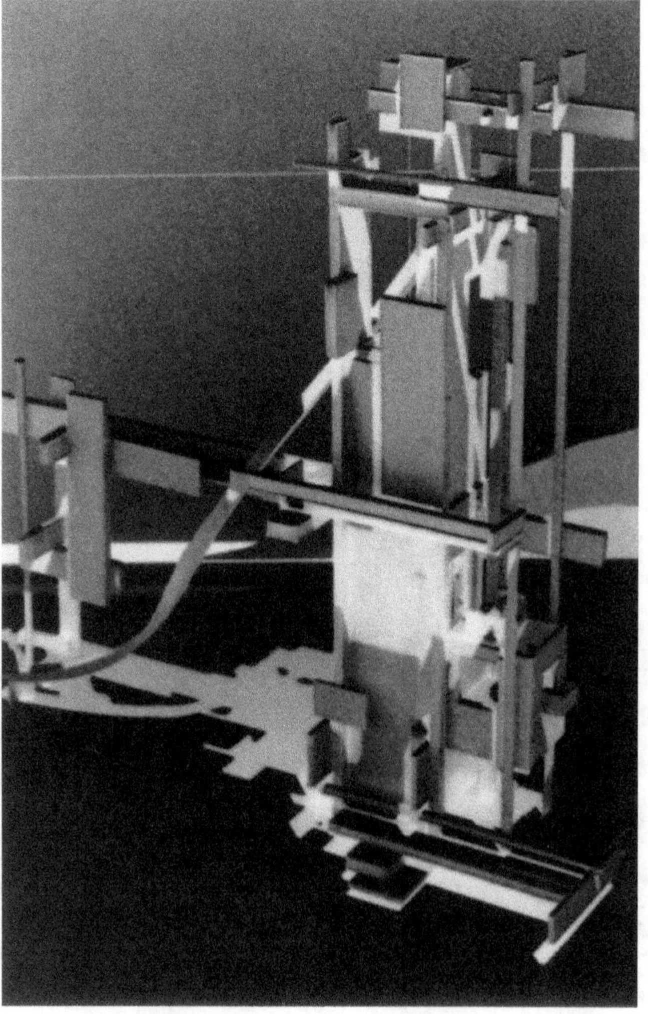

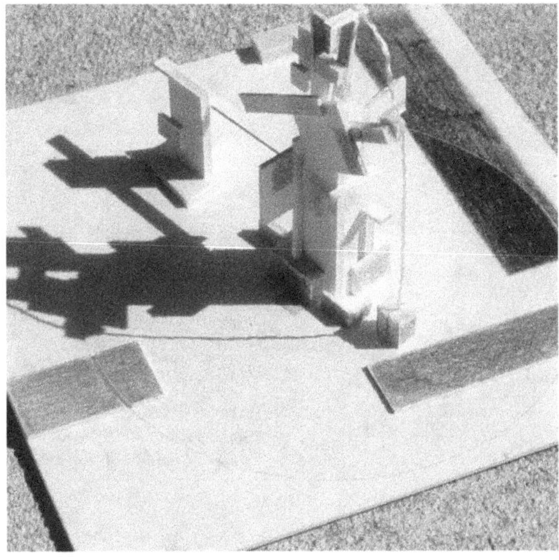

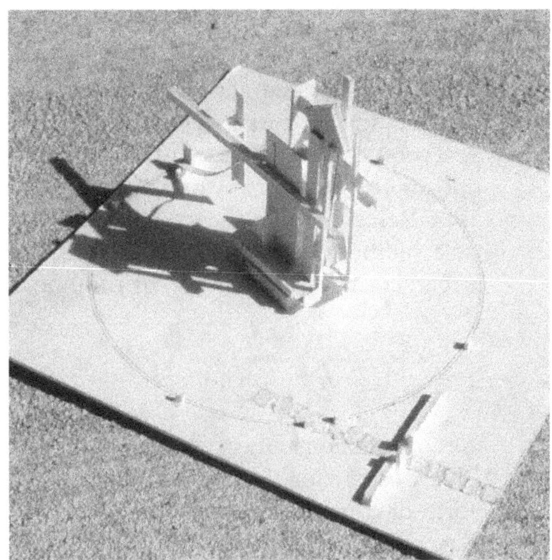

Transformation of ideas; going beyond De Stijl style period

TIME

That which was	Past	History Theory base
That which is	Present	Now Ideas
That which will be..	Future	Synthesis of Past and Present

PROJECT

observation space: symbolizing that which is, the present, ascending,
reaching the summit, sky, bright light, perfect for cloud counting...

meditation space: that which was, the past, descending at the same time, going into oneself, earth, comforting darkness, provides nice atmosphere for yester-day dreaming...

path: real and imagined. a steel wire connecting both spaces, creating movememt or change which translates into

LIFE

synthesis:
developments in two directions
1. rational
further abstraction, away from the human being straight lines, no colors, only black, grey, and white.
2.irrational
element of chance, the unexpected, complement to a one-sided dilemma,
a curve ---- a
s
l
i
d
e, as a Finale and
EXIT

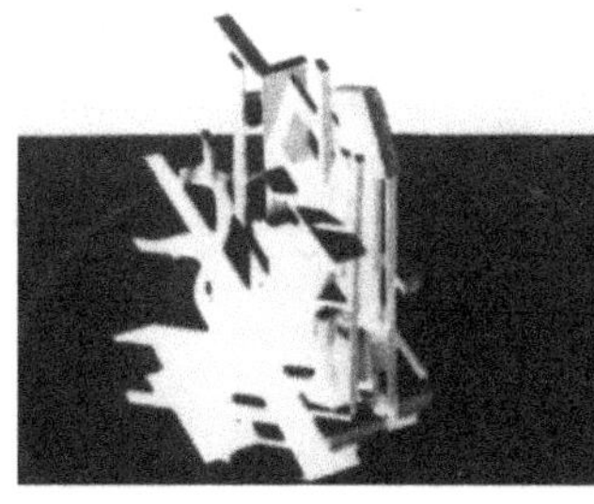

Monument to Commemoration and Condemnation

A Rural Field

Task: Design a monument for commemoration and condemnation. Each shall be a distinct space of its own to accommodate ten people each. Use the theory base of futurism, expressionism, and deconstructivism. Research your theory base and use it as a methodology. Pick one of three sites: urban corner, suburban lot, or rural field.

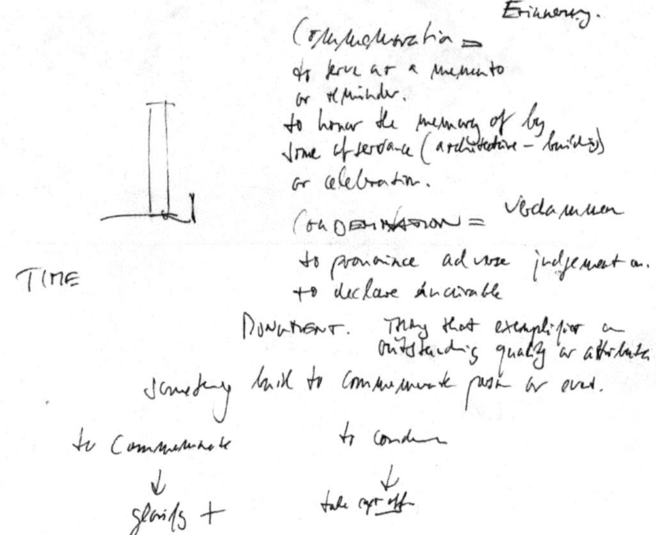

Deconstruction as theory base.
"Deconstruction is not a method, but a form of consciousness to some object."
Suspension of past + future; not one way of moving through space but infinite possibilities.

A Monument to Time

Situation: a rural field

Visitors to the monument approach it via a loosely defined path. There is only one space to be in, namely the NOW. Past space and Future space are, depending on belief system, either below or above; out of reach but not out of sight. The ideas underlying this design stem from the theory of deconstruction, combined with my own understanding of what existence, space, and time are.

Both ideas for this monument address thought or memory, and both can be viewed as intangible qualities. Thus the monument can not be occupied physically but only intellectually. It can not be built, hence it is not a monument. Yet it can exist as a sign which refers to the real thing. Two constructed cubes, one in the ground, the other above ground, separated by a glass plate that allows visual access but prevents concrete experience.

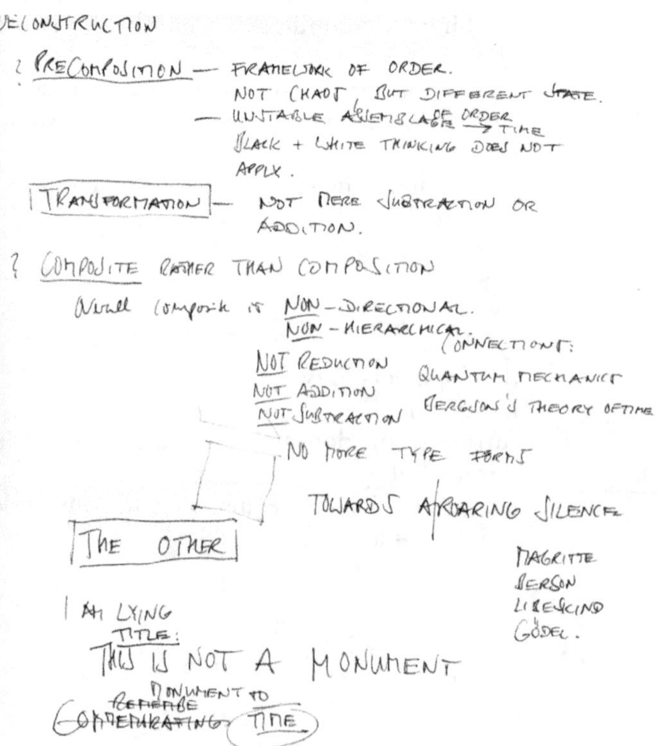

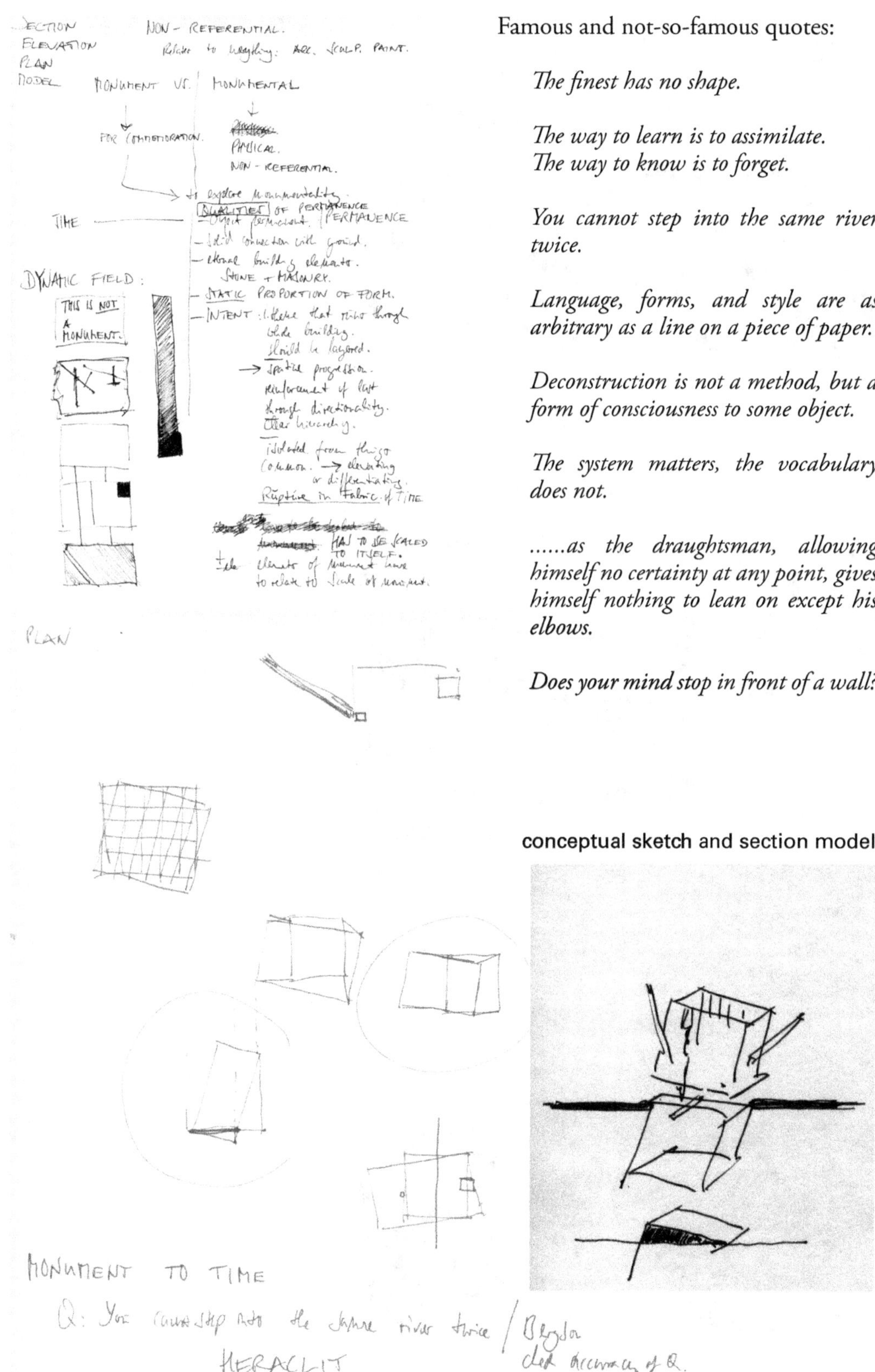

Famous and not-so-famous quotes:

The finest has no shape.

The way to learn is to assimilate.
The way to know is to forget.

You cannot step into the same river twice.

Language, forms, and style are as arbitrary as a line on a piece of paper.

Deconstruction is not a method, but a form of consciousness to some object.

The system matters, the vocabulary does not.

......as the draughtsman, allowing himself no certainty at any point, gives himself nothing to lean on except his elbows.

Does your mind stop in front of a wall?

conceptual sketch and section model

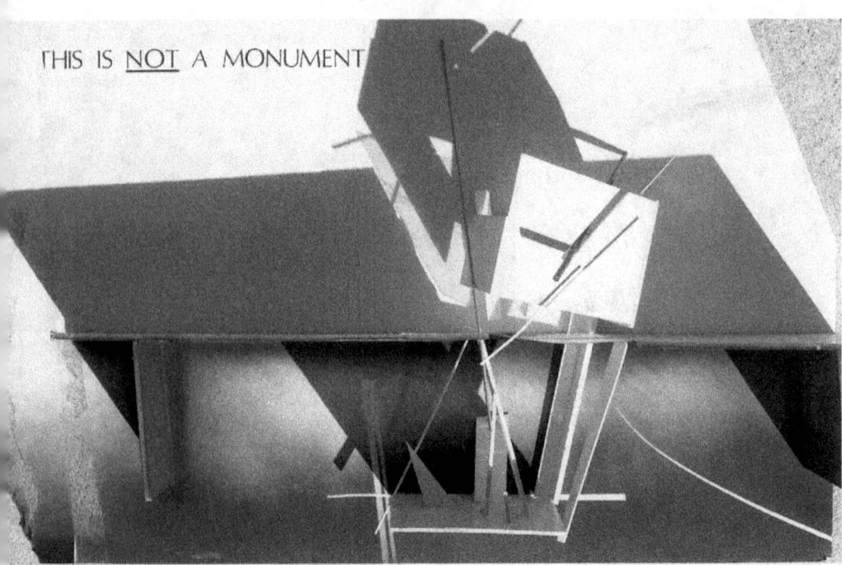

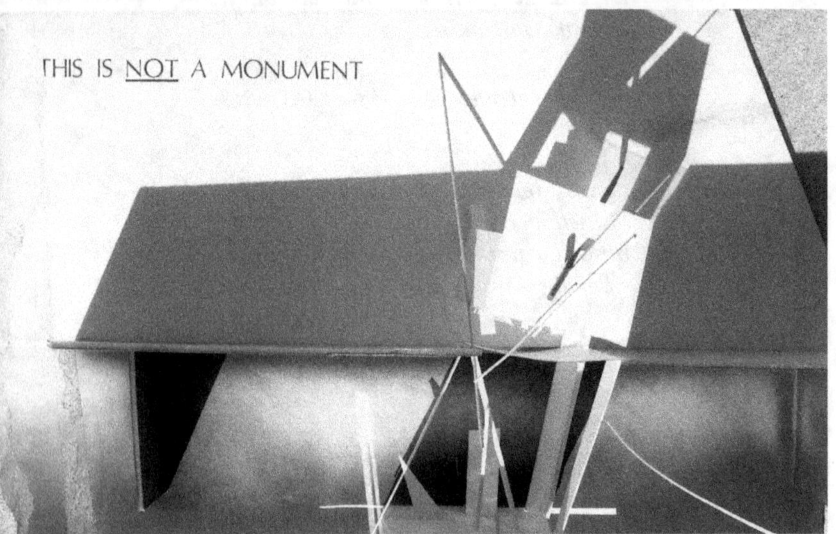

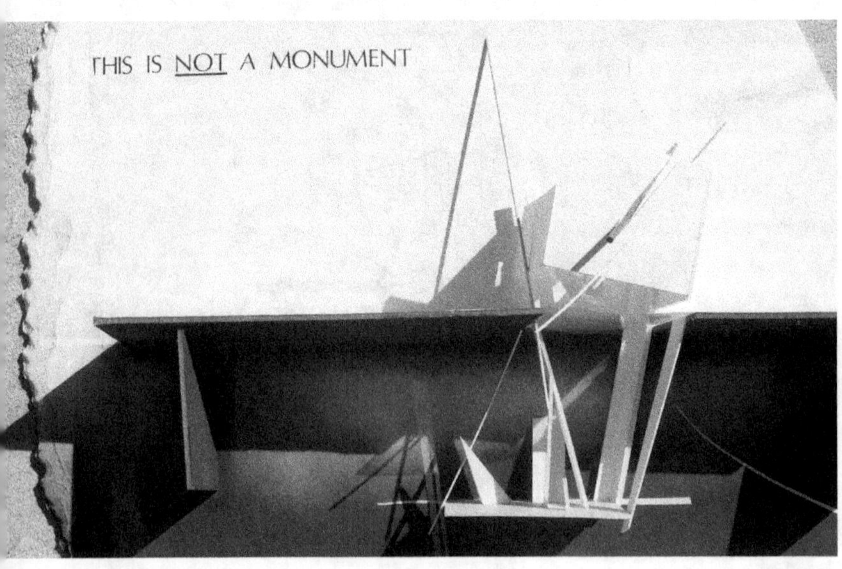

Final section model of the monument to commemoration and condemnation under different lighting conditions. Following Magritte's ideas about the arbitrariness between word and thing, this (the model) is *not* a monument

Section model

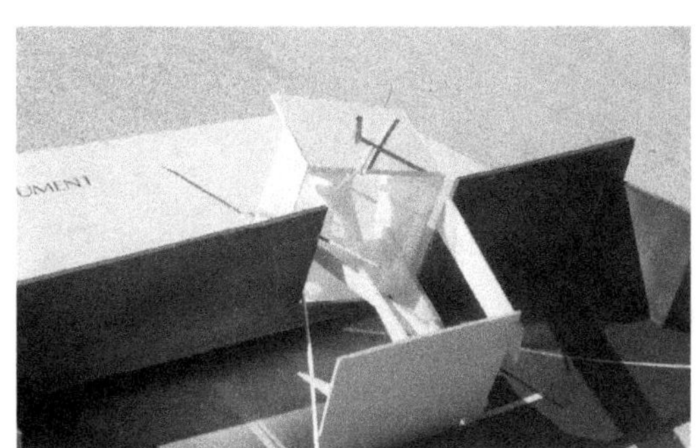

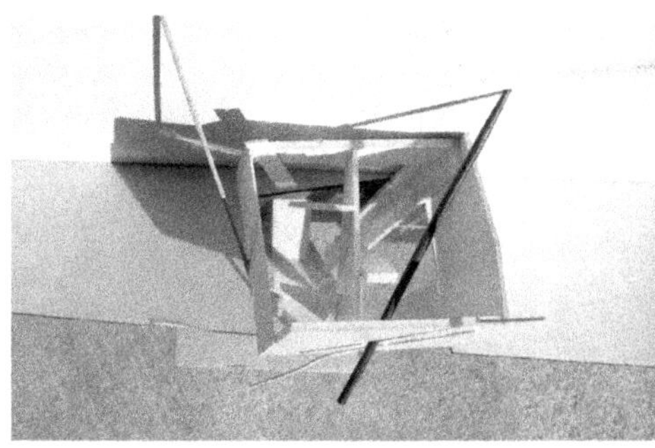

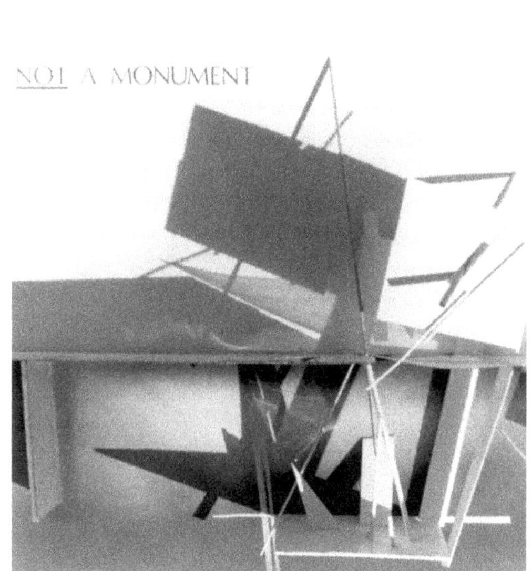

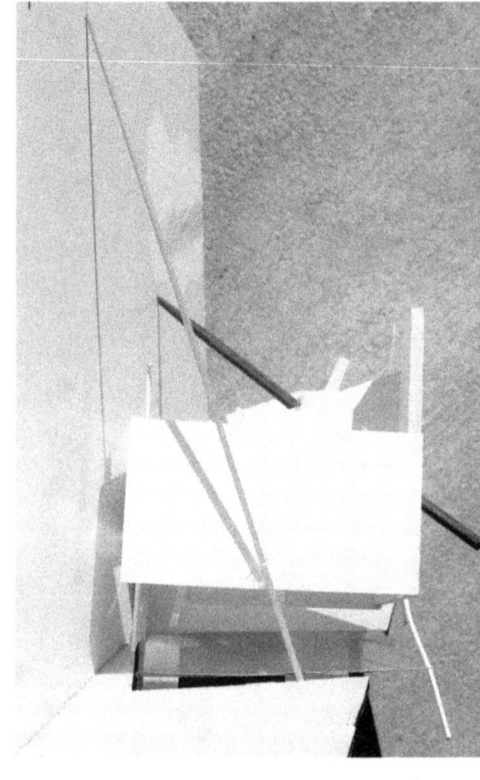

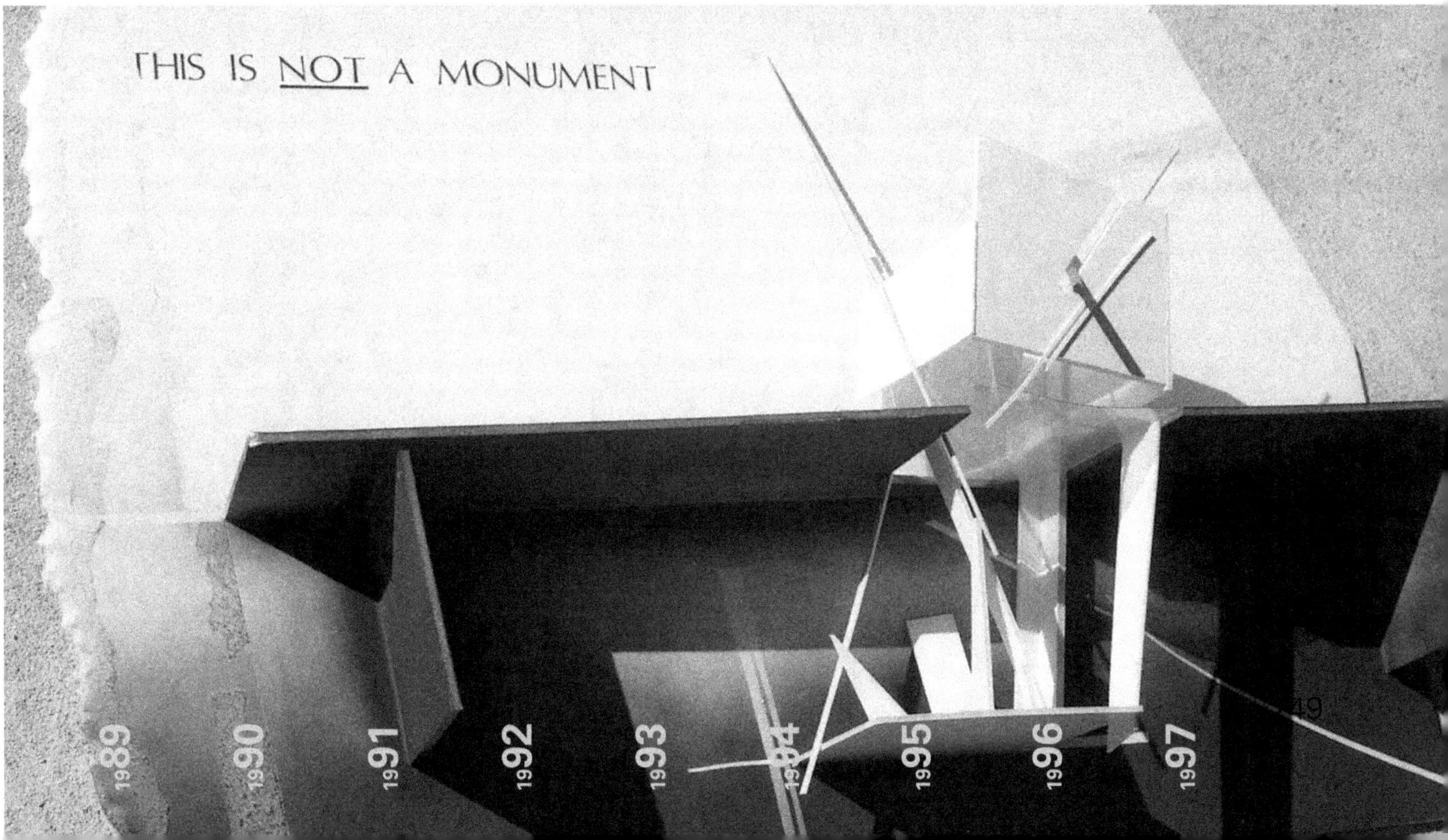

THIS IS NOT A MONUMENT

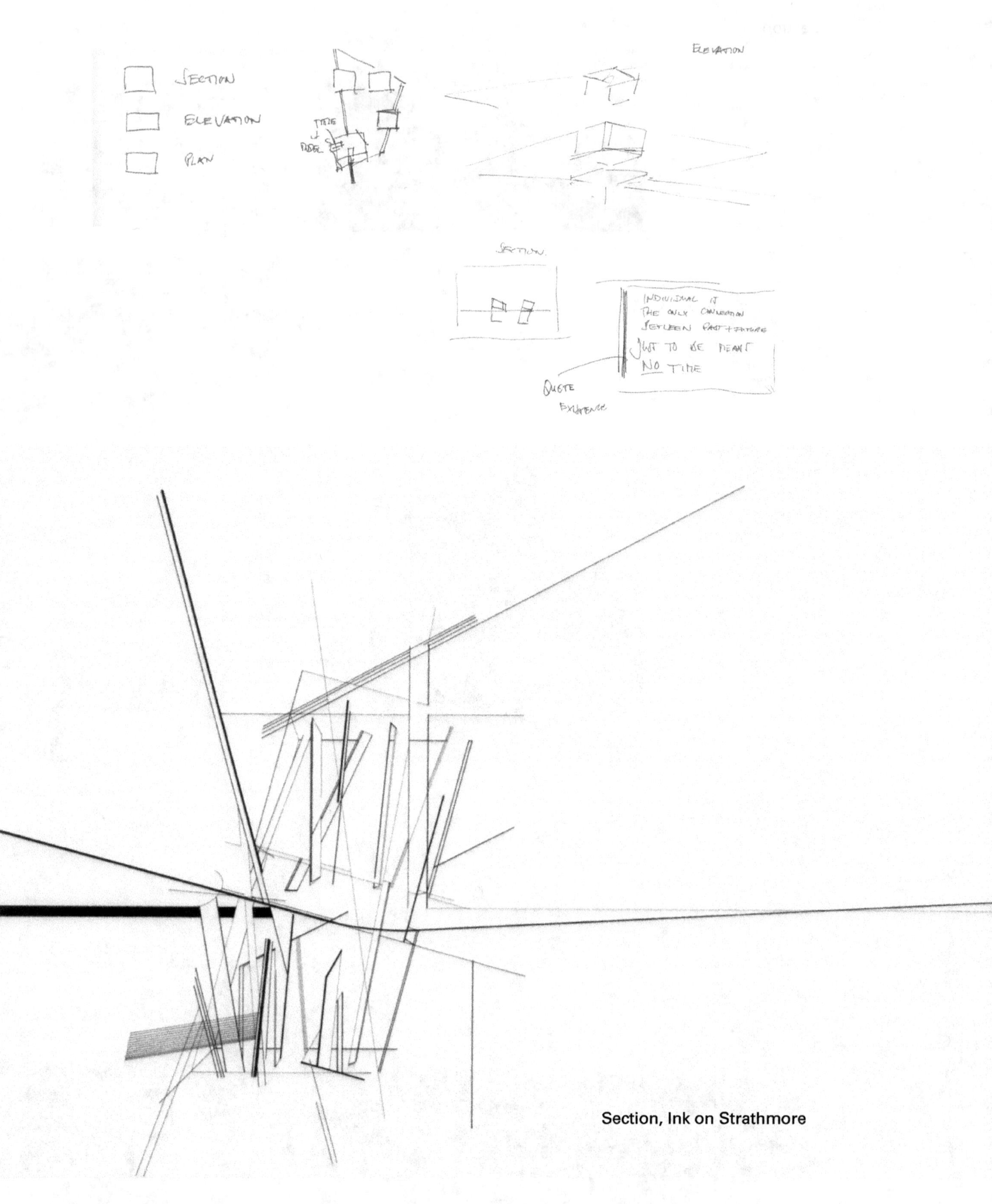

Section, Ink on Strathmore

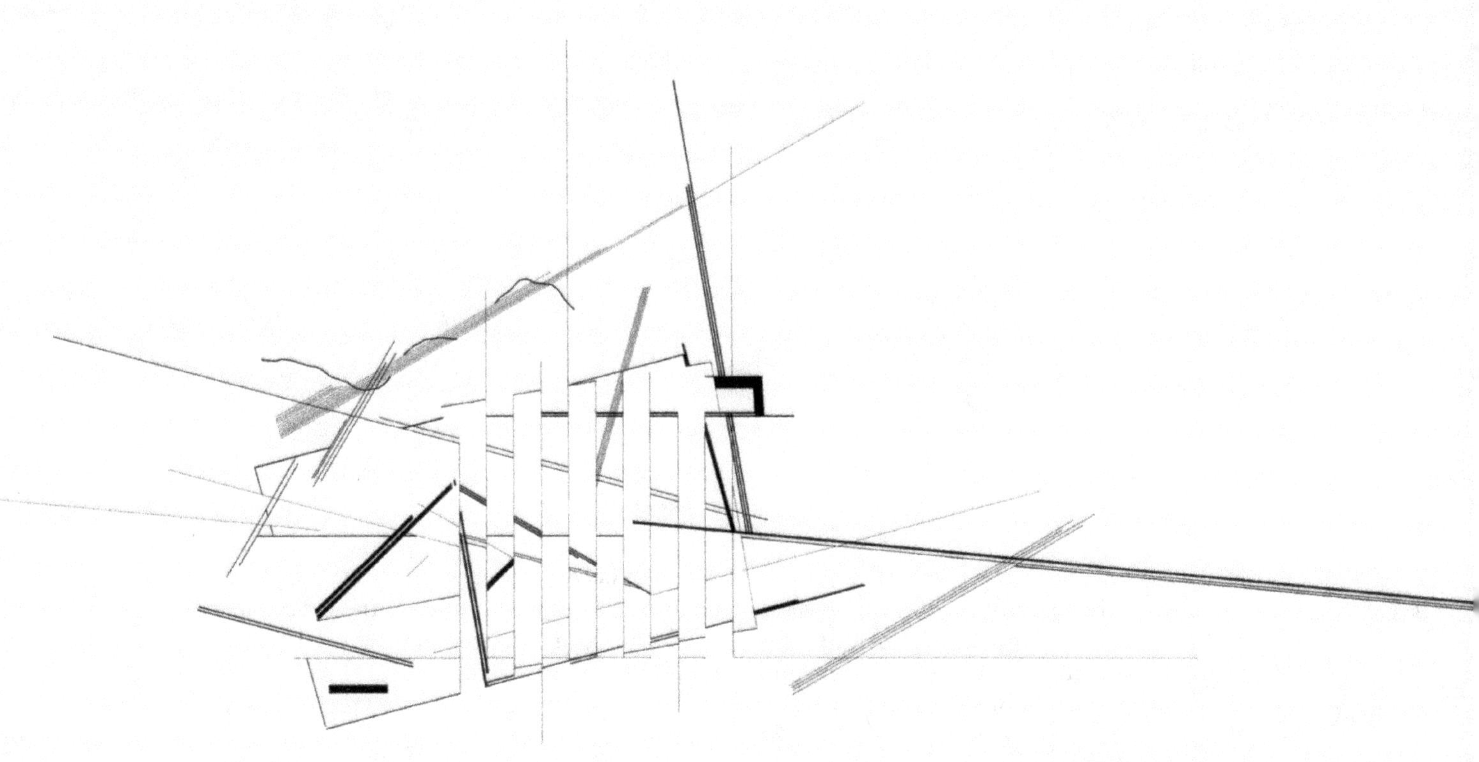

Plan, Ink on Strathmore

Savannah School of Design

Savannah, Georgia

Program: A Design School for 120 students

Studio	4 DBL Studio @ 1500 (each)		6000
Crit (areas)	4 @	500 each	2000
Labs	2 @	500 each	1000
Seminar (class)	4 @	500 each	2000
Gallery		2000	2000
Library			
Admin		500	500
Faculty Off 10 @ 150			1500
Public RR 2 @ 150			300
5 Faculty Townhouses @ 1000 each			5000
Dorms (60 students rms @ 150 each)			9000
Baths (4 group baths @ 250 each)			1000
Dining (2000 including kitchen) 500			2500
30% Circ + Mech			9700
Exterior Space(s)			8000
Total			50000

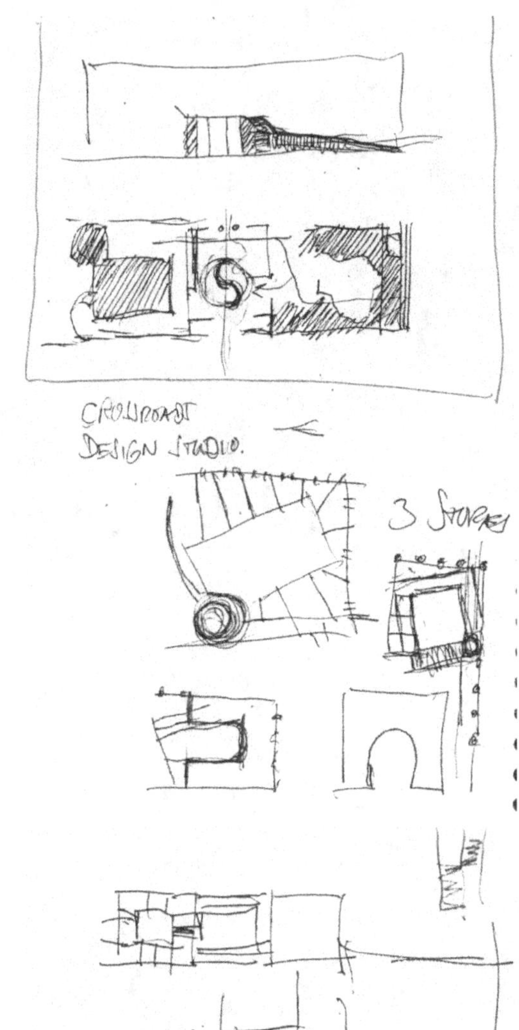

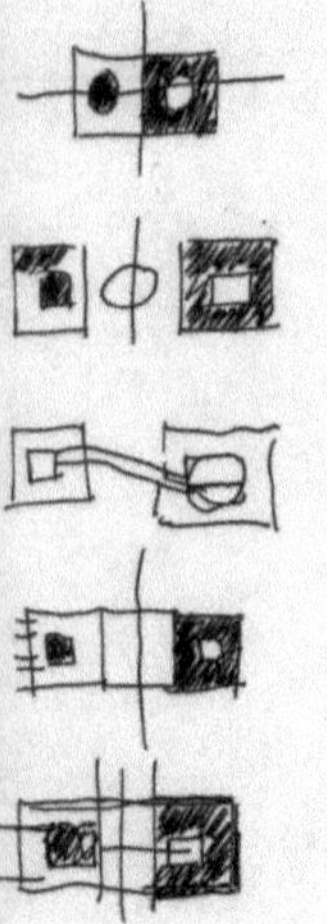

I arrived at the design for this project through the study of Savannah's architectural typology which includes the ideas of the square, the walled street, and the inherent duality of the Savannah house (front + back, representational towards the square and utilitarian toward the alley).

The Design School is sited on one of the 'set piece' lots fronting Monterey Square. Thus the building has a definite front addressing the square, and a back oriented towards one of the through streets.

The sides of the building were kept as solid as possible to address the street as a space without becoming oppressive. for example an arcade runs around the southwest corner of the building to mediate between street and built environment.

The Design School itself is conceived as a tri-partite scheme. An object surrounded by space (1. studios and galleries), and a space carved out of an object (2. dorms and offices), separated by a meeting space (3. cafeteria) which in Savannah's typology becomes the separator between the historical servant's housing and owner's quarters.

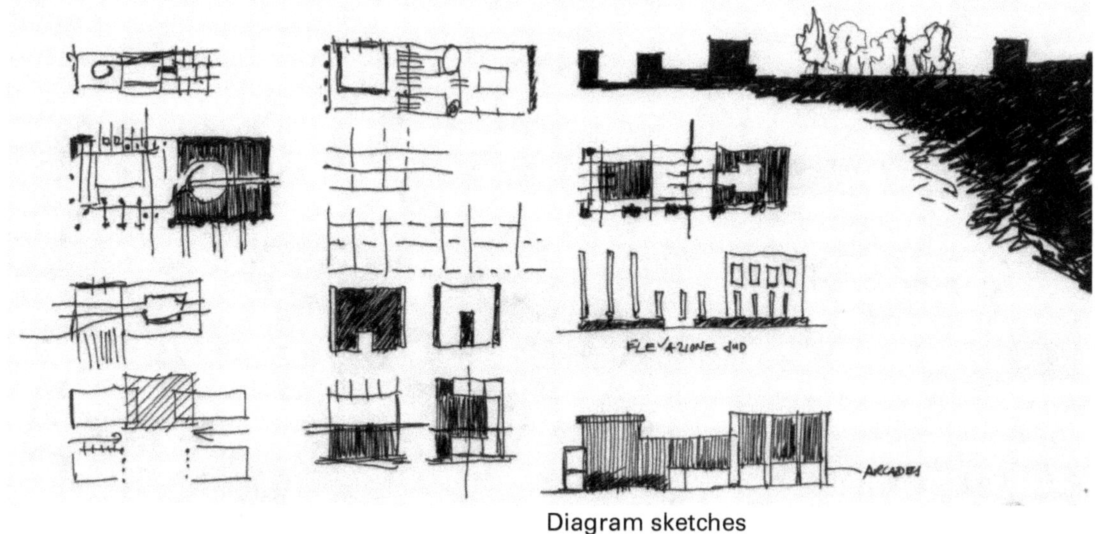

Diagram sketches

Figureground drawing of downtown Savannah site (ink on mylar)

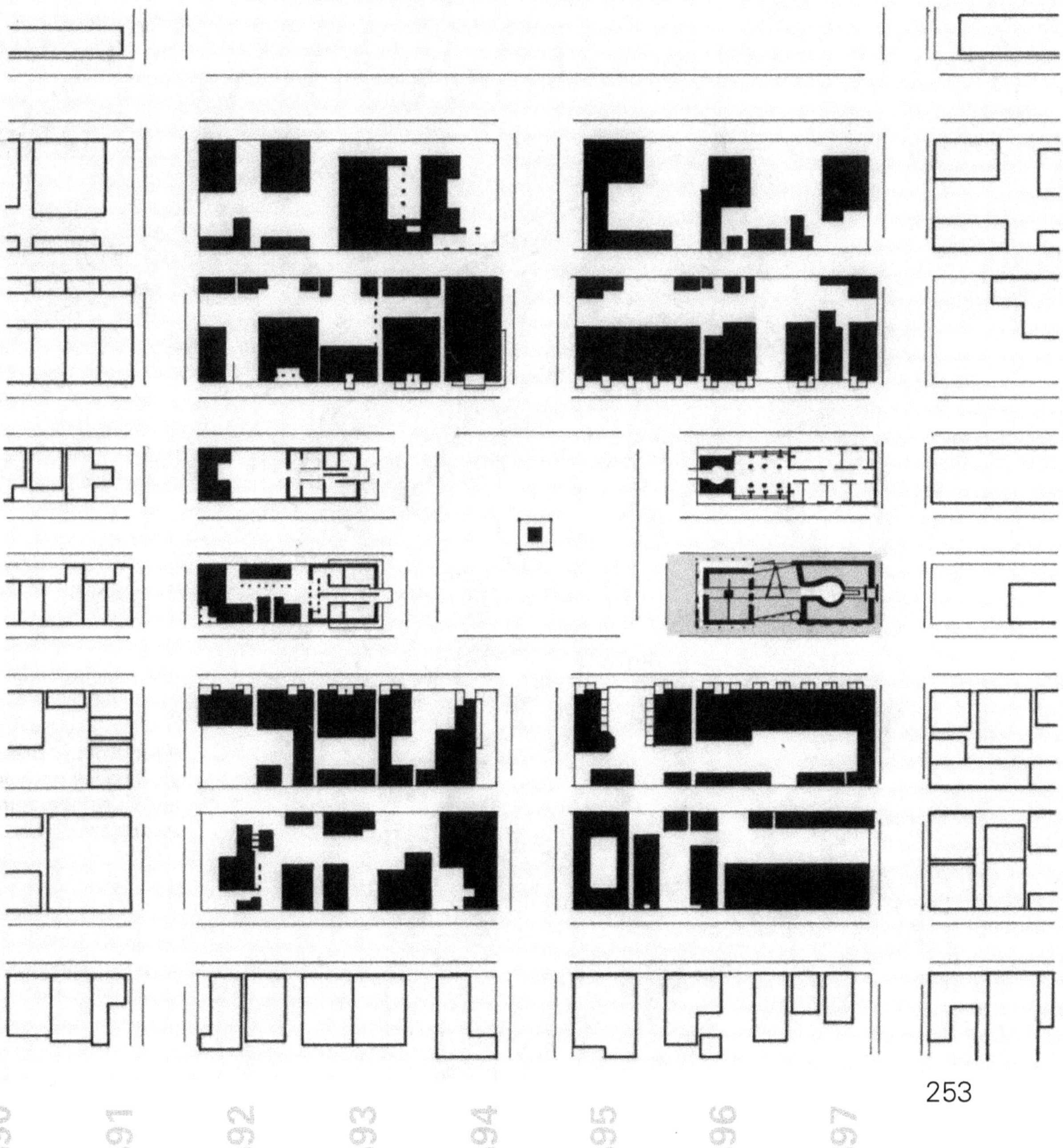

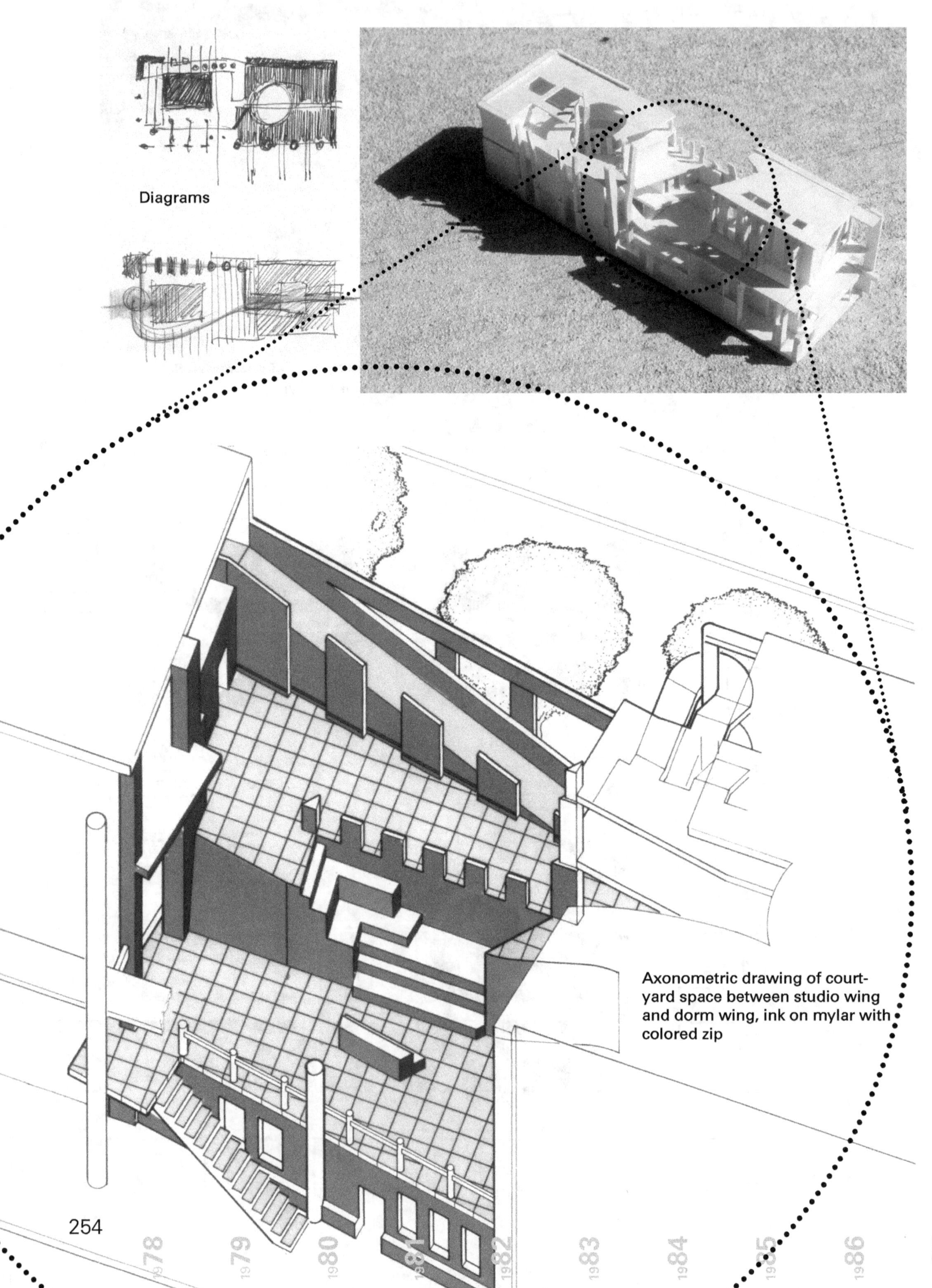

Diagrams

Axonometric drawing of courtyard space between studio wing and dorm wing, ink on mylar with colored zip

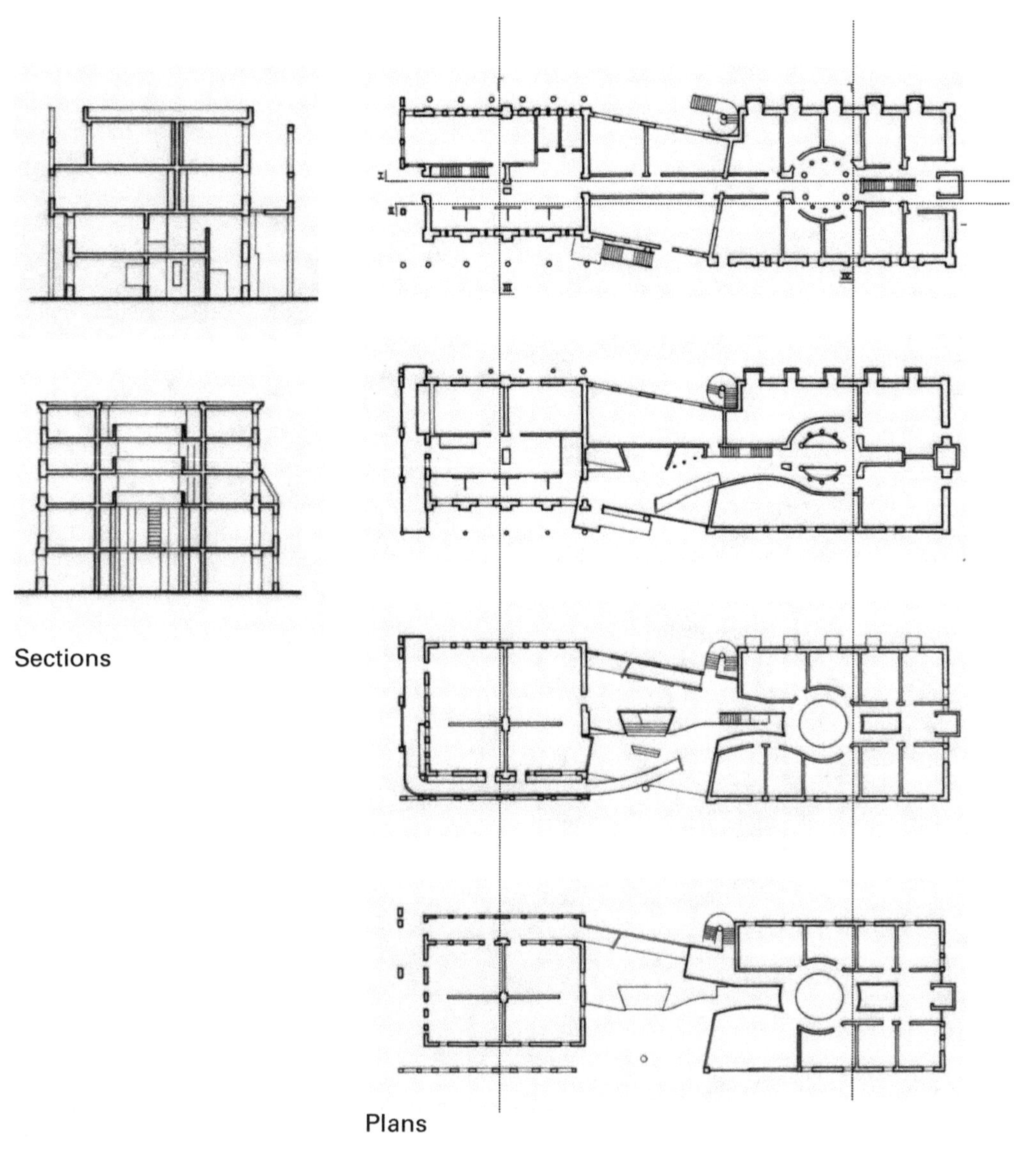

Sections

Plans

Sections

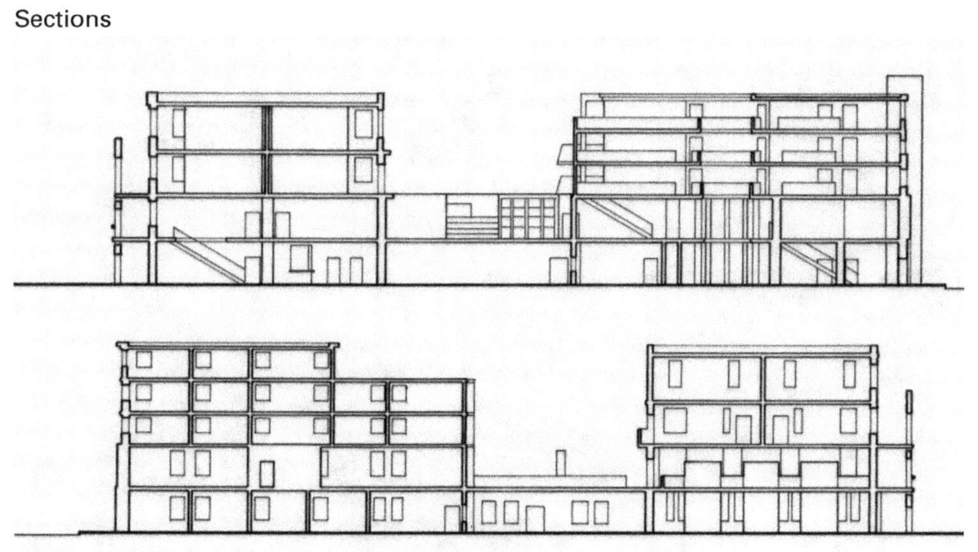

First Floor

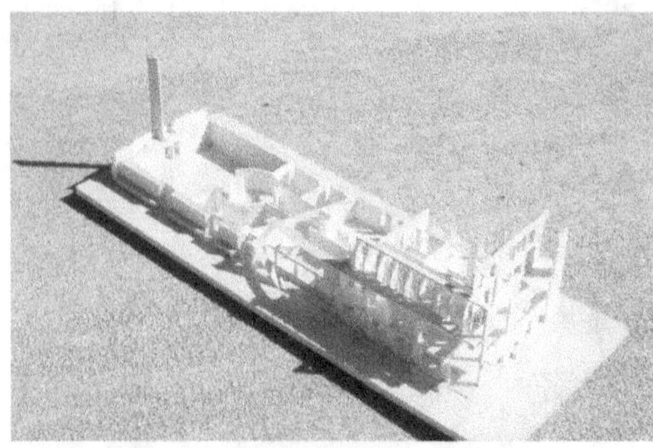

Second Floor

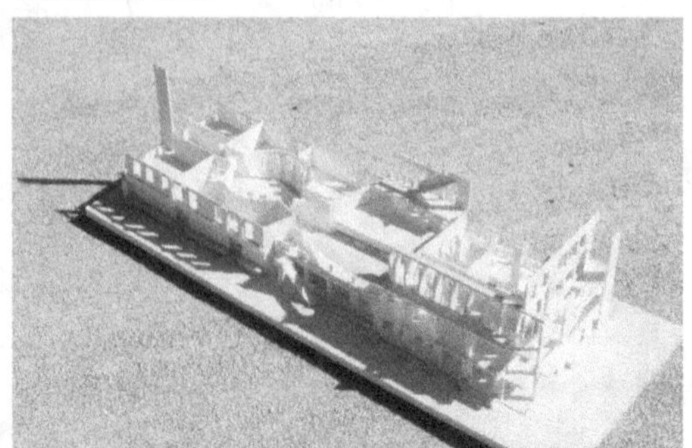

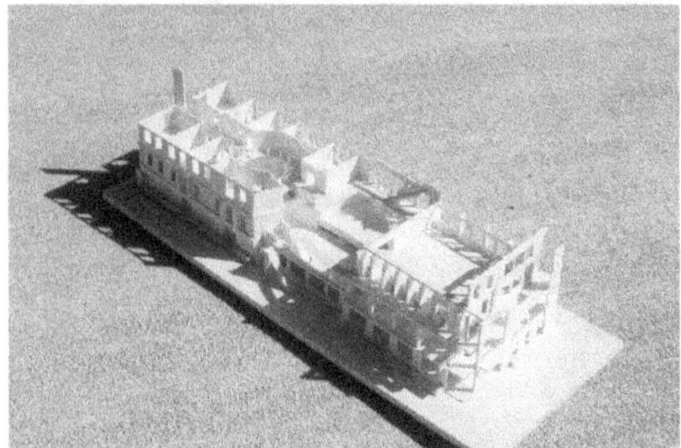

Third Floor

Final Model from Northwest

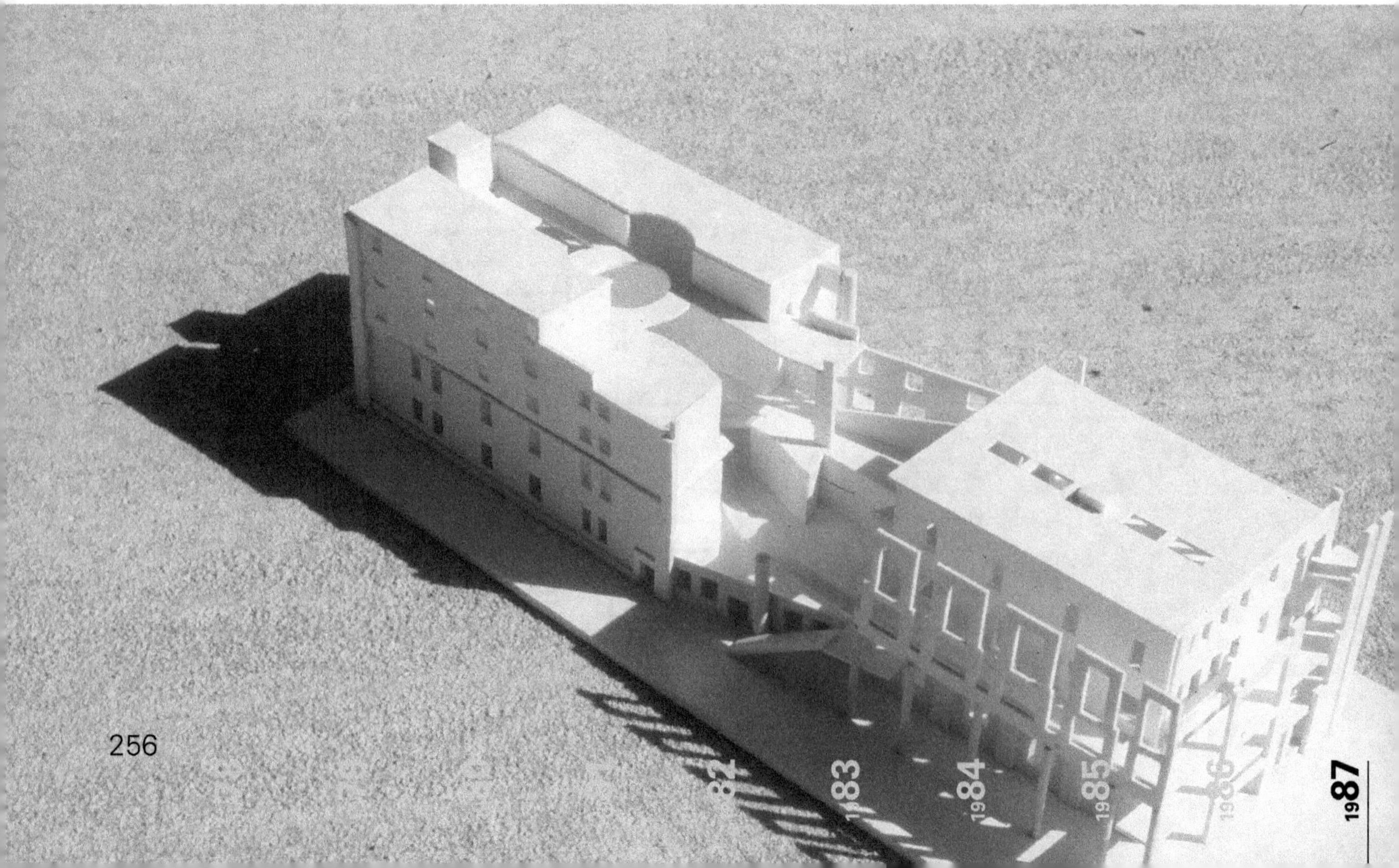

Elevations

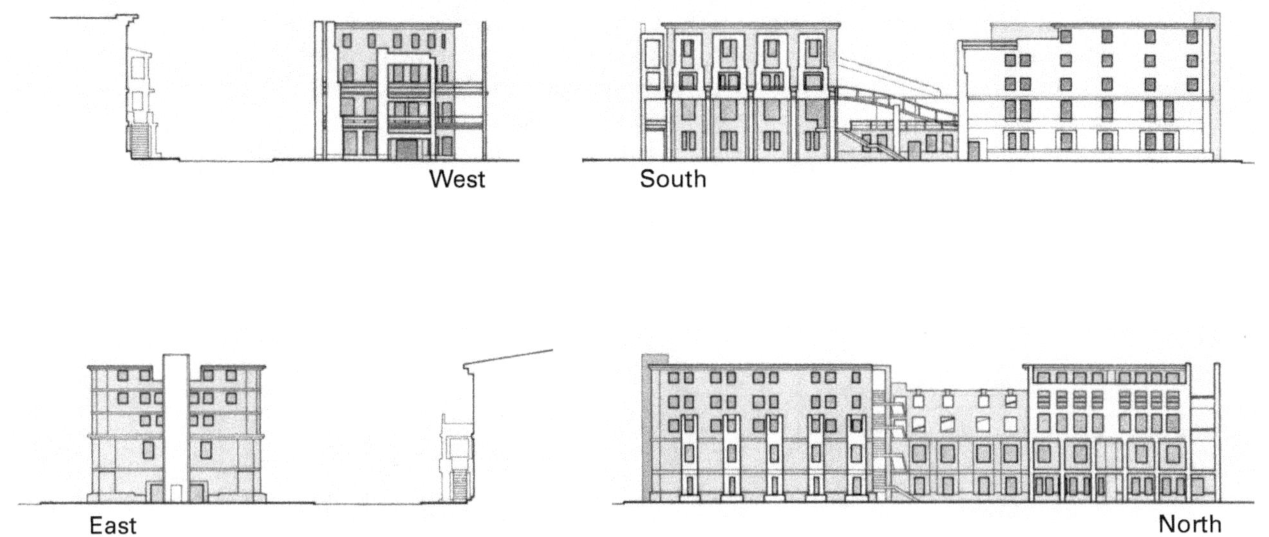

Final Model from Southwest

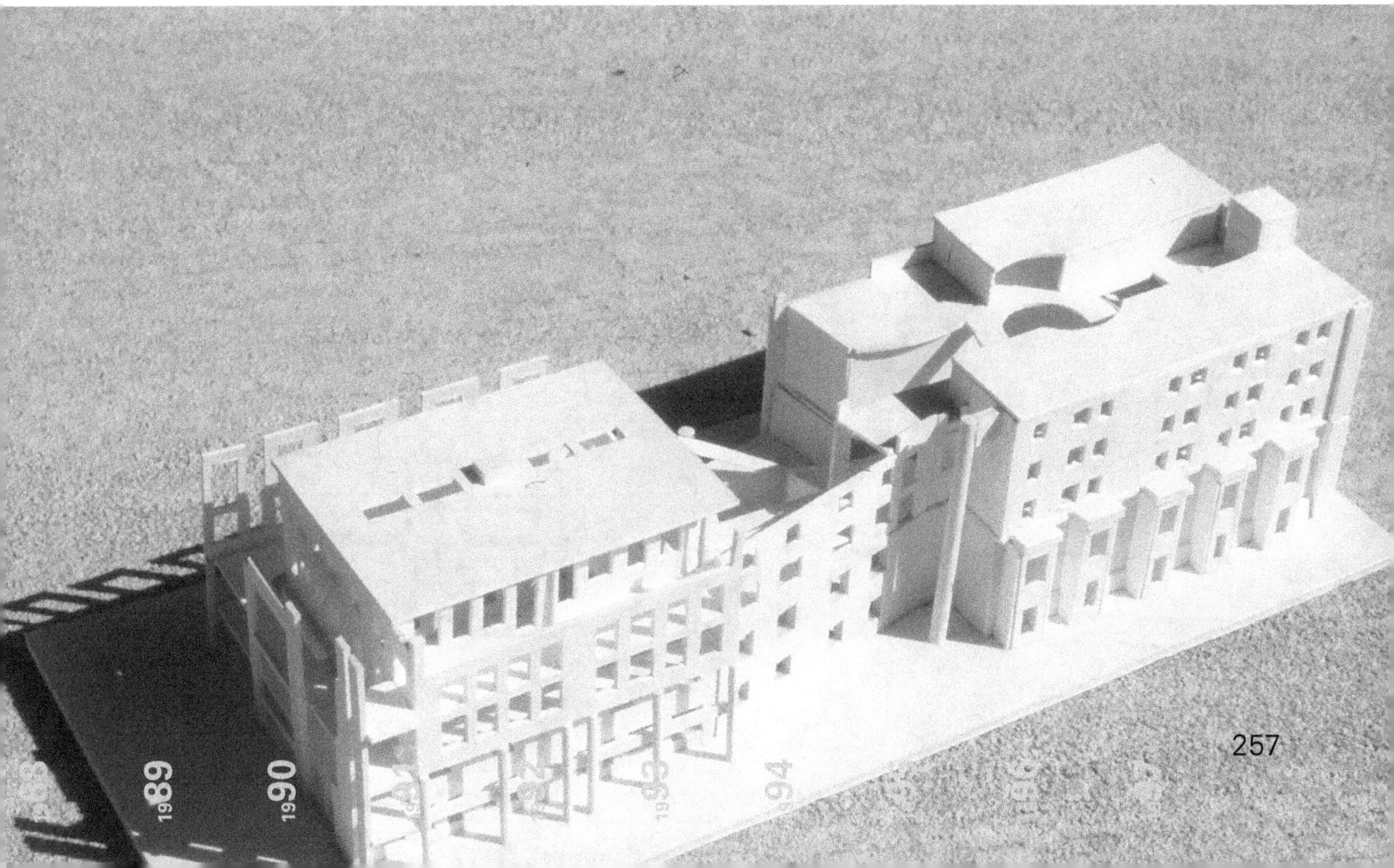

Project: Boston Infill

Newbury Street, Boston, MA

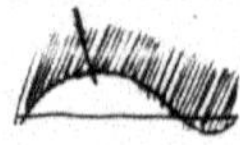

Scenario: Ms. Genevieve Hue, harpsichord builder and painter. Born in 1941 in Senlis, France. Received an M.A. in painting from the Art Institute of Chicago in 1966. Studied harpsichord building with Richard Kingston in Marshall, North Carolina. Freelance work as an artist in New York until 1982, then move to Boston. In the fall of 1986 Ms. Hue inherits a not unsubstantial sum of money and decides to buy some property off Newbury Street, and to build a combined workshop/gallery/studio with two apartments in the back to rent to students.

The character of the client obviously influenced the design of this project which deals with the following issues: continuity of Newbury Street as a wall, the narrow cross section of the building, and music notation as form giver.

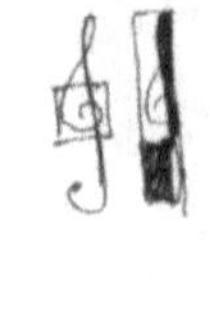

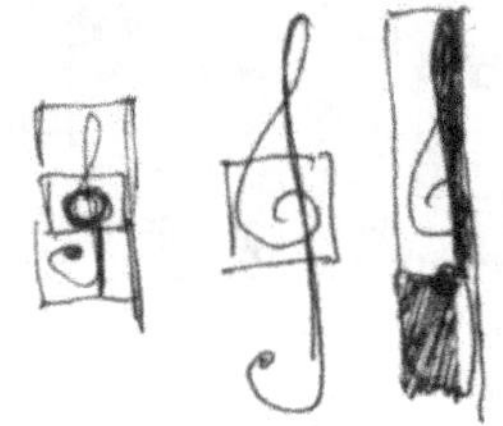

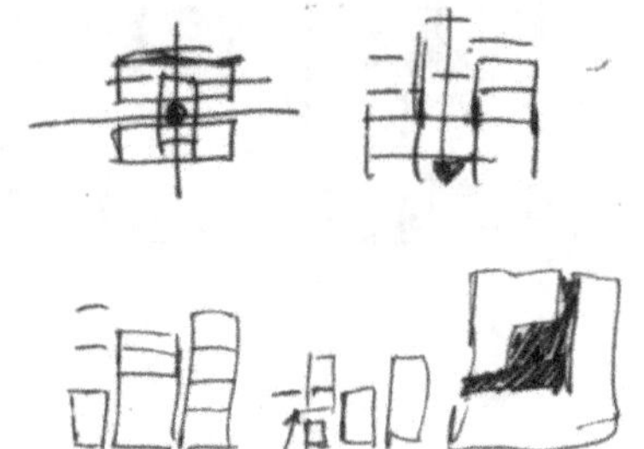

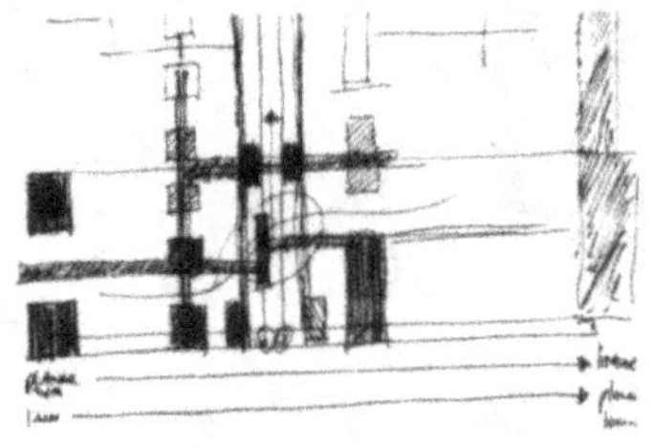

Design sketches

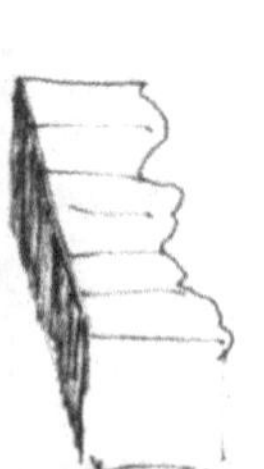

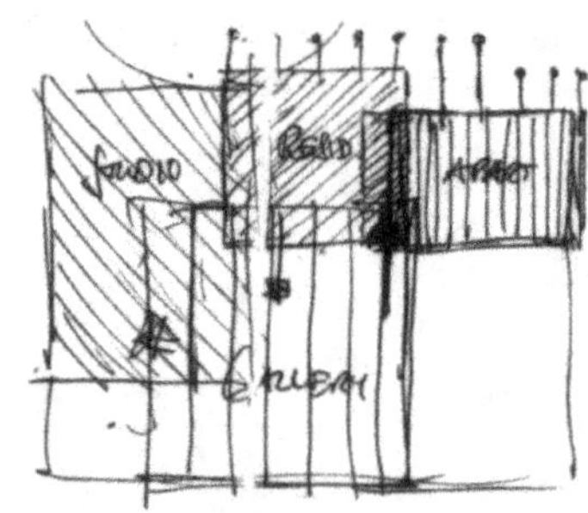

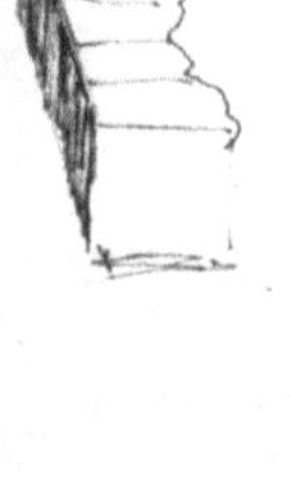

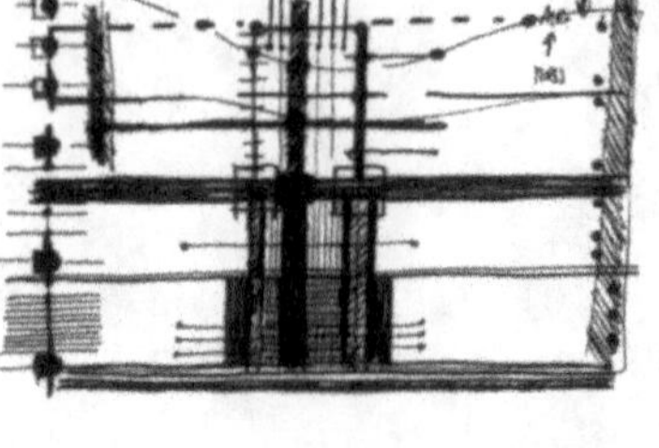

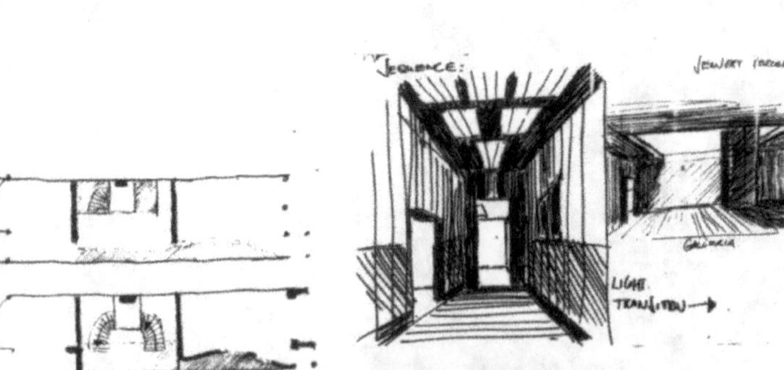

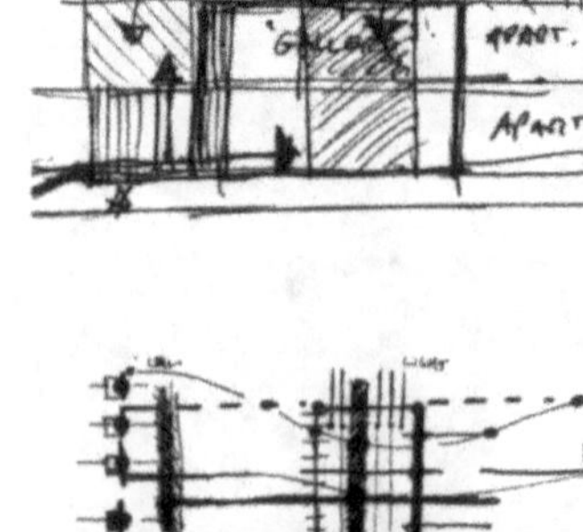

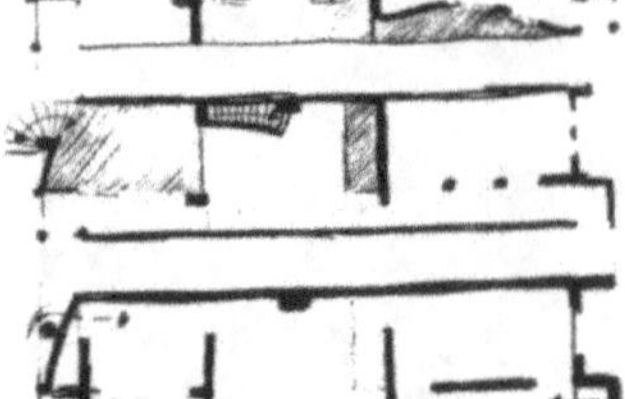

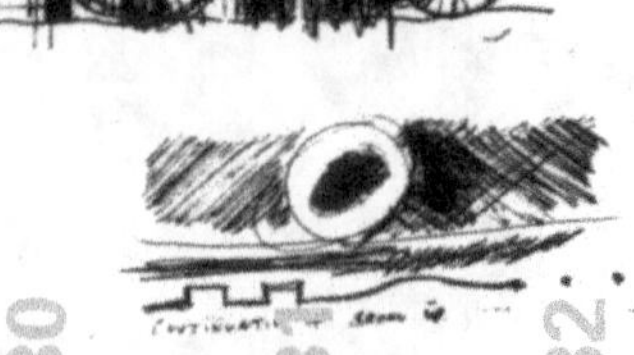

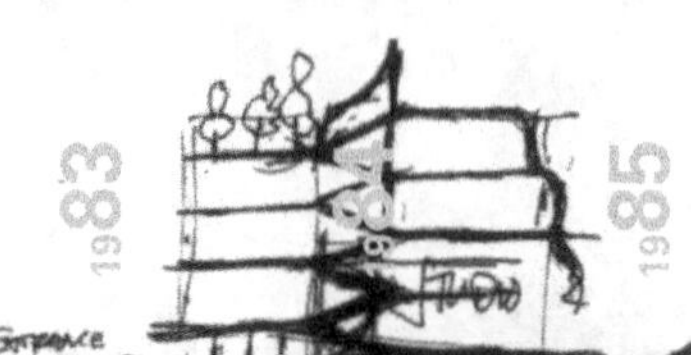

ARTICULATION STEPS:
DO MEIER DIAGRAMS
STRESS STRUCTURE
→ SPACE

MUSIC: INTRODUCIONE
CHANGE
BACK TO BEGINNING

LINK BETWEEN
RESIDENCE
+ PUBLIC.

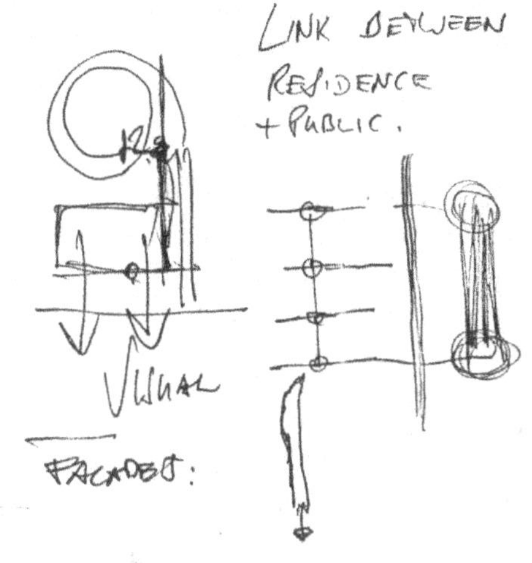

VISUAL

FACADES:

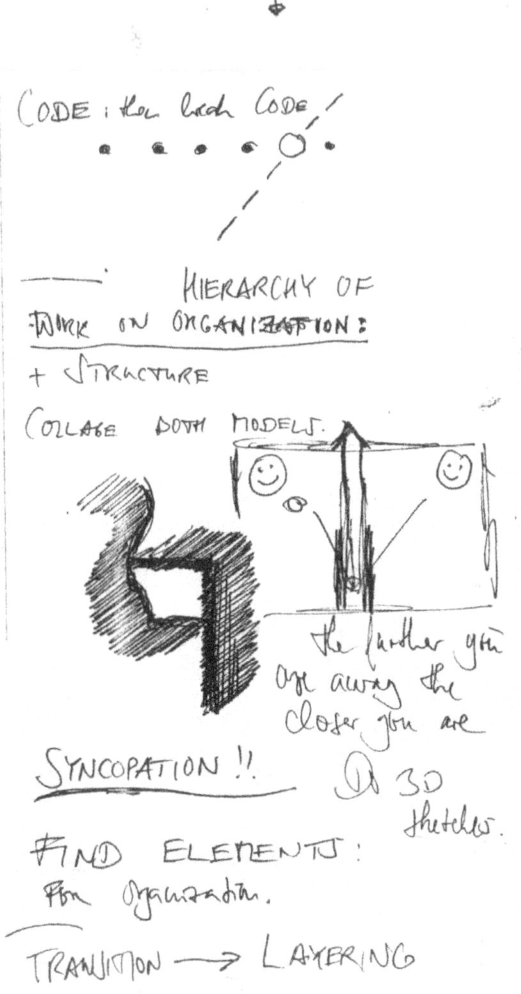

CODE: the brick CODE

HIERARCHY OF
WORK ON ORGANIZATION:
+ STRUCTURE
COLLAGE BOTH MODELS.

the further you go away the closer you are

SYNCOPATION !!

DO 3D sketches.

FIND ELEMENTS:
for organization.

TRANSITION → LAYERING

CURVES: INFLUENCE ON DESIGN

STAIRS!!

FACADE

STRESS HORIZONTALITY.

SHADED BY SHALLOW HORIZONTALS

STRAIGHT STAIRS ↔ CURVED LINE

TRANSITIONS:
DO SOMETHING ONCE, CHANGE
NO REPETITIONS; IF, THEN TRANSFORMED.

OBJECT IN SPACE: MONUMENT.
HOW DOES FACADE END?
LOOK AT SUGGESTIONS OF SPACE
~~CURVES CONNECTING LIGHT~~
SOFT VS. HARD.

8 p.m. University Gallery Opening of Exhibition.

PROCESS

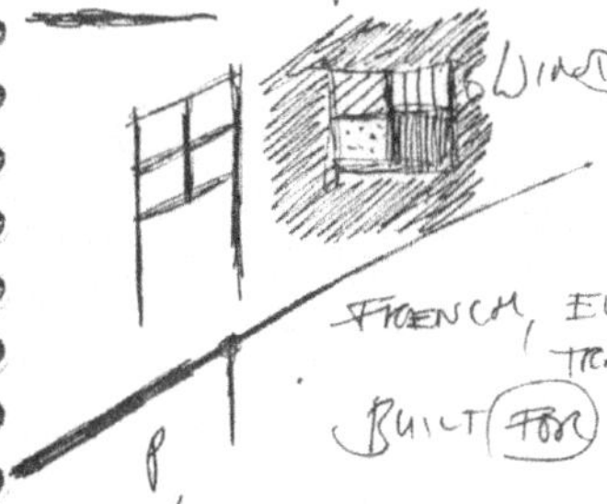

WINDOW DIAGRAM.

FRENCH, EUROPEAN TRADITION
BUILT FOR GENEVIEVE.

LIFE ARTISTE
PRIVATE VS. PUBLIC
RATIONAL VS. IRRATIONAL.

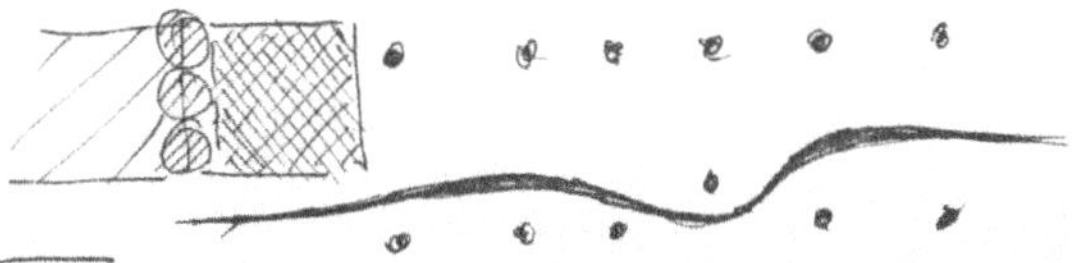

MAKE MORE COMPLICATED DIAGRAM
MAYBE

REGULATING LINES. NOT VIP NOW.

flip up.
BARCELONA PAVILION FROM to

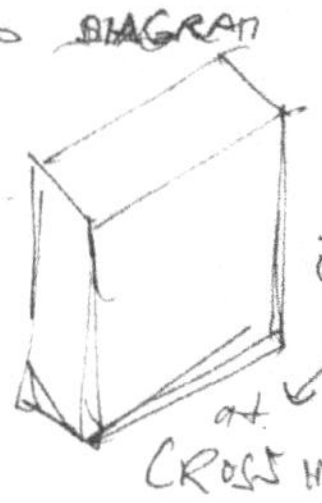

OPPOSING GRID
ROTATE → MOVEMENTO
at JUXTAPOSING CROSSING POINTS

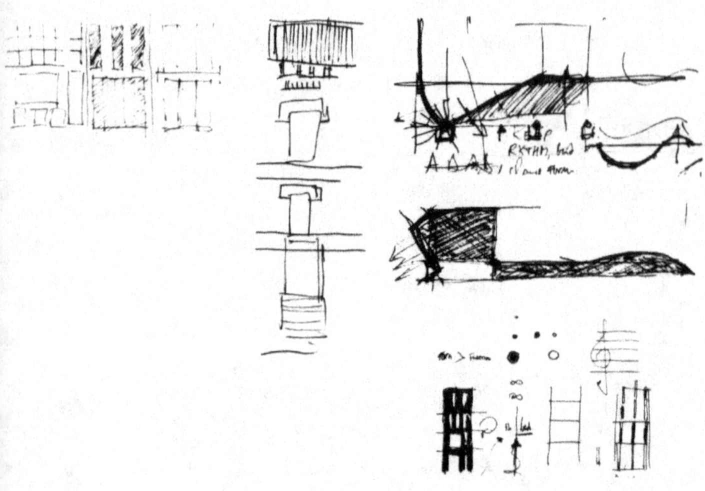

Other Data:
Ms. Hue would like her residence to occupy the upper two stories facing Newbury Street. The lower floors are to be used for the gallery and the studio. The two apartments are to face the back alley that runs parallel to Newbury Street on the north side. The studio has to have good natural light from the north. The gallery could be two-story connected by a stairway.

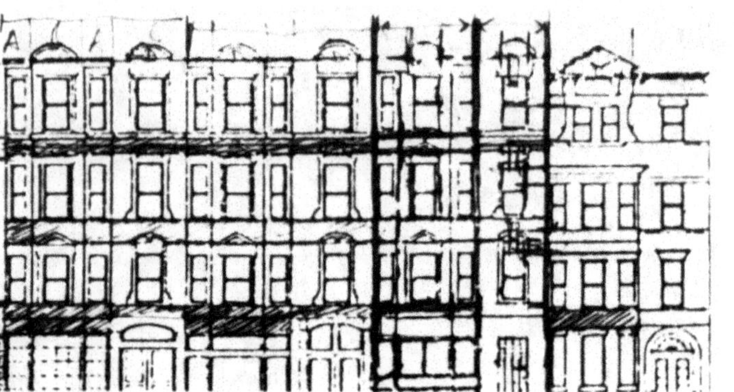

Elevational studies

Ms. Hue's Character:
Her skills as a harpsichord builder identify her as being both an artist as well as a rationalist. Harpsichord music was written in the 17th century, i.e. baroque era. The instrument itself is a synthesis of curved and straight lines, of form being more important than structure. These opposing ideas (systematization + dynamization) should carry through the whole structure because they reflect the character of Ms. Hue.

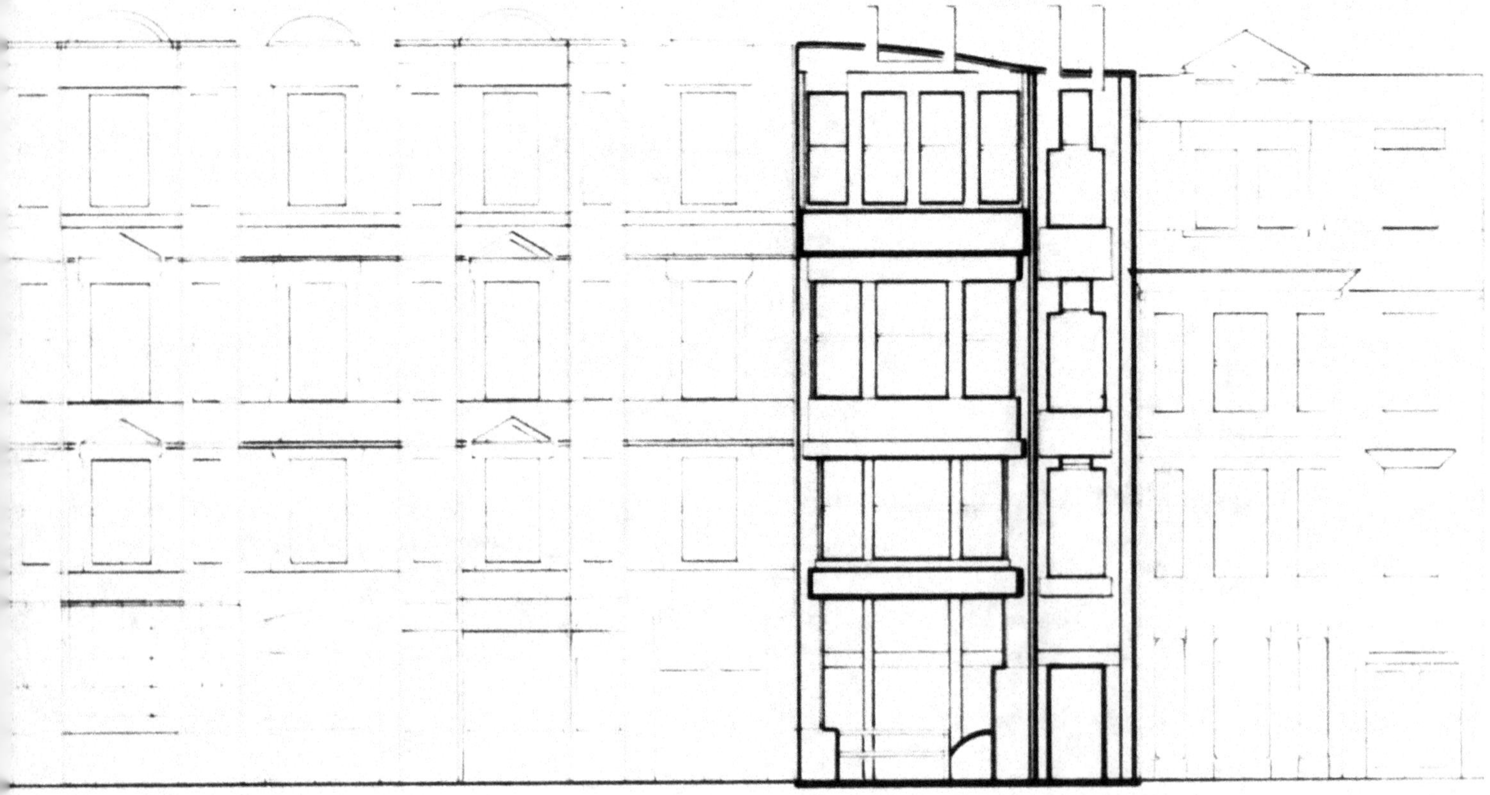

Program:
Residence, 2500 sq/f
Studio space with north light, 2000 sq/ft
Gallery for exhibit and sale of harpsichords and paintings 3000 sq/ft
Two apartments to be rented to M.I.T. students to pay off part of the mortage 1800 sq/ft

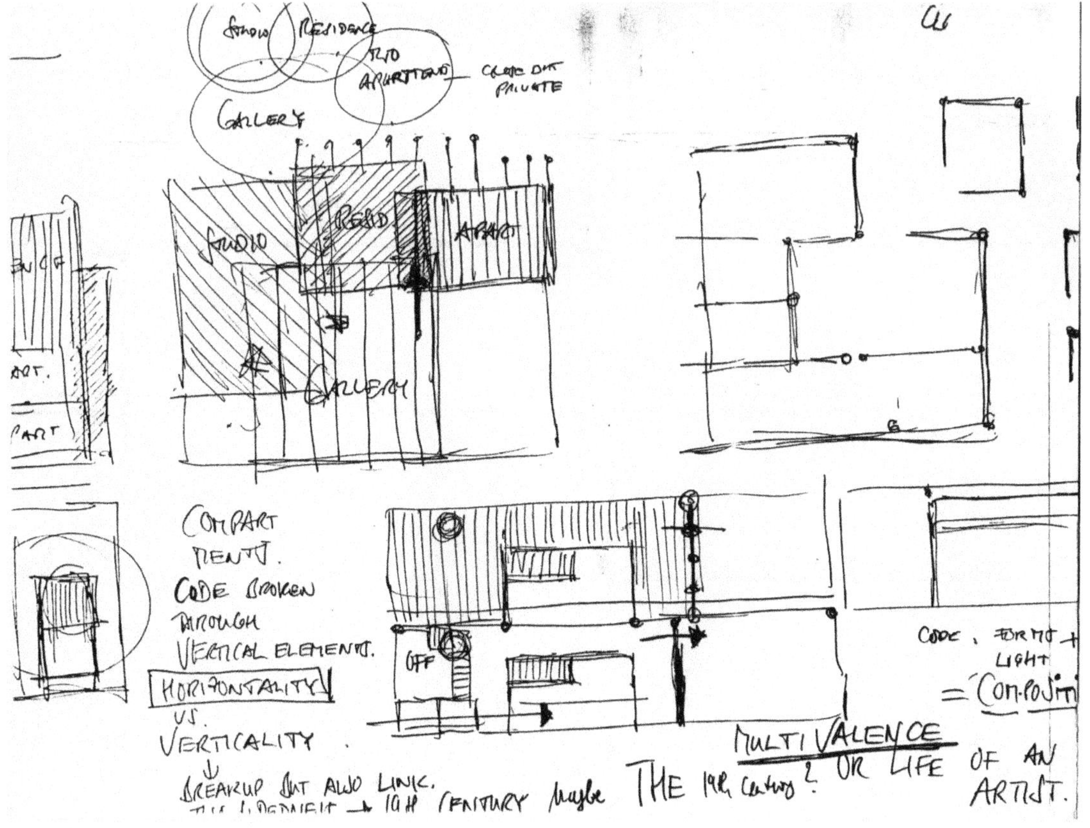

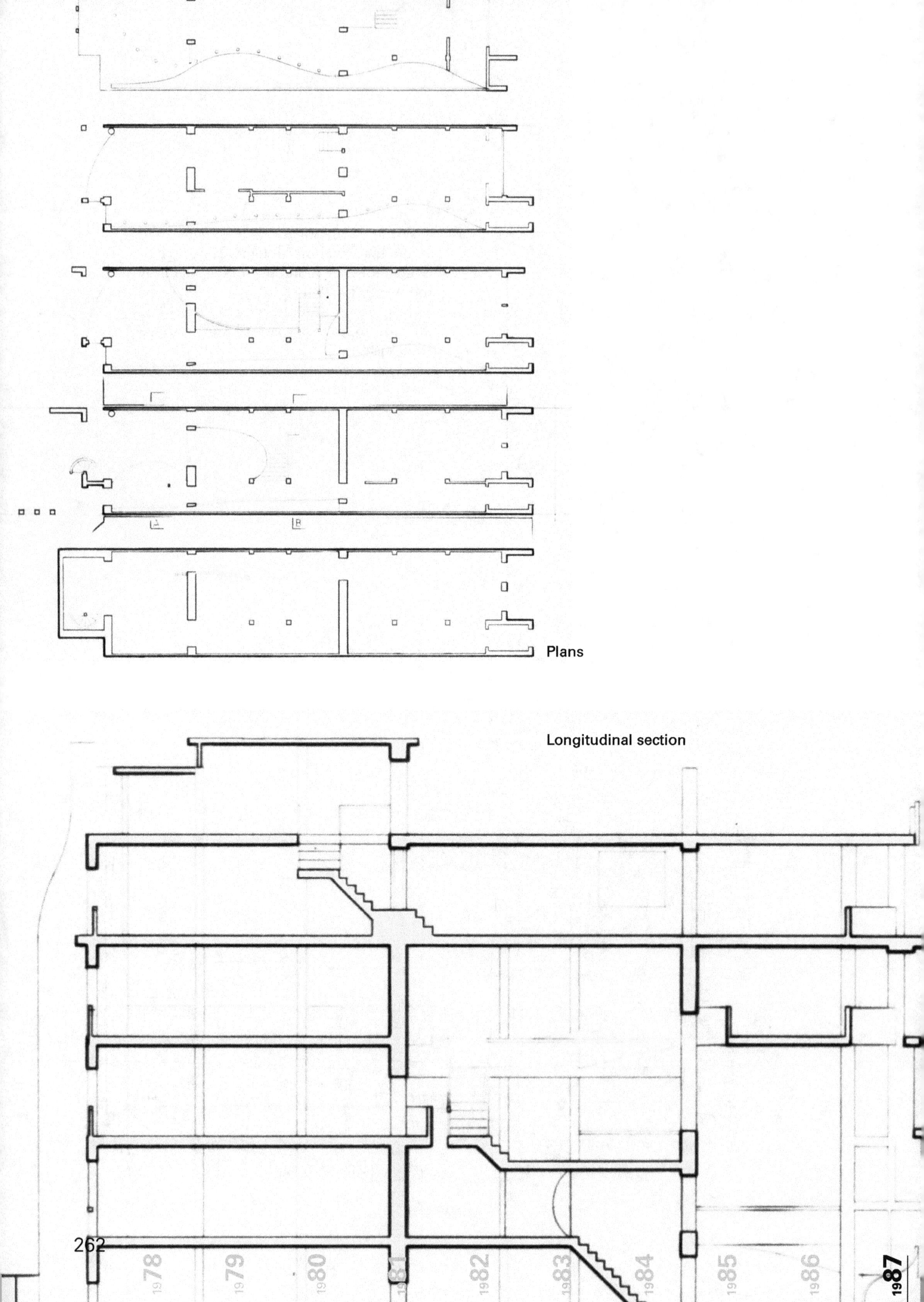

Plans

Longitudinal section

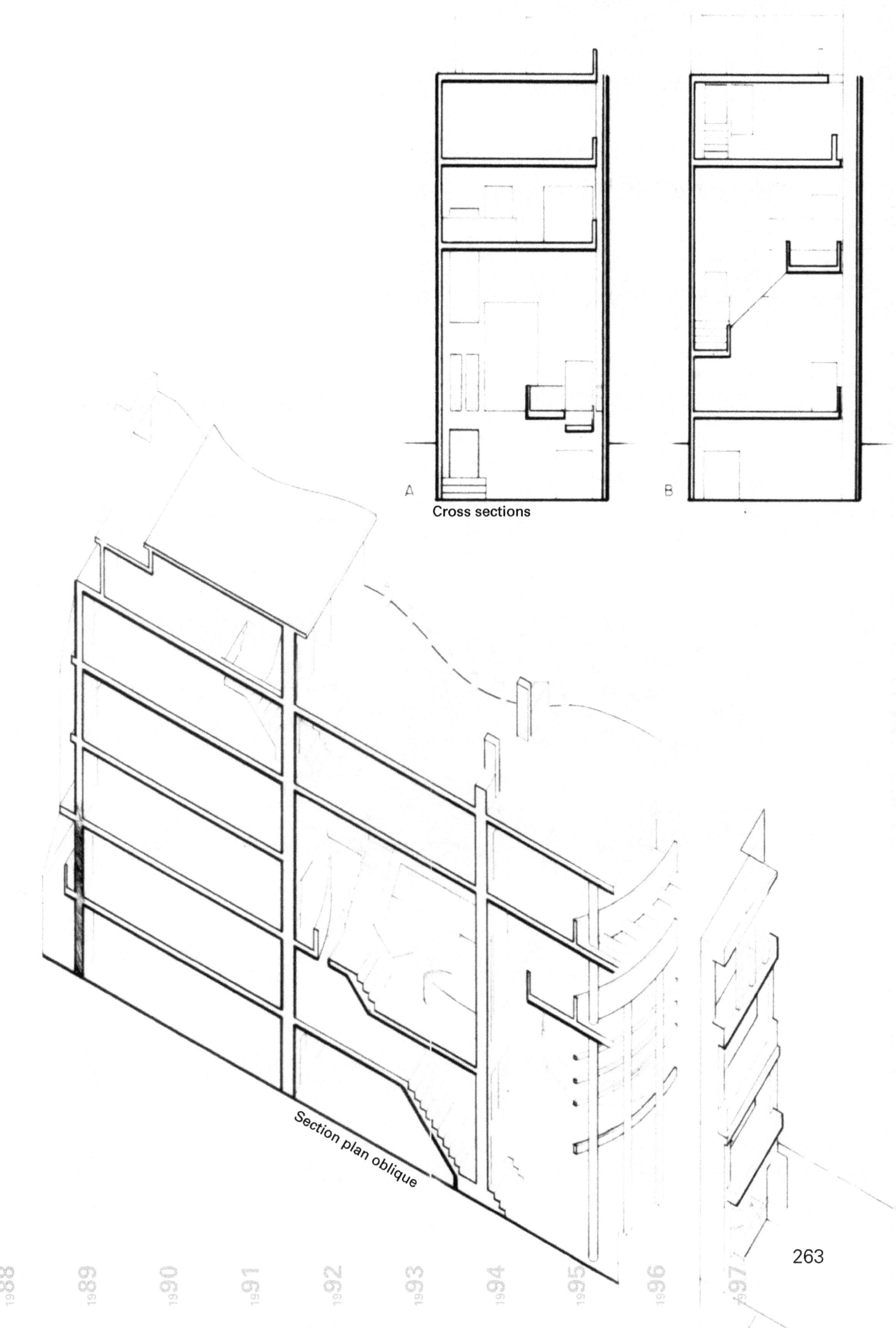

Cross sections

Section plan oblique

University of Florida Marine Biology Laboratory

Seahorse Key, Florida

The task was to design a Marine Biology Laboratory on Seahorse Key, a small island off of Cedar Key, in the Gulf of Mexico. With an old lighthouse that had been converted into dorms, and existing buildings that were no longer adequate for laboratory use, the program called for new living and working facilities, and the conversion of the lighthouse into a visitor center.

Section of Gulf of Mexico with topo map overlay

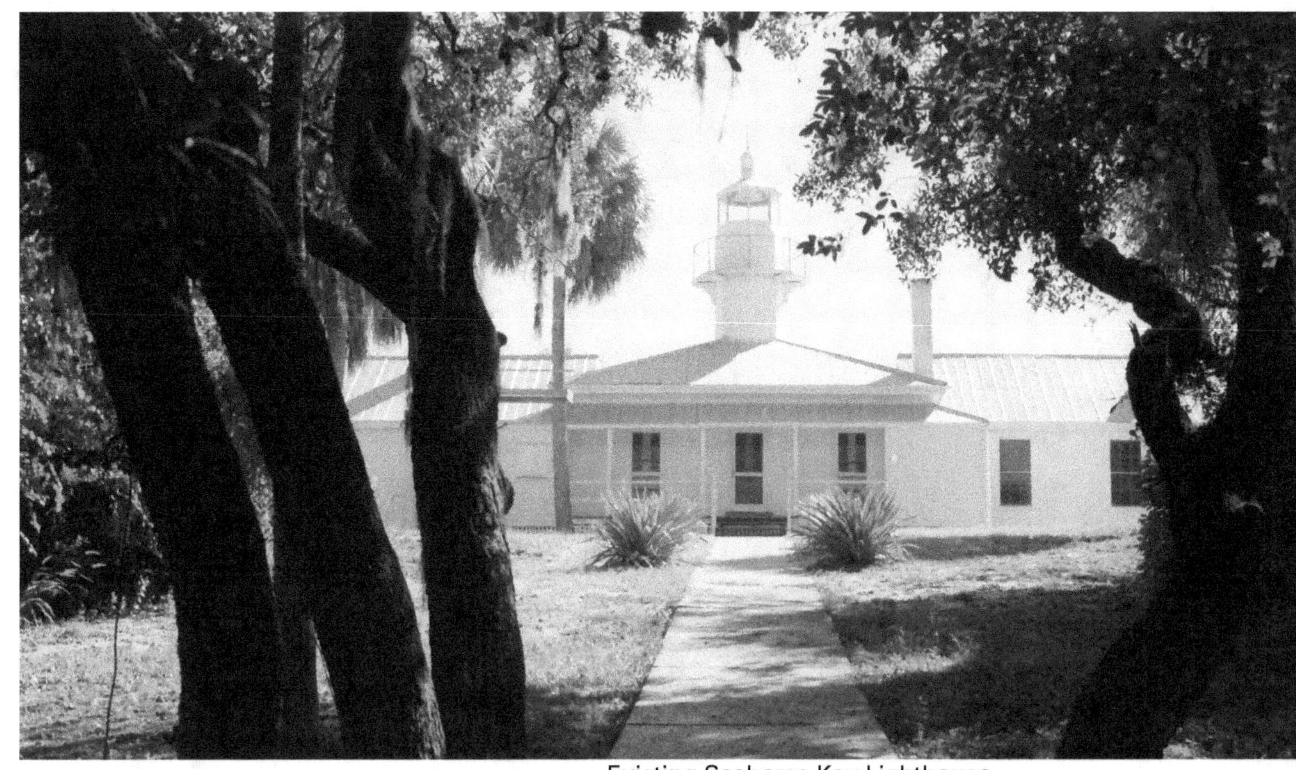

Existing Seahorse Key Lighthouse

Vegetation on Seahorse Key

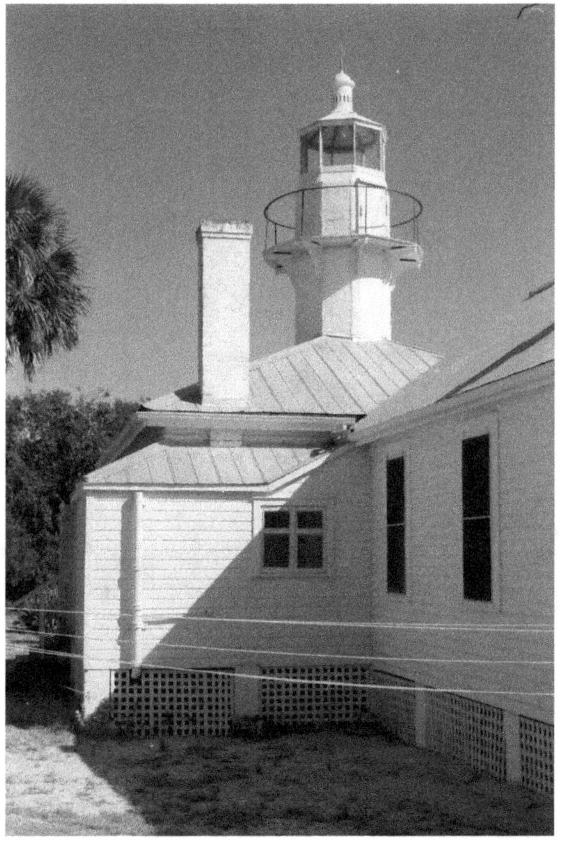

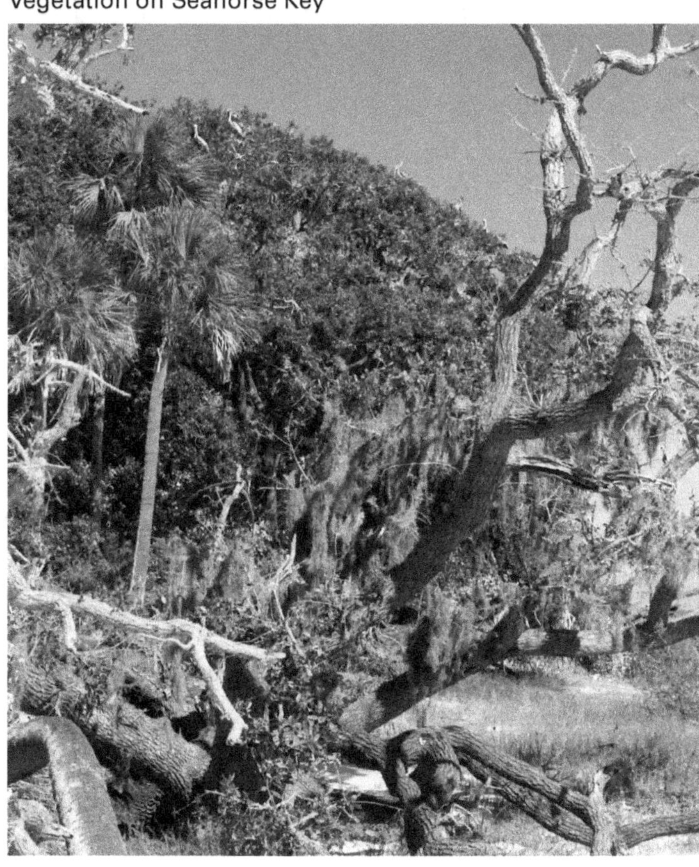

Developmental sketches

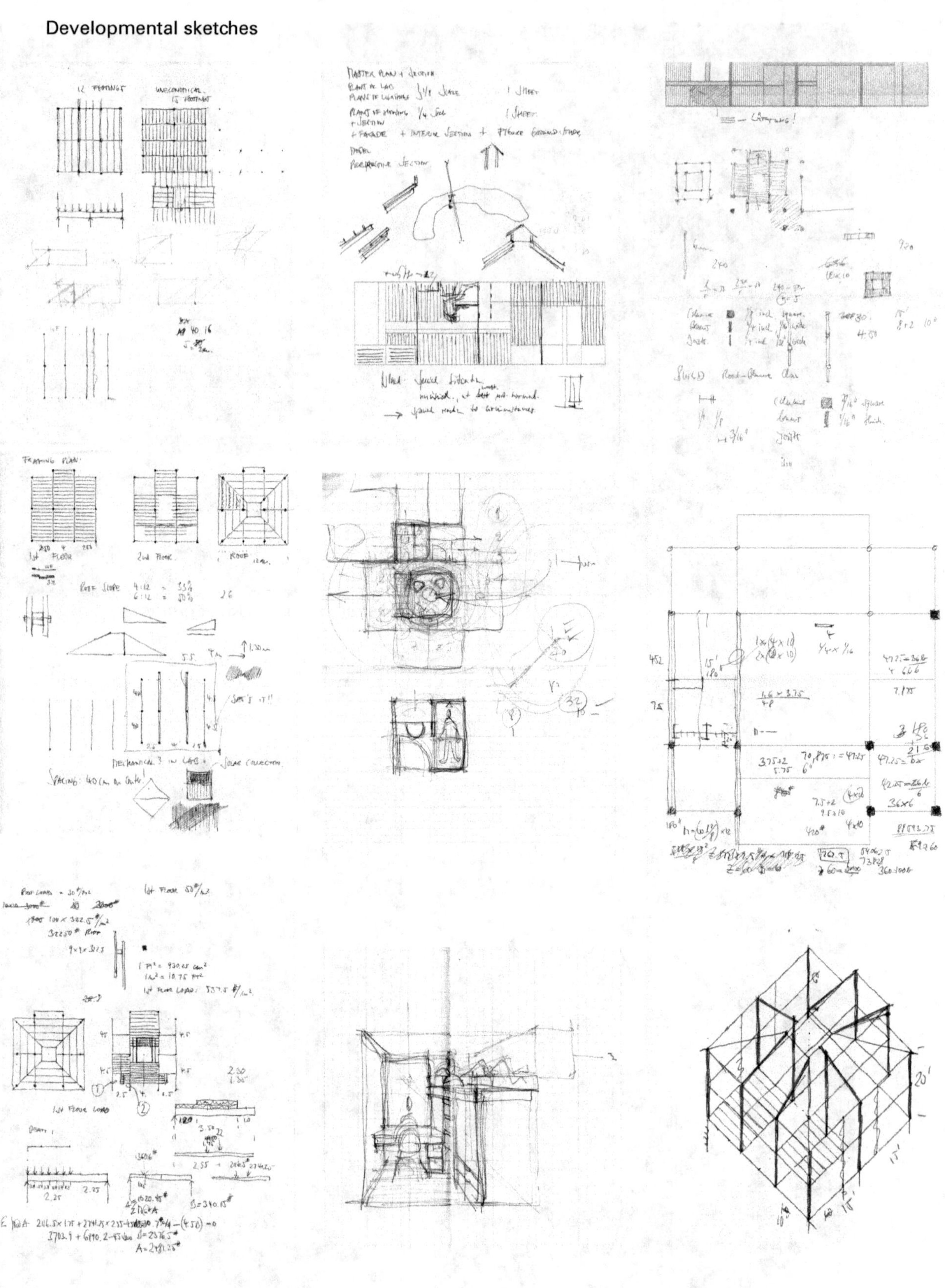

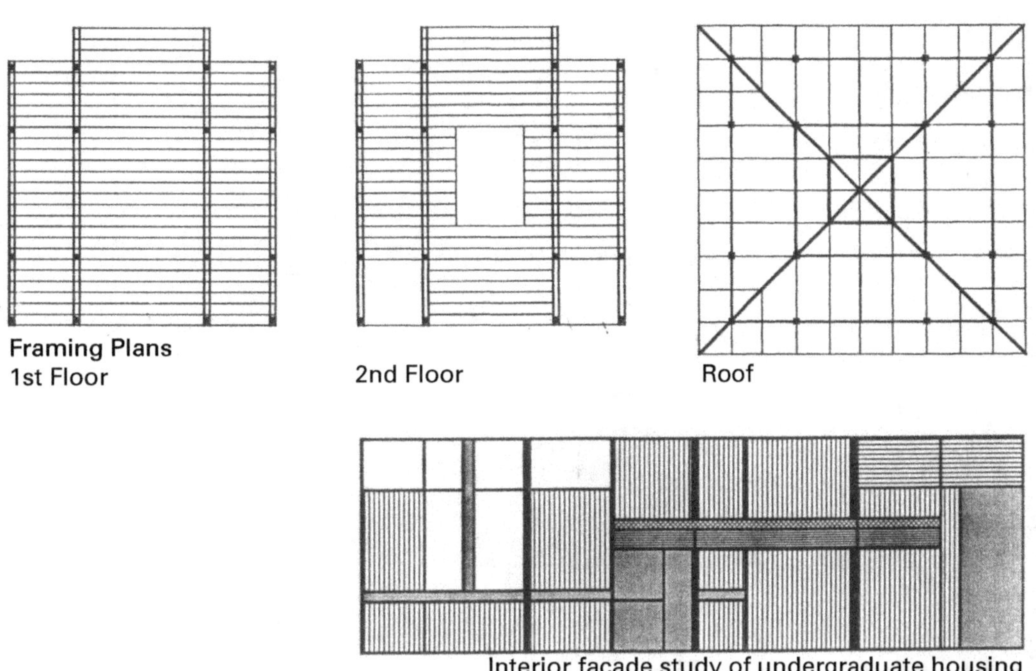

Framing Plans
1st Floor

2nd Floor

Roof

Interior facade study of undergraduate housing

Section perspective through housing unit showing approach up to the lighthouse

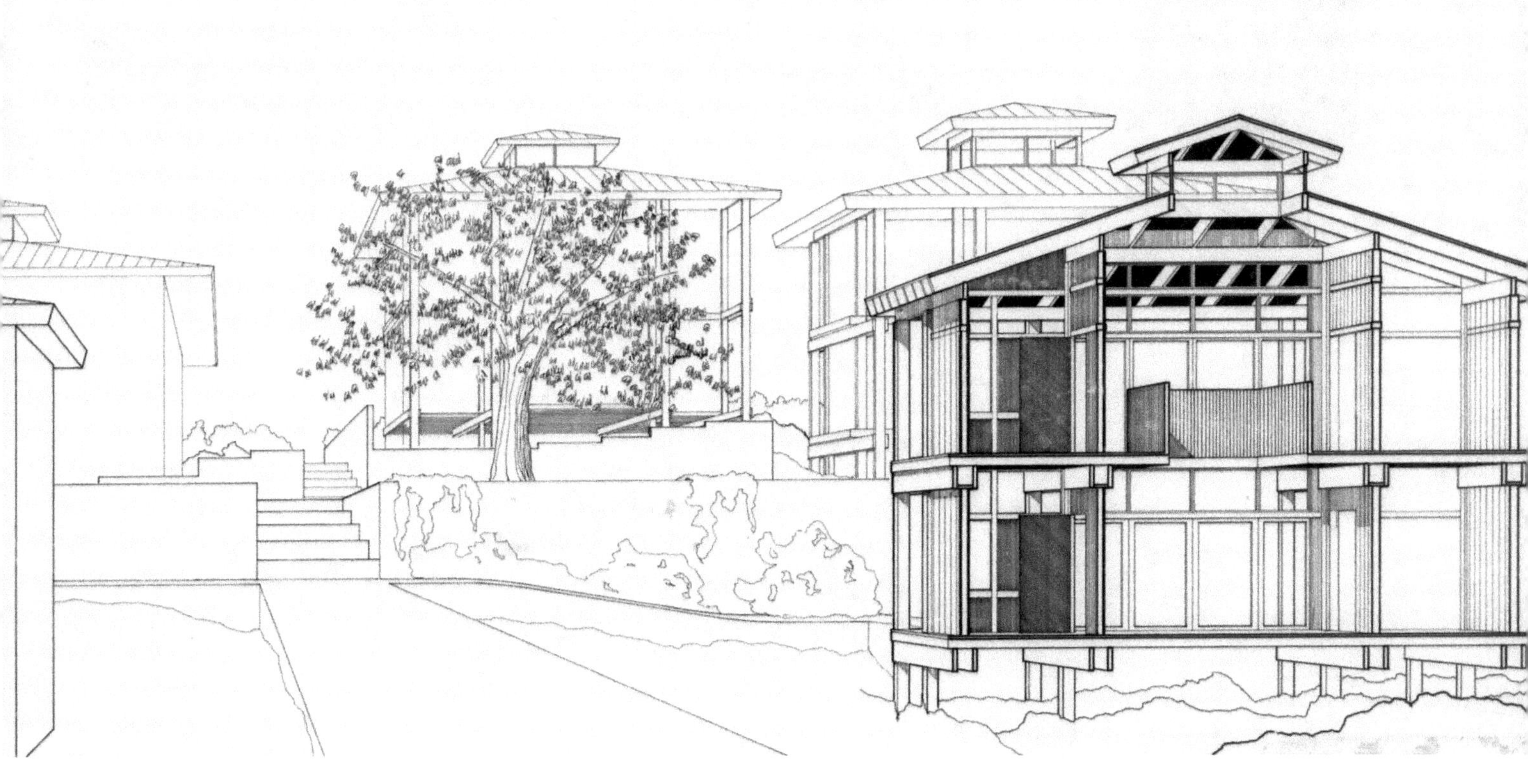

Architectural Projects

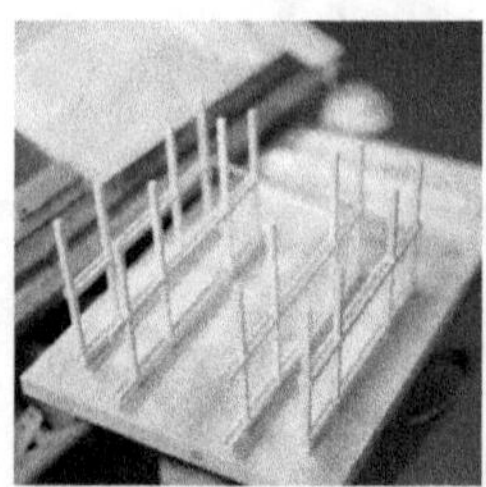

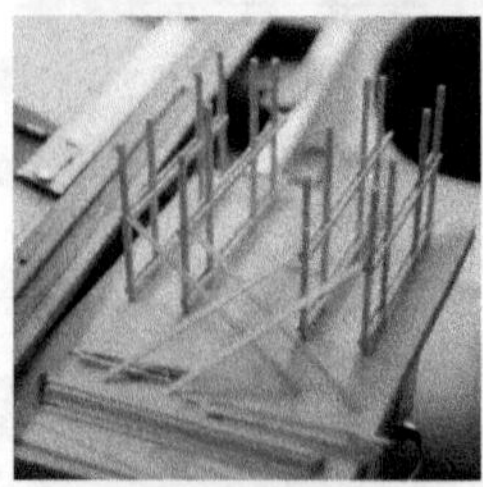

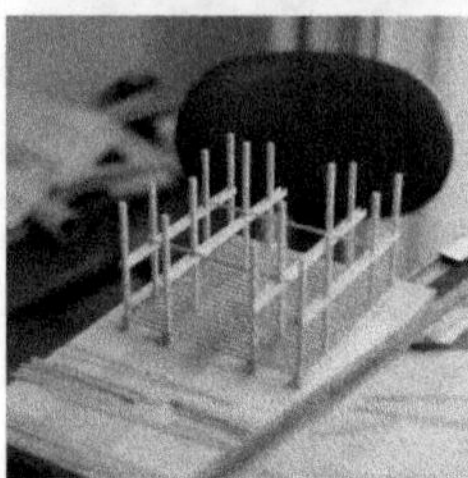

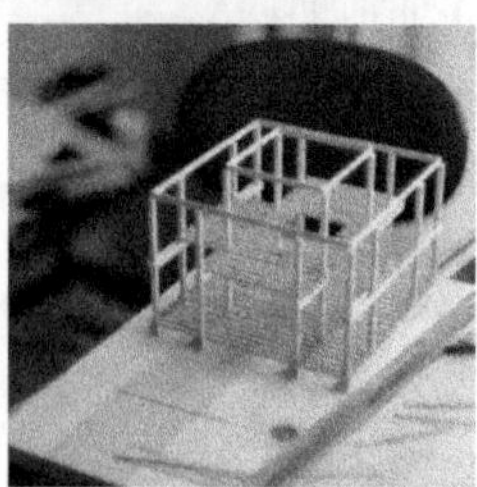

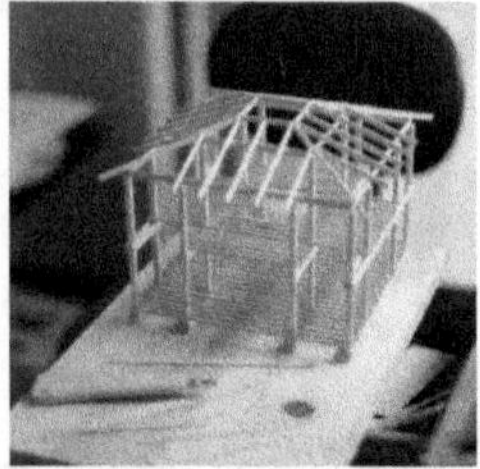

Model construction

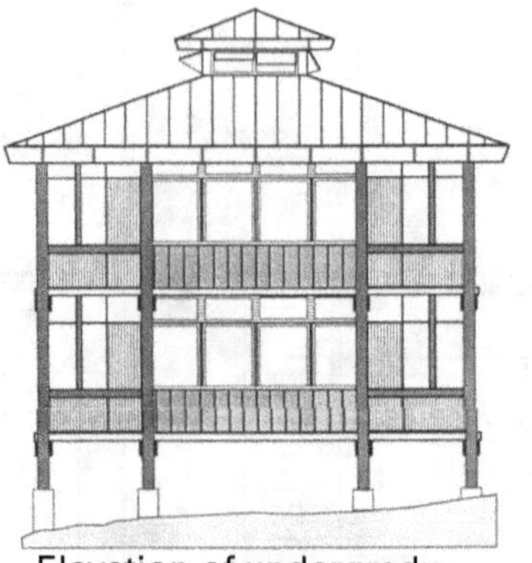

Elevation of undergraduate housing unit

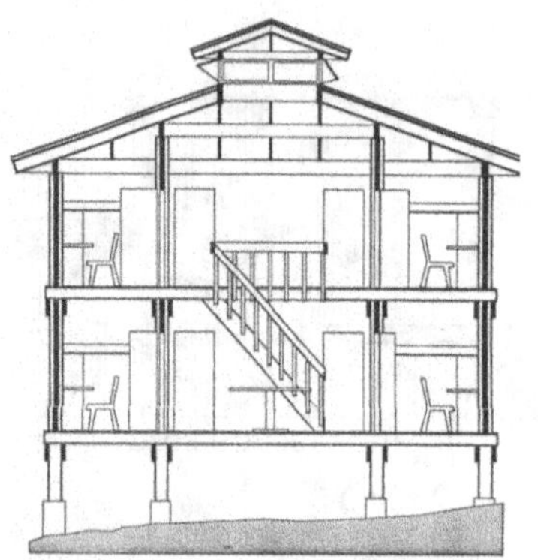

Section through undergraduate housing unit

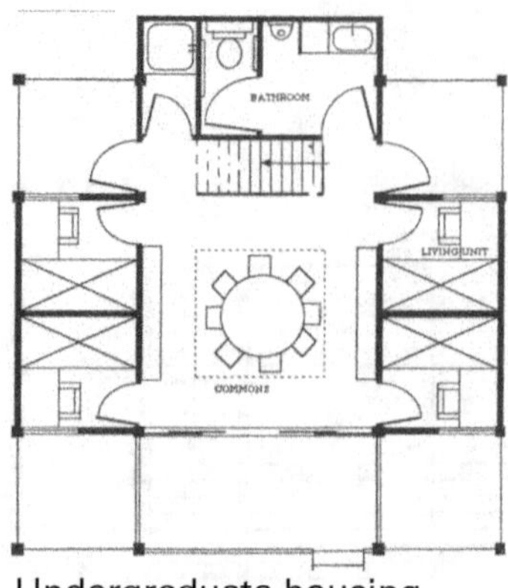

Undergraduate housing

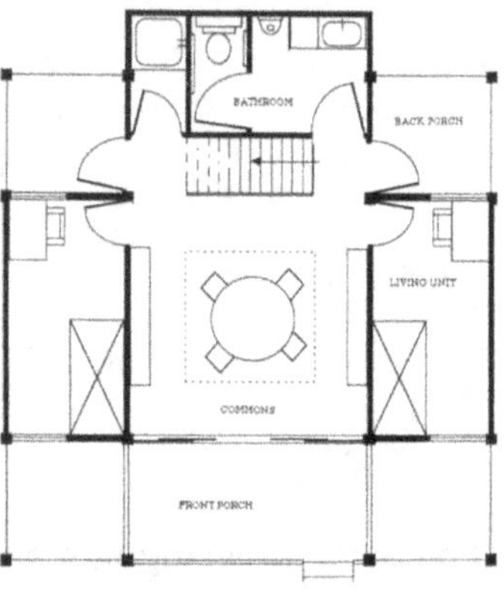

Graduate housing

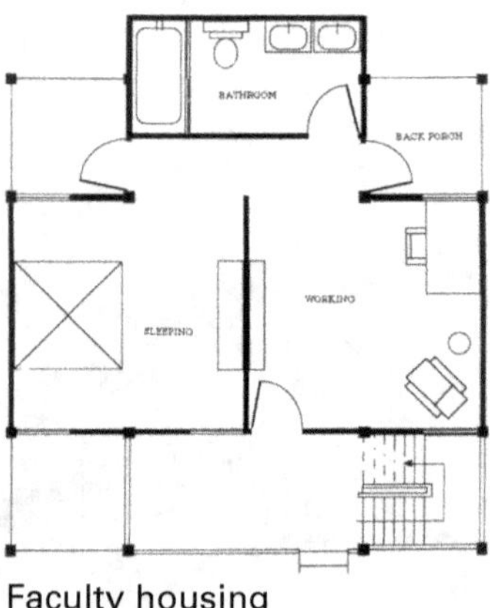

Faculty housing

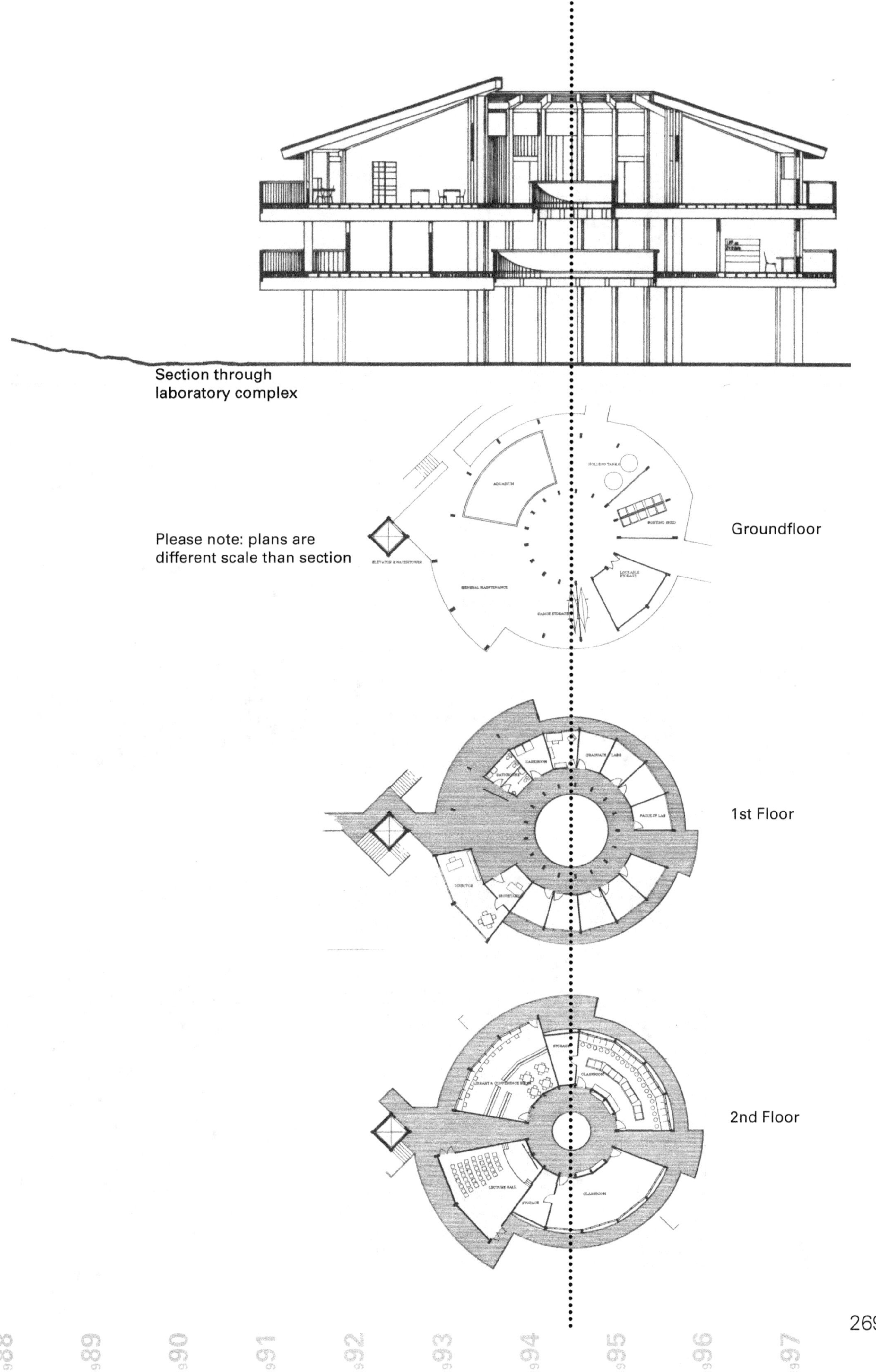
Section through
laboratory complex
Please note: plans are
different scale than section
Groundfloor
1st Floor
2nd Floor

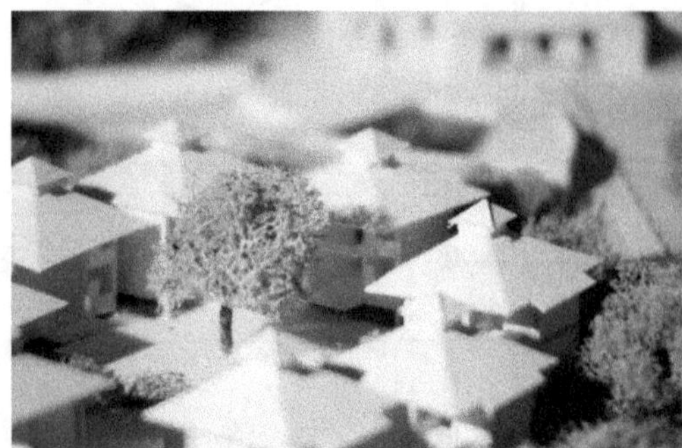

Final models in site model (1/8″ = 1′)

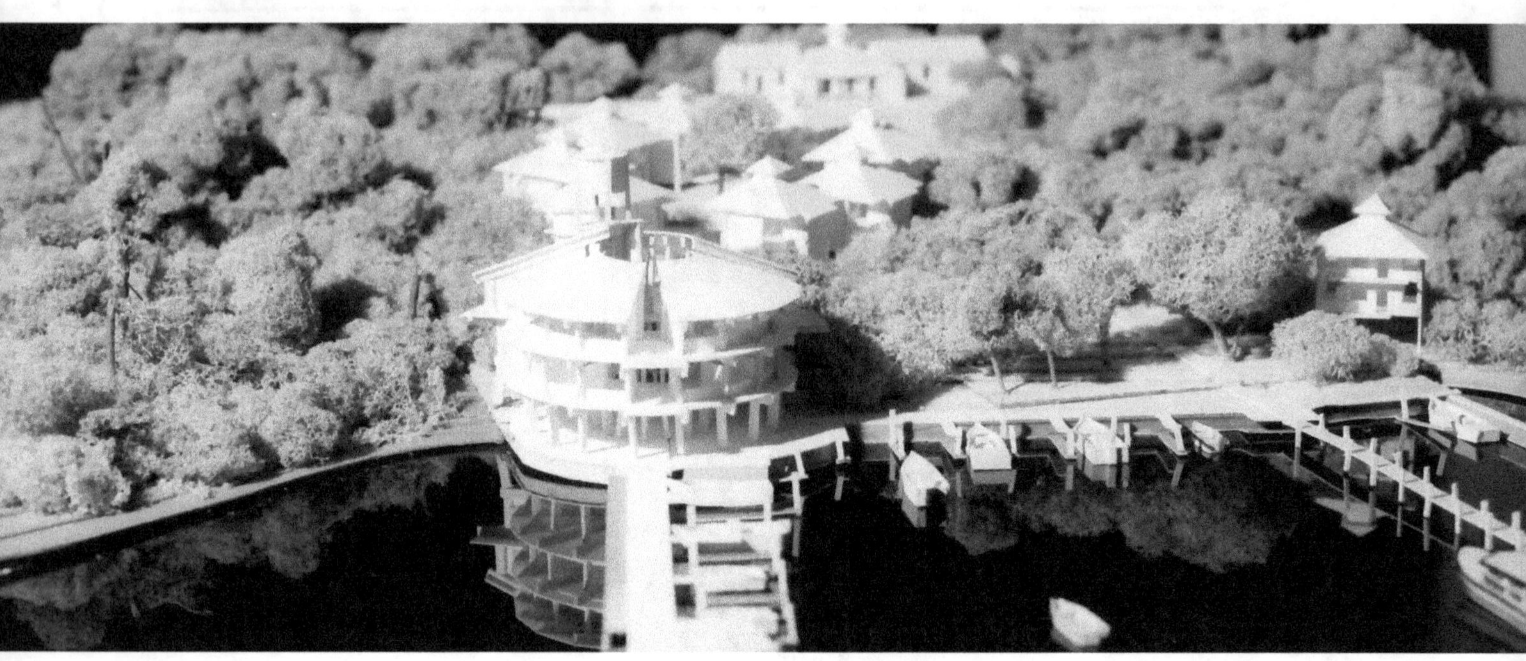

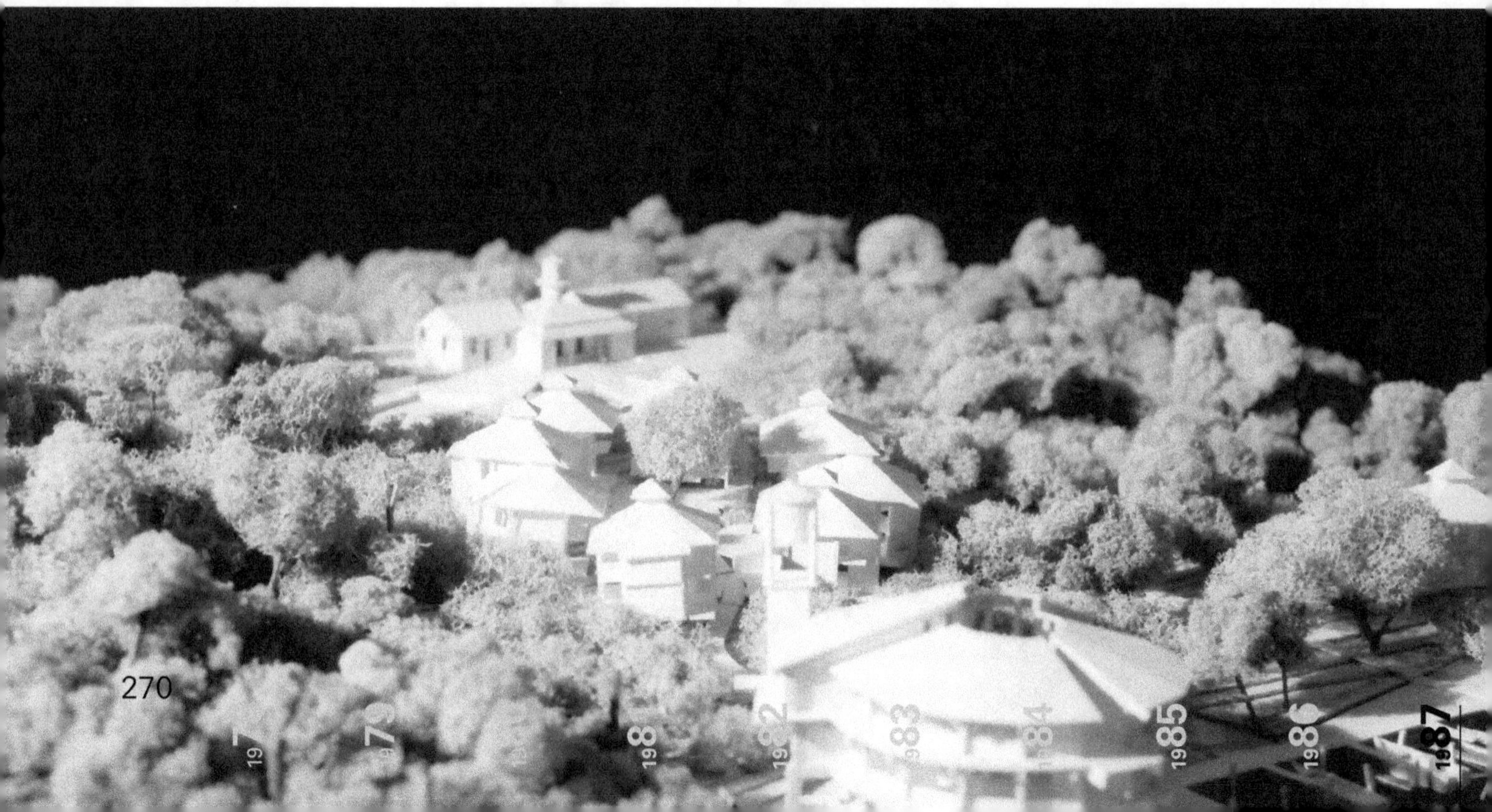

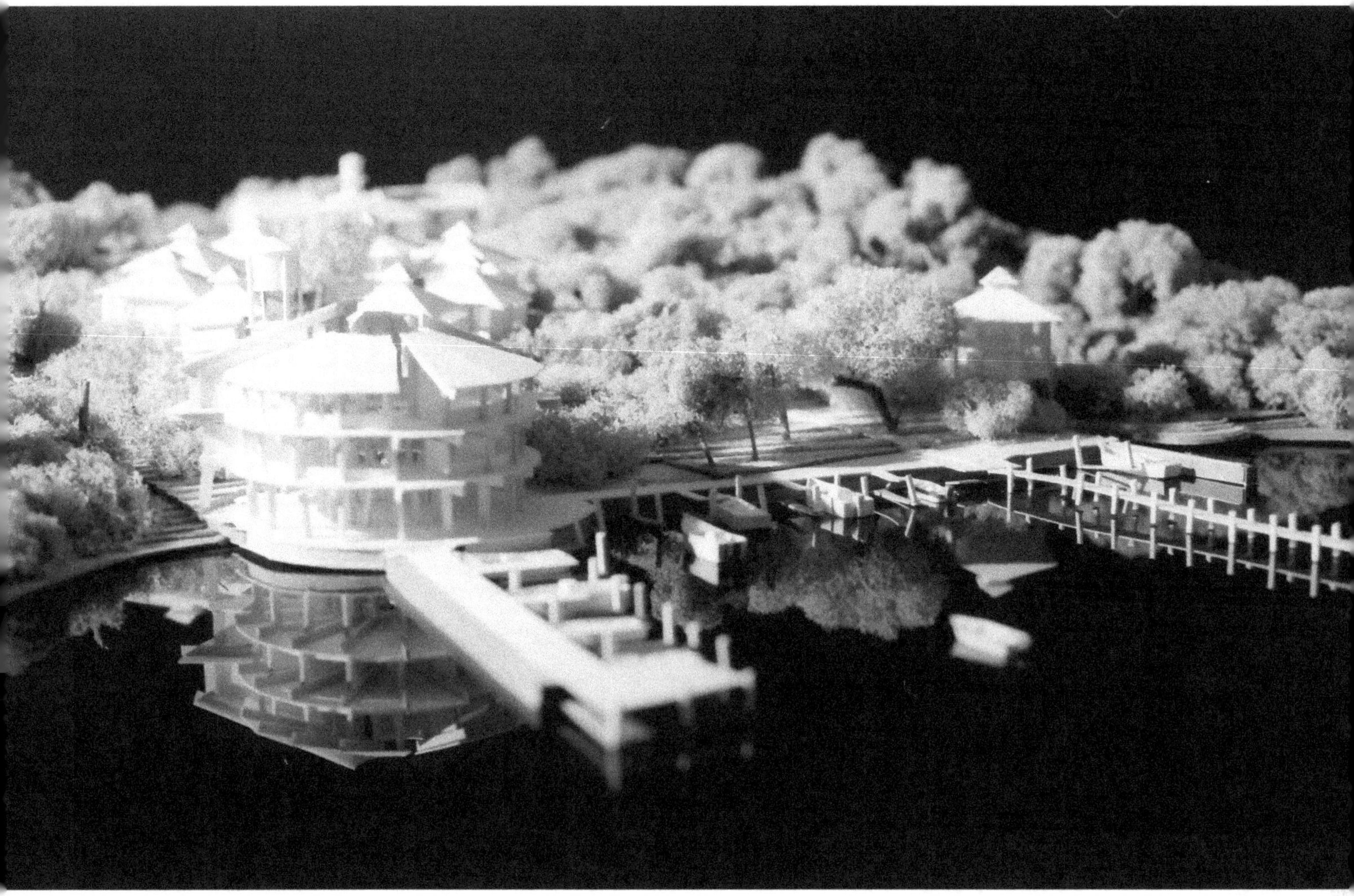

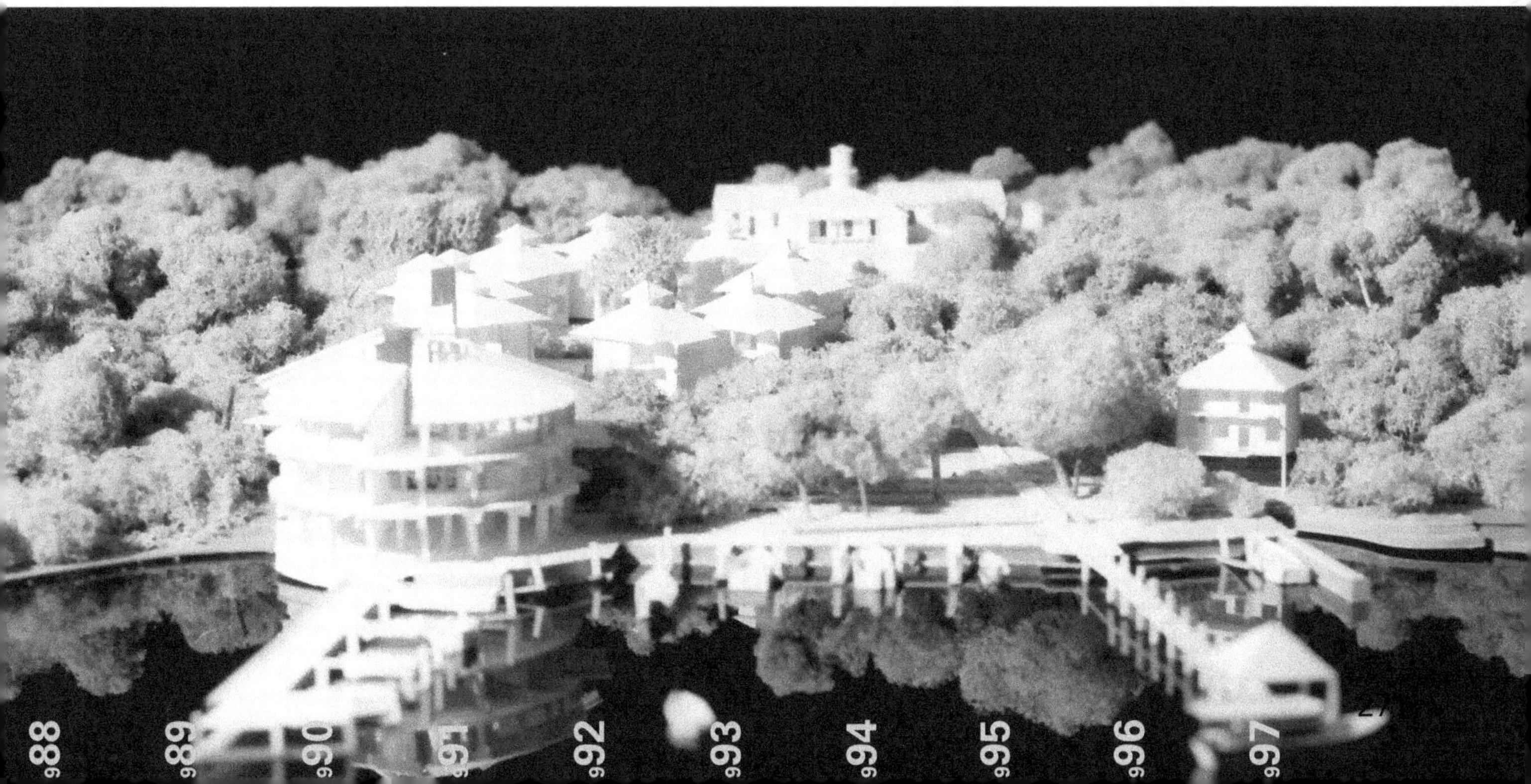

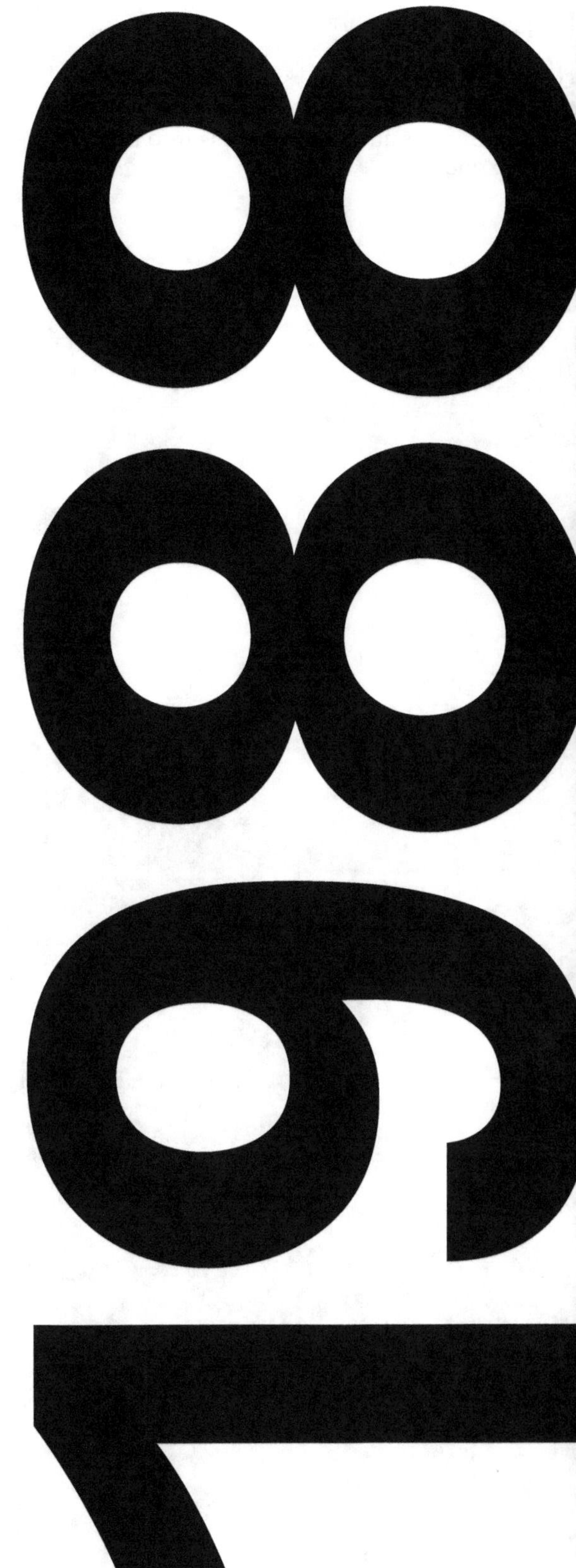
1988

Junkerhaus

Lemgo, Germany

A trope of loneliness and a journey through despair and hopelessness into a creative endeavor

Junkerhaus approach

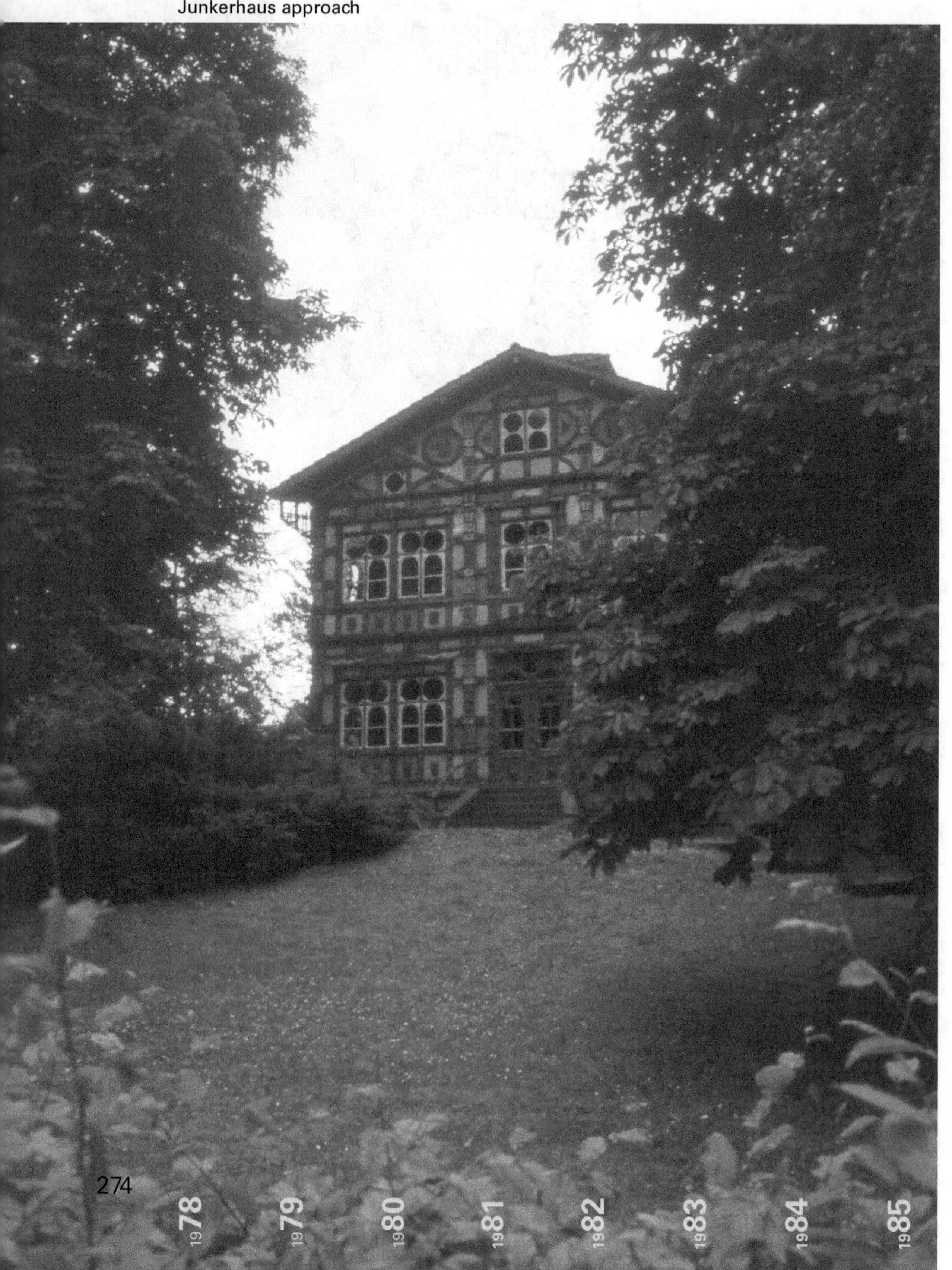

Junkerhaus entry

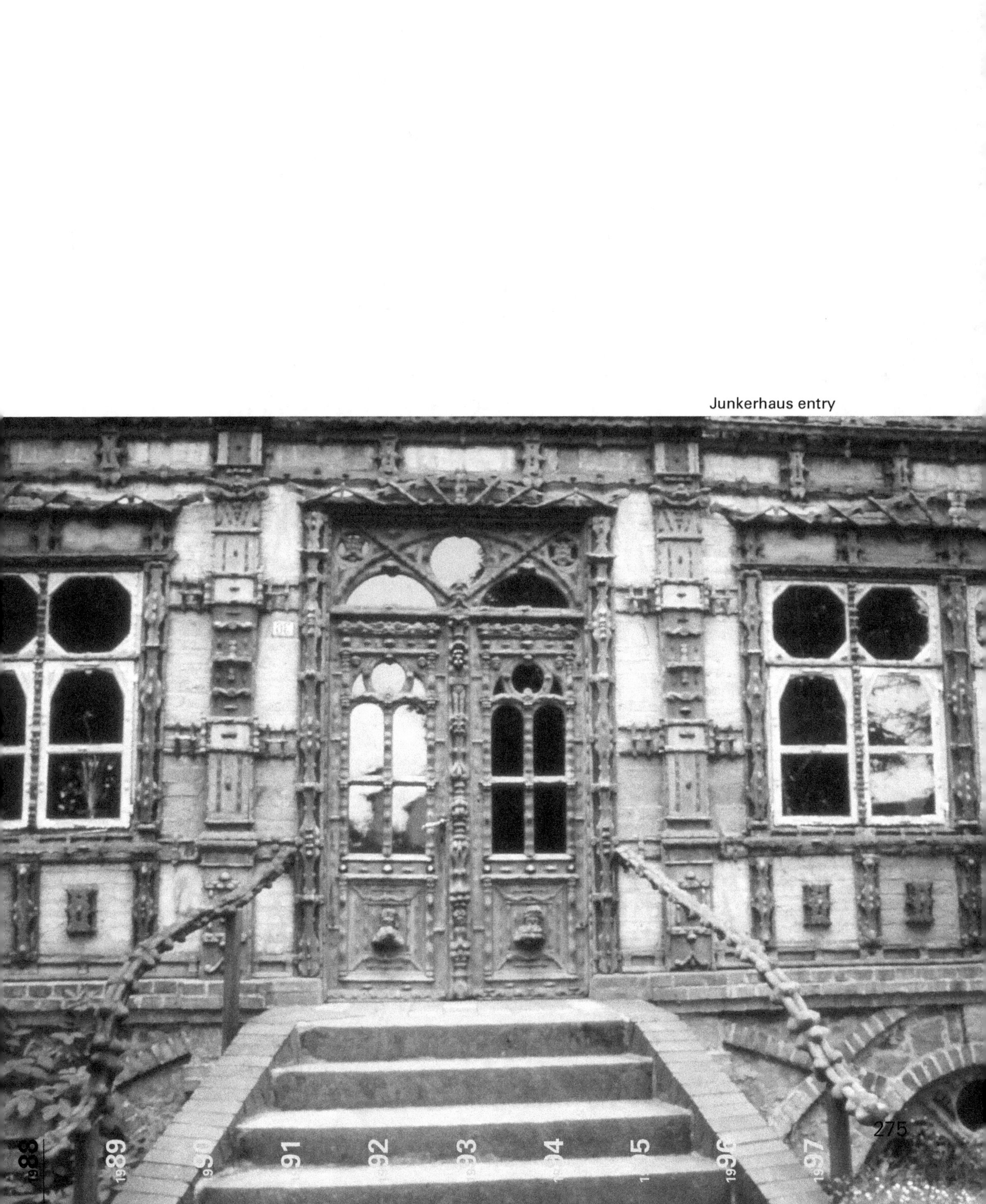

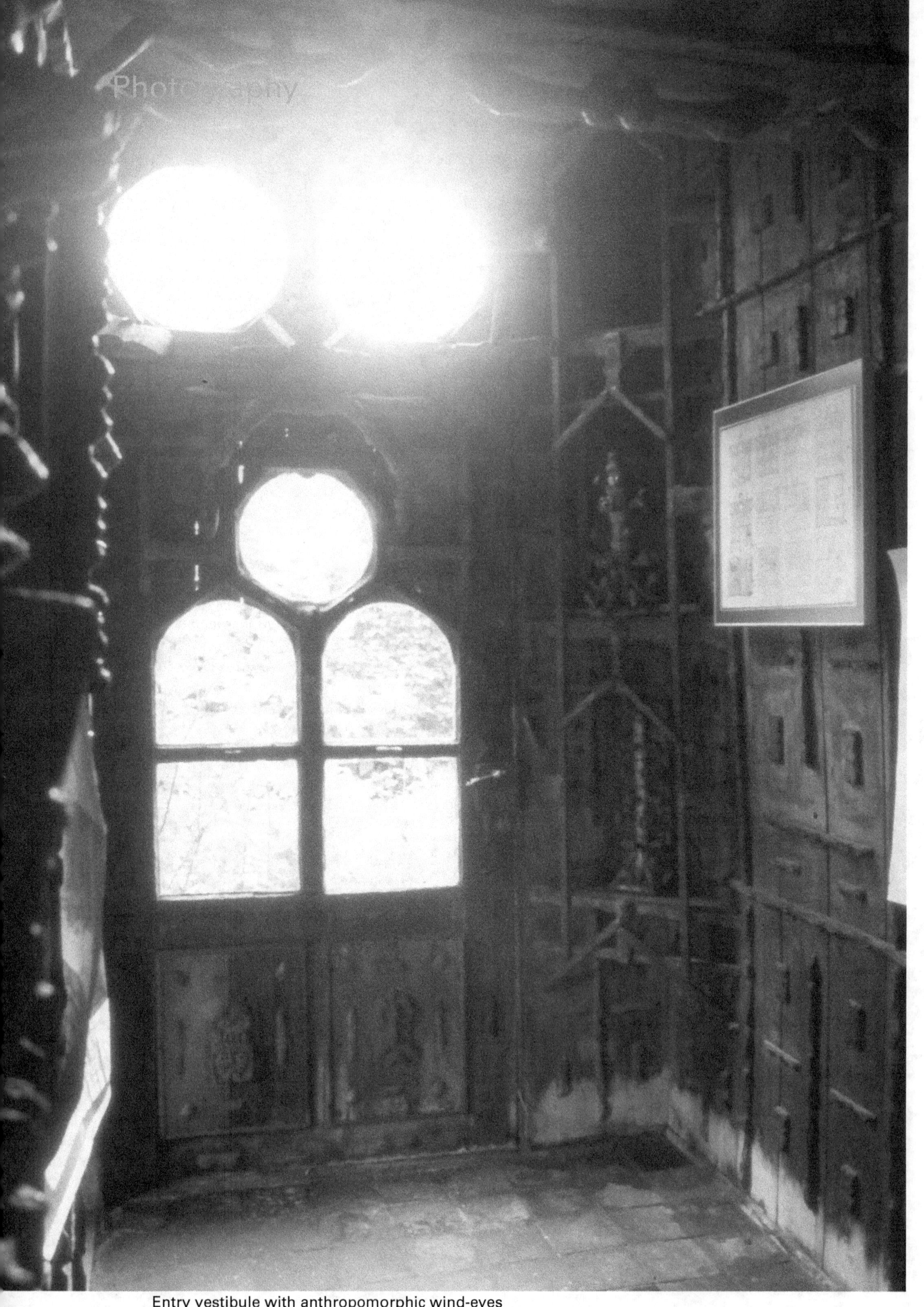

Entry vestibule with anthropomorphic wind-eyes

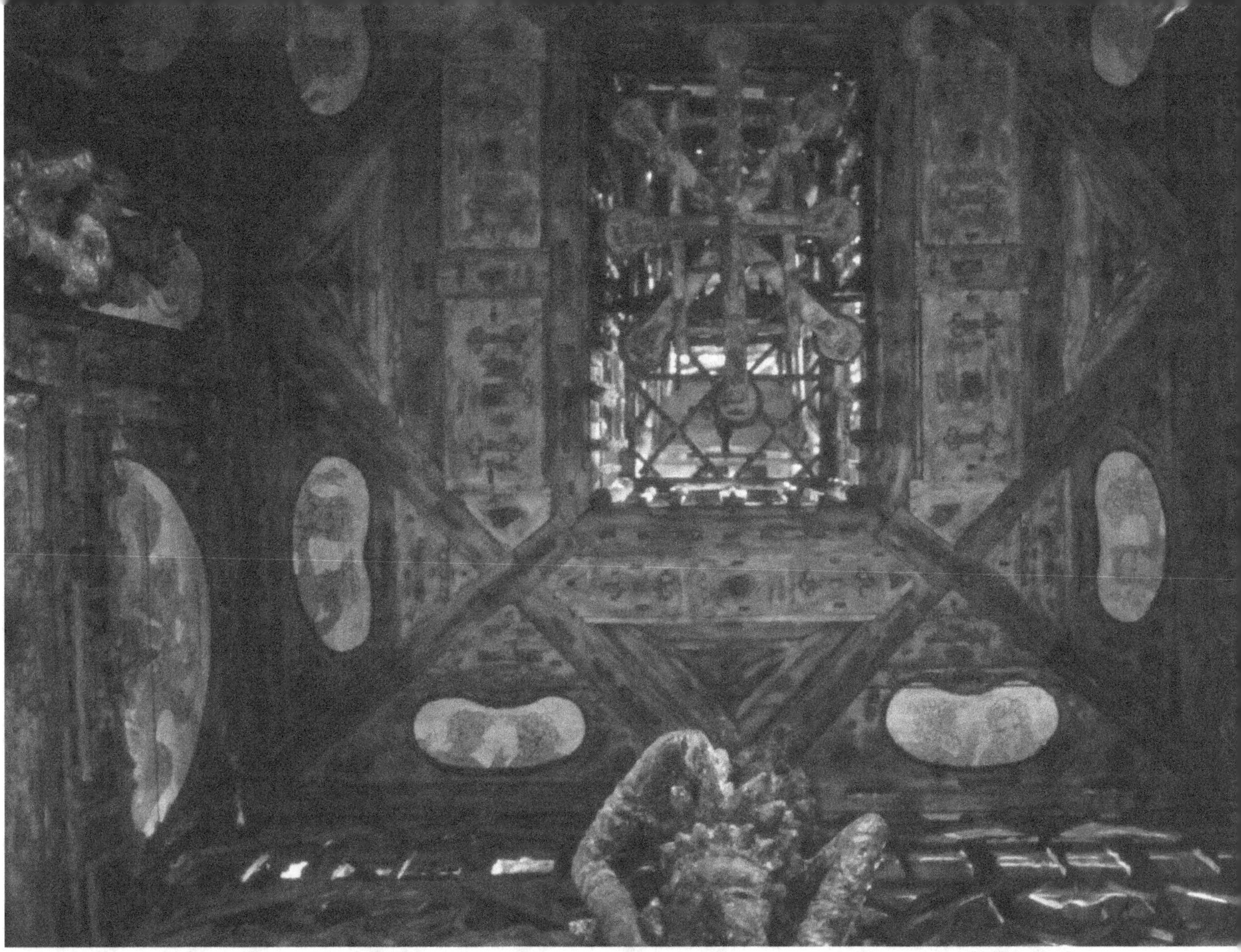

Ceiling

Atelier

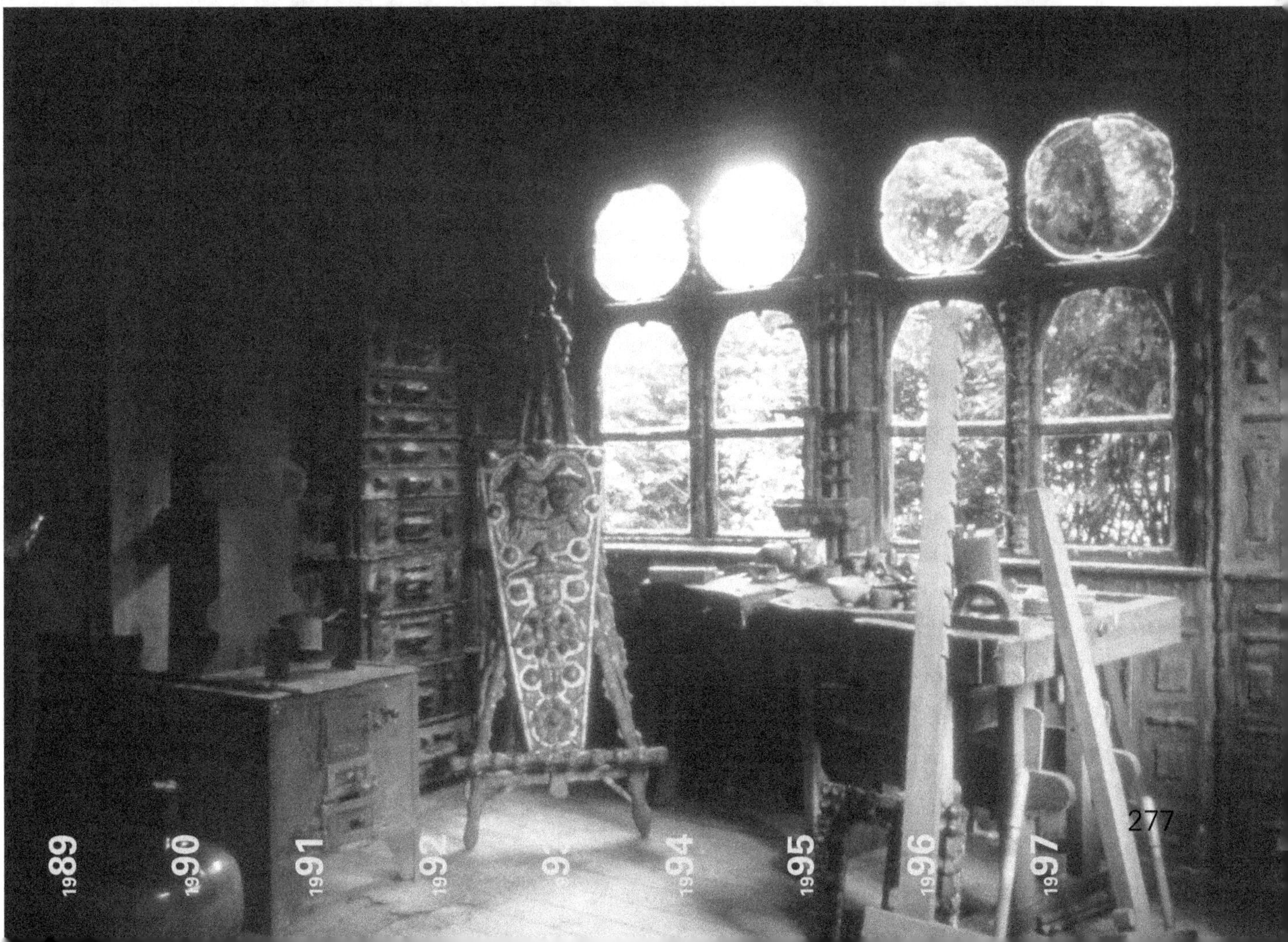

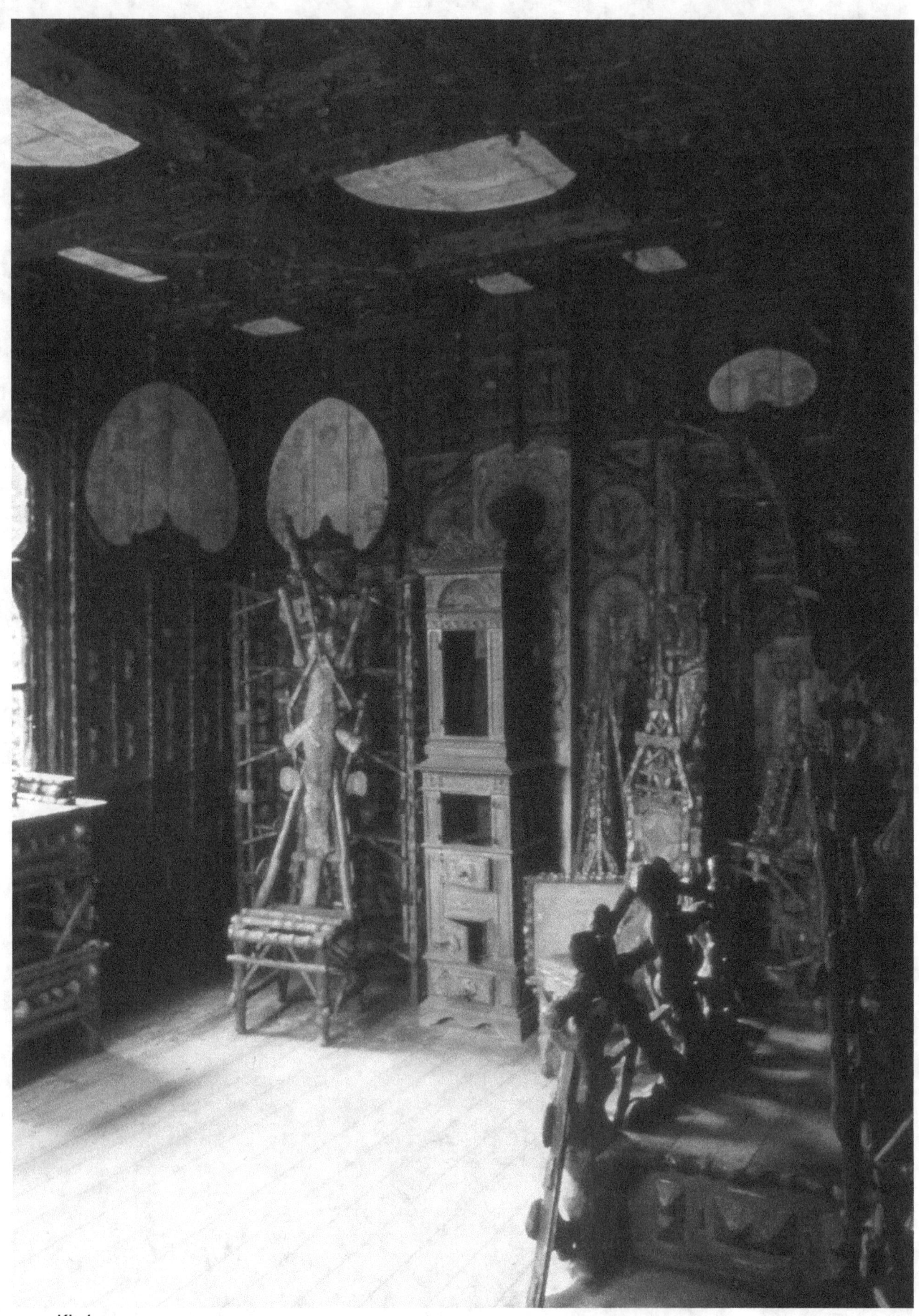

Kitchen

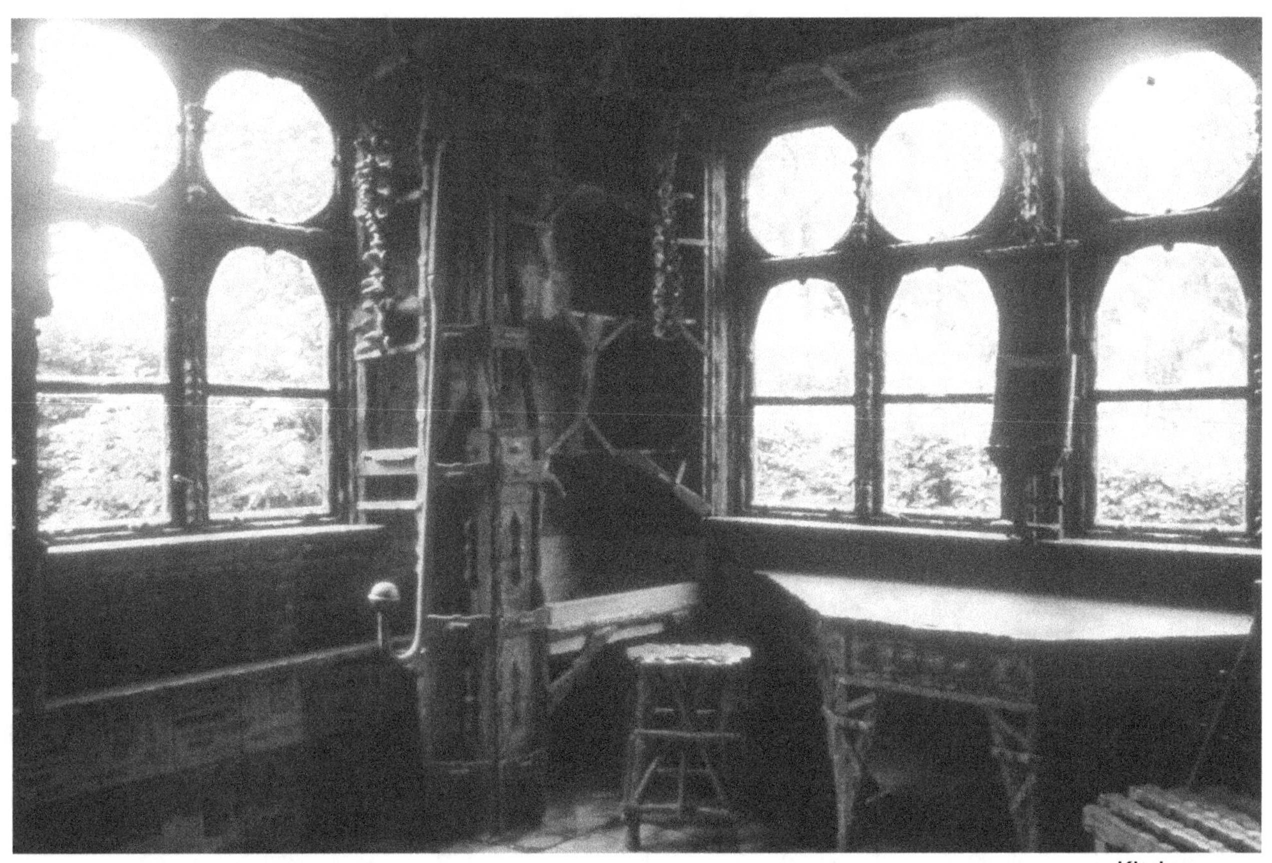

Kitchen

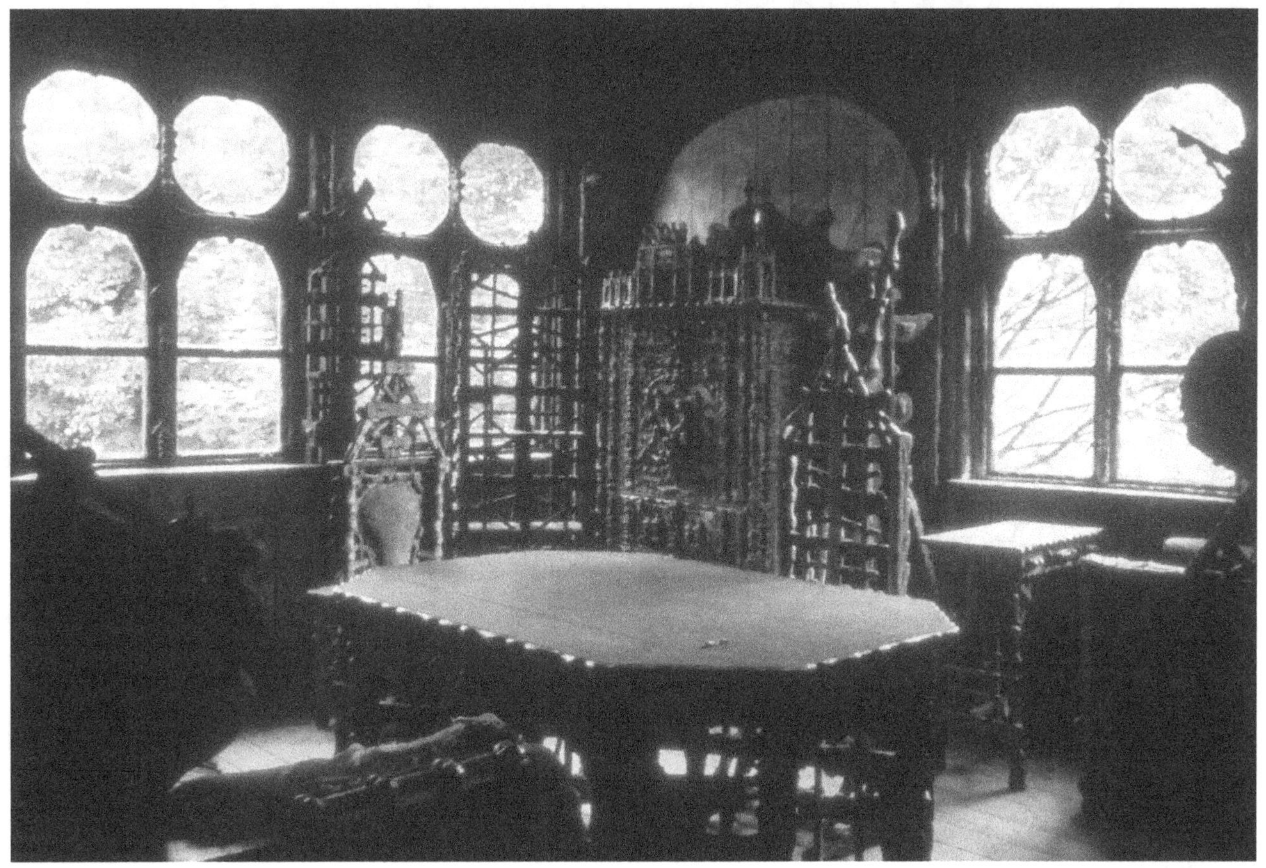

Dining room

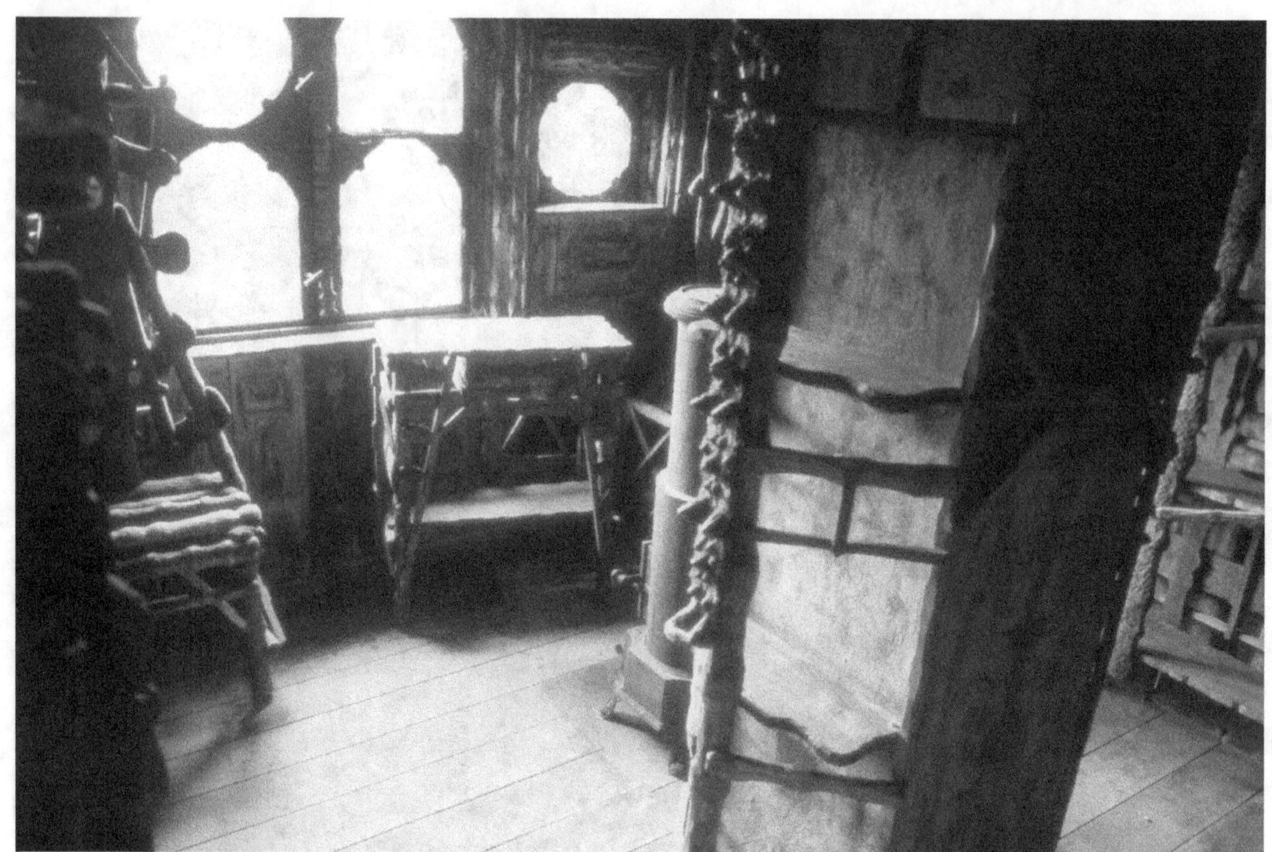

Bedroom

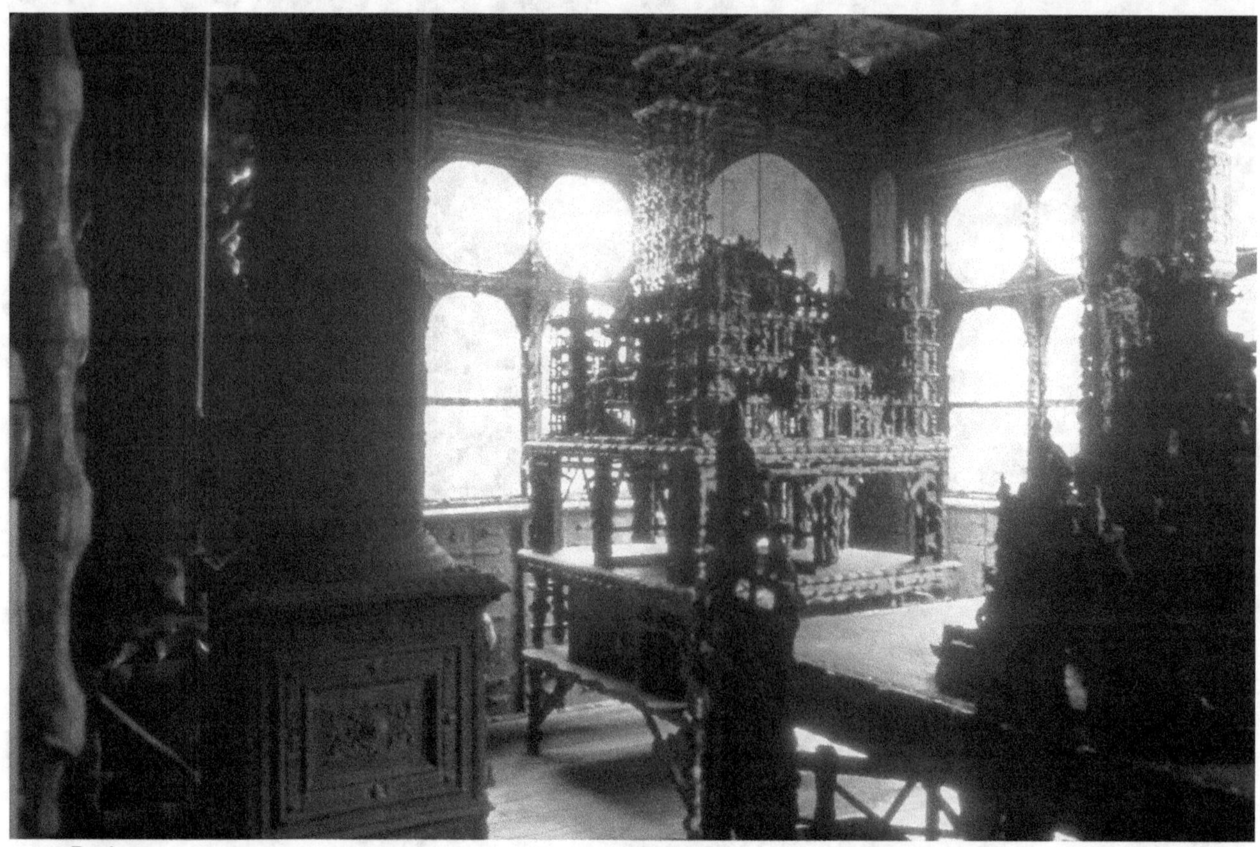

Bedroom

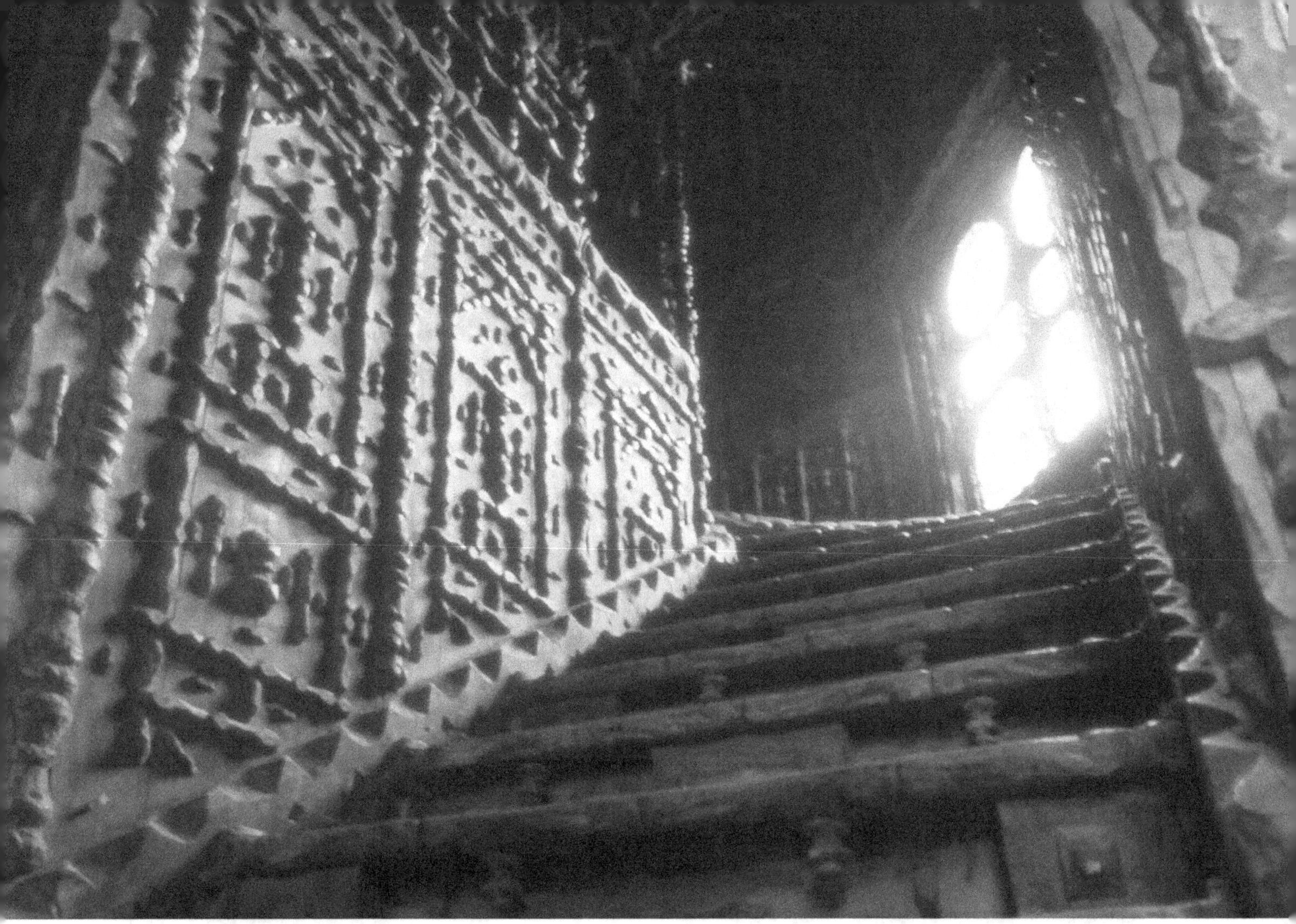

Stair to second floor

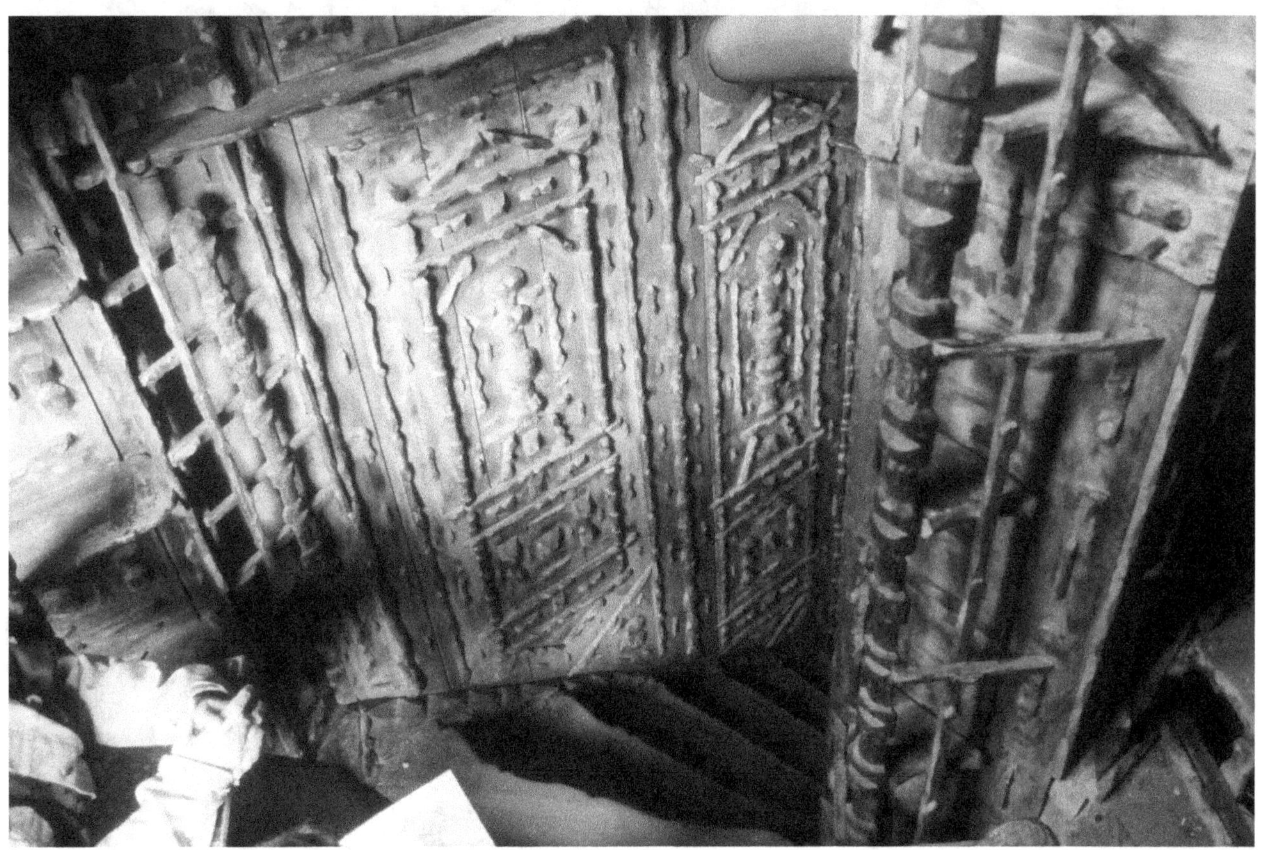

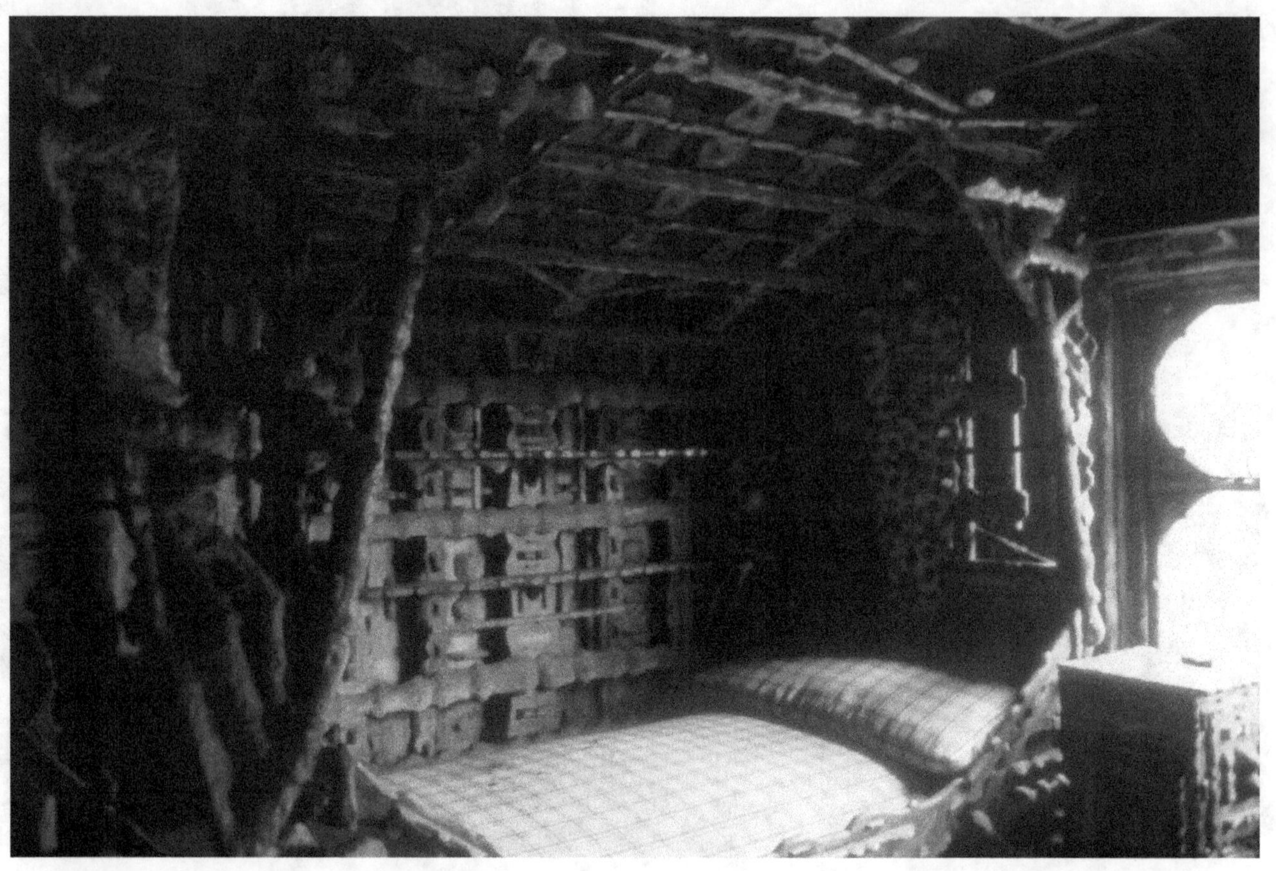

Bedroom

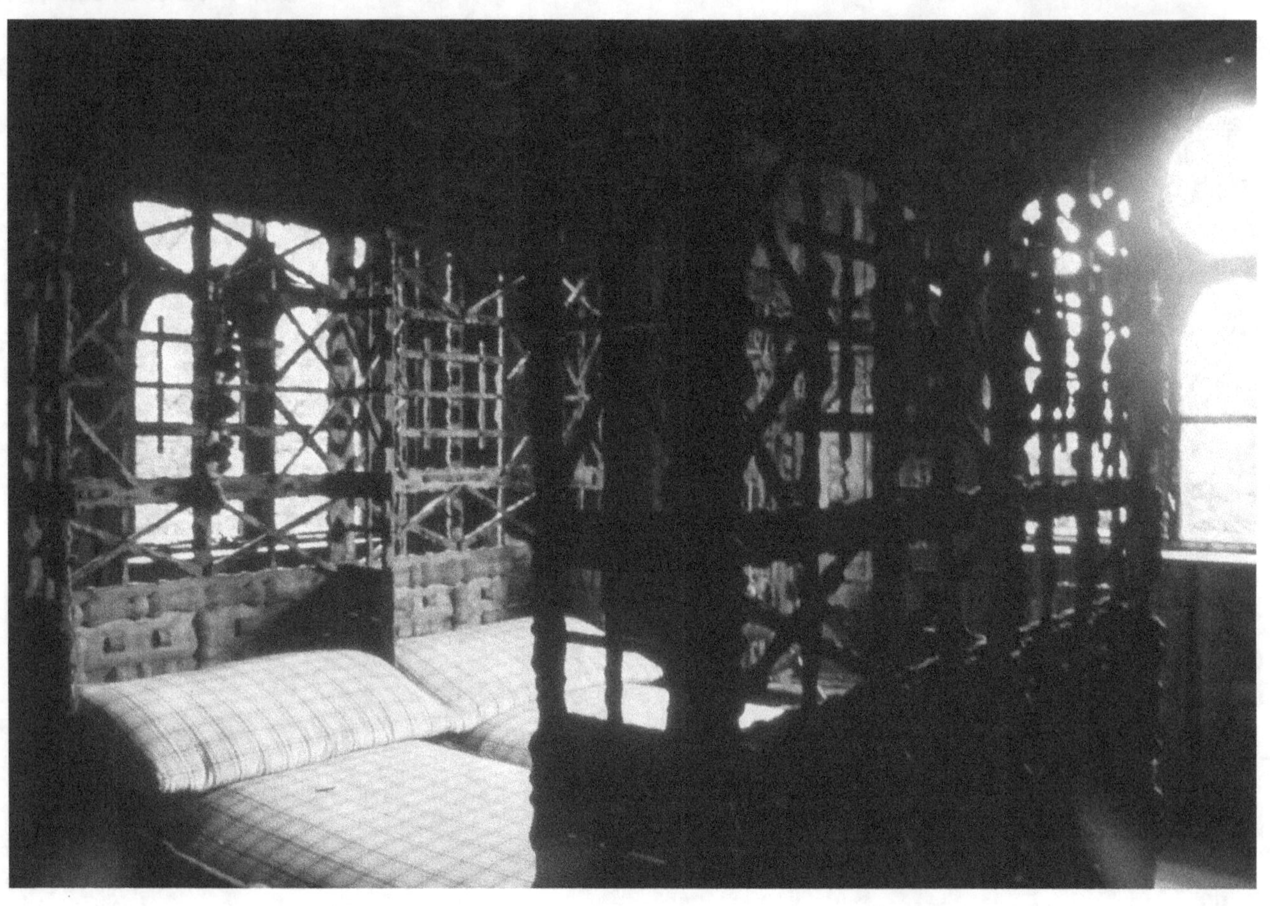

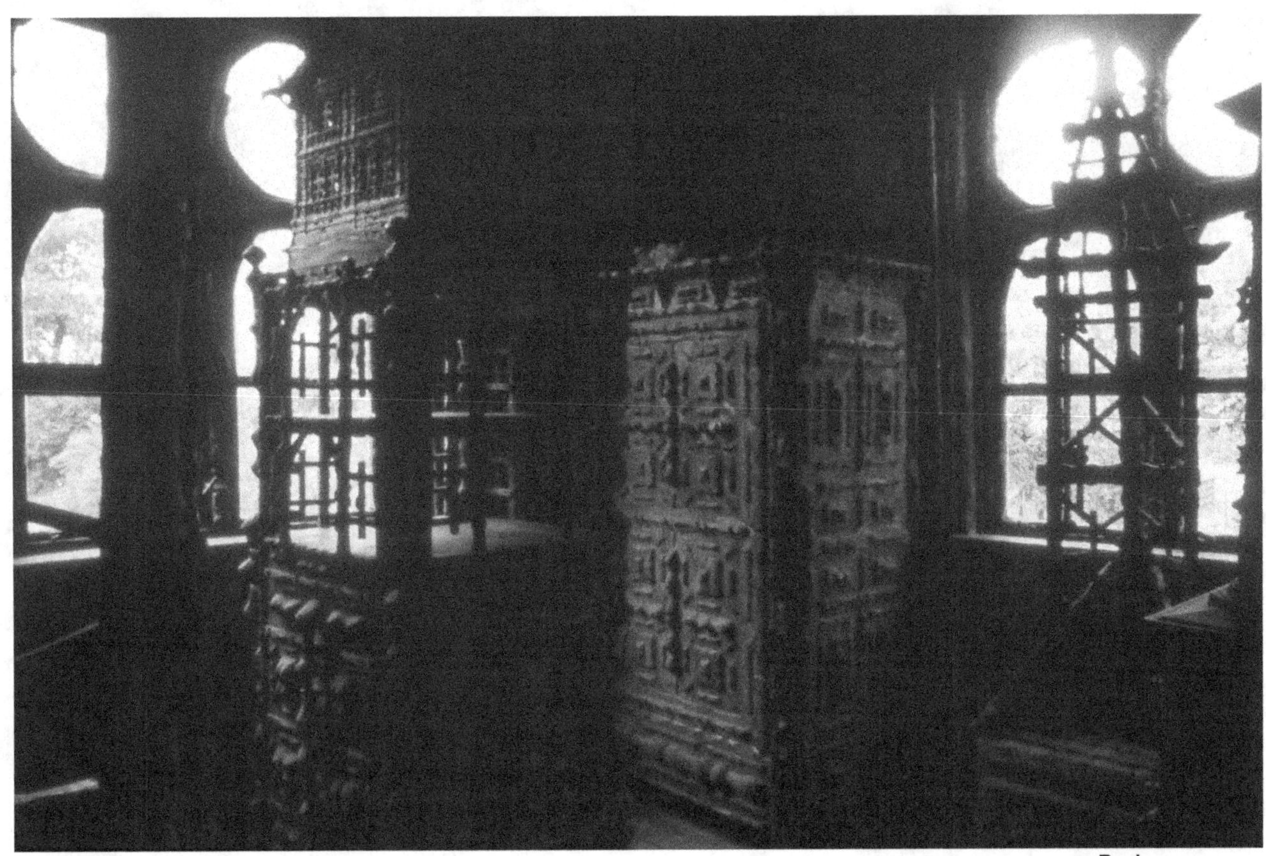

Bedroom

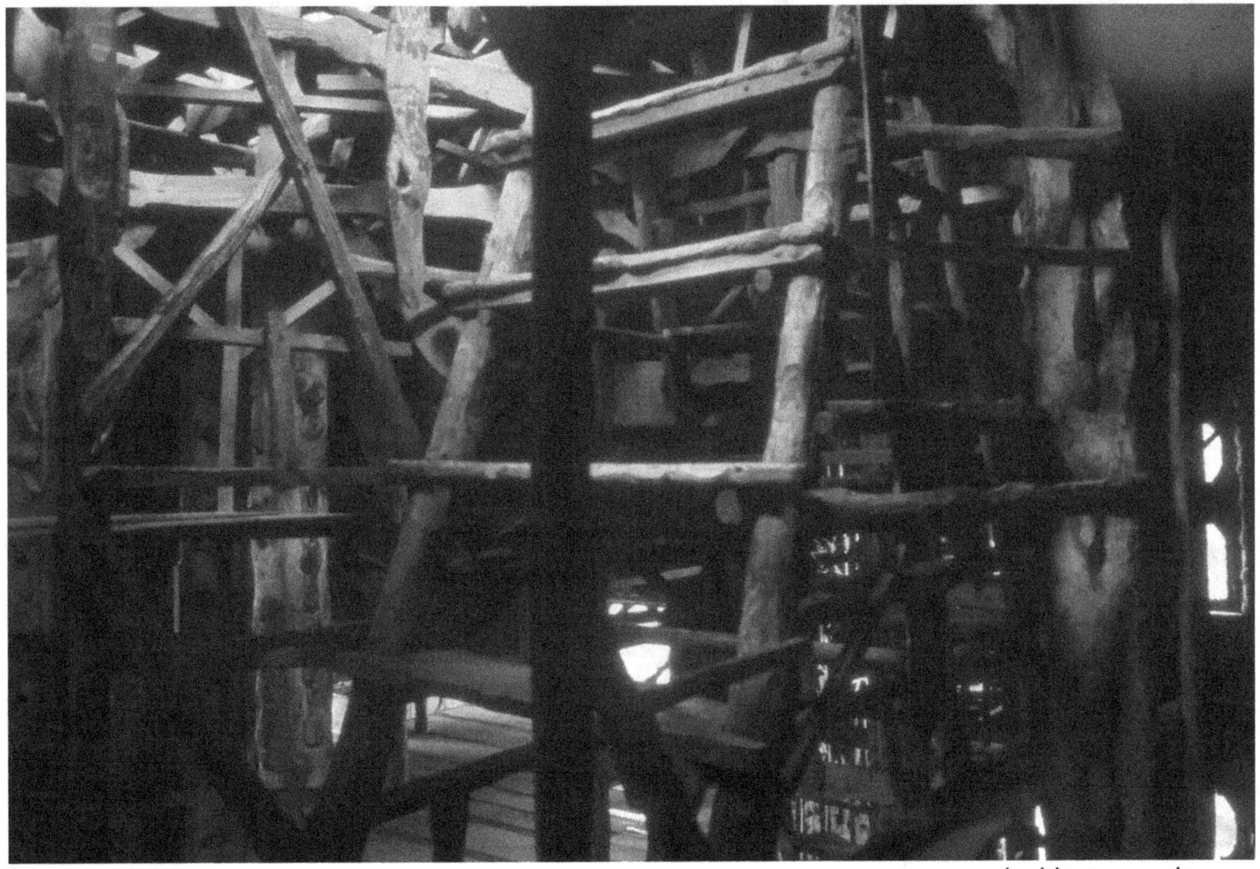

Ladder to cupola

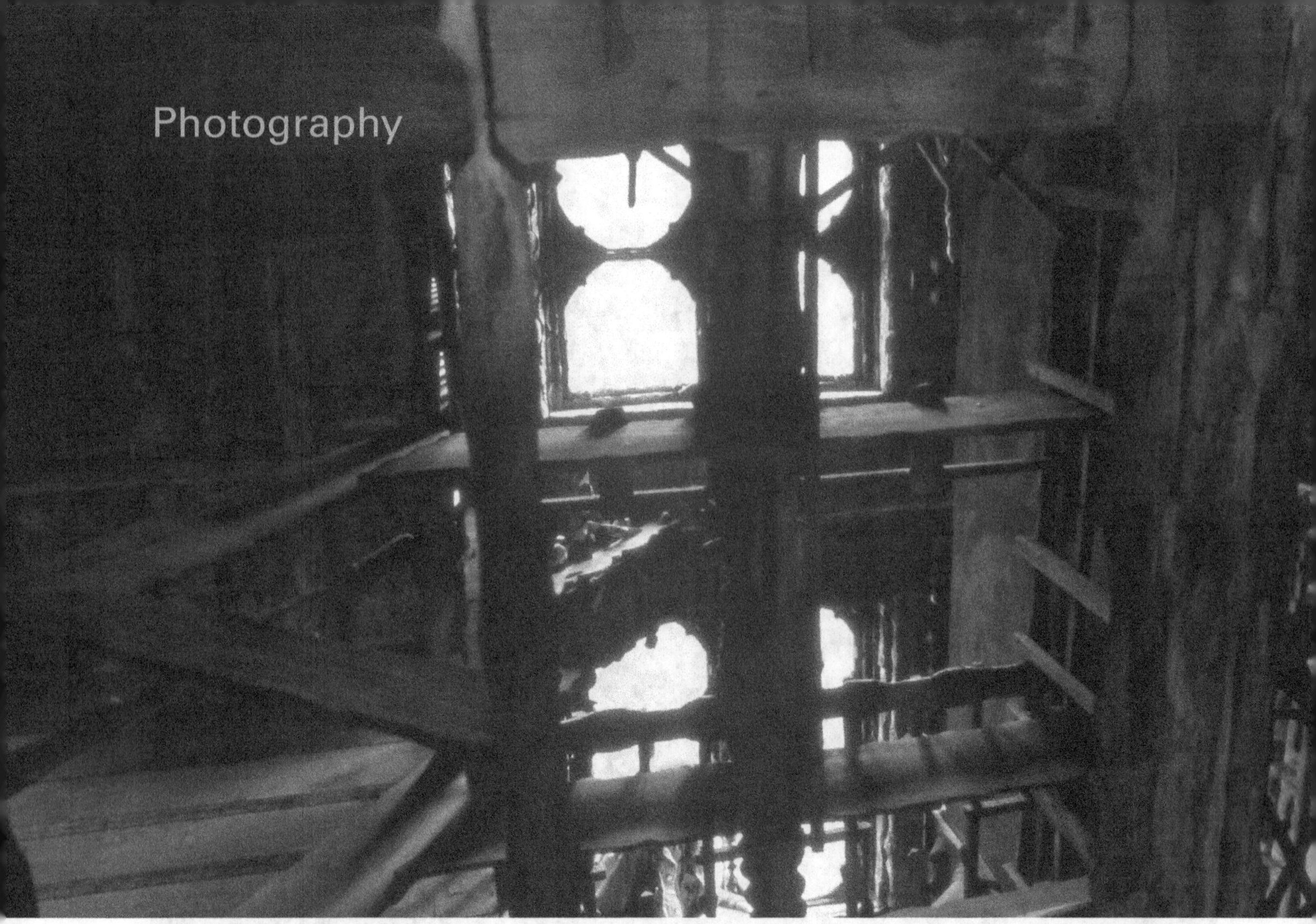

Photography

Attic

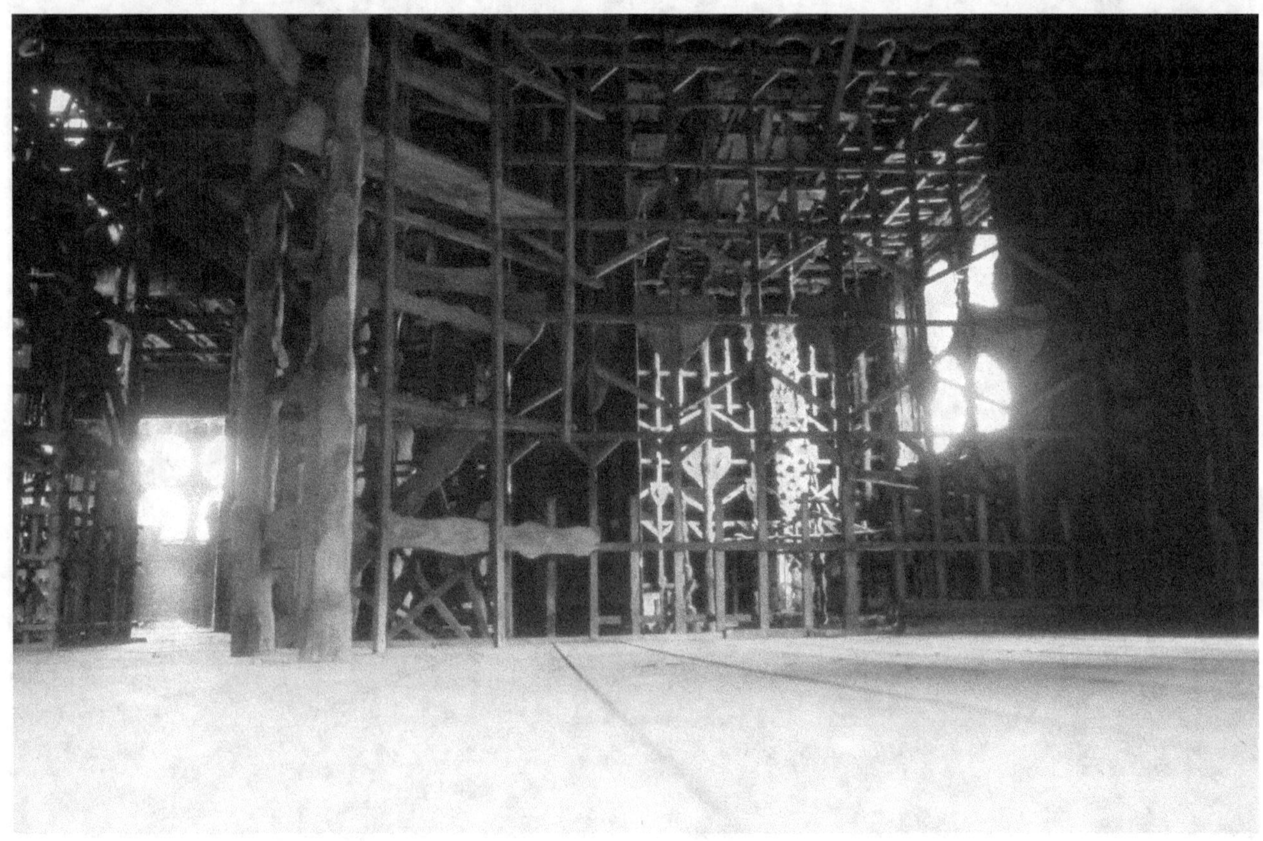

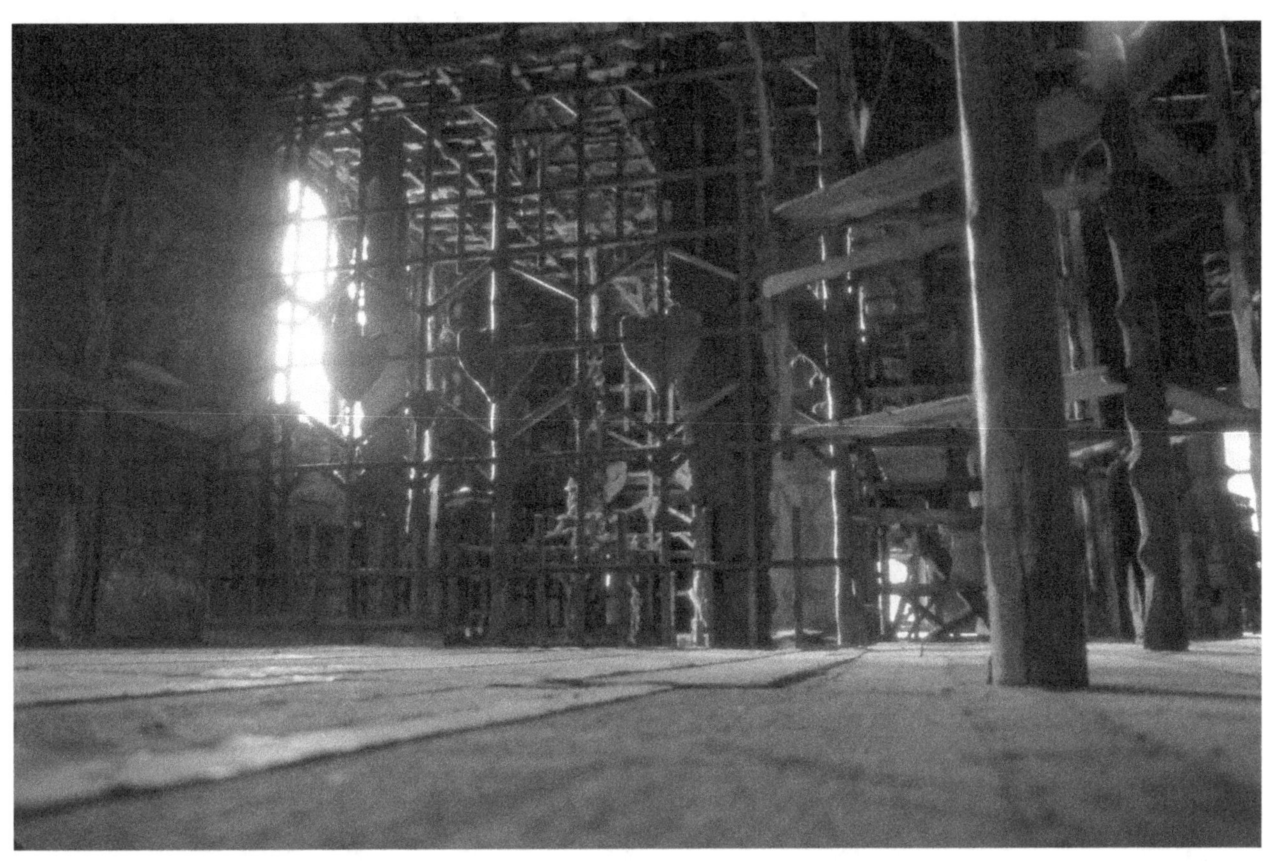

Attic

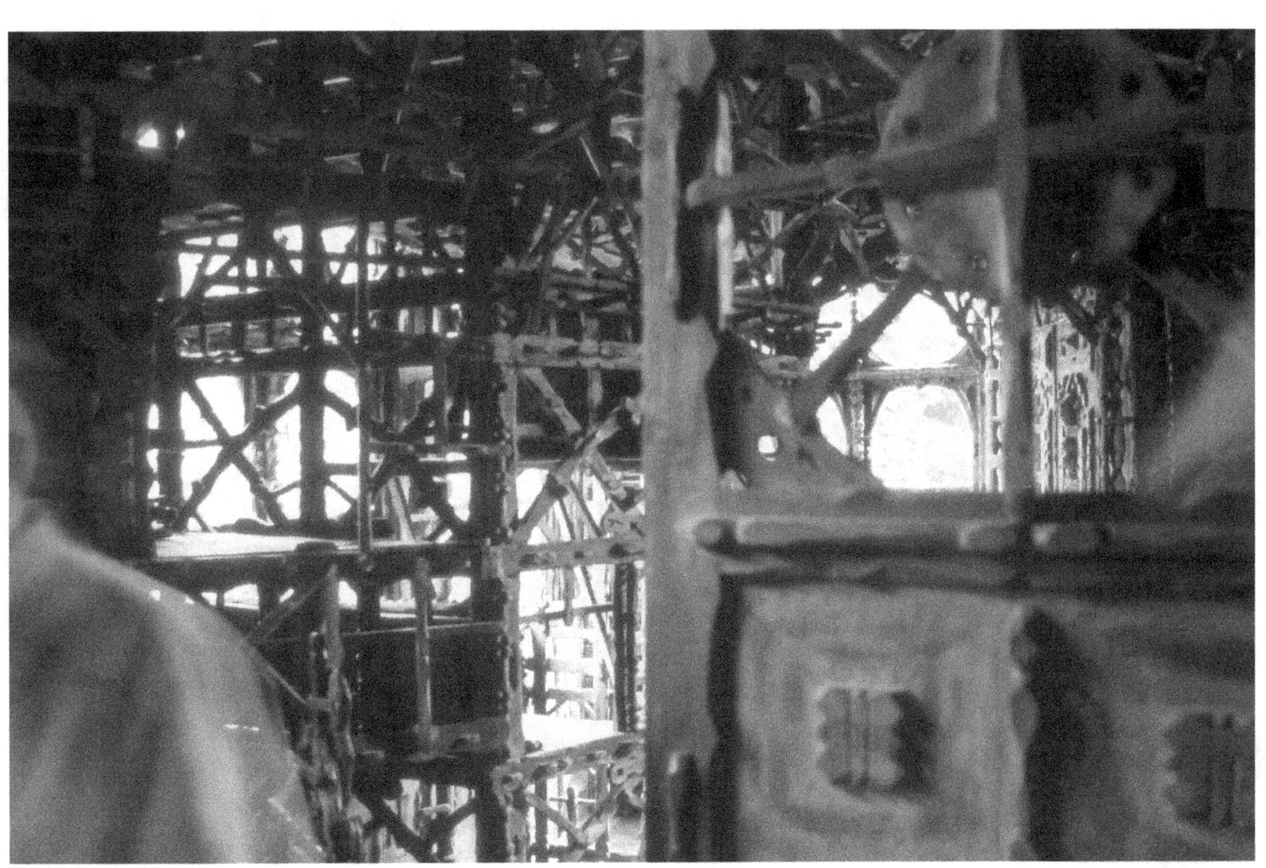

Prague

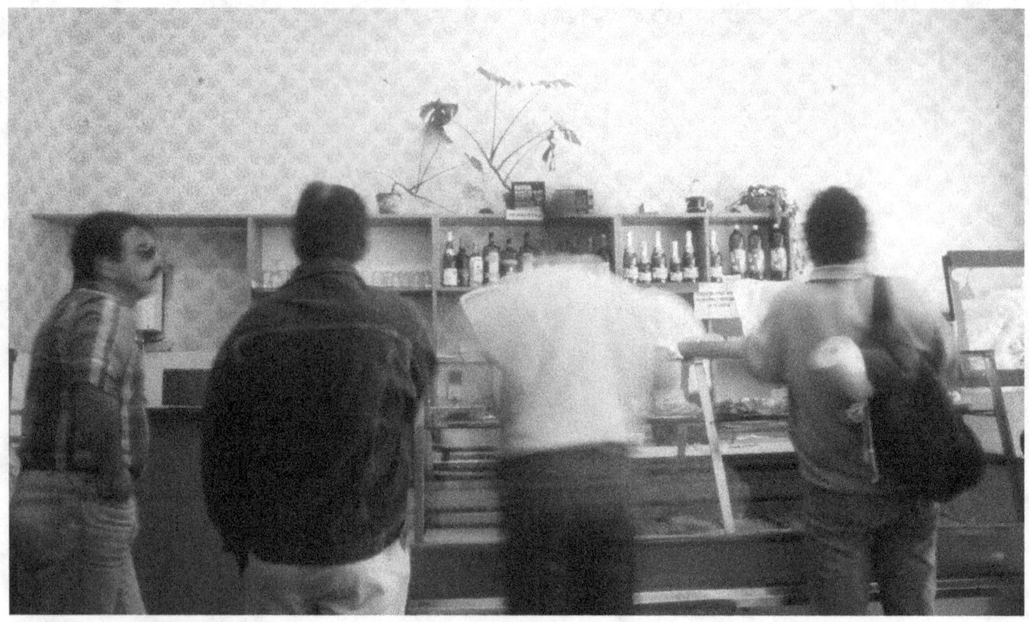

Beer bar at rush hour

Soluna jewelry store window display

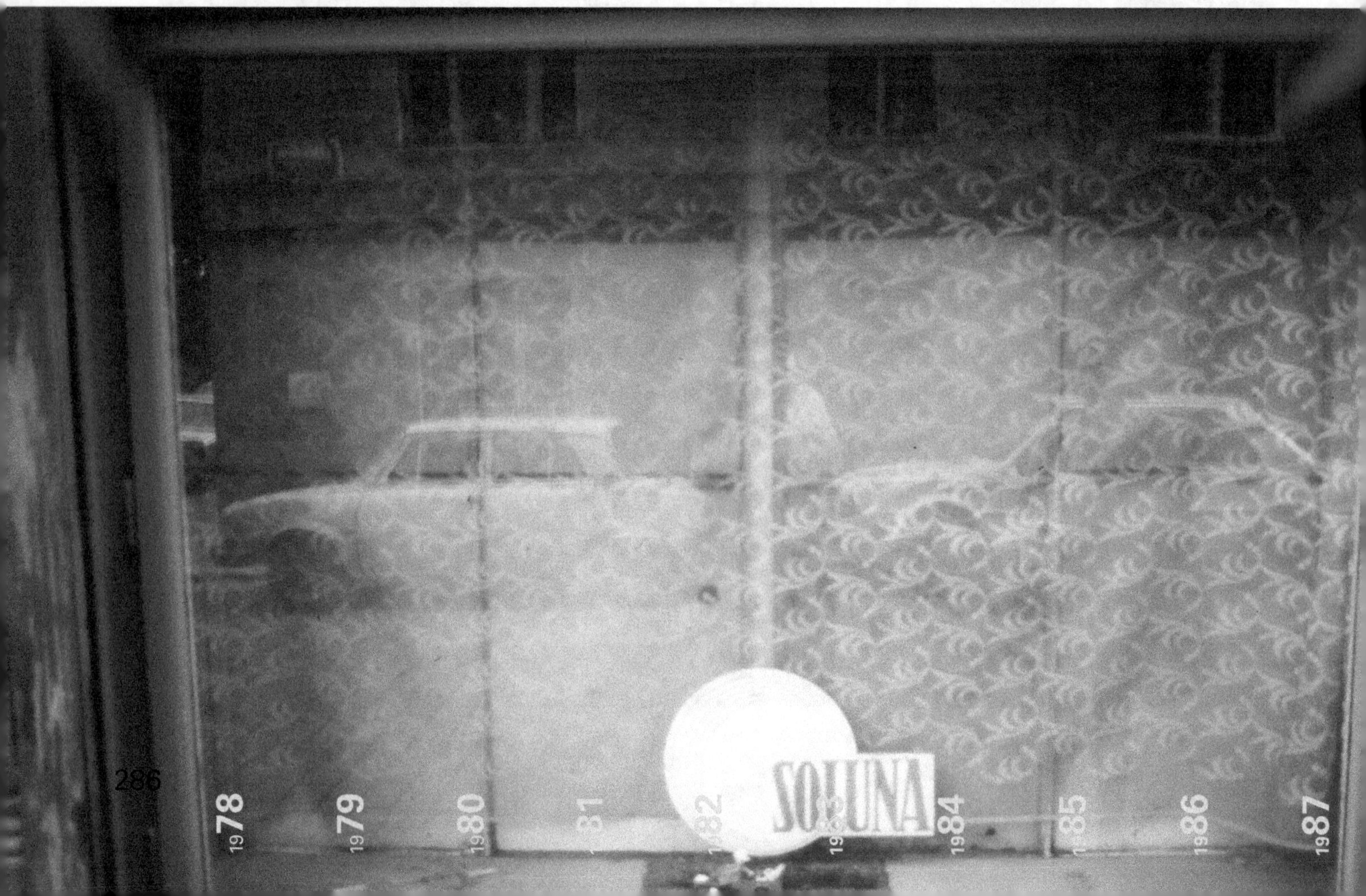

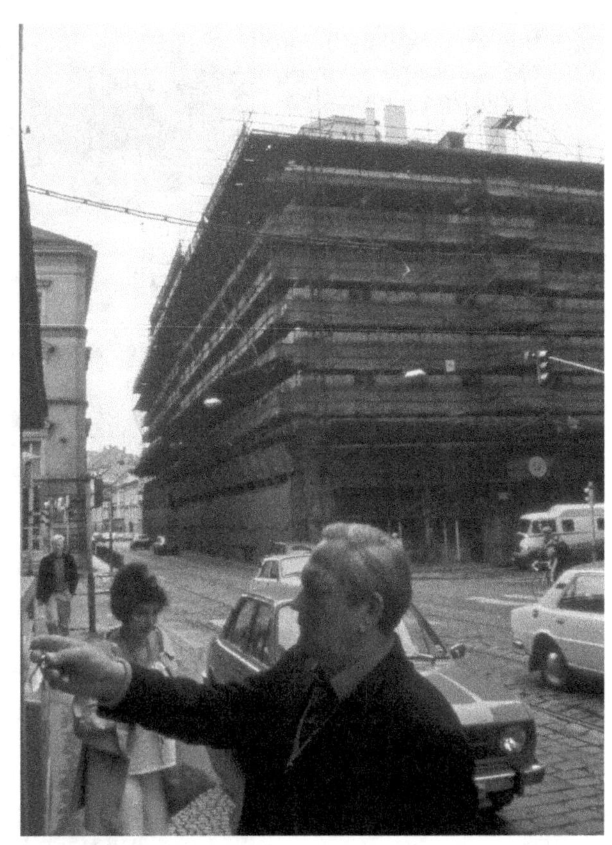

Street scenes

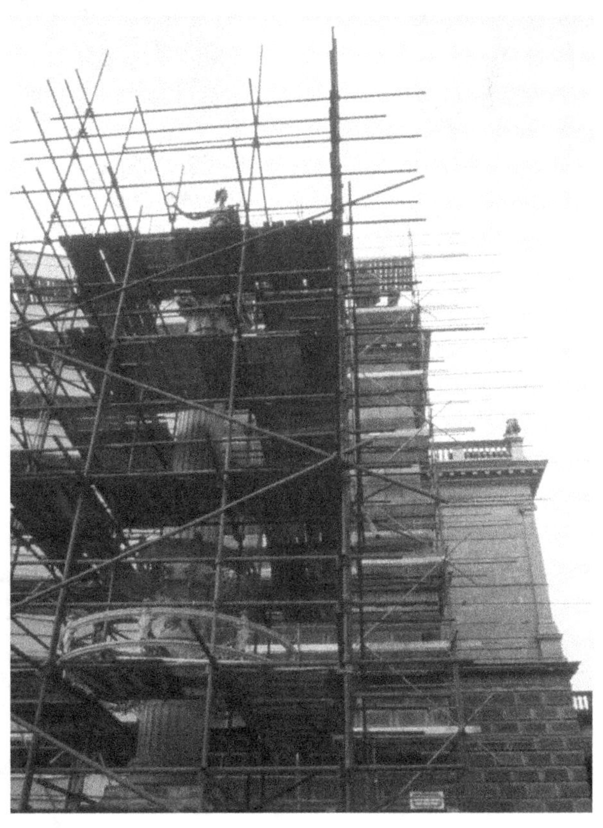

When we were visiting the city in 1988, with a proper visum for the Czech Republic since this was the time before the wall came down in Berlin, Prague seemed to be hiding under scaffolds

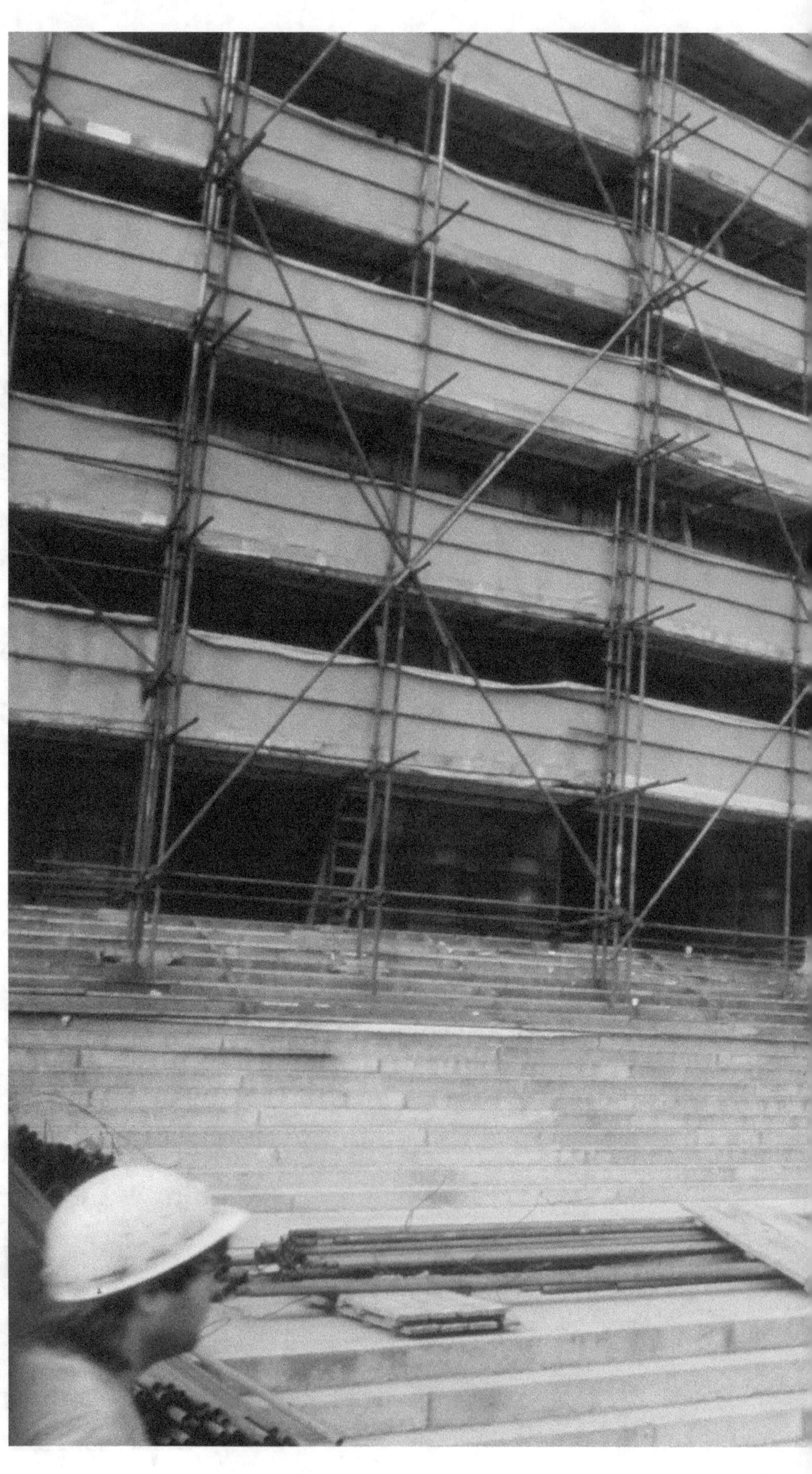

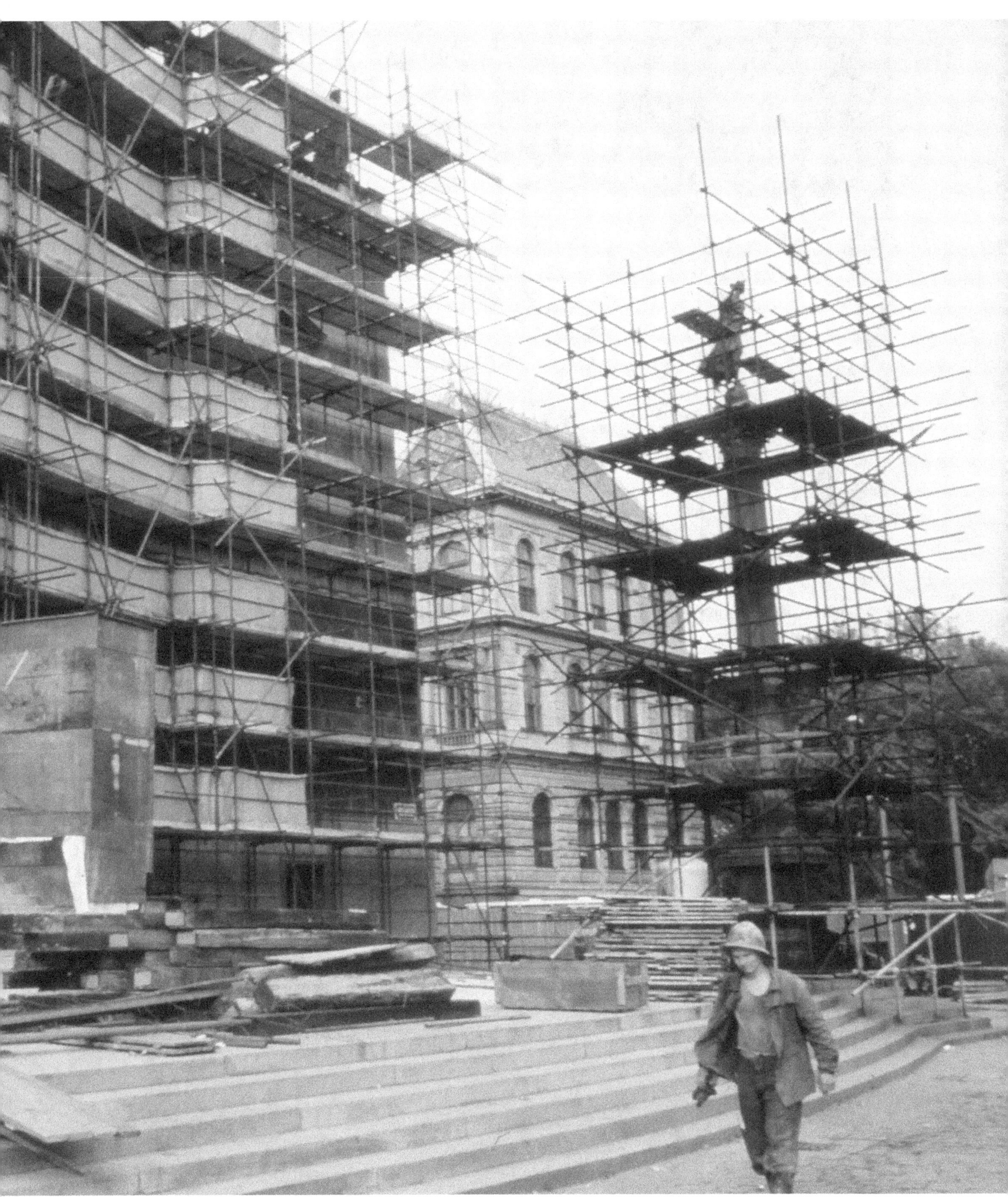

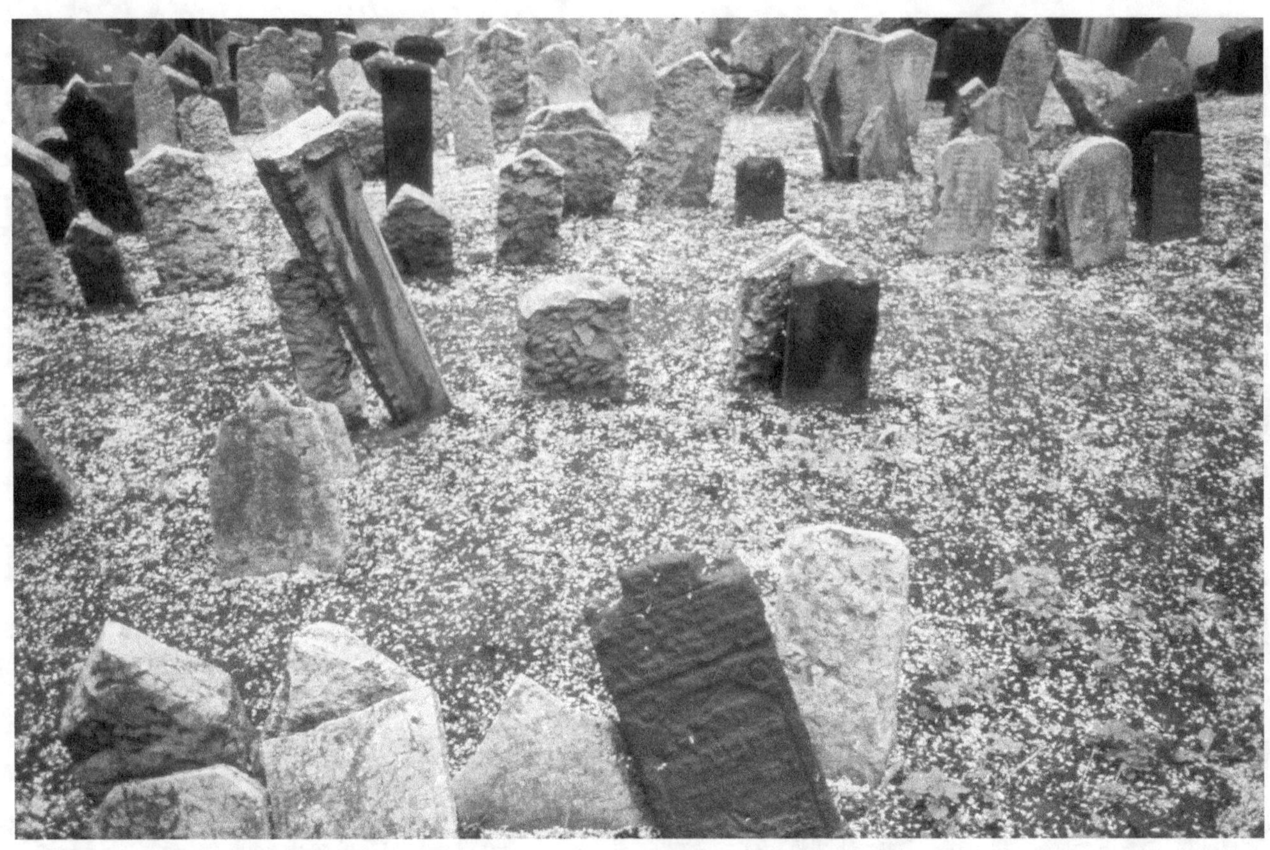

Jewish cemetery in Prague: history made manifest; what is left are rocks for the remembrance

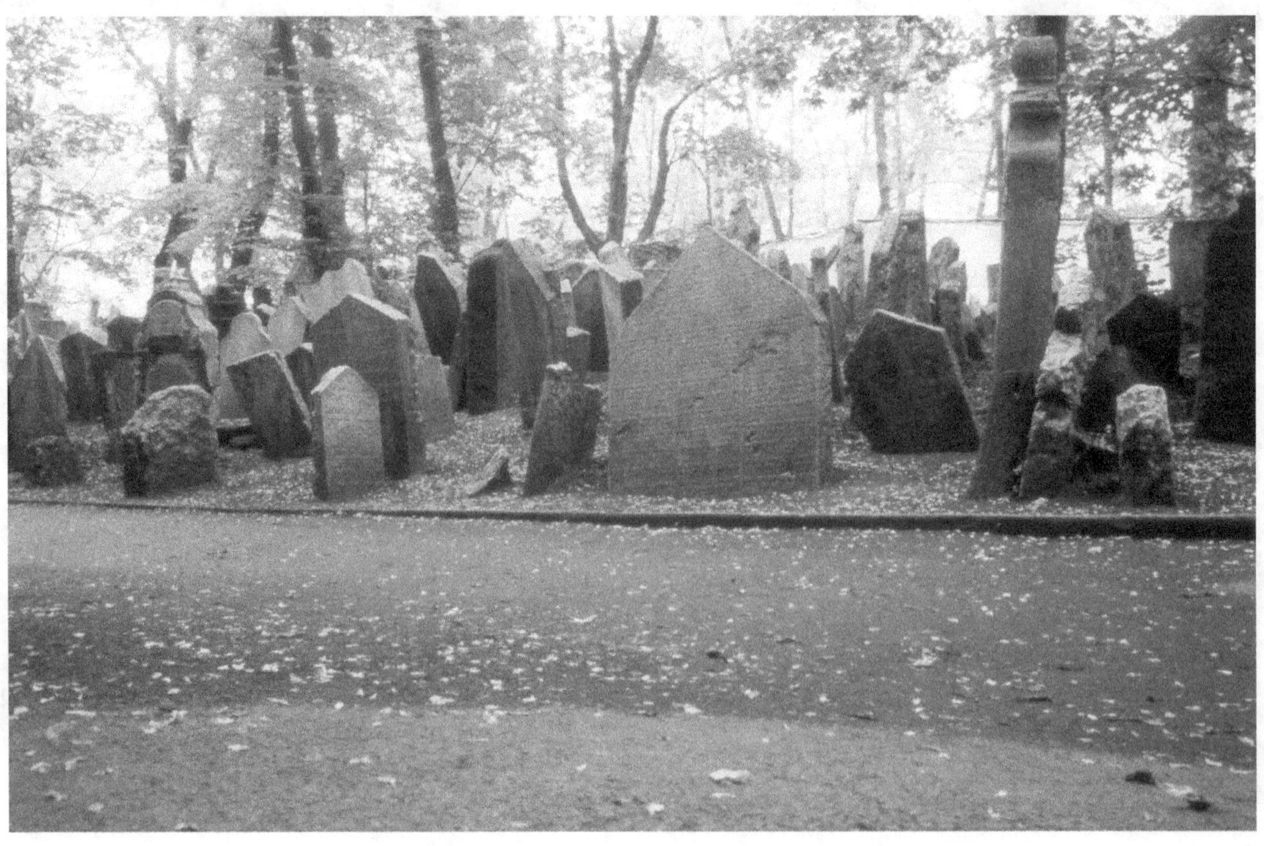

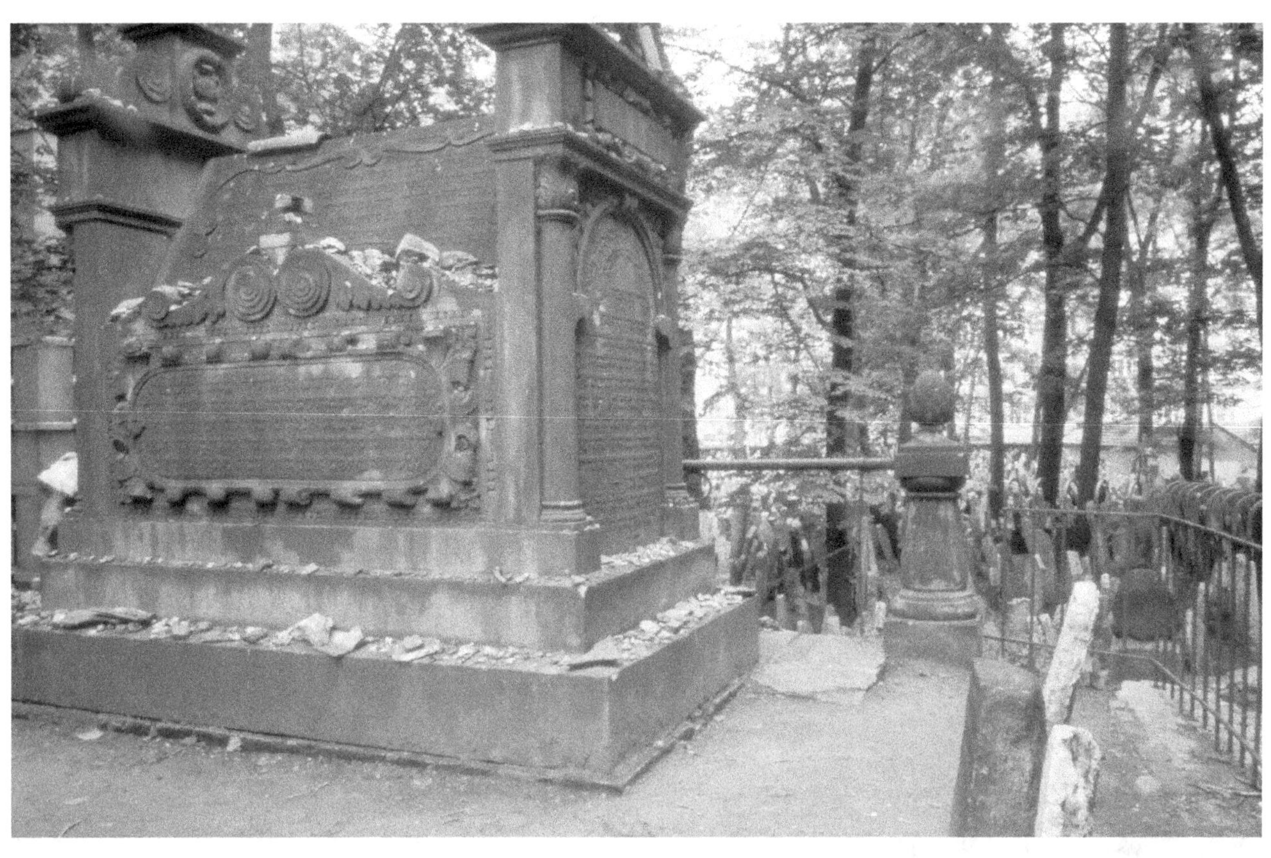

Jewish cemetery

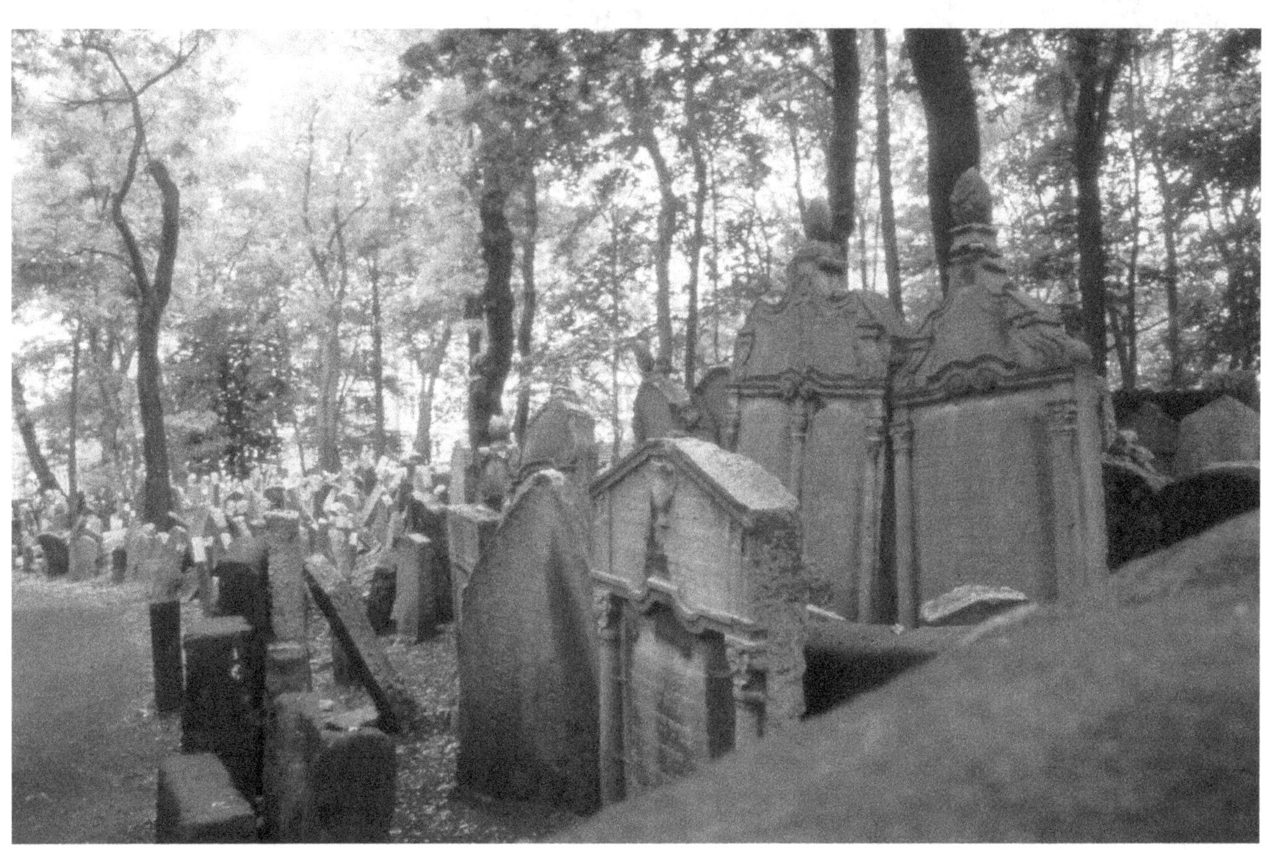

Nina and Beate in front of a house in the Golden Lane, Prague
next to Dr. Franz Kafka's house (Nr. 22) >

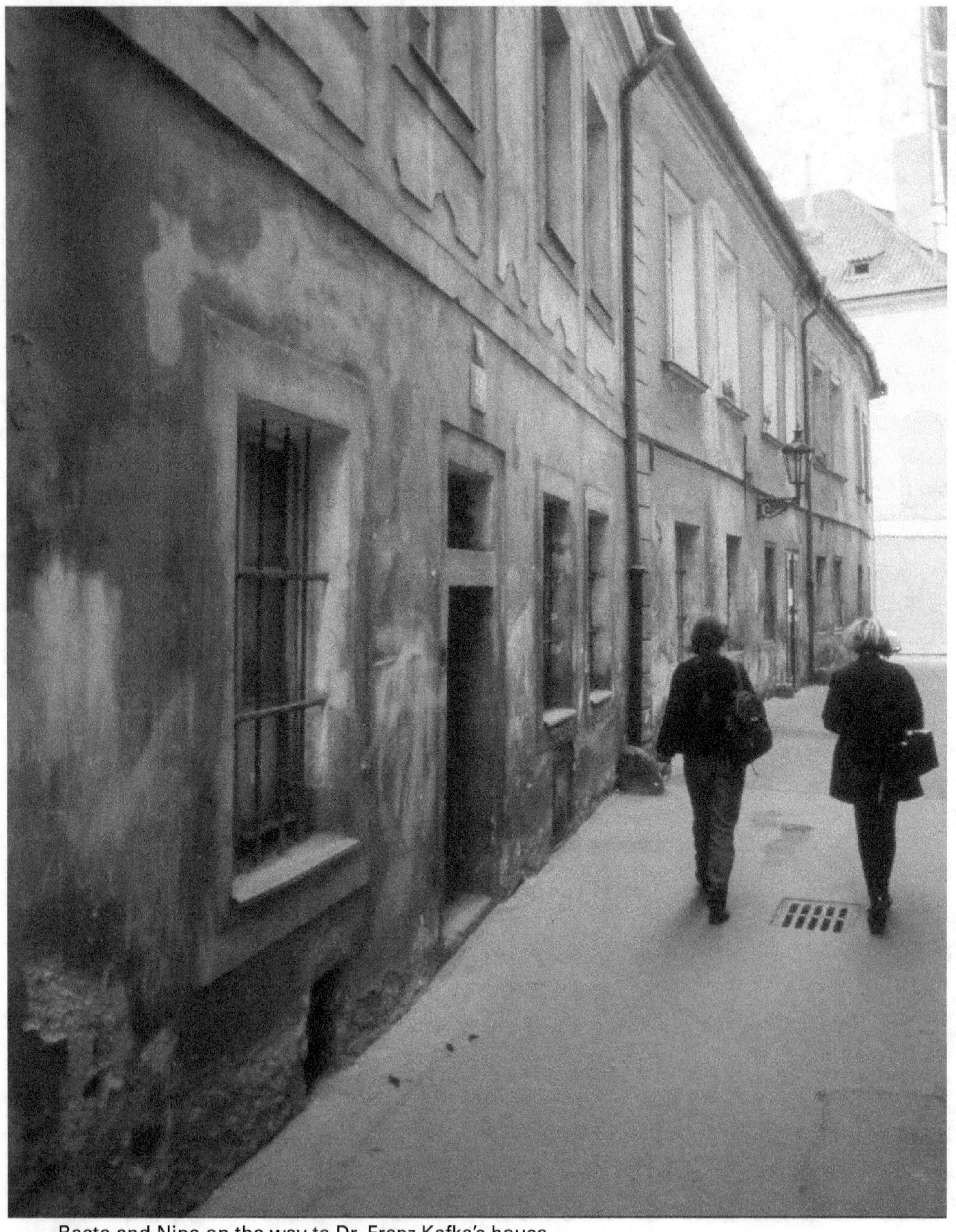

Beate and Nina on the way to Dr. Franz Kafka's house

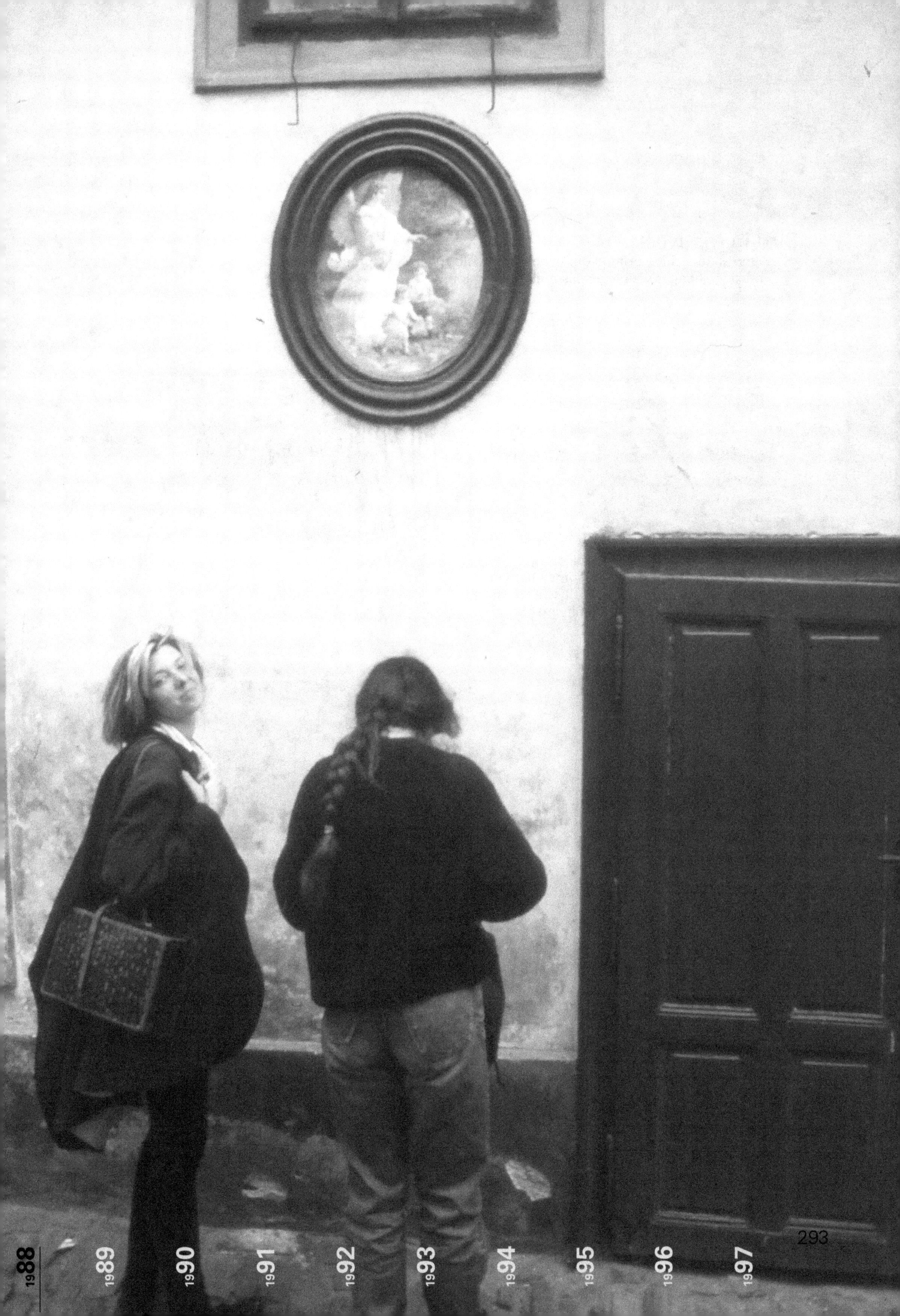

Etching

zinc plate, black ink, and paper

Bird in the Nest

Zinc plate etching printed on Arches watercolor paper; the process is iterative design: making changes visible across multiple versions

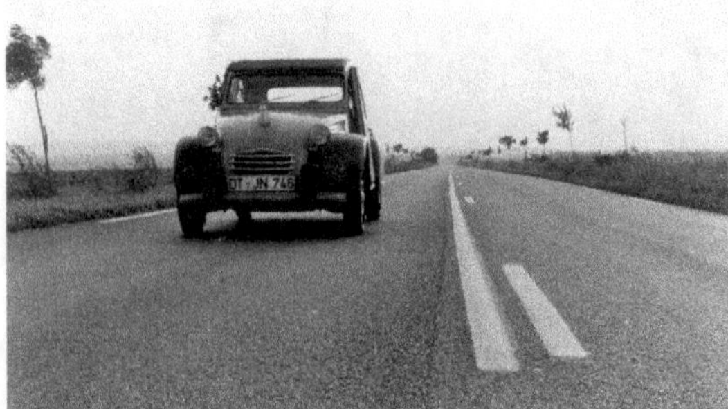

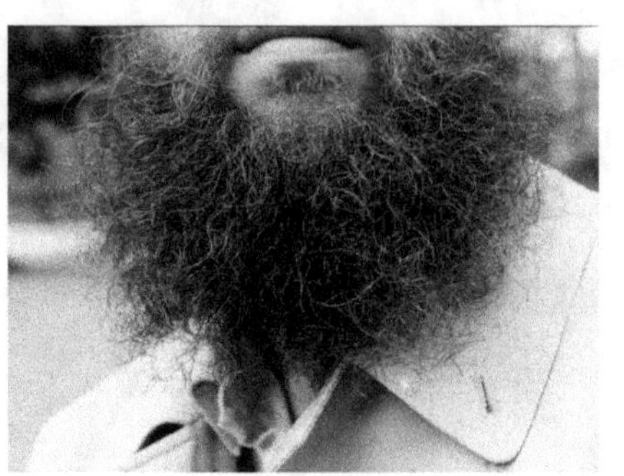

Sources: A photograph I took of my brother in our Citroën 2CV somewhere in France, and my beard, as well as a rooster, an egg, Miriam, and a magnifying glass

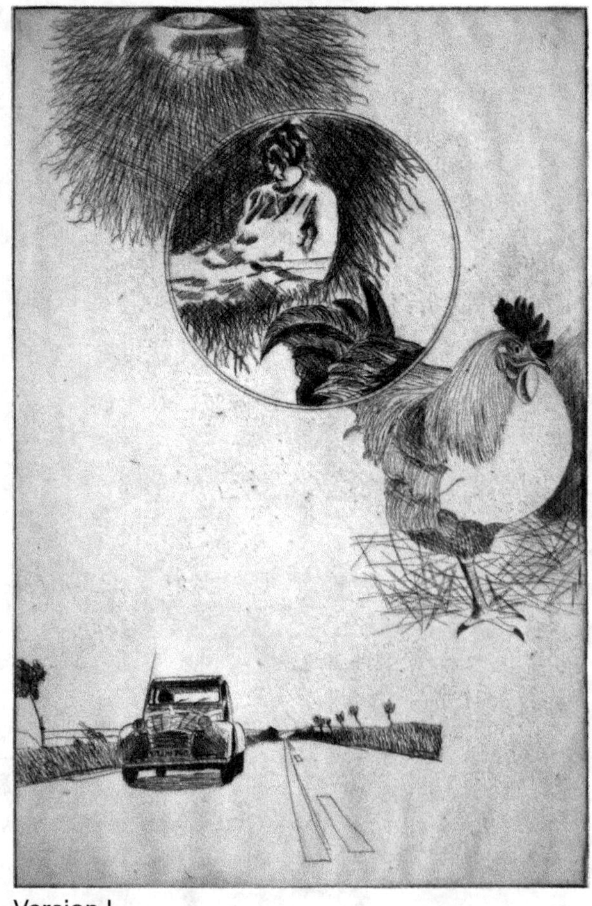

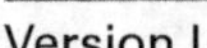

Version I

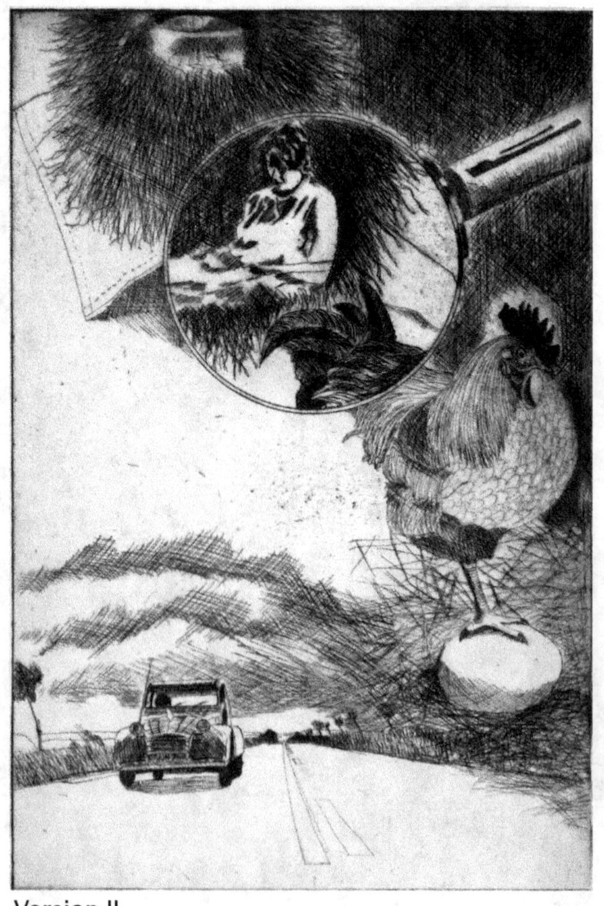

Version II

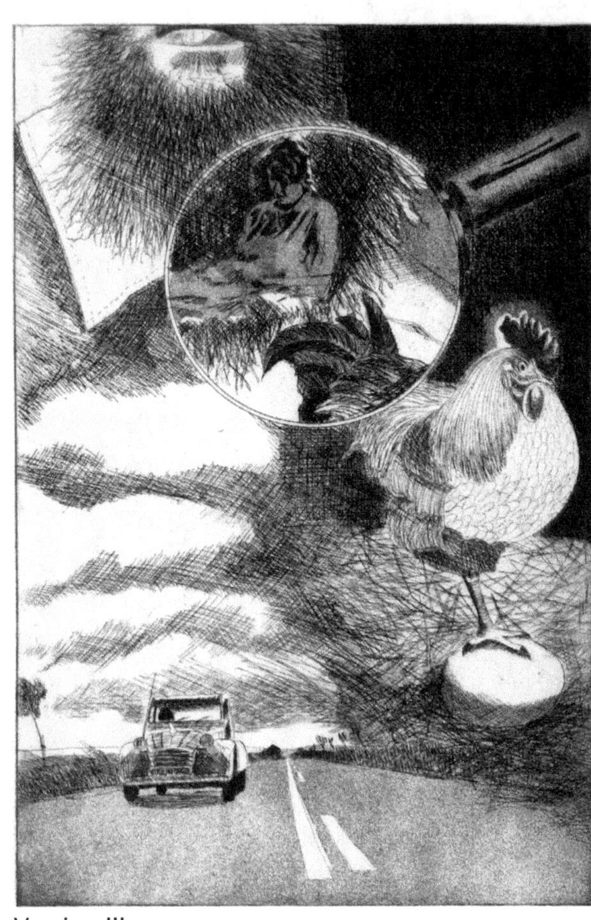
Version III

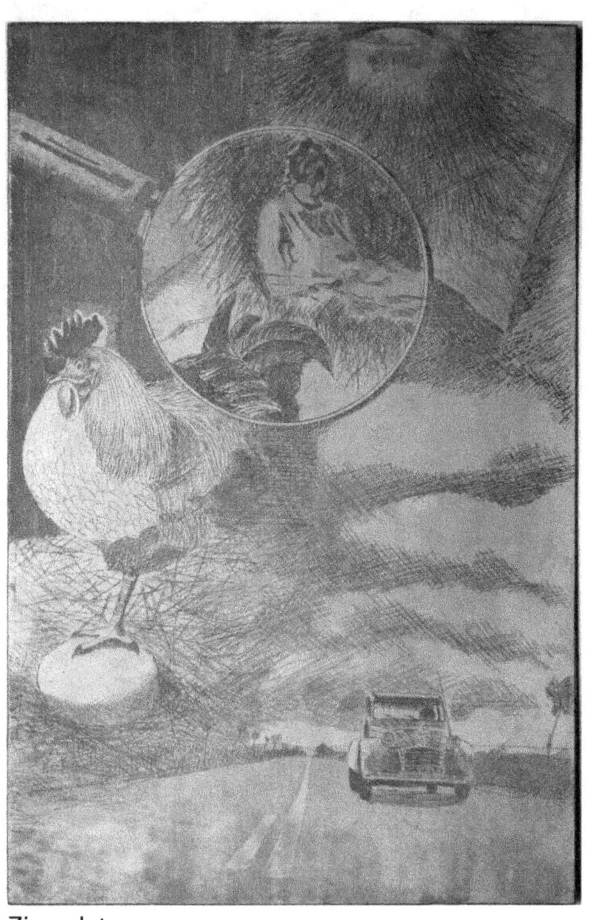
Zinc plate

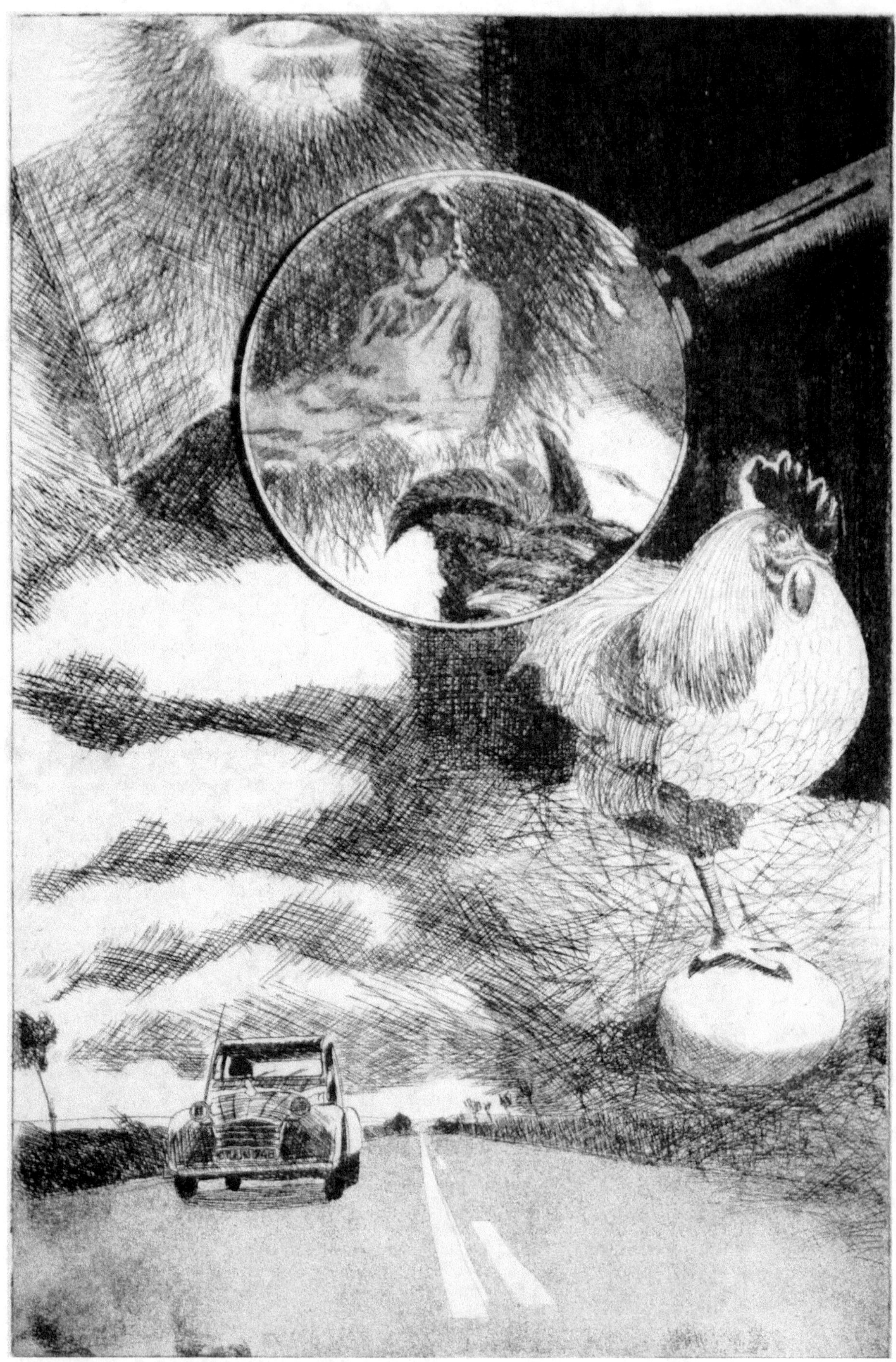

Bird in the Nest, final version (12″ x 18″)

Etching

zinc plate, black ink and paper

Perpetuum Mobile

Zinc plate etching with aquatint and drypoint technique

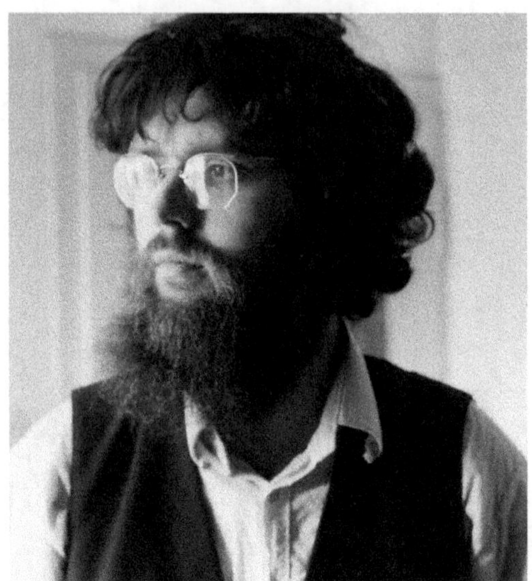

Source: self portrait, street scene, hot air balloon

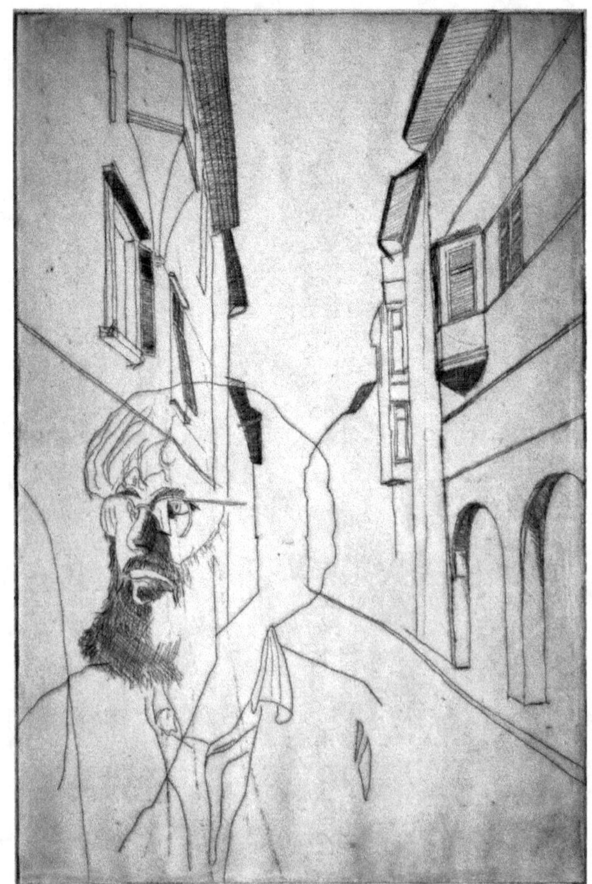

Version I

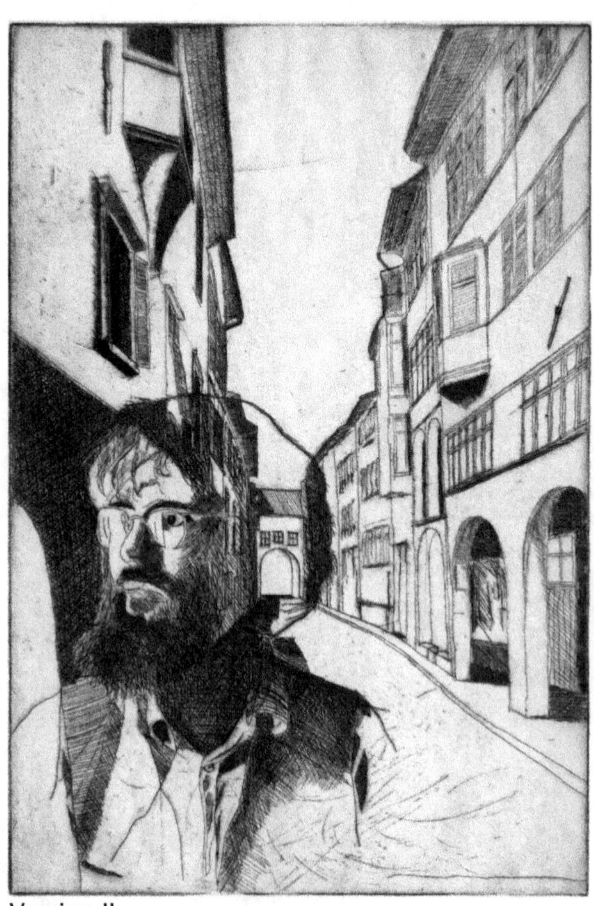

Version II

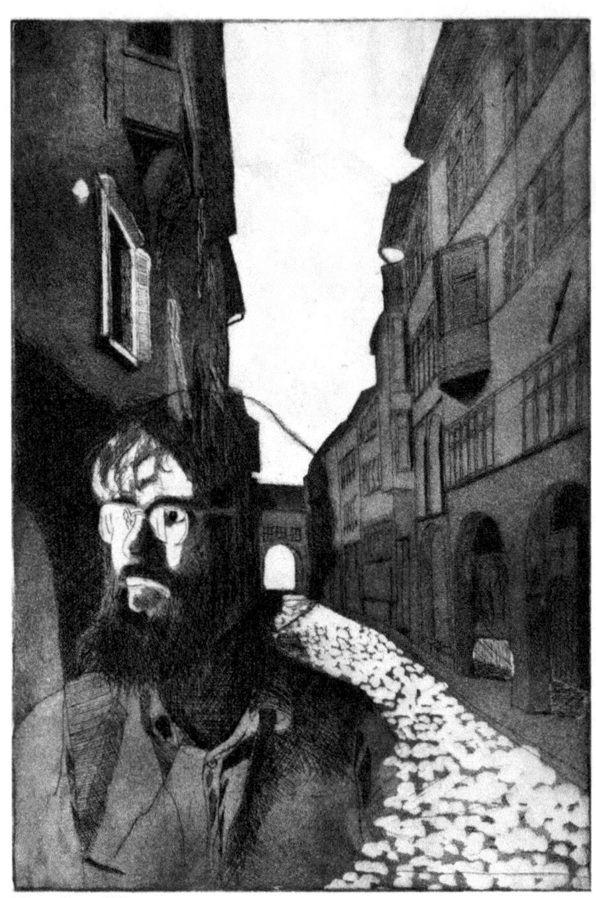

Version III

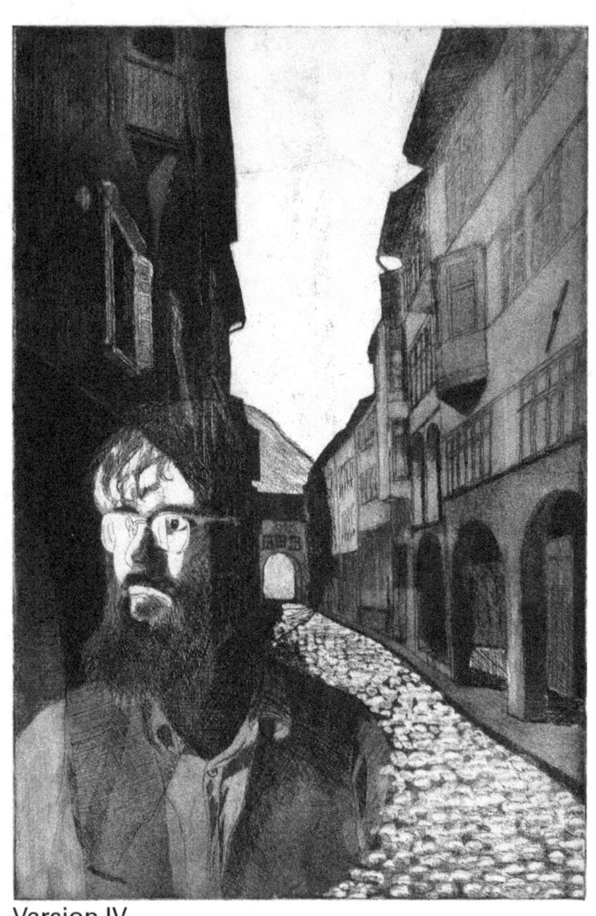

Version IV

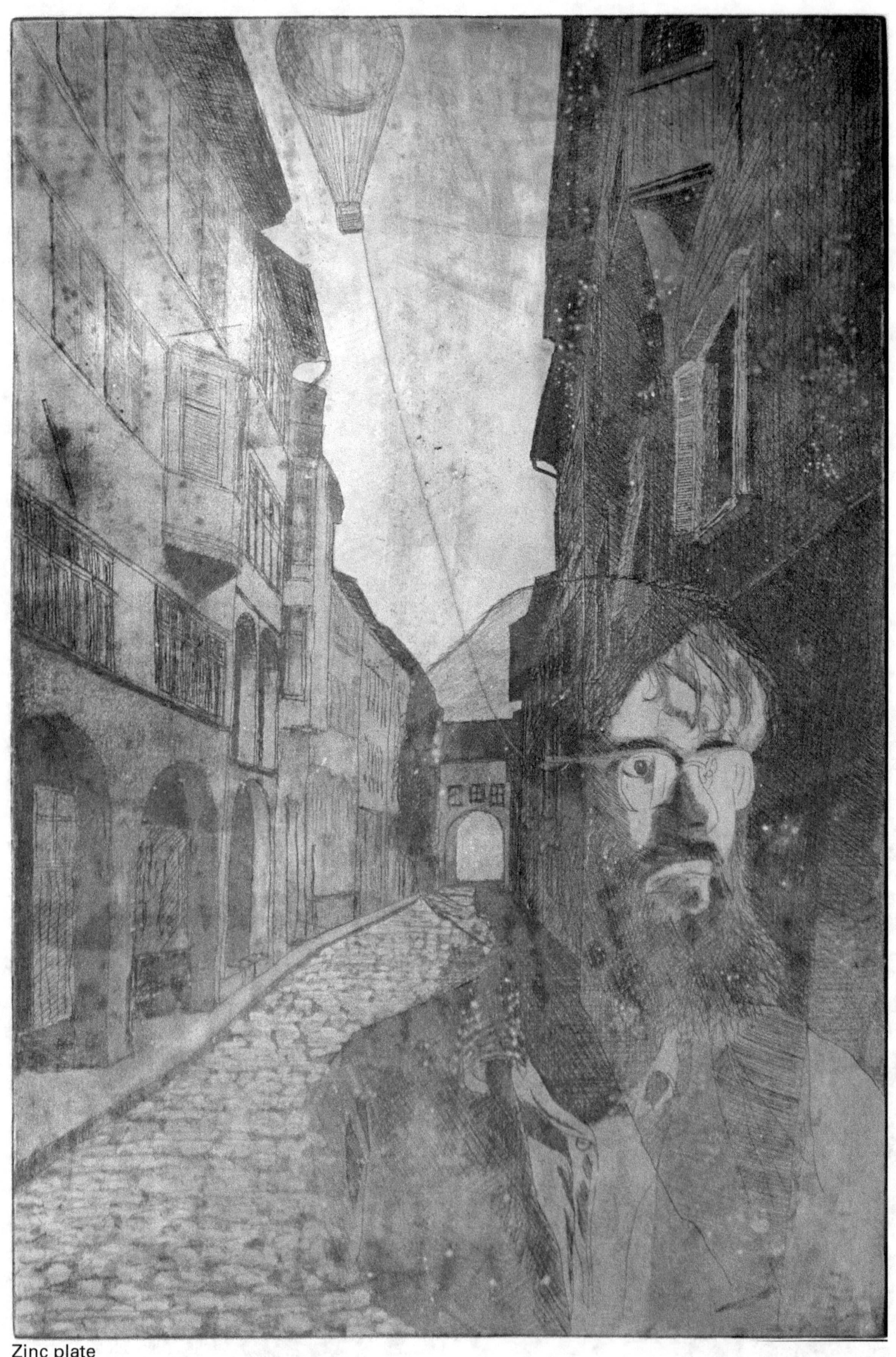

Zinc plate

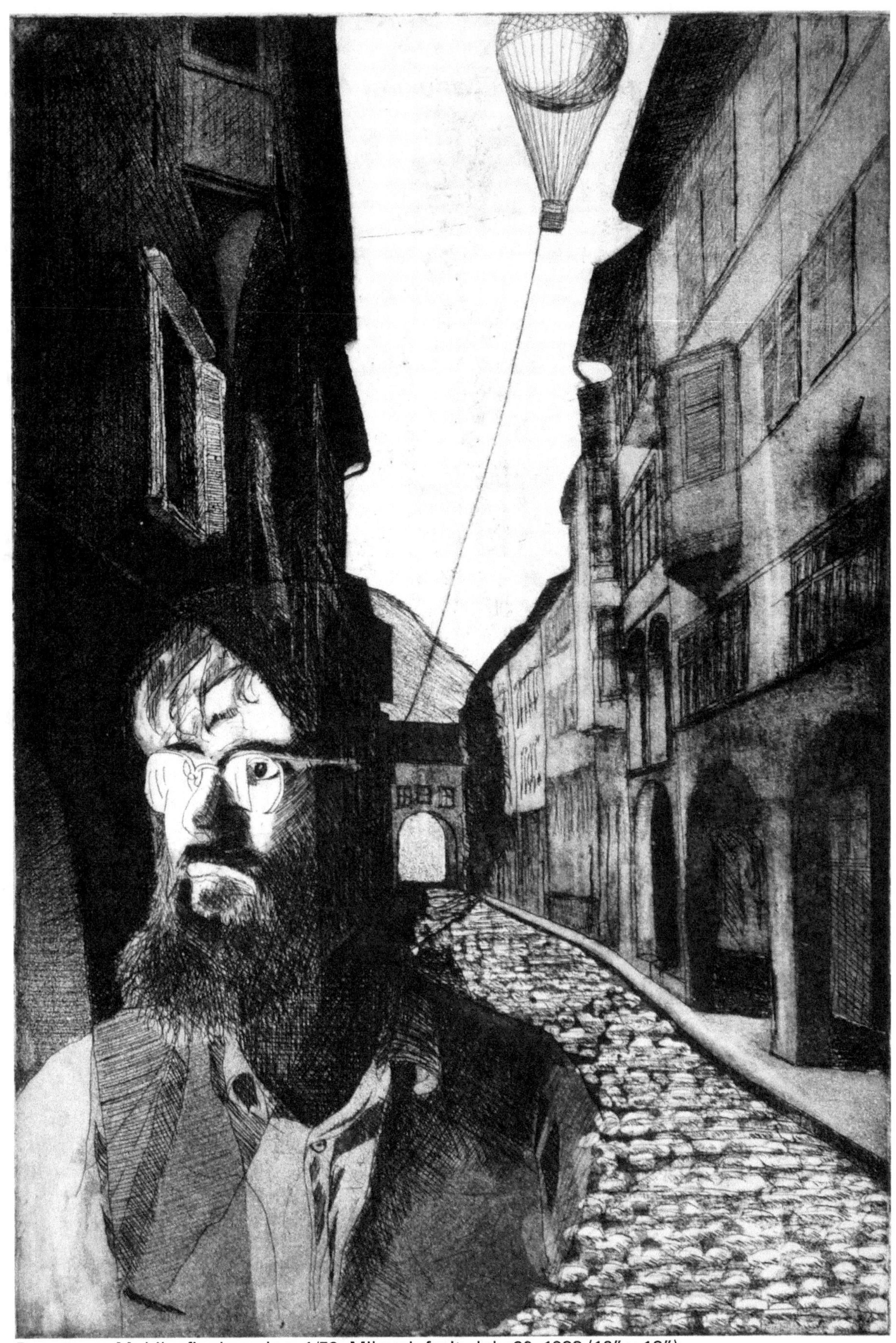

Perpetuum Mobile, final version, 1/59, Mikesch fecit, July 30, 1988 (12" x 18")

zinc plate, black ink, water color, and paper

Urban Design Competition, Milwaukee, WI

Etchings on zinc plate

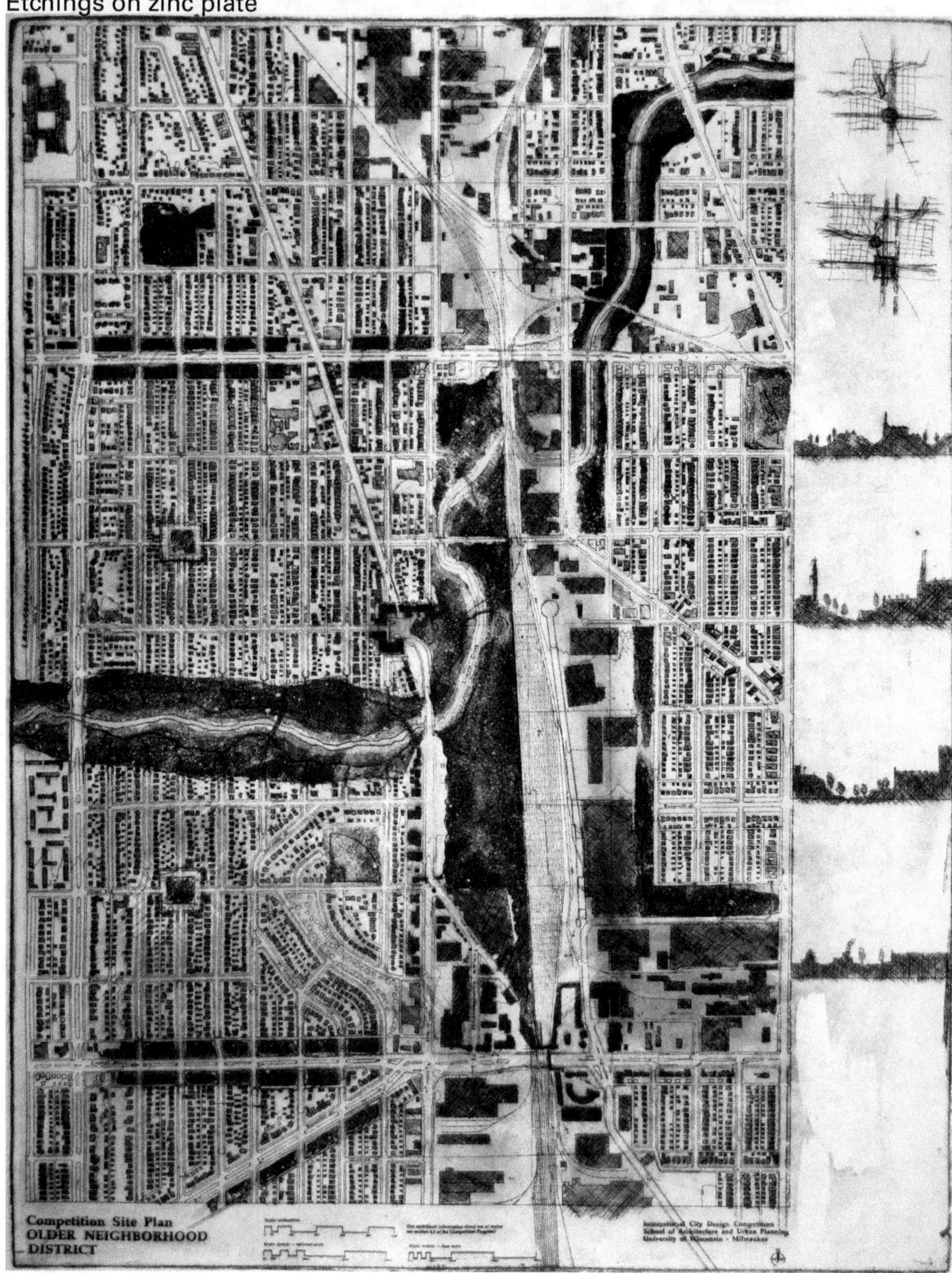

Overall site strategy

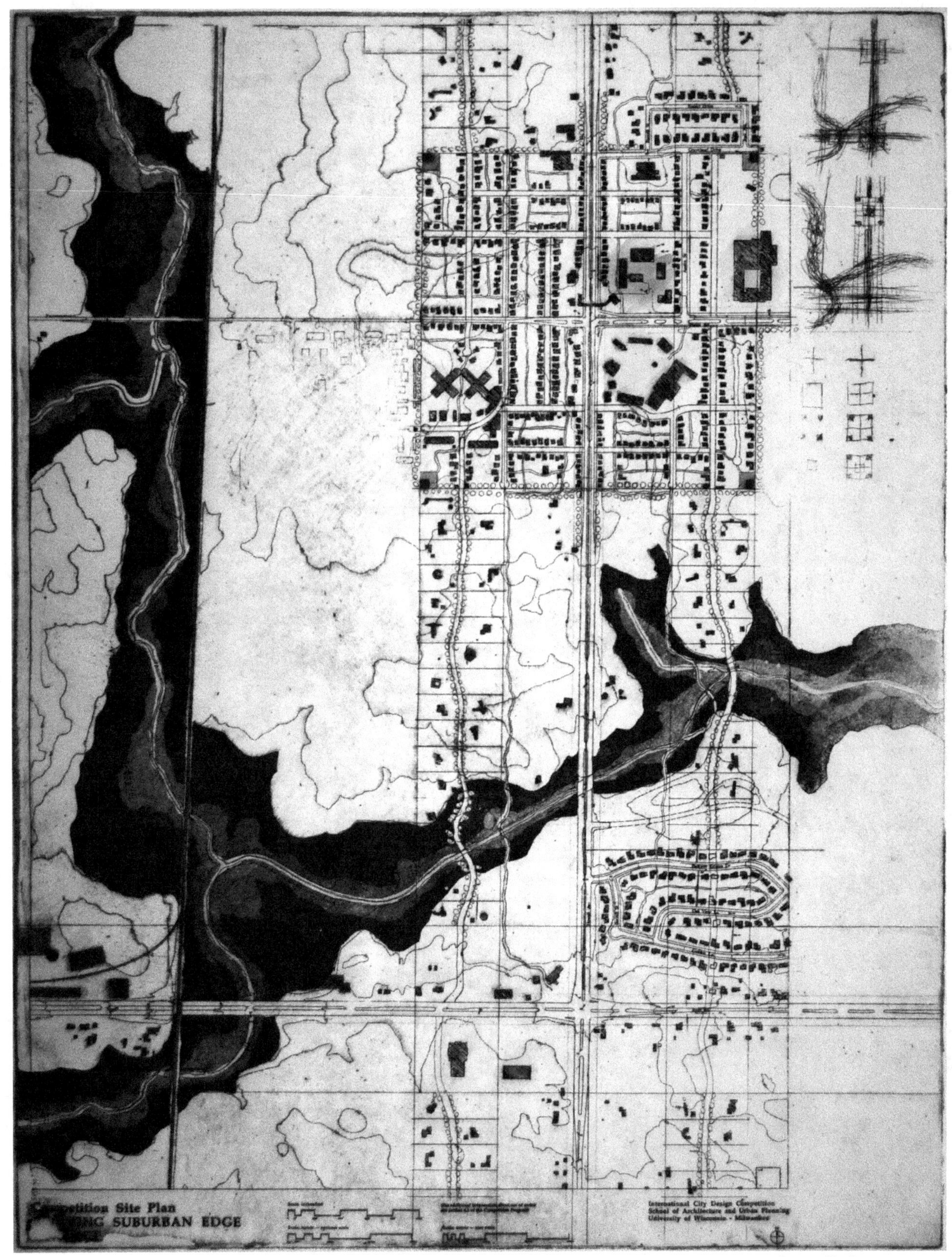

Overall site strategy

Etching

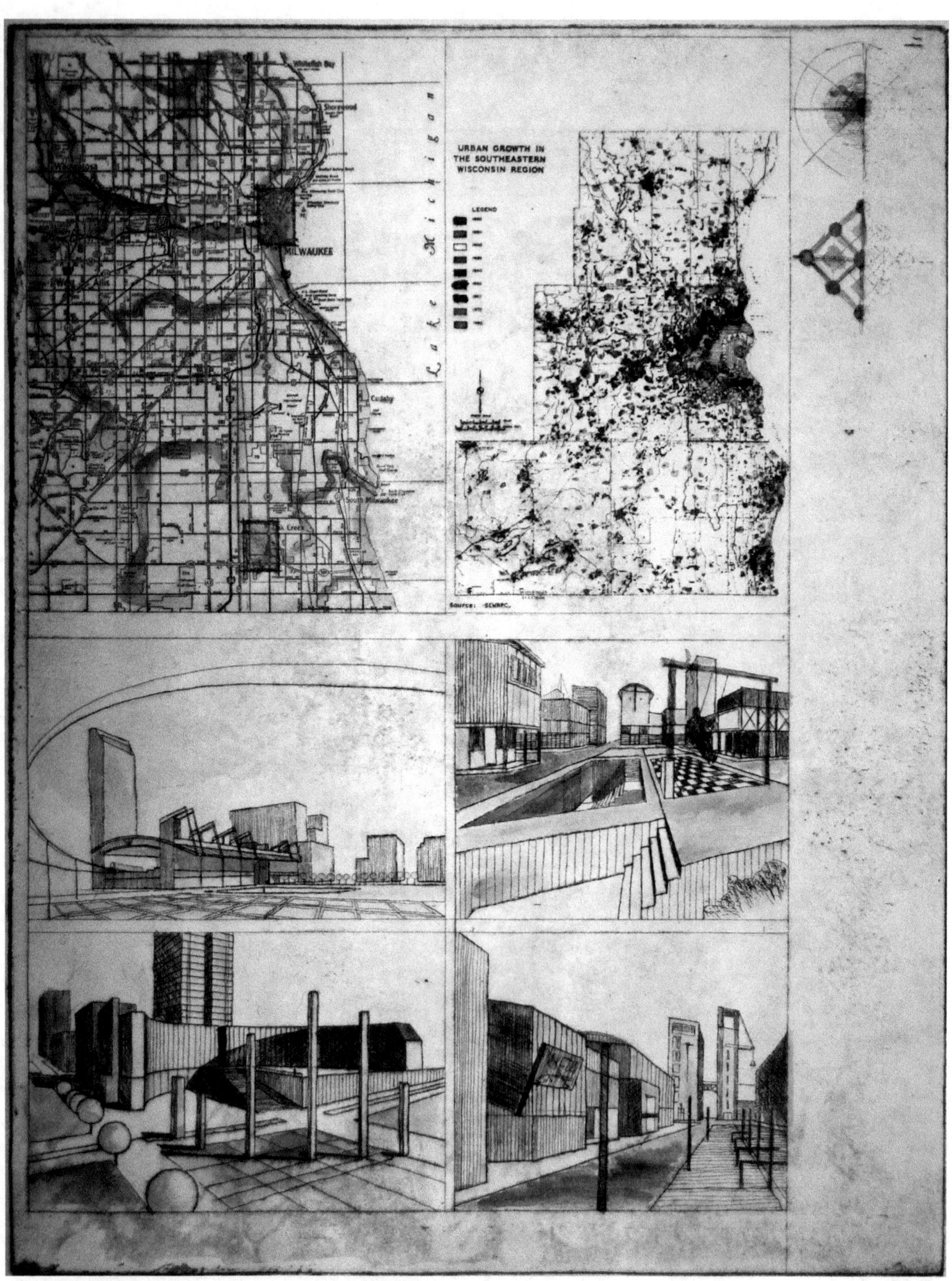

Perspective views of urban design interventions

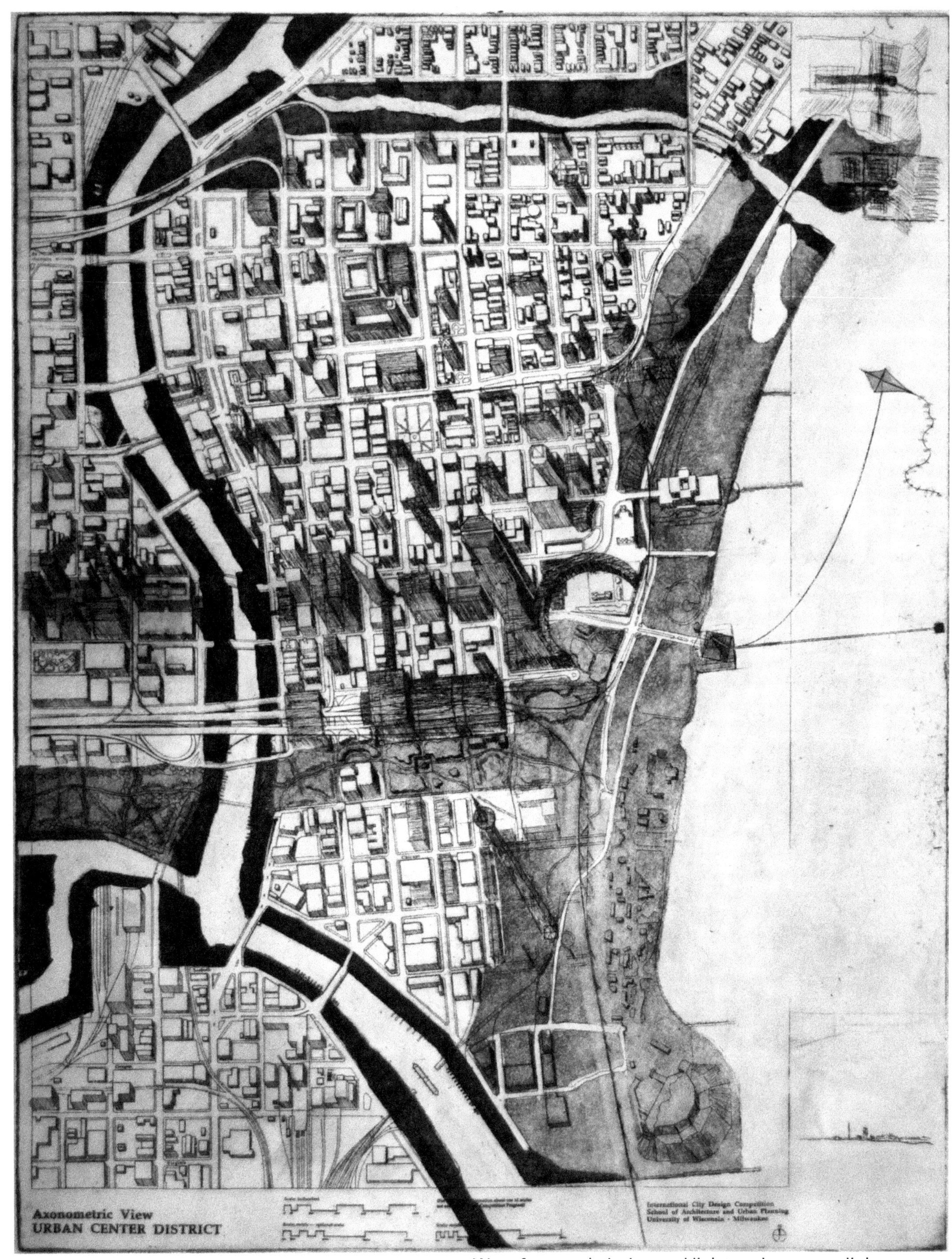

Waterfront park design and link to urban green links

Final version, detail

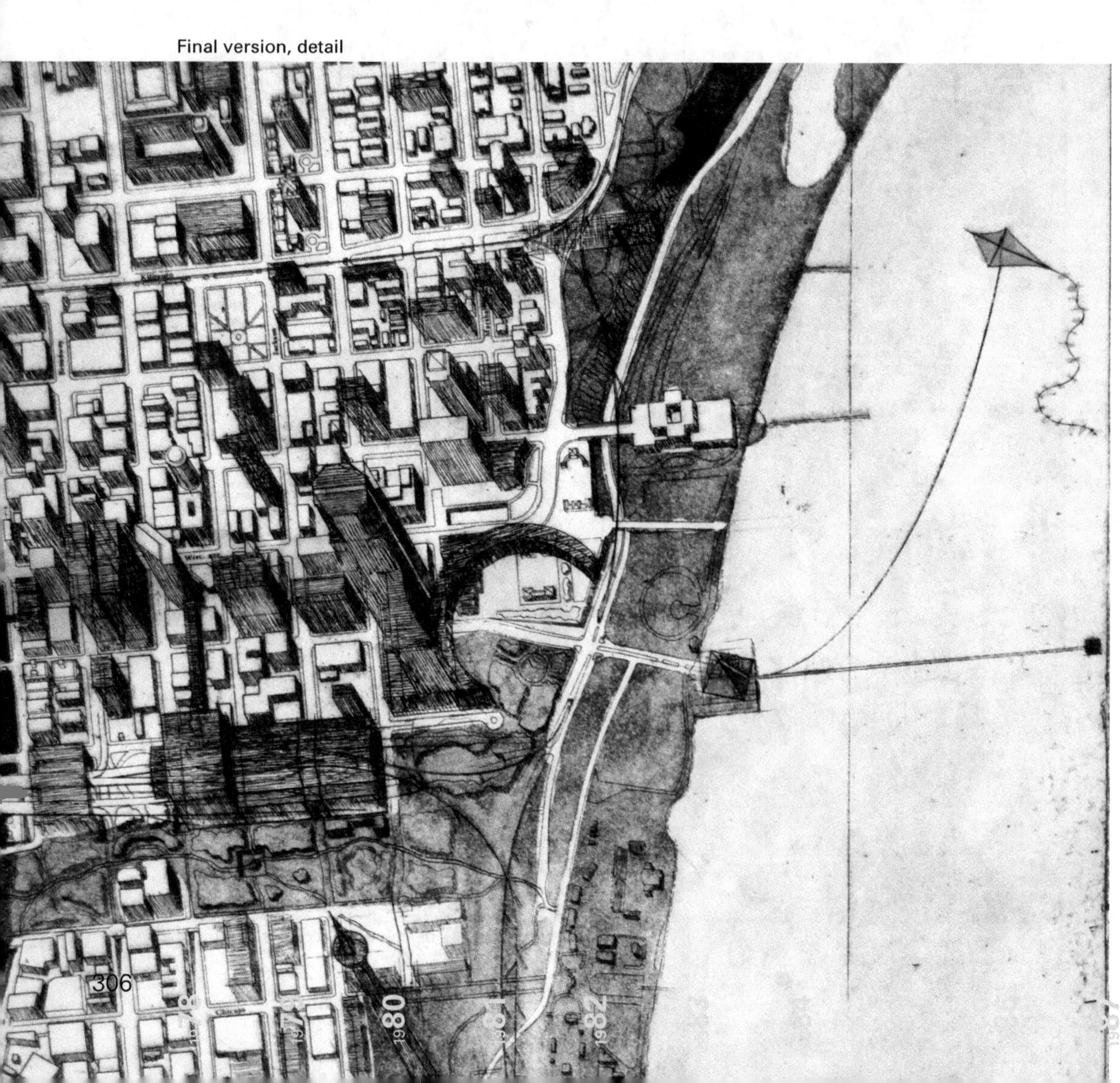

Etching

copper plate, black ink and paper

Duke of Clubs

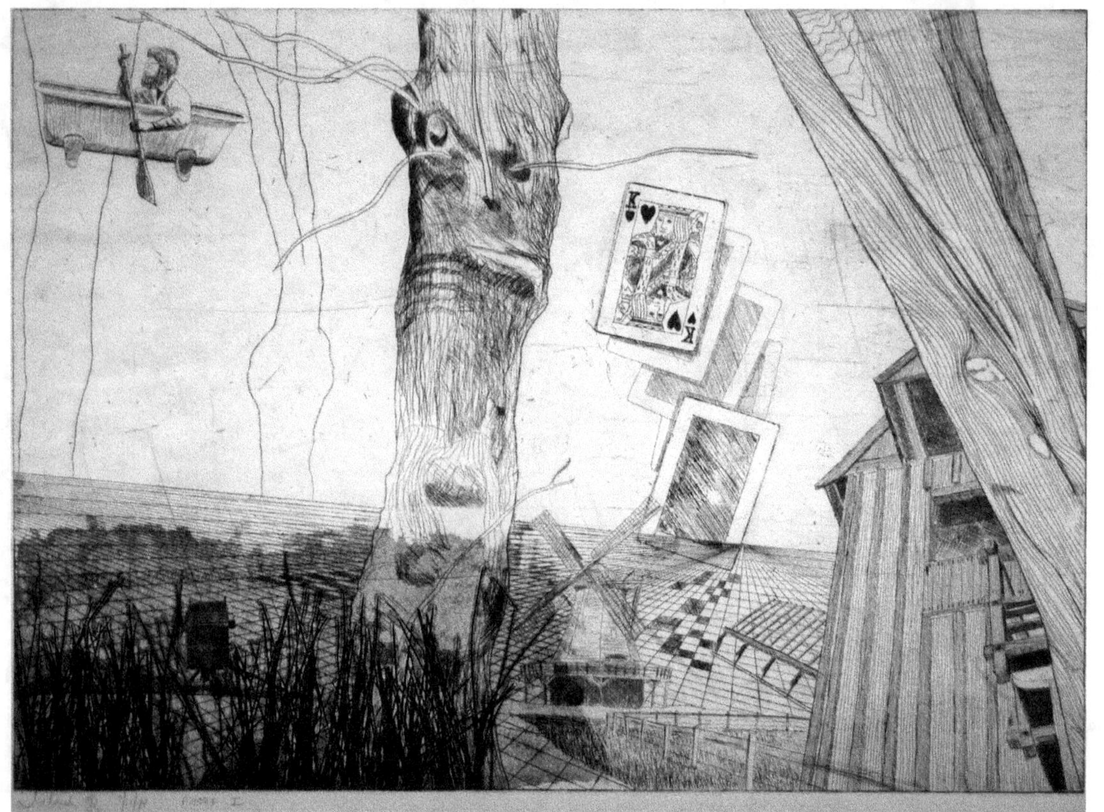

Version I

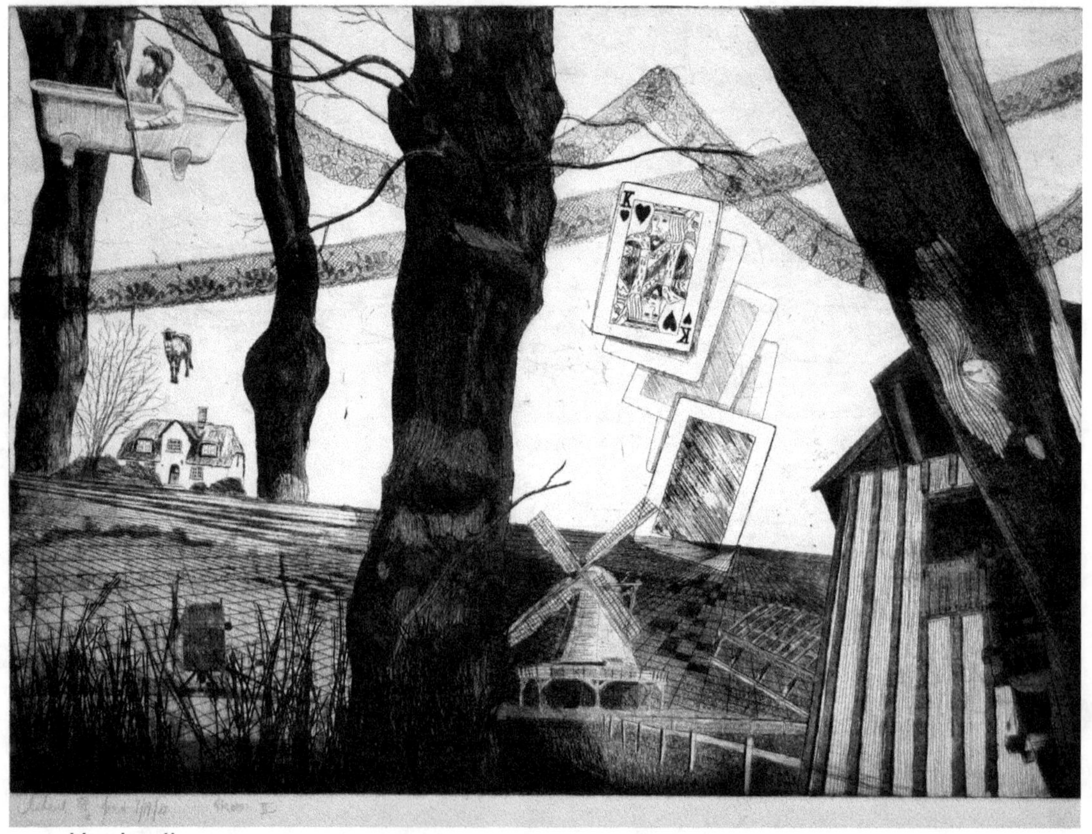

Version II

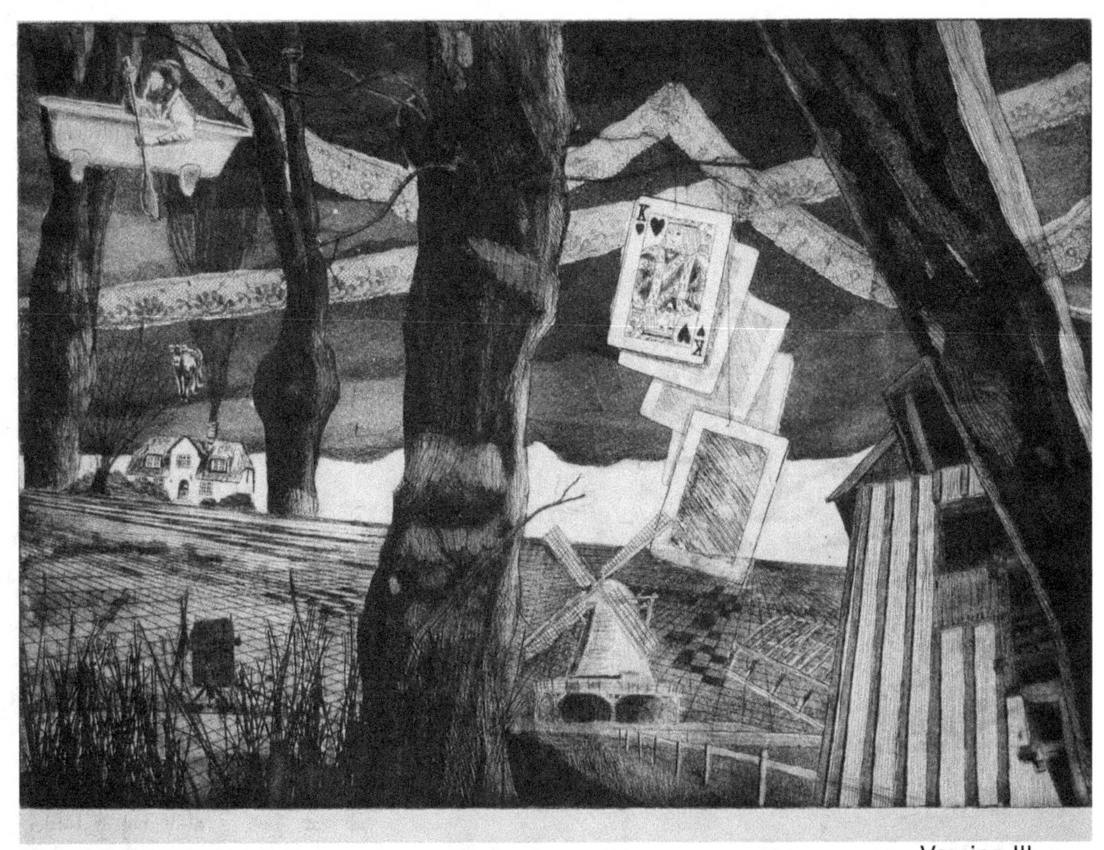

Version III

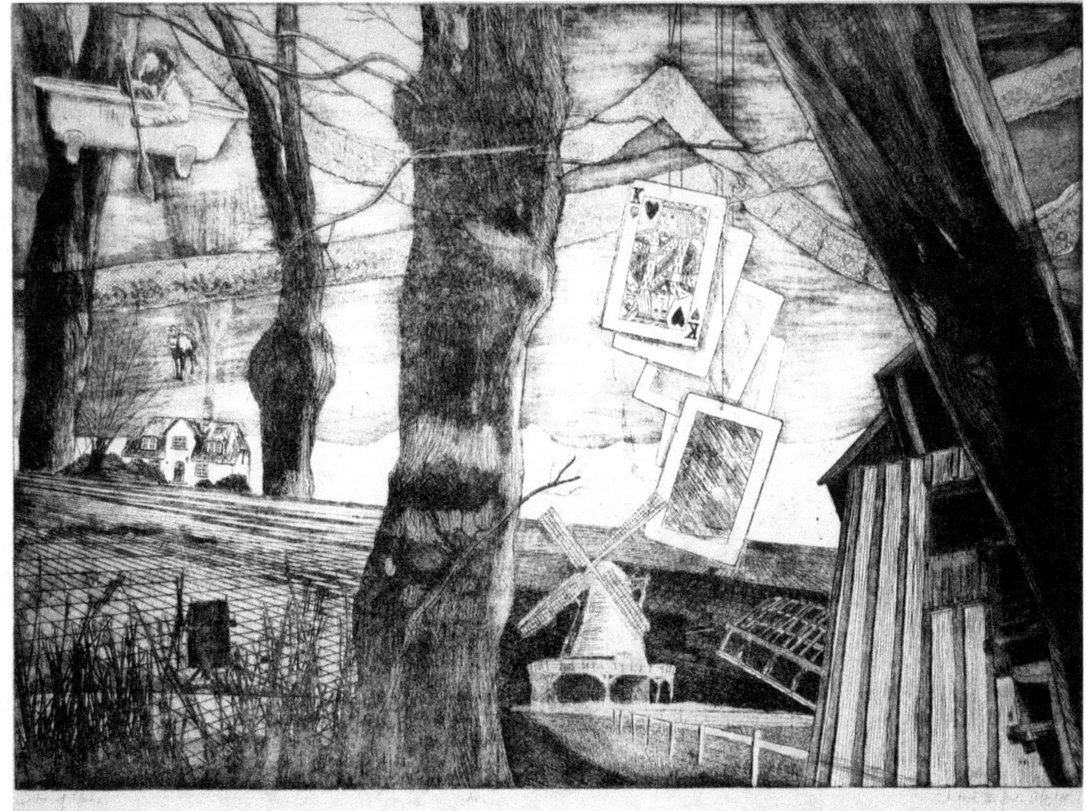

Version IV

Final version showing details

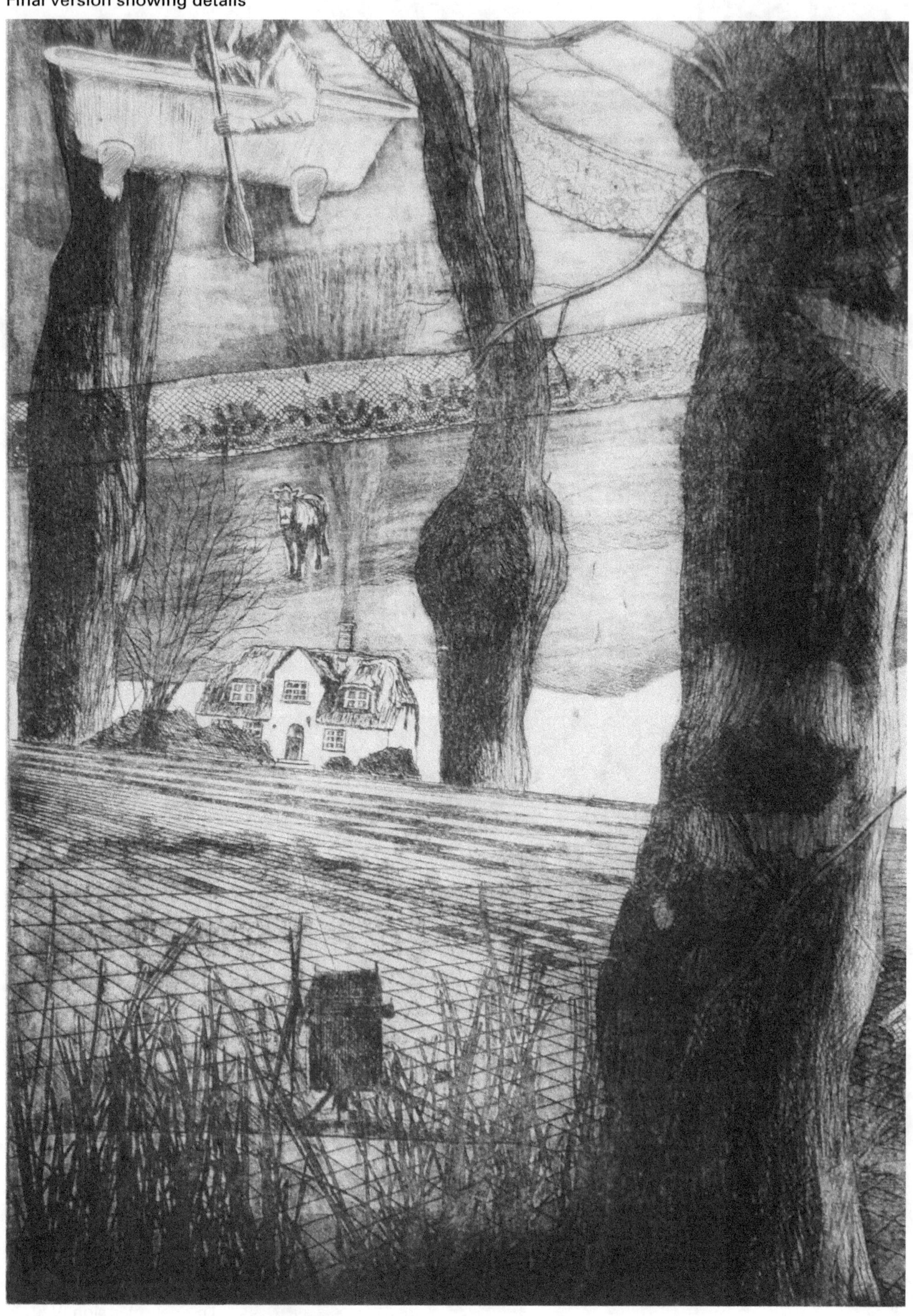

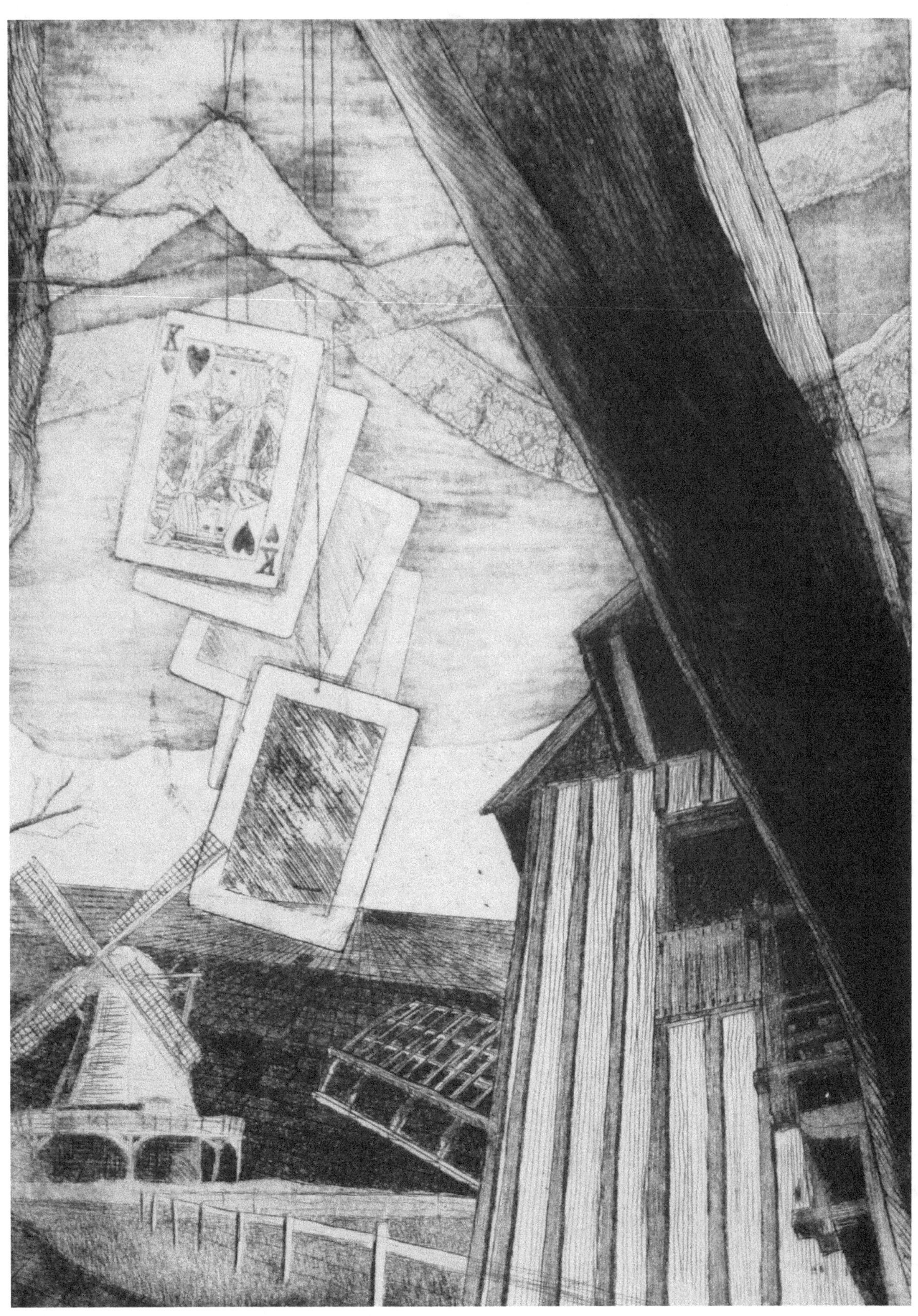

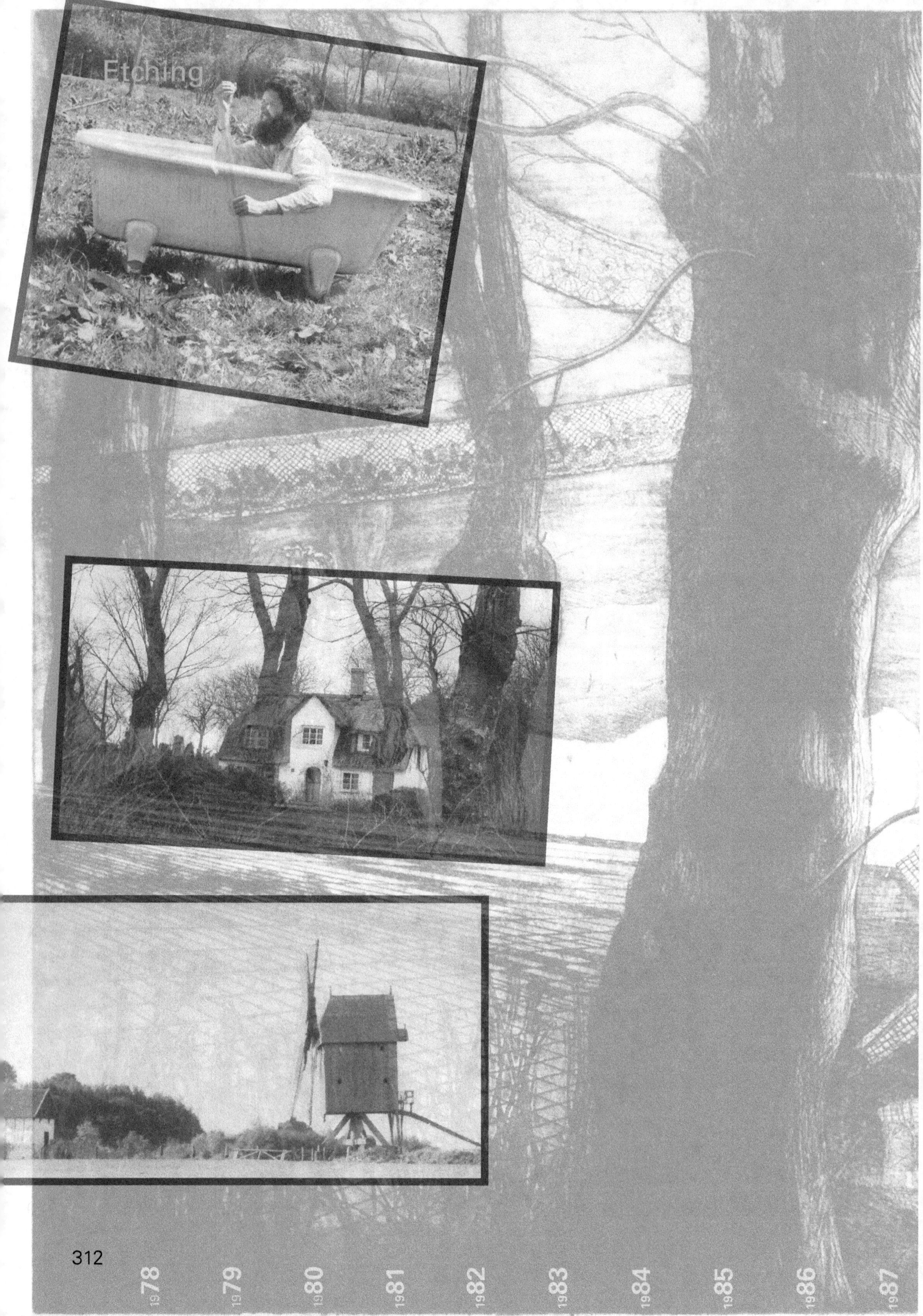
Etching
1978
1979
1980
1981
1982
1983
1984
1985
1986
1987

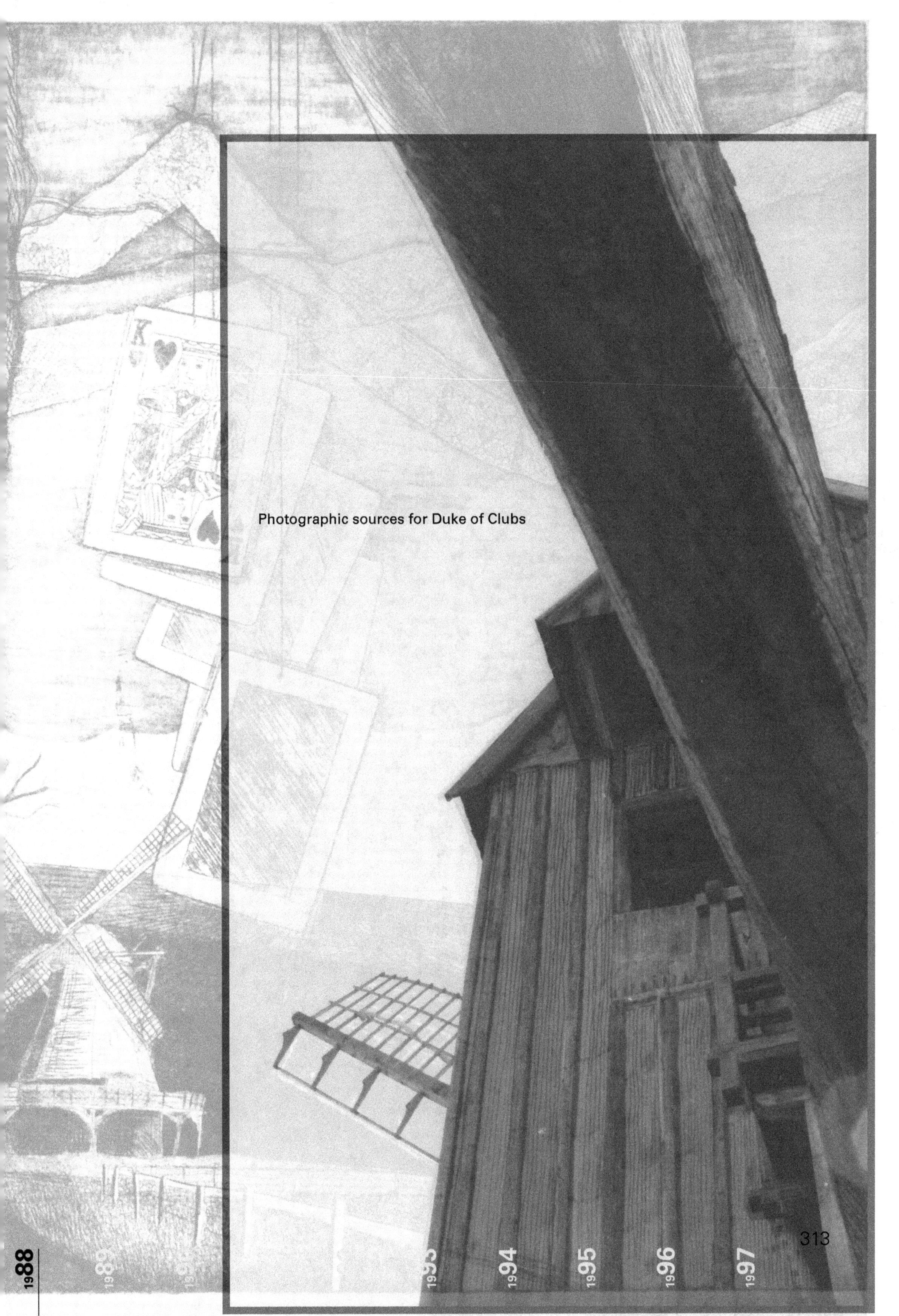

Photographic sources for Duke of Clubs

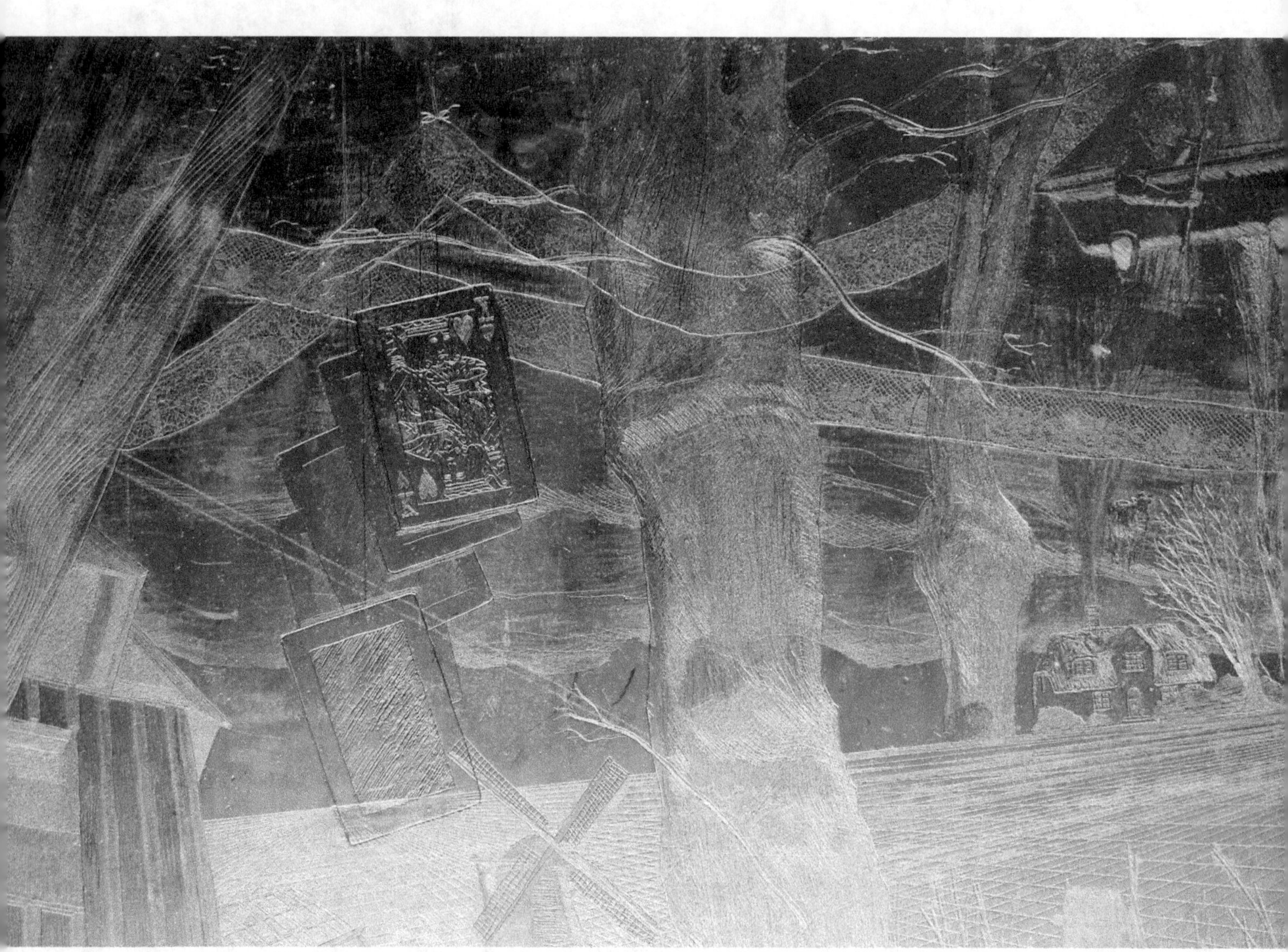

Duke of Clubs
Final version copper flate

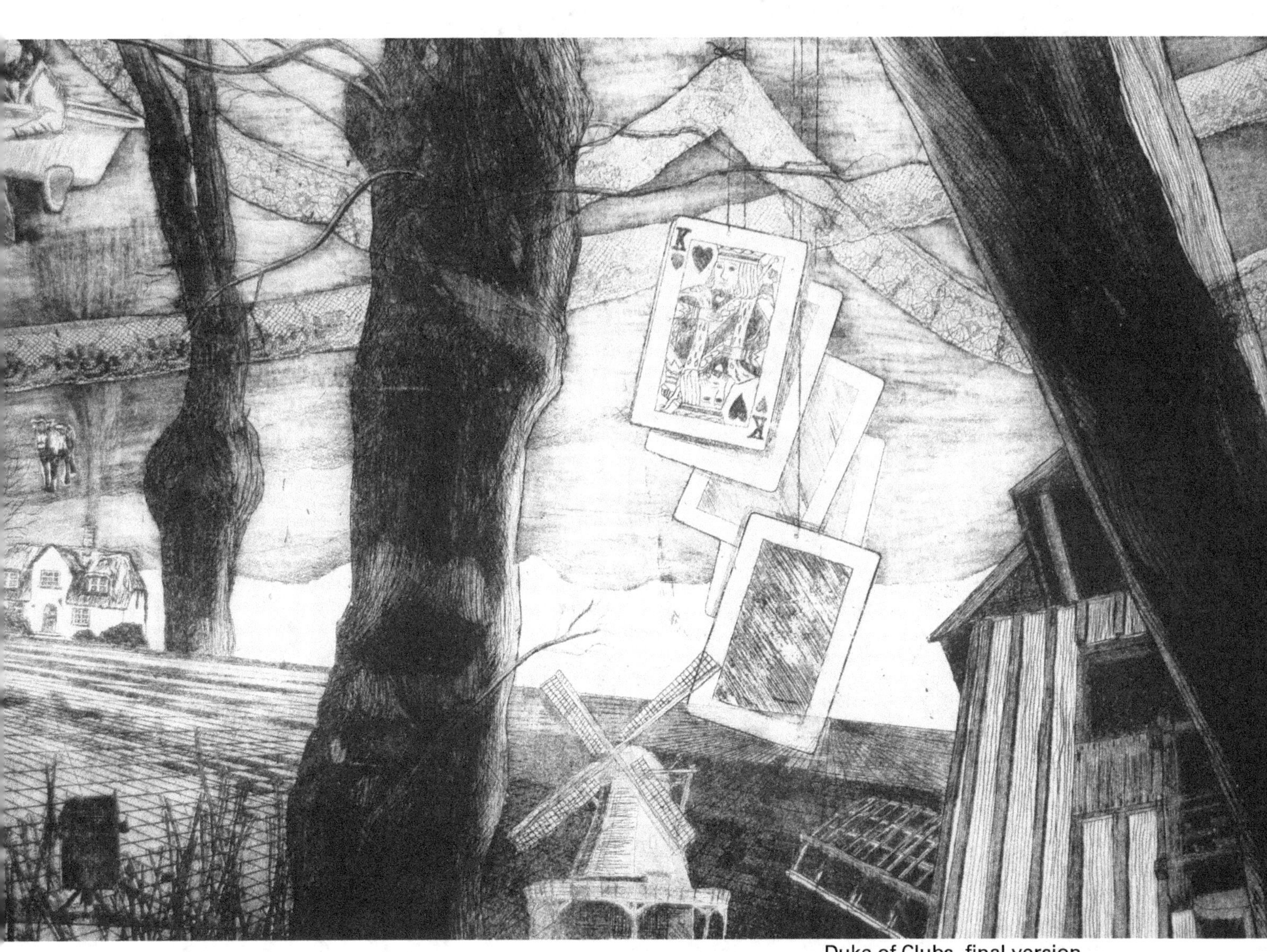

Duke of Clubs, final version
Etching and aquatint on copper plate
Summer 1988 (18″ x 30″)

Etching

The Acrobat

four zinc plates; CMYK ink, and paper

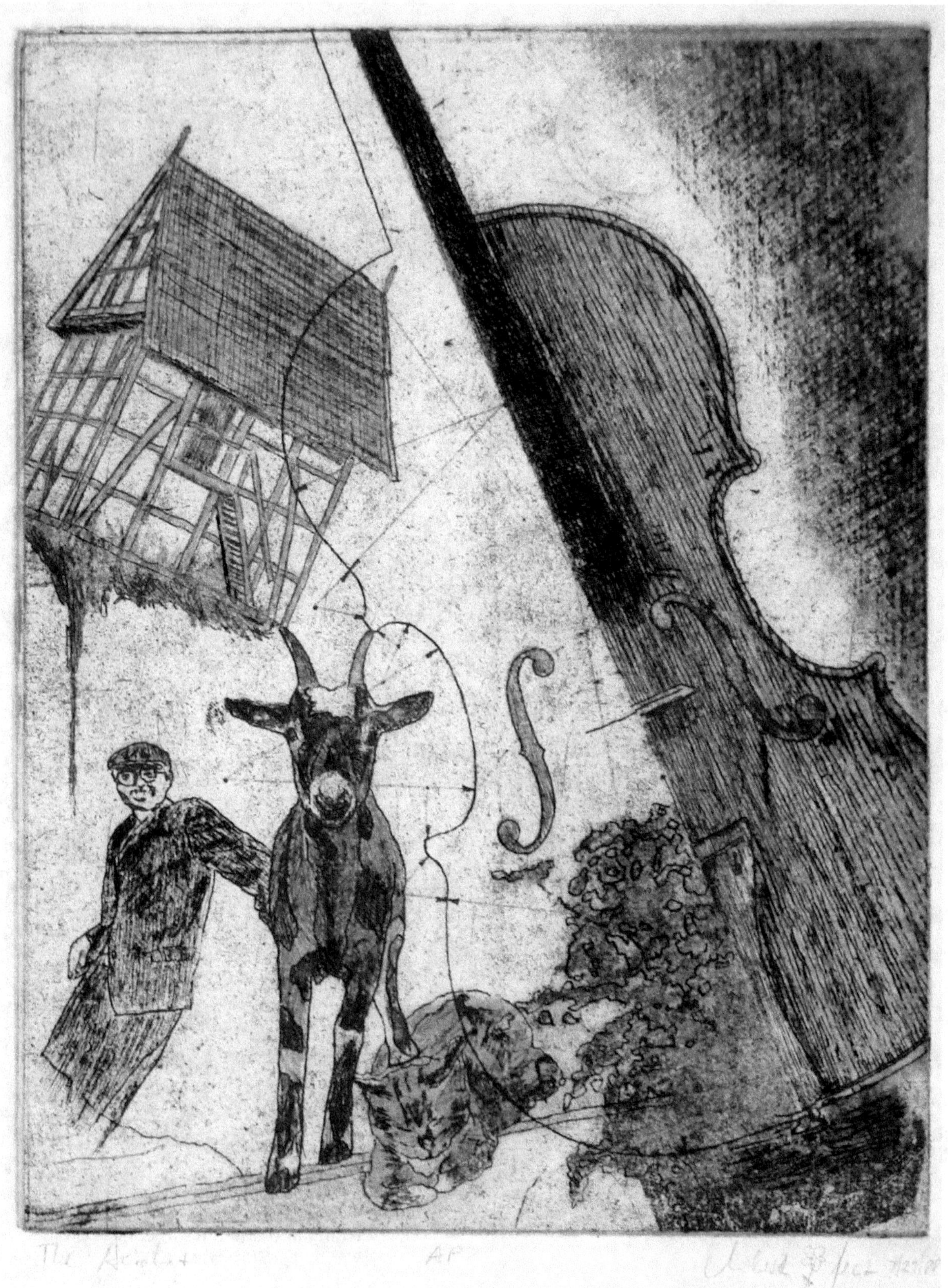

The Acrobat, Artist Proof I, Mikesch fecit, July 29, 1988

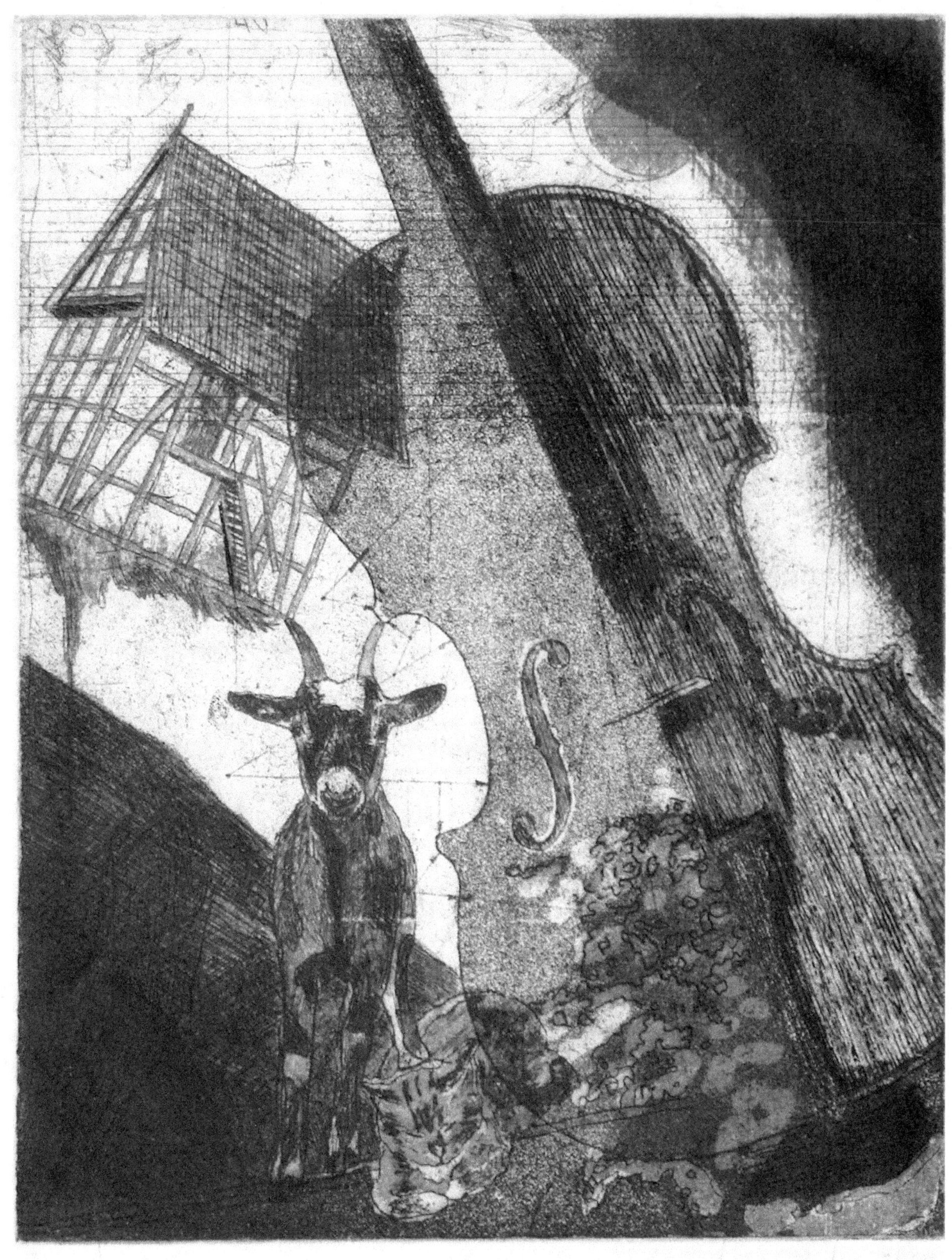

The Acrobat, Artist Proof II, Mikesch fecit, August 2, 1988

Viking Museum

Hyde Park, Chicago, IL

This project attempts to create a space for the Gokstad, a Viking ship buried about 1000 years ago, discovered in 1880, and a replica of it sailed to the Chicago World's Fair from Norway in 1893. Critical ideas dealt with the siting of the museum, the space for the ship itself (after the fair the boat was stored in a shed in Lincoln Park), and the geographical peculiarities of Norway.

The site is part of the original World's Fair property and presents approximately where the Gokstad replica landed in 1893. This brought up the idea of arrival but also the action of departure from across the Atlantic prior to arrival in the new world. The

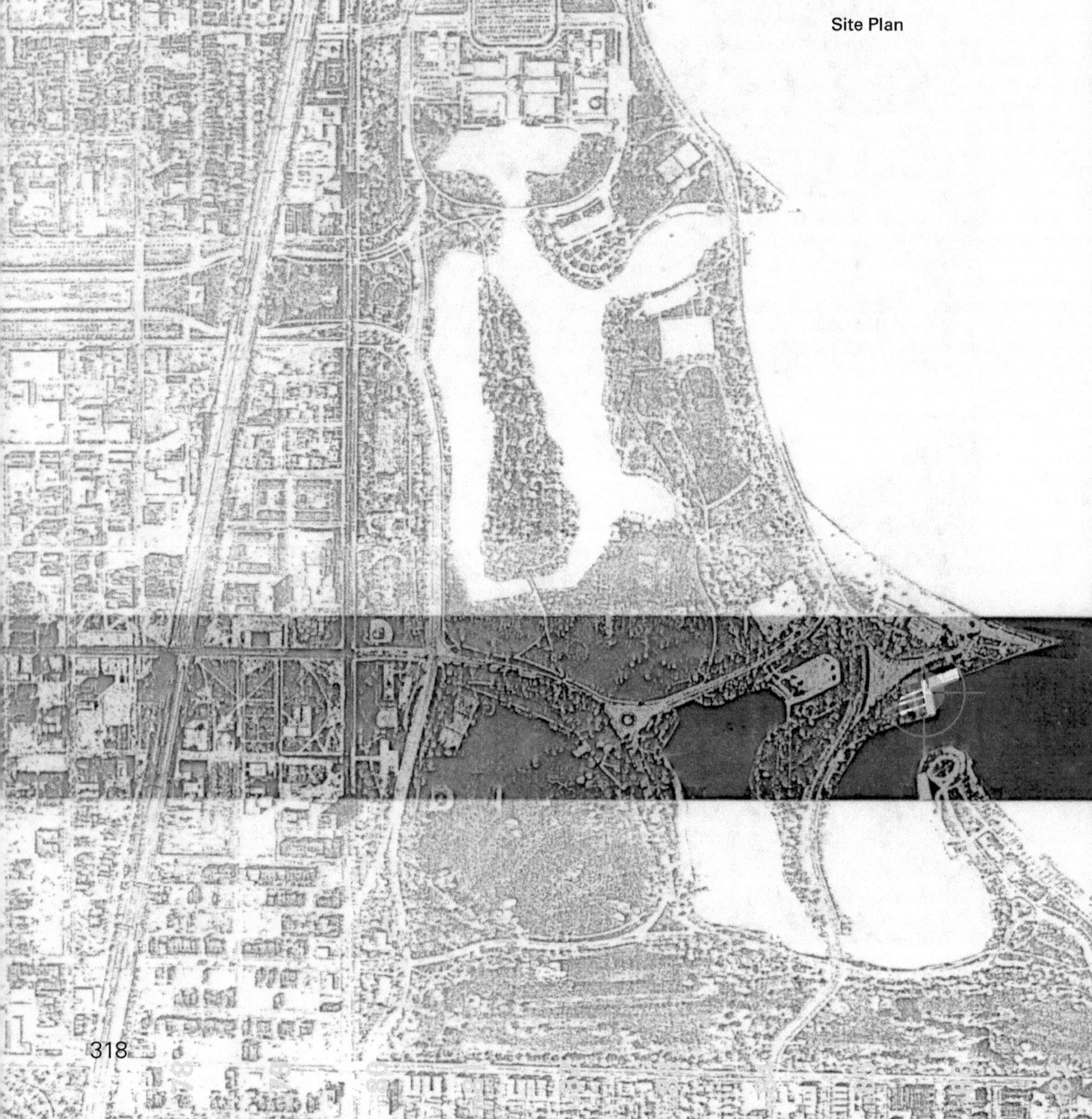

Site Plan

leaving of Norway by ship, sailing through a long and narrow fjord before reaching the open sea was transformed into a building with high walls or canyons that reflect the geography of Norway. The interior was conceived as an anti-climatic experience to the Gokstad ship. A simple space to accentuate an elegant object. To prepare the visitor for this emotional experience she is subjected to spatial extremes by ascending along the blank face of the monumental north wall, turning and entering the actual building only to turn again and participate visually in the long exhibit space for the ship. On the south the building breaks down to a more human scale and relates to the Atlantic, the joint between Europe and America. This act of joining, the sailing of the Gokstad from Norway to Chicago is expressed by placing the museum at the extreme eastern edge of the site, addressing again the idea of arrival and departure.

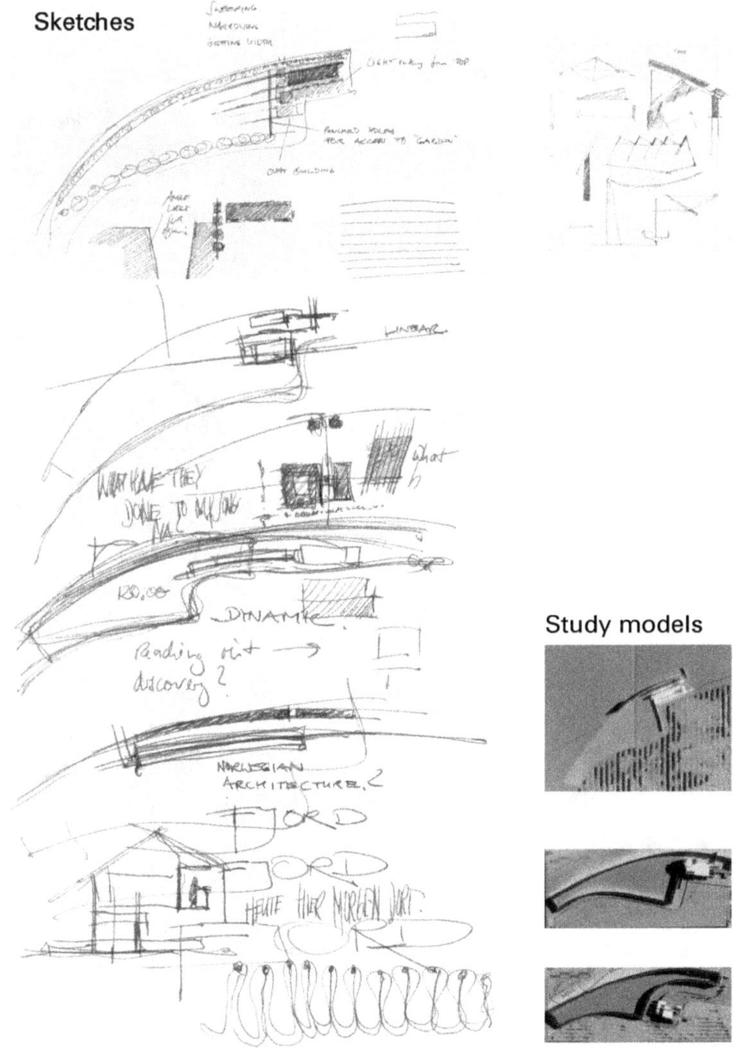

Sketches

Study models

Interior layout sketches

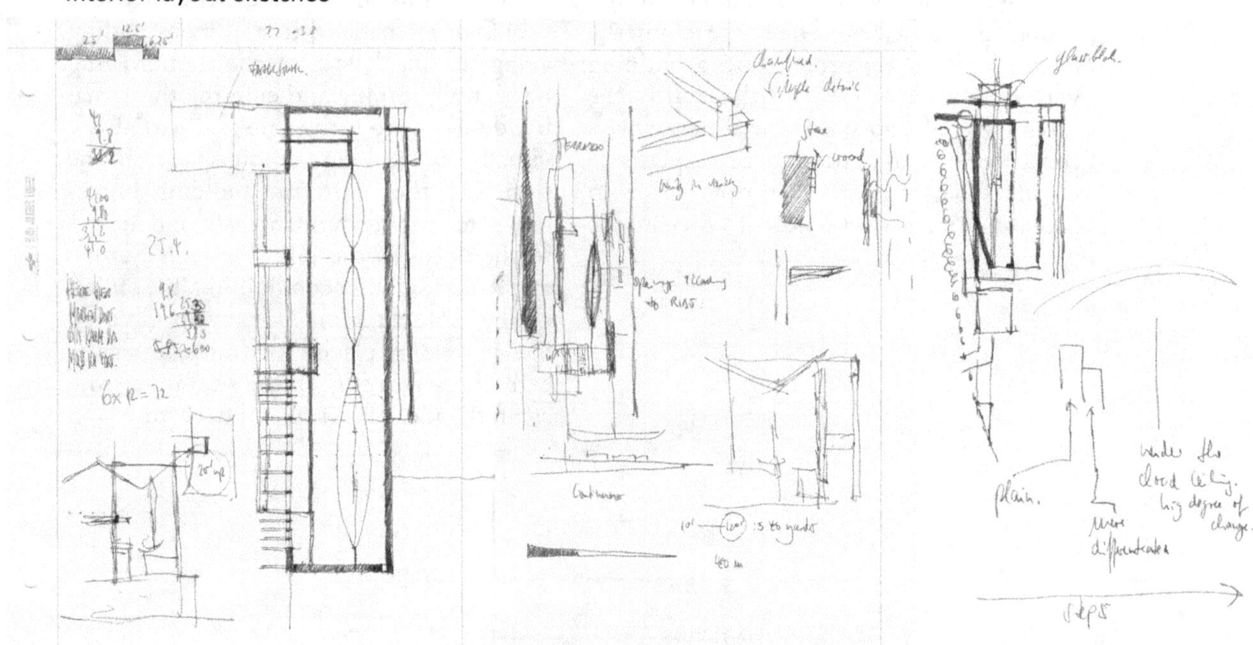

Model and site collage

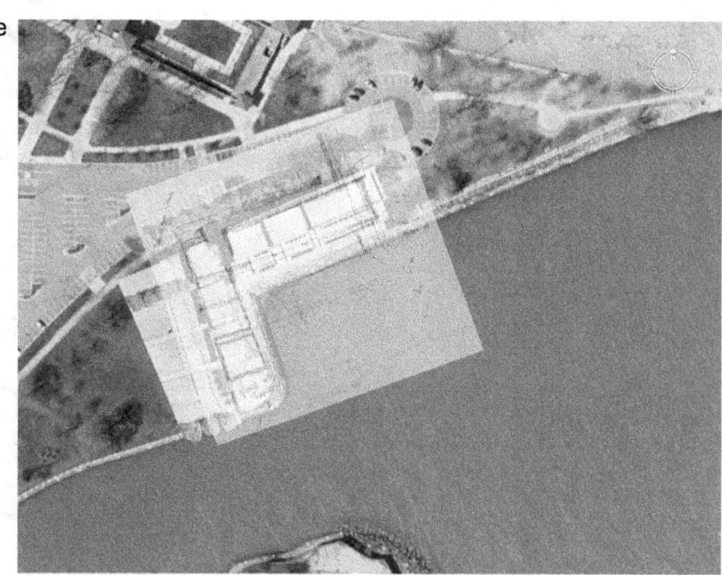

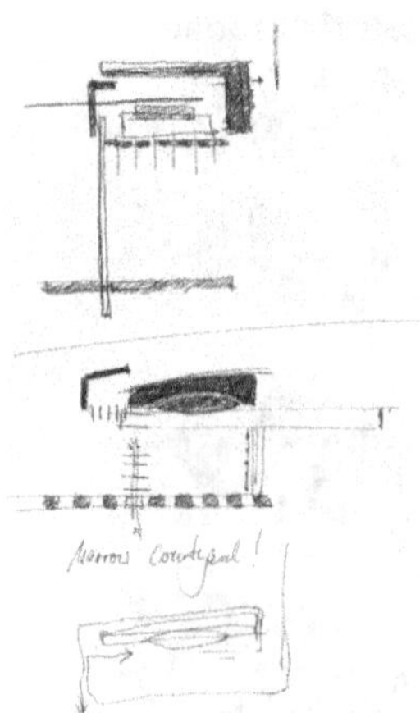

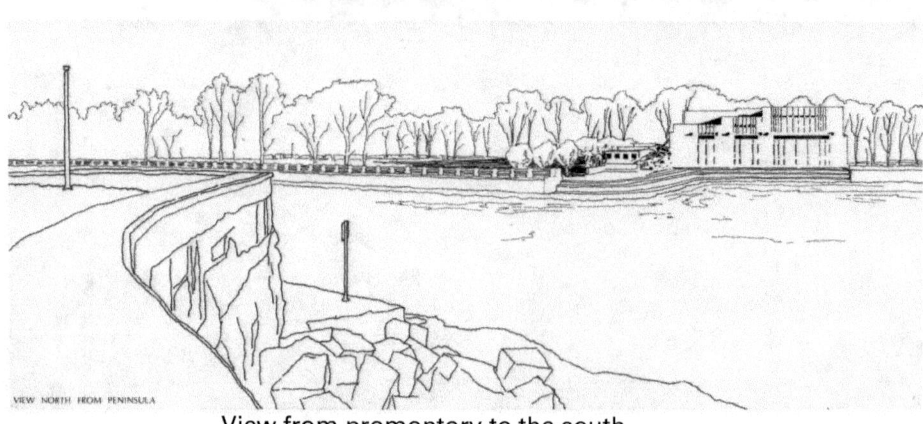

View from promontory to the south

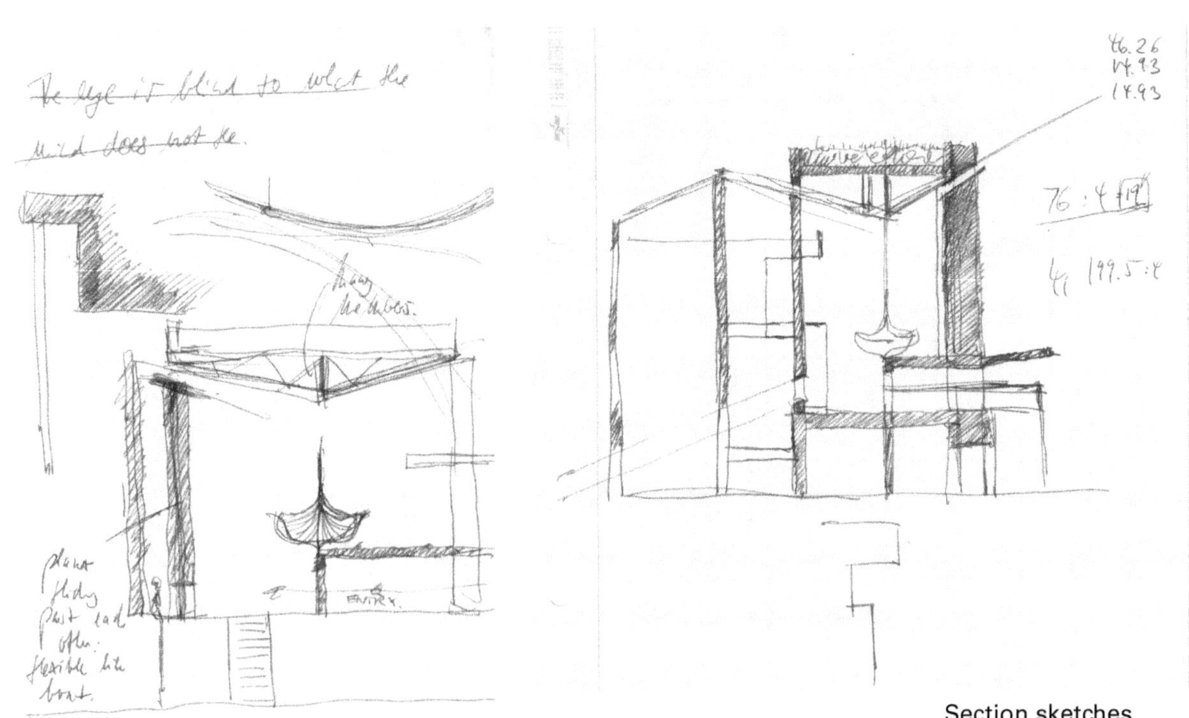

Section sketches

Design section

C–C

0 12 feet

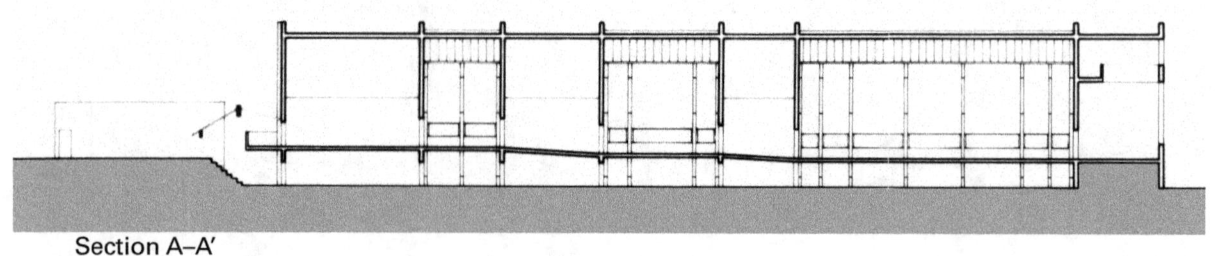

Section A–A′

Section perspective (ink on mylar)

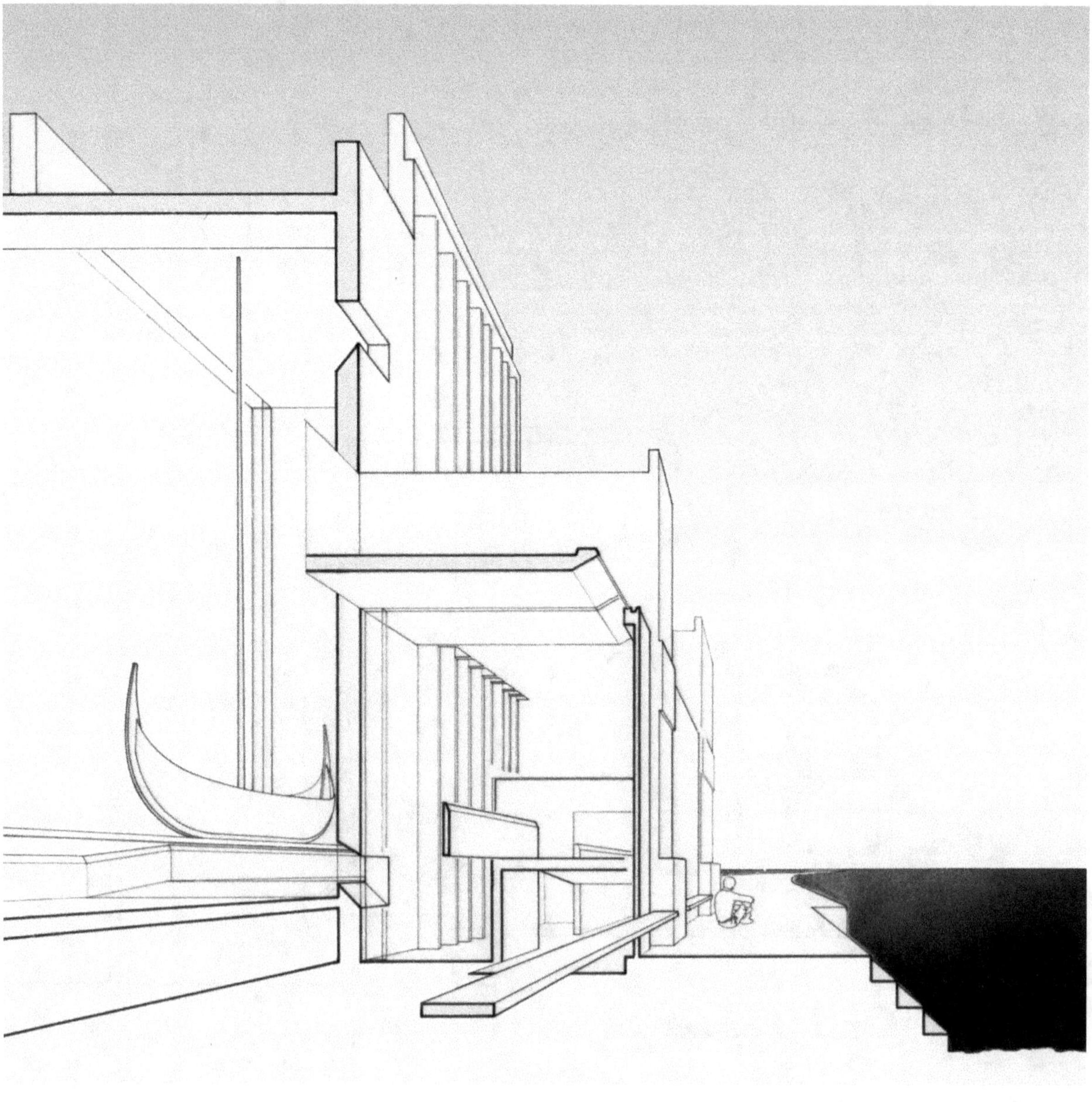

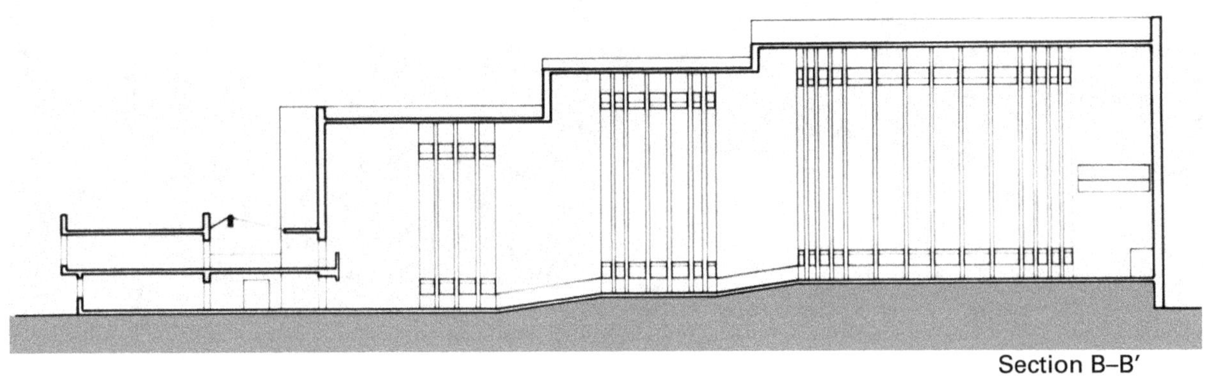

Section B–B′

Plan (ink on mylar)

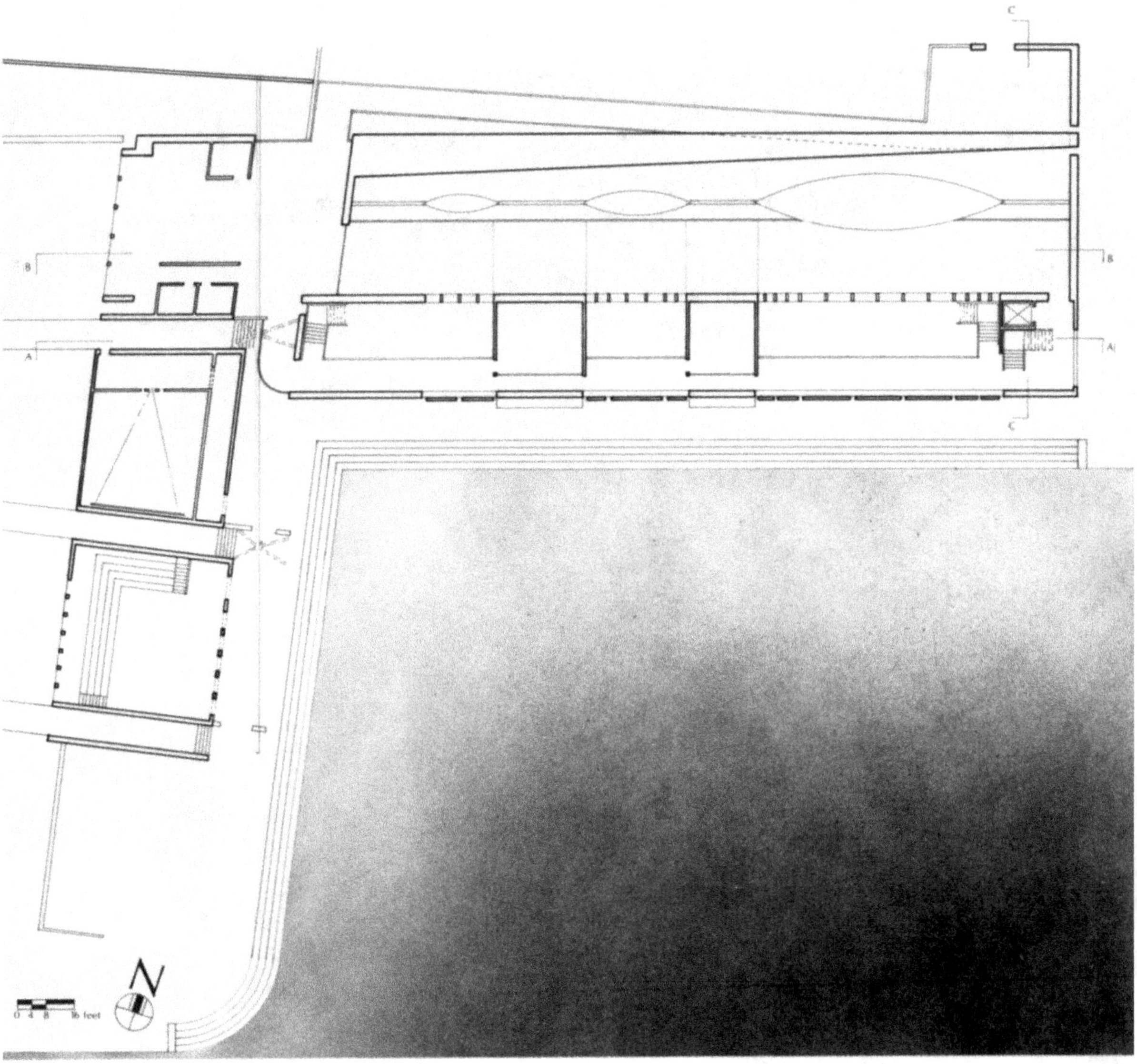

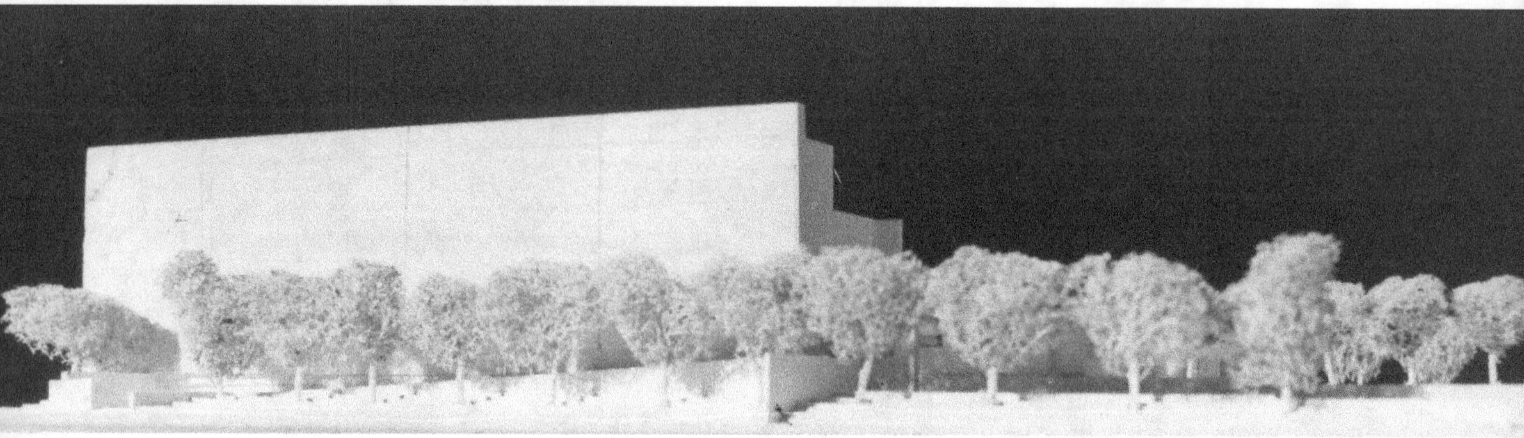

View from the north

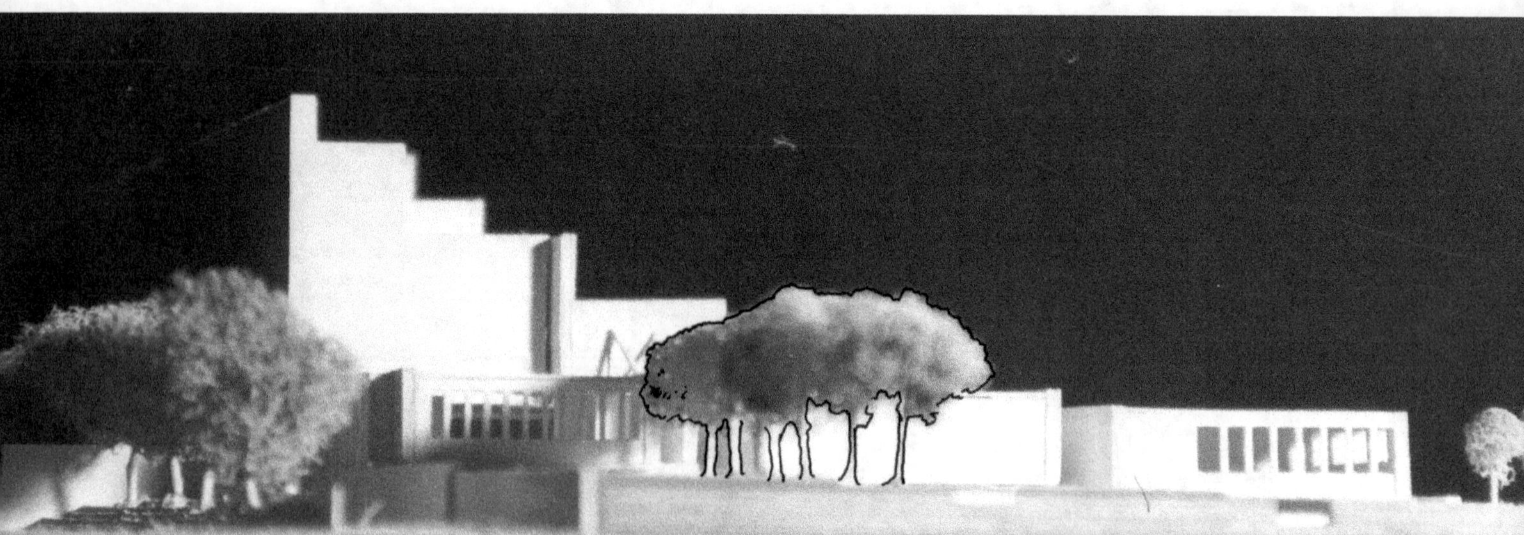

View from the west

View of the workshops toward the north

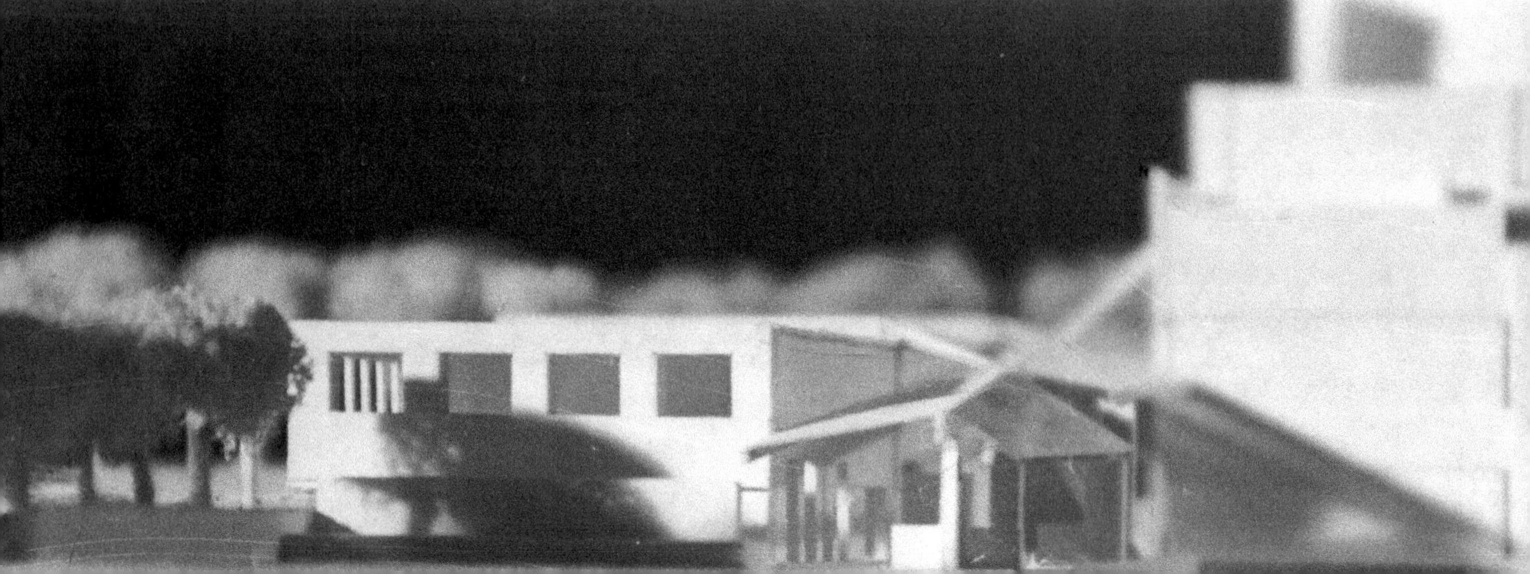

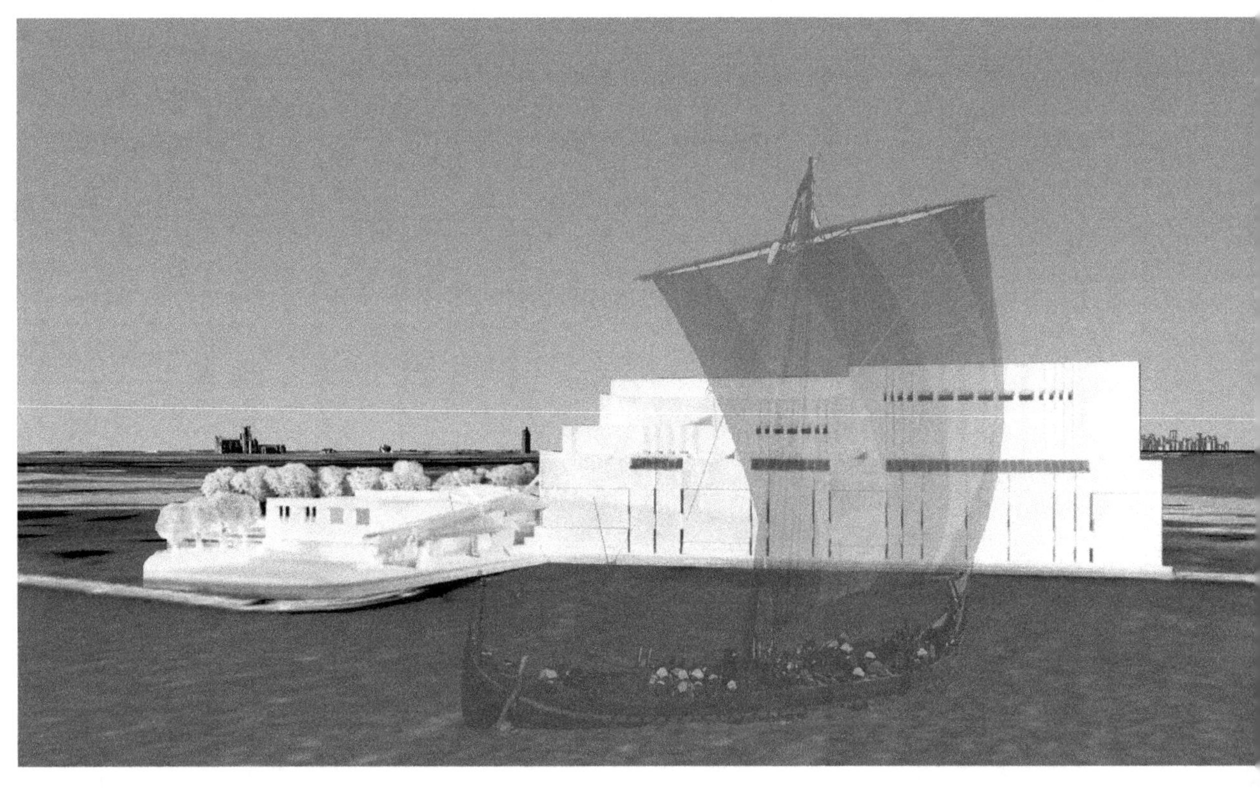

Views from the south

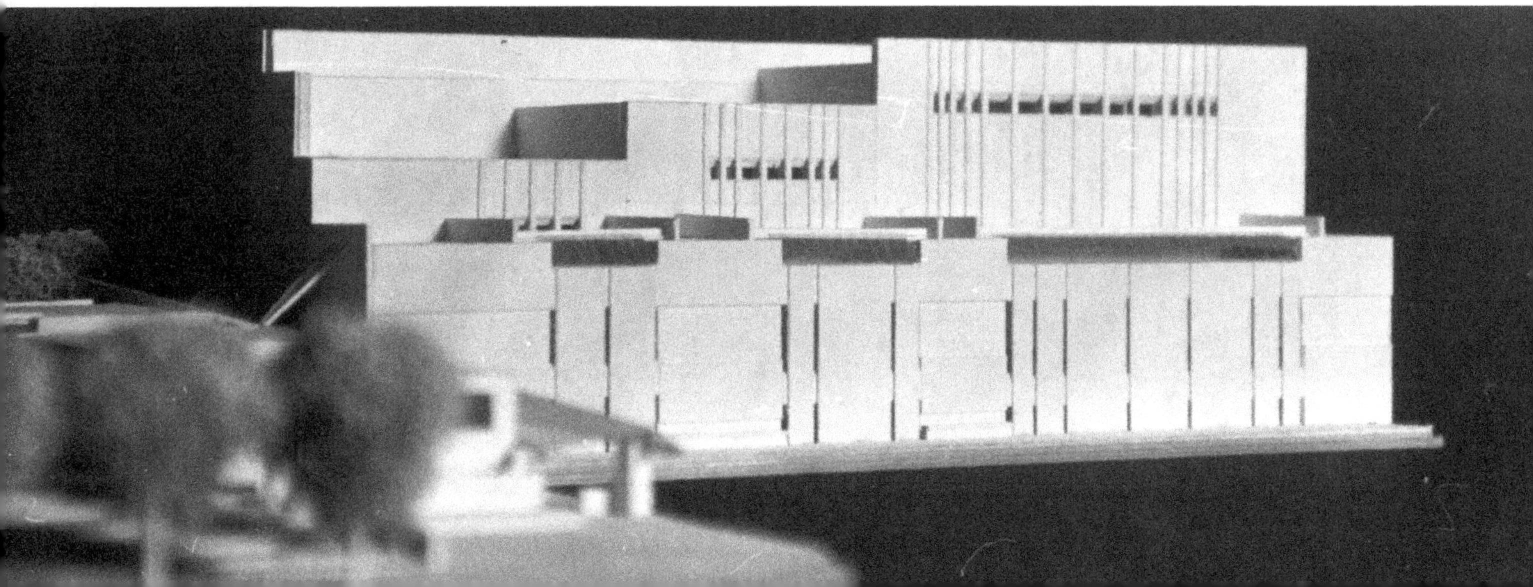

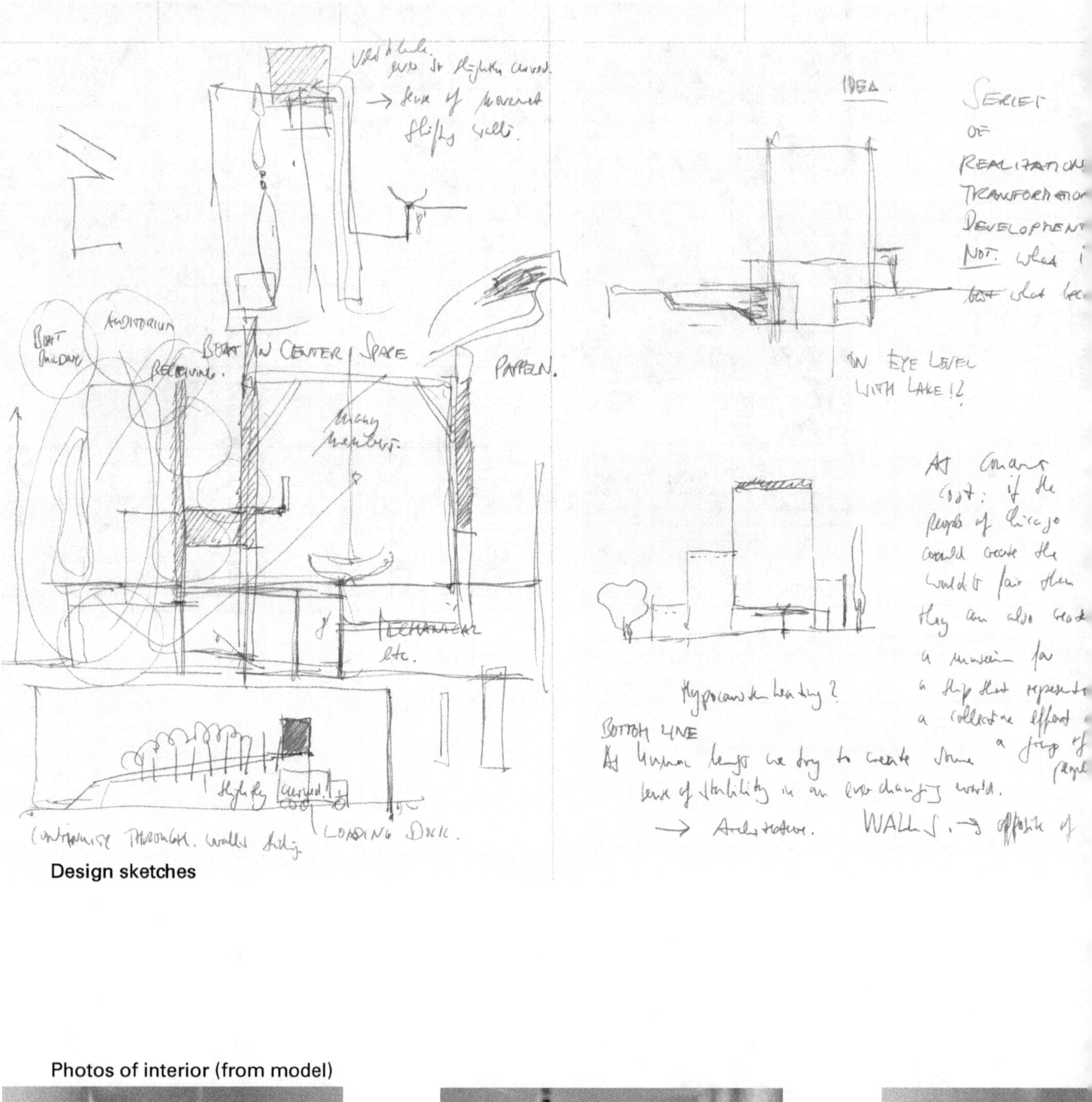

Design sketches

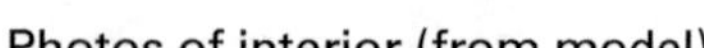

Photos of interior (from model)

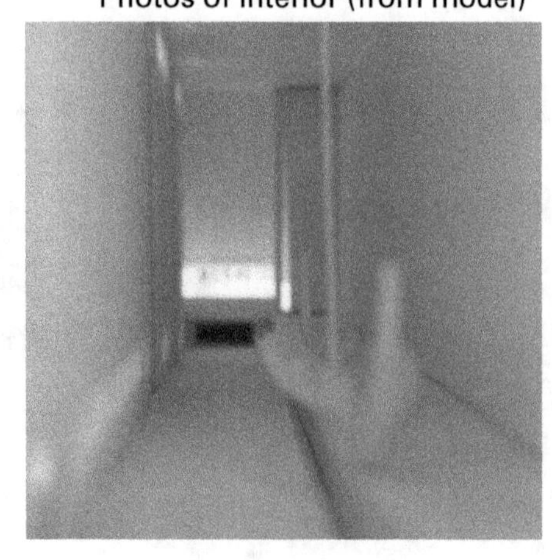

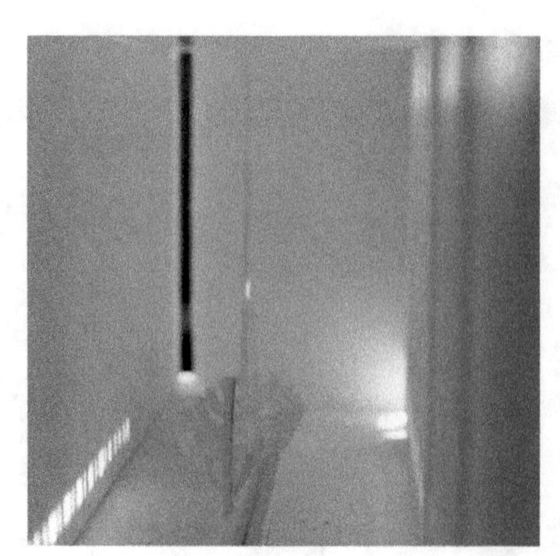

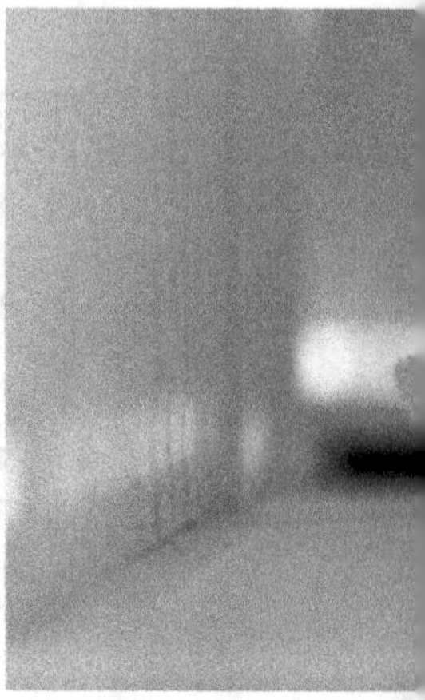

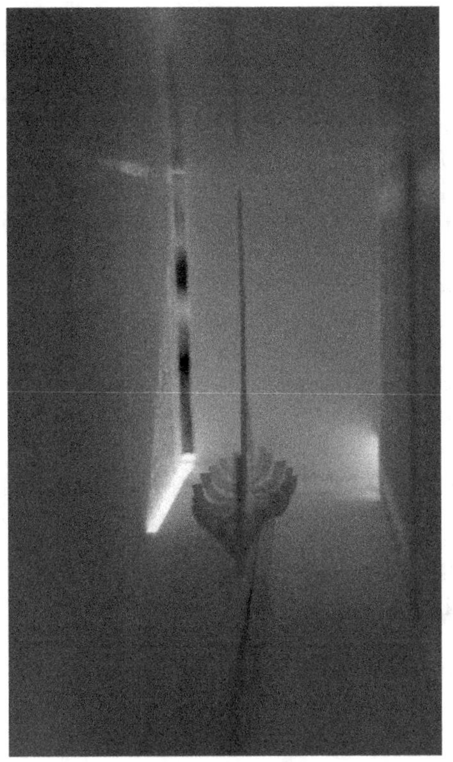

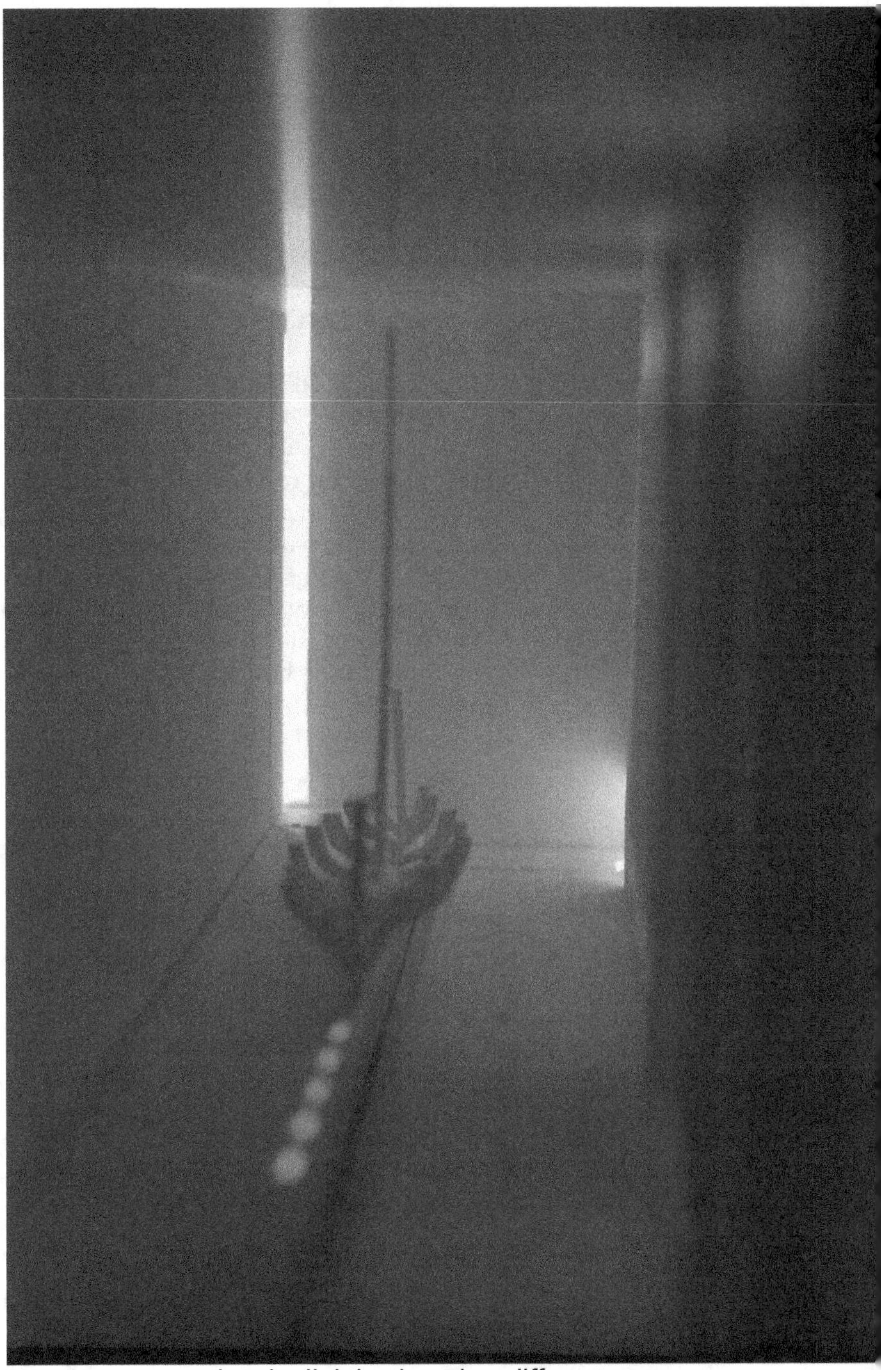

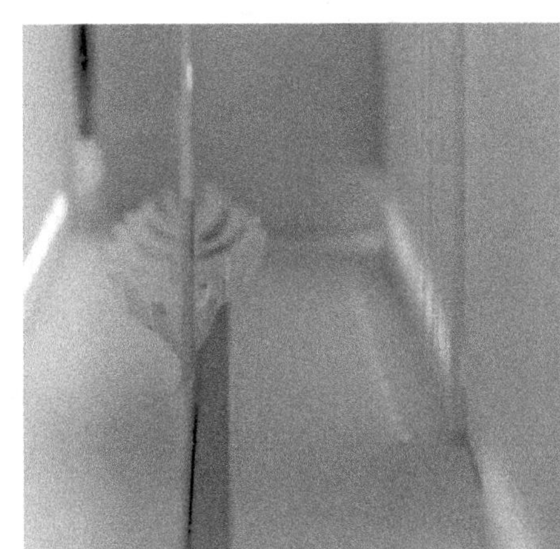

Interior lighting based on different sun positions (from model)

Boston Urban Design and Mayor-James-Curley Library

Boston, MA

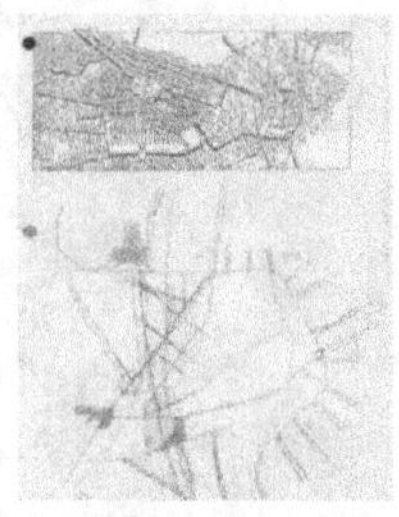

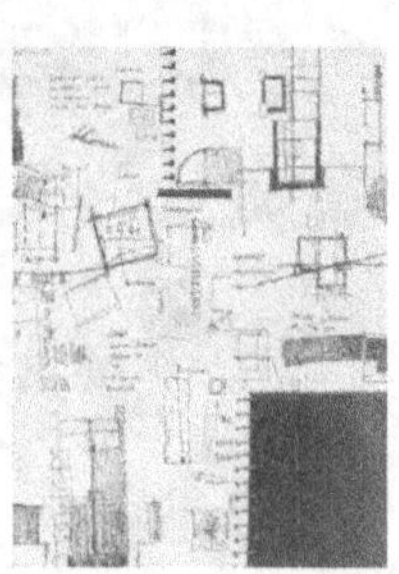

Boston is about the absence of history. History in the sense of cocealed layers (the German word for history is *Geschichte* = literally 'layering'). My design then is about an archaeology of Boston where its citizens can reëstablish their contact with an-other part of the city.

I started by overlaying the existing city with a map from 1794. Realizing the amount of artificial growth the city went through over time, I decided to reverse the development of the land encroaching upon water by cutting canals—that terminate at the historic coast line—into the existing fabric. Now the history of the city is more than the two-dimensional red line painted on the sidewalk; it becomes spatial, and thus architectural.

In some parts the old coastline turns into buildings that are here not further defined. Another task in the urban design part of this project was to deal with the depression of the interstate artery that cuts the head of Boston in half. My strategy was to link the North End with the Government District, yet let both of them keep their own identity through the insertion of the new Haymarket Square as a buffer in between. This square became also the site for the Curley Research Library.

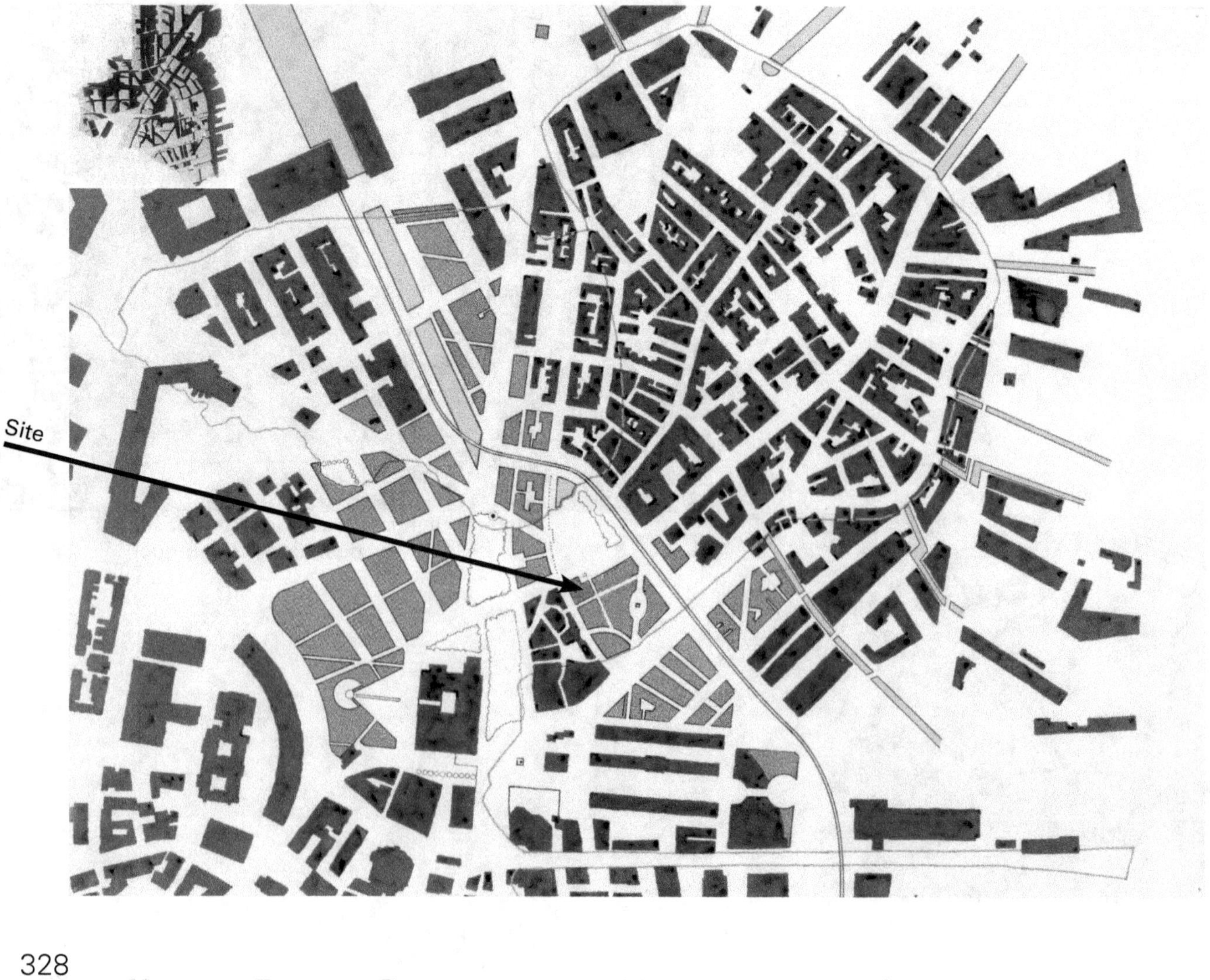

In the library I am investigating the idea and implications of time and ambiguity. This library is a body of knowledge for researchers. Knowledge is acquired over time and is as such always incomplete, i.e. in a state of becoming. This ambiguity between becoming and being is expressed in the siting of the building. There is a dry moat surrounding the libary at the base, surrounding the ancient layers in the ground, making entry possible only via a bridge that, when the library is closed, folds back and becomes part of the wall.

The program for the library also suggests a schism in that the largest part of the building is not accessible to the general public but only to researchers. Only the auditorium/ gallery and the Curley Memorial Room can be entered by the general public.

The two basement levels appropriately hosue the reserved stacks, the forbidden library, the underground past, simultaneously exposed and hidden, accessible only by special permission ("Do you have the password?" - "No." ['No' is the password]). The open stacks share the two floors above ground level with the Curley Memorial Room. The shifted cube above the open stacks is the reading room, one large volume whose edge is eaten away by the central vertical pendulum space that shows the reading room's dependency—or for that matter everything's dependency—on time. The tilted and shifted gallery/auditorium at the top of the library symbolizes the current state of confusion and instability in the body of knowledge.

The truss houses the elevator, a tentative link between below and above, past and future. Towering above everything else is the crane, a symbol of change in every city...

row of tall buildings
grey sky with thin trusses; cranes
that don't fly anymore

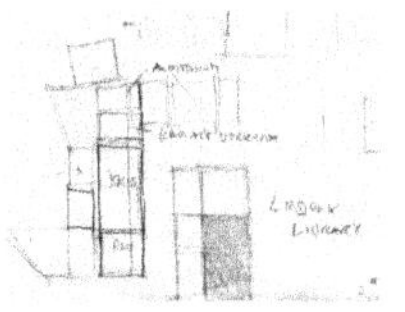

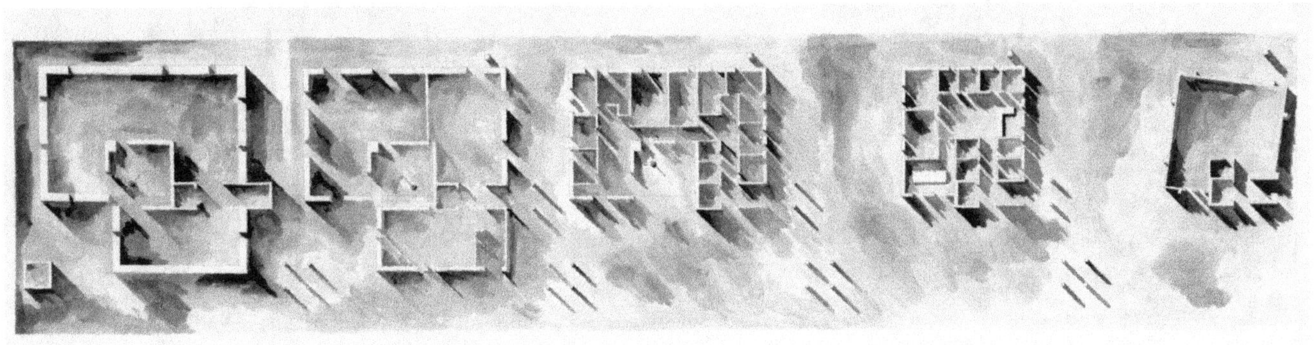

Plans (ink on water color paper)

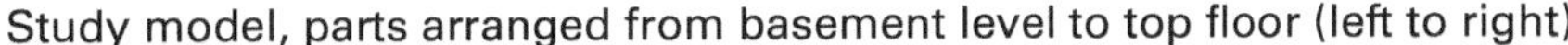

Study model, parts arranged from basement level to top floor (left to right)

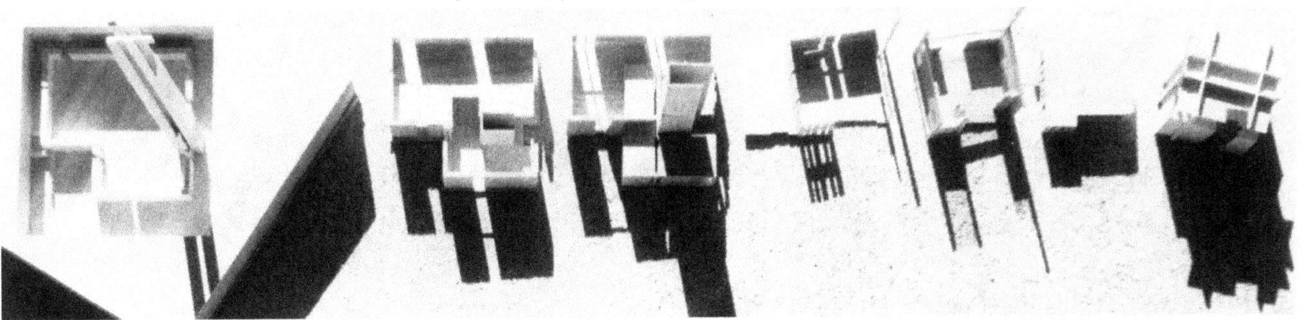

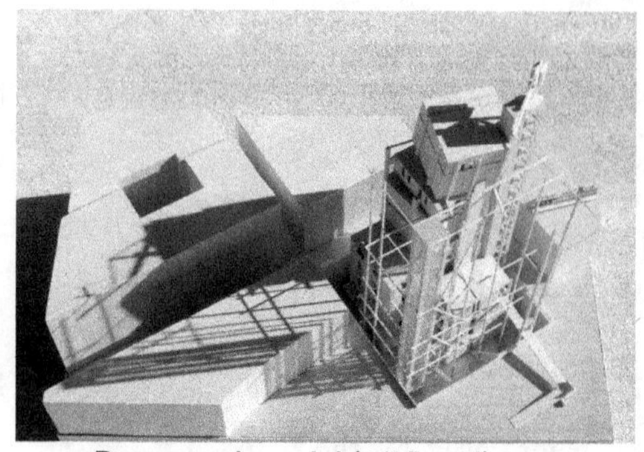

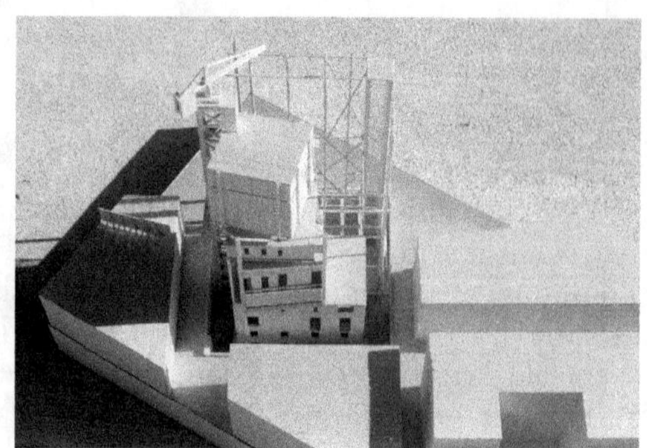

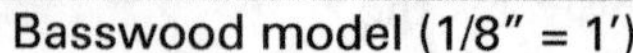
Basswood model (1/8″ = 1′)

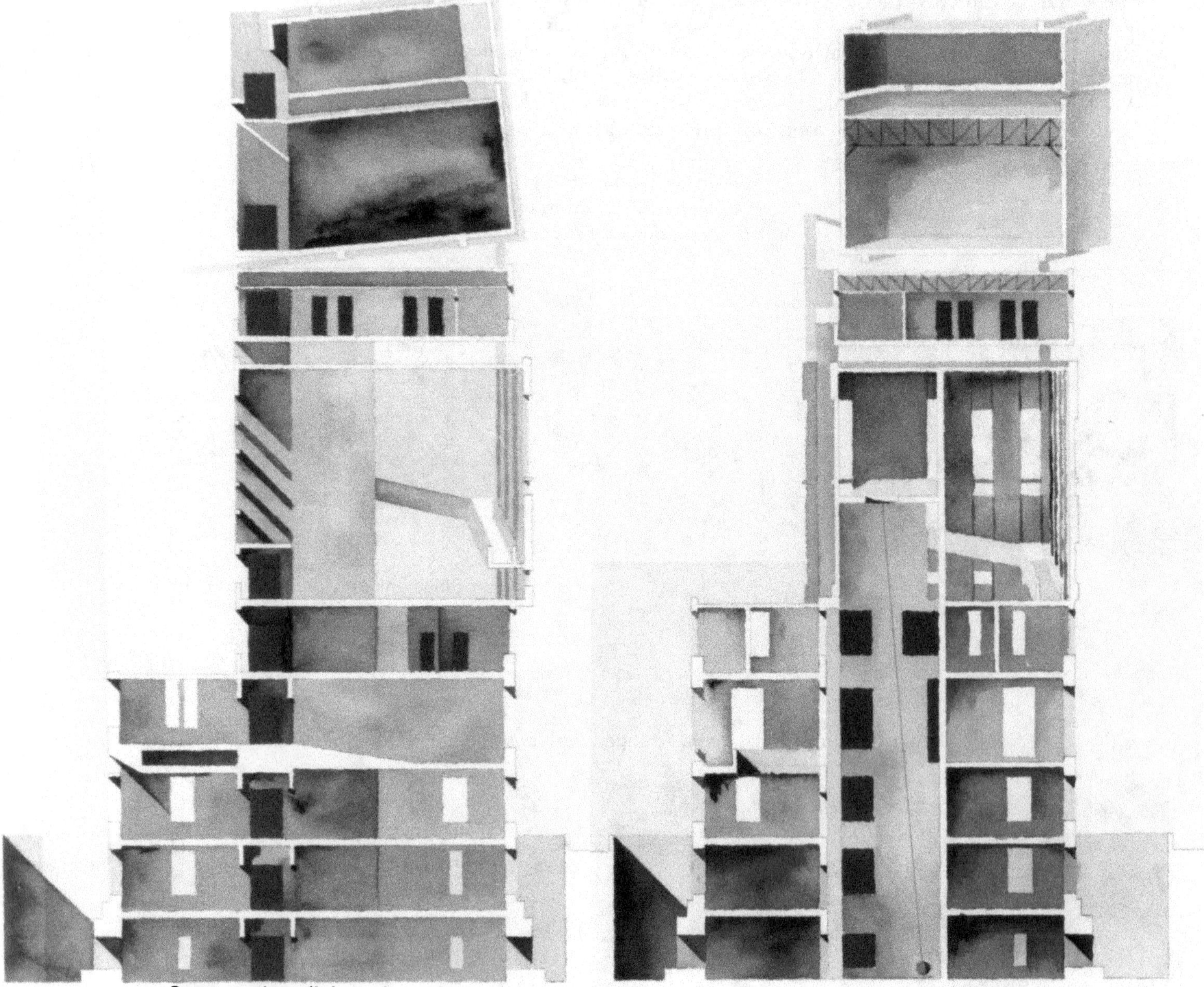

Cross sections (ink wash on water color paper)

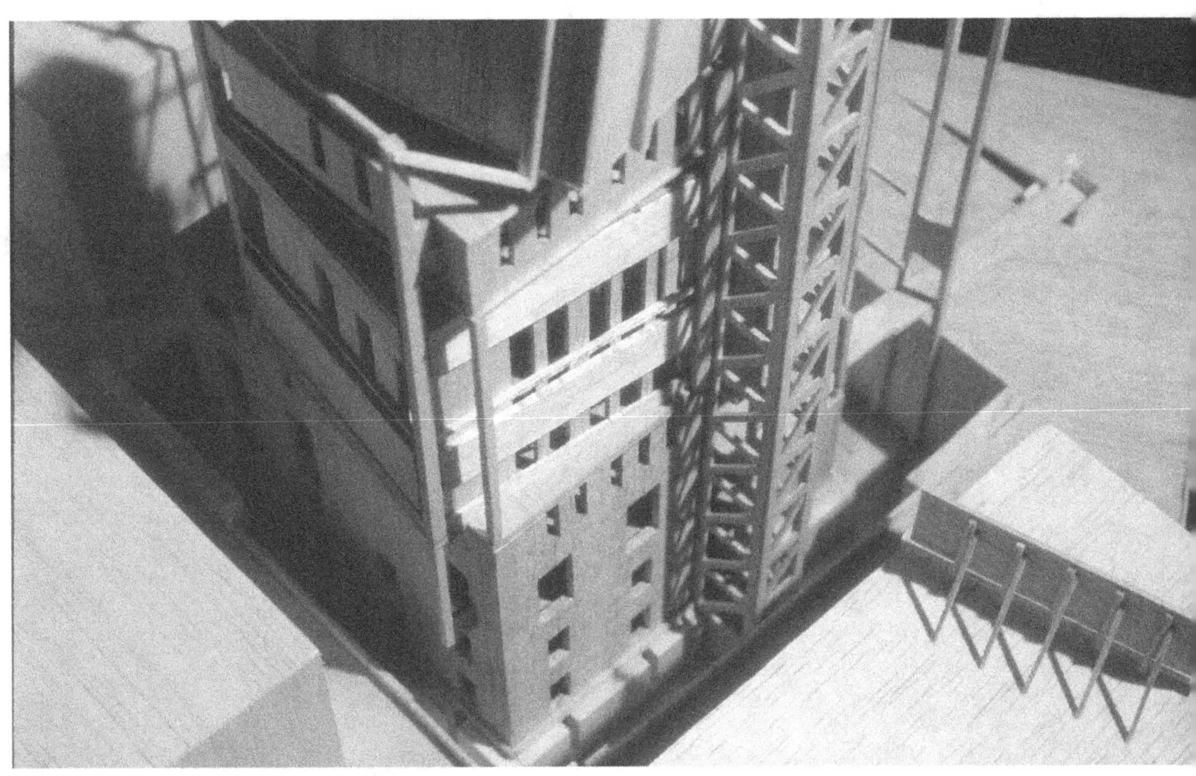

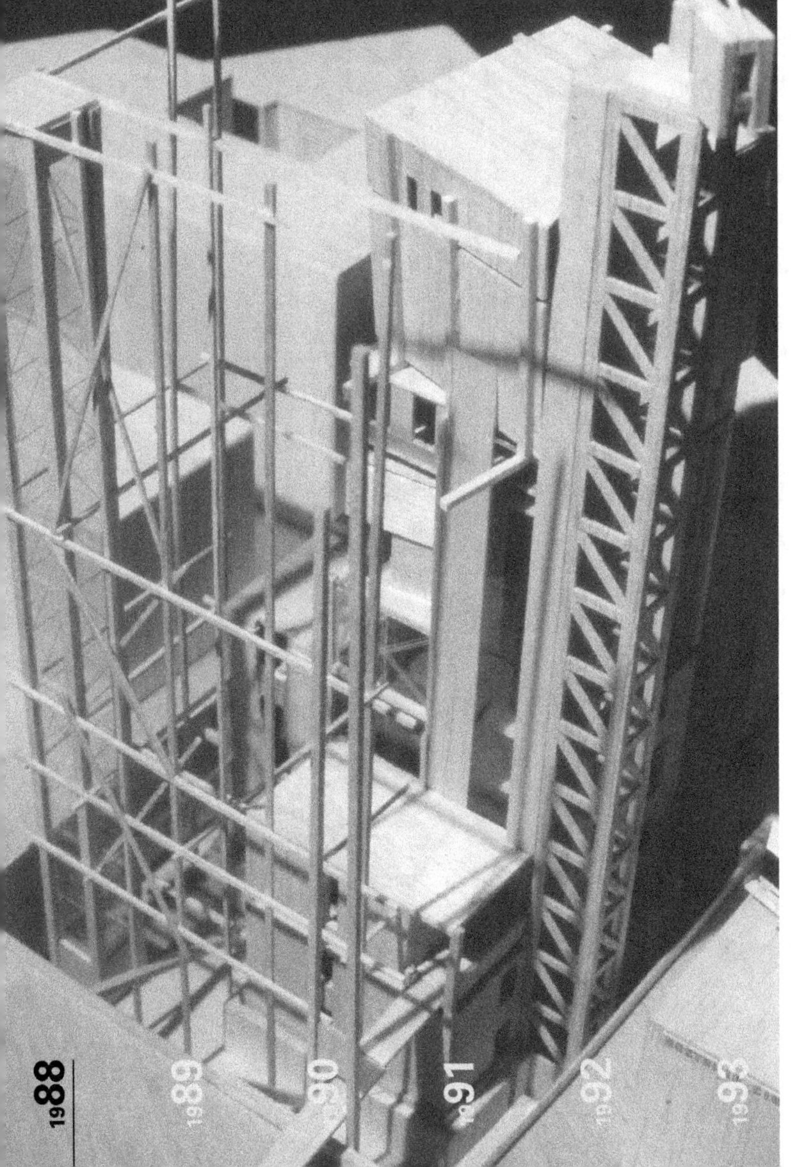

Basswood model (1/8″ = 1′)

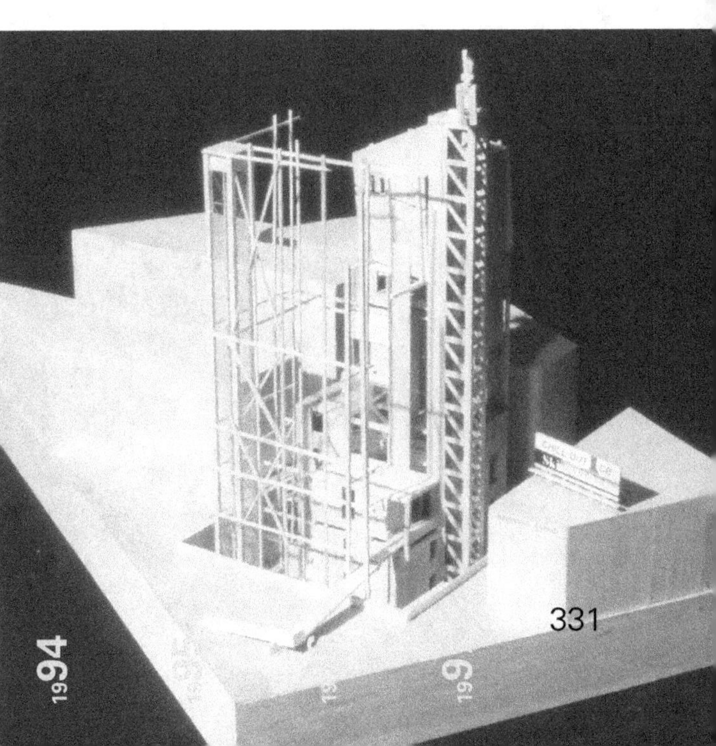

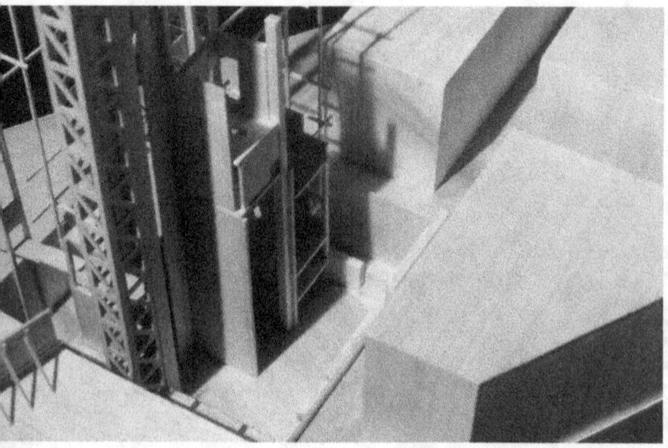

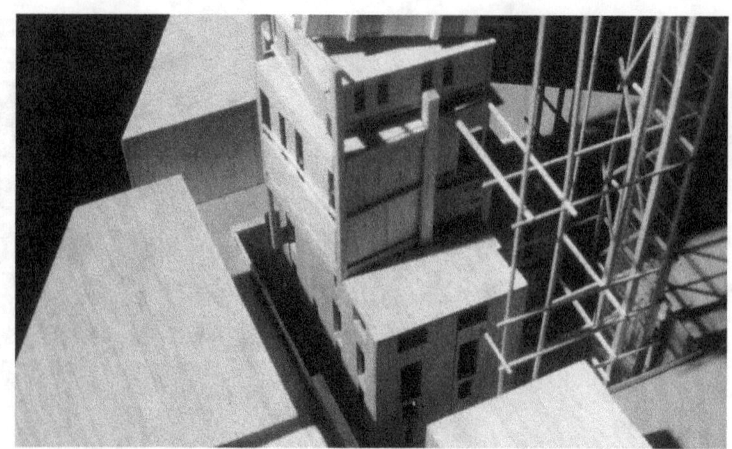

Basswood model (1/8″ = 1′)

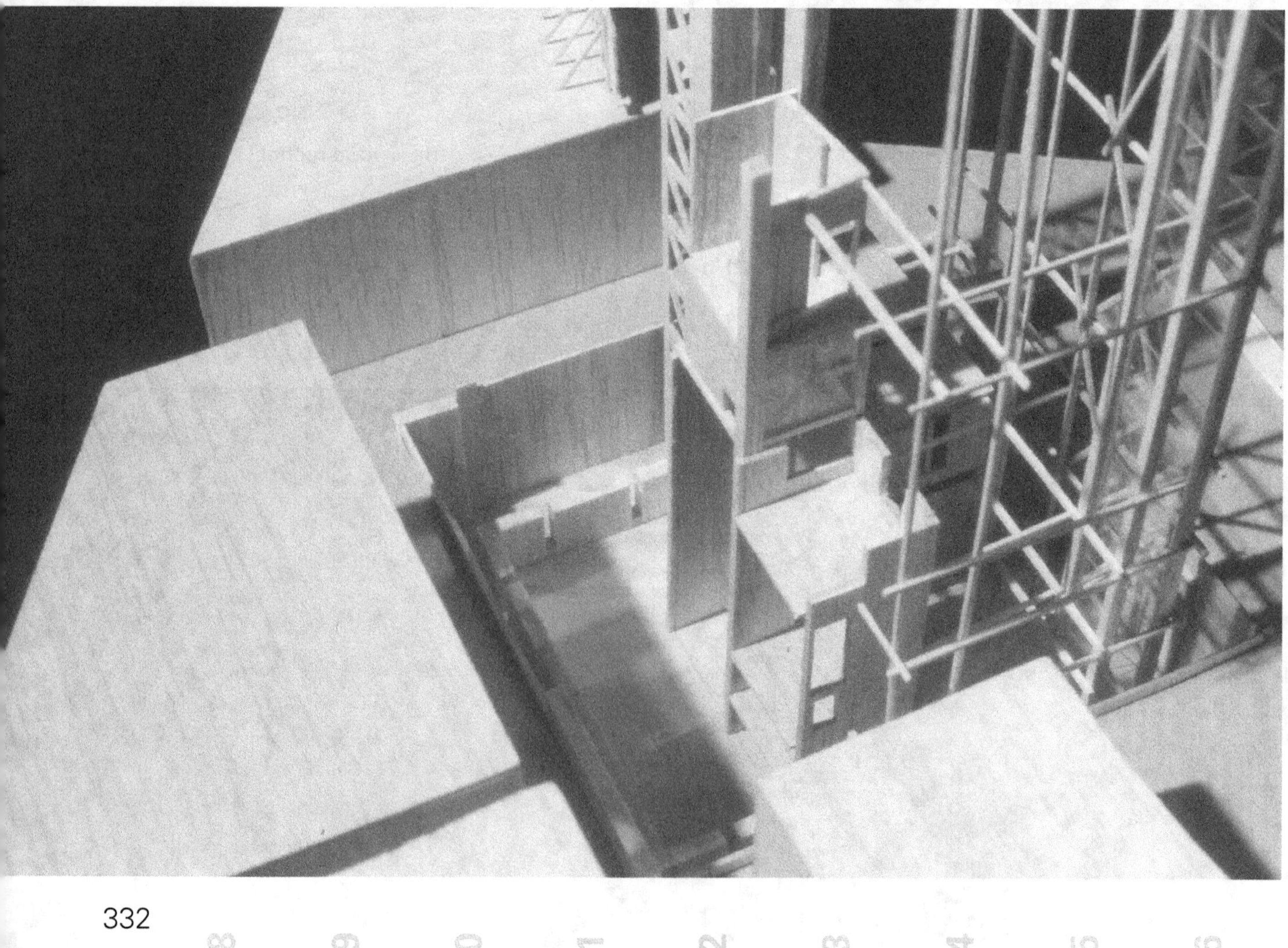

Shadow + Light study

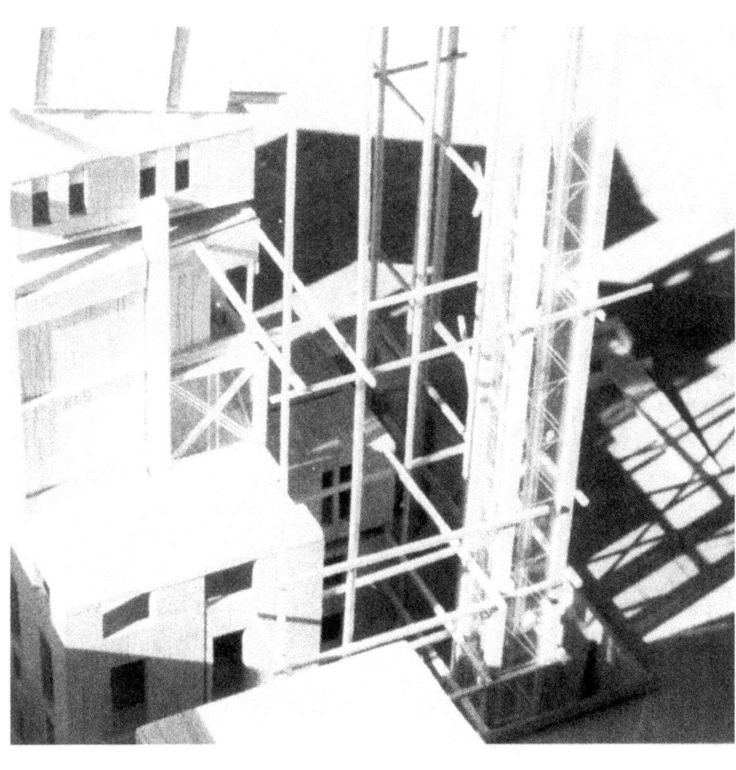

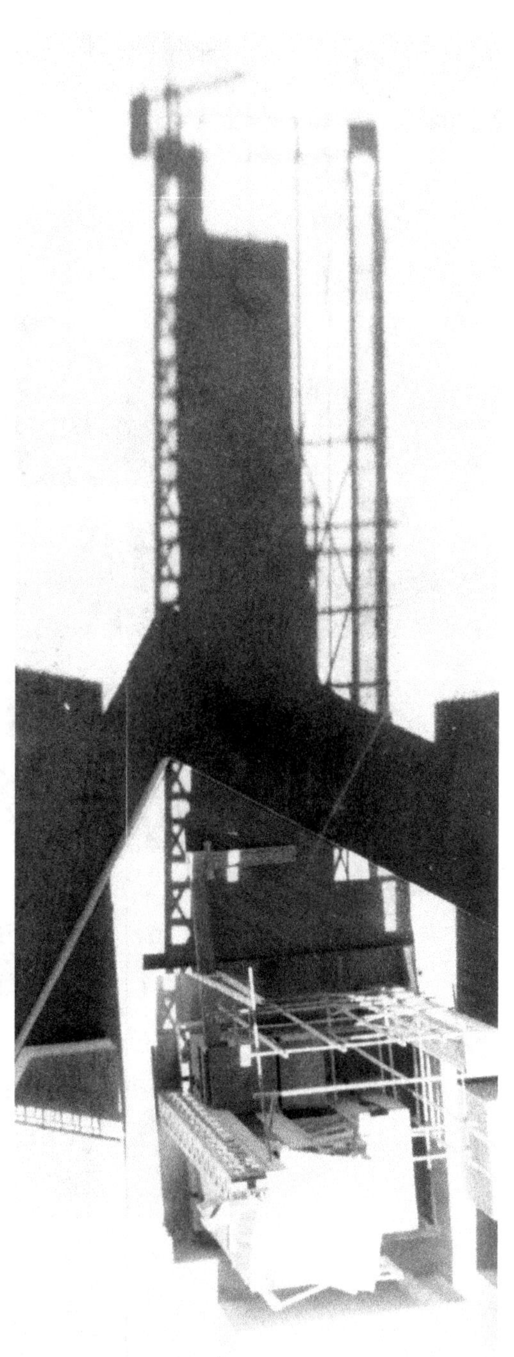

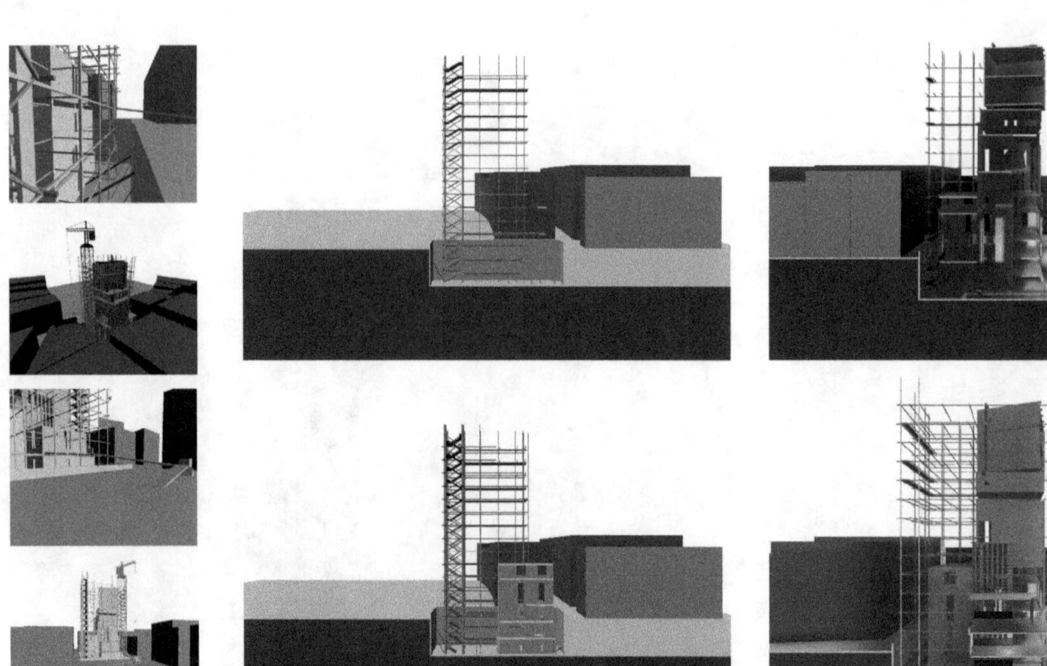

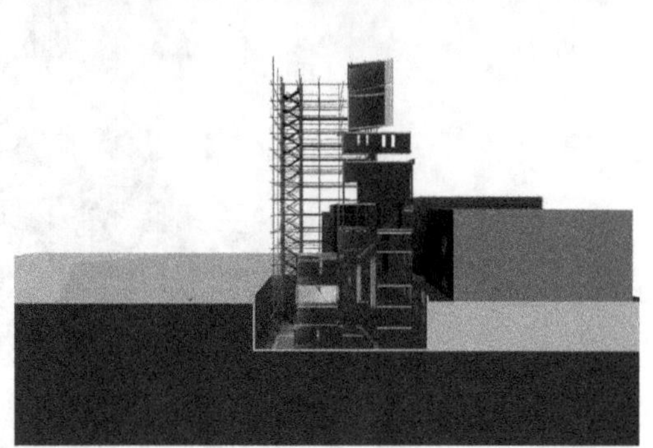

Digital section perspectives
(modeled in Architrion)

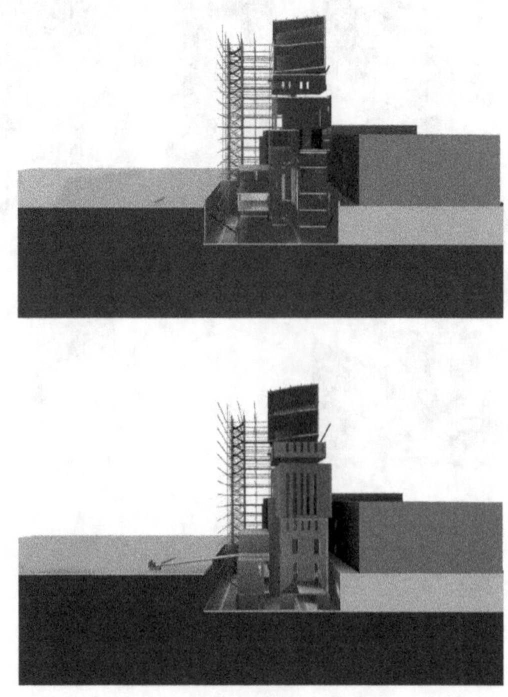

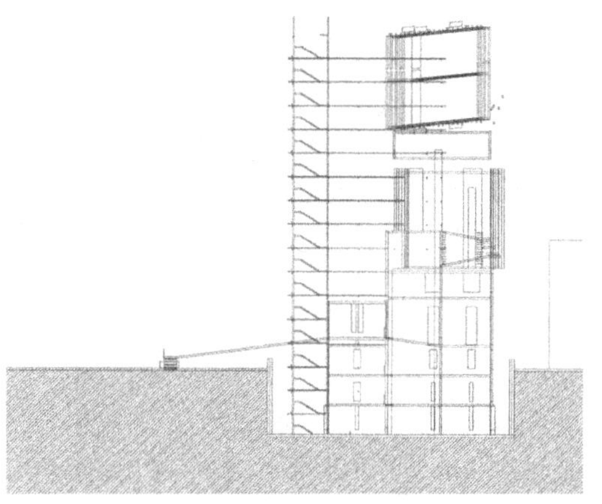

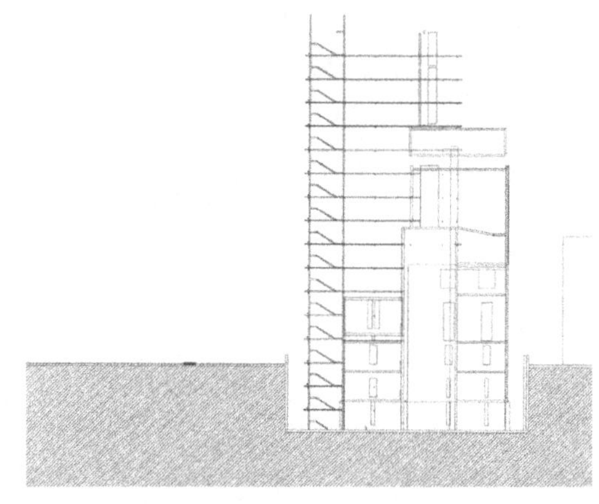

Digital sections
(modeled in Architrion)

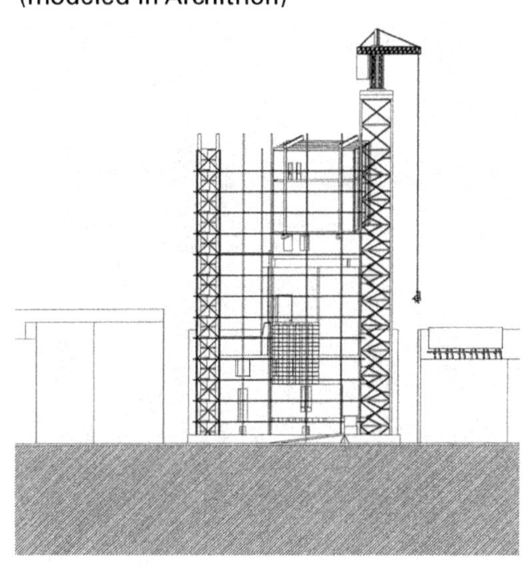

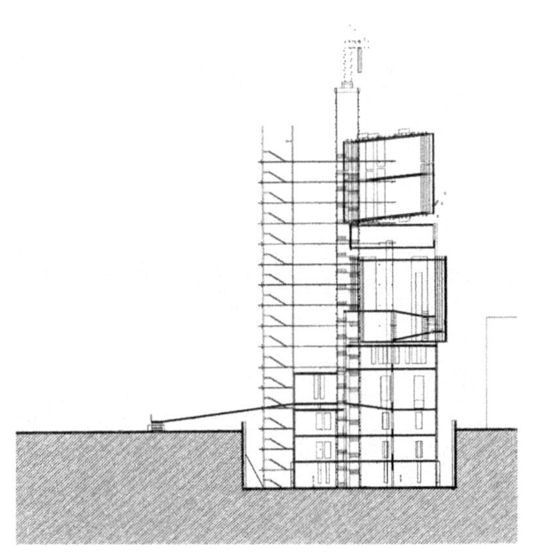

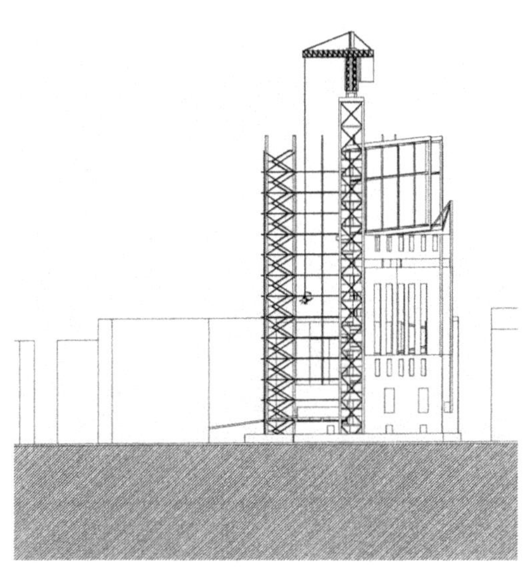

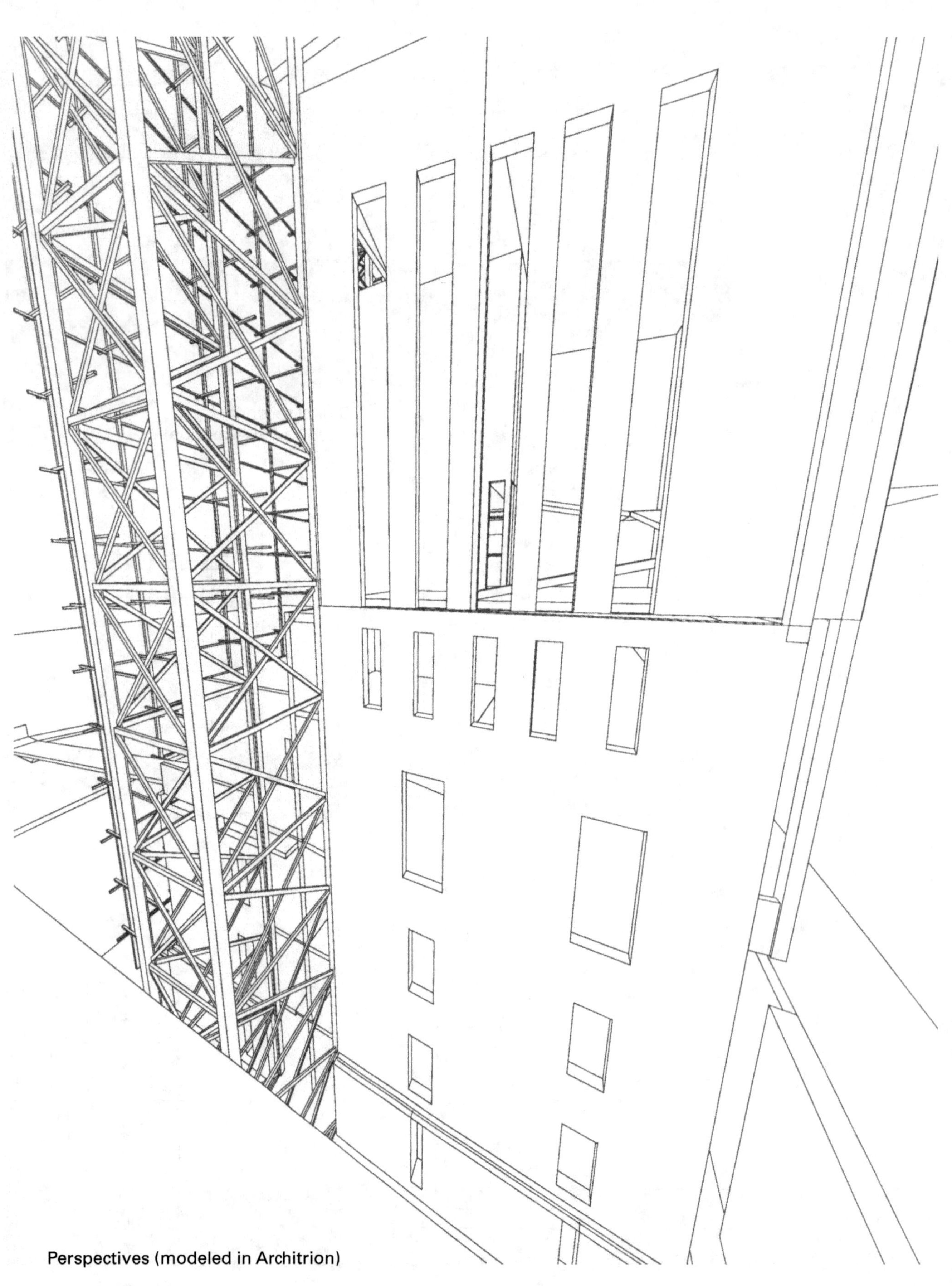

Perspectives (modeled in Architrion)

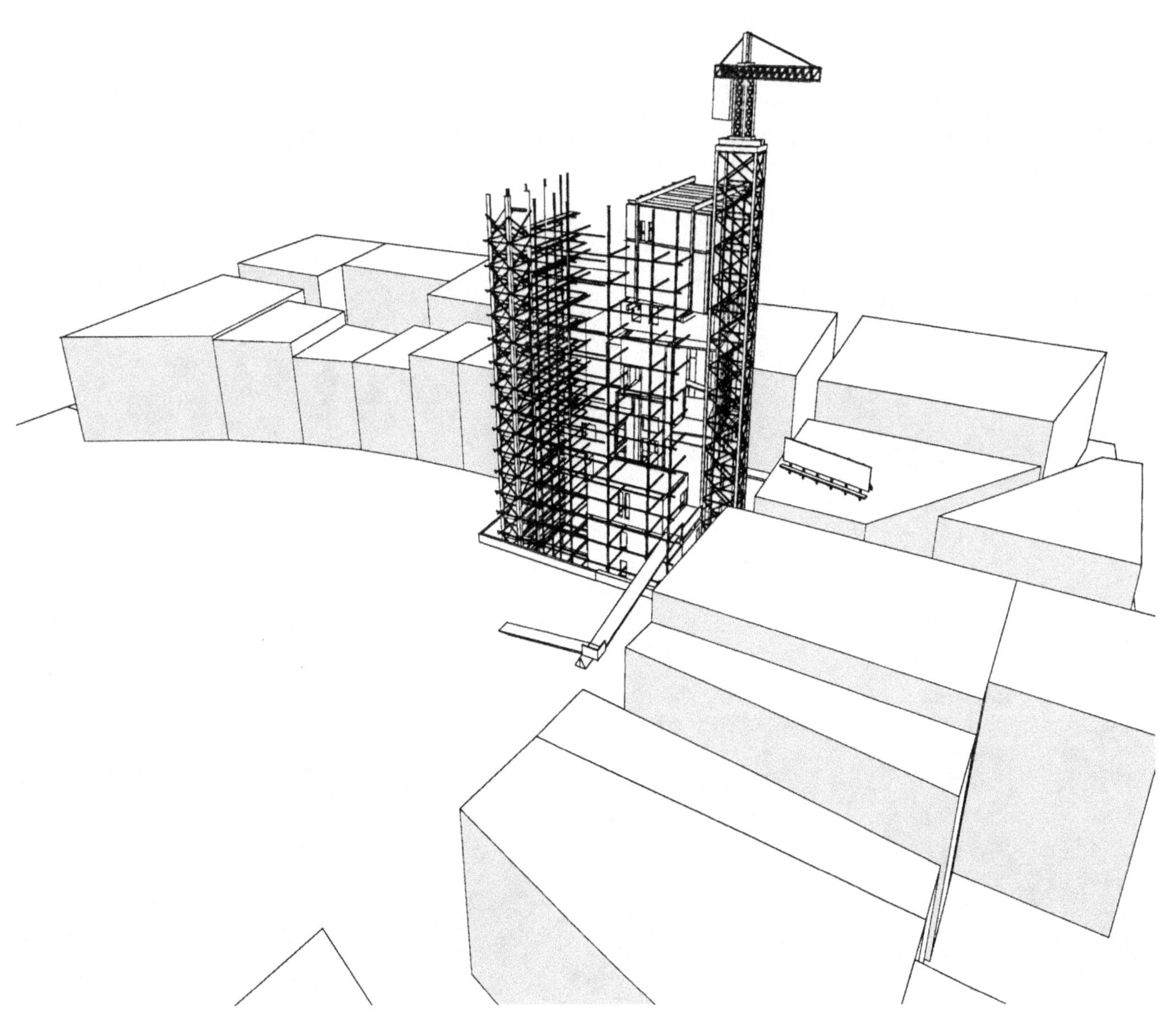

1989

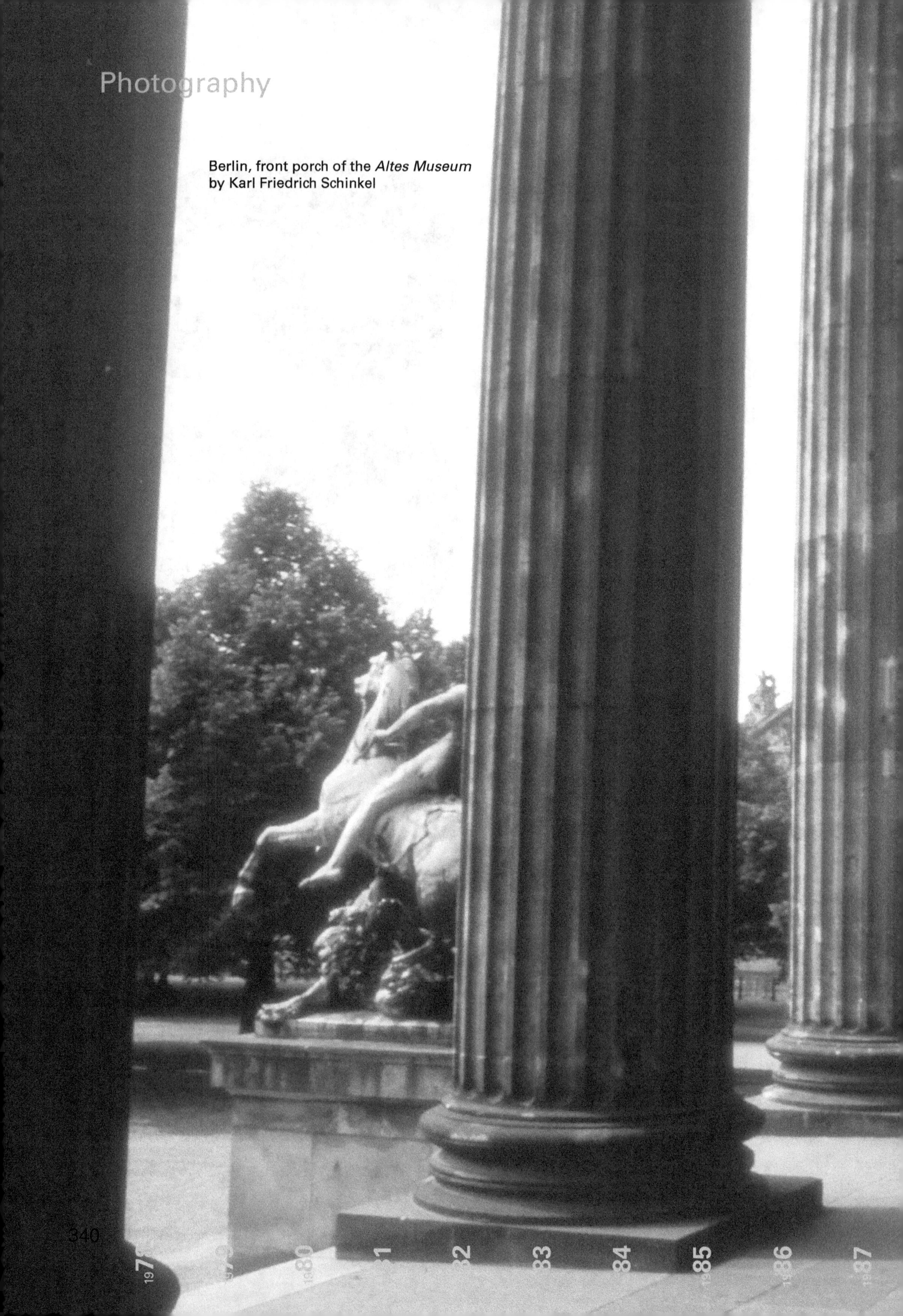

Berlin, front porch of the *Altes Museum*
by Karl Friedrich Schinkel

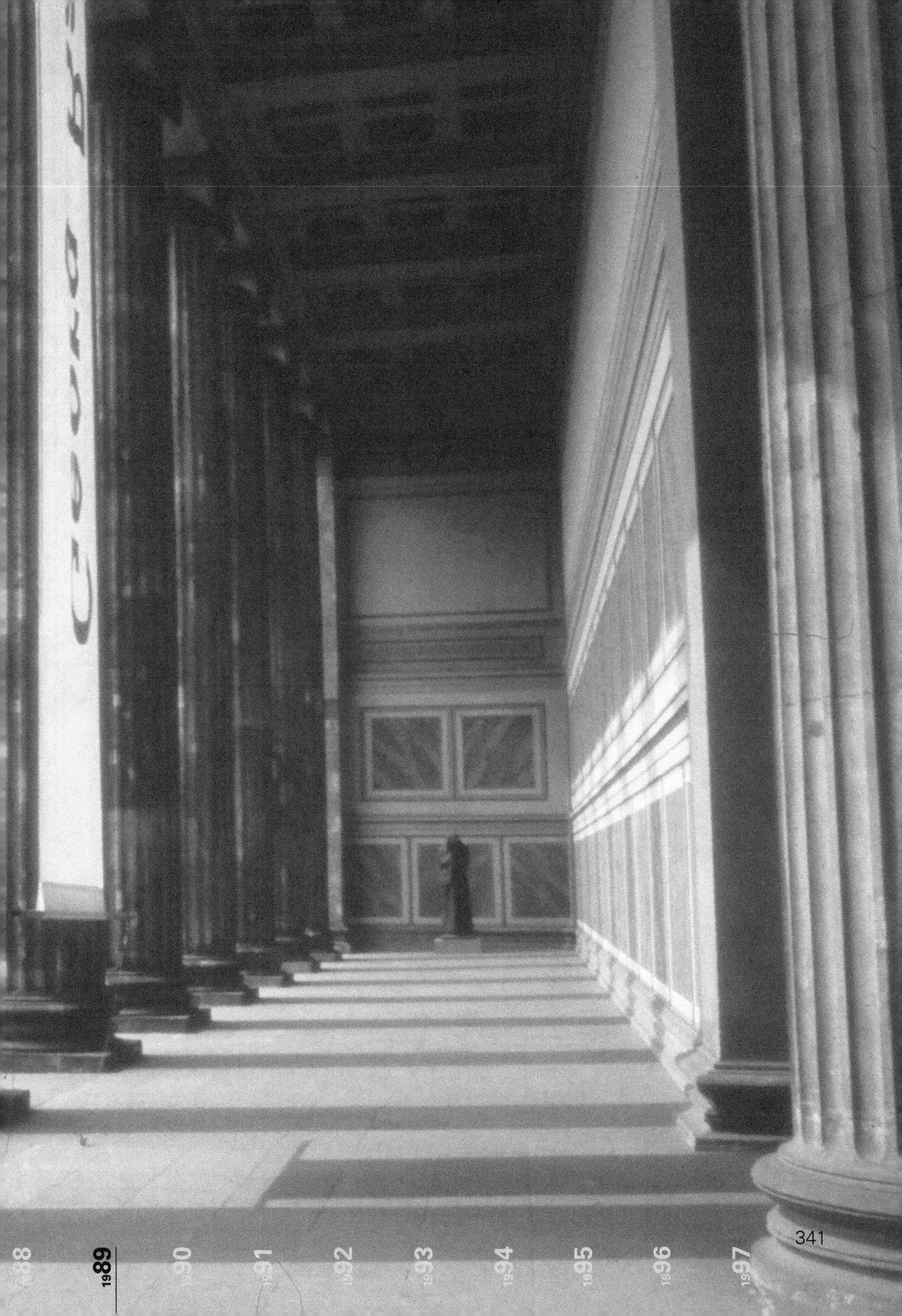

Berlin, *Brandenburger Tor*, all scaffolded up. Notice the restauration service (*Denkmalpflege*) from Berlin/DDR (German Democratic Republic). This was right after the border had been opened

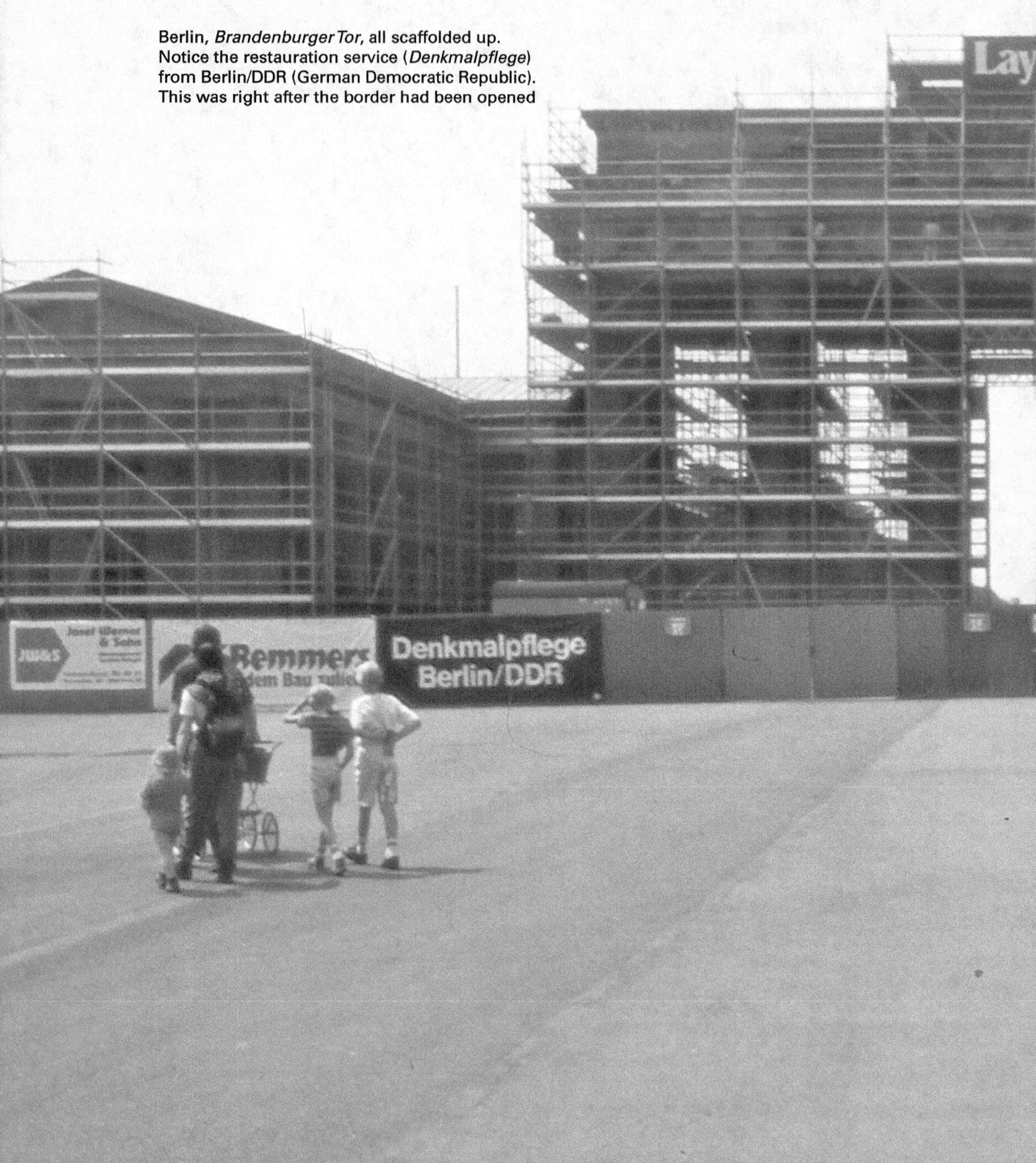

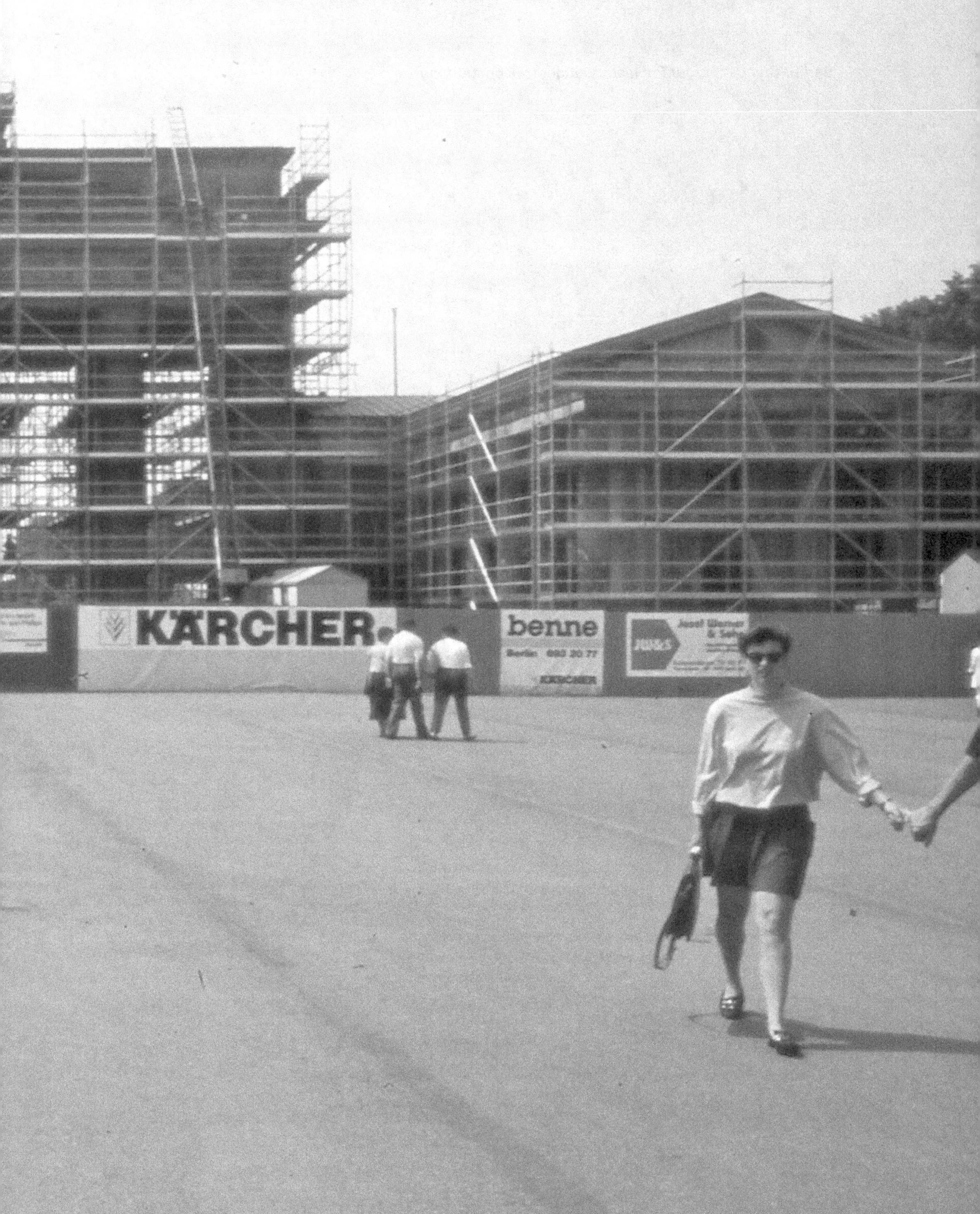
KÄRCHER
benne

Photography

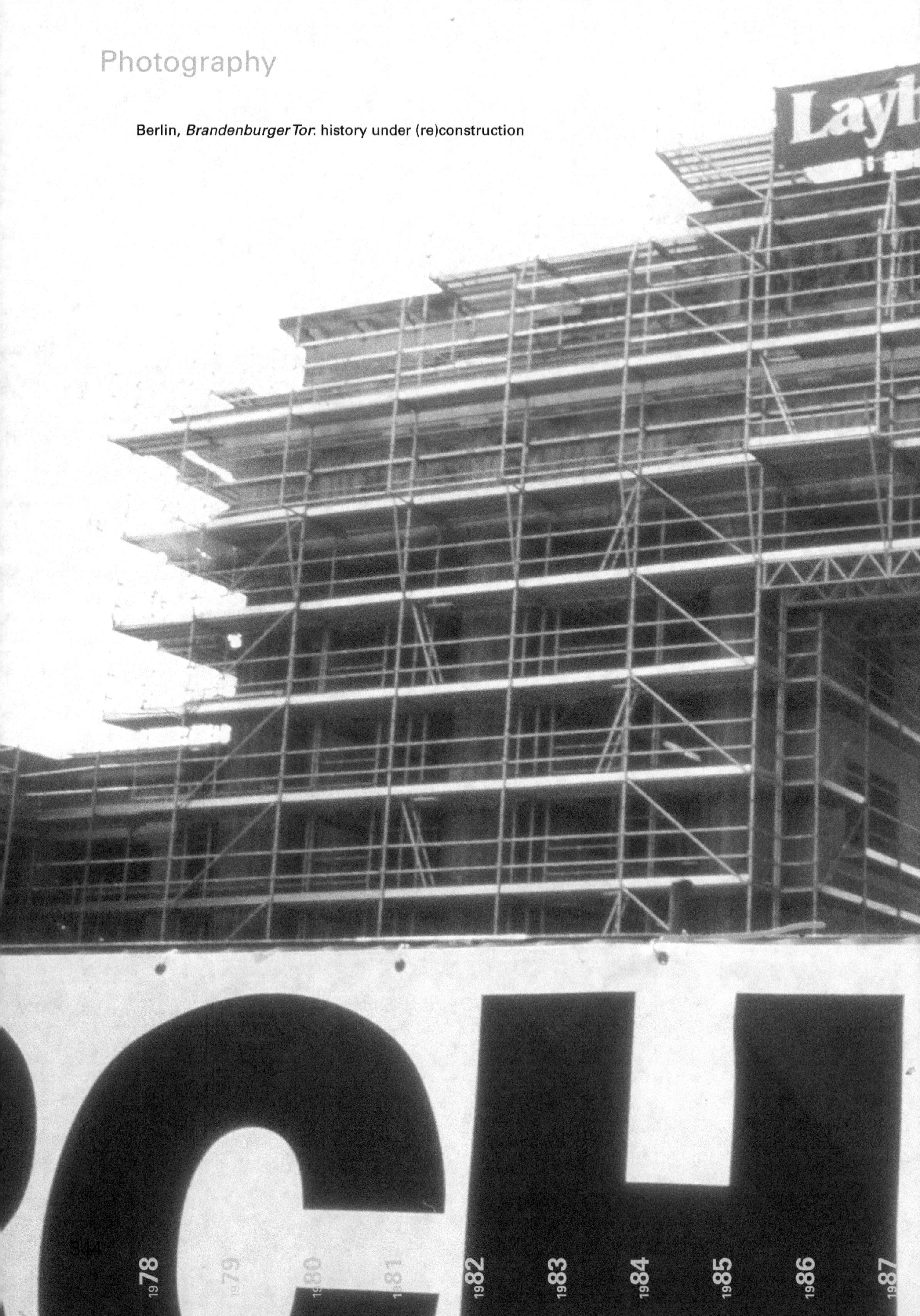

Berlin, *Brandenburger Tor*: history under (re)construction

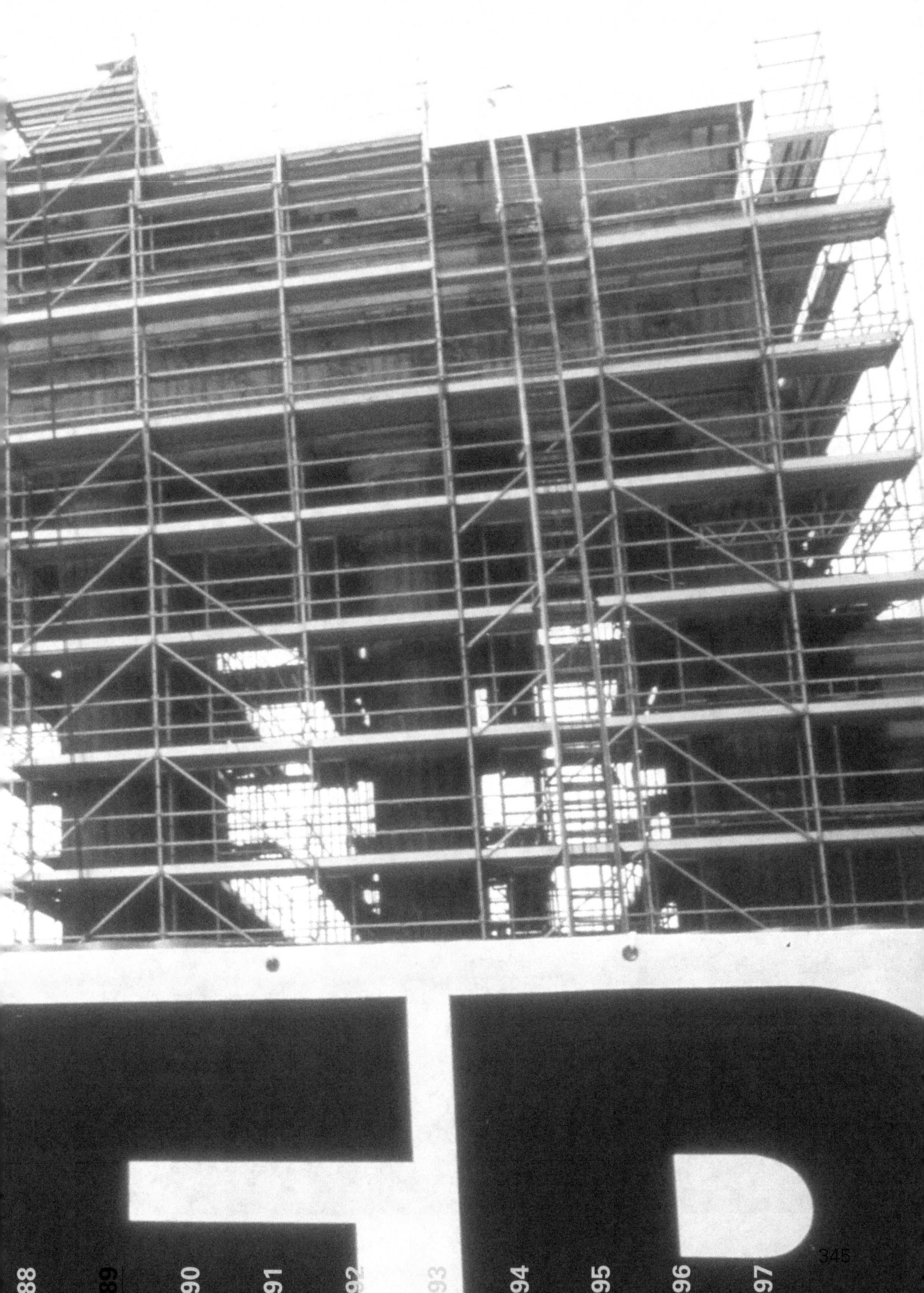

1988 1989 1990 1991 1992 1993 1994 1995 1996 1997

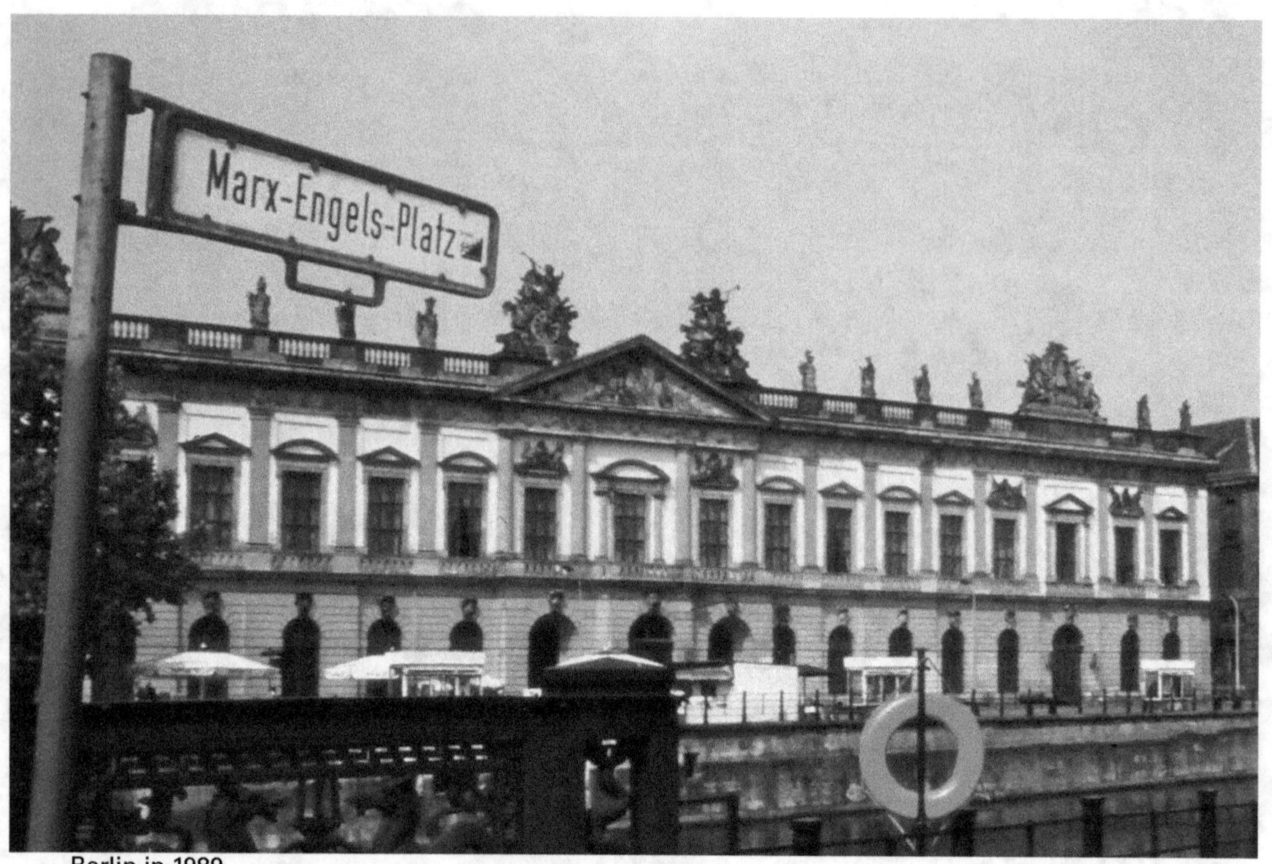

Berlin in 1989

On the way back to the West

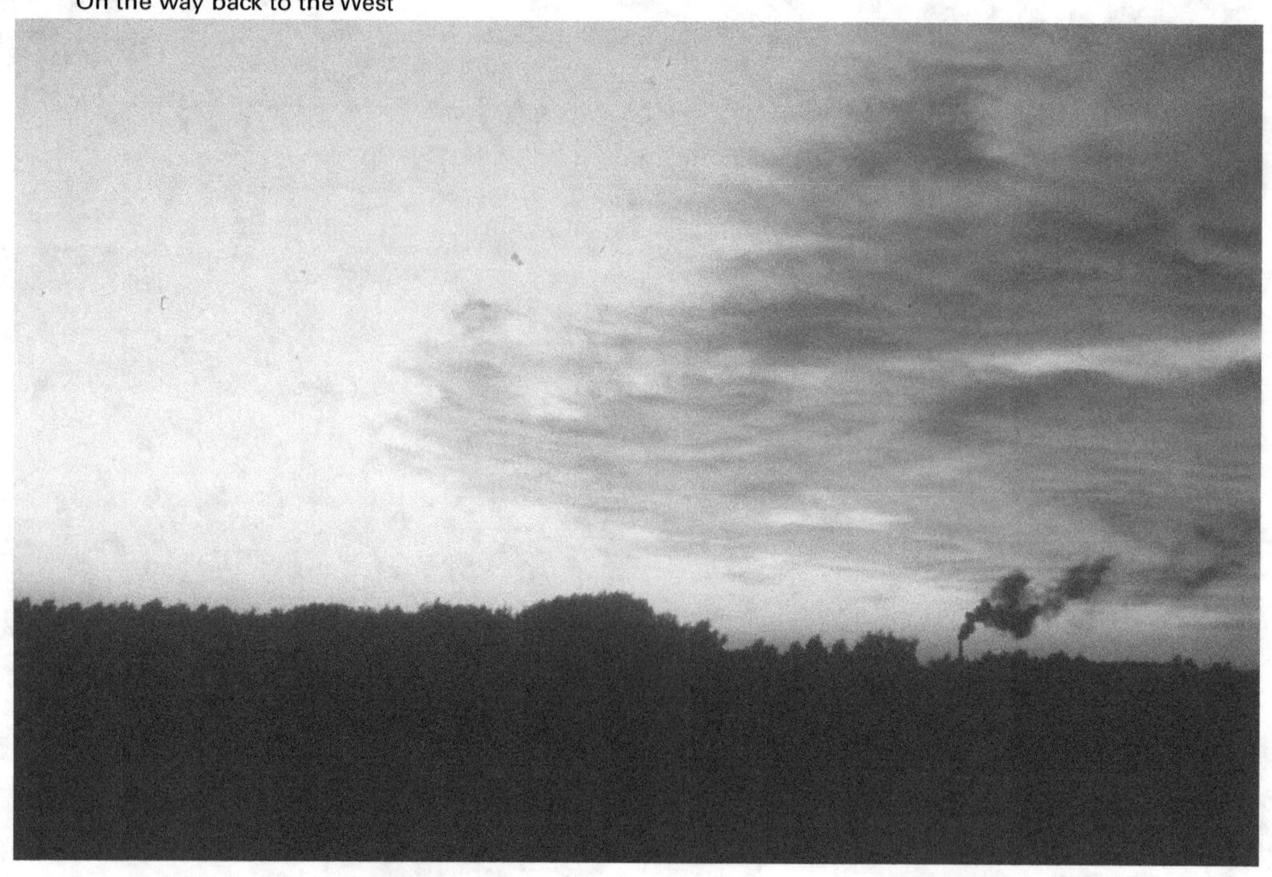

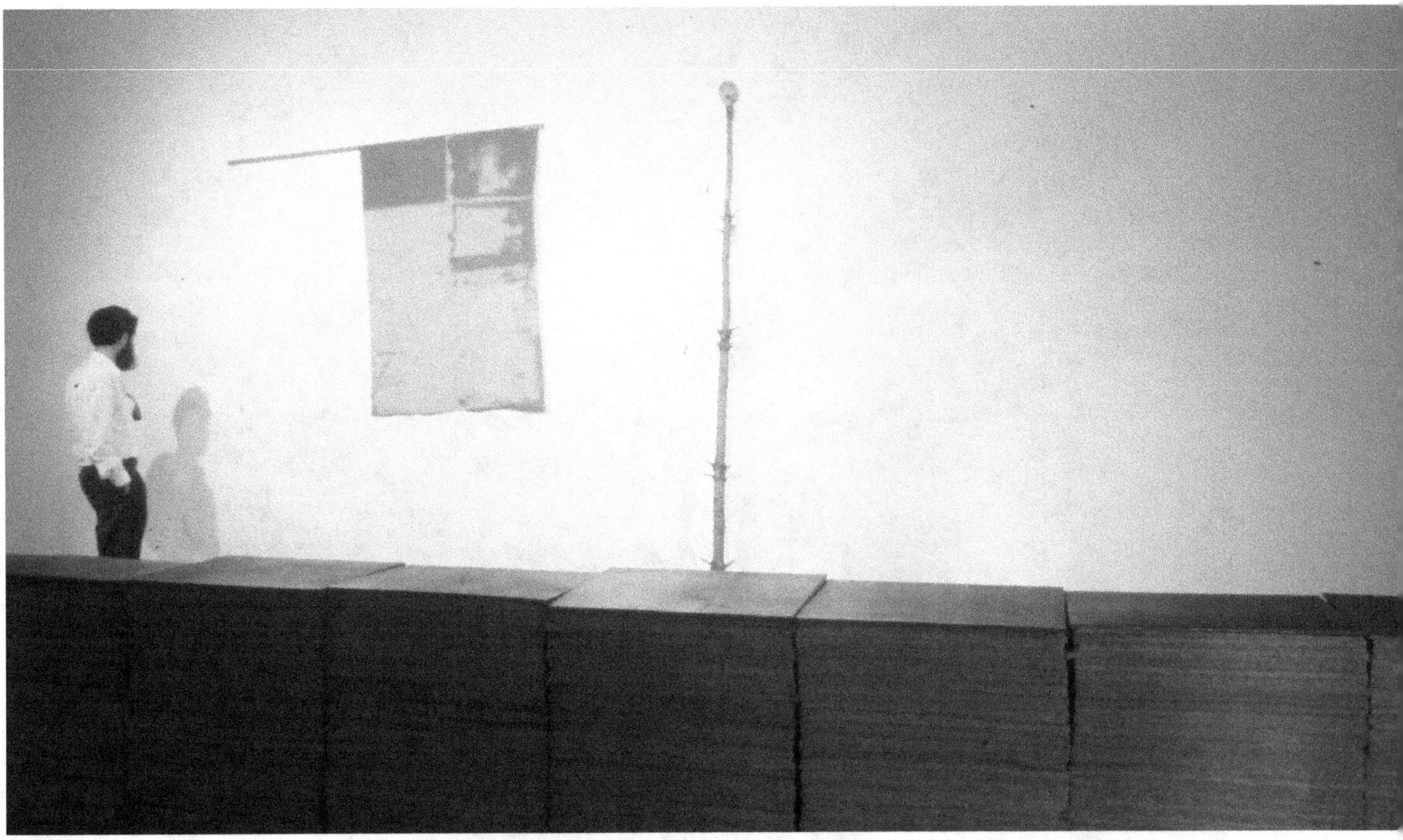

Mikesch and Walter Mücke contemplating Joseph Beuys' work in the *Bergisches Museum*, Mönchengladbach, by Hans Hollein (photo by Walter Mücke [above] and the camera [below])

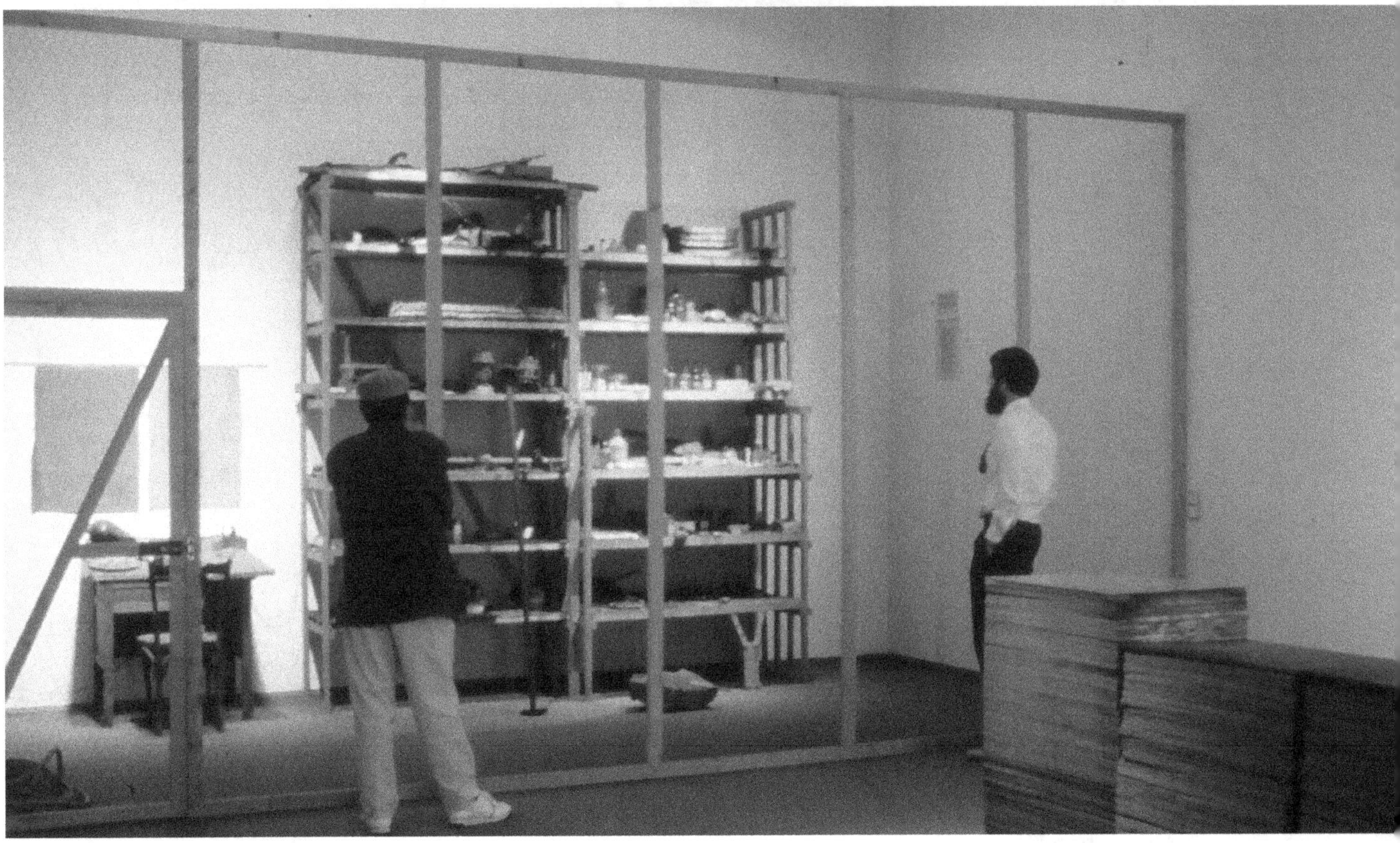

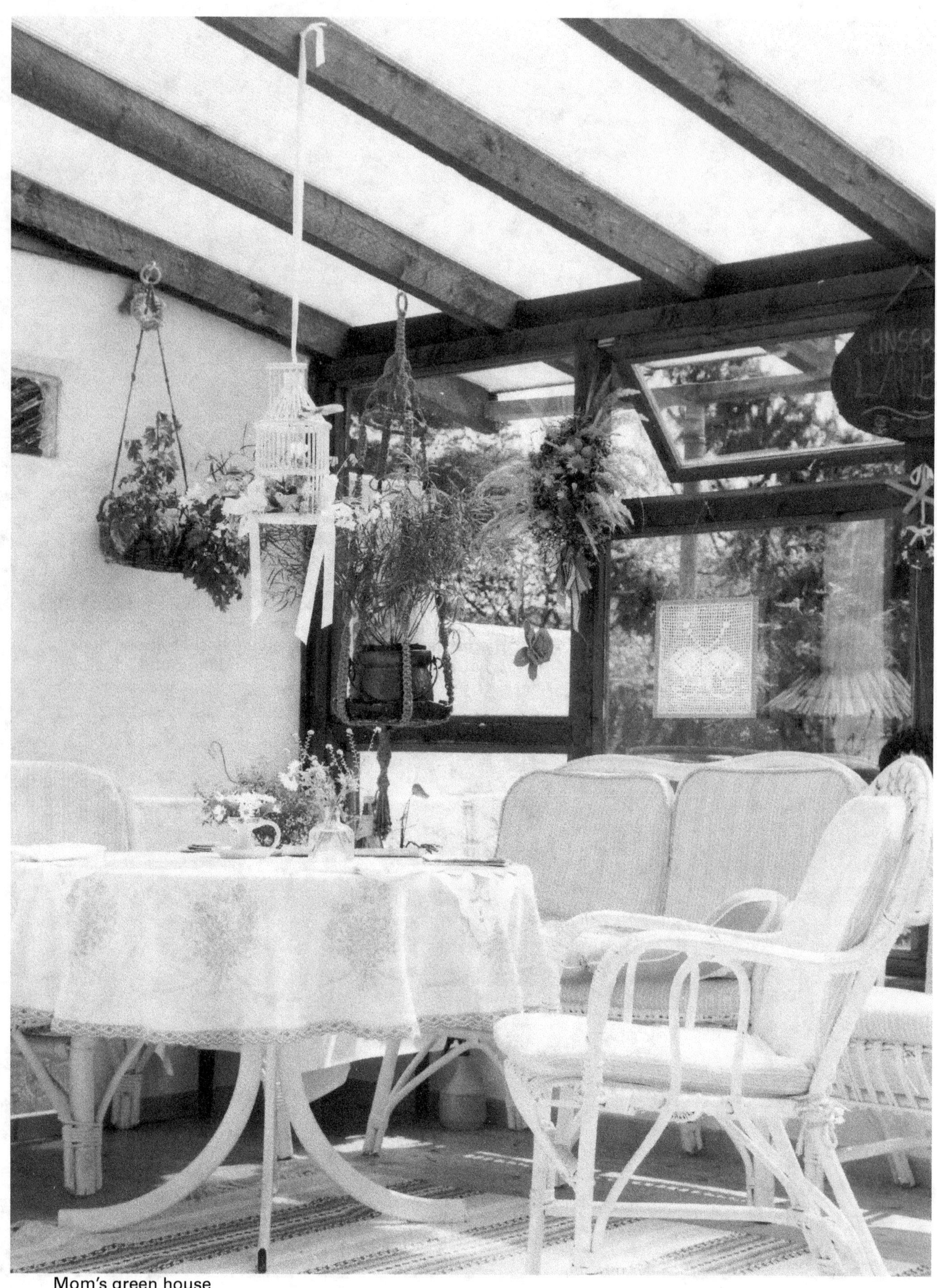

Mom's green house

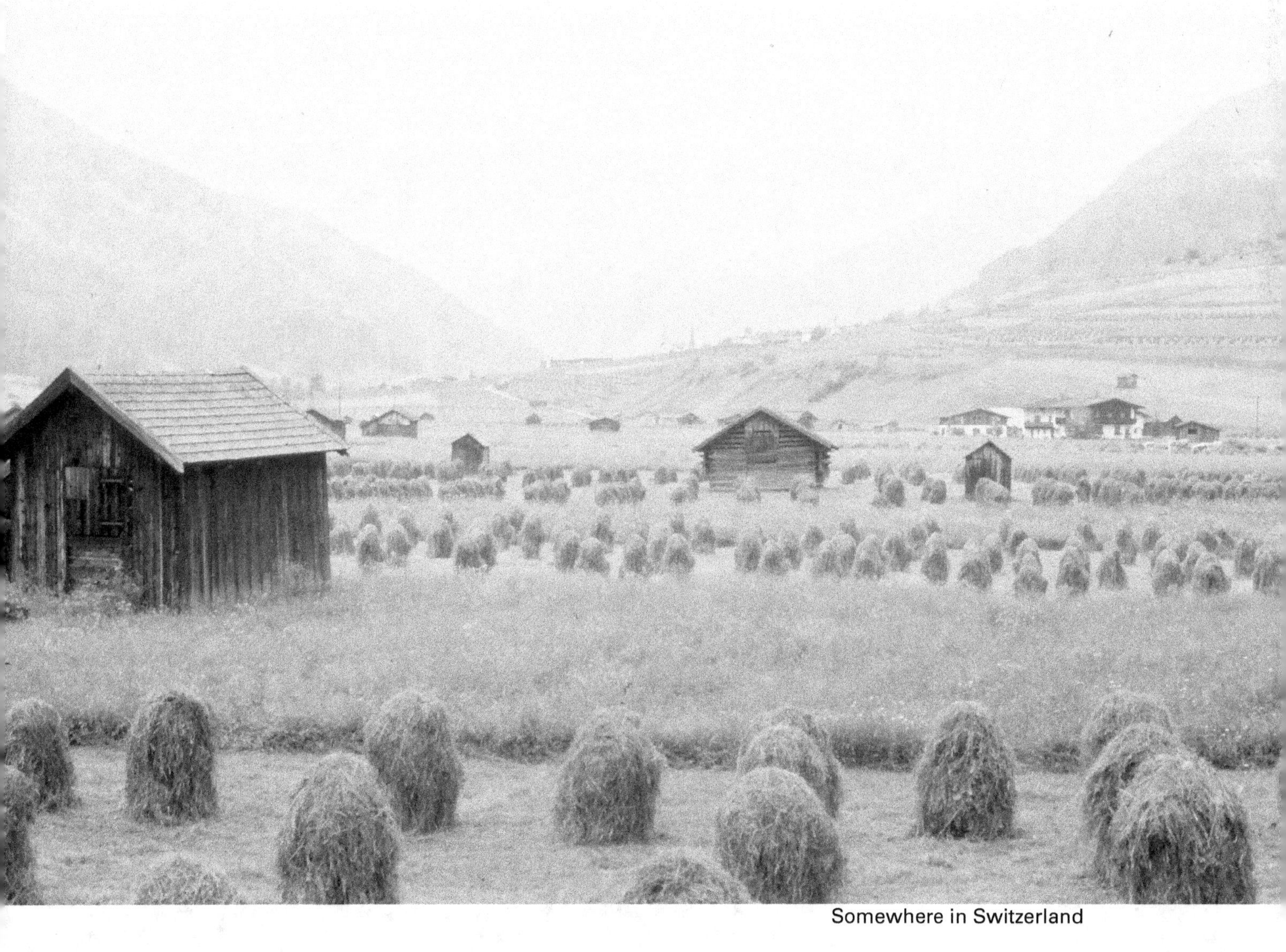

Somewhere in Switzerland

Ceramics
Wheel Throwing

Between finishing my Bachelor of Design and starting a professional MArch degree, I took some time in the summer to explore ceramics.
It was therapeutic to work with my hands, forming shapes out of mud, and sharing stories with my colleagues while focusing on the making of simple shapes.
The pieces on these and the following pages show the loot of vessels I produced during an intense eight-week session, starting from scratch, and with no prior experience of wheel throwing.

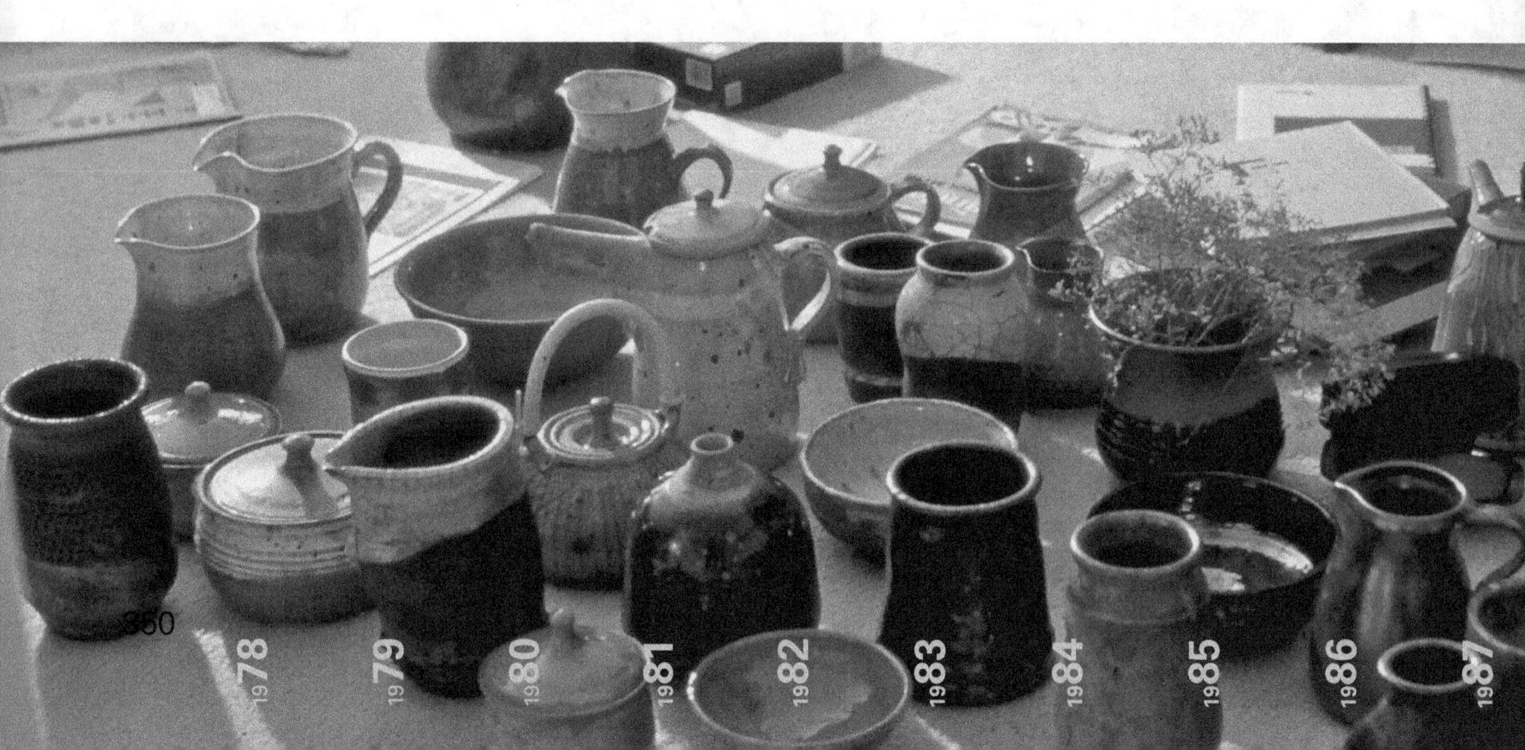

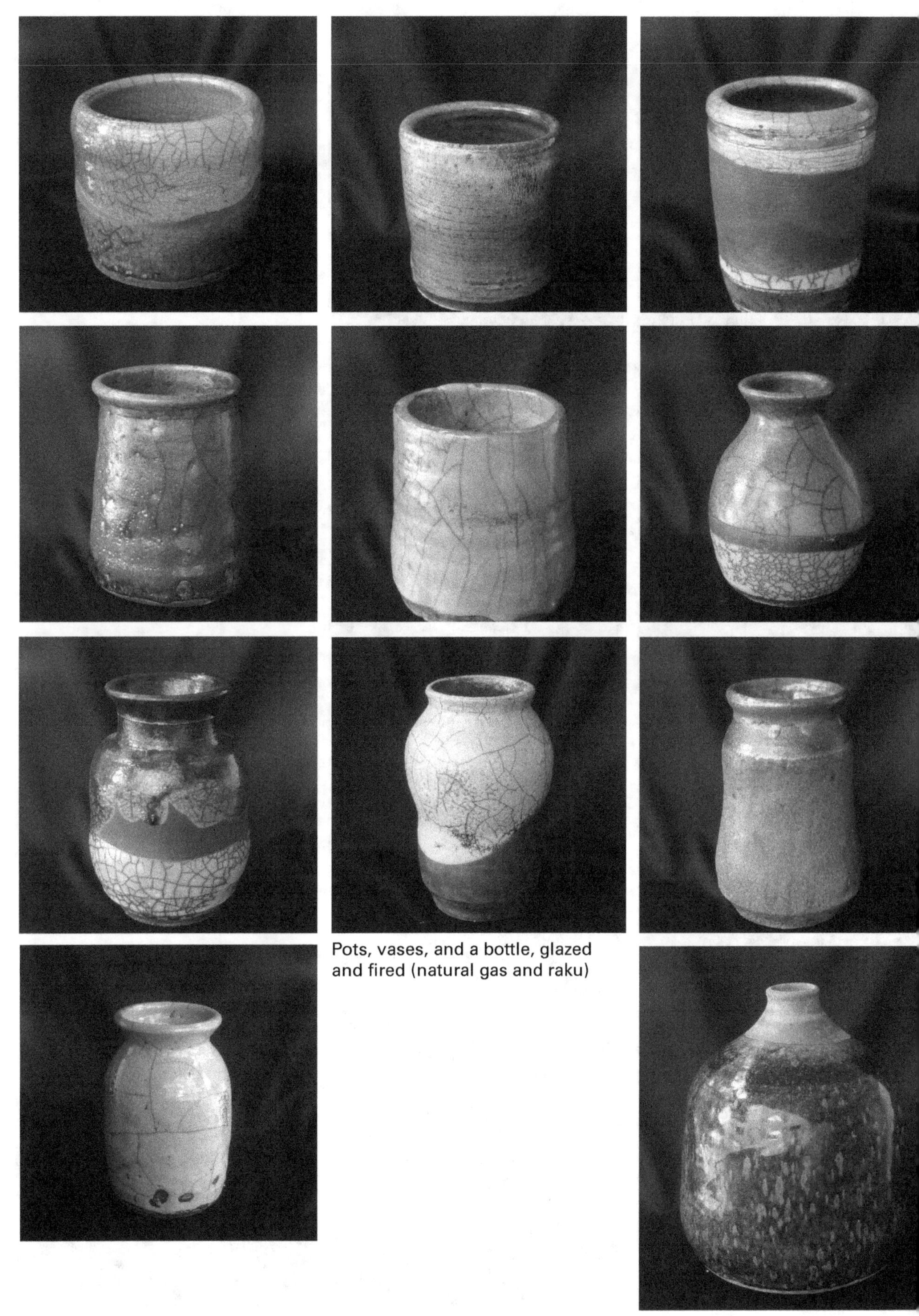

Pots, vases, and a bottle, glazed and fired (natural gas and raku)

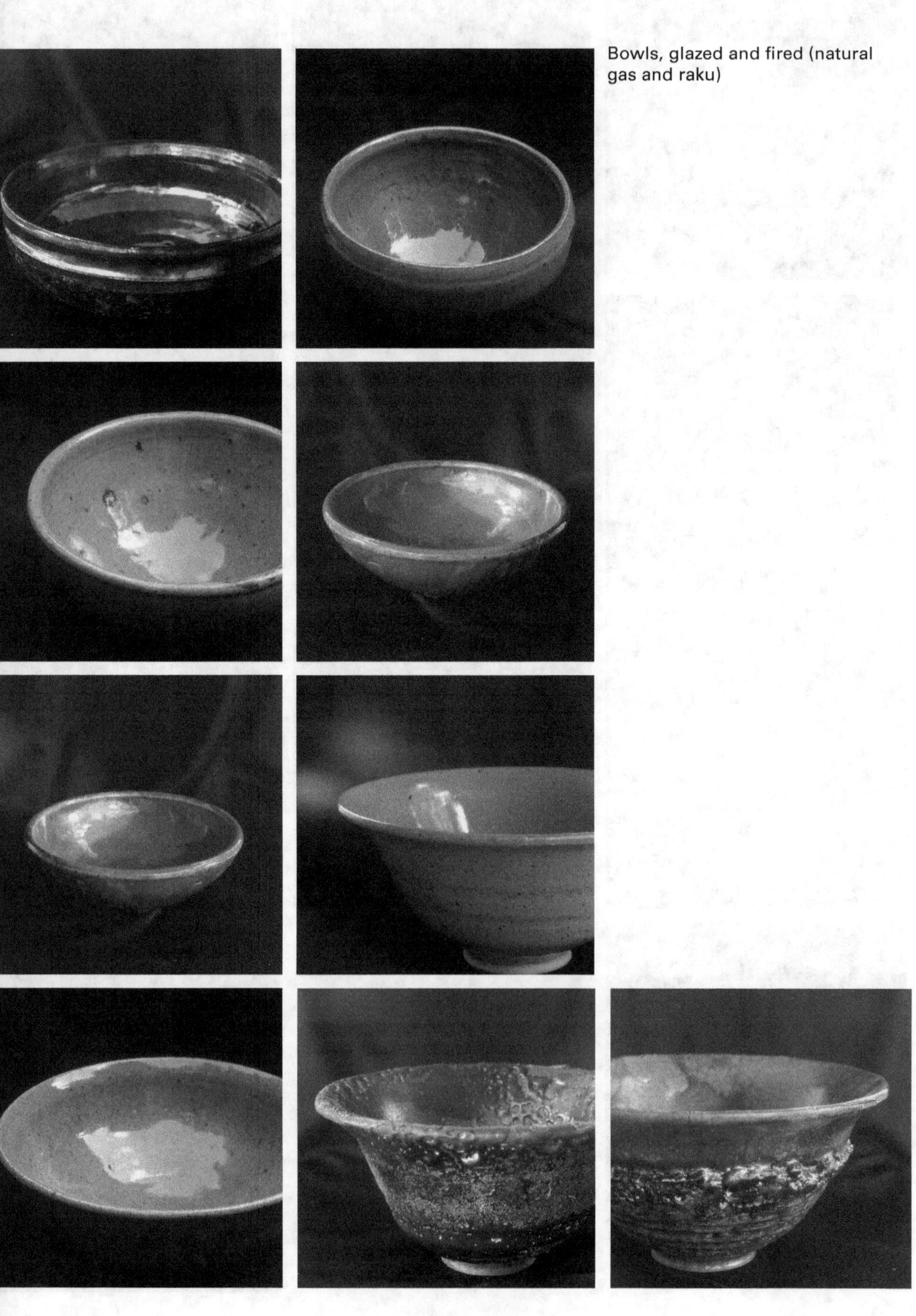

Bowls, glazed and fired (natural gas and raku)

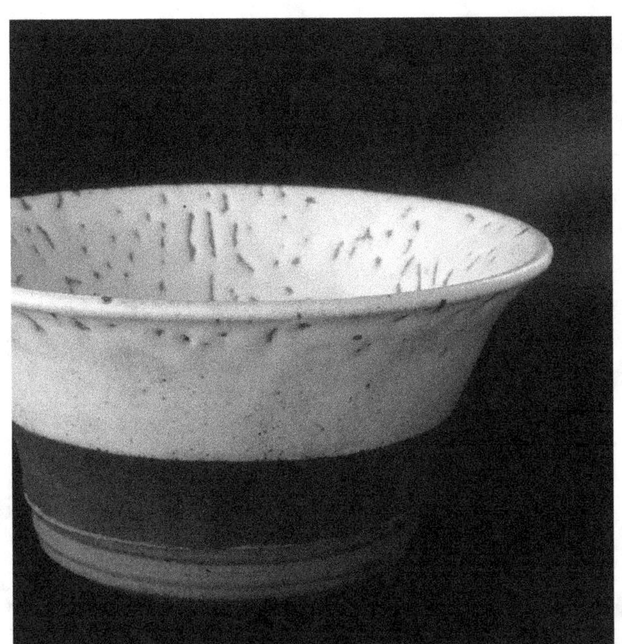
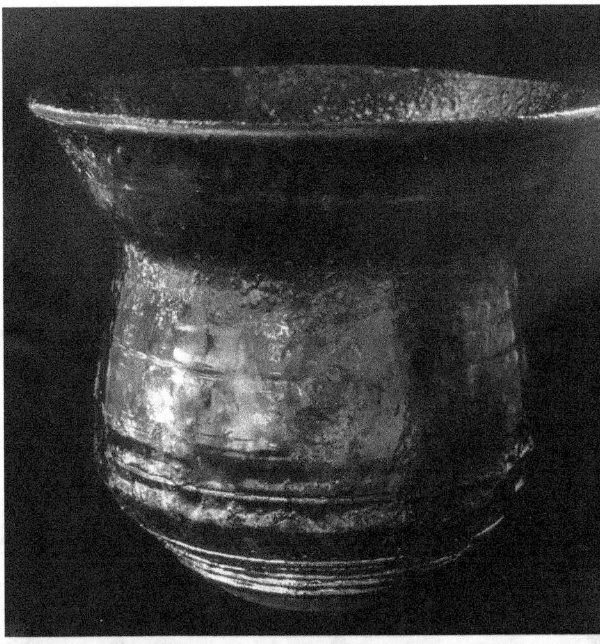
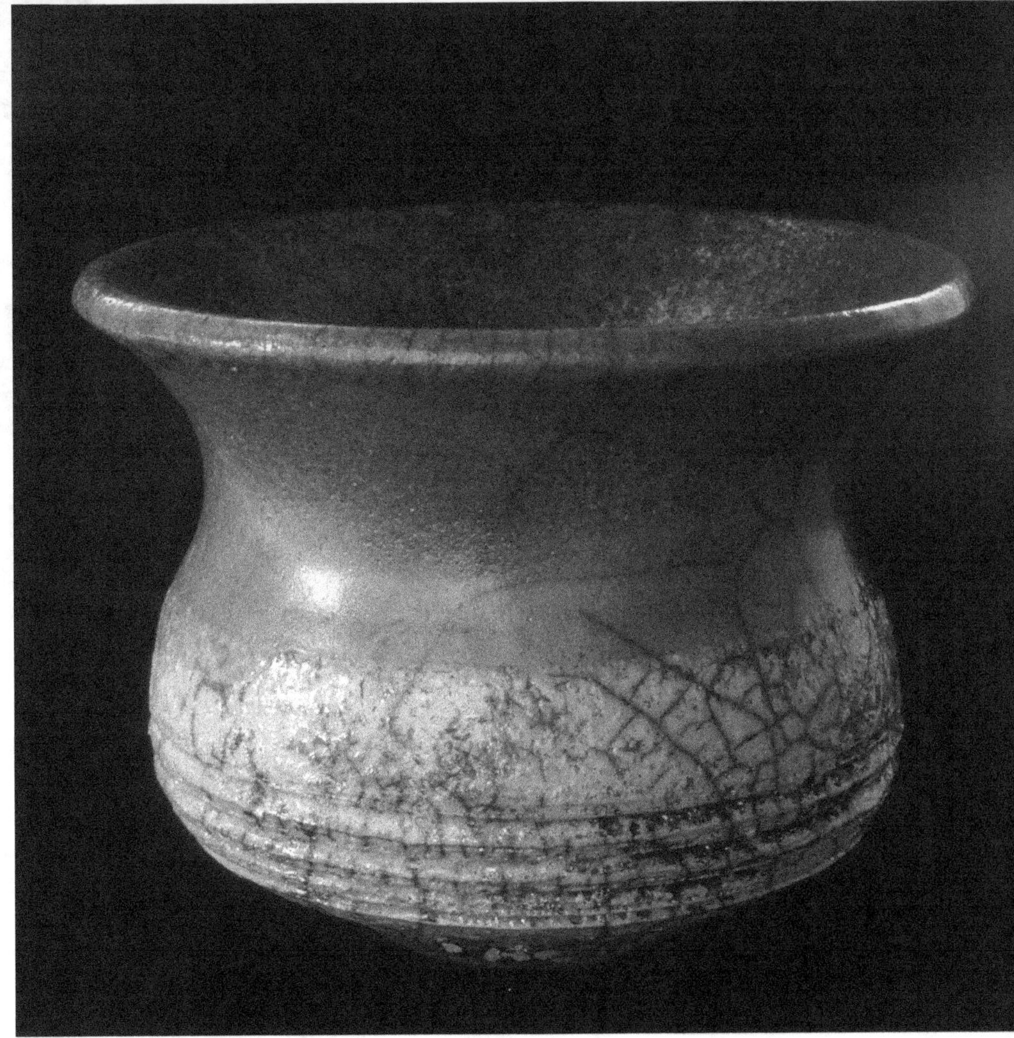
A bowl and two pots, glazed and fired (natural gas and raku)

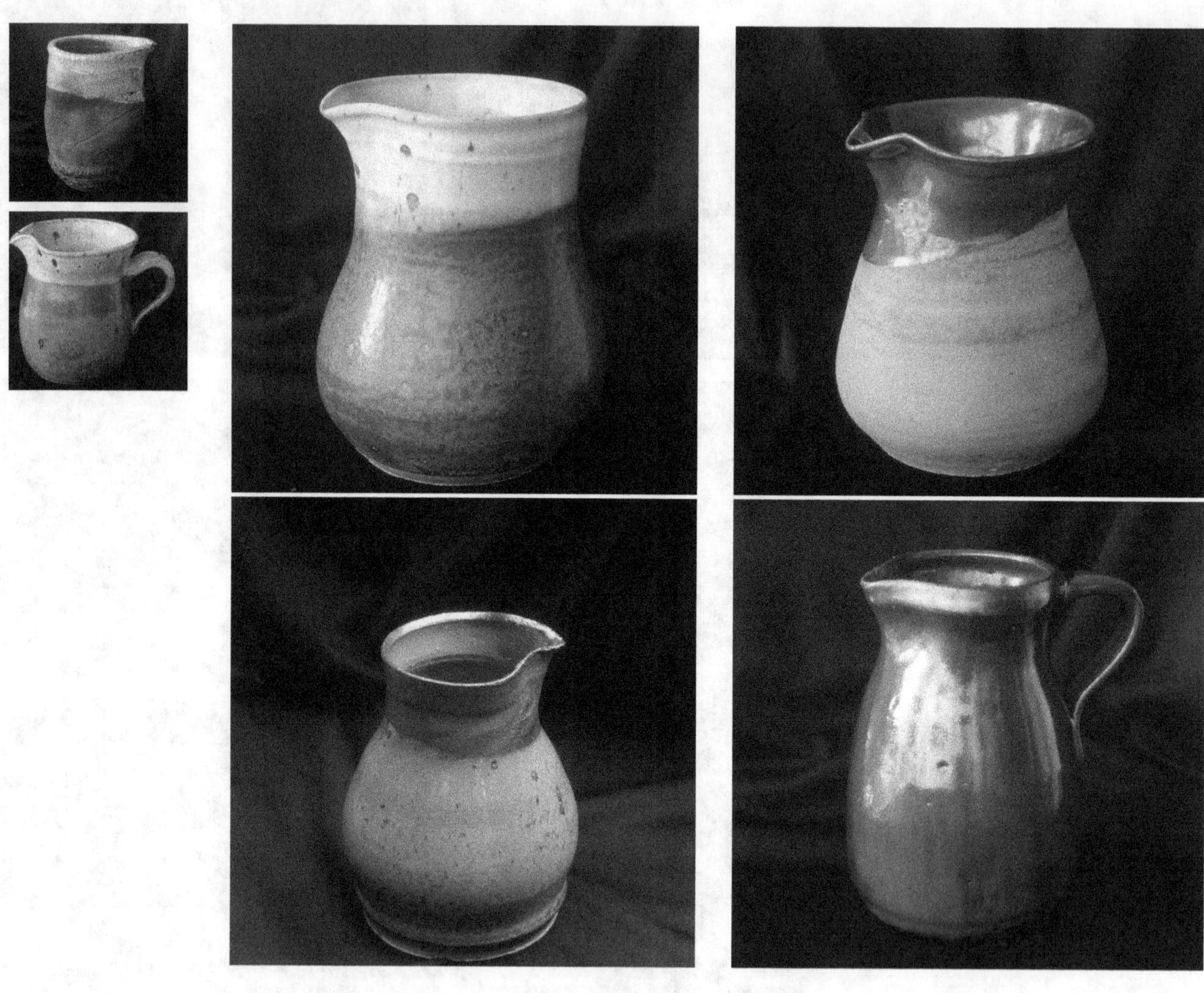

Pitchers, with and without handles, glazed and fired (natural gas)

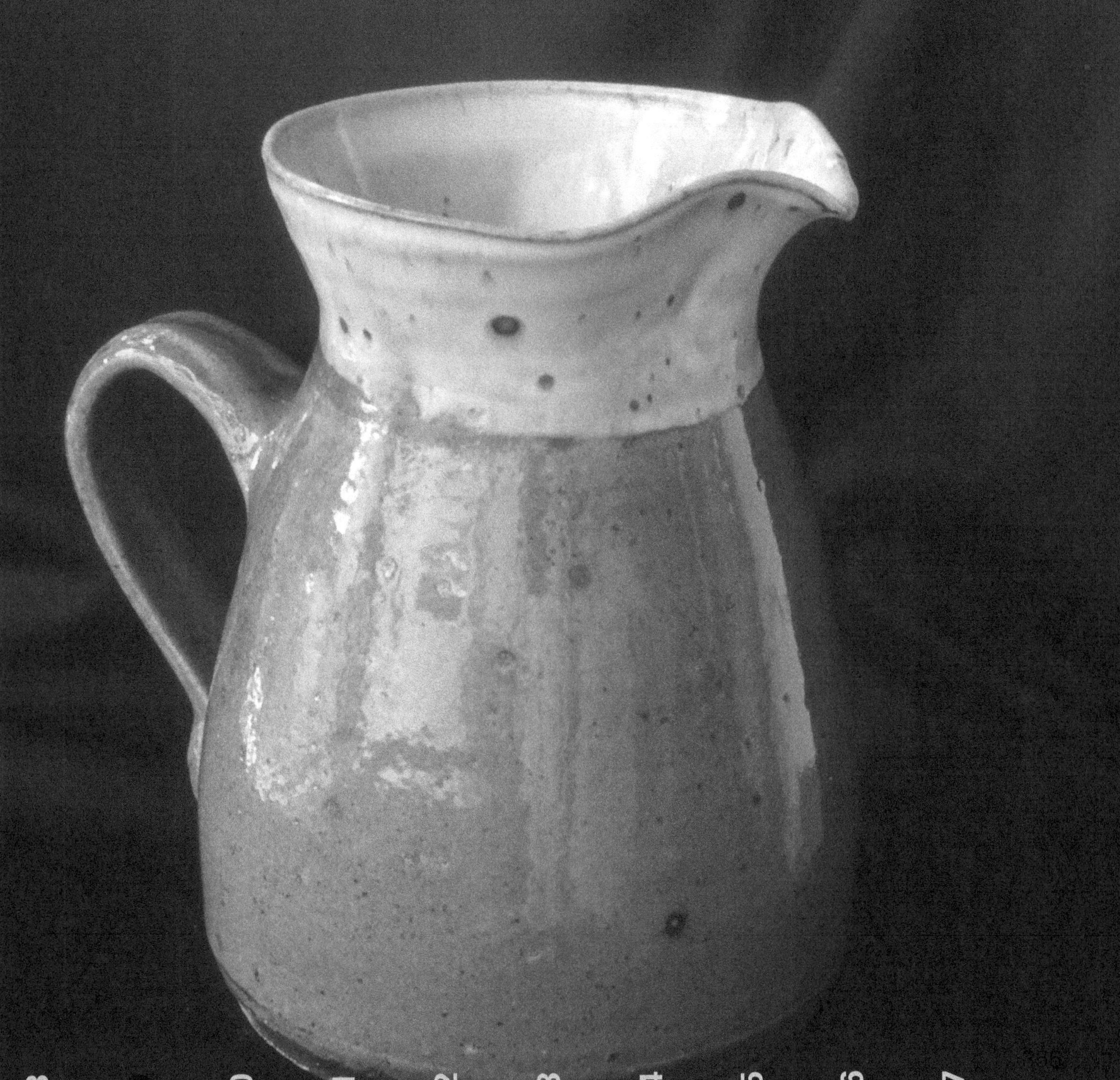

1988 1989 1990 1991 1992 1993 1994 1995 1996 1997

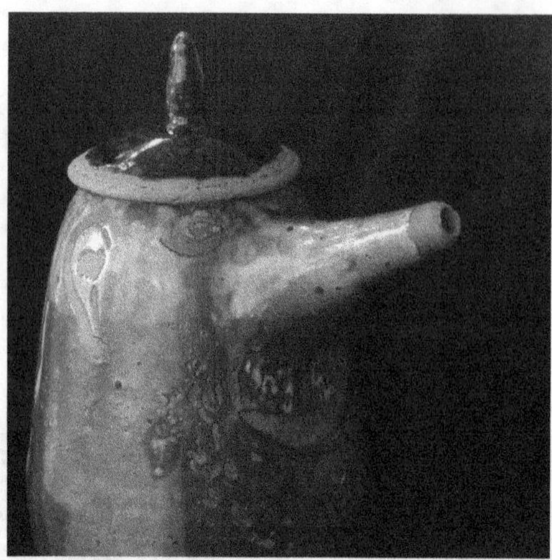

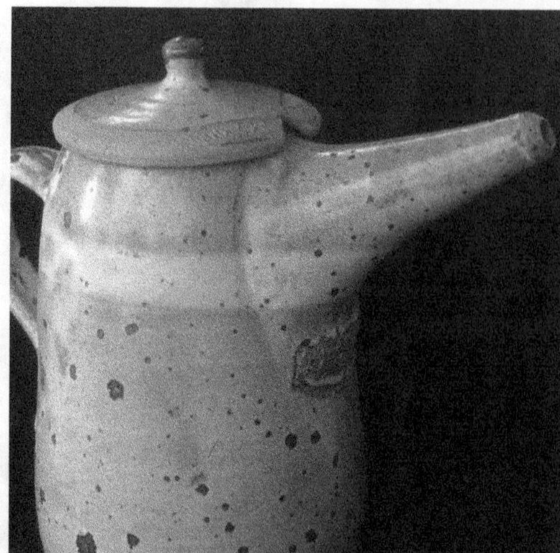

Two pots with lids and spouts makng funny faces, with and without handle, glazed and fired (natural gas)

Pot with lid, spout, and handle, glazed and fired (natural gas)

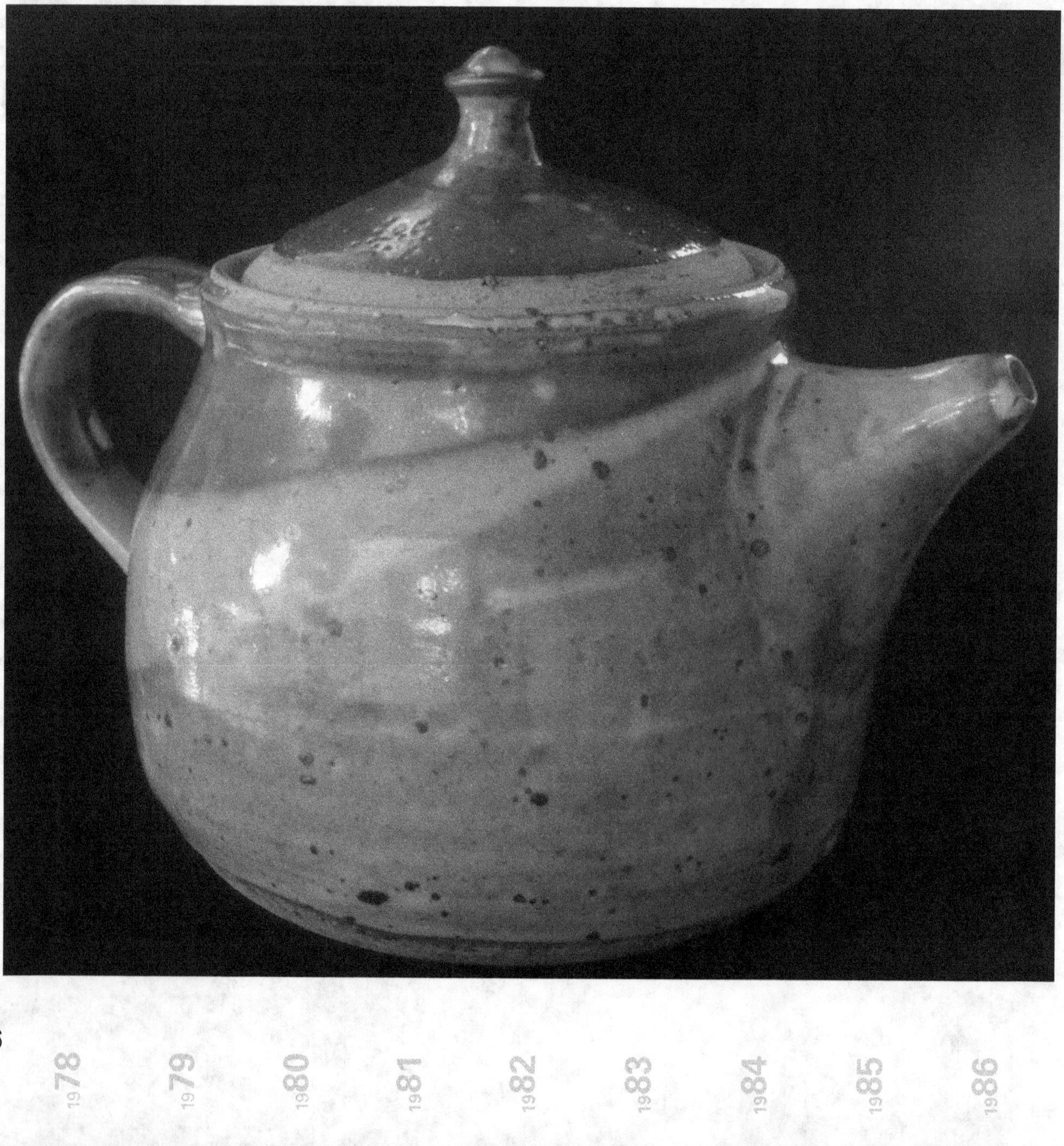

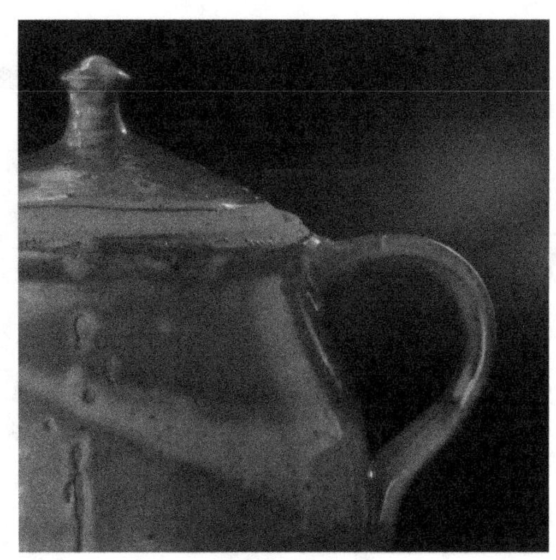

Details of pot with lid, spout, and handle, glazed and fired (natural gas)

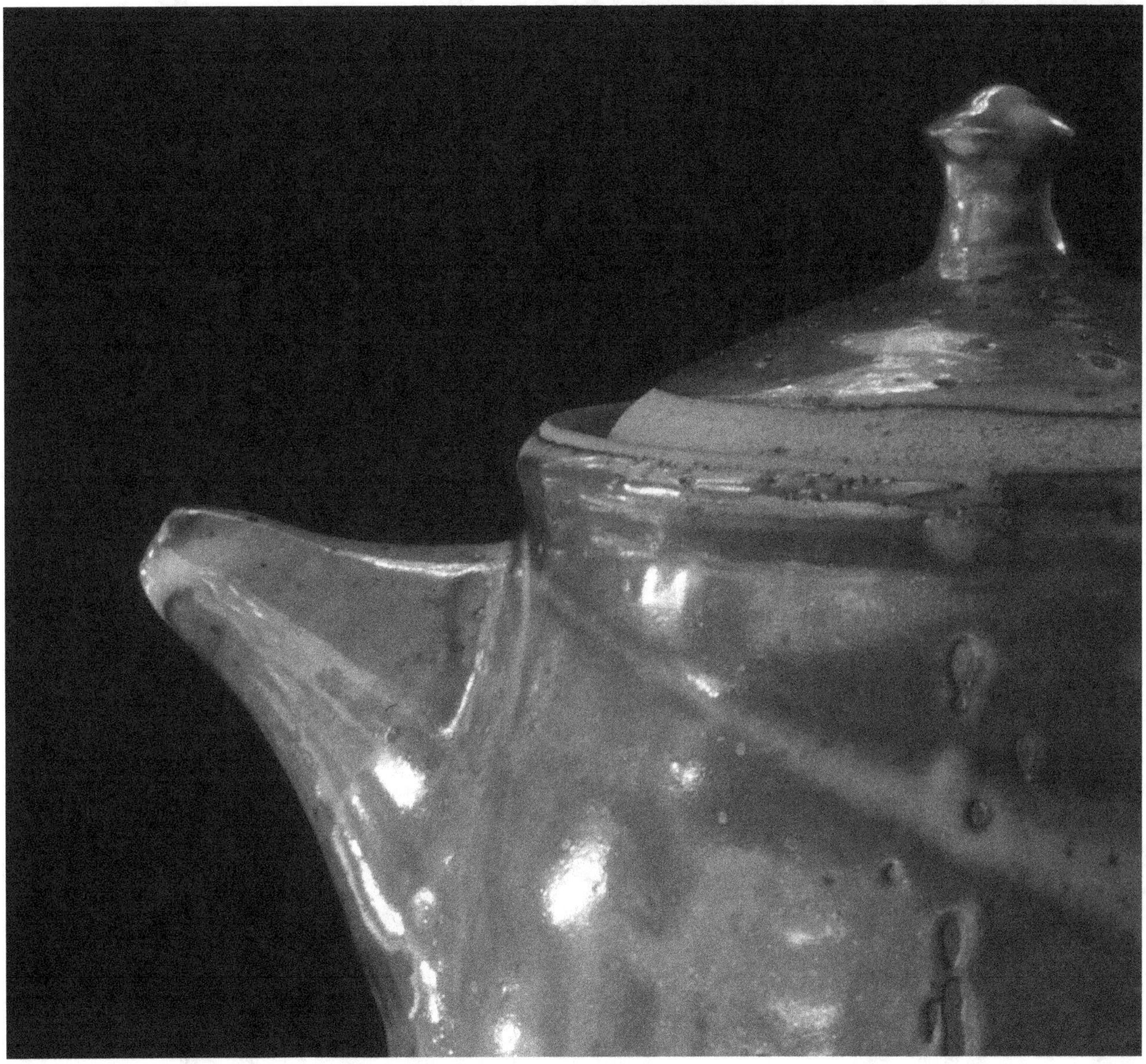

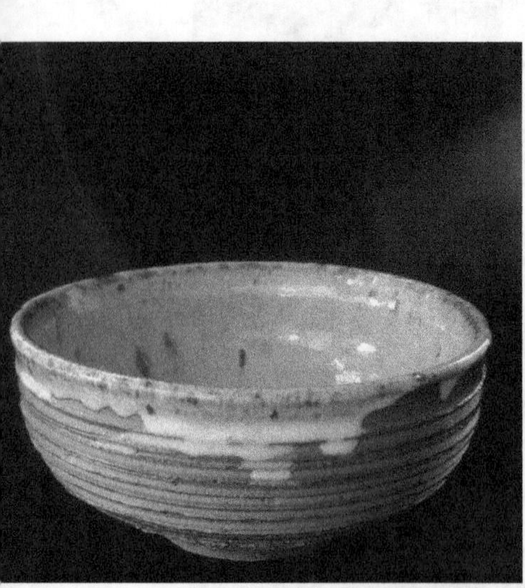

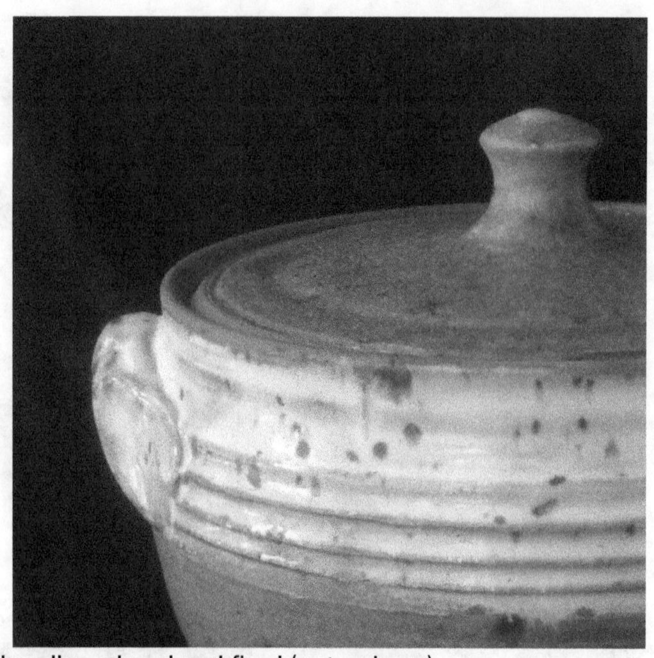

Two bowls, one with lid and integrated handles, glazed and fired (natural gas)

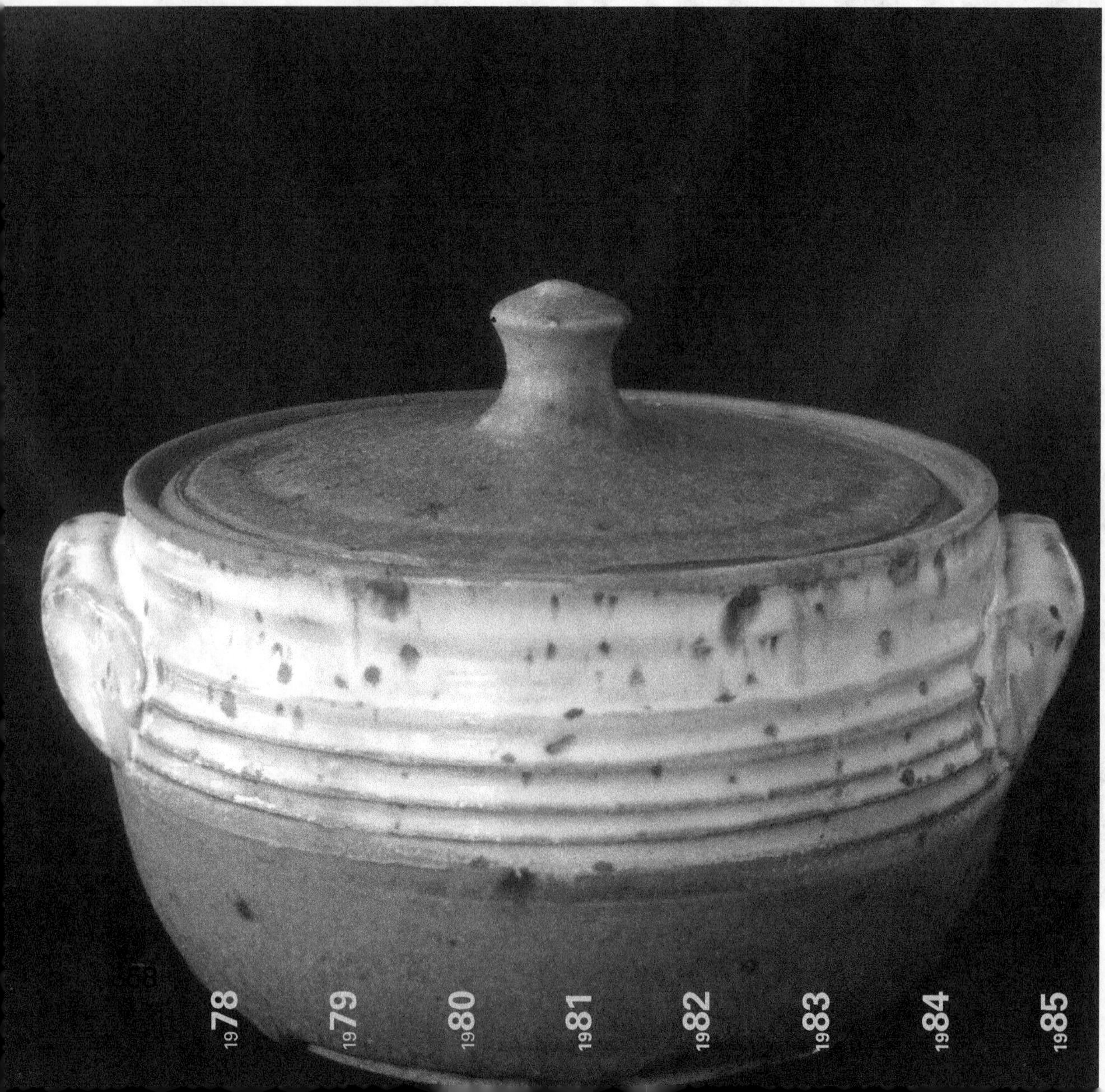

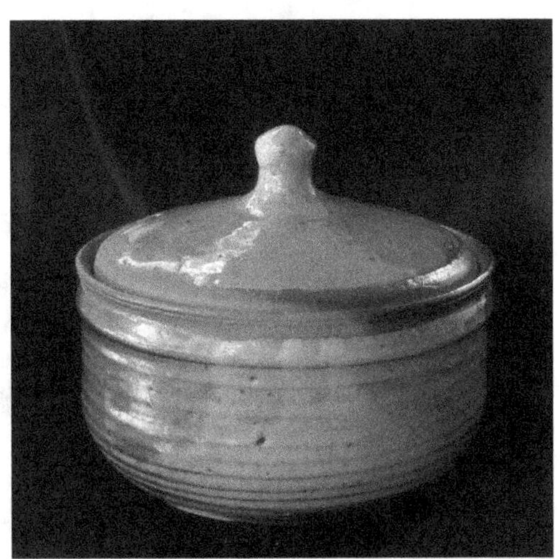

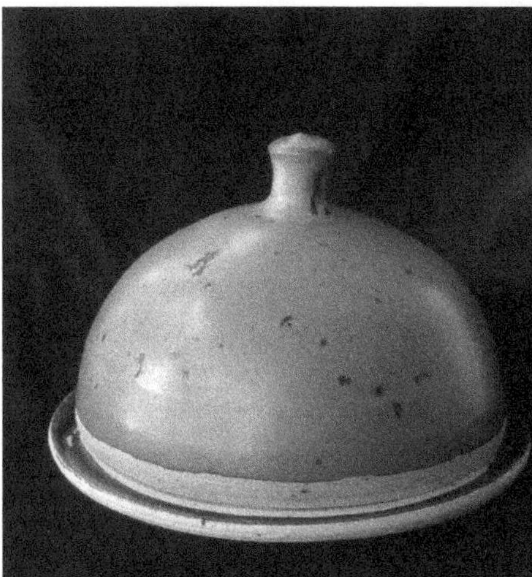

Two bowls, and a covered cheese bell, with lids and integrated knobs, glazed and fired (natural gas)

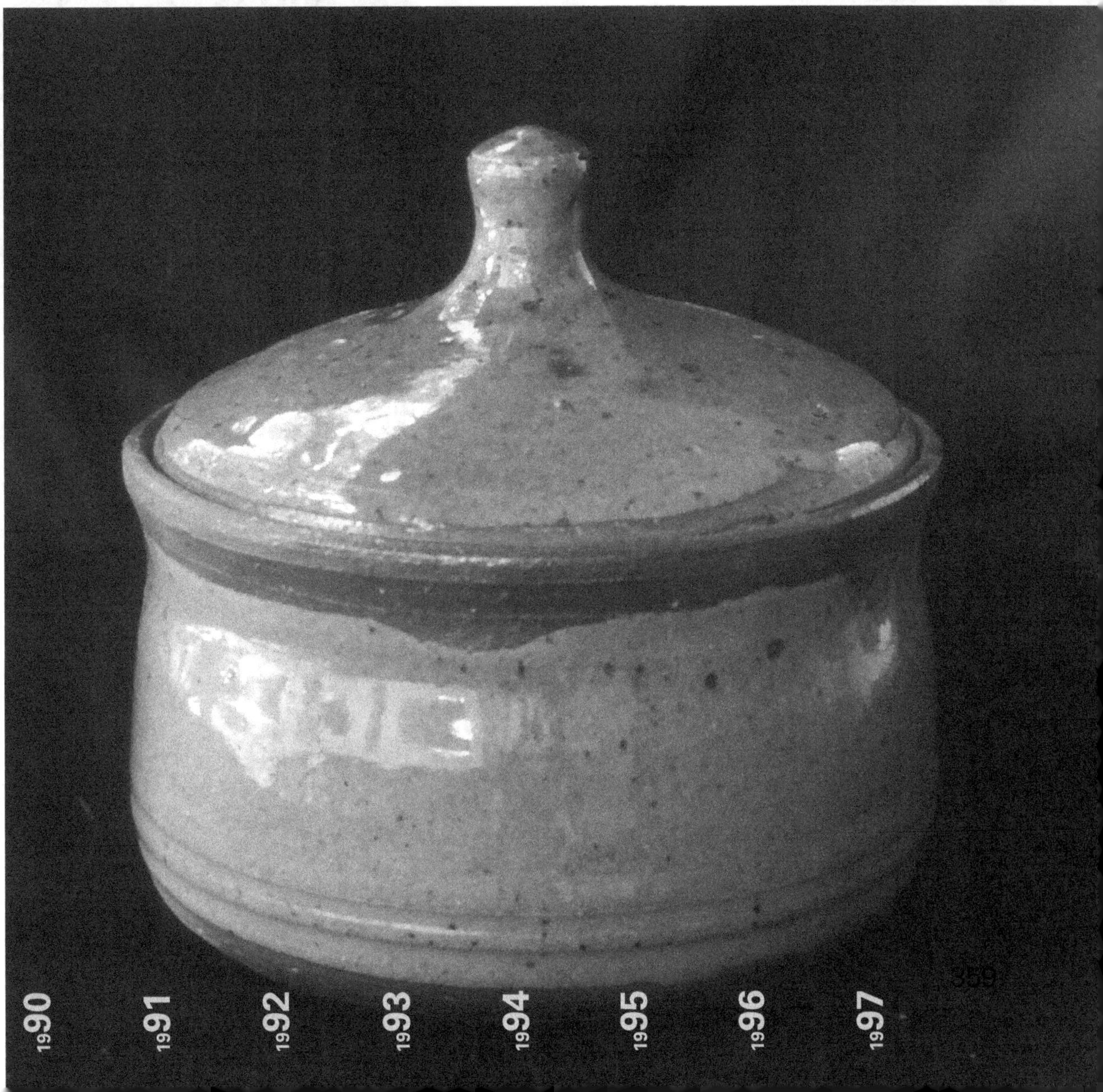

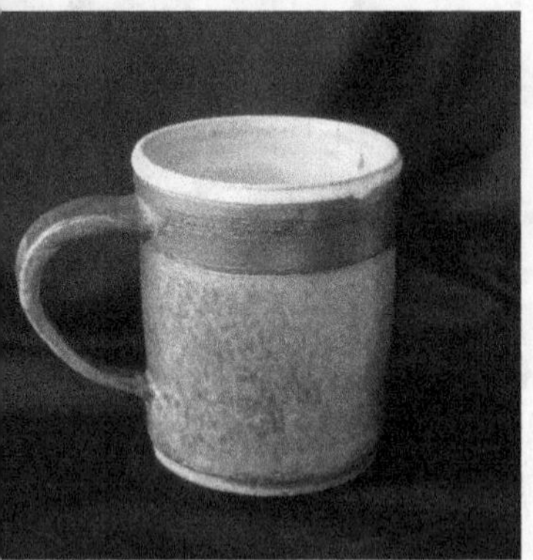

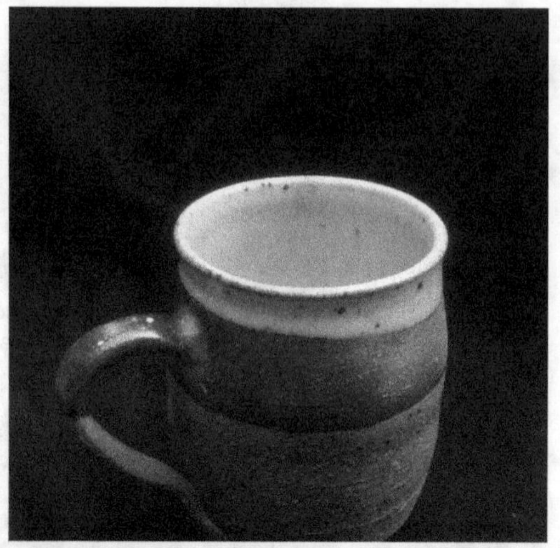

Various cups with handles, glazed and fired (natural gas and wood)

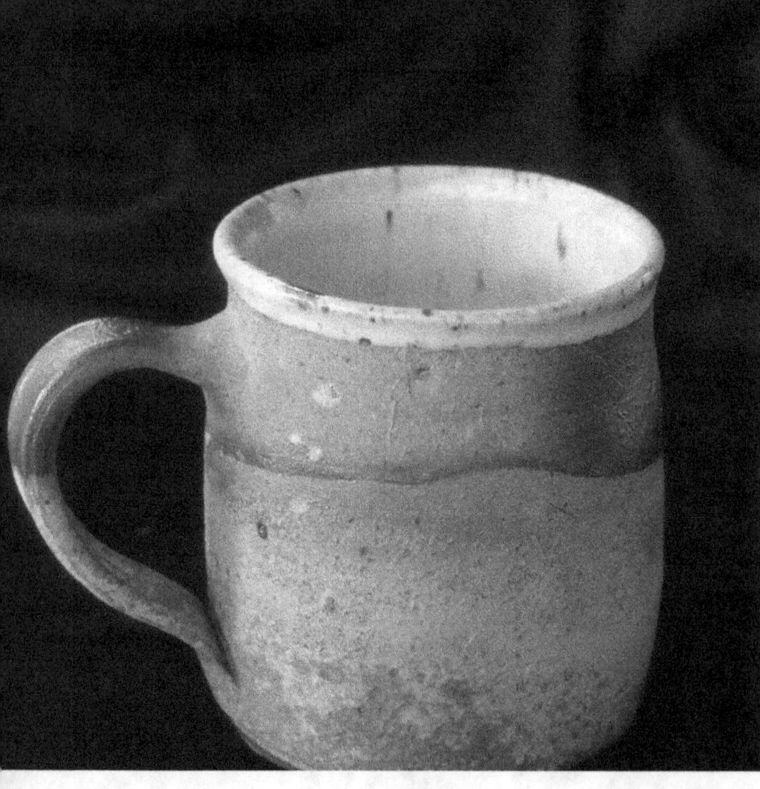

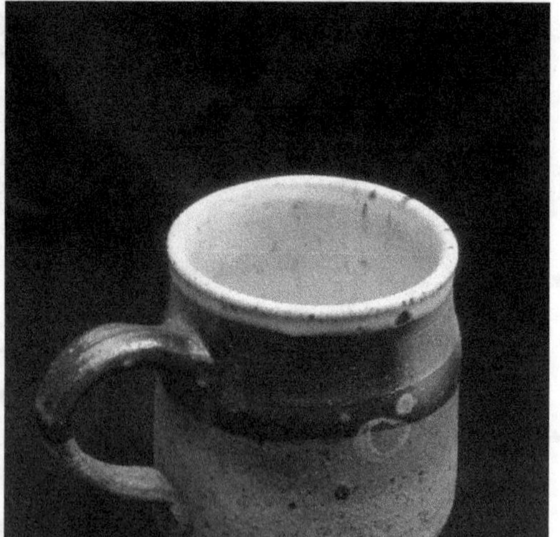

Beer Stein with large handle, glazed and fired (natural gas)

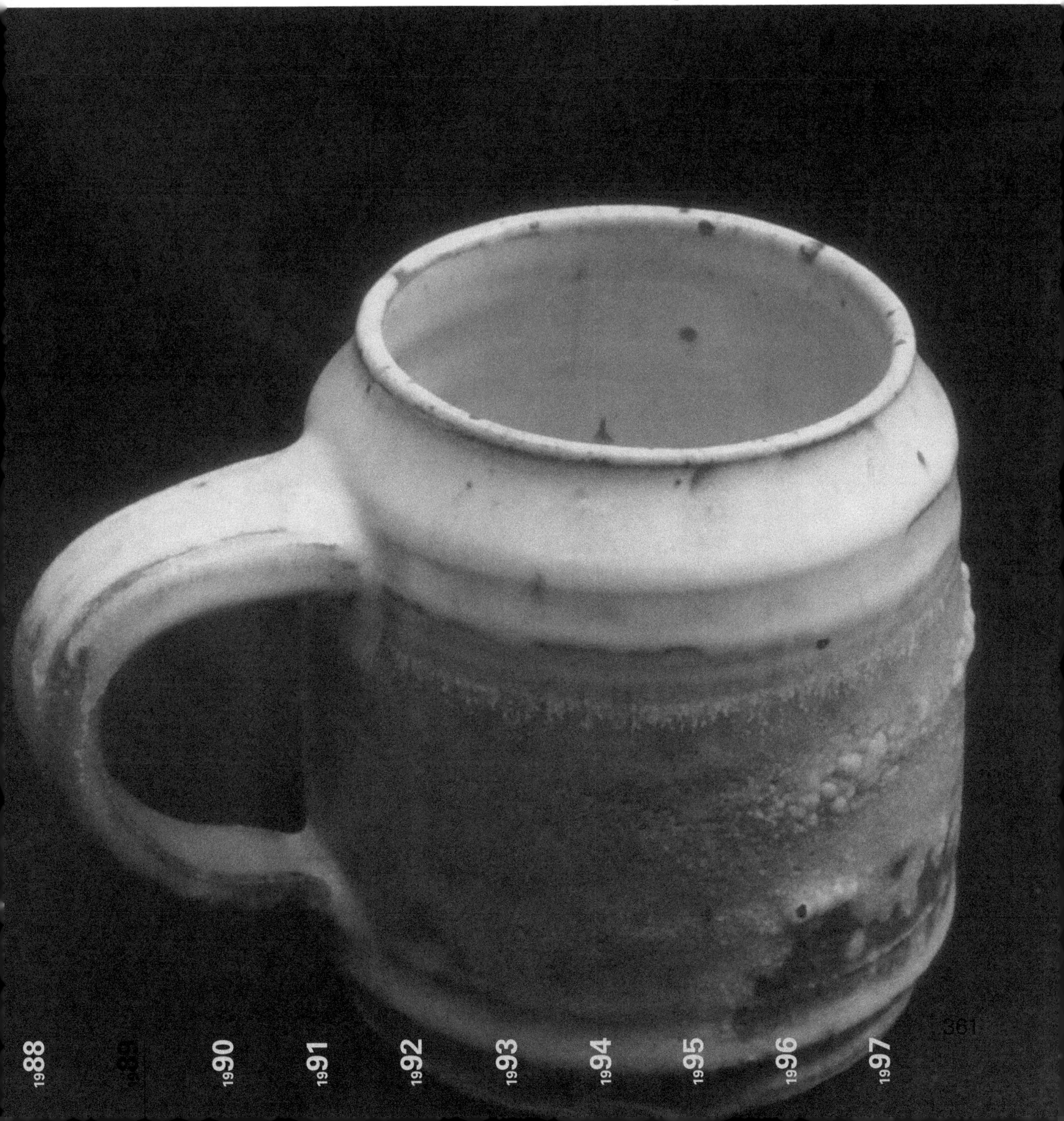

Design sketches for tea set

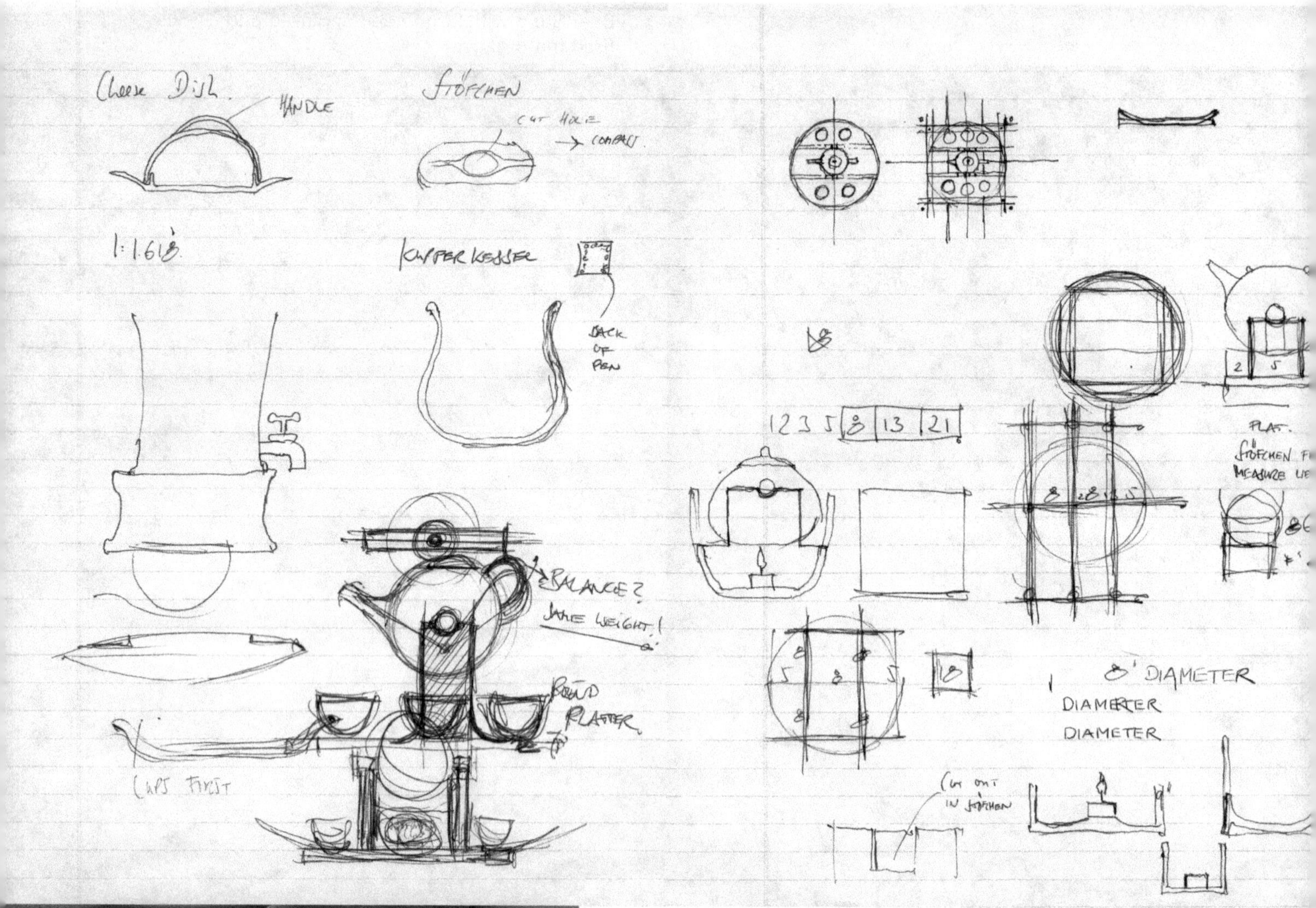

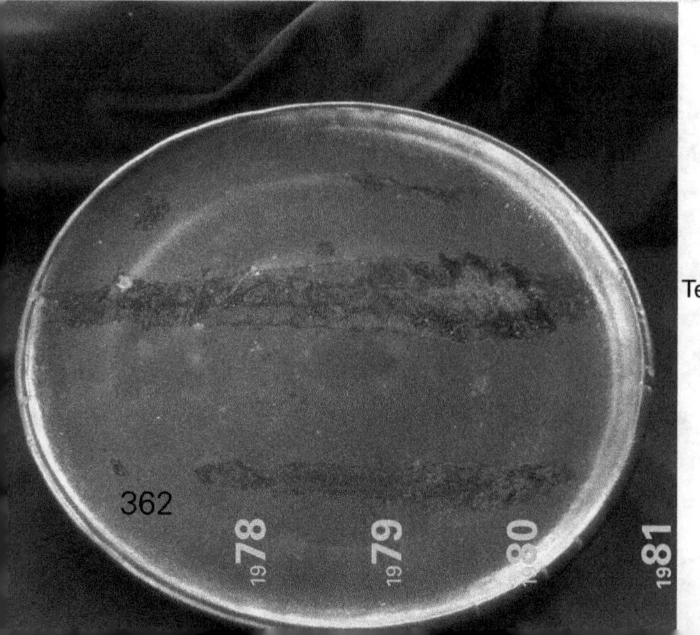

Tea set plate

Tea set consisting of one plate, six cups, suspended teapot with integrated warmer, glazed and fired (natural gas)

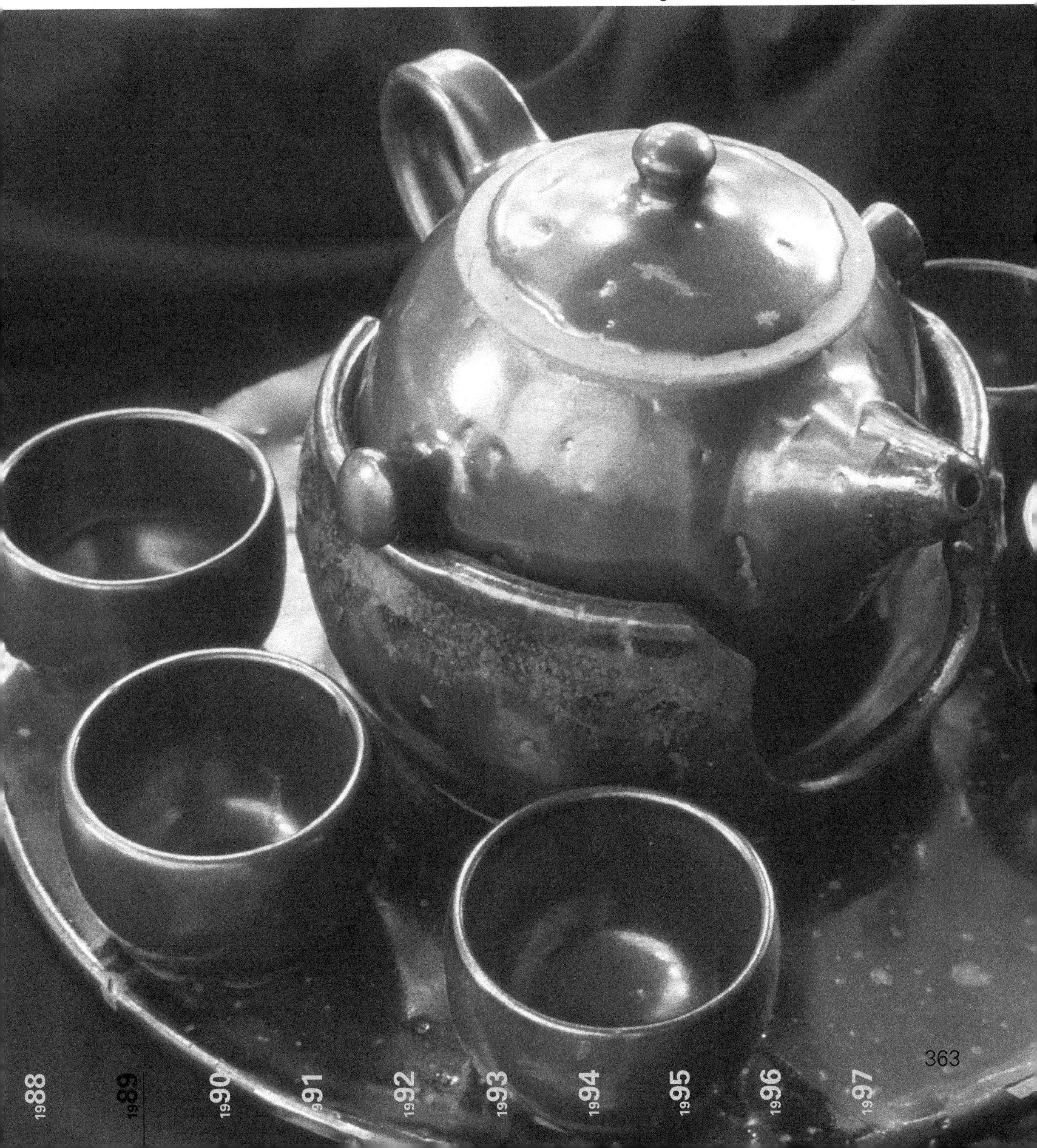

Design sketches for tea pot with bamboo handle, glazed and fired (natural gas)

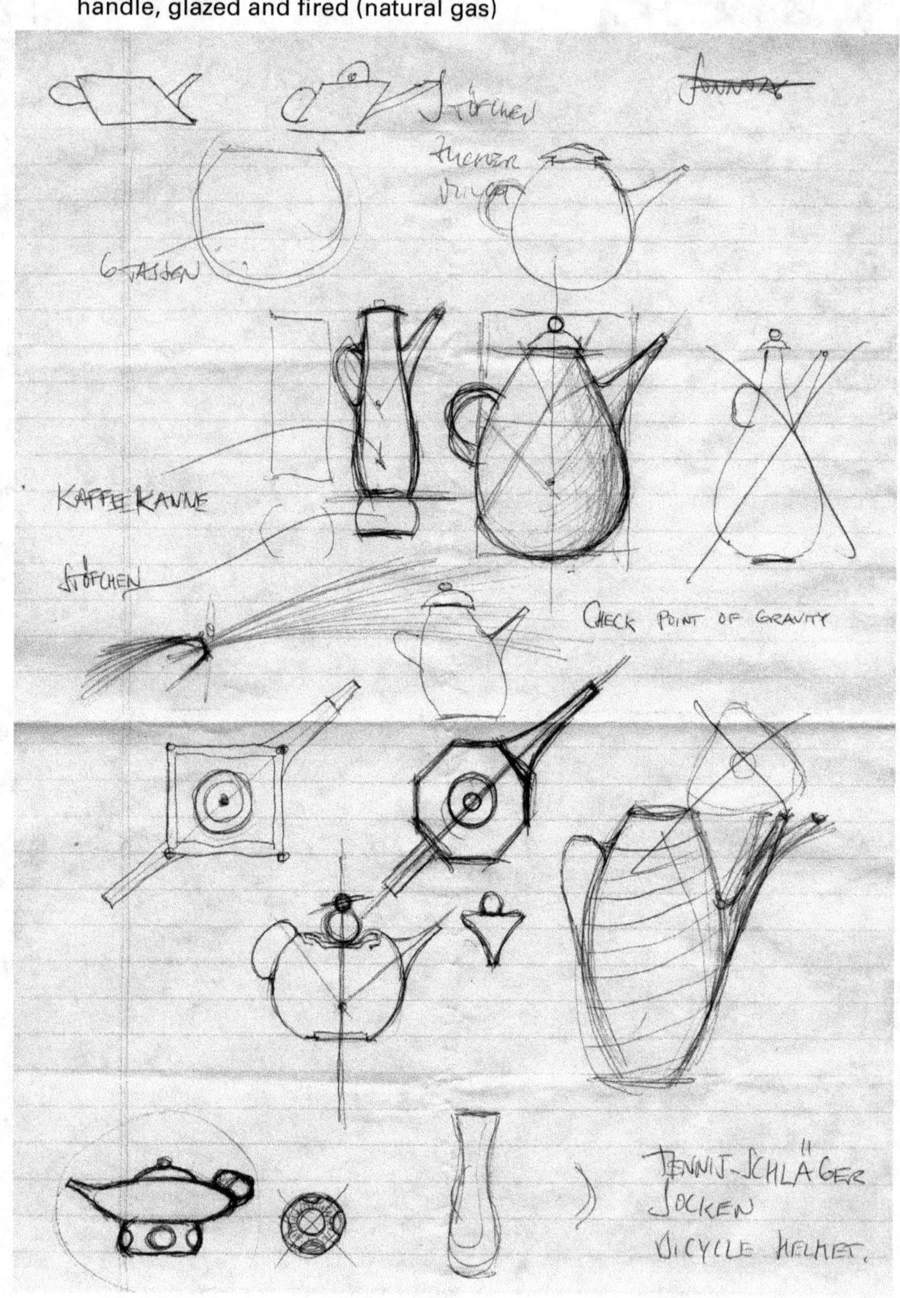

Tea pot with bamboo handle, glazed and fired (natural gas)

Parking Garage

University of Florida, Gainesville, FL

Programme:	
parking:	900-1000 automobiles
	5% reserved/secured stalls
private maintenance:	gasoline pump and oil change
	maintenance/security office with toilet
retail space:	12000 square feet
self-service car wash:	six stalls with vacuum
drive-thru bank:	four bays
	bank office (not public) with safe and toilet
disabled parking:	1:75 spaces

This project developed out of the consciousness of a difference between the car as a non-moving mass, when parked, and the traces cars leave or the traces architecture leaves in their absence. These presences of absence include the parking bay markings on the ground, fire barrels filled with sand, signs that allow or prohibit certain groups of people from parking their car in a particular space, security phones, car tire traces from abrupt breaks or acceleration, etc.

I interpreted this present absence with regard to the program as a design in which the building could be seen as a construction that allows different functions to take place simultaneously or in sequence. The simultaneity of actions becomes apparent in the markings as well as the physical structure of the parking garage. The 12000 square foot retail space was conceived as an outdoor market that disappears when it closes. The absence is marked by a collection of concrete boxes that contain utilities (water and electric hookup) as well as fold-out tables. The drive-thru bank with its bays serves in the evenings and on weekends as a car wash. The top floor of the garage is marked with both car bays markings and volley- and basket ball fields which are activities that take place currently on the unbuilt site.

On a larger scale the design is conceived as a differentiated field of vertical columns and horizontal planes. The five percent reserved/secure stalls were moved to the north-west corner. They are strategically placed for people who can afford the price for a short walking distance to the surrounding campus buildings. At the same time the mass of the non-reserved parking structure is placed in such a way that it appears to crush the relatively small but privileged reserved-parking volume.

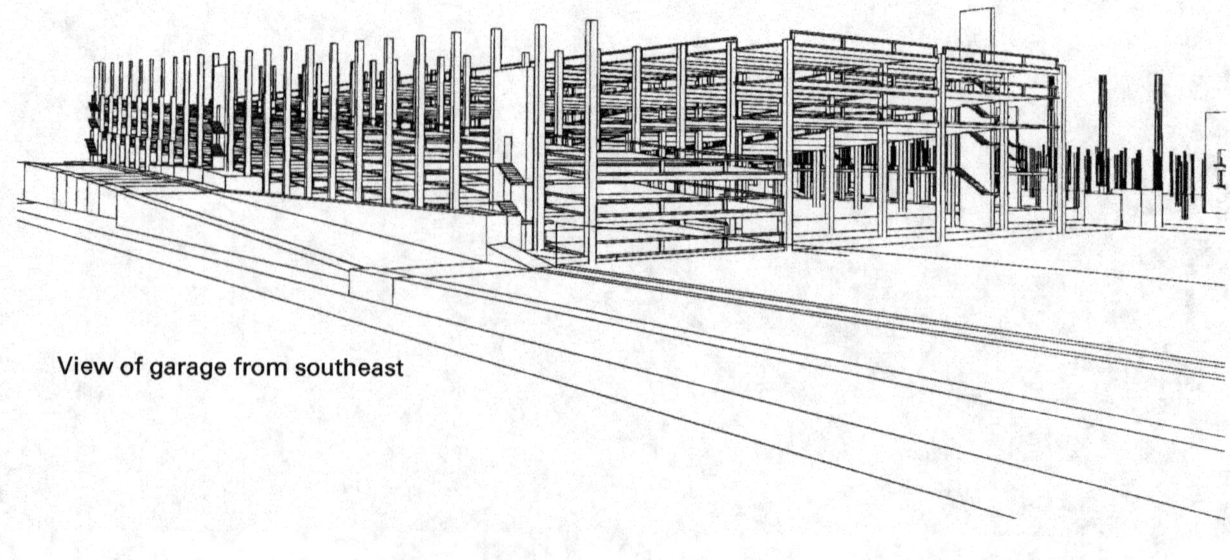

View of garage from southeast

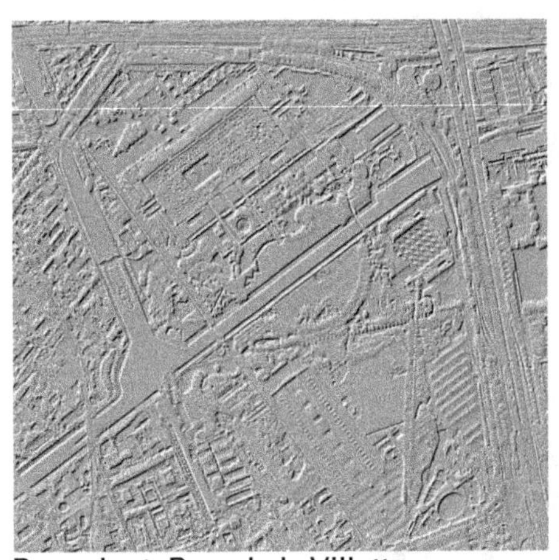

Precedent: Parc de la Villette

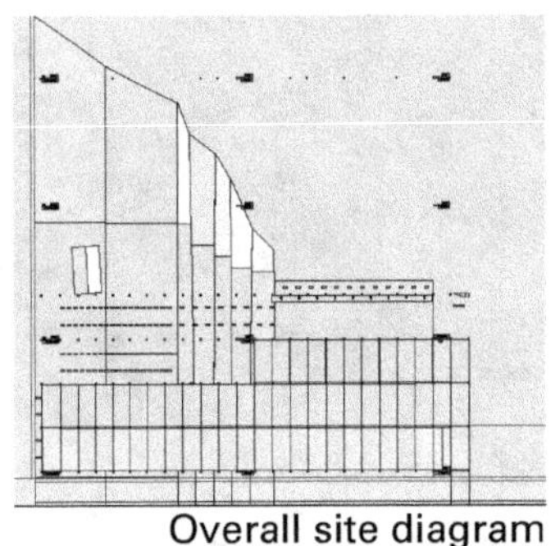

Overall site diagram

Wireframe of site

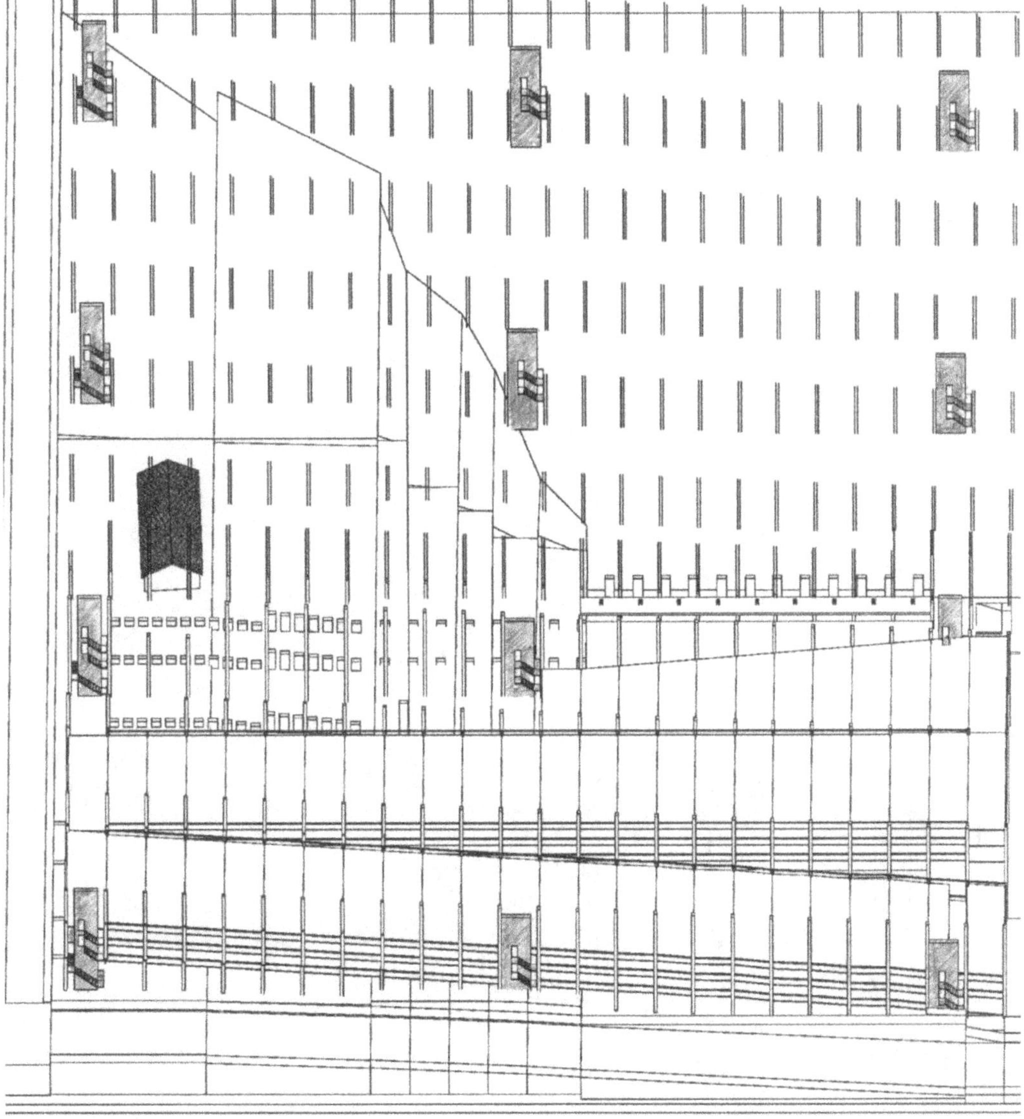

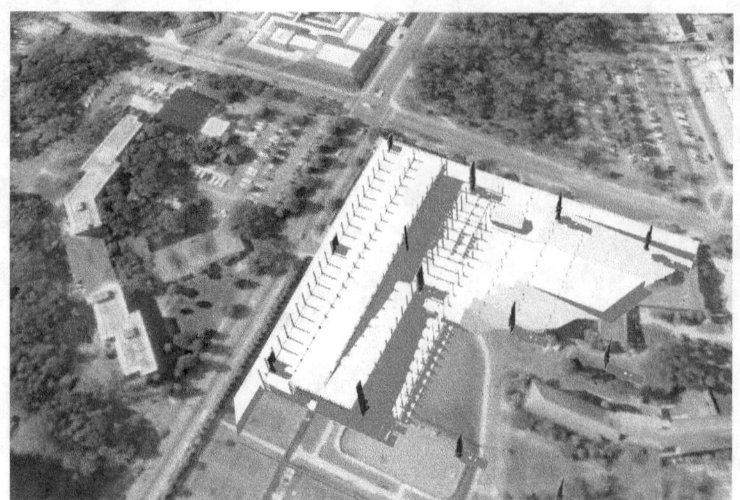

Site photo montage

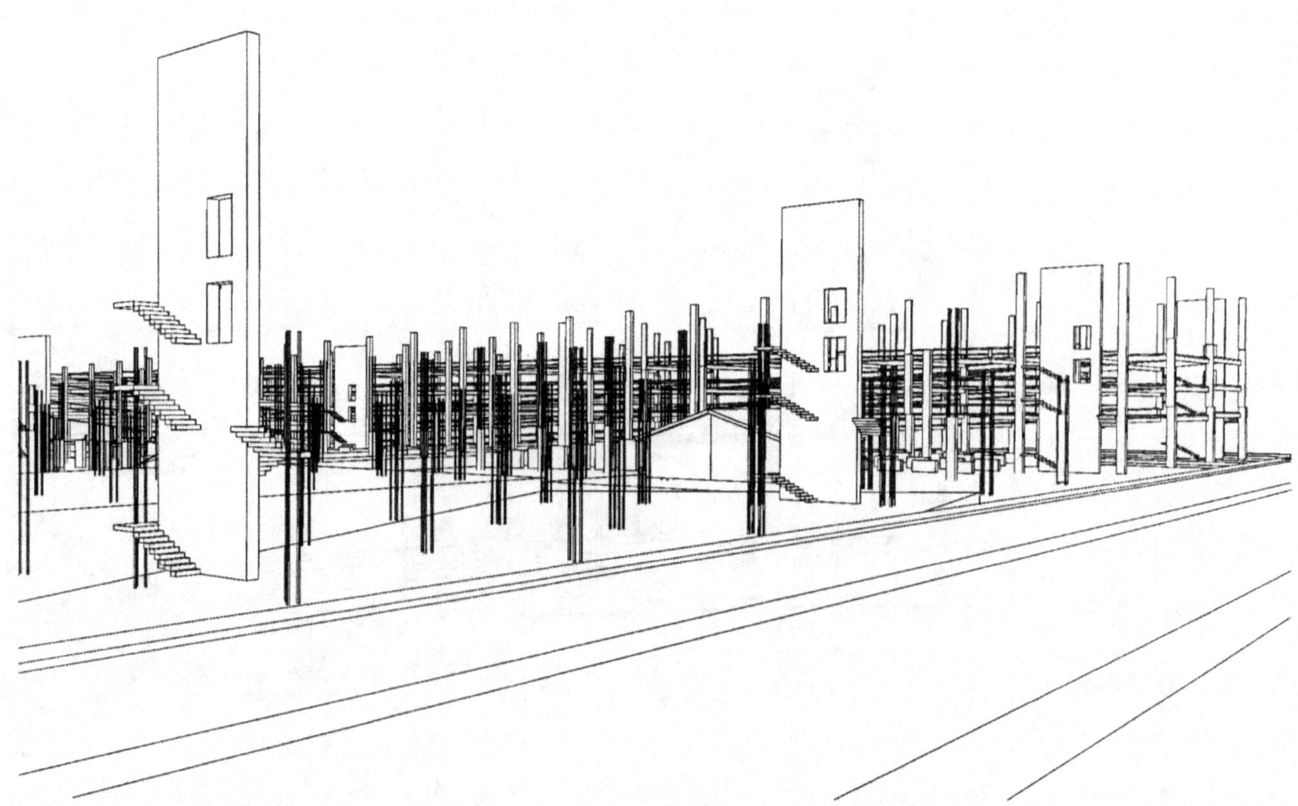

Ground level perspective looking toward the northeast, showing stair towers and column grid

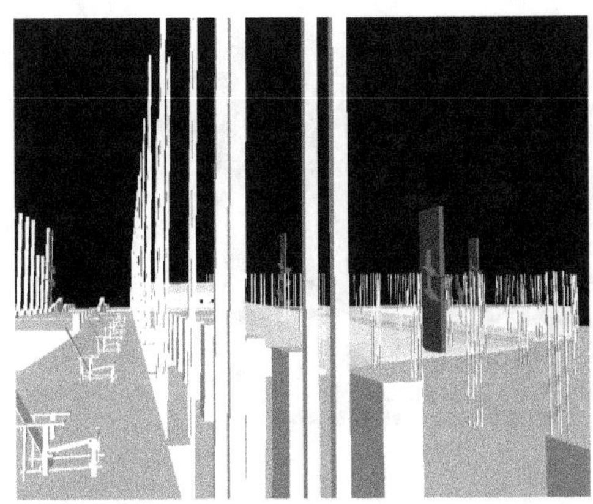

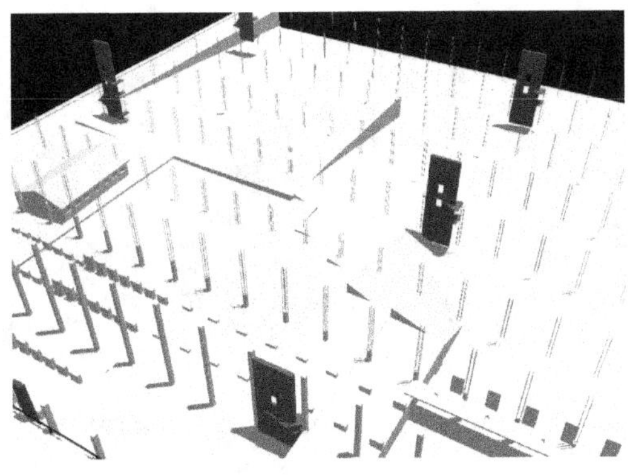

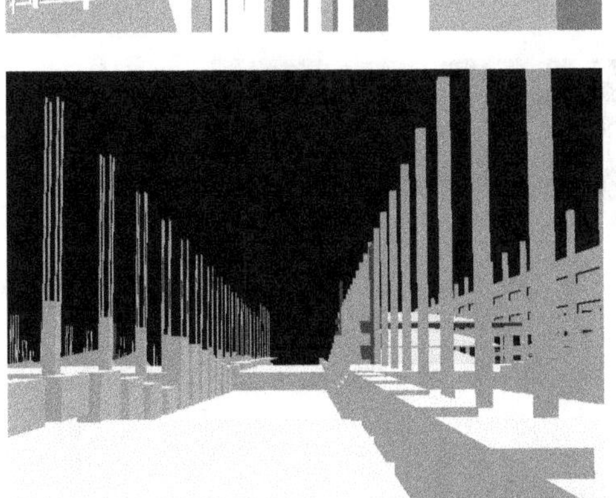

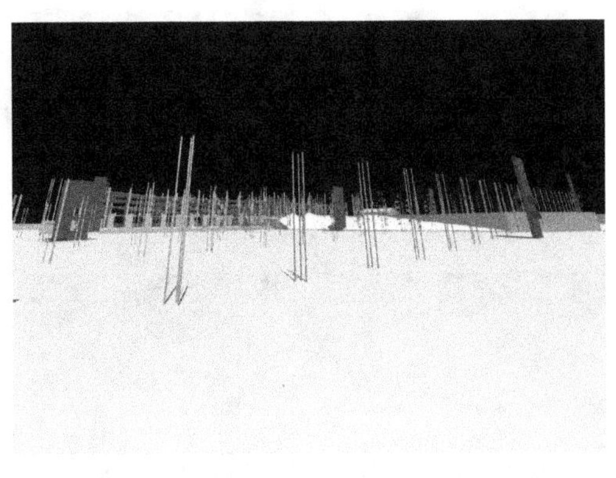

Perspective views

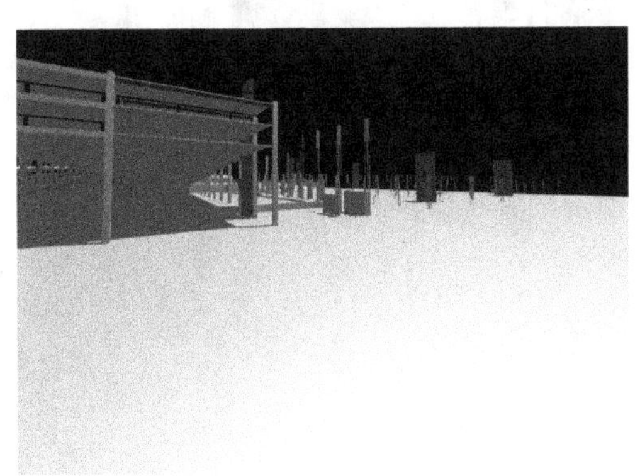

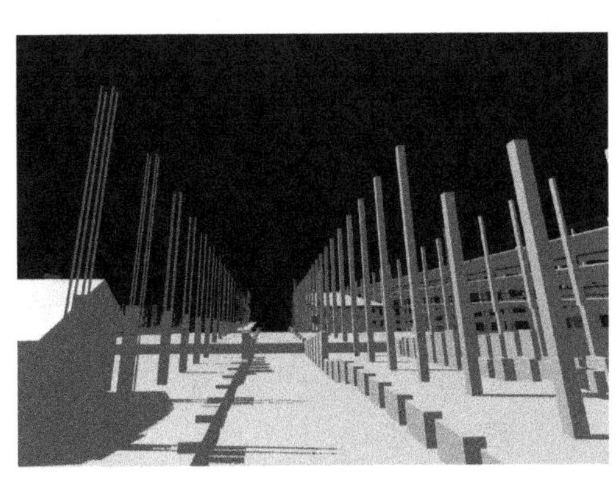

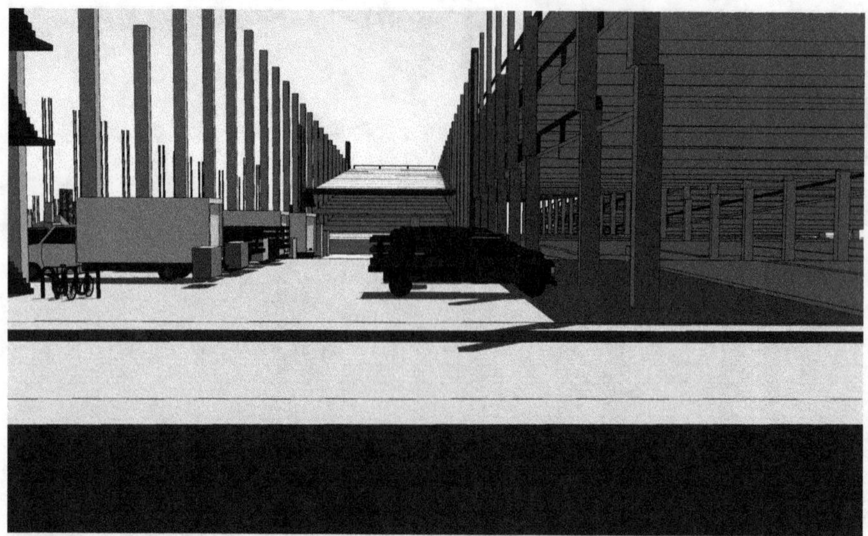

View of farmer's market

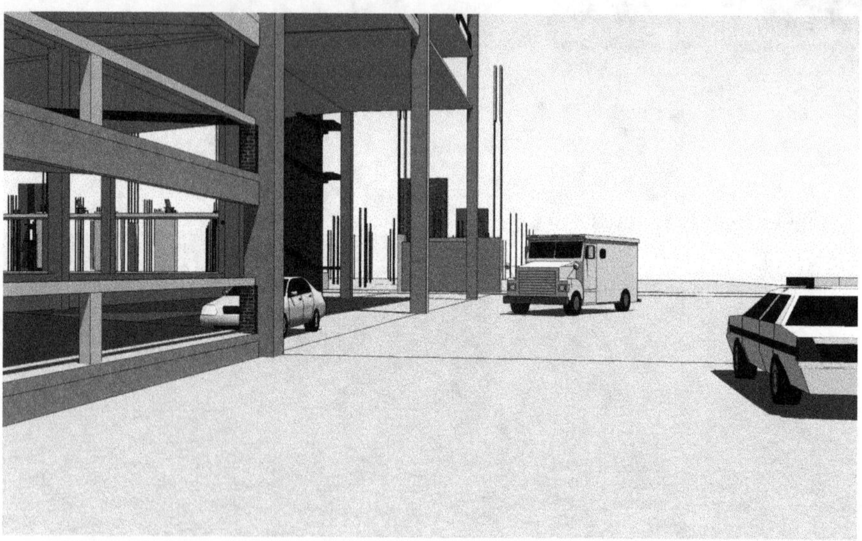

View of drive-thru bank

Reading Room for an Executive

Marquette Building, Chicago, IL

Programme:

size:	approximately 2500 square feet
permanent collection of books:	1000 square feet
current periodicals and newspapers:	500 square feet
two offices:	300 square feet
small exhibition room:	200 square feet
six computer terminals:	200 square feet

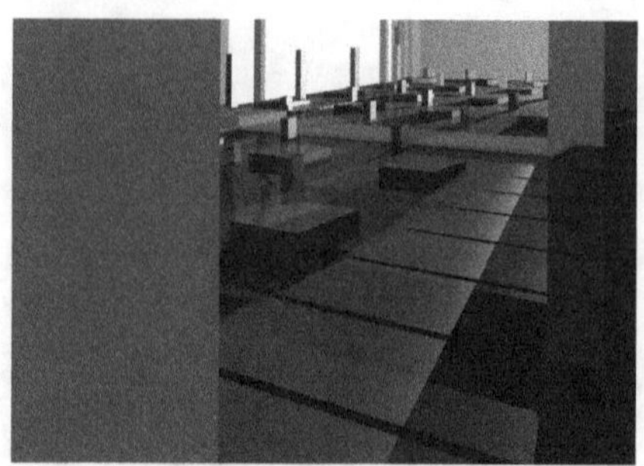
View into storage room

This project became the beginning of a series of investigations into the realm of storage, containment, and occupation in extreme sites.
In this case the macro site was the Marquette Building in Chicago's loop. I was given a long section of one floor along the east facade on the third floor of the building. However, in the process of analyzing the steel frame potential of the structure I decided to develop the reading room vertically in the south-west corner. The resulting five-storey volume makes formally a spatial and structural reference to sacred Gothic architecture. The supports are only partially revealed. The height of the volume can be experienced directly with an open elevator/cage that simultaneously functions as a mobile personal reading room within the larger, vertical reading room.

With respect to sacred Gothic architecture the reading room emphasizes the relationship between the material and the immaterial.
I consider the idea of a reading room for an executive an oxymoron. I assume that few CEOs have the time to go to a reading room, much less spend the day perusing books. In my interpretation an executive is concerned with the material world. On the other hand, someone who is concerned with the immaterial is the poet. The vertical organization, computers and magazines on the ground floor, offices on the second, and the reading room proper on the third floor, reinforces the difference between the executive's approach to attain information (efficient, speedy, etc.) and the poet's. However, this programmatic difference is blurred by the physical occupation of the spaces. The spiral staircase and the reading cage, which is the instrument for reaching the books in the reading room, are vertical links, both physically and spatially.

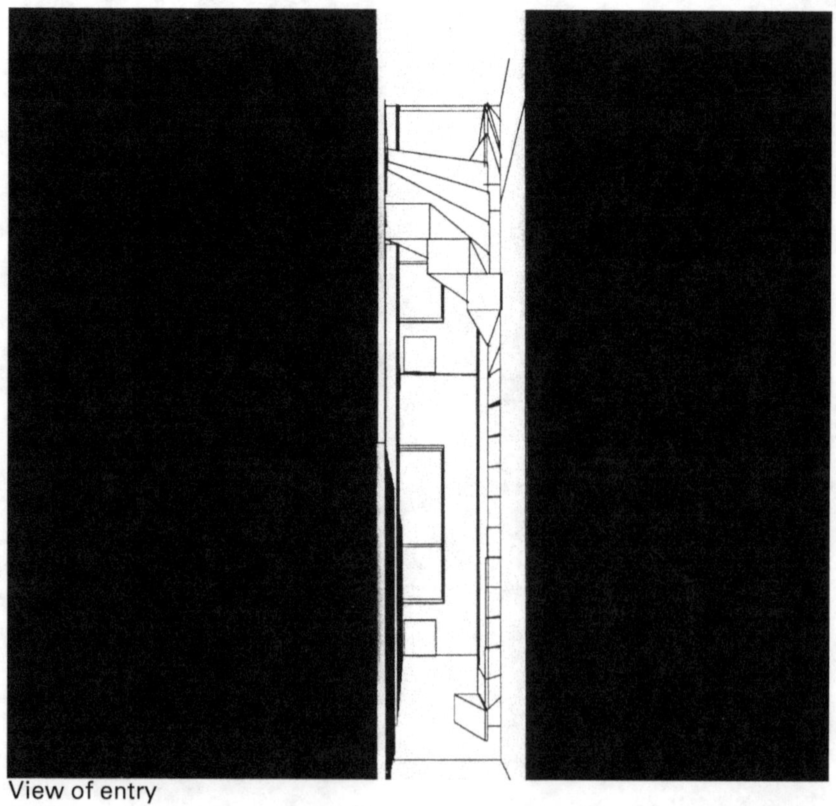
View of entry

Three readings can be made:

1: Site Specific
The reading room's position in the corner suggests a sensitivity to the loss of control in the center. This loss of power is further emphasized by the dependency of other elements on the corner. The elevator/cage for example is hung from a maneuverable boom that uses the corner as its hinge point. The relation of the parts to the whole is self-similar: the parts of the elevator/reading-cage conform proportionally to the whole reading room.

2: Idea Specific
The differentiation between information (data, numbers, objective) and knowledge (personalized, internalized, subjective) is expressed in section via the physical separation of efficient data retrieval from the six computer terminals and the more cumbersome but personal knowledge collection in form of the books in the stacks above. The medieval reference can be read in the computer alcoves as as well as in the three-storey stack space. While in medieval times religion succeeded in suppressing criticism by controlling knowledge, in the twentieth century the same process continues, only under reversed signs. Rather than limiting knowledge outright, there exists today a flood of information which makes it difficult if not impossible to discern what is important to know what is not. Both the access to the computers and the access to the books is difficult. In the former case the user has to know the right password, in the latter, the potential reader is subjected to an instrument of transport (the reading cage) which allows access to the books but simultaneously exposes the user to the danger of falling. The urge to know is countered by the fear to fall and fail.

3: Work Specific
By working at least in the initial stages of this project only on a computer using a CAD program (Architrion), visual space is prioritized when viewed on the computer screen. The information about the project resides on a data diskette and is virtually non-existent. Its space is poetic, dense, and almost immaterial. Its code is comprehensible only to a machine.

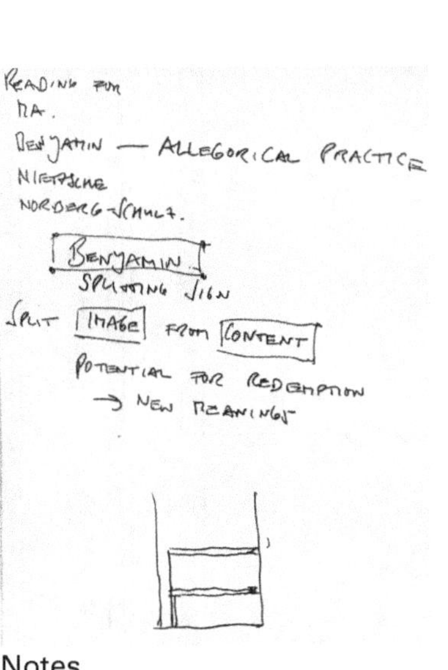

Notes

3D-Diagrams

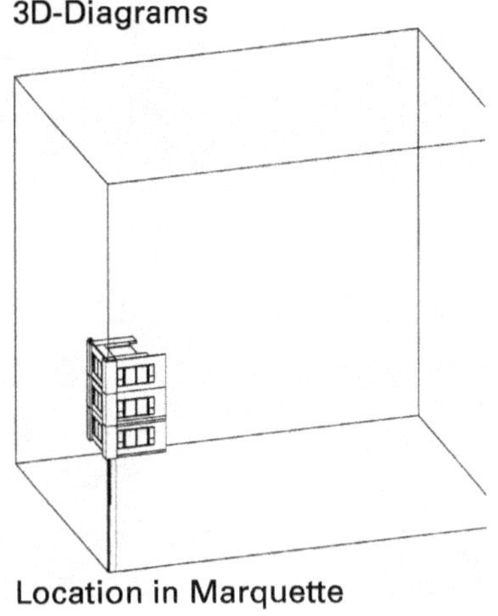
Location in Marquette building

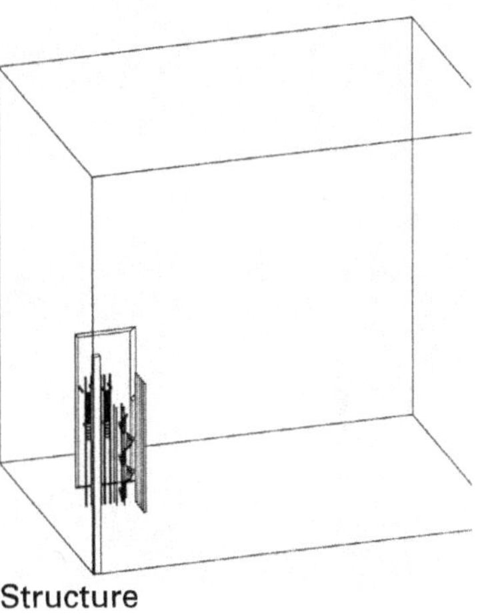
Structure

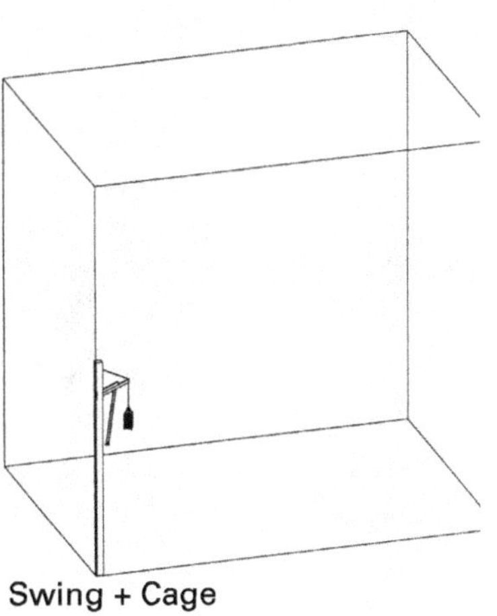
Swing + Cage

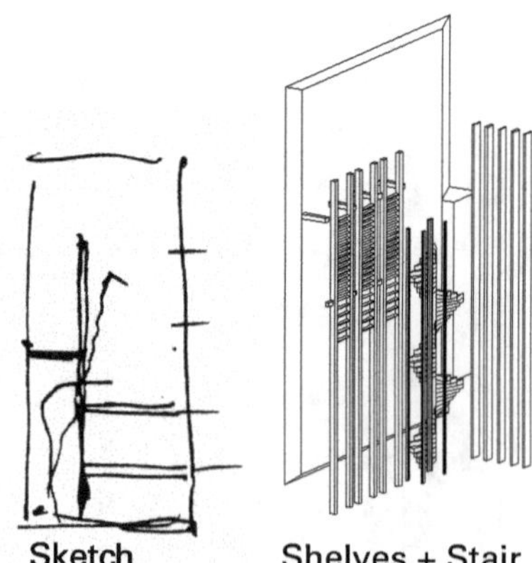

Sketch

Shelves + Stair

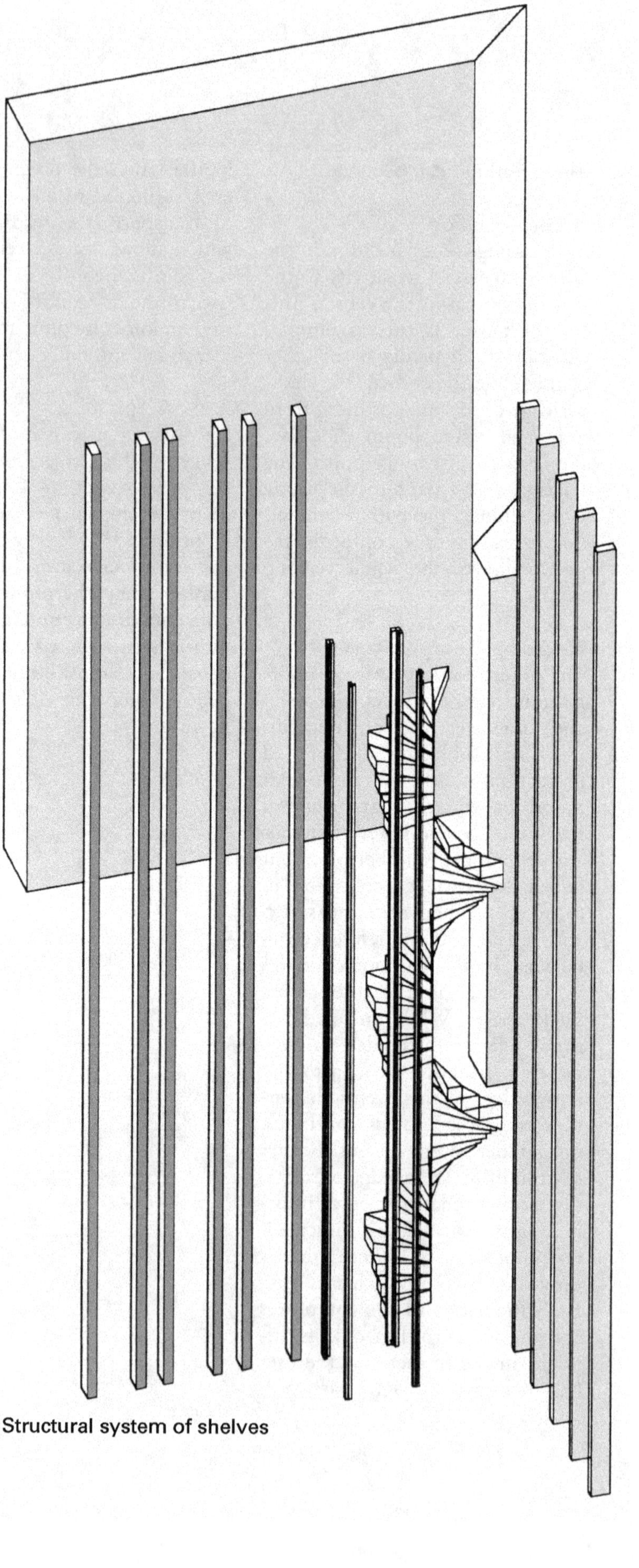

Structural system of shelves

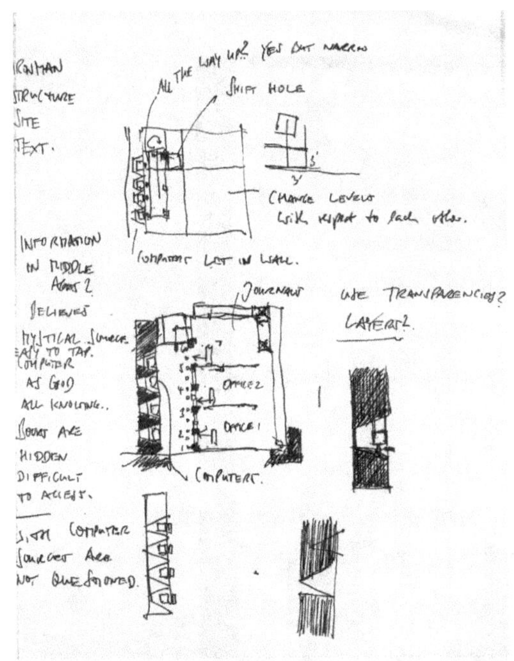

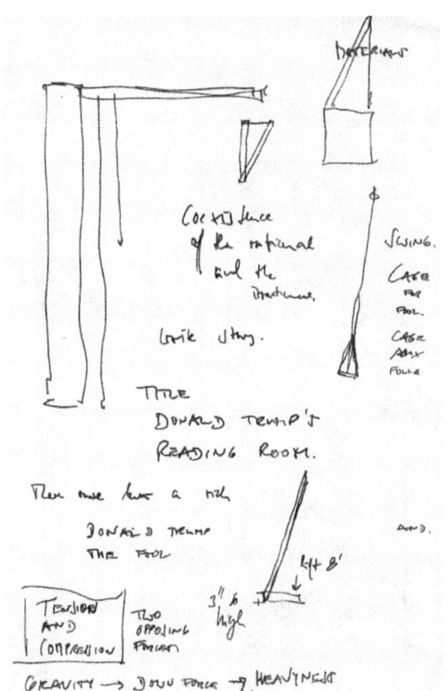

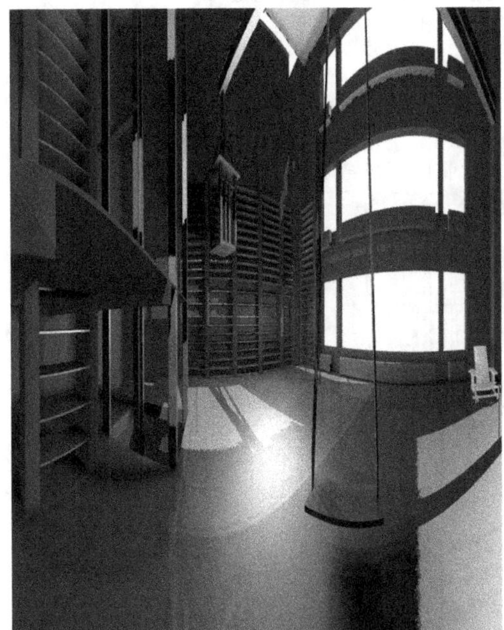
Wide-angle view of swing space

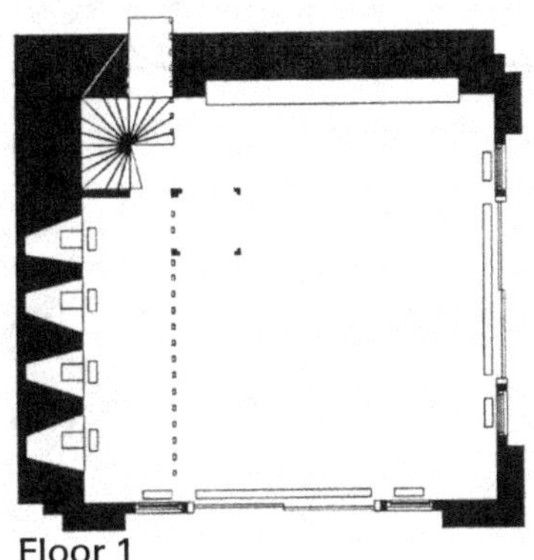
Floor 1

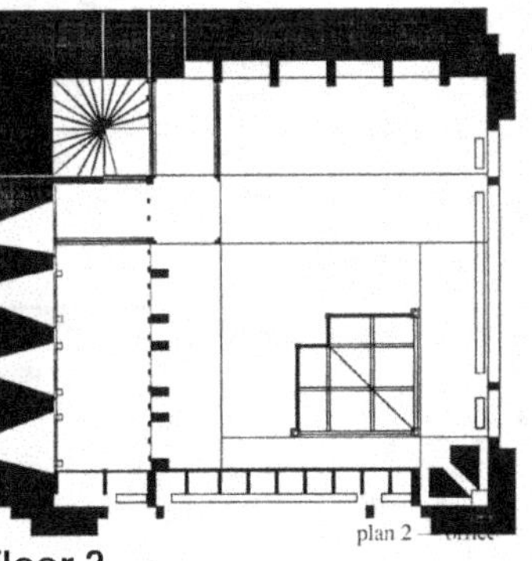

Floor 2

Floor 3 with perspective overlay

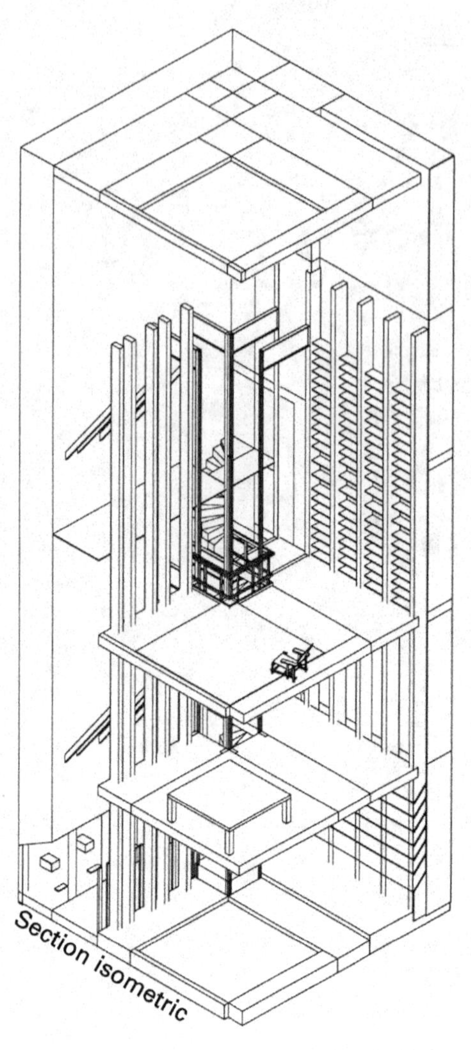

Section isometric

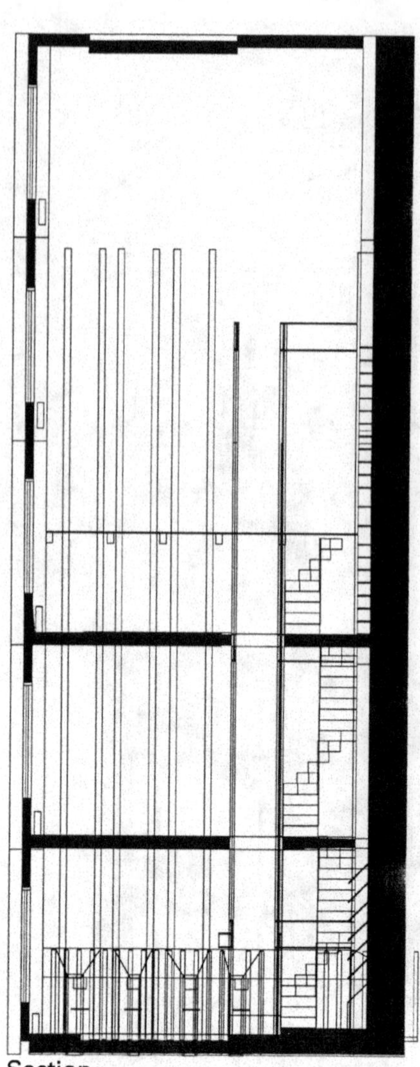

Section

On the stair approaching cage space

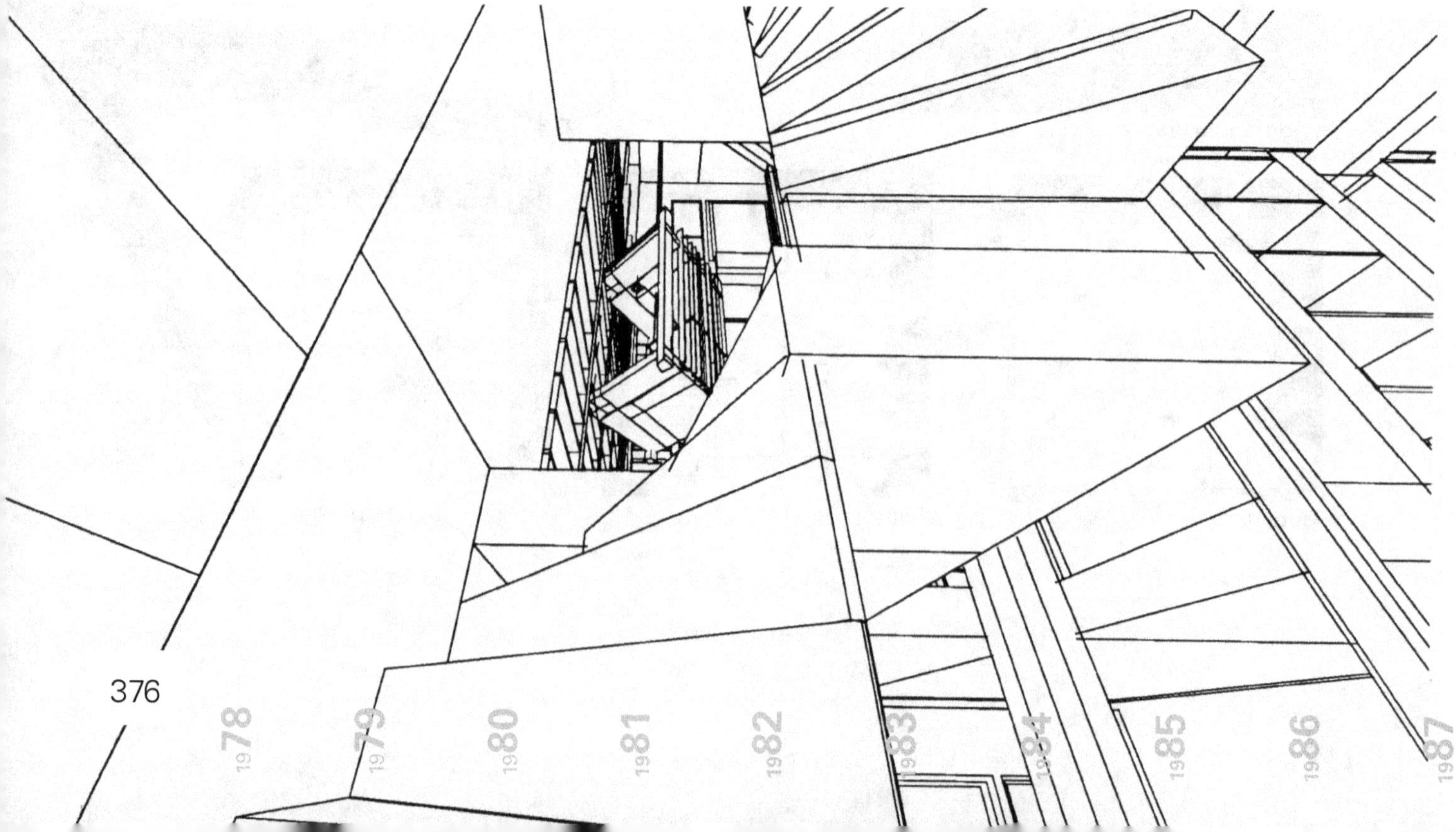

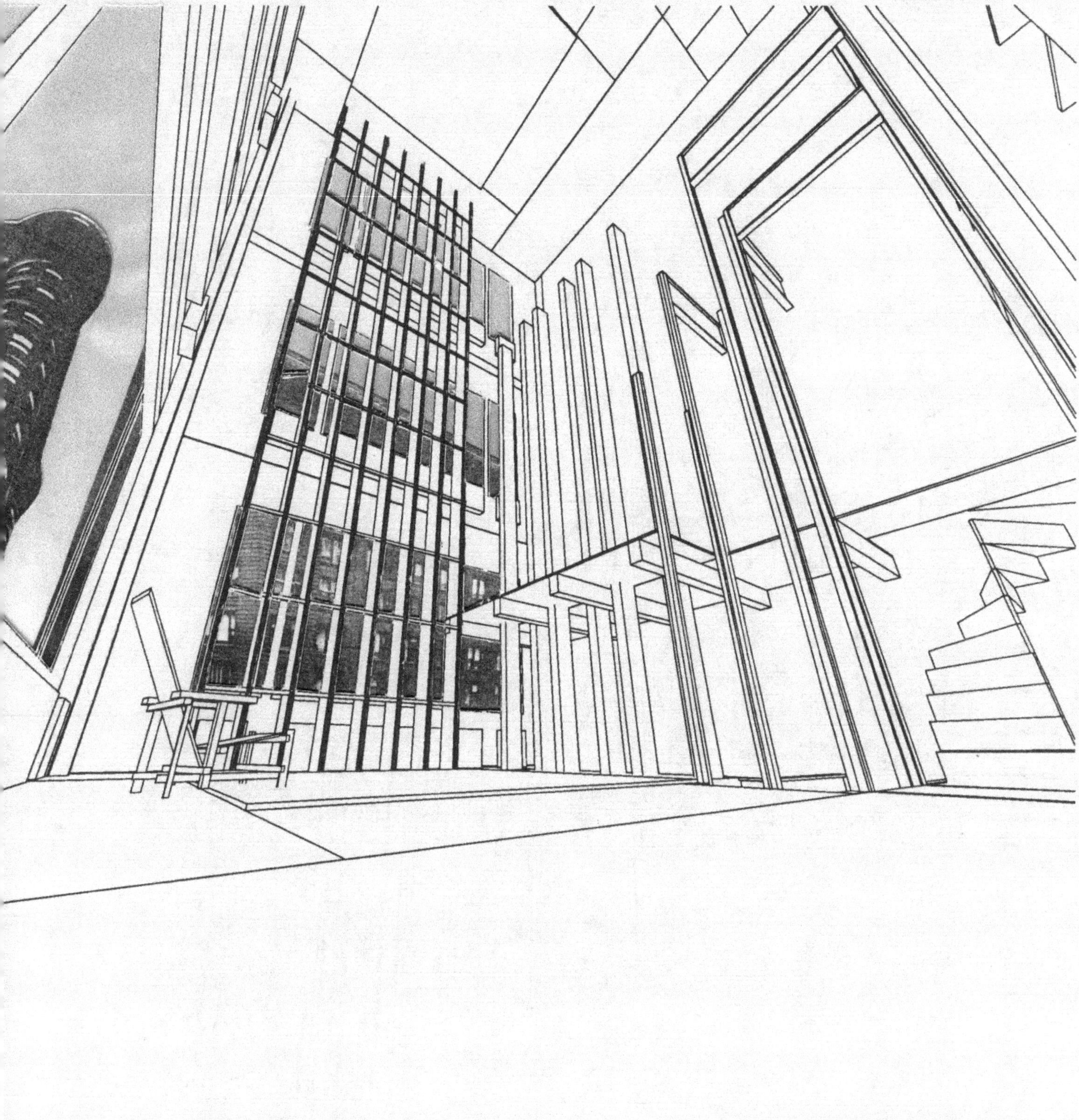

Reading room with Chicago context

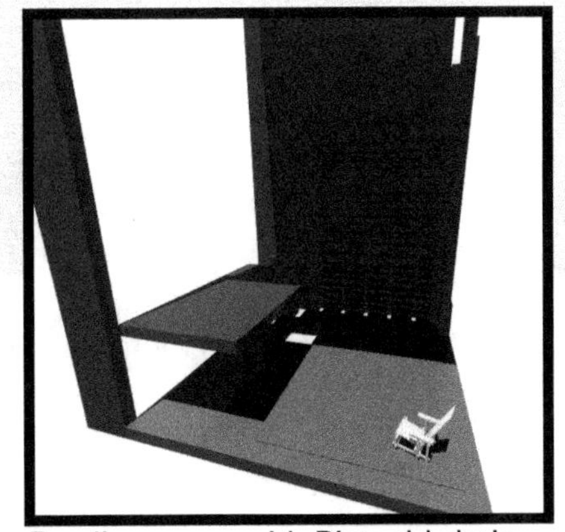

Reading room with Rietveld chair

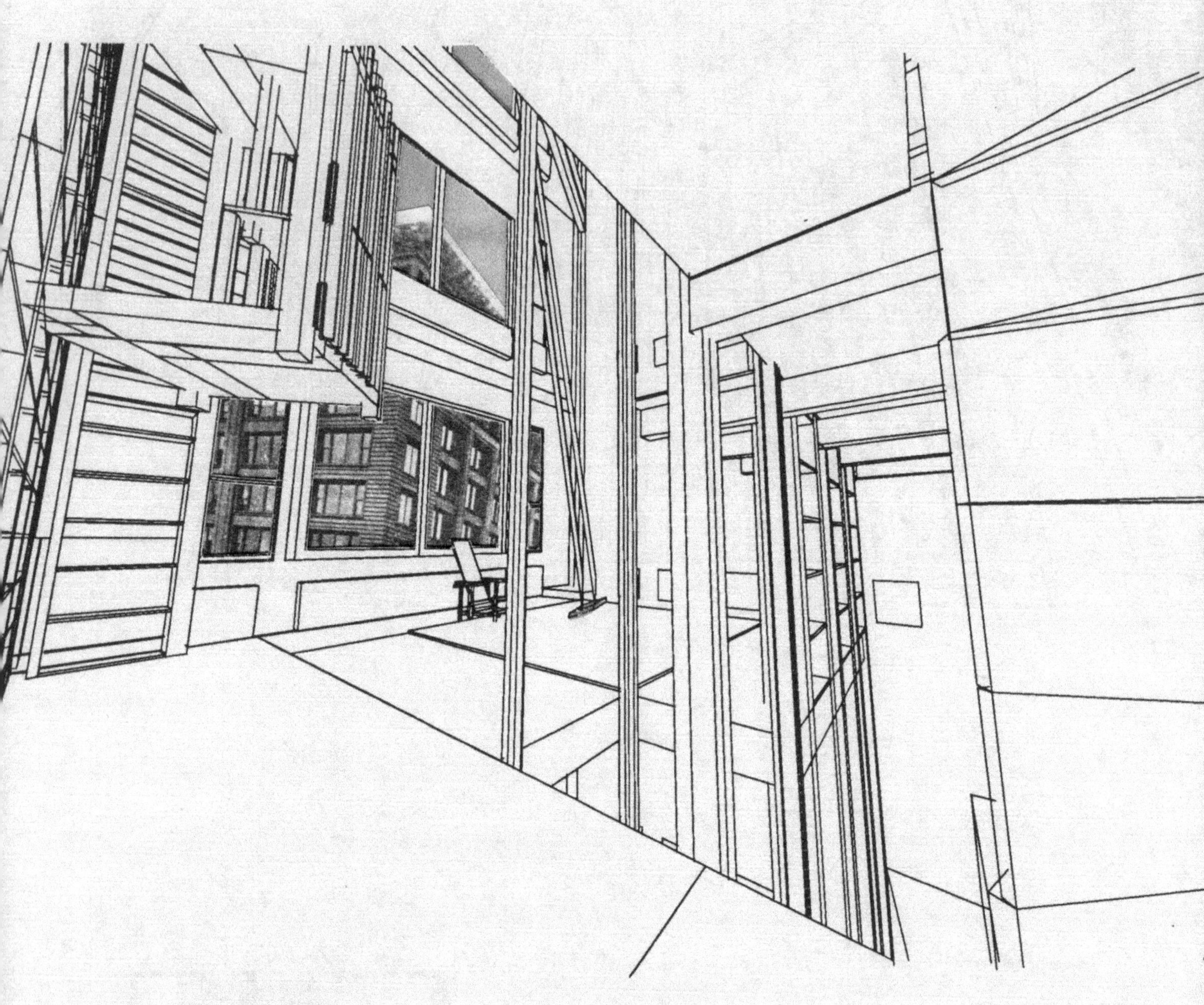

View from reading room

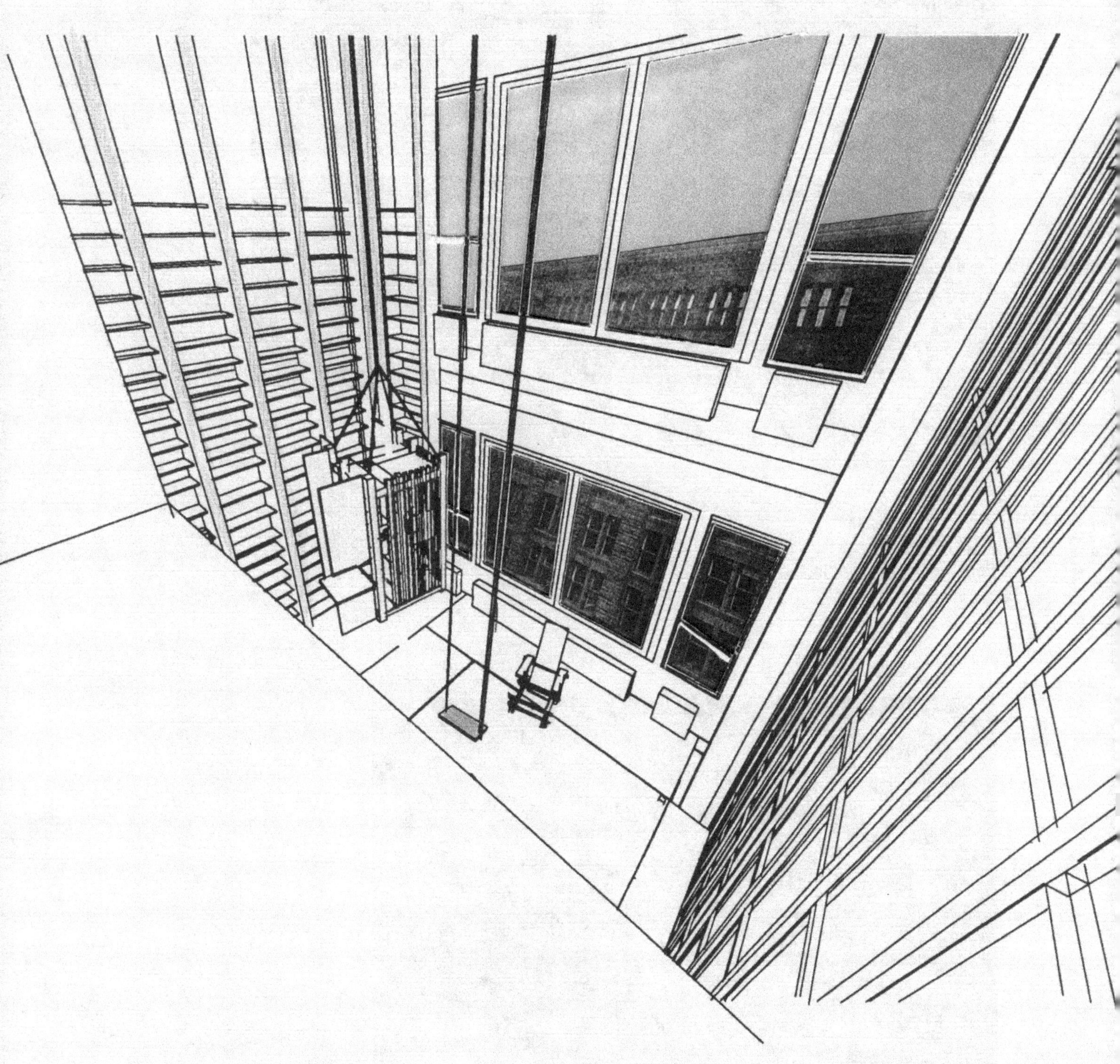

View a book might have as it looks at a potential reader

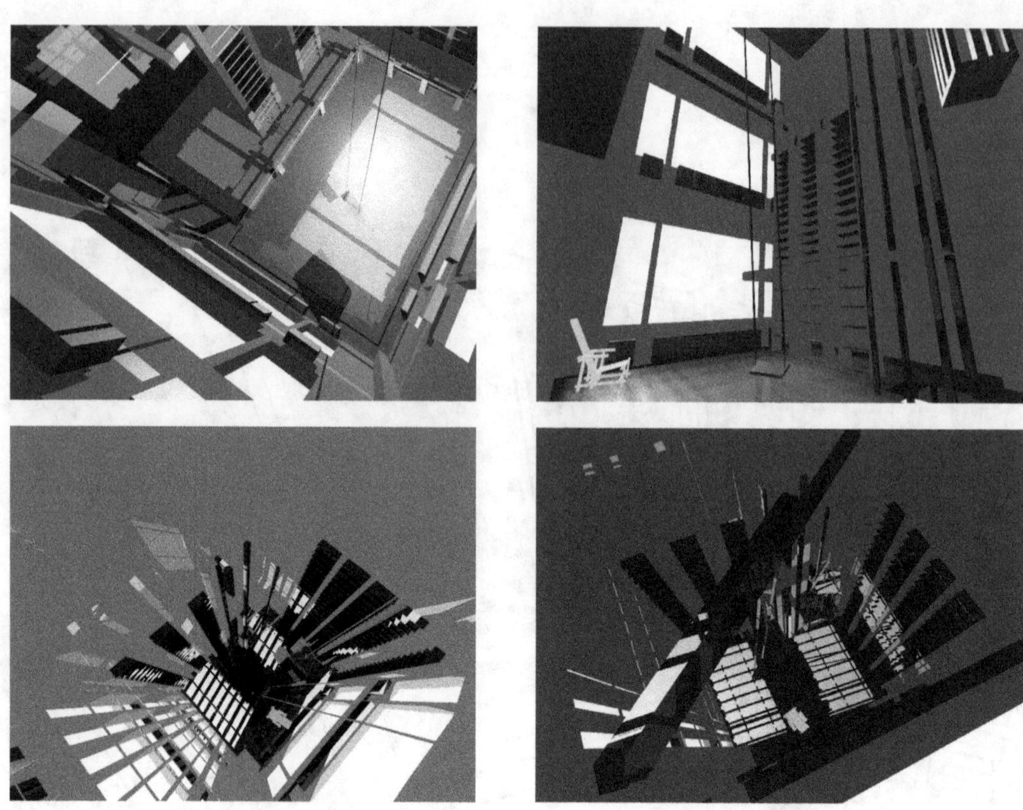

Perspectives of reading space

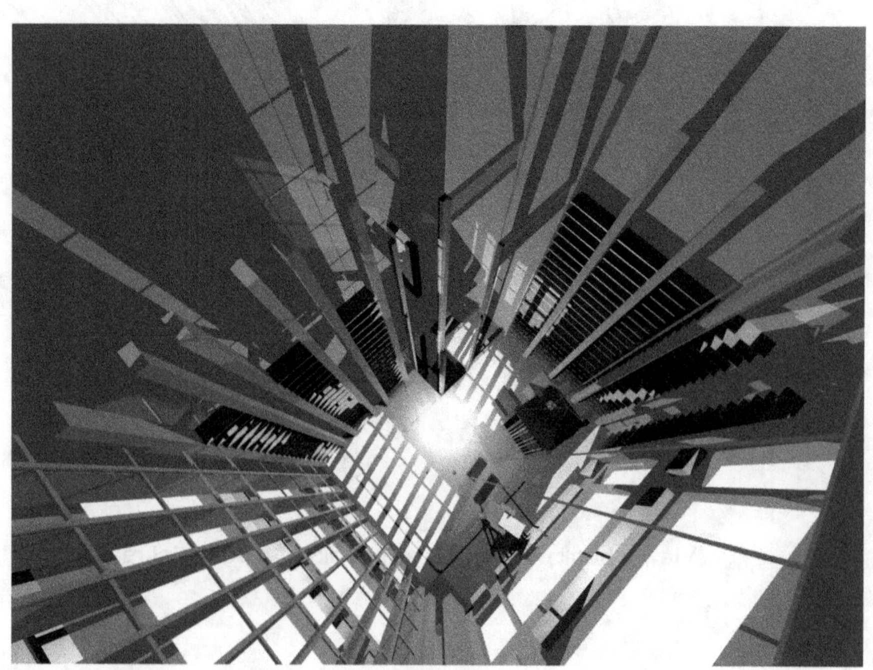

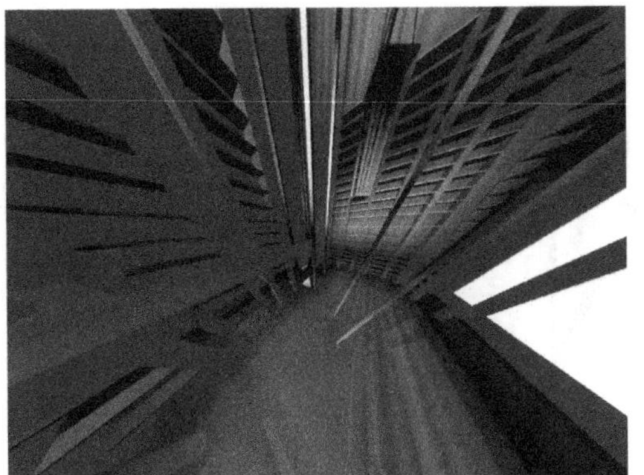
Wide-angle view into reading room

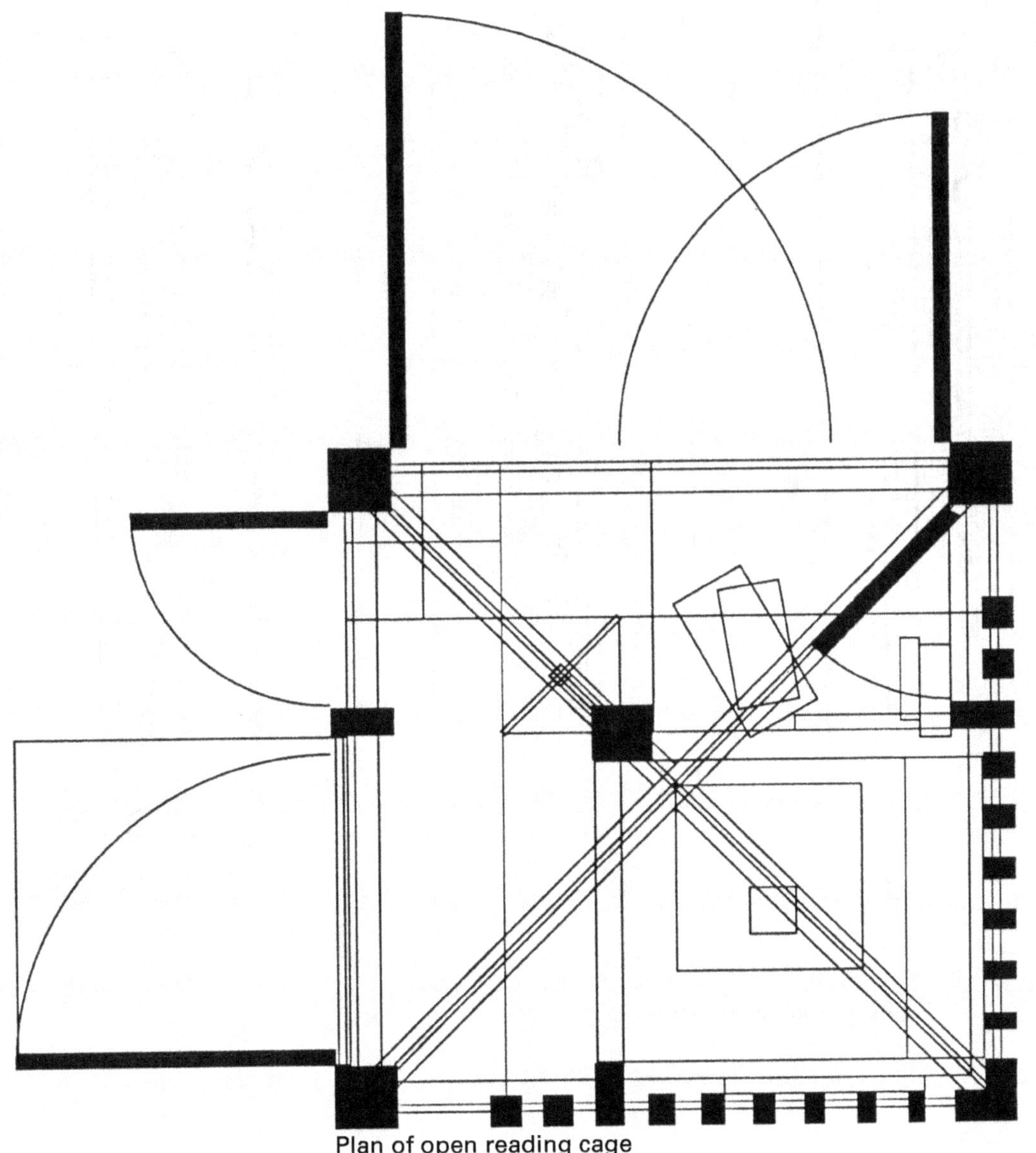
Plan of open reading cage

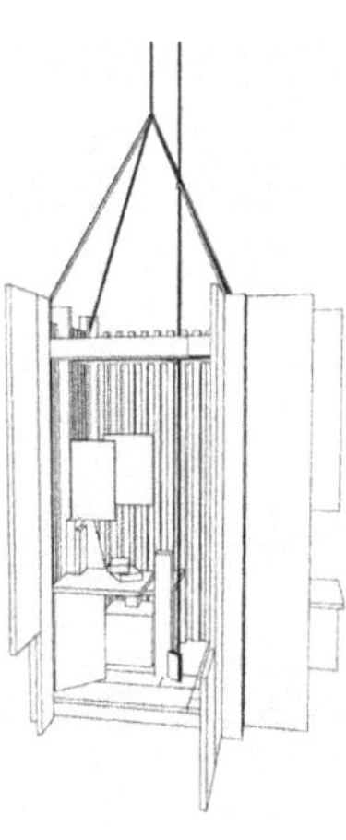

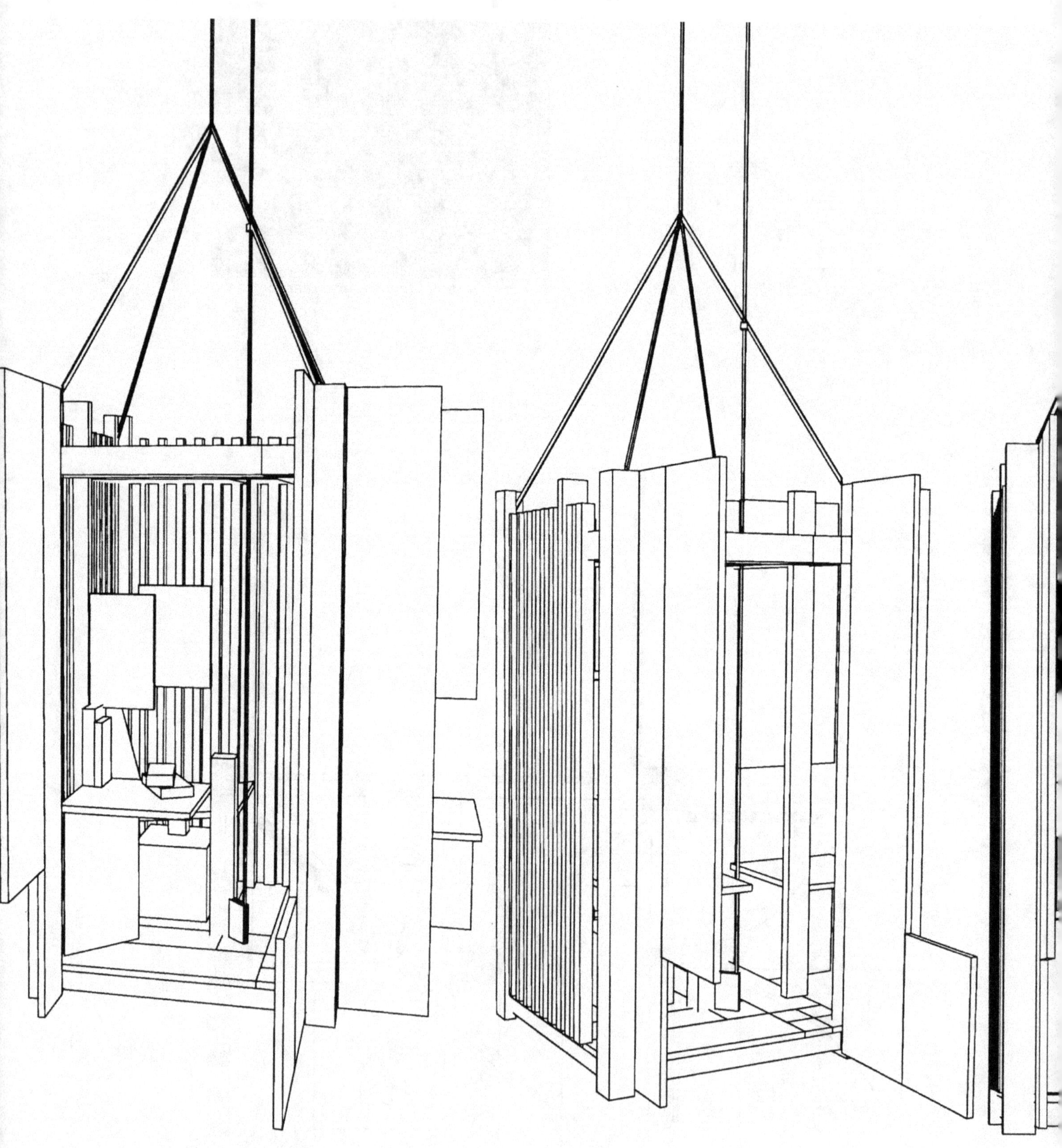

Reading cage rotating from open to closed

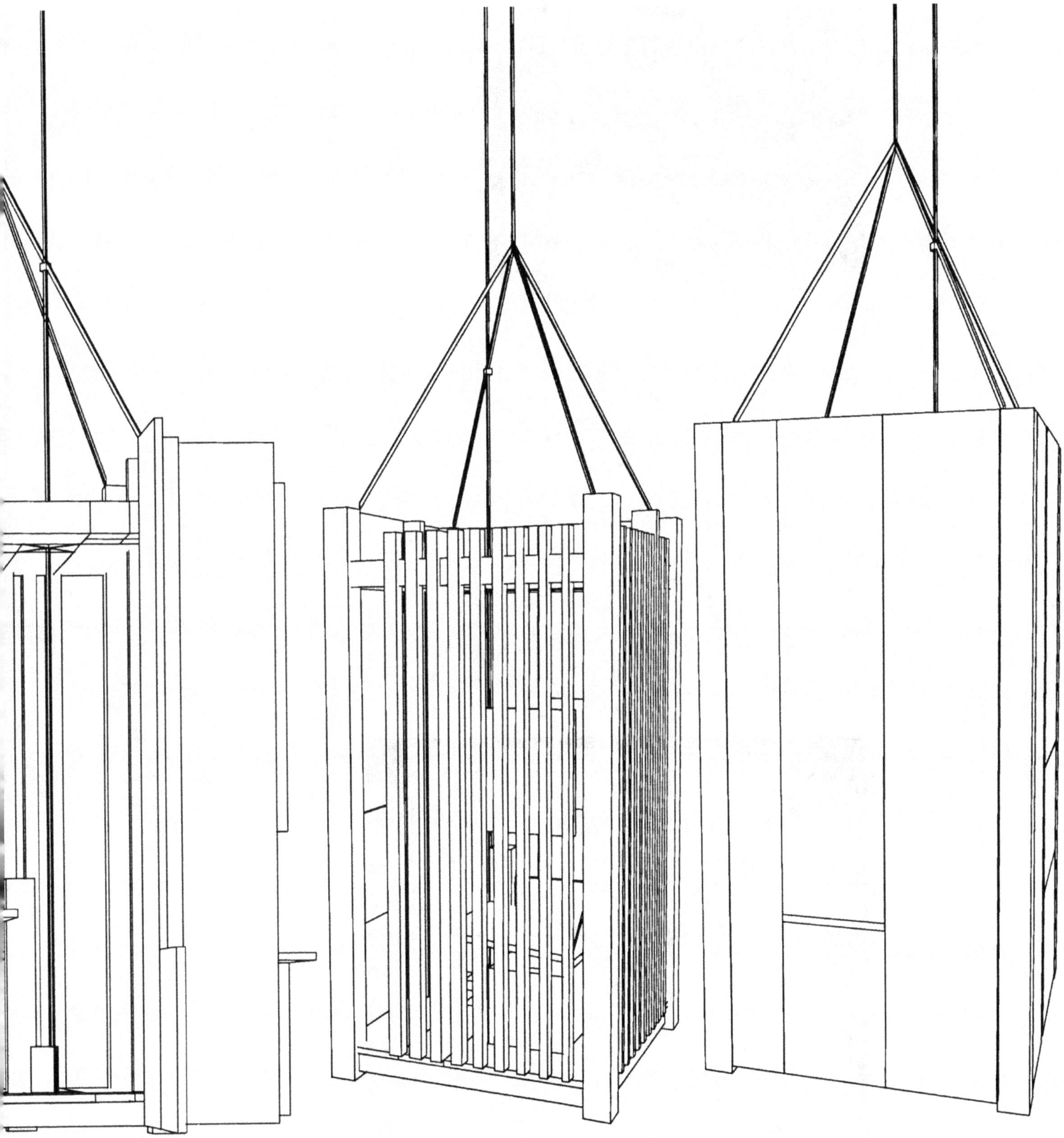

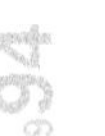

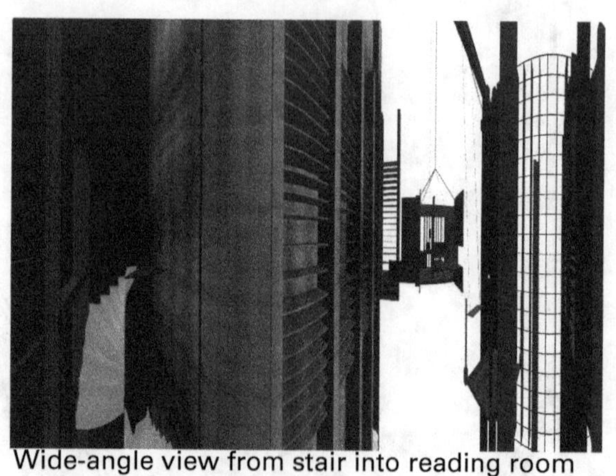
Wide-angle view from stair into reading room

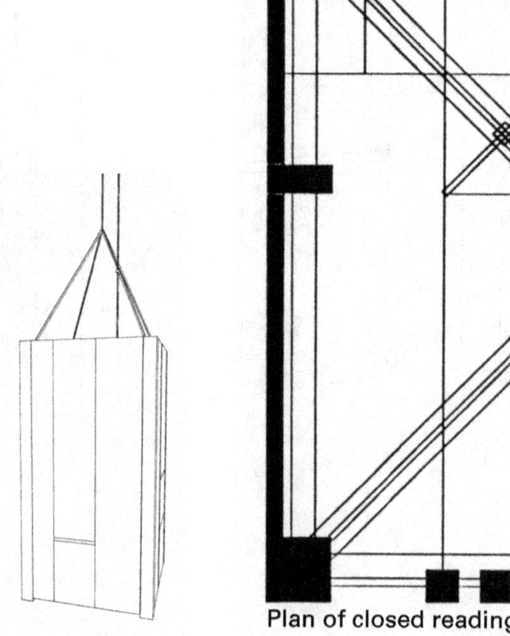

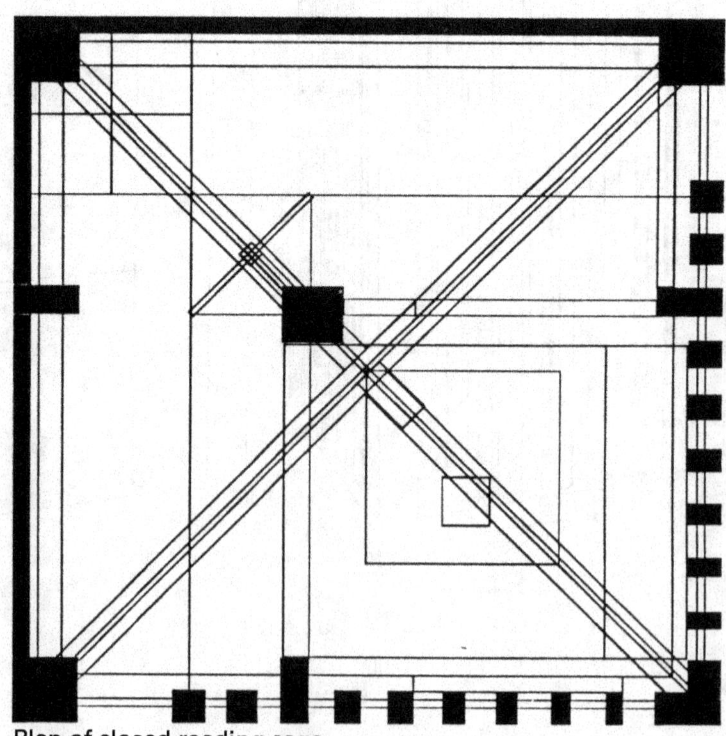
Plan of closed reading cage

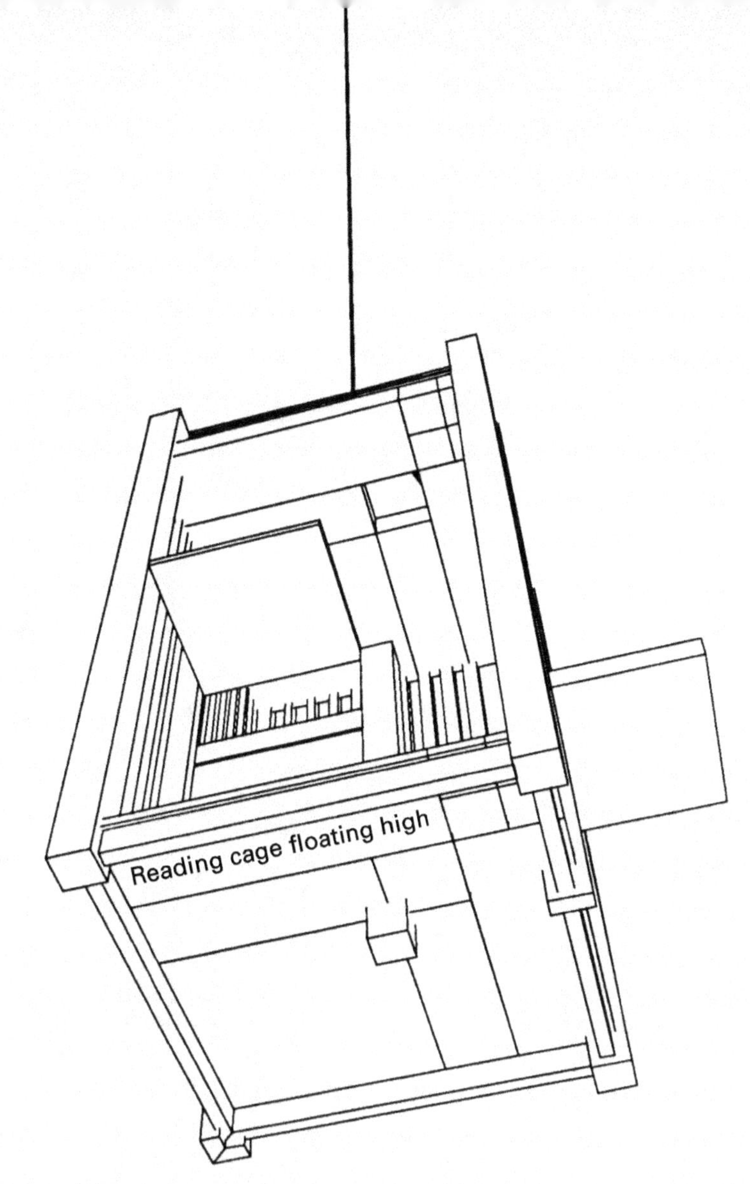
Reading cage floating high

www.ingramcontent.com/pod-product-compliance
Lightning Source LLC
LaVergne TN
LVHW082354100826
845155LV00025B/156

* 9 7 8 1 9 4 1 8 9 2 3 1 2 *